GUERRILLA MOVEMENTS
IN LATIN AMERICA

GUERRILLA MOVEMENTS
IN LATIN AMERICA

RICHARD GOTT

CALCUTTA LONDON NEW YORK

Seagull Books

Editorial offices:

1st floor, Angel Court, 81 St Clements Street, Oxford OX4 1AW, UK

1 Washington Square Village, Apt 1U, New York, NY 10012, USA

26 Circus Avenue, Calcutta 700 017, India

© Richard Gott 1970

First published by Verso in 1970

Seagull Books 2008

ISBN-13   978 1 90542 258 6 (Hardback)

ISBN-13   978 1 90542 259 3 (Paperback)

British Library Cataloguing-in-Publication Data

A catalogue record for this book is available from the British Library

Typeset by Seagull Books, Calcutta, India

Printed and bound in the United Kingdom by Biddles Ltd, King's Lynn

For Inti

'America will be the scene of many big battles sought by mankind for its liberation. In the framework of that struggle of continental scope, the struggles currently being waged in an active manner are mere episodes, but they have already provided martyrs who will figure in American history as having contributed their share of the blood needed in this final phase of the struggle for man's complete freedom. That history will feature the names of Comandante Turcios Lima, Father Camilo Torres, Comandante Fabricio Ojeda, Comandantes Lobatón and Luís de la Puente Uceda, central figures in the revolutionary movements of Guatemala, Colombia, Venezuela and Peru.

But the active mobilization of the people creates new leaders. César Montes and Yon Sosa have raised the standard in Guatemala, Fabio Vásquez and Marulanda in Colombia, Douglas Bravo in the west and Américo Martín in the Bachiller area command their respective fronts in Venezuela. Fresh outbursts of war will arise in these and other American countries, as has already occurred in Bolivia, and they will continue to grow with all the vicissitudes involved in this dangerous business of a modern revolutionary.'

Extract from the letter written by Che Guevara
to the Tricontinental, April 1967

CONTENTS

12. Héctor Béjar, leader of the 'Javier Heraud' detachment of the Ejército de Liberacíon Nacional (ELN); captured 1966.

13. Albino Guzmán, guerrilla in Luís de la Puente's detachment.

14.1. Hugo Blanco; Trotskyist peasant organizer; captured in 1963 and imprisoned in El Frontón.

14.2. Bridge at Comas dynamited in June 1965 by guerrillas under the command of Guillermo Lobatón.

15.1. Roberto 'Coco' Peredo, leader of the Ejército de Liberacíon Nacional (ELN); killed 1967.

15.2. Jorge Masetti, leader of the Argentinian Ejército Guerrillero del Pueblo; killed 1964.

16.1. Tamara Bunke, known as 'Tania'; killed 1967.

16.2. Régis Debray, sentenced by a military court in Camiri to thirty years' imprisonment for his part in the Bolivian guerrilla campaign.

between pages 314–5

17. Régis Debray, during his trial at Camiri, with Captain Hurtado of the Bolivian Navy.
(*Granada TV*)

18. The grave of Tania at Vallegrande.
(*Granada TV*)

19.1. Poster on the streets of Camiri attacking Debray: 'He who lives by the sword shall die by the sword'.

19.2. Che Guevara at the camp at Nancahuazú.

20–24. Nine photographs probably taken by Che Guevara himself during the course of the Bolivian campaign. They come from the roll of film that was found in his rucksack.

between pages 408–09

25. Ernesto Che Guevara with two peasant children.

26.1. Colonel Zenteno Anaya (*right*) and General Alfredo Ovando Candia (*foreground*), Vallegrande, 9 October 1967.
(*Granada TV*)

26.2. Major 'Pappy' Shelton of the US Army, at the US training camp at La Esperanza, near Santa Cruz.
(*Granada TV*)

27.1. A CIA agent, Eduardo González, climbing into a jeep at Vallegrande, 9 October 1967.
(*Granada TV*)

27.2. CIA man Gonzálcz nervously looks around, apparently aware that he is being photographed with a telephoto lens.
(*Granada TV*)

28–31.2. Five photographs taken by Brian Moser of Granada Television at Vallegrande on Monday, 9 October 1967, about 6 hours after Guevara was shot.
(*Granada TV*)

32. Defeat of the Revolution? From the roll in Guevara's rucksack.

LIST OF MAPS

ACKNOWLEDGEMENTS

This book was written at the Instituto de Estudios Internacionales of the University of Chile, perhaps the only centre in Latin America—or indeed elsewhere—where it would have been possible to engage in this type of research in a completely free and unfettered manner. I am enormously grateful to its director, Dr Claudio Véliz, who invited me to Chile to help him set up the institute and who shares my enthusiasm for contemporary history. I am also greatly indebted to my colleagues at the institute, particularly John Gittings and Alain Joxe, both of whom have written on various aspects of the guerrilla scene in Latin America. Innumerable Chileans made my stay in Santiago a delight, and I owe special thanks to the institute's librarian, Sandra Barbosa, and to my secretary, Ines Maria Leighton. Richard Hawkes kindly drafted translations of many documents for me at great speed, though the final versions, of course, remain my responsibility. Late in 1969, Richard Hawkes was killed in a climbing accident in Chile. He was one of the brightest young Latinamericanists in England and will be greatly missed.

The friendship and interest of a large number of journalists specializing in Latin American affairs have also been a great help; Christopher Roper of Reuters, Brian Moser of Granada Television, Mario Bianchi of Agence France Presse, Carlos Jorquera of Prensa Latina, Richard Wigg of *The Times,* Michael Field of the *Daily Telegraph,* Alfonso Varela of Radio Portales, Sven Lindquist of the *Dagens Nyheter,* and Gustavo Sánchez and Luís Gonzales of *El Diario.* Manuel Cabieses, editor of *Punto Final,* and Enrique Zileri, editor of *Caretas,* kindly lent me photographs, while Geoffrey Taylor, foreign editor of the *Guardian,* greatly encouraged me by printing virtually everything I cared to send from the guerrilla front. Jordan Bishop and Arthur Domike helpfully plied me with press cuttings, and Ricardo Luna made available his magnificent collection of material on contemporary Cuba.

My wife, Ann Zammit, would have preferred me to join the guerrillas rather than to write about them. At great cost to herself she allowed me to finish the book, for which I shall always be grateful.

Richard Gott

This book, first published in 1970, contains a first-hand account of the principal guerrilla movements formed in Latin America in the decade between the victory of the Cuban Revolution in January 1958 and the death of Che Guevara in October 1967. It gives details of their story and the ideas that they generated and discussed, and it provides a description of the polarized societies within which they operated. A second edition, published largely unchanged by Penguin Books in 1972, was titled *Rural Guerrillas in Latin America*, to indicate that the text did not cover the much publicized urban guerrilla movements that were developing in the early 1970s, notably in Brazil, Argentina and Uruguay.

Written during the climate of revolutionary euphoria that existed throughout the world in the late 1960s during the Vietnam War, the book reflects the general belief of that time that the customary rules of historic development might perhaps, just for a moment, be suspended. The actions of small guerrilla groups, welding disparate factions into a coherent and unstoppable political force, could, it was thought, overturn military dictatorships or corrupt civilian regimes, and promote radical change.

This was not just the optimistic view (or the hope) of the radical Left in the west. It was also the opinion subscribed to by the authorities in Washington and in Moscow, although both sides in the cold war were anxious in their various ways to ensure that these changes did not happen. The Americans from the time of Eisenhower and John F. Kennedy were perplexed and fascinated by guerrilla warfare, and this obsession has continued from that day to this, cold war or no cold war, through the Johnson and Nixon administrations, on to those of Carter and Clinton, and to those of the Bush family.

The Russians, for their part, were also concerned lest the guerrilla advocates should triumph. After an initial period in which Nikita Khrushchev expressed considerable enthusiasm for the Cuban

Revolution, the Russians in the Brezhnev era became alarmed by Latin America's schismatic guerrilla groups, often perceiving them to hold unacceptably Trotskyist or pro-Chinese views. They were also worried by the prospect of having to support future revolutionary governments with economic subsidies on the Cuban scale. Even the elected socialist government of Salvador Allende received little Soviet assistance. The Russians in the last 25 years of the cold war preferred diligently to pursue détente with the west.

For the Americans, guerrilla movements meant counter-guerrilla operations, and for nearly half a century this strategy was imposed on Latin America, implemented by pliant civilian regimes and, more often, by brutal military dictatorships. The result in many countries was war, not just against the guerrilla pinprick but against the entire population. The war against the indigenous peoples of Guatemala in the two decades after 1970 led to 200,000 deaths, mostly of innocent indigenous peasants. The endless civil war in Colombia produced a similar figure. The 'dirty war' in Argentina, waged by the armed forces between 1976 and 1982, led to tens of thousands of dead and 'disappeared', as did the war unleashed in El Salvador. All over Latin America individuals were targeted by death squads, while entire villages were slaughtered by soldiers operating under orders. When President Clinton visited Guatemala in March 1999 he finally felt called upon to apologize, declaring that US support for the military forces that had engaged 'in violent and widespread repression' was wrong.

Forty years after Guevara's death, the international climate and discourse about political change has changed out of all recognition. The heroic guerrillas in the mountains and jungles of Latin America, fighting for a better life against repressive dictatorships, would today, in the world after 9/11, be demonized as 'terrorists'. Yet they were once seen to belong to that long-established and honourable tradition of those who picked up arms to fight for national liberation.

This book has long been out of print, though it is often sought after by students researching into the origins of today's world. This new edition has been reprinted according to the original text, but in a postscript I have sketched in the details of what happened after 1970.

Richard Gott

London, January 2007

At 8.30 in the warm evening of Sunday, 8 October 1967, 1 was walking round the main square of Santa Cruz in eastern Bolivia with an English friend, when a man beckoned to us from a cafe table.

'I have news for you,' he said. And we said 'Che?', for the possible capture of Guevara had been on our minds for a week. Some days earlier we had been in the small town of Vallegrande and had heard Colonel Joaquín Zenteno Anaya, the commander of the Eighth Division of the Bolivian army, express confidence that his troops would have Che within their power before the week was up. He explained how they had been reinforced by 600 'Rangers', fresh from the training camp run by United States Special Forces north of Santa Cruz. He told us how the guerrillas had been encircled. Only on one side was there a possibility of escape, and there the army had planted soldiers dressed as peasants who would swiftly give the alarm if the guerrillas passed that way. From the evidence of the inhabitants of a village which the guerrillas had entered at the end of September, and from that of two captured guerrillas, there was no doubt that Che was the leader of this encircled band.

'Che has been captured,' our cafe contact told us, 'but he is severely wounded and may not last the night. The other guerrillas are fighting desperately to get him back, and the company commander is appealing by radio for a helicopter so that they can fly him out.' The company commander had been so excited that his words came out in a jumble. All those listening could hear was 'We've got him, we've got him'.

Our contact suggested that we should hire a helicopter and fly immediately to the guerrilla zone. He did not know whether Che was alive or dead, but he felt that there was little chance of his surviving long. We did not have the money to hire a helicopter even if there had been one available, and in any case it is impossible to fly in Bolivia after dark. So we hired a jeep instead and set off at four o'clock in the morning of Monday, 9 October, to drive to Vallegrande.

We arrived there five and a half hours later, and drove straight to the airfield. There half the population of the small town seemed to be waiting, the school children in white dresses and amateur photographers anxious to secure pictures of dead guerrillas. For, only two weeks before, the bodies of the Bolivian guerrilla, 'Coco' Peredo, and of the Cuban 'Miguel' had been brought there. And in the cemetery close to the airfield lies the body of 'Tania', the beautiful girl guerrilla who died with nine others on 31 August after being treacherously led into an ambush in the Río Grande. The inhabitants of Vallegrande had by now become accustomed to the comings and goings of the military.

The most excited in the crowd were the children. They were pointing to the horizon and jumping up and down, for children's eyes can see further than those of adults. Within seconds a speck appeared in the sky and it soon materialized into a helicopter, bearing on its landing rails the bodies of two dead soldiers. They were unstrapped and unceremoniously loaded into a lorry and carted into the town. But as the crowd melted away, we stayed behind and photographed the crates of napalm provided by the Brazilian Armed Forces that lay around the periphery of the airfield. And with a telephoto lens we took photos of a man in olive-green uniform with no military insignia who had been identified to us as an agent from the CIA.

Such temerity on the part of foreign journalists—for we were the first to arrive in Vallegrande by 24 hours—was ill-received, and the CIA agent in the company of some Bolivian officers tried to have us thrown out of the town. But we were equipped with sufficient credentials to show that we were bona fide journalists, and after much argument we were allowed to stay. The one and only helicopter then set off again to the fighting zone, some 30 kilometres to the south-west, bearing with it the figure of Colonel Zenteno. Shortly after one o'clock in the afternoon, it returned with a triumphant colonel, barely able to suppress an enormous grin. Che was dead, he announced. He had seen the body, and there was no room for doubt. Colonel Zenteno is an honest man, not accustomed to revealing more than is absolutely necessary, and there seemed no reason to disbelieve him. We rushed to the tiny telegraph office and thrust our dispatches to the outside world into the hands of a startled and unbelieving clerk. None of us had much confidence that they would ever arrive at their destination.

Four hours later, at exactly five o'clock, the helicopter came back once more, bearing this time a single small body strapped to the outside rail.

But instead of landing close to where we were standing, as it had done on previous occasions, it came to a halt out in the middle of the airfield, far from the eyes of prying journalists. We were forbidden to break through the cordon of determined soldiers. But very speedily the distant corpse was loaded into a closed Chevrolet van, which began a hectic run up the airfield and away. We leapt into our jeep, which was standing near, and our enterprising driver followed close. After about a kilometre the Chevrolet turned sharply into the grounds of a tiny hospital, and although the soldiers tried to shut the gates before we could get through, we were close enough behind to prevent them from doing so.

The Chevrolet drove up a steep slope, and then reversed towards a small colour-washed hut with a bamboo roof and one side open to the sky. We leapt out of the jeep and reached the back doors of the van before they had opened. When they were eventually thrown open, the CIA agent leapt out, yelling unappropriately in English, 'All right, let's get the hell out of here.' Poor man, he was hardly to know that there were two British journalists standing on either side of the door.

Inside the van, on a stretcher, lay the body of Che Guevara. From the first moment I had no doubt that it was he. I had seen him once before almost exactly four years previously in Havana, and he was not a person one would forget easily. Since then, my personal memory of him had doubtless become mingled with the frequent photographs in the press, and I must confess that I had forgotten the blackness of his scanty beard. He seemed smaller, too, and thinner than I had remembered. But months in the jungle had clearly taken their toll. In spite of these lingering questions in my mind there could be no real doubt that this was Guevara. When they carried the body out, and propped it up on a makeshift table in the hut that served as a laundry in less troubled times, I knew for certain that Guevara was dead.

The shape of the beard, the design of the face, and the rich flowing hair were unmistakable. He was wearing olive-green battledress and a jacket with a zippered front. On his feet were faded green socks and a pair of apparently home-made moccasins. Since he was fully dressed, it was difficult to see where he had been wounded. He had two obvious holes in the bottom of his neck, and later, when they were cleaning his body, I saw another wound in his stomach. I do not doubt that he had wounds in his legs and near his heart, but I did not see them.

The doctors were probing the wounds in his neck and my first reaction was to assume that they were searching for the bullet, but in fact they were merely preparing to put in the tube that would conduct the formalin into his body to preserve it. One of the doctors began cleaning the dead guerrilla's hands, which were covered with blood. But otherwise there was nothing repellent about the body. He looked astonishingly alive. His eyes were open and bright, and when they took his arm out of his jacket, they did so without difficulty. I do not believe that he had been dead for very many hours, and at the time I did not believe that he had been killed after his capture. We all assumed that he had died of his wounds and lack of medical attention sometime in the early hours of Monday morning.

The humans around the body were more repellent than the dead: a nun who could not help smiling and sometimes laughed aloud; officers who came with their expensive cameras to record the scene; and of course the agent from the CIA. He seemed to be in charge of the whole operation and looked furious whenever anyone pointed a camera in his direction. 'Where do you come from?' we asked him in English, jokingly adding, 'From Cuba? From Puerto Rico?' But he was not amused, and curtly replied in English, 'From nowhere.' Later we asked him again, but this time he replied in Spanish. '¿Que dice?' he said and pretended not to understand. He was a short stocky man in his middle thirties, with sunken piggy eyes and little hair. It was difficult to tell whether he was a North American or a Cuban exile, for he spoke English and Spanish with equal facility and without a trace of an accent. Subsequently I discovered that his name was Eddie González. He had been a night-club owner in Havana before the Cuban Revolution.

Long before the death of Che Guevara, the capture and subsequent trial of the French Marxist philosopher, Régis Debray, in the small south-eastern Bolivian oil town of Camiri, had given enormous publicity to the guerrillas operating in that part of the country. As a result we probably know more about them than about any other guerrilla band on the continent. But in general, although Latin America is often regarded as a revolutionary continent, little is known about the revolutionaries who, inspired by the Cuban example, have been fighting in the mountains of half a dozen countries for almost a decade.

We know more about what happens elsewhere. In parts of Asia guerrilla warfare has been an almost continuous phenomenon since the Japanese first spread beyond their islands. In southern Africa the fierce internal struggle by the black majority against their white oppressors is still in its infancy, but the pattern of the future has already been etched out in battle. Even in Europe, when the Nazi menace made it necessary, the most improbable people took to the hills. Armed resistance to tyranny, whether under foreign or indigenous guise, is part of our global human heritage.

Latin America is no exception. Guerrillas, it is true, were not really central to the defeat of imperial Spain in the nineteenth century, and until recently internal violence was largely confined to traditional class conflicts—the shooting of strikers, peasants and miners—and the slaughter of the Indian population. Contrary to the generally accepted belief, deliberate political violence has played a comparatively minor role in Latin America. World wars initiated in Europe have been more prodigal of human life than the frequent *coups d'état* for which Latin America is renowned.

Nevertheless, 'Our America', as Fidel Castro called it in the First Declaration of Havana in 1960, 'the America that Bolívar, Hidalgo, Juárez, San Martín, O'Higgins, Tiradentes, Sucre and Martí wished to see free', has had its share of revolutionary heroes. And not all in the nineteenth century either. Zapata in Mexico and Sandino[1] in Nicaragua maintained and reinforced a tradition of rebellion that nourishes the revolutionaries of today—a tradition to be found in what Fidel describes as:

> The genuine voice of the people: a voice that breaks forth from
> the depths of coal and tin mines, from factories and sugar mills,
> from feudal lands where rotos, cholos, gauchos, jíbaros, the heirs
> of Zapata and Sandino, take up the arms of liberty; a voice heard
> in poets and novelists, in students, in women and children, in
> the old and helpless.

The richness of his historical tradition, inflated by such splendid
rhetoric is not equalled anywhere else in the world.

At a liberal estimate, the world has seen five genuine revolutions
in the last 200 years: in France, Russia, Vietnam, China and Cuba. And
so the question arises, what do revolutionaries—men with a mentality
capable of encompassing profound and significant changes—do
between whiles? The answer obviously is that they spend the time
organizing revolutions that fail. Although these revolutions fail, a cor-
pus of folk myth is made out of them which serves to nourish a revolutionary tradition that may eventually triumph.

In the aftermath of the successful Cuban Revolution, Latin
America, like much of the rest of the Third World, has been moving
through a profoundly counter-revolutionary phase. With Cuba isolated and blockaded, the United States has felt free to work its will on the
rest of the continent. Wherever independent-minded governments
have raised their heads, the United States has been there ready, with
the most suitable type of chopper always at hand. Through an all-
embracing aid system that not only trains the Latin American soldier
but also recommends what textbooks his child shall read—thus effectively governing the cultural environment in which the bulk of the lit-
erate population must live—the United States controls Latin America
as absolutely as any previous metropolitan power in its relations with its
empire. In this situation it is a matter for rejoicing that there are in some
countries some people in rebellion, even if for the most part they are
organizing revolutions that fail.

When I first began thinking about this book, the only guide in
English to the subject was an article in the *New Left Review*[2] entitled
'Latin America: The Long March' by a then unknown Frenchman
called Régis Debray. From his detailed and first-hand knowledge of
the various revolutionary movements in Latin America, it seemed that

Debray had it in him to produce the kind of book I had in mind—a book that would collect together the pitifully inadequate material available, for the purpose of enlightening a wider and uncommitted audience as to the nature of Latin America's guerrilla movements, their programmes, personalities and the actions in which they had been involved.

However, it was clear from Régis Debray's next major effort in this field, 'Revolución en la Revolución?' ['Revolution in the Revolution?' *Casa de las Américas* (Cuadernos series)], published in January 1967 in Havana, that he felt his prime concern to be that of a philosopher and thinker, communicating his ideas to fellow revolutionaries. They, of course, would know exactly what he was talking about. He felt no need to pad the book out with unnecessary historical material. But, as I wrote in a review of the book when it appeared in an English edition later that year, 'such is our ignorance of Latin America, the Englishmen in a position to query the factual basis upon which his theories are erected can be counted on the fingers of one hand'. This book, then, is designed to help remedy that ignorance.

It is in no sense a complete or definitive history of the guerrilla movements that have sprung up in Latin America in the aftermath of Fidel Castro's revolution in Cuba. Such a task is probably at this stage beyond the resources of any single researcher. Documentary material, which often began life only in mimeographed form, is hard to come by. Crucial participants are often dead, in hiding, or unavailable in the hills.

Yet a large research team, financed inevitably by an American foundation, would have little success either. Academic research into the social sciences is regarded, quite rightly, with the greatest suspicion by the Left in Latin America. Too often its purposes are political rather than purely academic. Consequently anyone who travelled around the continent making a great song and dance about investigating guerrilla movements would soon find the most useful doors were closed to him. Even a bearded English radical can run into unsuspected obstacles. As the ex-President of Bolivia, Dr Paz Estenssoro, explained to me on one occasion, 'I've always been told to be careful of bearded men. Half of them are Castroites, and the other half are employed by the CIA.'[3]

Nevertheless, a beginning has to be made. As F. W. Deakin writes in the preface to his monumental study of the fall of Italian Fascism:

> The study of contemporary history is fraught with the temptation of uttering premature personal judgments, and with the snare of the uncritical assembly of excessive material. In spite of the uneven wealth of written sources, much has been destroyed by chance of war, and perhaps more buried by the death of leading witnesses or withheld by the living. In spite of such hazards, which are the lot of the historian, it seems that the prime and humble duty of the student of contemporary history is to establish the elementary record before it is dissipated.[4]

So this book is by way of being an English audience's introduction to a subject that absorbs the interest of a large percentage of the politically aware in Latin America, and creates headaches of varying kinds for the denizens of the Pentagon and the State Department. The information gathered together here comes from a variety of sources, mostly from the pages of obscure left-wing periodicals, from newspapers, occasionally from people and books. There are three publications in Spanish that deserve to be singled out as being especially useful: *Marcha*, published fortnightly in Montevideo; *Punto Final* published fortnightly in Santiago; and *Sucesos*, published in Mexico City.[5] All three are exceptionally good magazines by any standard, besides being broadly speaking pro-Cuba and carrying a certain amount of material about guerrilla movements. Since it first appeared in 1967, the Cuban magazine *Pensamiento Crítico* has proved indispensable.

In addition, any foreign student of contemporary Latin America owes an enormous debt to *Le Monde* and its infatigable correspondent Marcel Niedergang. *Partisans*, the magazine of François Maspéro's publishing house, is also very useful. In English there is virtually nothing, apart from the publication in translation of Régis Debray in the *New Left Review*, and the regular, if rather tendentious, articles from the guerrilla front published in Huberman and Sweezy's *Monthly Review*. *Ramparts* has recently begun to take a more eager, if somewhat untutored, interest in the subject.

When Castro was first successful, many people believed that Latin America was about to enter upon a period of revolutionary ferment. From the beginning of the presidency of John Kennedy, the United States began to take enormous interest in examining the cause of social unrest, and in devising methods of combating the threat of guerrilla warfare. But in spite of this widespread belief in the imminence of revolution, the fact remains that since 1959 only five countries in Latin America have produced guerrilla movements of any significance: Venezuela, Guatemala, Colombia, Peru and Bolivia.

Only in the first three countries have these groups managed to survive. In Peru the guerrilla outbreak of 1965, though well-planned, was crushed within six months. And had it not been for the presence of Che Guevara and Régis Debray, the disastrous Bolivian *foco* of 1967, which lasted less than a year, would have been ignored by the world's press in the same way that comparable abortive uprisings in Paraguay,[6] Ecuador[7] and Argentina[8] were neglected.

I have not chosen to include these last three in this study, partly because the inadequacy of the material available makes it impossible to draw any worthwhile conclusions, and partly because they were each effectively crushed by the armed forces while they were in the process of moving from the stage of clandestinity. I have also omitted the chiefly urban-based movements in the Dominican Republic,[9] and the Peasant Leagues of Brazil,[10] partly out of a desire to restrict the length of the book (both, in any case, have been more widely publicized and studied than the movements dealt with here), and partly because I felt that neither completely fulfilled my concept of what a guerrilla movement is. Such a movement, according to my narrow and rather ponderous definition, is a political organization that seeks by means of armed warfare in the countryside to change the political and social structure of a country. The assumption of supreme power by the organization concerned may come before, after or during the achievement of this objective.

In his book on guerrilla warfare, Che Guevara wrote that, 'in the conditions that prevail, at least in Latin America and in almost all countries with deficient economic development, it is the countryside that offers ideal conditions for the fight'.[11] But this does not mean that all peasant

movements must be classified as guerrilla uprisings. Many such movements—perhaps most—have a vision of what they are fighting for that is
strictly limited to their village, their valley or their region.[12] It is doubtful in my view, though I have included it here to give the background to
a later guerrilla outbreak, whether Hugo Blanco's efforts to organize the
peasants in the Peruvian valley of La Convención in the early 1960s can
be correctly classified as a guerrilla movement.[13]

And although I have dealt at some length with the situation in
Colombia prior to 1964 when the army launched its major attack
against the Communist 'independent republic' of Marquetalia, my
own feeling is that the Colombian *violencia* should be categorized
more as a civil war than as a war involving politically motivated movements of the kind I have tried to define.[14] (One can hardly ignore the
period of the *violencia* when Liberal and Conservative peasant guerrillas tore each other, rather than their landlords, to pieces—at a cost of
between 200,000 and 300,000 lives.)

I have adopted this narrow definition largely in order to counter-
act the impression left by the writings of Régis Debray and others
(including Guevara himself) to the effect that, with armed revolutionary groups springing up all over the continent in the wake of Fidel
Castro's victory in Cuba, one can refer to 'the essential unity of the
Latin American revolution'. Debray, for example, having happily gathered together all signs of insurrectional activity throughout Latin
America, draws all kinds of continent-wide conclusions from this
scanty evidence. First, when writing in 1964, he referred to 'the ordeal
of that immense, scattered "1905" which Latin America has undergone since the victory of the Cuban Revolution'.[15] Then, in a second
essay in 1965, he concluded that since the Venezuelan revolutionaries
had turned to the countryside after their failures in the cities, so the
rest of Latin America must continue along this historically ordained
path.[16] (The Venezuelans, he suggested, had followed the pattern laid
down by Mao Zedong who, in 1927, after bloody battles in Canton and
Shanghai, took his followers on the Long March through the countryside that led to eventual victory.)

Unfortunately, though I have the greatest admiration and respect
for Régis Debray as a committed revolutionary philosopher, I cannot

but conclude from my own researches that his writings are littered with numerous errors of fact and that consequently his theories may need to be substantially modified. You cannot lump together peasant rebellions, officers' revolts, strikes by miners and student riots, and conclude that they are all part of the same phenomenon and are all fighting for the same objective, especially since the ideology motivating the guerrilla groups has been, on occasion, Communism of the Soviet or Chinese variety, Castroism, Trotskyism or just plain nationalism. The historical experience of each Latin American country has been so different—from the attitude of the Communist parties to the nature of the repression—that few generalizations about the continent can ever be sufficiently valid to provide the basis for a viable philosophical theory.

Nevertheless, in spite of the fragmentary nature of the Latin American guerrilla experience since 1959, it is possible to isolate three distinct periods through which it has passed:

1 1959–61. A period of utopian efforts, described by Debray as the 'years of effervescent heroism', in which guerrilla movements were led principally by students, who believed that victory was a matter of months.

2 1962–65. A period in which certain important guerrilla movements were supported, and sometimes controlled, by the orthodox Communist parties.

3 1966–69. The period since the Tricontinental Conference in Havana in January 1966, in the course of which the Communist parties gradually abandoned their guerrilla interests.

When, on 8 January 1959, Fidel Castro marched triumphantly into Havana at the head of a ragged, bearded band of amateur soldiers, it seemed to many sympathizers throughout Latin America that the Latin American Revolution had begun. The Cuban revolutionaries themselves were not slow to proclaim themselves as the precursors of a wider continental upheaval. As Régis Debray wrote in 1965, 'the Cuban Revolution has, from its earliest days, always presented itself as the vanguard detachment of the Latin American Revolution, and the Cuban people and its leaders, after six years of struggle, have abandoned none of their proletarian internationalism.'

From the very beginning, too, there was an emphasis on the fact that, given the similar conditions in all the Latin American countries, the methods used by the guerrillas in Cuba could be successfully repeated elsewhere. The presidential candidate of the Socialist–Communist alliance in Chile, Salvador Allende, wrote in 1960:

> Cuba's fate resembles that of all Latin American countries. They are all under-developed—producers of raw materials and importers of industrial products. In all these countries imperialism has deformed the economy, made big profits and established its political influence. The Cuban Revolution is a national revolution, but it is also a revolution of the whole of Latin America. It has shown the way for the liberation of all our peoples.[17]

The man in Cuba most closely associated with this view that the Island revolution represented but the first step in a historic movement that would eventually and inevitably spread to the mainland was Che Guevara. As an Argentinian caught up in the tangle of Cuban revolutionary nationalism while in Mexico, it was inevitable that his thoughts should not remain limited to the confines of Cuba. As early as 27 January 1959, in a talk to the Nuestro Tiempo association in Havana, he outlined the implications of the Cuban Revolution for the rest of Latin America:

> The example of our revolution for Latin America and the lessons it implies have destroyed all the café theories: we have shown that a small group of resolute men supported by the people and not afraid to die if necessary can take on a disciplined regular army and completely defeat it. That is the basic lesson. There is another, which our brothers in Latin America in economically the same position agriculturally as ourselves should take up, and that is there must be agrarian revolution, and fighting in the countryside and the mountains. The revolution must be taken from there to the cities, and not started in the cities without overall social content.

Although there is no evidence that Castro or Guevara at this early stage had formulated any clearly conceived plan for 'exporting' the revolution, the success of the guerrilla struggle in Cuba certainly helped to trigger off other revolutionary attempts during the rest of 1959, especially in the Caribbean. Castro allowed exiles from several countries to use Cuba as a base, and he made no attempt to disguise where his sympathies lay. Three weeks after taking power, he flew to Caracas in Venezuela and called for the formation of a 'democratic bloc' within the Organization of American States (OAS), and suggested that dictatorial governments should be expelled from it. He singled out the governments of Somoza, Trujillo and Stroessner (in Nicaragua, the Dominican Republic and Paraguay) as being particularly objectionable. Exiles from these countries, he later declared, could count on his aid and sympathy.

The first revolutionary attempt in the wake of the Cuban Revolution occurred, however, not in these countries but on the shores of Panama—the centre, symbolically enough, of United States military activity in Latin America. According to one commentator markedly hostile to Castro, the American journalist Tad Szulc, 'the expedition was armed, equipped, and organized by the Castro régime and led by a Castro army officer. It included more Cubans than Panamanians among the hundred-odd men who landed or tried to land in Panama. The local authorities smashed the "invasion" within a few hours.'[18]

A more objective historian points out that in fact the invaders surrendered on 1 May to a five-man investigating committee appointed by the OAS, insisting that they had done so 'only as the result of an appeal from Castro'.[19] The Panamanian government never accused the Cuban government of complicity in the invasion, and Castro himself condemned it.[20]

A month later there was another attempt to set up a revolutionary beachhead in the Caribbean, this time in Nicaragua. On 1 June, two planeloads of rebels flew into the country from Costa Rica, and the next day the Nicaraguan government alleged to the OAS that yachts full of armed men were on the way to help. By chance there was a clash with the rebels in the territory of Honduras, and the Hondurans allegedly captured a letter from Guevara, then the commander of La Cabana fortress in Havana, urging the Cuban authorities to give 'all forms of co-operation and help' to the Nicaraguan authorities.[21]

Later in June, anti-Trujillo rebels launched an operation in the Dominican Republic. Castro was particularly hostile to Trujillo since he had harboured Batista and other wanted war criminals who had fled from Cuba. Tad Szulc gives the following description:

> Here Castro could use legitimate Dominican exiles who had been trained in Cuba by his Rebel Army officers in guerrilla tactics. His idea had been to drop in the Dominican Republic a guerrilla force to establish itself in the mountains, as he had done in Sierra Maestra, while another group was to land on the northern coast. A planeload of rebels landed at Constanza, while two launches tried to disembark raiders near Puerto Plata. But the scheme failed because the population, terrorized by thirty years of the Trujillo dictatorship, did not rally to the invaders' aid. In fact, peasants helped the Trujillo troops flush out the would-be liberators, and the whole episode ended in a matter of days.[22]

Few of the potential guerrillas got beyond the beachhead. They had copied the Cuban pattern too faithfully, allowing themselves to be picked off as the passengers on the *Granma* had been in December 1956, but without leaving survivors to struggle on to a new Sierra Maestra.

Finally, on 13 August 1959, there was a report that 30 men had invaded Haiti. President Duvalier's secretary told reporters that the leader of the invasion was an Algerian who had served in Castro's revolutionary army. The force allegedly consisted entirely of Cubans, and the operation had been financed by a former Haitian senator, Louis Déjoie—an arch-enemy of Duvalier—with the full support of Che Guevara.[23] It was no more successful than any of the other previous uprisings in the Caribbean that year.

In Caracas in January, Fidel had specifically attacked the regimes in Nicaragua, the Dominican Republic and Paraguay. But it was not until the end of the year, in November, that a group of 80 guerrillas crossed from Brazil into northern Paraguay. They were all picked up within a week, though a few managed to escape into Argentina. There was no evidence of Cuban involvement.

These early movements believed fundamentally that it was enough just to copy the more obvious characteristics of the Cuban example. In two short years, Castro and his followers had outmanoeuvred and finally defeated the professional army of Fulgencio Batista, an army trained and assisted by a military mission from the United States. The post-Cuban guerrillas expected that their mere existence would topple their governments in similar fashion, as the Israelites had once overthrown the walls of Jericho with a few blasts of the trumpet.

In spite of these early setbacks, the bulk of the guerrilla movements continued to believe that the Cuban Revolution had sparked off the 'second independence' of Latin America and indicated the way in which this new independence could be won. Although this is an article of faith with the guerrillas, it is bolstered by a not unimpressive series of arguments, most of which were laid out by Che Guevara himself in an article entitled 'Cuba: Exceptional Case or Vanguard in the Struggle against Colonialism?', published in April 1961 in *Verde Olivo*, the publication of the Cuban Revolutionary Army.[24] In this article Guevara sought to criticize those who have 'affirmed that the form and paths of the Cuban Revolution are a unique product and that the historic transition of the peoples in the other countries of America will be different'.

While recognizing that 'there were exceptional factors giving peculiar characteristics to the Cuban Revolution', Guevara placed the emphasis on the factors 'that are common to all the peoples of America'. Among the exceptions he listed the following: (1) the personality of Fidel Castro, a man to be ranked with 'the greatest figures in the history of Latin America'; (2) the fact that North American imperialism was 'disoriented and could not measure the true depth of the Cuban Revolution'; (3) the fact that the national bourgeoisie 'up to a certain point' showed itself 'favourable to the revolutionary war'; (4) the fact that 'in most parts of Cuba the country people had been proletarianized by the operation of big capitalist, semi-mechanized forms of cultivation and had entered a stage of organization that gave it a stronger class consciousness' (but having admitted this, he points out that the Sierra Maestra was in fact 'inhabited by a class of peasants different in its cultural and social roots from those that dwell in the regions of extensive, semi-mechanized Cuban agriculture').

Guevara then states flatly that in his opinion 'no other factors of exceptionalism exist'. And he goes on to look at what he calls 'the permanent roots of all social phenomena in America'—the *latifundia* system, underdevelopment and 'the hunger of the people'.

Guevara's belief that the Cuban example could be followed elsewhere in the continent has been shared by most observers writing from the United States. American writers, of course, are normally more preoccupied with why Castro 'went communist' than with why the guerrillas were able to defeat Batista's army. Thus when Ernst Halperin writes, 'Yes, the Cuban experience can be repeated elsewhere in Latin America', he is referring to the 'communist' rather than the 'revolutionary' experience.[25] Guevara, on the other hand, was more concerned with the revolution that occurred in January 1959 than with what has been called the 'second' revolution in 1960 or thereabouts when Cuba became closely associated with the Soviet Union.[26]

It is important to note, however, that Guevara's belief in the 'unexceptionalism' of Cuba is not shared by everyone, especially by academics less heavily engaged in the cold war than those in the United States. Two English writers, Robin Blackburn and Professor Hugh Thomas, by no means hostile to the Cuban Revolution, have, by studying it in its specific historical context, isolated further unique characteristics. Robin Blackburn, for example, rightly points out that 'Cuba is strikingly and immediately set apart from the rest of Latin America by its late independence'.[27] He also suggests that in the degree of violence 'the wars for independence in Cuba were clearly qualitatively distinct from the Latin American revolts of the early nineteenth century'.[28]

He also has some interesting observations about the Cuban aristocracy and the sugar industry—Cuba's basic crop. He reveals that the foreign companies in Cuba survived the 1929 slump far more successfully than the Cuban ones. Consequently, by the beginning of the 1930s the *per capita* value of the United States' stake in the Cuban economy was 'seven times as great as for the continent as a whole. It had reached dimensions where it no longer supported and secured the local landowning class, as it did everywhere else in Latin America; it had largely replaced this class.' Nor was the landowning aristocracy the exception. So tied up with foreign interests were the Cuban capitalists that Blackburn also concludes that 'the Cuban capitalist class could not properly be described as a "national" bourgeoisie'. Hugh Thomas, who has arrived independently at many of Blackburn's conclusions, points out that by the time of Castro's revolt, such traditional institutions as the army, the bureaucracy and the Church 'had either withered away or had not properly developed Cuban roots at all'. His conclusion is that 'most of the forces traditionally a restraint on revolution had in Cuba collapsed *before* Castro rose against Batista'.[29]

In these circumstances it may well be that the nature of the war against Batista, as Blackburn indicates, is best suggested in a remark of Engels, in a letter written to Vera Zasulich in 1885. In it he speaks of 'exceptional cases where it is possible for a handful of people to *make* a revolution, i.e. with one little push to cause a whole system . . . to come crashing down and thus by an action in itself insignificant to release explosive forces that afterwards become uncontrollable'. This is one of the chief attractions of the Cuban Revolution. Arthur Schlesinger Jr describes the delight of the undergraduates at Harvard when Castro came to address them in the spring of 1959: 'They saw in him, I think, the hipster who in the era of the Organization Man had joyfully defied the system, summoned a dozen friends and overturned a government of wicked old men.'[30]

The arguments provided by Robin Blackburn and Hugh Thomas are not entirely conclusive in proving the exceptionalism of Cuba. Detailed research might well reveal comparable, though not identical, structural weaknesses in other countries of Latin America. Hugh Thomas himself agrees that although 'the origins of the Cuban Revolution must be sought in the state of the Cuban sugar industry', nevertheless, 'similar conditions may exist in other countries of Latin America, in respect to other crops'.[31] But it is probably right to conclude, as guerrilla experience elsewhere has shown—and the guerrillas themselves admit it—that something more than the 'one little push' mentioned by Engels is needed if the Cuban success is to be repeated elsewhere. The nature of the 'pushes' that have been tried so far are described in this book.

Although from 1962 onwards a number of guerrilla movements were supported by the local Communist party, notably in Venezuela,

Guatemala and Colombia,[32] it is as well to emphasize at the outset that guerrillas in Latin America have had remarkably little help from the orthodox Communist parties. In fact no Latin American Communist party has ever regarded a guerrilla movement as an essential item in the struggle to secure power, or as the only one. It has never suggested that a guerrilla movement should be set up. Invariably it has sought to utilize or control one that already exists. In addition, not a single Latin American Communist party, with the exception of the Venezuelan one, has ever admitted that 'a revolutionary situation' exists in their country. Since they use the extremely narrow Leninist definition—which certainly would not have fitted the Cuban case—there is very little prospect that they will.[33]

The same is true of Peking. In spite of their theoretical enthusiasm for the armed struggle, the pro-Chinese organizations in the continent have by and large adopted a similar passive attitude. But while the pro-Chinese groups have rejected the electoral road, the pro-Russian parties have never lost an opportunity—except when banned from participating in elections—of supporting a Centre-Left candidate, however disastrous the result. In 1958–59 the Venezuela Communists were supporting the coalition government of Rómulo Betancourt; yet by the middle of Betancourt's term of office they were all in prison. In Peru, although Fernando Belaúnde Terry was elected President in 1963 with Communist support, he savagely turned against them on numerous subsequent occasions to prove to the army that he was not their dupe. In Guatemala, the election in 1966 of the civilian President Mario Montenegro—with support from the Communists—brought in its trail an unparalleled increase in right-wing violence. In Colombia, the Movimiento Revolucionario Liberal (Liberal Revolutionary Movement, MRL), led by Alfonso López Michelsen and supported by the Communists, was always deeply committed to the electoral process. It neither supported the guerrillas, nor even the campaign of Father Camilo Torres for electoral abstention.

This is not the place for a sustained critique of the way in which, as the American writer Ernst Halperin puts it, the Communist parties have managed 'to carve out for themselves a modest niche in the Latin

American political establishment'. But it is difficult to dissent from Halperin's conclusions that these parties consist of

> small, urban-based groups of intellectuals with some student backing and a minimal working-class following, led by professional politicians who hire out their services, not for money but for small political favours such as the permission to hold closed meetings, to publish a news-sheet or literary journal and to occupy a few trade union posts. These men are not venal. Their corruption is of a more insidious kind. They can be bought, not by money, but simply by providing the minimal conditions needed to allow them and their followers to maintain the illusion of being the 'vanguard' destined to lead the proletariat to victory in its struggle for the liberation of mankind.[34]

Nevertheless there have been occasions—notably in the three or four years following 1962—when the orthodox Communist parties have supported the armed struggle as a useful political tactic. Although it is fashionable to believe that the Latin American Communist parties take their orders from Moscow, the experience of each country has been so different that it is difficult to draw any hard and fast conclusions about a Communist 'line' in Latin America. Strictly speaking, for example, the Venezuelan Communist party did not decide to give priority to the legal struggle until April 1965. The Colombian Communist party still favoured the armed struggle in January 1966, and the Guatemalan Communists did not part company from the guerrillas until January 1968. Throughout the period under consideration in this book, however, the orthodox Communist parties have in fact displayed a marked reluctance to consider the armed struggle as an essential component in the revolutionary process—a reluctance which predates the Cuban Revolution.

The basic problem for the Communists in the early 1960s was that they were in danger of being outstripped by three distinct elements: (1) the pro-Peking extremists within their own ranks; (2) the splinter organizations that split off from failed reformist parties like Acción Democrática of Venezuela and the Alianza Popular Revolucianaria Americana (American Popular Revolutionary Alliance, APRA) party of

Peru; and (3) the military. Guerrilla movements in Latin America have in fact usually had their origins either in army revolts or in these splinter parties, which have political programmes to the left of the Communists. On no occasion have they resulted from a conscious decision of the orthodox Communist party, although they have often been joined or led by individual Communists.[35]

The Venezuelan guerrillas that began early in 1962 were organized largely by the Movimiento de Izquierda Revolucionaria (Revolutionary Left Movement, MIR), which had split off from Acción Democrática in 1960. The Peruvian guerrillas that began in the middle of 1965 were organized entirely by the MIR, which broke away from APRA in 1959. (The Peruvian MIR was openly hostile to the Communist party.) In Colombia, too, the Ejército de Liberación Nacional (National Liberation Army, ELN), which began operating in 1965, owed more to dissident elements from the old Gaitanist wing of the Liberal party than to the Communist party.

Although the Venezuelan guerrillas began in the early months of 1965, the military who rebelled at Carúpano and Puerto Cabello in May and June brought an important influx of army officers into the guerrilla ranks before the Fuerzas Armadas de Liberación Nacional (Armed Forces of National Liberation, FALN) was formally constituted in February 1963. Another guerrilla movement with military origins was that of Guatemala, where a revolt on 13 November 1960—in protest against the presence of a CIA training base that was preparing Cuban exiles for the Bay of Pigs invasion—included two officers, Marco Antonio Yon Sosa and Luís Turcios Lima, who in 1962 were to launch the guerrilla Movimiento Revolucionario 13 de Noviembre (Revolutionary Movement of 13 November, MR13).

Anxious that these various movements should not slip out of their control, the Communists inevitably took an interest in them. In particular, they made great efforts both in Venezuela and in Guatemala not to antagonize the army. They had no desire, after all, to repeat their Cuban experience, where Castro's 26 July Movement had achieved power independently of the Communists—with disastrous repercussions on the Cuban Communist party. It was not until the middle of 1958 that a representative of the party, Carlos Rafael

Rodríguez, joined Castro in the Sierra Maestra, and ever since the Revolution the 'old guard' Communists have been fighting a losing battle to retain their influence.

In Venezuela, for example, in 1962—the year in which the Communist party officially decided in favour of the armed struggle—there did seem a definite possibility that the revolutionary groups might prove victorious. A Venezuelan Communist, writing in the *World Marxist Review* in September 1967,[36] states quite baldly that 'in 1962, a revolutionary situation matured in the country'. He hastily qualified this by adding that in fact this did not develop into a victorious revolution. The Central Committee admitted its mistake in 1966. They had 'assessed as a "revolutionary war for national liberation" a movement which had not yet acquired such a character and which was directed chiefly at overthrowing the government'.

By the beginning of 1962, Betancourt's all-party coalition had completely collapsed. The *MIRista* split in 1960 had deprived Acción Democrática of 14 deputies, and a further 26 deputies led by Ramón Jiménez split away in 1962, depriving Betancourt of this parliamentary majority. The three Cabinet Ministers of the Unión Republicana Democrática (Democratic Republic Union, URD) had already abandoned Betancourt in 1960 in protest against Venezuelan participation in the OAS condemnation of Cuba at San José. In 1962, one of their most important leaders, Fabricio Ojeda, who had led the struggle against Pérez Jiménez from within Caracas itself, resigned from parliament and joined the guerrillas. In addition, Betancourt, a passionate anti-Communist, played into the hands of the activist elements within the Communist party by suspending the operations of both the party itself and of the MIR. In these circumstances, effectively deprived of liberty to operate legally, it was not surprising that in December 1962 the Fourth Plenum of the Venezuelan Communist party came out officially in favour of the armed struggle. It is, incidentally, curious that whereas the great betrayal by APRA of the anti-imperialist cause which it was supposed to represent has now been fully recognized by historians, Acción Democrática on the whole has escaped such harsh judgement. Yet Betancourt's betrayal of the popular movement that overthrew Pérez Jiménez, which deprived him within two years of the support of half his party, is at least comparable with that of Haya de la Torre.

The Venezuelan party's decision to support the guerrillas was also made, one may surmise, because among its ranks, as among those of all the Latin American Communist parties at that time, there were a significant number of activists favourable to the armed struggle who were eventually to split away and join separate pro-Peking organizations. The Chinese decision to split the world Communist parties was taken at the end of 1963—being announced in a speech by Chu Yang entitled 'Everything Tends to Divide into Two', published in the *People's Daily*, 27 December 1963.

Just how large were these pro-Peking groups? According to the few figures available, the founding conference of the pro-Peking Peruvian Communist party, in January 1964—the first to be formed in Latin America—was convened by *a majority* of the Central Committee members of the old Moscow party and representatives from 13 out of 17 regional committees.[37] The conference was also attended by observers from the Communist Youth League. In Bolivia, the party split in 1965. Pro-Soviet sources have admitted that nine of the 44 members of the Central Committee were involved in the secession, and that the secessionists had considerable strength in three departments of the country. The new group was able to set up a parallel organization in six of the 14 departments where the pro-Russian party had regional committees. In Paraguay, the Communist party, which survived in exile with its headquarters and most of its members in Argentina, split in 1965 as well. It appears that the *majority* of the party leadership, including the Secretary-General, went over to join the pro-Chinese organization. No figures exist to assess the dimensions of the splits in other countries, but it is reasonable to assume that they were of comparable size.

By January 1968 the Chinese were able to announce that 'Marxist–Leninist parties and organizations' with Maoist orientation had been established in 'more than 10 countries' in Latin America. But in practice they were noticeably cautious in according recognition to these groups. Only those of Brazil, Peru and Colombia were officially recognized as parties by Peking. The split with the Soviet Union did not therefore involve an increase in revolutionary activity on the part of the pro-Chinese. Their revolutionary aims had been largely achieved by the break with the Russians.

In fact the chief results of the split, which involved the withdrawal of the more militant members from the pro-Moscow parties, were a swing to the Right on the part of the orthodox Communist parties in favour of legality, and the abandonment of the armed struggle. Once the *Pekinistas* had split away they were no longer an internal menace to the Communist party: their work of disruption had been done and they became what they are today, essentially powerless and irrelevant, more of a menace to the guerrillas and to the pro-Cuban movements in the continent than to the orthodox Communist parties. The pro-Peking groups, it is worth adding, have been consistently hostile to the Cuban line ever since the end of 1964. Not only did they oppose the guerrilla movements in Colombia, Peru and Bolivia, but at the Plenum of the pro-Chinese Albanian Communist party in 1967, it appears that a Colombian delegate actually called for an anti-Castro front to be created in Latin America.[38] It should be noted in this context that to this day the Communist party of the People's Republic of China has neither acknowledged nor mourned the death of Comandante Guevara.

With the *Pekinistas* outside, and effectively neutralized, the only important opposition to the orthodox Communist leadership as the fount of revolutionary wisdom came from the guerrillas themselves, some of whom were *MIRistas* or former army officers, while others were actually members of the Communist party's Central Committee—as in Venezuela, Colombia, Guatemala and Bolivia. Inevitably and crucially, the argument arose as to whether the leadership of the guerrilla group should be in the town or in the mountains—an argument which has been discussed at length in the writings of Régis Debray. Had the Communist parties been prepared to support the armed struggle with more vigour, this problem might never have been posed in such an acute form.

The fact remains, however, that the Communist party of Venezuela, at its Seventh Plenum in April 1965, decided to give priority to the legal struggle. The other parties in the continent followed suit during the course of the next three years. In December 1965, as a consequence of the Venezuelan party's attitude, two of the most important guerrilla leaders, Douglas Bravo of the Communist party and Fabricio Ojeda—formerly of the URD—set up a political directorate for the guerrillas in the countryside, with themselves in control. In effect they had cut their links with the Communist party, and Bravo was formally suspended from the Central Committee in May 1966.

Why the Venezuelan Communist party chose the particular moment of April 1965 to make their decision against the armed struggle is not altogether clear. The possible reasons for the change in policy include, firstly, a split in the Venezuelan MIR, hitherto a staunch supporter of guerrilla action, both in the mountains and in the towns. Its most important member, Domingo Alberto Rangel, who had been in prison since 1963, came out in favour of abandoning the armed struggle during the course of the following year. This meant that the Communists no longer had to face serious opposition from a non-Communist leftist group. Secondly, in December 1964, the new Venezuelan President, Raúl Leoni, began a new policy of 'rehabilitating' the Communists, and allowing them to undertake their normal activity on condition that they put a stop to using violent methods. The Communists, who had been banned from participating in the elections of December 1963, were eager to be allowed to return to legality. It is worth adding that throughout the brief years in which the Venezuelan Communists supported the armed struggle, their most important leaders were in prison.

The Colombian party is somewhat exceptional in that it favoured the armed struggle well on into 1967. This arises from the peculiar circumstances associated with the 'Independent Republic' of Marquetalia. The Communist party was committed to the defence of Marquetalia, because of all the peasant leaders thrown up by the *violencia*, its commander, Manuel Marulanda, known as Tiro Fijo, was their man: he was a member of the party's Central Committee. Consequently, when the army moved to destroy Marquetalia in 1964, and subsequently Marulanda announced his intention of continuing the fight, the Communist party was virtually obliged to support him.

In January in the following year, the Cuban-inspired ELN went into action and, surviving the initial period, had a number of successes—including the important psychological victory of enticing Father Camilo Torres to join their ranks at the end of 1965.

Afraid that the ELN would prosper and yet be out of their control, the Communist party formally turned Marulanda's peasants into the Fuerzas Armadas Rebeldes de Colombia (Revolutionary Armed Forces of Colombia, FARC), early in 1966. The decision to do this was taken at the 10th Congress of the Colombian Communist party in January 1966. This congress, where the attendance was apparently 48 per cent peasant, 'centralized the leadership of armed action in the rural localities . . . to meet the requirements of the revolutionary process in our country'. At least four of the guerrilla leaders were members of the Central Committee. This remarkable decision seems to have been made as a concession to the belief of the ELN that the leadership should be exclusively in the mountains. Of course, the political decisions involving the FARC continued to be taken in the city, but the Colombian Communist party was certainly more flexible than its Bolivian counterpart, which refused to countenance a politico-military command that would be out of the direct control of the Communist party in La Paz. So, too, was the Guatemalan Communist party, which did not abandon the armed struggle until 1968.

The Peruvian party, on the other hand, has never shown any interest in guerrillas at all. This is partly explained by the fact that the potential guerrilla movement of Hugo Blanco was inspired by Trotskyism, and the later efforts of Luís de la Puente were supported by the Peruvian MIR, which had inherited some of the anti-Communist characteristics of APRA.

The very different attitudes of the Communist parties in various countries suggest that they were not following any master plan outlined in Moscow. The Communist Party of the Soviet Union (CPSU) seems to have been reasonably favourably disposed towards supporting guerrilla movements, at least until the end of 1964. In August that year, *Communist*, the theoretical journal of the CPSU, had come out in favour of the armed struggle, and as late as December the Latin American Communist parties, meeting in Havana, had, albeit rather reluctantly, agreed to support the revolutionary fighters of the continent, specifically mentioning Venezuela, Colombia, Guatemala, Honduras, Haiti and Paraguay. By 1965, however, the Russians were

opposing the idea. Why they changed their mind is a subject for speculation. It may have had something to do with the fall of Khrushchev
in November 1964. More probably it had to do with a desire to
improve relations with the United States in view of the ever-widening
split with China.

Guerrilla movements in the third and most recent period, that is
to say, in the years since the Tricontinental Conference in January
1966, have been characterized not just by the absence of Communist
party support, but also by a significant change of programme.

Up till then there had been a general belief that it was possible to follow the Cuban example: this was not just an emphasis on guerrilla warfare, and the possibility of creating revolutionary conditions through the
guerrilla *foco*, but also a desire not to antagonize the bourgeoisie. The
middle classes were regarded as a potentially revolutionary force as they
appeared to have been in Cuba. Virtually all the guerrilla groups
believed that it was possible to follow the Cuban road in this sense. It was
this that made possible the temporary alliances with the Communists,
who also believed in the virtues of the national bourgeoisie.

The first to rebel against this idea was Yon Sosa in Guatemala. He
came out in December 1964 with the 'First Declaration of the Sierra
de las Minas'—a full-blooded appeal for a Socialist programme and
the abandonment of any alliance with the bourgeoisie. It was written
under the influence of the Trotskyists, and consequently caused a
break with the Communists in March 1965. For more than two years
the guerrilla movement in Guatemala was divided between Trotskyists
and Communists.

The last movement which appears to have believed that it was pos-
sible to secure the support or the neutrality of the bourgeoisie was the
Peruvian MIR, which ended in disaster in the last months of 1965.
Camilo Torres, too, seems to have had similar illusions.

But, in December 1965, the break with this position was made
explicit by the action of Douglas Bravo and Fabricio Ojeda in splitting
from the Venezuelan Communist party and setting up a new directorate
in the countryside. One of the first documents issued by this new organization (also called the FALN/Front de Libération Nationale or the
National Liberation Front, FLN) in February 1966, includes this passage:

'Today, for example, it seems that what happened in Cuba is unlikely to be repeated in exactly the same way. Liberation movements cannot count on the factor of surprise nor on the expectant attitudes of former times.

Apart from the fact that imperialism has learnt from its mistakes and is blocking the roads to revolution as much as it can, the national bourgeoisie is also now aware that the end of the Latin American revolutionary road is Socialism; that is to say, everybody knows that the ills which afflict the continent can only be cured by Socialist measures, so that even if we can talk at the beginning of a bourgeois revolution, in fact the move to Socialism cannot be long delayed. Under the circumstances, assertions about the Latin American situation must be made with many reservations. What happened in Brazil—basically—showed that today the bourgeoisie cannot fulfil the revolutionary traditional role assigned to it in the early stages of the movement.[39]

In this situation, it is clearly superficial to think of the Latin American struggle in other terms than those of the so-called 'long war'. To think that the Cuban feat can be copied in Venezuela, is to overlook the particular conditions of the country, to act blindly without any kind of proper analysis of the situation.

By the middle of the 1960s the guerrillas were seeing themselves as part of a Latin American and global struggle against the United States. They believed that unless that struggle was won, there would be no Socialist or nationalist programme in Latin America or anywhere else. Thus these new guerrillas differed from the Communists, not just on tactics (armed struggle) but also on their programme. The Communists talked vaguely about imperialism, but, as Guevara pointed out in his letter to the Tricontinental, 'in speaking of the destruction of imperialism, we must identify its head—which is none other than the United States of America'.

Earlier the guerrillas had talked in strictly nationalist terms: their foreign allies were the Socialist world in general and the new radical Third World countries—Algeria, the Congo and Tanzania. As the struggle grew more intense, they allied themselves only with movements that were actually involved in armed revolution. The only foreign capitals they looked to were Havana, Hanoi and Pyongyang.

The internationalism of the struggle became crucial. The Venezuelan FALN/FLN, in the document already quoted, points out that 'we must return to the old and well-tried principle of striking the enemy in his most sensitive spots and in many places at the same time. These were the tactics which brought success in the struggle against Spain.'

And in his last letter Guevara made the point that the only form of solidarity with Vietnam was to fight at its side: 'it is not a question of wishing the victim success, but of sharing his fate; going with him to death or victory'. Nowhere in his later writings did Guevara suggest that the Cuban road had to be followed. No, today, 'it is the Vietnam road which people should follow, this is the road which America will follow'.

Debray, of course, asked that his readers should look more closely at the Cuban experience. But he did not do this merely in order to support his argument in favour of the armed struggle. Essentially, he sought to prove, firstly, that the guerrillas should create their own vanguard party, as had been done in Cuba, and not rely upon the old Communist party; and secondly, that the emphasis should be put on the destruction of the old armed forces—also an important characteristic of the Cuban Revolution.

There was a belief in the early period—at least until October 1962—that the only problem facing the revolutionary was that of achieving the initial revolution—that of seizing power. After that the revolutionary changes in society would be made under the protection of Soviet power. But after the Cuban missile crisis, which indicated the limits of Soviet interest in Latin America, there was a shift in emphasis to the 'long war', and a tendency to think in terms of creating the type of society through guerrilla struggle that would be able to defend itself against outside attack when the final victory had been won. 'The more time we have to prepare the people now,' the Guatemalan guerrilla leader, César Montes, explained in 1966, 'the less difficult will be the transformation to Socialism later.'

It would seem, in fact, from an examination of later statements by guerrilla leaders and from the writings of Debray, that the new generation of guerrillas were not just advocating guerrilla warfare as the best means of achieving a certain objective widely agreed upon by differing groups. Rather it would seem that the objective itself was not in fact shared by other political organizations of the Left. The guerrillas in fact were talking about an objective that could only be achieved through guerrilla warfare. This attitude, consciously or not, owed much to Franz Fanón, who emphasized the desirability of creating a new type of society through violent, revolutionary struggle. To paraphrase Marshall McLuhan, the method had become the programme.

This last period has also coincided with an increased Cuban interest in Latin American guerrilla movements. Curiously enough, in view of American claims that the Cubans were attempting to subvert the rest of Latin America from the very first months of the Revolution, the United States has produced precious little solid evidence to back up its assertion. The subject has been studiously avoided by American scholars. Although a plethora of books has appeared on Cuba's relations with the Communist world, virtually nothing has been written on Castro's policy towards Latin America. It is interesting to note, too, that although American policy for the past decade has been dedicated to repressing liberation movements in Latin America, not a single serious study of any of these movements has appeared in the United States. The American tax-payer is thus paying for his army to crush movements of which he has virtually no knowledge.

The evidence seems to suggest that during the early years of the Revolution Castro leant over backwards not to give his southern neighbours cause for grievance. He made tremendous propaganda speeches—especially the two Declarations of Havana—prophesying the imminent downfall of the oligarchies at the hands of the dispossessed. In 1960 he suggested that the Andes range could become the Sierra Maestra of South America. Revolutionaries flocked to Havana for inspiration, and doubtless many received money and training. But all this took place within a Caribbean context, where revolutionary groups in exile had for years made plans to return in triumph to their countries. Governments normally turned a blind eye to their activities, hastily disowning any connection with them when the revolutionary attempt ended in failure. Castillo Armas invaded Guatemala from Honduras in 1954; Castro himself invaded Cuba from Mexico in 1956; and the Cuban exiles invaded Cuba in 1961 from Guatemala. Castro did not have help from the Mexican government, but he did get a planeload of arms from Admiral Wolfgang Larrazábal's government in Venezuela.[40]

General Alberto Bayo, the Spanish Republican general who trained Fidel's forces in Mexico, has described what he thought after his first meeting with the Cuban revolutionary:

> The idea seemed impossible. I had had thousands of similar conversations with utopian idealists who dreamt of organizing guerrillas to overthrow Franco, Somoza, Trujillo, Pérez Jiménez, Péron, Carias, Odría, Batista, Stroessner, Rojas Pinilla, and so many others. But all these conversations, once spoken, dissolved in the air like cigarette smoke.[41]

But many, like Fidel, went on to launch their forlorn expeditions, though none achieved this success. When Castro came to power, he could hardly disallow his origins. He could hardly refuse permission for revolutionaries to leave Cuba to attack Somoza in Nicaragua, Trujillo in Santo Domingo or Duvalier in Haiti. Doubtless he turned a blind eye to their activities, but no other government in the area with a claim to popular backing could have done less. When an attack came against Panama—a less dubious regime than that of the three dictators—Castro roundly condemned it.

Cuban support for the Latin American Revolution, therefore, in the early years, was distinctly limited. Castro preferred normal diplomacy. He flew to Caracas in 1959 to thank the Venezuelan people for their help. He flew to the United States to explain his policies. He went to a conference in Buenos Aires. Che Guevara attended the Punta del Este meeting in 1961 that set up the Alliance for Progress. He was notably moderate. He then had interviews with President Frondizi of Argentina and President Quadros of Brazil. The Cubans at that time had no prejudices against getting together with bourgeois regimes.

But as the years went by the United States tightened its blockade of Cuba and, through the resolutions of the OAS, persuaded its Latin

American allies to do likewise. Diplomatic relations and trade relations were broken off. Cuba became increasingly isolated.

It was at this moment that the regime, in 1963–64, appears to have begun to take more seriously the prospect of encouraging revolutionary movements in Latin America. To some within the government it must have seemed that Cuba's survival depended to a large extent on a successful revolution on the mainland. For Cuba, cut off from the continent, was becoming dangerously dependent on the Soviet Union—thousands of miles away. And the nuclear crisis of October 1962 had seemed to indicate that Russian support was of a strictly limited kind.

But even when the Cubans did expand their guerrilla interests, the degree of support was still small. A subcommittee reporting to the United States House of Representatives in 1967 could only find 'four proven instances of direct Cuban support to insurgent groups'.

In November 1963, a cache of several tons of weapons and ammunition, discovered in western Venezuela, was conclusively traced to Cuba.

Large quantities of small arms were provided to Guatemalan insurgents between February and September 1966 by a Cuban-supported ring based in Mexico City and Tapacula on the Mexican–Guatemalan border. The ring has since been broken up by the Mexican authorities.

In July 1966, some 20 to 30 armed insurgents, at least some of whom had received guerrilla training in Cuba, were landed on the Venezuelan coast in a boat probably provided by Cuba.

The . . . May 8 1967, clandestine landing in Venezuela was the first instance in which there was proof of direct Cuban army involvement. Two members of the Cuban armed forces were killed; and two were captured.[42]

And as a study prepared for the United States Senate Committee on Foreign Relations in January 1968 indicates, the extent of Cuba's financial involvement was also strictly limited:

From published sources, it is impossible to give an accurate quantitative summary of Cuban direct and indirect aid to

Latin American insurgents. None will be attempted here. However, two assertions seem in order. One is that in the United States and Latin America the tendency has been to exaggerate the monetary value of Cuban aid. In part, this arises from the unfounded assumption that the Soviets have provided a blank cheque for Cuban subversive activities. Though the Soviets may have given some aid for this purpose, circumstantial evidence suggests that they prefer to disperse funds directly or through agents more amenable to their commands . . .

Castro's monetary contributions have been small. Subversive groups in Venezuela, Guatemala and Colombia have been forced to rely on robbery and kidnapping to raise money. It is not that Castro doesn't wish to give more but, put simply, he can't afford the expense. Castro has made at least three shipments of material to Venezuela, but these represented only a limited shot in the arm for the FALN, which has suffered from lack of resources.

Cuba has probably invested more in training of Latin Americans in Cuba and in propaganda than on other kinds of aid. . . . The Castro government has also sent a few individuals to serve with, train, or lead guerrillas in the field, most notably in Bolivia and Venezuela.[43]

Nevertheless, by the time of the Tricontinental Conference in January 1966, Cuba had definitively committed itself to supporting a continental revolution. The following year, after the 8 May 1967 landing in Venezuela, in which four Cubans were captured, the Cuban Communist party came out with the strongest statement of solidarity and responsibility it had ever made:

They accuse us of helping revolutionary movements. In fact we are lending assistance and we shall continue to do so as often as we are asked, to all movements that are struggling against imperialism in whatever part of the world.[44]

This new-found Cuban enthusiasm for Latin American guerrilla movements began to manifest itself at the very moment when the Russians, and the local Communist parties which depended on them, were beginning to emphasize the virtues of peaceful coexistence and a rapprochement with the United States and its client governments in the southern continent. A vicious debate between Castro and the Venezuelan Communist party led to the exclusion of the Venezuelan Communists from the conference of the Organization of Latin American Solidarity (OLAS) held in Havana in August 1967.

At the Tricontinental, the Chilean Socialist party had suggested the creation of a new, specifically Latin American, organization that would link the revolutionary movements of the continent. This was strongly opposed by the Communist delegates at the conference, and indeed by Castro himself, who was only convinced of the need for such a new organization by the arguments of the Chilean Socialist leader, Salvador Allende. Even so, it took more than 18 months to get this new organization—OLAS—into being.

The OLAS conference, which brought together 27 Communist and revolutionary groups in the continent (with the absence of the Communist parties of Venezuela, Brazil and Argentina, and with no pro-Chinese parties present), was important for its revelation of the by now implacable hostility of the orthodox Communist movement for the revolutionaries who favoured the armed struggle, and also because, with the presence in Havana of the American Negro leader, Stokeley Carmichael, the revolutionary organizations of the Third World were linked for the first time with the radical movement in the United States. For the first time, indeed, it seemed that the anti-imperialist struggle had joined hands with the race war.

Much of the enthusiasm aroused by OLAS was created by the existence of the Bolivian *foco*, which had begun earlier that year. Although the participation of Che Guevara in that struggle was not widely known at the time, he was the absent inspiration of the conference. He was elected the Honorary President of the organization. OLAS in fact was so closely identified with him, that it was difficult for it to survive his death.

In the two years that have passed since that conference and since the death of Guevara, much of the passion has gone out of the debate between Communists and revolutionaries in Latin America. They have gone their separate ways more in sorrow than in anger. But it is a deep and disastrous division, for the guerrillas need the

Communists—for where else will they find their manpower—and the
Communists need the guerrillas—for how else can they maintain
their claim to be revolutionaries?

Notes

1 The most recent book on Sandino is Neil Macaulay, *The Sandino
   Affair*, Quadrangle Books, Chicago, 1967.

2 October–December 1965.

3 One of the charges used against Régis Debray by the pro-Moscow
   faction in the Cuban Communist party, led by Anibal Escalante, was
   not only that he had been expelled from the French Communist
   party, but also that he was employed by the French Intelligence
   Service.

4 F. W. Deakin, *The Brutal Friendship*, Weidenfeld & Nicolson, London,
   1962.

5 *Sucesos* came to an end in 1968. Its editor, Mario Menéndez
   Rodríguez, founded a new, similar magazine called *¿Por Qué?*

6 Guerrilla movements were active briefly in Paraguay in November
   1959, and again early in 1962. A new metalled road from Asunción
   to the Brazilian frontier at Puerto Stroessner has opened up to
   Japanese colonists an area that was formerly suitable for guerrillas.

7 In March 1962 a movement of Ecuadorean students managed to last
   out for two days in the mountains.

8 There was a guerrilla movement in Tucumán in December 1959
   organized by dissident Peronists led by Comandante Uturunco. Little
   is known about it. In 1963–64, the Ejército Guerrillero del Pueblo
   (Guerrilla Army of the Town, EGP), led by Comandante Segundo,
   operated clandestinely in the Salta area. Segundo (Jorge Masetti) was
   a friend of Guevara. Also in his group was a Cuban known as Papi or
   Ricardo who was a member of Guevara's Bolivian expedition and
   killed in July 1967. The EGP was crushed before it went into action.
   Segundo's fate is unknown, thought it is assumed that he is dead. See
   further, Ricardo Rojo, *Mi Amigo el Che*, Editorial Jorge Alvárez,
   Buenos Aires, 1968, pp. 175–93.

9 See Franklin J. Franco, *República Dominicana, Clases, Crisis y
   Commandos*, Casa de la Americas, Havana, 1966.

10 See especially the following: Francisco Julião, *¿Que son las Ligas
   Campesinas?*; Antonio Callado, *Os industriais da Seca e os 'Galileus' de*

Pernambuco, Civilização Brasileira, Rio de Janeiro, 1960; Josué de Castro, *Sete Palmas de Terra e um Caixão*, Editora Brasiliense, São Paulo, 1965; Irving Louis Horowitz, *Revolution in Brazil; Politics and Society in a Developing Country*, E. P. Dutton & Company, New York, 1964, pp. 13–34; Anthony Leeds, 'Brazil and the Myth of Francisco Julião', in Joseph Maier and Richard W. Weatherhead (eds), *Politics of Change in Latin America*, Praeger, New York, 1964, pp. 190–204; Benno Galjart, 'Class and following in Rural Brazil', *America Latina*, NO. 7, July–September 1964; Gerrit Huizer, 'Some Notes on Community Development and Rural Social Research', *America Latina*, NO. 3, July–September 1965.

11 Che Guevara, *La Guerra de Guerrillas*, Department of Instruction of MINFAR (Ministry of the Revolutionary Armed Forces), Havana, 1960; translated by J. P. Morray, *Guerrilla Warfare*, Monthly Review Press, New York, 1961.

12 See Gerrit Huizer, *On Peasant Unrest in Latin America*, a collection of notes for the ILO–CIDA study on the role of peasant organizations in the process of agrarian reform in Latin America countries. CIDA–Panamerican Union, Washington, D.C., June 1967.

13 See Víctor Villanueva, *Hugo Blanco y la Rebelión Campesina*, Editorial Juan Mejía Baca, Lima, 1967.

14 See Germán Guzmán Campos, *La Violencia en Colombia*, Ediciones Tercer Mundo, Bogotá, 1962, and Orlando Fals Borda, *La Subversión en Colombia*, Ediciones Tercer Mundo y Departamento de Sociología, Universidad Nacional, Bogotá, 1967.

15 Régis Debray, 'Le Castrisme: la longue marche de l'Amérique Latine', *Les Temps Modernes*, Paris, NO. 224, January 1965.

16 Régis Debray, 'América Latina: algunos problemas de estrategia revolucionaria', *Casa de las Américas*, Havana, NO. 31, July–August 1965.

17 Preface to J. Tabares del Real, *La Revolución Cubana* (1960), quoted in Boris Goldenberg, *The Cuban Revolution and Latin America*, Allen & Unwin, London, 1965, p. 311.

18 Tad Szulc, 'Exporting the Cuban Revolution', in John Plank (ed.), *Cuba and the United States*, Brookings Institution, Washington D.C., 1967, p. 79.

19 Geoffrey Warner, 'Latin America', in Geoffrey Barraclough (ed.), *Survey of International Affairs 1959–1960*, Oxford University Press, Oxford, 1964, p. 471.

20 *New York Times*, 20 April 1959. Guevara himself said later, in a speech at the United Nations in December 1964: 'A group of adventurers,

headed by a café *barbudo*, who had never been in the Sierra Maestra and who is now in Miami, or some base or somewhere, managed to fire the enthusiasm of a group of boys and carry out that adventure. Cuban government officials worked with the Panamanian government to destroy it. It is true that they left from a Cuban port, and that at the time we had a friendly discussion.'

21 Geoffrey Warner, 'Latin America', p. 471.

22 Tad Szulc, 'Exporting the Cuban Revolution', p. 79.

23 Geoffrey Warner, 'Latin America', pp. 478–79.

24 An English translation appeared under the same title in *Monthly Review* (July–August, 1961). See Ernesto Che Guevara, *Obra Revolucionaria* (Prólogo y selección de Roberto Fernández Retarmar), Ediciones ERA, SA, Mexico City, 1967, pp. 515–26. This is the most comprehensive collection of Guevara's writings to have appeared in any language, though it is by no means complete.

25 See Andrés Suárez, *Cuba: Castroism and Communism, 1959–1966*, M.I.T. Press, New York, 1967, Foreword by Ernst Halperin, p. xi. Curiously enough, Halperin maintains that Cuba joined the Soviet camp, not because Castro was afraid that the United States might invade, in which case he would need protection from the other great power (an oversimple if not unreasonable point of view), but specifically because Soviet support 'opened the perspective of spreading the revolution to the Latin American mainland . . . under the protection of the Soviet nuclear umbrella'. This now seems to be United States official and academic orthodoxy, and is based on a complete ignorance of revolutionary movements in Latin America.

26 See, for example, J. P. Morray, *The Second Revolution in Cuba*, Monthly Review Press, New York, 1962.

27 Robin Blackburn, 'Prologue to the Cuban Revolution', *New Left Review*, NO. 21, October 1963. Cuba secured its independence from Spain in 1898.

28 The Spanish army sent to deal with the Cuban situation was comparable proportionately with 3,000,000 United States soldiers sent to Vietnam in 1968: 218,000 Spaniards against a Cuban population of 1,570,000.

29 Hugh Thomas, 'Why Democracy Failed in Cuba', *Observer*, 9 February 1964; and see also, 'The Origins of the Cuban Revolution', *World Today*, October 1963.

30 Arthur Schlesinger Jr, *A Thousand Days*, André Deutsch, London, 1965, p. 199.

31 One American writer, for example, has pointed out that 'all Castroite guerrilla insurgencias in Latin America, including Castro's own rising in Cuba's Sierra Maestra, have occurred in or very near coffee-growing areas with dispersed hill-billy populations living on *minifundio* [tiny subsistence plots] where endemic conflicts between landlord and peasant have been aggravated by declining world coffee prices' (Bolivia, of course, was an exception). The writer goes on to suggest that a high stable world coffee price might be more effective in combatting guerrillas than more normal methods of 'counter-insurgency'.—Norman Gall, 'The Legacy of Che Guevara', *Commentary* (New York), December 1967.

32 Colombia, of course, is an exception. Throughout the period of the *violencia*, the Colombia Communist party—like the Liberal and Conservative parties—had their own guerrillas. This, however, was more an example of their conformity with the standards of the time than an indication of revolutionary enthusiasm.

33 A 'revolutionary situation', according to Lenin, presupposes certain objective conditions: a political crisis which makes it impossible for the old ruling classes to continue ruling in the old way; a substantial deterioration in the conditions of the masses; and the rise of a genuinely mass movement.

34 Ernst Halperin, 'Peking and the Latin American Communists', *China Quarterly*, NO. 29, January–March 1967.

35 With the exception already mentioned of Colombia.

36 Juan Rodríguez, 'The New in the Political Line of the Communist Party of Venezuela', *World Marxist Review*, September 1967.

37 In fact, a pro-Peking party had been set up before this date. A group of Stalinists in Brazil who had never accepted the changes in policy implicit in the declarations of the 20th Congress of the CPSU in 1956—and who were finally expelled from the Brazilian party in 1961—formed their own rival party in February 1962, with some financial support from Peking. See Ernst Halperin, 'Peking and the Latin American Communists'.

38 See, in this context, the Open Letter to Fidel Castro by Oscár Zamora, leader of the pro-Peking wing of the Bolivian Communist party, published in *Los Tiempos* (Cochabamba), July 1968. This letter attacks Fidel, and, by implication, Guevara, for having relied on the pro-Russian party in Bolivia to help launch the guerrilla campaign. In January 1968 a new guerrilla movement began in Colombia, called the Ejército Nacional del Pueblo (National Army of the Town).

It has expressed pro-Chinese sentiments, but there is no evidence so far that the Chinese themselves have expressed any interest in it.

39 In 1964 in Brazil, the left-leaning reformist 'bourgeois' government of João Goulart was overthrown by Marshal Castelo Branco with the blessing of the United States Embassy.

40 Apparently these weapons were not of great importance. According to Fidel, 'they were 150 weapons that came when our troops were advancing on Santiago de Cuba, in December [1958], when the columns of Camilo Cienfuegos and Ernesto Guevara had already taken an important part of Santa Clara'.—speech by Castro, 10 August 1967.

41 General Alberto Bayo, *Mi aporte a Ja Revolución Cubana*, Imp. Ejército Rebelde, Havana, January 1960.

42 *Communist Activities in Latin America, 1967*, Report of the Subcommittee on Inter-American Affairs of the Committee on Foreign Affairs, House of Representatives, July 1967, p. 7.

43 *Survey of the Alliance for Progress: Insurgency in Latin America*, a study prepared at the request of the Subcommittee on American Republics Affairs of the Committee on Foreign Relations, United States Senate, by Professor David D. Burks, Indiana University, January 1968, pp. 5–6.

44 See Richard Gott, 'When Castro's Men and Communists Fall Out' and 'Charting the Revolutionary Course', *Guardian*, 1 and 3 August 1967 (respectively). This was, of course, a very different attitude from that which had obtained earlier. At Punta del Este in 1961, Guevara had said: 'We cannot promise that we will not export our example as the United States asks us to, because an example is a matter of spirit and spiritual element can cross frontiers. But we will give our guarantee that no arms will be transported from Cuba to be used for fighting in any Latin American country.'

I

Soldiers and Peasants in Guatemala

1. The Fall of Arbenz and the Origins of the Guerrillas

'It wasn't we who were in the government; it was Colonel Arbenz,
who was merely a friend of ours.'

Guatemalan peasant

In June 1954, the constitutionally elected government of Jacobo Arbenz Guzmán, President of Guatemala, was overthrown by the United States Central Intelligence Agency. The history of the guerrilla movements in Latin America, indeed the contemporary history of Latin America itself, cannot be understood without reference to this cardinal event. For the overthrow of Arbenz seemed to show—at least to a later generation of revolutionaries—that no government in Latin America which attempted to put through even the mildest economic and social reforms could survive the hostility of the United States. A powerful myth was created to the effect that no revolutionary movement could hope to succeed while the United States chose to topple governments at will.[1]

The myth was broken four and a half years later when the Cuban Revolution triumphantly proved it wrong. This was perhaps one of the most important results of Castro's victory for the rest of Latin America. The dangerous belief was created that the United States was not invincible and could be challenged successfully. But in 1965, 11 years after Colonel Arbenz was deposed, the United States' invasion of Santo Domingo once again seemed to indicate that, in spite of the rhetoric of

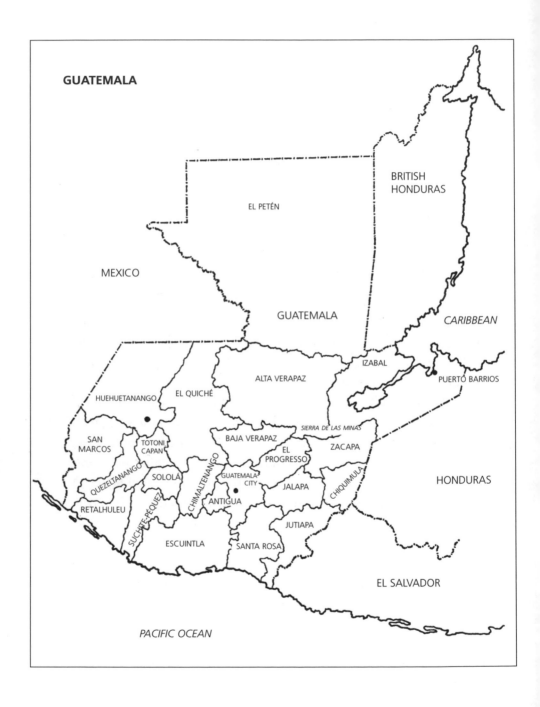

GUATEMALA

BRITISH
HONDURAS

EL PETÉN

MEXICO

GUATEMALA

CARIBBEAN

IZABAL

PUERTÓ BARRIOS

ALTA VERAPAZ

HUEHUETANANGO   EL QUICHÉ

SIERRA DE LAS MINAS

SAN
MARCOS   TOTONI
CAPAN   BAJA VERAPAZ   EL
PROGRESSO   ZACAPA

HONDURAS

QUEZELTANANGO   SOLOLÁ   CHIMALTENANGO   GUATEMALA
CITY   JALAPA   CHIQUIMULA

RETALHULEU   SUCHITE-PEQUEZ   ANTIGUA

JUTIAPA

ESCUINTLA   SANTA ROSA

EL SALVADOR

PACIFIC OCEAN

the Alliance for Progress, the United States was not prepared to tolerate even the most modest moves towards radical change. Perhaps the myth was not a myth after all.

The revolutionaries in the continent were to draw important lessons from the experience of Guatemala in 1954. They concluded that a revolution which did not go 'all the way' in terms of dispossessing the wealthy and giving the peasants and poorer classes a solid stake in the revolution, could be expected to fail.[2] Colonel Arbenz himself was the inheritor of the Guatemalan Revolution of 1944 that had overthrown the dictator Jorge Ubico. Although this revolution had made important reforms, they were too small to appeal to the dispossessed and too large to be tolerated by the rich and powerful. In a polarized society where the power retained by the rich was threatened, counter-revolution was inevitable. And counter-revolution with United States support, in a situation where those who had benefited from the revolution had nothing to defend themselves with, could not fail to be effective.

The causes of United States anger with Arbenz were explained in a statement made on 25 May 1954 by the Secretary of State, John Foster Dulles.

Firstly, said Dulles, Guatemala was the only Latin American country that had voted against a resolution passed by the Organization of American States in March 1954 which declared that the 'domination or control of the political institutions of any American state by the international Communist movement . . . would constitute a threat to the American states, endangering the peace of America'. Secondly, Guatemala had failed to ratify the Río Defence Pact of 1947—an agreement which effectively ensured that all Latin American armies came under United States control. And thirdly, President Arbenz had been buying arms from Eastern Europe.

This latter charge was hardly the fault of Arbenz, since his government had been the victim of a United States blockade which the American government had successfully persuaded many of its allies to join. The British Foreign Office, for example, issued a statement on 18 July 1954 which said that 'Her Majesty's Government strongly disapproves of the sale of arms to Guatemala, and for several years has been refusing licences for the export of any arms to that country'.[3]

At the time, many critics of the United States' involvement in the internal affairs of Guatemala believed that the American government was motivated chiefly by anger at the expropriation of the uncultivated lands of the United Fruit Company, a United States enterprise that played a key role in the Guatemalan economy.[4] With the advantage of hindsight, however, it seems reasonable to conclude that the blind ideological hatred and distrust of Communism which characterized United States' foreign policy throughout the cold war years was a more important factor in the State Department's decision to act than the minor misfortunes of a small United States firm. John Foster Dulles thought that Arbenz was 'soft on Communism': no further argument for intervention was necessary.

In fact, neither Colonel Arbenz nor his predecessor, Juan José Arévalo, had Communist or even Socialist sympathies. The Arbenz land reform, for example, which so annoyed the United Fruit Company, had been specifically designed to improve conditions for capitalist farming.[5] But both Arbenz and Arévalo did attempt to secure a minor degree of political independence from the United States. For this, their 'revolution' had to be stopped.

The CIA candidate to take over the presidency of Guatemala was Colonel Carlos Castillo Armas, himself an unsuccessful contender in the elections of 1950 from which Arbenz had emerged victorious. He was also the organizer of a previous unsuccessful coup. Invading from Honduras in the middle of June 1954, Castillo Armas had little difficulty in overthrowing the Arbenz regime.[6] One of Arbenz's supporters, an Argentinian named Ernesto Guevara, hoped that the regime would arm the workers and peasants in order to repel the invading forces.[7] But Arbenz did not have sufficient fire in his belly to perform such a revolutionary act. At the end of June he resigned meekly, leaving the road open to a government of military colonels.

With the overthrow of Arbenz, Guatemala began a long period of counter-revolutionary government. 'Castillo Armas,' wrote a correspondent some years later, 'proved to be something less than a democratic crusader. Instead of pushing land reforms, he earned the indignation of many peasants by returning to the big landowners virtually all of the estimated 1.5 million acres expropriated by the Arbenz régime.'[8]

It was this reversal of the admittedly limited land reform of Arbenz that seems to have created conditions in which guerrillas were later able to flourish.

Castillo Armas, however, did not live to see the full results of his coup. On 22 July 1957 he was shot dead by one of his palace guards, who was immediately accused by the government of having Communist affiliations. President Eisenhower, true to form, declared that the death of Castillo Armas was 'a great loss to our nation and for the whole free world'.

Elections to find a presidential replacement were held on 20 October and, although the winner appeared to be Ortíz Pasareli, a former justice of the supreme court, the man who ran second, General Miguel Ydígoras Fuentes, immediately declared the election to be invalid. A further election on 19 January 1958 showed General Ydígoras Fuentes as the winner. The first election had not been a particularly fair one, since neither the Communists nor even the vaguely left-wing Revolutionary party had been allowed to participate. But in the second election the Revolutionary party was allowed to stand, putting up as their candidate a lawyer called Mario Méndez Montenegro who made a reasonable showing at the polls.[9] Ydígoras won largely because Méndez split the vote.

In 1960, the United States once again involved itself in the affairs of Guatemala. President Eisenhower, who had been informed by Vice-President Nixon in April 1959 that Fidel Castro was 'either incredibly naïve about Communism or under Communist discipline',[10] had become increasingly concerned about the potential threat posed by the Cuban regime. Consequently, on 17 March 1960, after a trip through Latin America, he set in motion the machinery to destroy it. The following passage appears in his autobiography:

> I ordered the Central Intelligence Agency to begin to organize the training of Cuban exiles, mainly in Guatemala, against a possible future day when they might return to their homeland. More specific planning was not possible because the Cubans living in exile had made no move to select from among their number a leader whom we could recognize as the head of a government in exile.[11]

The Guatemalan Ambassador in Washington, Carlos Alejos, had a brother, Roberto, who owned large coffee plantations in remote areas of Guatemala, and who was also one of President Ydígoras' most prominent backers. Roberto Alejos became the chief intermediary between the CIA and the President and, conveniently, was able to offer one of his coffee ranches, at Helvetia de Retalhulen, as a base for CIA operations. Here, Cuban exiles were trained as pilots and communications experts and given general training to prepare them for an invasion of Cuba scheduled for the following year.[12] Arthur Schlesinger, Jr describes the scene:

> It was the rainy season, and they had to build their own camp in sticky volcanic mud five thousand feet above the sea. In their spare time, they received training from a Filipino colonel who had organized guerrillas against the Japanese during the Second World War.[13]

But such activities, which of course soon became widely known in Guatemala—but not outside—were by no means unanimously approved of by the Guatemalan army.[14] A number of nationalist officers who had no hostile feelings towards Fidel Castro (who had not at that stage declared himself to be a Marxist–Leninist) saw no reason why Guatemala should be used as a springboard for a United States-sponsored invasion of Cuba.[15] In particular, they disliked having to pretend that the Retalhulen base was being used for nothing more sinister than the training of Guatemalan recruits.

Consequently, a coup was planned. On the night of 13 November 1960, a military uprising led by Colonel Rafael Sessan Pereira took place at the barracks of Fort Matamoros, outside Guatemala City. Among those who supported him were two young lieutenants, Marco Antonio Yon Sosa and Luís Augusto Turcios Lima. Turcios was in Petén Department at the time, but he returned to the city to help the uprising. The revolt was designed essentially to prevent the Cuban exiles and the CIA from using Guatemala as a base for their operations against Cuba. But the nationalist officers also hoped to end corruption and inefficiency in the army and the government.

The presence of Cuban exiles training in Guatemala, Turcios later declared, 'was a shameful violation of our national sovereignty. And why was it permitted? Because our government is a puppet.' But he emphasized that his reasons for joining the revolt were essentially 'the traditional ones of younger officers; fed up with corruption, desiring structural changes in the army; nothing really different.'[16]

It was in fact a typical nationalist officers' revolt, though according to the government it also had the support of Mario Méndez Montenegro. It marked the culmination of several months of political and military unrest. Bombings in Guatemala City had been going on for more than a year, and there had been rumours for a long time that left-wing groups in the country were in touch with Colonel Carlos Paz Tejada who had been President Arévalo's defence minister and who was in open opposition to the post-Arbenz governments.[17]

Inevitably, President Ydígoras accused the opposition of being financed and organized from Cuba, and he was able to give more substance to this argument when, on 2 August, ex-President Arbenz announced on Havana television that in future he intended to make his home in Cuba. (Hitherto he had lived in exile in Uruguay.)[18]

At Fort Matamoros, Colonel Pereira's rebel group, consisting of about a hundred men, killed a colonel and a captain and escaped, according to a government statement, 'taking with them troops and armament'.[19]

Another group managed to take over the military base at Zacapa, and also the banana port of Puerto Barrios on the Atlantic coast, 150 miles north-east of the capital. On their arrival at Zacapa barracks, according to an account by Adolfo Gilly, 800 peasants presented themselves 'and asked for arms with which to fight against the government. This was not in the programme, nor was it even anticipated by the rebels, who could not make up their minds to arm the peasants.'[20]

Puerto Barrios was in the very part of the country where the Cuban exiles were training and, in view of the delicacy of the situation, the Guatemalan government immediately cabled Washington.[21]

Hearing from his Secretary of State, Christian Herter, that the situation was 'not good', President Eisenhower decided (as he later recalled) that 'if we received a request from Guatemala for assistance, we would move in without delay. At that moment, Cuban exiles were training in Guatemala, and we had to consider the possibility of

Castro's sending forces of his own to attempt an overthrow of the Guatemalan government.'[22] Consequently, five United States naval vessels were immediately sent down to the Guatemalan coast. At the same timem freshly trained Cuban exile pilots from the Retalhulen base were called in to help suppress the Guatemalan officers' revolt. One of them tried to land with a planeload of troops at the airport of Puerto Barrios but was repelled by hostile fire.[23] Another bombed the town and the airfield from the air. The runway was bombed, a Guatemalan army communiqué announced, to prevent the landing of Cuban planes that might have attempted to supply the rebels.

In these circumstances, the revolt could not last long. On 17 November, President Ydígoras declared a victory, announcing from the balcony of the presidential palace in Guatemala City that:

> we shall be merciful to the soldiers who have been deceived, but we shall apply the full force of the law to the traitorous officers. We shall not pardon these leaders of treason who have been paid with Castro's money. We shall not pardon them here, nor in Honduras, nor wherever they have hidden themselves.[24]

But it had been a near thing. The correspondent of the *Christian Science Monitor*, writing from Guatemala City in December, pointed out that:

> the fact that the rebels could take over two garrisons before the government learnt of the revolt and that it took four days for huge government forces to put down ill-equipped men, is cause for much comment here. This indicates a greater degree of discontent than most people imagine. It is believed by many here that the presence of the United States Navy on the coast did discourage any intentions that local Communists might have had of taking advantage of the rebellion and potential help from Cuba.[25]

But the rebels had themselves to blame as well. According to Adolfo Gilly, of the 150 leaders and officers who were sworn members of the secret group that had begun plotting earlier in the year, only 45 revolted on 13 November. Four years later, when some of them were more politically motivated, they produced a document giving a further reason for failure:

It was the very limited scope of the movement's political orientation that caused its military downfall; having a huge arsenal and a military zone under its control signified nothing, so long as the military leaders did not understand clearly why they were fighting and towards what goal they were moving.[26]

Faced with military defeat and the prospect of execution if captured, the rebel officers retired to the mountains and then into exile. Colonel Pereira managed to escape to Mexico, while Yon Sosa crossed the border into Honduras. Turcios Lima made his way to El Salvador.

After four months of exile, the last two, together with another officer, Alejandro de León, returned to Guatemala where, inevitably separated from the army, they began looking for ways of continuing the struggle against the regime. Adolfo Gilly, in his account of the origins of the guerrilla movement in Guatemala, describes in some detail how during their flight the rebel officers were welcomed by the peasants. Alejandro de León, for example, was hidden and protected by a peasant who, 'seeing him on the run, realized that he was a rebel officer and offered him refuge. It was raining that night and there was no food in the house. At one point the peasant began hacking away at some of the wooden wall-boards of his hut. "It's to make a fire with. I don't have any dry wood and you're soaking wet. I can fix the wall tomorrow." '[27] Yon Sosa in Honduras and Turcios Lima in El Salvador had similar experiences in their encounters with the peasantry. Although Gilly's stories are obviously more in the nature of propaganda than strict history, they go some way to providing an explanation of how rebel officers from the Guatemalan army gradually turned into left-wing guerrillas:

> In Guatemala, as in Honduras, and El Salvador [writes Gilly], all the peasants helped and protected the rebels, tried to influence them and win them to their side. The peasants' motive was not only to offer their solidarity but also to win allies and leaders in their struggle for the land. The peasantry has done this with many rebel fighters, over and over again; they have been doing it for years, for centuries. Many of the rebels did not respond, but the effort was not in vain; the influence was felt by some, although not immediately. Yon

Sosa and Alejandro de León and their *compañeros* did not jump to conclusions; but, little by little, the peasants won them over.[28]

At the time, Second-Lieutenant Turcios Lima was barely 19. He had been born on 23 November 1941, and came from what he himself described as a lower-middle-class family. His father was a watch repairman and his mother worked in an office. His father died when he was young. In an interview in 1966, Turcios described his mother as a 'reactionary'. She had approved of the United States-supported rebellion of Castillo Armas in 1954.[29] He was educated at a private Catholic school and later, at a government vocational college.

His mother had wanted him to be an army officer; so at the age of 15, he was sent to the Polytechnic School, Guatemala's military academy. He graduated in 1959 with the rank of second-lieutenant. Subsequently, he spent six months at the Ranger training school at Fort Benning, Georgia, in the United States, in late 1959 and early 1960.

Asked on one occasion to describe his experience in the United States, he replied that 'from the military point of view it was very good'. And to another interviewer he explained why he had liked it: 'We had the officers' club, 15-ounce Texas steaks, good clothes, the best equipment. Plenty of money, too: every month I sent $150 to my mother. What worries did I have?'[30]

It is difficult, in fact, to understand the Guatemalan guerrillas without taking their military origins into account. Alan Howard, an American journalist who talked to Turcios early in 1966, underlines his nationalist outlook:

> Though he suddenly found himself in a position of political leadership, Turcios is essentially a soldier fighting for a new code of honour. If he has an *alter ego*, it would not be Lenin or Mao or even Castro, whose works he has read and admires, but Augusto Sandino, the Nicaraguan general who fought the U.S. Marines sent to Nicaragua during the Coolidge and Hoover administrations.[31]

Lieutenant Yon Sosa was three years older than Turcios and of Chinese extraction. He too had had the benefit of United States military training—at Fort Gulick in the Canal Zone—but he had not been impressed. Later, he told an interviewer, 'I was able to put to good use the little I had learned in Panama—little, because the courses were poor, to tell the truth, and I learned a lot more here in the sierra, fighting against imperialism.'[32]

During the course of 1961, Turcios Lima spent some time negotiating with the leaders of a number of political parties 'to find out what they stood for'. He seems to have been unimpressed by them all until finally, in July, he met the leaders of the banned Partido Guatemalteco del Trabajo (PGT), the Guatemalan Communist party. 'They were different from the others,' he told an interviewer some years afterwards, 'they really cared about the people.' From these first meetings, there began what Turcios was later to describe as 'close collaboration' between his group of military rebels and the PGT. But the Communists by no means dominated the group of Turcios' supporters. One guerrilla leader, Camilo Sánchez, recalls that when he joined up with the rebels at this stage, he found 'not only Communists, but also sincere revolutionaries, Catholics, and people whose only aspiration was to overthrow the régime in order to replace it by something more equitable'.[33]

Even at this early stage in the struggle, the lives of the members of the movement of Turcios and Yon Sosa were constantly in danger. At the same time as political discussions with the PGT were going on, in July 1961, Alejandro de León was captured by the chief of the political police, Ranulfo González Ovalle, and murdered. According to Gilly, 'the shock produced by the death of Alejandro de León . . . acted as a powerful stimulus in leading the movement to put an end to its negotiations with the opposition parties and to decide to launch guerrilla warfare.' In addition, they appear to have been impressed by the initiative of a group of peasants who, in December 1961, offered them their support provided that they began an armed struggle for the land.

The fact is that, given their character as outlaws, the officers who had survived the revolt of the previous year had very few alternatives open to them. It was easier to survive capture in the country than in the town, and the peasants they had encountered—notably in their flight after 13 November—seemed friendlier than the politicians in the town. Given the Cuban example, guerrilla action seemed a logical choice. Consequently, Yon Sosa and Turcios Lima abandoned their negotiations with the bourgeois politicians and took to the hills.

Notes

1   It was not always even necessary to overthrow a revolutionary government. The Bolivian Revolution of 1952, led by Paz Estenssoro, and later by Siles Zuaso, was subverted by the United States from within.

2   At a Latin American Youth Congress held in Havana in August 1960, Che Guevara explained the importance of Arbenz's failure: 'We should also like to extend a special greeting to Jacobo Arbenz, President of the First Latin American country which fearlessly raised its voice against colonialism; a country which, in a far-reaching and courageous agrarian reform, gave expression to the hopes of the peasant masses. We should also like to express our gratitude to him, and to the democracy which gave way, for the example they gave us and for the accurate estimate they enabled us to make of the weaknesses which that government was unable to overcome. This allows us to go to the root of the matter and to behead those who hold power and their lackeys at a single stroke.'—Che Guevara, *Obra Revolucionaria*, p. 309. The essential lesson of Guatemala was that in any revolutionary process the old army had to be destroyed. Only the Bolivian Revolution of 1952 and the Cuban Revolution actually got rid of the army. In a document of the Central Committee of the Guatemalan Communist party of June 1955, which analysed the failure of Arbenz, it stated clearly that 'it is an error to try to secure revolutionary changes while leaving the old army intact'.—Alain Joxe, *El conflicto chino-soviético en América Latina*, Editorial Arca, Montevideo, 1967, p. 35.

3   *Keesings Contemporary Archives*, p. 13677. Britain did not technically support the blockade.

4   Colour was given to this argument by the fact that Secretary of State John Foster Dulles had been a member of the law firm that drew up the pre-war agreement between United Fruit and the Guatemalan government, and his brother Allen Dulles, then head of the CIA, had formerly been President of the company.

5   The preamble to the reform law stated that 'the agrarian reform of the Revolution aims to liquidate feudal rural property and the rela-

tions of production arising from it, in order to develop capitalist methods and forms of production in agriculture and to prepare the way for the industrialization of Guatemala'. See the study, *Tenencia de la Tierra y desarrollo socio-económico del sector agrícola en Guatemala*, produced by the Comité Interamericano de Desarrollo Agrícola (CIDA), Panamerican Union, Washington, D.C., 1965.

6 One writer on guerrilla warfare considers that the Castillo Armas' invading army should be classified as a guerrilla band, and he chalks up its success as a success for guerrilla warfare in general. See Andrés Cassinello Pérez, *Operaciones de Guerrillas y Contra-guerrillas*, Compañía Bibliográfica Española, Madrid, 1966, p. 154.

7 Guevara had in fact only been in Guatemala since February 1954— though apparently this was long enough for him to become known as 'agitator' to the anti-Arbenz forces. After Arbenz's fall, he was forced to spend a month's asylum in the Argentine embassy in Guatemala City. See Ricardo Rojo, 'Mon ami Guevara', *L'Express*, 29 April 1968; and Rojo, *Mi amigo el Che*, 1968, pp. 59–71.

8 Dan Kurzman, *Washington Post*, 13 March 1966.

9 Although in the post-1954 period Méndez Montenegro had a reputation for being left of centre, he had in fact been one of the leaders of the attempted coup against Arévalo in 1949.

10 Dwight D. Eisenhower, *Waging Peace*, Heinemann, London, 1966, p. 523.

11 Ibid., p. 533.

12 David Wise and Thomas B. Ross, *The Invisible Government*, Jonathan Cape, London, 1965, pp. 23–9.

13 Schlesinger, *A Thousand Days*, p. 206; and see also Haynes Johnson, *The Bay of Pigs*, W. W. Norton and Co., New York, 1974.

14 In October, a student group in Quezaltenango issued a statement denouncing the fact that anti-Castro Cubans and North Americans were preparing an invasion of Cuba in Guatemalan territory—*New York Times*, 26 October 1960. In spite of articles by Professor Ronald Hilton in *The Nation* and the *Hispanic American Report* in November, the use of Guatemala as a springboard for a Cuban invasion did not become widely known until the following year. See the *New York Times*, 8 April 1961, where the paper finally screwed up its courage to mention the existence of a secret base.

15 President Ydígoras announced on 14 May that the Guatemalan armed forces would conduct continuous guerrilla warfare training

manoeuvres until further notice. Diplomatic relations with Cuba were suspended in April—*New York Times*, 15 May 1960.

16 Interview with Alan Howard, *New York Times*, 26 June 1966.

17 *New York Times*, 23 July 1960.

18 *New York Herald Tribune*, 4 August 1960.

19 *New York Times*, 14 November 1960.

20 Adolfo Gilly, 'The Guerrilla Movement in Guatemala', *Monthly Review*, Part I: May 1965, p. 14. (This is an important source for a study of the Guatemalan guerrilla movement. A second article was published in the *Monthly Review*, Part II: June 1965. Adolfo Gilly is a Uruguayan Trotskyite who tends rather to romanticize the role of the peasantry.)

21 See John Gerassi, *The Great Fear in Latin America*, Collier Books, New York, 1966, pp. 184–5, for an account of how these cables became public.

22 Eisenhower, *Waging Peace*, p. 613.

23 Wise and Ross, *The Invisible Government*, p. 33.

24 *Le Monde*, 19 November 1960.

25 *Christian Science Monitor*, 12 December 1960. The revolt did have the effect of giving President Ydígoras second thoughts about the political wisdom of allowing the Cuban exiles to continue training in Guatemala. In March 1961, Roberto Alejos was dispatched to President Kennedy with a letter requesting that the exiles should be removed by the end of April. They were. They left for Cuba in the middle of the month and were resoundingly defeated at the Bay of Pigs.

26 Document produced by MR13 on the fourth anniversary of the revolt.

27 Gilly, 'The Guerrilla Movement in Guatemala', Part I, p. 15.

28 Ibid., p. 16.

29 Interview with Henry Giniger, *New York Times*, 18 March 1966.

30 Interview with Alan Howard, *New York Times Magazine*, 26 June 1966.

31 Gilly, 'The Guerrilla Movement in Guatemala', Part I, p. 16.

32 Ibid., Part II, p. 31.

33 Camilo Castaño, 'Avec les Guérrillas du Guatemala', *Partisans*, NO. 38, July–September 1967, p. 150.

2. The Guerrillas go into Action

'The 6th of February 1962 marks the conscious beginning of
guerrilla warfare in our country, in the sense of an armed struggle
taking place in the countryside, with the political and social
support of the peasantry, initially carried out by a small,
unsophisticated, irregular military force.'

César Montes

In February 1962, after scanty preparation, the meagre guerrilla
forces of Yon Sosa and Turcios Lima, together with Luís Trejo
Esquivel, went into action from their hideout in the mountains of
Izabel, in the Sierra de las Minas. They gave themselves the name
Guerrilla Movement Alejandro de León-November 13—a name that
was designed to commemorate both their fallen comrade and the
abortive uprising of 1960. In their opening statement, the guerrillas
declared that:

> Democracy vanished from our country long ago. No people
> can live in a country where there is no democracy. That is why
> the demand for changes is mounting in our country. We can
> no longer carry on in this way. We must overthrow the Ydígoras
> government and set up a government which respects human
> rights, seeks ways and means to save our country from its hard-
> ships, and pursues a serious self-respecting foreign policy.

The statement called on the Guatemalan people to join the struggle and not tolerate tyranny and humiliation for one more day.[1]

The moment appeared to be propitious. As one of the later guerrilla leaders, César Montes, wrote, 'The national impact that was produced ripened the conditions for popular rebellion.'[2] As usual, the first social group to be aroused were the university students. The immediate roots of student disquiet lay in the congressional elections of the previous December. The elections were for half the seats in Congress and, although the government won only one of the four seats in Guatemala City itself, it won overwhelmingly in the country districts. It was widely assumed that the results had been falsified.

The atmosphere of crisis in the aftermath of these elections was heightened by the assassination on 24 January of the Secret Police Chief, Ranulfo González, who was gunned down by a passing car while leaving his home. President Ydígoras promptly declared a state of siege, and said that the killing was the work of 'Guatemalan and international gunmen in the service of Marxism directed from Cuba'.[3]

But although this new rebel movement had organized itself to engage in guerrilla warfare, it was in essence much the same as the group of officers that had rebelled in November 1960. The strategy of the guerrillas consisted in planning an attack on military installations, much as Colonel Pereira had done. The first guerrillas were formed with a view to swiftly overthrowing the government, not for a long war of attrition.

The revolt began with an attack by guerrilla forces on two army posts and the robbery of a United Fruit Company office on 6 February 1962. According to a press report, 'about fifty men took part in the attack on the military outposts in the town of Bananera and Morales. The President said the attacking group had arrived in several trucks. They seized arms and money from the military posts and also from the United Fruit Company office.'[4]

On 10 February the rebels claimed that they had shot down a Guatemalan Air Force plane, and on 26 February rebel sympathizers captured two radio stations in the capital itself.[5] In an interview on 14 February, President Ydígoras said that an intelligence report put the number of men involved in the revolt at about a hundred. Pointing out that both rebel and loyalist officers had been trained at the United States guerrilla warfare training school at Fort Gulick in the Canal Zone, he added that 'one of our great difficulties is that both sides have been trained in the same tactics by the same experts. Our commanders are very smart, but the rebels are very smart too.'[6]

In March, a new guerrilla group led by Lieutenant-Colonel Paz Tejada was formed. It was called 'The October 20th Front', to commemorate the Revolution of 20 October 1944 which had led to the overthrow of the dictator Ubico and the rule of Juan José Arévalo. In a statement issued in March, this group denounced the Ydígoras government as being chiefly responsible for the grave political and economic crisis, and accused it of trampling on human rights and increasing poverty. The parliament which had been elected in December, 'could no longer fulfil its functions as a constitutional organization but had become an organization of government stooges'. Condemning the foreign policy of the government, the statement said 'we are indignant over the foreign military bases in our country and the military treaties with foreign powers'. Foreign military bases, it added, had seriously infringed the country's sovereignty, while the existing military treaties threatened new international provocations and the suppression of Central American peoples.

The Guatemalan people, continued Colonel Paz Tejada, had made use of all possible peaceful and legal methods, but the dictatorial regime continued its policy of persecution.

> The only road left is the road of uprising. The only way to end the calamities torturing our country is to overthrow the despotic rule of Ydígoras and set up a government which proves by deeds that it is worthy of the people's trust.
>
> Conscious of our responsibility for the motherland and having listened extensively to the views of the people and believing in their patriotic support, we have set up the 'October 20th Guerrilla Front'. We declare that we will embark on an open uprising.
>
> No matter in which part of our motherland we may be, we will take up arms. We will never recognize the Ydígoras government's right to rule the country.
>
> We reaffirm that our struggle is a national struggle. At this critical moment, we point out once again in this statement that the motive of our movement is that which spurred the

patriotic officers of the Alejandro de León–November Thirteenth movement to engage in struggle. Our purposes are the same as those of these young officers. On our side are university students, workers, peasants, patriotic professionals, and upright soldiers in the army and security forces.[7]

Although the revolt at Bananera in February was crushed within a week, riots, strikes and student demonstrations continued in Guatemala City itself. Three political parties, the National Liberation Movement, the Christian Democrats and the Revolutionary party, issued a joint manifesto calling for the resignation of President Ydígoras and the formation of a joint civil–military junta, to restore order.

On 16 March, the President ordered the army to take control of the city. At least 20 students had been killed in the previous two days and more than 200 injured. After bringing in 2,000 reservists from the interior of the country, the government announced plans to flood the city with a total of 40,000 soldiers. And the following month, recognizing that repression was the only policy that could keep him in power, President Ydígoras reorganized his Cabinet. With the exception of the Foreign Minister, he staffed it completely with military officers.

The revolutionary situation was at an end. The rebellion, as César Montes wrote later, effectively lacked 'definite direction, clear-cut orientation and adequate organization'.[8] There was nothing further for the rebels to do except to retire to the hills to lick their wounds. The existence of guerrillas had certainly provoked a crisis situation in Guatemala's political life: the forces opposed to the government, however, were not strong enough to take advantage of the crisis.

For the second time in two years, Turcios Lima and Yon Sosa found themselves facing defeat. And this time defeat was serious, for more was involved than the fate of a handful of soldiers. Students and peasants, as well as soldiers, had all joined in the general uprising from February to April. It would take a long time to replace those who had been killed; and, with an increase in repression, any hope of organizing something fresh in the towns would have to be postponed for some considerable period ahead. Once again the guerrilla leaders had to fall back to the country where, amidst the peasantry, they could escape the worst of the urban repression.

One more attempt was made later that year to set up a guerrilla front, but it seems to have been doomed to failure from the first. Turcios Lima described this effort as follows:

> In November 1961, the 13th to be more precise, to commemorate the rising of 1960, an attempt was made to set up another guerrilla front in the Huehuetenango region, in the west of the country. It is a very mountainous yet densely populated area. The leaders of the movement had made no political preparations; they barely knew the terrain and they had no support from peasant organizations. They went round and round in circles, vainly trying to explain to the peasants in lightning meetings what they were fighting for. A setback. They were all captured and shot. . . .[9]

Little is known of what happened to the guerrillas during the rest of the disastrous year of 1962, but it appears that the political discussions of the previous year were resumed. For in December the decimated group from the Alejandro de León–13 November Front promoted the formation of a politico-military alliance between themselves, the Partido Guatemalteco de Trabajo (PGT), and the '12 April Movement'. (This latter grouping was primarily organized by students and had arisen as a result of the student demonstrations at the beginning of the year.)[10] The new alliance was called the Fuerzas Armadas Rebeldes (FAR)—Rebel Armed Forces—and was designed to be chiefly responsible for planning and co-ordinating the military activity of the various guerrilla fronts which still existed in embryo.

It was about this time that Turcios Lima first met César Montes, a young law student who was later to become an important guerrilla leader. Together with two others, Turcios Lima and César Montes began wandering around the region of the Sierra de las Minas making contact with the peasants. They talked with the peasants and organized them, but it was not the FAR's purpose at that time to form military units until they could be certain of peasant support, adequate information and supply lines.[11] According to Gilly, 'the FAR's role was merely executive. It was a "mailed fist", while political direction remained in the hands of the Frente Unido de Resistencia (FUR), organized by the PGT and other groups, in which MR13—the guerrillas—were not represented.'[12]

Gilly also gives an account of the political attitude of the FAR at this stage:

> Its programme was provided by the PGT; the goal was not a Socialist revolution, nor a workers' and peasants' government. It called for a national democratic revolution that would carry to power a bloc of four classes: workers, peasants, national bourgeoisie, and petty bourgeoisie. The programme of the government would be based on industrialization and the development of Guatemala within a capitalist framework; certain measures would be taken against imperialism while preserving the property, social position, and participation of the national bourgeoisie.

From the very first, the seeds of later internal conflict were sown. The PGT made it quite clear that guerrilla action was not in any circumstances to be allowed to dominate the political choices made by the party.

At the end of the year, in November, at the very same time as the FAR was set up, the PGT decided to support the candidature of Jorge Toriello as Mayor of Guatemala. Later, the guerrillas were to use this in their arguments against the Communists. César Montes wrote, in 1968, that 'support for Jorge Toriello, a liberal politician from the local bourgeoisie with little popular support, not only distracted attention and revolutionary effort, still in a state of ferment from the rising of March–April 1962, but also brought Toriello and the forces which supported him to a sad and foreseeable political defeat'.[13]

At the time, of course, the use of the electoral tactic seemed justified but three months later, in March 1963, when President Ydígoras was overthrown by a soldier even more conservative than he, prospects for any sort of democracy in Guatemala involving free elections seemed uncommonly remote.

On 30 March 1963, Ydígoras's Defence Minister, Colonel Enrique Peralta Azurdia, took over control of the country. A statement issued by the armed forces said that they had acted because Guatemala was 'on the brink of an internal conflict as a result of subversion promoted by pro-Communist sectors, and because of the infiltration of Communists that had become more alarming each day'. In a press statement the following day, Colonel Peralta said that the army had no intention of remaining in power and had only intervened in order to restore tranquillity to a 'confused' political situation, and to prepare the atmosphere for general elections. He emphasized that, when political activities were allowed to begin again, any party with pro-Communist sympathies would be banned.

Before Peralta's coup, General Ydígoras had in fact been preparing the atmosphere for presidential elections. They were originally scheduled to be held in October 1963. The likely winner was ex-President Juan José Arévalo, who had secretly returned to Guatemala just a few days before Peralta's coup, after nearly 10 years of exile in Mexico City. Quite why Ydígoras had allowed him back is not known, though rumours suggested that it had been done 'in the belief that it would redound eventually to the benefit of Robert Alejos, who General Ydígoras hoped would be chosen as his successor'.[14] Alejos, it will be recalled, was the man who had lent his coffee ranch to the CIA for the purpose of mounting the Bay of Pigs operation.

Whatever the reasons, there is no doubt that the presence of Arévalo in the country, and the prospect of his winning the election, was too much for certain sections of the military. They had to intervene to stop such a development.[15]

The Peralta coup, which meant the postponement of any possibility of free elections, made the guerrilla path seem more sensible if also more dangerous. And in April 1963 the three principal guerrilla organizations issued a joint statement, the three groups being the Alejandro de León–13 November Revolutionary Movement, the 20 October Revolutionary Movement and the 12 April Revolutionary Movement. The statement was blunt.

The Guatemalan people are forced to resort to armed action, it said, as the 'only form of opposing the Peralta Azurdia dictatorship today. The guerrilla groups, which are operating in the Zacapa and Izabal mountainous areas, are patriots and people's forces. . . . The Insurgent Armed Forces (FAR) are ready to lay down their lives for the noble and just cause of turning the fatherland into a land free from tyranny, poverty, capitulationism and corruption.'

The statement called on all Guatemalans, whatever their political belief, to unite and coordinate their efforts with the common goal of reforming the country. It also denounced the Azurdia dictatorship for ruthlessly persecuting the residents in those areas where the guerrillas were active. Aircrafts, it said, were sent into these regions to attack the peasants with rockets and incendiaries, causing casualties and damage to crops.

The document pointed out that the guerrillas had continuously dealt blows at the government troops. In an engagement on 22 March, five government troops were killed (including a lieutenant), and 28 were wounded. In a battle between 18 and 19 April, the government troops sustained further casualties. Signs of vacillation, it said, had already appeared among the officers and men of the government troops.

The statement affirmed that the ruling circles could never wipe out the guerrillas, who had both the people's support and cooperation. The insurgent movement, it concluded, was sure to end in victory, and 'the criminals who are now enslaving the people will certainly be punished'.[16]

Nevertheless, victory was still very far off. Inexperience, as much as anything else, told heavily against the guerrillas. Régis Debray tells of how in July 1963, an entire guerrilla *foco*—21 men—in the Izabal zone was liquidated owing to a lack of vigilance.

> A guerrilla messenger was picked up in the city and forced, at the point of a machine-gun, to lead a detachment of the Central American army to the camp. The messenger leading the column took the most difficult path, thinking it to be guarded by a sentry. He revealed his presence by a shout before reaching the place where he expected to find the sentry. No one answered. The messenger was killed, and the detachment entered the encampment in the dead of night. The sentry had been relieved earlier in the evening, because this access was considered to be impenetrable.[17]

Although during the early years of the guerrilla struggle in Guatemala, many of the errors and mistakes can be explained by a lack of experience, in the long run the political differences which arose within the guerrilla movement caused more havoc.

Notes

1   The only source for this statement that I have been able to find is the *Hsinhua News Agency*, 20 February 1962. Hence the rather curious English.

2   César Montes, 'Una ruptura lógica y necesaria', *Punto Final*, NO. 53, 23 April 1968.

3   *New York Times*, 26 January 1962.

4   *New York Times*, 7 February 1962.

5   *Hsinhua News Agency*, 28 February 1962.

6   *New York Times*, 16 February 1962.

7   *Hsinhua News Agency*, 4 April 1962.

8   Montes, 'Una ruptura lógica y necesaria'.

9   *Le Monde*, 7 February 1966.

10 The 'April 12 Movement' withdrew from the FAR in 1965. See *Information Bulletin of the World Marxist Review*, NO. 56, 20 October 1965, pp. 42–3.

11 *New York Times*, 26 June 1966.

12 Gilly, 'The Guerrilla Movement in Guatemala', Part I, p. 18. See also, José Milla, 'Problems of a United Democratic Front in Guatemala', *World Marxist Review*, December 1964.

13 Montes, 'Una ruptura lógica y necesaria'. Another candidate was Dr Villagran Kramer, Director-General of the Unidad Revolucionaria Democrática (Revolutionary Democratic Union, URD), who was later to enter into negotiations with the guerrillas.

14 *New York Times*, 28 April 1963.

15 In a letter dated 4 May 1963, Che Guevara made the following comment on the Guatemalan situation: 'In Guatemala the guerrillas are fighting. The people have to some extent taken up arms. There is only one possibility of slowing the development of a struggle that shows all signs of developing toward a Cuba or Algerian-type revolution. Imperialism has that possibility, although I am not sure if they will bother to use it: "free elections" with Arévalo. That is how we see the matter. Can you think it is otherwise?'—letter printed in Ernesto Che Guevara, *Reminiscences of the Cuban Revolutionary War*, Grove Press, New York, 1968, p. 265. Guevara was almost certainly right. The United States would undoubtedly have preferred an Arévalo–Alejos government. Colonel Peralta was a typical anti-American right-wing nationalist.

16 Once again, the curious phraseology of this document is explained by the source: *Hsinhua News Agency*, 30 April 1963.

17 Debray, *Revolution in the Revolution*? Joint Publications Research Service, United States Government (JPRS 40, 310), 20 March 1967; also, Monthly Review Press, London and New York, 1967, translated from the author's French and Spanish by Bobbye Ortíz, p. 44.

3. Yon Sosa, The Trotskyists and MR13

Under the Peralta Azurdia dictatorship, which lasted from 1963 to 1966, it was not only the Communists who suffered; other political parties were either banned or saw no future in electoral activity. Consequently, it was possible for the guerrillas to resume with the opposition political parties the negotiations that had begun in 1961 and been broken off by the over-hasty rush to man the barricades early in 1962.

Yon Sosa, in particular, seemed anxious to get some kind of organized political support for his guerrillas. He made approaches to a left-wing but anti-Communist party called the Revolutionary Democratic Union (URD), led by Villagran Kramer. At one time, Villagran Kramer later recalled, a union between his party and Yon Sosa's guerrilla group was seriously considered. Representatives of the two organizations held a number of meetings but these were broken off when Kramer's party finally decided, in May 1964, to go in for electoral action. 'This decision,' said Kramer, 'was made over the heated objections of the Yon Sosa group, which maintained that a revolutionary overthrow of the Peralta government was Guatemala's only political solution.'[1]

Yon Sosa was so desperate for support from an existing organized group that, in November 1963, he told Villagran Kramer he would accept assistance from 'the Communists or anyone else'. Kramer's party, as a typical Latin American anti-Communist Social Democratic party, of course jumped to the conclusion that the Communists were already controlling Yon Sosa's guerrillas.[2] At that time, Kramer recalled, his party was convinced that the Yon Sosa group was 'under Communist domination'. He feared that if his party joined up with the guerrillas it too would become 'dominated' by the Communists.

In fact, as events were to show, the guerrillas had no difficulty in steering clear of such a fate. But political negotiations, whether with the Communists or with Villagran Kramer, inevitably led to differences arising between the guerrillas, both within Yon Sosa's MR13, and between it and the other groups in the FAR. The immediate grudge of Yon Sosa was that although MR13 participated in the FAR, the FAR's political and military strategy was decided by the FUR in which it had no representation. And of course the group in the FUR with the strongest voice was the Partido Guatemalteco del Trabajo— the Guatemalan Communist party.

Adolfo Gilly, who at the time was a firm partisan of Yon Sosa, explains the situation as follows:

> Lacking a programme of their own, adhering only to the idea that there was no way out but armed struggle, the men of MR13 were obliged to accept this division of labour in which their armed struggle was carried out under outside political leadership, in whose decisions they had no direct participation.
>
> But inside FAR the same contradiction that had earlier led MR13 to break with the bourgeois opposition groups was at work. The FUR leadership always kept open the possibility and the hope of eventual negotiations leading to a shift from armed to electoral struggle. The guerrilla actions which MR13 planned to carry out were considered by FUR to be, not a means of toppling the system, but an instrument of pressure which could force the government to negotiate and yield on the electoral, democratic level.
>
> Meanwhile, the leadership of MR13, having taken the armed struggle into the mountains, was—in spite of vicissitudes, dilemmas, and impasses—under continuous pressure from the peasant masses. Guerrilla warfare, fighting with arms in hand and side by side with the peasants, had its own

logic. While the political leadership of FUR, committed to democratic negotiations, moved in the direction of conciliation, the leadership of the armed struggle moved in a revolutionary direction. The activity of the *guerrillero* who is fighting alongside the peasant masses, who sees poverty and exploitation on all sides, who is under constant pressure from the peasantry to advance—receiving meanwhile its solidarity and support, its endless demonstrations of revolutionary dedication—is not negotiation but struggle. And he feels that negotiation and the programme that exalts it as a goal are constant brakes on his initiative.[3]

Yon Sosa's guerrillas were not just becoming more radical in their appreciation of the need for a strategy of the armed struggle, but, in addition, the whole emphasis of their programme had begun to change. During the period 1963–64, writes Adolfo Gilly:

> the leadership of MR13 underwent a period of internal transformation. From a nationalist and anti-imperialist orientation, it moved to an acceptance of Marxism as a method of analysis and action, and socialism as the goal of the struggle. From the concept of anti-feudal, democratic revolution, it moved to a programme of anti-imperialist and anti-capitalist revolution, of Socialist revolution and, following the path of the Socialist revolutions of China and Cuba, of a government of workers and peasants as the goal of the revolutionary struggle. This transformation opened new horizons for the guerrilla struggle, which had reached a dead end; it opened the way for organization of the masses; at the same time it transformed the conception of the guerrilla force's own role and its relation to the masses.[4]

Gilly does not point out, as he should have done, that it was also at this juncture that MR13 and Yon Sosa came under the influence of certain Trotskyist ideologues, sent by the Fourth International to fill the political vacuum that undoubtedly existed within the guerrilla movement. As Debray put it, the Latin American Bureau of Buenos Aires—a section of the Fourth International—run by Posadas, 'took advantage of MR13's abandonment by and lack of assistance from other political organizations'.[5]

Though hostile towards the position of the Trotskyists, Debray gives a reasonably fair account of their attitude towards the conduct of guerrilla warfare:

> The Trotskyist ideology has reappeared today from several directions, taking as its pretext several transitory defeats suffered by revolutionary action, but always proposing the same 'strategy for taking power'. Let us summarize it:
>
>> The worker and peasant masses everywhere crave Socialism, but they don't yet know it because they are still in the power of the Stalinist bureaucracies. Hence the latent spontaneity of the workers must be awakened. For the attainment of this goal, the guerrilla movement is not the highest form of revolutionary struggle; 'dual power' must be instituted at the base, that is, a call must be made for the formation of factory and peasant committees, the proliferation of which will ultimately permit the establishment of a single United Confederation of Workers; this confederation, by means of instantaneous and generalized risings in the mountains and the cities, will be the instrument for taking power. From now on the work of agitation must aim at unleashing strikes and workers' demonstrations. In the countryside the aim should be the organization of peasant unions; occupation of the land; organization of localized insurrections, which will gradually spread to the cities, with the rallying-cry of Socialist Revolution. The workers must, step by step, take control of the means of production. They must rise up immediately and directly against the state power, without intermediaries or specialized detachments. The Revolution will arise from existing or latent economic struggles, which will be sharpened to the point of becoming a mass insurrection—a direct passage from union action to insurrection.[6]

Francisco Amado Granados, a Trotskyist who became a national director of MR13, made the same point rather more enthusiastically in an interview with Adolfo Gilly early in 1965:

We plan to organize underground committees of armed workers and also students similar to these now existing among the
peasants; we shall promote trade unionism, legal or underground; and we shall prepare the conditions and the mental-
ities of the masses for a revolutionary workers' *central*.[7] And
our slogan, which is already spreading, will become a reality
for important sectors of the population: 'Workers, peasants,
students, arm yourselves.'[8]

With this perspective for action, Yon Sosa's group dropped
Alejandro de León from their title and simply began calling themselves the Movimiento Revolucionario 13 de Noviembre. Within the
new MR13 there were a number of guerrilla fronts. One, led by Yon
Sosa himself, retained the name of Alejandro de León. Another, by
Luís Turcios, took the name of the Edgar Ibarra Front. Turcios never
seems to have swallowed the Trotskyist doctrine with as much gusto as
Yon Sosa and, as time went by, the two fronts began to diverge ideologically. But in the beginning all was harmony. In December 1964,
the new Trotskyist MR13 drew up its first major policy statement. An
expanded meeting of the 'National Directorate' of MR13 was held
between 10 and 22 December 1964, at a guerrilla encampment in the
Sierra de las Minas called 'The Orchids'. From this meeting emanat-
ed the 'First Declaration of the Sierra de las Minas', first published in
MR13's publications, *Revolución Socialista*, in February 1965.

The declaration emphasized that nothing could be done in Guatemala 'without arming the masses and without destroying the
machinery of the capitalist state . . . that is, making a Socialist revolution as in Cuba'. The minimum programme of the revolution was to
include expropriation without compensation of foreign companies,
especially United Fruit, and a land reform that would distribute land
to the peasants.

The declaration made clear that 'North American imperialism'
was a major enemy of the Guatemalan Revolution, but MR13 was also
opposed to the 'pacifist, revisionist, conciliatory line of Khrushchev'
(who had been deposed two months previously).

Within Guatemala, the declaration called on students and soldiers to collaborate with MR13. Soldiers who engaged in repression,

it warned, would be 'implacably punished', either before or after the triumph of the revolution. In fact the guerrilla movement in this period took particular care to try to convert the army. The military origins of Yon Sosa and Turcios Lima were probably responsible for this. Doubtless they felt that the army was a suitable place to begin looking for recruits. The following leaflet indicates the type of propaganda that MR13 aimed at the military:

> Soldier: Refuse to fire against your peasant brothers. Refuse to burn down villages, refuse to torture!
>
> Soldier: Turn your guns on those who plunder and persecute the peasantry. Our struggle is yours: it is the struggle for land and for a government of workers and peasants!
>
> Soldier: Support the organization of peasant committees in the villages; organize, together with other soldiers, underground committees in your barracks, garrisons, and posts, to discuss how you can help the peasant and guerrilla struggle!
>
> Soldier: Support land seizure by the peasants! The land belongs to him who tills it, not to the *latifundistas* or the United Fruit Company!
>
> Soldier: Bring to trial those of your officers who have tortured and murdered your peasant brothers!
>
> Soldier: Unite with the peasant guerrilla force, join the peasant militia!
>
> Soldier: The *guerrilleros* are not your enemies. They are workers, students, and peasants who fight for the land.
>
> Forward with the alliance of peasants, workers, and soldiers!
>
> Forward in the struggle for the land, against peasant evictions, against military repression of the peasantry, and for the expropriation of the *latifundios*.
>
> Workers, students, peasants, arm yourselves!
>
> Revolutionary Movement of 13 November
Guatemala, 27 October 1964[9]

Details of the MR13 during its Trotskyist phase are to be found only in the two long and illuminating articles by Adolfo Gilly, entitled

'The Guerrilla Movement in Guatemala' and that already cited. Gilly spent several weeks with Yon Sosa's guerrillas earlier in the year and, although he is committed to the particular ideology that MR13 was then espousing and would appear to be somewhat over-optimistic about the revolutionary potential of the Guatemalan peasantry, his articles give a valuable insight into the outlook and activities of the guerrillas at that time.

Gilly's thesis, which he attributes to the peasants themselves, is that 'the counter-revolution (of 1954) triumphed because the people were not armed'. He cites numerous instances when peasants demanded arms from the Arbenz government and were denied them. One peasant told the following story:

> I was working in Tiquisate at the time. Government representatives came to us, at the time of the Castillo Armas uprising, asked our leaders if, among the six *fincas* [farms] we were working on, we could gather 300 men, who would then be armed. We told them yes. We each returned to our *finca*, and when we called for 50 volunteers from each one, the peasants were angry and told us that they were all volunteers; the next day, instead of 300 there were 3,000 men assembled, waiting for arms. But the government representatives never came, and then the Arbenz government collapsed.[10]

Lieutenant-Colonel Augusto Vicente Loarca, an MR13 leader who had been a member of Arbenz's general staff in 1954, told a similar story: two days after the Castillo Armas uprising had begun he had said to Arbenz: 'Colonel, let's get a thousand men together. It would be easy; and with you at their head, the whole country will rise up.' Arbenz said it was too late, there was nothing to be done, and he had already resigned. 'If only he had followed my advice, the masses would have crushed Castillo Armas, and we would not have to be doing what we are doing today,' Loarca added.[11]

In addition, Gilly suggests that since the Arbenz land reform was a half-hearted affair, many peasants had received little to defend. 'The land over there,' said one peasant, 'was distributed. Then came the "liberation" and it was taken away from us. The land over there,' he pointed in another direction, 'they didn't distribute. It's the best land, belonging to rich people, so it wasn't touched.' It is for these reasons, Gilly concludes, that:

> The Guatemalan guerrillas of MR13 fight today for the Socialist revolution and for a government of workers and peasants. Neither the method nor the programme was drawn up by a group of pure theoreticians, as a kind of parlour game. If, for the first time in Latin America, a guerrilla movement has sprung up in Guatemala that openly declares its Socialist objectives, this is without doubt due to the influence of the world revolutionary process and the Cuban Socialist revolution. But it is also due—especially due—to the deep collective experience of the Guatemalan people, to the defeat suffered in 1954, and to the fact that, since then, workers and peasants, instead of lapsing into resignation or retreat, have gone on fighting as best they can.[12]

The actual organization of the guerrilla band itself during the Trotskyist period is of interest since it differs somewhat from what has obtained elsewhere and at other times. Evaristo Aldana, one of the leaders of the Alejandro de León Front, explained the system to Adolfo Gilly:

> In the first place, we organized what we call a 'centre' for our guerrilla units. This 'centre' constitutes the directorate. We then organized 'groups'; each member of the 'centre' is active in his 'group' and responsible for it. The position of 'group' leader is a rotating one. In organizing a 'group' we take into account such facts as the literacy of its members, level of political discussion, and military potential. This system has produced excellent results.
>
> . . . [The 'centre' provides] military and political leadership for the Front. Experience has taught us that the functioning of 'groups', and consequently of the Front as a whole, depends on the functioning of the 'centre'. The positions of responsibility in the 'centre' are held by *compañeros* who, in action and discussion, show the greatest determination to

move ahead, the highest sense of responsibility, and the finest collective spirit.

. . . Given the tasks that we must fulfill and the conditions under which the struggle is developing, we are obliged to base ourselves on what is called 'democratic centralism'. We cannot subject ourselves to 'pure democracy' (*democraticismo*), nor to the more backward sectors of the masses and the Movement; we must base ourselves on those sectors possessing the highest determination, and the greatest degree of understanding and boldness. This does not mean that we disregard the *compañeros* and the sector of the masses whose understanding is still limited. They will advance and mature by observing the resolution in action of those having greater comprehension and sense of purpose.[13]

Aldana pointed out that since 90 per cent of the unit were peasants, the majority could neither read nor write. They had learnt within the guerrilla band.

Faced with an ignorant and politically backward peasantry, the objective of the guerrillas was to secure converts by means of 'armed propaganda'—an attempt to turn the peasants into revolutionaries by means of meetings and arguments. The organizers, of course, arrived with gun in hand. Alan Howard has described the method in the way that he saw it in operation in 1966:

The village would be secured militarily. All inhabitants would be required to attend a meeting at which several rebels would talk on different themes: reform, exploitation, the people's army, security measures. During this initial contact with the community the rebels would seek out the village leaders, hoping to make them the nucleus of a Local Clandestine Committee—a tightly organized unit that, in its most advanced stage, acts as the final political authority of the village.

Often, the rebels win over the local government official to their cause. If they fail, the rebels try to persuade him to remain neutral. And if he actively opposes rebel authority, he will probably be executed. In the past year the rebels had executed, by their own count, thirteen men in the region and scores of police and army officials in other areas who had allegedly tortured and killed rebel partisans. The army usually retaliates by rounding up a number of suspects, jailing them for interrogation and eventually releasing them. Torture is more or less standard practice and sometimes a suspect doesn't come home.[14]

Alan Howard was, in fact, talking about the system operated in 1966 by Turcios Lima's group. But Yon Sosa's guerrillas had a similar tactic.

Gilly comments:

Our struggle is not primarily military [Yon Sosa explained to Gilly early in 1965], but social. It's not our intention to destroy the government by military means; we intend to dissolve it through social action. This means that at the same time we must be organizing the bases of the government that will replace the old one, a government of workers and peasants. Our guerrilla force organizes on the social level. True, we fight with arms in hand, but we also organize the peasant masses and the city workers. They are the ones who'll topple the capitalist dictatorship.

The principal task of the Guatemalan guerrilla force today is peasant organization; all military actions are subordinate to it. When a guerrilla squad marches through the mountains, its machine-guns, rifles, and grenades are not its principal weapons of struggle; these are necessary, indispensable, providing the basis of security. But the principal weapon is the word—written and spoken, especially spoken.[15]

A further objective of the guerrilla face at this period was to make itself indispensable to the peasantry. Gilly writes:

The guerrilla force unites the peasantry. Unlike workers, peasants don't have the facilities to organize for concerted action; they are scattered, each one on his plot of land or in his village, surrounded by an enemy whose power is embodied in the army and other instrumentalities of repression.

The guerrilla force, going from village to village, from region to region, is the embodiment of the common struggle and of the common aspirations of the peasants to possess the land. And there is a key fact to be remembered: the *guerrilleros* go with gun in hand. The peasants see in these rebel arms a symbol of their own unconquerable dignity.

When a guerrilla patrol passes through a village, it is not as a squad of armed men that they are welcomed but as the representatives of hundreds of peasants of other villages; the patrol communicates the content of their many discussions throughout the province, brings the villages closer together by constant marches back and forth, and carries new suggestions for action.[16]

Gilly quotes from a speech by a guerrilla leader, Evaristo Aldana, given on one of these visits to a village:

You have noticed that we have weapons. We have them so that we can struggle against the government and the landowners; against the capitalists who live off the toil of workers and peasants; and against the army which defends them and represses you. We are fighting for the land, so that each peasant shall have the land he tills, so that no peasant shall be obliged to pay rent or taxes to the big landowners. But we alone are not going to win the land. You must take it over, with our assistance. We will help you with our weapons, but you must organize and prepare to take possession of the land. You must prepare well; you must talk to all the peasants in the area. And you must have arms if you are to take the land and defend it. We should organize this undertaking together and launch the attack when we are completely prepared. You surely remember that land was distributed here, during the Arbenz régime; but then came the so-called 'liberation' and it was taken away from you.

Therefore it is not enough for the lands to be given to you; you must have arms to defend them with. Each peasant must have his weapon. Furthermore, we must have a government that will defend us, the workers and peasants, instead of defending the *latifundistas*. We must prepare ourselves, uniting with peasants in other regions and with city workers, if we are to establish our own government.[17]

This guerrilla technique of entering a village, gun in hand, to explain to the population the motives of the guerrilla struggle has become known as 'armed propaganda'. Its principal characteristic is that it does not necessarily involve clashes with the armed forces of the state. As a tactic it has, however, been considerably criticized by a later generation of Latin American guerrillas. Debray, in particular, is of the opinion that although armed propaganda has its role, it must follow and not precede military action:

> To consider armed propaganda as a stage distinct from and prior to military operation is, it seems, to provoke the enemy needlessly, to expose the comrades working as propagandists to assassination or the need to escape, and to expose a future or possible zone of guerrilla action. Given the social, ideological, and psychological conditions of the peasantry in the majority of Latin American countries, given the diverse intelligence agencies at the enemy's disposal (strongly reinforced since the Cuban Revolution), an agitational group, whether armed or not, will be watched, uncovered, and liquidated; in embryo if necessary. What is worse, its contacts, the cells it has organized, the people who have 'worked' in the rural areas, in the villages, and in the neighbouring towns will perhaps meet the same fate. If their enemy is astute enough to wait, it will not make a move until even later, so as to permit its espionage services to infiltrate. A 'peasant' will be planted in the organization: the whereabouts of the entire guerrilla group will thus be known from the beginning and promptly liquidated.[18]

The importance of Yon Sosa's movement, however, is not the emphasis that it placed on 'armed propaganda', but rather that it was the first guerrilla movement in Latin America to adopt an outright Socialist programme. This was an important break with the precedent that had been established by the Cuban guerrillas, and a recognition

of the fact that the ruling classes and the United States could not be
fooled into supporting a radical movement with apparently limited
aims, as they had been in Cuba. As the American Ambassador in
Guatemala, John O. Bell, explained to a journalist in the middle of
1965, 'the most politically susceptible element here is the middle
class, composed of men of industry, commerce and the professions—
a very unlikely group, after the experience of Cuba, to be giving support to the Communists.'[19] In the following interview, recorded by
Adolfo Gilly early in 1965, Yon Sosa explains his position in more
detail:

> YON SOSA: In the process of fighting, living with the peasants,
> and encountering many frustrations, we reached the conclu-
> sion that in Guatemala the only real revolution of the masses
> that can be made is a Socialist revolution. And how we've
> advanced since reaching that conclusion. A multitude of
> things that formerly seemed confusing have been clarified.
> There were *compañeros* who agreed in theory for the need for
> Socialism but who were afraid the peasants would not under-
> stand a Socialist programme and would be frightened off by
> the idea of such a drastic step. It was they who didn't under-
> stand the peasants. To those peasants who are looked to as
> leaders in their communities the idea of a Socialist revolution
> appears to be so simple and logical that they are impatient
> with anyone who attempts to propose some other solution.
> This is our strength, and it constitutes not only material
> strength but also strength of programme.

> ADOLFO GILLY: And no one told you that with such a programme
> you would antagonize the bourgeoisie?

> YON SOSA: Of course we were warned of this eventuality.
> Everything was done to make us hesitate, to intimidate us.
> But what convinced us was observing how the peasants
> responded to our programme. The programme passed the
> test of the masses, and from that point on we were adamant.
> Anyway, what does it matter what the bourgeoisie says?
> They're already against us. Have you found a single bourgeois

who supports the *guerrilleros* or the militant peasant leaders? And what force does the national bourgeoisie have, anyhow? In Guatemala, none. Furthermore, since we have taken up arms and gone to the mountains, they are more closely linked than ever to imperialism, and more vehemently against us . . .

ADOLFO GILLY: How did you all become Socialists?

YON SOSA: While we were dodging the bullets. It's impossible to fight for very long, side by side with peasants, and not become a Socialist. An armed revolution must become a Socialist revolution. Which countries, similar to ours, have been able to emerge from backwardness? Cuba, China, North Vietnam, North Korea—they have all taken the Socialist path. A backward country cannot advance along the capitalist path, and there is no third alternative. All you have to do is look around and see what's happening in the world. How could we not be for Socialism?

But it's not enough to be for the Socialist revolution, you have to say so. There are *compañeros* who think that, although they themselves can understand it, the masses cannot, and therefore one must not speak of it. This shows lack of confidence in the masses. These *compañeros* think that the peasants are concerned only with problems of crops; whereas peasants today are interested in Cuba, China, the Congo, and everything that's happening in the world. You need only to talk to them to find this out. But you must talk to them in simple language, not in abstract formulas; and there's nothing simpler than the idea of a government of workers and peasants.

ADOLFO GILLY: What do you think about Vietnam?

YON SOSA: But why do you ask? You heard the discussion last night with the other *guerrilleros*; you even added your two centavos worth! But if you like, I'll answer you as a guerrilla commander to a journalist. I think that the imperialists are a bunch of bastards; you can get rid of them only with guns and that's what the Vietnamese *guerrilleros* are doing. In doing so, they're helping us, however far away they are. And I think that the workers' states have to help the Vietnamese with arms, with soldiers, with everything, if necessary with atomic weapons. The workers' state must give them arms, not permitting themselves to be intimidated by the nuclear blackmail of imperialism; they must also mobilize all the peoples of the world in support of the Vietnamese. We are supporting them, as much as we are able, by attempting to overthrow capitalism in Guatemala and by combating imperialism—not with declarations, but with guns. The Congolese *guerrilleros* are doing the same. When we have a workers' state in Guatemala, you can be sure that we won't equivocate—we shall extend the revolutions, helping all the other countries of Latin America to make theirs, if they haven't already done it.[20]

It has often been suggested that Yon Sosa was pro-Chinese. When asked in 1966 with which of the Socialist countries MR13 identified itself most, he replied: 'We identify ourselves more with China and her political line. We cannot accept the Soviet "peaceful co-existence".'[21] Nevertheless, there is no evidence that Yon Sosa was at any stage under Chinese influence, direction or domination.

Early in 1965 Adolfo Gilly asked one of the MR13 leaders, Francisco Amado Granados, what the position of the movement was towards the Sino-Soviet split. He received the following reply:

We don't share the attitude of those who claim that the conflict is irrelevant to us and that we must remain neutral. This subject is of concern to revolutionaries throughout the world; vital questions of revolutionary strategy are involved. We do not share the position of the Chinese *compañeros* in all aspects, but we think that their general revolutionary line of opposition to peaceful coexistence and peaceful transition serves to activate the revolution and can provide a basis for discussion and the re-grouping of all revolutionary forces, proletarian and national, throughout the world, on the path of violent armed struggle against capitalism and imperialism.[22]

This was more or less the orthodox Trotskyist position towards the Sino-Soviet split. It bears some similarity to the Cuban attitude towards the Chinese theoretical stance, although Granados' first sentence is a rebuke aimed directly at the Cubans. Cuba's position has always been that the Sino-Soviet dispute was a disaster for the Third World, and that it is better for those not involved to remain neutral.

Notes

1   *New York Times*, 20 December 1964.

2   Villagran Kramer classified his own group 'as belonging in the same category as such well-known Latin American "democratic-leftist" organizations as Costa Rica's *National Liberation Party*, headed by ex-President José Figueres, Venezuela's ruling *Democratic Action Party* and the *Popular Action Party* of Peruvian President Fernando Belaúnde Terry'. Villagran Kramer's party, however, did not consider itself to be 'anti-Communist', since in Guatemala this term is 'synonymous with ultra-conservative' and military rule.

3   Gilly, 'The Guerrilla Movement in Guatemala', Part I, p. 16.

4   Ibid., p. 19.

5   Debray, *Revolution in the Revolution?* p. 37. Organized Trotskyism is stronger in Latin America than anywhere else in the world. It has had a hand in political agitation in the countryside in Guatemala, Peru and Brazil. It is very divided, and its activities are often difficult to trace. It has had no historian—but deserves one.

6   Ibid., p. 36. Debray adds, more cruelly, that 'Trotskyism attributes great importance to the Socialist character of the revolution, to its future programme, and would like it to be judged by this purely phraseological question, as if declaring a thousand times that the revolution should be Socialist would help call it into existence.'

7   This is the same as the United Confederation of Workers to which Debray refers.

8   Gilly, 'The Guerrilla Movement in Guatemala', Part II, p. 29.

9   Ibid., Part I, p. 31.

10 Ibid., p.10.

11 Ibid., Part II, p. 32. Guevara's idea had been somewhat similar. According to Ricardo Rojo, 'Guevara's proposal was that the city should first be tightly controlled, then the invasion force, whose offensive capacity was militarily very small, could easily be kept isolated. This dual operation would have sealed the fate of Castillo Armas's adventure, but it went right against Arbenz's military training. Giving arms to the civilian organizations, to the many parties who professed loyalty to the revolution as well as to unions and peasant groups, was an absolutely essential step.'—Rojo, *Mi Amigo el Che*, p. 70.

12 Gilly, 'The Guerrilla Movement in Guatemala', Part I, p. 11.

13 Ibid., Part II, pp. 36–7.

14 *New York Times*, 26 June 1966.

15 Gilly, 'The Guerrilla Movement in Guatemala', Part I, p. 20.

16 Ibid.

17 Ibid.

18 Debray, *Revolution in the Revolution?* p. 56. Eduardo Galeano, a Uruguayan journalist who interviewed César Montes early in 1967, reveals the latter's opposition to Debray's views about armed propaganda: 'In the course of our conversation, César Montes disagreed violently with what Debray says about armed propaganda in *Revolution in the Revolution?* "Undoubtedly," Montes told me, "Debray is well informed about the Cuban experience. He had access to many wholly unknown documents. But he knows little about the Guatemalan experience. He only knows some aspects, from people who were in our movement but who had lived abroad for some time. I don't think he knows much about other movements either. Calling him an adventurer for what he says is not to belittle him, but I think that the situation in each country and the use made of certain measures which he criticizes should be examined more thoroughly. In Cuba the guerrillas never held armed propaganda meetings. But they didn't need to." These remarks did not prevent César Montes from recognizing Debray's valuable contribution to the self-awareness which the Latin American revolution is acquiring.'—Eduardo Galeano, *Guatemala, Clave de Latinoamérica*, Ediciones de la Banda Oriental, Montevideo, 1967, pp. 29–30.

19 *Latin America Times*, 27 July 1965.

20 Gilly, 'The Guerrilla Movement in Guatemala', Part II, pp. 29–35.

21 *La Época* (Montevideo), 10 August 1966.

22 Gilly, 'The Guerrilla Movement in Guatemala', Part I, pp. 37–8.

4. Turcios Lima and The FAR

'Military training without political understanding is as useless as a gun
with damp ammunition. With it, even a machete is enough.'

Turcios Lima

The extremely advanced ideas of Yon Sosa—and his Trotskyist advisers—were by no means shared by all members of the guerrilla movement. Turcios Lima, in particular, had grave doubts, not so much
about the Socialist objective as about the methods of achieving it. His
particular group, the Edgar Ibarra Front, began to have ideas of its
own that were substantially different from those of Yon Sosa. And as
early as 16 October 1964 (that is, before Yon Sosa's 'Declaration of the
Sierra de las Minas'), the leadership of this front had written a letter
drawing attention to the differences that had arisen between it and
Yon Sosa. The letter was addressed to both the Central Committee of
the PGT and to the national leadership of MR13. It contained the following comments:

> This entire [Trotskyist] position leads, by means of a clever
> manoeuvre, to the removal of revolutionary content from the
> guerrilla movement: to the denial that it can become the army
> of the people; to the denial of the role of the peasantry in our
> countries' revolutionary wars; to the denial of the need for the
> military defeat of imperialism and its lackeys as a precondi-
> tion to seizing power from them; to the concealment of the
> prolonged duration of the armed struggle; to the deceptive
> presentation of the insurrectional outlook as a short-term

matter; to the splitting of the people's forces and the diversion of revolutionary efforts into the peaceful organization of unions and mass organizations. . . .

The slogan calling for occupation of the land and factories, which could be helpful at certain stages of the struggle, provokes, when used anarchically, massacres, and tremendous setbacks for the peasants and workers who do not yet have the strength to sustain these invasions. The famous 'dispute' with the bourgeoisie over the ownership of the means of production is inconceivable so long as the ruling classes control the whole apparatus of repression. This tactic could be applied in zones where the development of guerrilla forces, or of the popular army, had proceeded to the point of being able to hold the wave of repression in check. Under other circumstances, it exposes the people's most vulnerable targets to the enemy's blows. Such actions can acquire the character of real provocations, causing defeats that oblige the people to retreat politically as the only way of protecting themselves against repression.[1]

With the publication of this letter, the Edgar Ibarra Front effectively defined itself as an entity with military and political views distinct from those of the MR13. But the letter was by no means an orthodox Communist rebuttal of Trotskyist methods, and it appears that Turcios, while disliking the trend within the MR13, was also anxious to keep his distance from the comrades in the PGT. In the circumstances he decided, as head of the Edgar Ibarra Front, that his front could no longer remain within the Trotskyist MR13. From then on the guerrilla movement in Guatemala was divided, with Yon Sosa running the MR13 and Turcios in control of the FAR. A year or so later, at the Tricontinental Conference in Havana, in January 1966, Turcios explained his differences with Yon Sosa to the French journalist Marcel Niedergang:

El Chino was trying to represent the revolution all by himself. . . . For him guerrilla warfare is a 'stimulant' to modify the political context. For us, guerrilla warfare is basic, and that's what brings us against the Communists, who are too often timid and cautious. . . . El Chino talks of a 'Socialist revolution' at a time when there is no evidence of any Socialist consciousness in the country. He talks of 'Soviets' of the 'Union of Caribbean Socialist Republics'. . . . He is a dreamer.[2]

Yon Sosa's radicalism was incorrigible and he reiterated his support for the Socialist revolution later in 1966 during an interview. When asked what the ideological difference was between the FAR and MR13, he replied:

FAR advocates a democratic revolution while MR13 is for the immediate march to Socialism. We want nothing to do with the bourgeoisie, but FAR seeks to make the bourgeoisie join this movement. The democratic revolution [of] FAR stands for a transition to Socialism, but who knows how long that transition will take when they conciliate the class enemy. It is possible to attain unity between MR13 and FAR provided it is under the programme of Socialist revolution. I am very glad that FAR is advancing. I believe that before long they will fight for the same objective that we do.[3]

An FAR commander, Camilo Sánchez, made the following comments about Yon Sosa in an interview with Camilo Castaño in February 1967:

Above all it is essential to make it clear that Yon Sosa is an honest comrade, really sincere towards the revolution and towards the people. He has worked with the Trotskyists without being a Trotskyist. He never was one, he isn't one now. As a result of his relations with the Trotskyists and of the course they wanted the revolutionary movement to take [they wanted to monopolize control of the struggle in Guatemala under the banner of the Fourth International], the FAR broke off relations with the November 13 Movement led by Yon Sosa. [The November 13 Movement had lost its influence amongst the people who originally supported it.] We believe—without falling into sectarianism—that the participation of the Trostkyists in the November 13 Movement resulted in its becoming a regional organization; earlier it had been a national Movement.[4]

It was this conflict between a national and a regional organization that eventually led Yon Sosa himself, in 1966, to break with the Trotskyists. He abandoned the Fourth International for a simple reason: 'Two Trotskyist comrades who were with us made improper use of the funds collected. Without consultation they sent to the Fourth International some of the funds forcibly exacted from the bourgeoisie (about 60,000 quetzales).'

Yon Sosa saw no reason why money collected in Guatemala should end up in Buenos Aires. When asked by a journalist whether the political line of MR13 had subsequently changed, Yon Sosa replied: 'No. Our line remains the same. We expelled these two comrades after we had tried them and we broke with the Fourth International, but we have not changed our principles of Socialist revolution.'[5]

But Turcios saw the light rather earlier than Yon Sosa and, once having decided to break with the Trotskyists, he was forced to begin to define his ideological position. For a former army officer, this was no easy task. He had not liked the Trotskyists, but he did not find the PGT very sympathetic either. Anxious to clarify his ideas, he convened a conference in March 1965 of the leaders of the PGT, the Communist Youth Movement (OPT), and the leaders of the various zones of resistance who had been operating in a more or less dislocated way ever since the split of the previous year. From this conference sprang the 'Provisional Revolutionary Leadership Centre' of the FAR, an attempt to give the revolutionary movement and the guerrillas centralized direction and leadership. According to Debray, this new movement crystallized round the ideas and sentiments expressed in the Edgar Ibarra letter of the previous October: 'It was on the basis of this remarkable formulation of the form and content of the Guatemalan Revolution that the new Fuerzas Armadas Rebeldes were organized, later in 1965, by agreement with the renewed and rejuvenated Partido Guatemalteco del Trabajo.'[6] The full programme was published later in 1965 as the result of a resolution passed by the Central Committee of the PGT, under the title 'Organize and Unite the Masses, Develop the People's Revolutionary War'. Like the October letter, it was by no means an orthodox Communist statement, and it contains an interesting indictment of Trotskyism: 'The formula of the socialist revolution,' says the resolution, 'is a general pattern into which the Trotskyists would like to fit the diverse and manifold realities of every country of the world.' Such 'pseudo-revolutionary talk' is false and dangerous. 'Socialism is not a state of consciousness but a scientific theory confirmed by history.'

But aside from theorizing, there was a definite call to action. It was necessary, said the resolution, to establish a Provisional Revolutionary Leadership Centre 'that would organize and press forward the people's revolutionary war'.

This remarkably outspoken document must have caused some eyebrows to be raised in the Soviet Union, for on almost every point it appeared to be a good deal closer to the Chinese than to the Soviet line. Nevertheless, the PGT's enthusiasm for the armed struggle and the revolutionary war was short-lived. César Montes, writing nearly three years later when the FAR broke with the PGT, had few illusions about the 'rejuvenated' party:

> The national conference of the PGT renewed the Central Committee with a certain number of young cadres who had distinguished themselves in the guerrilla struggle or in related tasks. But instead of carrying out the proclaimed purpose of bringing the whole PGT into the war, it was simply a manoeuvre to counteract the more radical points of view and swallow up the military leaders in a complicated disciplinary apparatus. It was not by chance that after this conference the FAR began to be mentioned in some international publications of European Communist parties as 'the Armed Forces of the PGT'.

César Montes also underlined the inadequate support by the Communist party:

> In none of those events which formed a trend or constituted determined stages and objective advances in the still brief history of our revolutionary guerrilla war—a series of positive and national characteristics of our revolution—in none of them was the initiative, far-sightedness, analysis, inspiration or organizational contribution of the PGT leadership present. The only exception was the founding of the FAR and the CPDR, in which they were forced to participate by the initiative of other forces. Their chief contribution was to slow down and distort the original impulse and aims, rather than to encourage and develop them. In other events they were wholly absent.[7]

But none of this was obvious in 1965, and when the invitations were sent out from Havana to the revolutionary movements of the world to attend the Tricontinental Conference in January 1966, Turcios Lima and the Communist FAR were asked to come and Yon Sosa and the Trotskyist MR13 were ignored.

In spite of Yon Sosa's decision to continue on his own without Trotskyist support—a decision that was made towards the end of

1965—he found himself at the receiving end of one of Fidel Castro's rare diatribes against Trotskyism. The occasion was Castro's closing speech to the Tricontinental. Castro had been goaded by the continual Trotskyist insinuations that he had murdered Che Guevara (who had 'disappeared' earlier in the year), and he was determined to launch a counter-attack.

Castro began by quoting from a long article by the head of the Latin American Political Bureau of the Fourth International, published in the Italian journal *Lotta Operaria*. This article all but accused Fidel of liquidating Guevara in order to put an end to the Latin American Revolution, and concluded with some favourable comments about the MR13 movement in Guatemala. After quoting the relevant passage, Fidel turned to the question of Guatemala:

> It is by no means a coincidence that this gentleman, leader of the Fourth International, mentions here very proudly the case of Guatemala and the November 13 Movement, because precisely in regard to this Movement, Yankee imperialism has used one of its most subtle tactics to liquidate a revolutionary movement, that is, the infiltration of it by agents of the Fourth International. . . .
>
> How did this happen? Yon Sosa was, undoubtedly, a patriotic officer. Yon Sosa heads the movement of a group of army officers—in fact, the mercenary troops who later invaded Giron took part in the crushing of this movement—and through an individual who was a merchant, who took charge of the political part of the movement, the Fourth International arranged matters so that this leader, lacking knowledge of the profound political and historical problems of revolutionary thought, allowed that agent of Trotskyism—who, we have not the slightest doubt, is an agent of imperialism—to take charge of editing a newspaper in which the programme of the Fourth International was copied from head to tail.
>
> What the Fourth International thus committed was a true crime against the revolutionary movement, to isolate it from the rest of the people, to isolate it from the masses, by corrupting it with the stupidities, the discredit and the repugnant and nauseating thing that is Trotskyism today within the field of politics. For, if Trotskyism represented at a certain stage an

erroneous position, if a position within the field of political ideas, Trotskyism became in later years a vulgar instrument of imperialism and reaction.

These gentlemen reason in such a way that, for instance, with regard to South Vietnam, where a vast revolutionary front has united the immense majority of the people and has closely grouped different sectors of the population around the liberation movement in the struggle against imperialism, to Trotskyites this is absurd, it is counter-revolutionary. . . .

Fortunately, the revolutionary movement in Guatemala was saved. And it was saved because of the clear vision of one of the officers who, together with Sosa, had started the revolutionary movement, and who, on understanding that folly, that stupidity, broke away from the November 13 Movement and organized, with other progressive and revolutionary sectors, the Rebel Armed Forces of Guatemala.

And this young officer, who had such a clear vision of the situation, is the representative of the revolutionary movement of Guatemala in this conference, Comandante Turcios. Comandante Turcios has to his credit not only the fact that he was one of the first in the armed struggle for the liberation of his oppressed people, but also the merit of having saved the Guatemalan revolution from one of the most subtle and perfidious stratagems of Yankee imperialism. . . .

And we hope that Yon Sosa, whose patriotic intentions at the beginning of the struggle are not in doubt, and whose condition as an honest man is not in doubt—although we do have very serious reservations about his attitude as a revolutionary leader—will not take too long to separate himself from those elements and rejoin the revolutionary movement in Guatemala. . . .

Turcios Lima, who now led the most significant guerrilla movement in Guatemala, had changed considerably from the youthful lieutenant who participated in the uprising five years earlier on 13 November 1960. He had become politically knowledgeable and, in particular, while benefiting from the support of the PGT, he had never lost his independence.

'I am not a Communist party member,' he told an interviewer in March 1966, though he pointed out at the same time that his philosophy was close to that of the party.[8] Although he had received Castro's nod of approval at the Tricontinental, he refused to take sides in the conflict between Moscow and Peking. He declared that he intended to keep his movement independent of world Communist currents. The FAR is 'a nationalist movement', he said, 'supported neither by Moscow nor Peking, nor Havana'.

Later, Turcios' second-in-command, César Montes, made the same point: 'Fidel Castro is not our supreme head. We realize of course that our struggle must take place on a continental level. We shall then need a leader on this level. We shall choose him ourselves when we need him. For us Fidel is no more than the living proof that our struggle can succeed. We admire him but we absolutely refuse to take orders from him.'[9]

Turcios explained that his group had neither the strength nor the desire to take over power at that moment in time. They were in the 'first stage'—one of 'survival'—in which they were trying to organize the peasantry. Later, in a second stage, which might not occur for some years, an 'equilibrium of forces' between the guerrillas and the army would be reached, and this would permit more direct and open warfare.

A reporter who interviewed César Montes in June 1966 explained that the rebels conceded that they had neither intention nor hopes of seizing power in the near future. Their aim was to build a resistance base in the countryside and a safe refuge by developing a highly conscious mass of *campesinos*. 'The more time we have to prepare the people now,' Montes explained, 'the less difficult will be the transformation to Socialism later.'[10]

Nevertheless the emphasis on the 'long war' and the qualities of the peasantry, was making a virtue out of necessity. The guerrillas simply found the countryside a more fruitful area for their ideas than the towns.

In an interview with Mario Menéndez Rodríguez, the editor of the Mexican paper, *Sucesos*, in the middle of 1966, Turcios gave a brief outline of what his movement was fighting for:

> We are fighting for land and against imperialism. In the first place, we must have freedom from intervention; we must have freedom in order to lead our country into the road of progress and take such measures as will suit the present reality. You cannot ignore the fact that we are essentially an agricultural country, with a most uneven distribution of land and a primitive system of production. It stands to reason that we must carry out

a general and thorough land reform; that is to say, not just by giving land to the peasants but providing them with the necessary credits and loans and implements. We must take such measures as will increase production and steadily lead the peasants to adopt voluntarily superior modes of production, co-operation and collectivization. But, first of all, there must be freedom, which cannot be won through elections or such other channels. There is only one road before Guate-mala, the road of armed force. In my opinion, the revolution will be made by the peasants, the workers and the urban middle strata, in other words, by the exploited who clearly realize that those who have everything, or almost everything, have not the slightest intention of surrendering and dividing up what they own on the principle of reasonable distribution. On the contrary, they are sure to leave no stone unturned to defend their all.

When asked whether an armed intervention by the United States of the type that had occurred in Santo Domingo was likely in Guatemala, Turcios replied:

We believe that there will be such an armed intervention when the puppet government, the army and police find themselves unable to control the people and find themselves too weak to protect the monopoly clique and when the régime, like that in Vietnam, begins to crumble. Yet, like the heroic people of Vietnam, we are ready, ready to shed our last drop of blood. Such a situation, a situation in which there will be large-scale intervention, is no pure hypothesis but an objective reality. But with the rising tide of the revolutionary movement of the people oppressed by imperialism, aggression will meet greater difficulties because aggression needs more marines, needs more millions of dollars and vast amounts of material of all descriptions. The struggle for liberation may be drawn out, but to defeat imperialism is the aim of not just one country. The dawn of victory is sure to break through in the end.[11]

The United States invasion of Santo Domingo in 1965, together with the occupation of South Vietnam, is a subject to which the guerrillas constantly return. Santo Domingo was, in the history of the continent, a turning-point which seemed to negate the possibility of following the Cuban road to revolution. The clock was turned back to 1954 when Arbenz was overthrown. But instead of returning to the defeatism of the era between 1954 and 1959, when the Latin American Left believed that little could be done in the face of the United States threat, the post-Santo Domingo revolutionaries began to develop a new theory. If invasion was inevitable, then perhaps it should be welcomed. While the revolutionary movement in Santo Domingo had been shattered by the landing of the Marines, in Vietnam it had been vastly strengthened. And if the Americans were forced to intervene in a number of places at the same time, the experience of Vietnam—rather than of Santo Domingo—might well be repeated. After 1965 this became a dominant theme in guerrilla theory.

Notes

1 Debray, *Revolution in the Revolution?* pp. 38–9.

2 *Le Monde*, 6 February 1966.

3 *La Época* (Montevideo), 10 August 1966. According to Turcios, another of the differences between the two groups was that 'Yon Sosa believed in an urban revolution that would spread to the countryside, while the FAR emphasized peasant action'.—*New York Times*, 18 March 1966.

4 Castaño, 'Avec les Guérrillas du Guatemala', p. 156.

5 Interview printed in *La Época* (Montevideo), 10 August 1966; reprinted in *Global Digest* (Hong Kong), VOL. IV, NO. 1, January 1967. Yon Sosa physically expelled his erstwhile Trotskyist friends from the country on 1 May, 1966; see 'Guatemala: País en Guerra', *Tricontinental* (Havana), NO. 6, 1968.

6 Debray, *Revolution in the Revolution?* p. 41.

7 Montes, 'Una ruptura lógica y necesaria'.

8 *New York Times*, 18 March 1966.

9 Jean Lartéguy, 'Les Guérrilleros: (2) portrait d'un maquisard', *Paris Match*, 26 August 1967.

10 *New York Times*, 26 June 1966.

11 *Sucesos* (Mexico City), 18 June 1966.

5. ELECTIONS AND THE DEATH OF TURCIOS

'We must view our struggle as a long-term one which will last perhaps ten,
perhaps twenty years. Our first objective is to last out, to survive.'

An FAR leader to Jean Lartéguy, 1967

The split in the guerrilla movement did not cause a measurable abatement in guerrilla activities. On 9 February 1965, the Chief of the United States military mission, Colonel Harold Houser, was shot at in his car while driving home. MR13 claimed responsibility and stated that the act 'constituted the response of the Guatemalan people to the criminal acts of Yankee imperialism in North and South Vietnam'.[1]

In May, the Deputy Minister of Defence, Colonel Ernesto Molina Arreaga, was shot dead as he left his car outside his home. And in November and December, several kidnappings of wealthy Guatemalans were organized which, according to the correspondent of the *New York Times*, 'in addition to netting more than $300,000 in ransom, struck terror in residents of the capital and came close to provoking an attempted *coup* against the régime by dissatisfied army officers'.[2]

After the attack on Colonel Houser, President Peralta declared a state of siege and suspended the constitution. Francisco Villagran Kramer and the organizers of his Revolutionary Democratic party (URD) were smartly bundled out of the country.

According to Villagran, the PGT and MR13 had 'exerted great pressure' at this stage on the URD in a further attempt to get it to join in a violent revolution against Peralta. 'It reached the point where they threatened to consider us "enemies of the people", and part of the military régime.'

He explained the situation further in an interview in July: 'Peralta is closing the door to a peaceful solution of the problem in Guatemala with his policy of persecuting democratic opponents. . . . He is falling into exactly the situation the Communists want to bring about, where no alternative but violent revolution will be left.'[3]

The policy of the Guatemalan Communists, Villagran Kramer continued, was to create 'a set of conditions which would force the United States to intervene, as it did in Santo Domingo, on the theory that that would unite the Guatemalan people behind them in a struggle against *imperialismo yanqui*'. He recalled that in January and February an intense debate had taken place within the URD about whether to support the guerrillas or whether to try to seek a peaceful political solution. 'The government resolved the whole debate by expelling us from the country,' he observed wryly. But a MR13 commander, referring to the URD, commented that 'they are paying the penalty for believing in a petty bourgeois utopia: a "peaceful" solution to dictatorship. Here there can be no peaceful solution, and there can be no elections.'[4]

Peaceful solution, perhaps not, but elections, to everyone's surprise, were apparently on Colonel Peralta's agenda. After a new Constitution had been pushed through on 15 September 1965, which declared Communism and other forms of totalitarianism to be illegal, elections for the Presidency were announced for the following March.

There were three candidates, two colonels and a civilian. The latter, Mario Méndez Montenegro who was the leader of the Revolutionary party, was found shot dead in his home on 31 October. Though attempts were made to explain it as suicide, it was subsequently admitted that he had been assassinated. The next day the Revolutionary party chose his brother, Julio César Méndez Montenegro, a former Dean of the University of San Carlos Law School, to be their presidential candidate.

One of the colonels was Miguel Àngel Ponciano Samayoa, who had been the army Chief of Staff. He had the backing of Castillo Armas' old National Liberation Movement. The other colonel, Juan de Díos Aguilar de León, was supported by Colonel Peralta himself.

The elections were to prove yet another major bone of contention between the PGT and the FAR. During the Tricontinental in January 1966, Turcios came out firmly against supporting Méndez Montenegro or indeed having anything to do with the electoral process:

We do not propose to prevent the elections from taking place, because as yet we do not have sufficient strength to do so.

Quite a lot of people remain who still naïvely expect something from the electoral game. So there will be elections. But let it be clear that when we are strong enough, and when the awareness of our people has better grasped the hollowness of elections with a reactionary government in power, we shall forcibly prevent this vile deceit of the people from continuing.

. . . If we revolutionaries were to participate in these elections, or if we called upon the people to participate in them by voting for the Revolutionary party or any of the other opposition parties, we would be giving our backing, our principled support, our revolutionary approval and the support of the masses who believe in us, to people who we know have no scruples, who we know are the accomplices of reaction and imperialism.[5]

This point of view was not welcomed by all the leaders of the PGT, and some of them had been considerably concerned by the outcome of the Tricontinental. While welcoming Fidel's attack on Trotskyism in general and Yon Sosa in particular, they were somewhat perturbed at the thought that Turcios Lima and the FAR might in future owe more allegiance to Cuba than to the Moscow-influenced PGT.

Consequently, while Turcios was still away in Havana, the Provisional Revolutionary Leadership Centre of the FAR (CPDR), at the instigation of the PGT, took a decision to support Méndez Montenegro and the Revolutionary party, in spite of the fact that the Edgar Ibarra Front, led during Turcios' absence by César Montes, voted against the decision.

On his return to Guatemala, Turcios did in fact loyally decide to abide by the decision taken in his absence. Later in the year, after the elections, he explained the FAR's attitude to an interviewer:

In the first place, it is necessary to explain the only real significance of the line towards the last election that was approved by the FAR. Even though the election took place in relative tranquillity, it was tinged with a variety of political colours which were the immediate outcome of the complicated situation in present-day Guatemala. One must not forget that in this country of ours, which has long been under dictatorial rule, it is unavoidable that not a few people are tired of so many deaths and so much bloodshed. Thus, these citizens sought and expected a final change of the system through peaceful means. It was precisely because of this that the revolutionary FAR leadership, aware of the situation and always attentive to satisfying in one way or another the needs, demands and aspirations of the people of all sectors, decided to vote for Julio César Méndez Montenegro—not because we supposed this distinguished lawyer would be able to modify the present situation; that, we know, is a task he could not tackle. The objective is very clear; voting for Julio César Méndez Montenegro represents a form of struggle against the arbitrary behaviour of the government and also a demonstration to public opinion—in this case, particularly international public opinion—of the complete and total repudiation of the dictatorial regime. Therefore the victory of the candidate of the Revolutionary party signifies a political victory of the FAR, for the Guatemalan people have through the voting expressed their irrepressible desire for changing the system.

However, it is necessary to repeat and stress the point that the guerrillas do not have the slightest doubt about what road to take, for there is only one road. This is by no means the road of elections but the road of armed struggle.[6]

Nevertheless, the PGT's decision to support Méndez Montenegro—and more particularly its growing belief that the armed struggle emphasized by Turcios was not the best way forward in the circumstances—created a serious division within the revolutionary ranks. The exact details are not known, but it appears that a number of PGT leaders who had been living in exile in Mexico, perturbed by the growing militancy of the guerrillas, decided to return to Guatemala before election day in order to sort things out.[7] It was a disastrous decision.

For on the eve of the elections, on 5 March 1966, the police surrounded a modest one-storey stucco house in Guatemala City.[8] After a gun battle, 26 Communists or Communist sympathizers were arrested, including the leader of the PGT, Victor Manuel Gutiérrez, and the Secretary-General of the National Peasants Federation, Leonardo Castillo Flores.

To many people's surprise, particularly that of the army, Méndez Montenegro won the election, though he failed to get an absolute majority over his military rivals. To be confirmed as President, he had to have the affirmative vote of the Congress. There was initially some doubt as to whether Peralta, who was due to relinquish power on 30 June, would actually do so. But this, and a similar fear that the disgruntled Colonel Ponciano would stage a coup, proved to be groundless. On 5 May Méndez Montenegro was duly elected by the Congress.

One of the reasons why the army allowed him to take power seems to have been that he agreed that the Minister of Defence should be appointed by the army and remain responsible to the armed forces rather than to the Presidency. From the very beginning of his period of power, therefore, Méndez was effectively controlled by his colonels. United States pressure on the colonels may also have been important.

Meanwhile, there was some concern about the fate of Victor Gutiérrez and his colleagues who had been captured by the police in March. The FAR mounted a big propaganda campaign, particularly in the university, in an attempt to get the government to reveal the whereabouts of the detained political prisoners.

On 4 May two important figures were kidnapped by the guerrillas, who indicated that they would not be returned until the government announced what had happened to the left-wingers who had disappeared. Those kidnapped were the presidential Press Secretary, Baltassar Morales Cruz, and the Chief Justice of the Supreme Court, Romeo Augusto de León. According to press reports, Morales was captured after a gun battle in central Guatemala City in which his son and chauffeur were killed.[9] In an interview in June with the editor of the Mexican paper *Sucesos*, Turcios explained the kidnapping:

> The purpose of kidnapping these two men is to compel the military government under Peralta Azurdia to make known the whereabouts of the twenty-eight political prisoners who disappeared several months ago. . . . The kidnapping of these two officials by no means implies that the FAR intend to threaten them with death. The FAR protect their lives even when the dictator refuses to meet the terms already put forward.
>
> We are not executioners like the ruling militarists. We are young people who are conscious of our role as social reformers. We merely pit revolutionary justice against counter-revolutionary violence.
>
> Morales Cruz, who is the Minister of Information and spokesman of the military government, is well aware that the

statement of the FAR on the question of political prisoners is perfectly correct. However, he knows nothing about the murders, at least it appears to be so. And since Peralta Azurdia has given orders to execute all those who have been captured, naturally he cannot make any statement in public. Therefore he resorted to denying everything.

On the other hand, leaving aside the fact that the kidnapping has demonstrated to opinion at home and abroad that the twenty-eight revolutionary leaders were executed by the armed guards of Peralta Azurdia, the political blows this action dealt to the military dictatorship on the eve of the restoration of the 'constitution' has no precedent in Guatemala. The most important conclusions in this regard are as follows:

1) For the first time the reactionary strata have taken a different attitude towards the FAR.

2) The illegal government under Peralta Azurdia is already in a state of war with them, no longer regarding the insurgents as 'bandits', 'mobs' and 'hooligans', etc.

3) Some organizations which originally stood aloof in the disturbed political situation have now taken an interest in the current situation. They have taken the proposals of the FAR into consideration and levelled strong charges against the ruling militarists. The Red Cross Society and the Archbishopric are a case in point.

4) The universities, University Students' Association, Lawyers' Association, Law Students' Association, Faculties of Law and other progressive bodies and their leaders are all inclined to the new political current. They have openly castigated the dictatorship as the source of all misfortunes in Guatemala and urged it to accede to the demands of the FAR.

5) In the past some of the Guatemalan newspapers adopted a slavish attitude towards every action of Peralta Azurdia and his followers, and even went so far as to refuse to publish reports about the capture of political prisoners, or paid no heed to the requests made by the mothers of the captured that their sons be put on public trial. But now they have made a complete about-turn and begun to publish in full all the bulletins issued by the leading centre of the FAR.

6) Public opinion supports us mainly because in the past many people knew nothing about the record of the military dictatorship. In the new Congress a section of opinion demanded that Colonel Maximiliano Serrano Cordova, the Minister of Internal Affairs, come forward to give an account of the facts exposed by the FAR. The authorities were so utterly shameless that they have even sown the seeds of hatred among the relatives of Morales Cruz and Romeo Augusto de León.[10]

After the kidnappings, the government imposed the customary state of siege. But in spite of this a further kidnapping took place on 26 May, this time of one of the two Vice-Presidents of the newly elected Congress, Héctor Méndez de la Riva. (He was later released, and, much shaken, retired to recuperate in Miami.) It was not until July, after Méndez Montenegro had formally taken over as President, that the truth leaked out.

On 16 July two former police agents told the University Students' Association what had occurred. The men captured in March had all been shot by a firing squad. Three of them, including the two labour leaders, were tortured in the police headquarters in Guatemala City and subsequently driven to a military base on the Pacific and shot. Their bodies were put in sacks and dropped into the sea from an army transport plane.

Others killed were said to include Kris Yon Cerna, the niece of Yon Sosa, and Eunice Campirán de Aguilar Mora, the wife of a Mexican student, David Aguilar Mora, who had disappeared after his capture in Guatemala in December. She had come to Guatemala to look for her husband. Both women were said to have been beaten to death with clubs and buried in shallow graves near the Zacapa military base.[11]

With the confirmation of the widespread rumour that those detained had been assassinated, the guerrillas released the two officials on 31 August in exchange for a student guerrilla, José Maria Ortíz Vides, who had been captured by the police in June.

In spite of these disagreeable events which characterized the last months of the Peralta dictatorship, many people believed that the advent of a civilian President might create an atmosphere of national unity in which a truce between government forces and the guerrillas might be possible.

Turcios rejected the idea from the very start. Interviewed in March to discover his views on the new President, he replied: 'In the final analysis nothing will change. The army will not stop its repressions. So we won't stop either.'[12]

César Montes was of a similar opinion. 'I have a great deal of respect for Méndez,' he told a reporter. 'He was my professor in law school and I believe he is an honest and intelligent man. But the army will never allow him to carry out the profound reforms our country needs.'[13]

On 1 July Méndez Montenegro formally took over as President. His Vice-President, Clement Maroquín Rojas, issued an appeal to the guerrillas to cooperate with the government. Yon Sosa's reply was as blunt as those of Turcios and César Montes:

> We have not asked for a truce. There is no truce. The period of temporary peace we have had has helped the moving of patrols to other provinces. There is no truce at all. . . . I think that any-one who has Marxist ideas will not accept, even in his dreams, an amnesty. If we accept that, all the past crimes and mistakes will be forgotten. Moreover, we are no criminals, we have committed no crimes, therefore we do not ask for pardon.[14]

The PGT were desperately anxious for the amnesty proposal to be accepted, but eventually the conditions that the government was forced to attach to it, under pressure from right-wing political groups and the army, were so onerous that even the orthodox Communists felt bound to oppose it. A party spokesman, J. M. Fortuny, explained why in the pages of the *World Marxist Review*:

> The right-wing conspirators want to see the President fail in his efforts to enter into a dialogue with the guerrillas. For this reason they blocked the amnesty which the government submitted to Congress. Paradoxically enough, the government was far more interested in an amnesty than the revolutionaries for whom it was intended. An amnesty without unacceptable conditions (and it was such an amnesty that the government proposed) would have given the President sufficient moral grounds for a dialogue with the guerrillas. But congressmen from the parties of the Right and the more reactionary wing of the Revolutionary party introduced a number of amend-ments, one of which stipulated that the guerrillas must sur-render their arms within eight days. In this way the reac-tionaries turned the amnesty proposal into an ultimatum of a

kind that might be presented to an enemy who had either been defeated or was on the verge of defeat, which certainly was not the case. In the circumstances the Rebel Armed Forces were quite justified in rejecting both the ultimatum and the amnesty.[15]

On 16 July, two weeks after Méndez Montenegro had taken over, the FAR issued a statement, signed by Turcios and Bernardo Alvarado Monzón, the guerrillas' chief civilian leader, stating that 'despite the popular attraction of the new régime, the army retains most of the effective power. The Guatemalan army is still the same reactionary tool of native plutocracy and foreign companies and therefore must be fought to the bitter end.'[16]

The army was in fact ready and waiting, and Guatemalan history since Méndez Montenegro assumed the Presidency is the story of how a small-scale localized guerrilla struggle developed into something approaching a civil war. But this chapter was not to be written by Turcios Lima.

Early in the morning of 2 October 1966, he was driving an Austin Cooper on the Roosevelt Highway on the outskirts of Guatemala City. With him was an 18-year-old student, Silvia Yvonne Flores Letona. According to press reports, the car hit an object in the road, over-turned and burst into flames. Later a broadcast by Havana radio alleged that there had been an 'explosion of an unknown character' in the car before it caught alight.[17]

Turcios was killed outright; the girl died on arriving at hospital. A third woman, travelling with them, escaped with burns and bruises. The following day an estimated 1,500 mourners attended his funeral at the cemetery in Guatemala City. 'I could die tomorrow,' he once said. 'Things would not change. Others will carry on.'

One of his friends made an oration over his grave:

Friends, Gautemalan *compañeros*. . . . Like all true revolution-aries, Turcios knew that life should be lived to the full in the service of a high and noble ideal. . . . Comandante Turcios loved life in order to build the coming victory of all Guatemalans by revolutionary means. . . . With him the Guatemalan revolution loses one of its youngest and most experienced leaders.[18]

Notes

1   Interview by Adolfo Gilly with Francisco Amado Granados (Gilly, 'The Guerrilla Movement in Guatemala', Part I, p. 34). The MR13 commander continued: 'It was not the military attaché as an individual whom we attacked, it was his role. He came here to organize repression against the Guatemalan masses, just as his counterparts are doing in Vietnam. Our action had the added purpose of focusing the attention of the United States people on us—it was a way of appealing for their support in our struggle. The military attaché was a criminal, forming part of a team of criminals, who are preparing in the name of the United States capitalism, a worldwide atomic war. They are dragging their own people towards such a war.'

2   *New York Times*, 18 March 1966.

3   *Latin America Times*, 22 July 1965.

4   Gilly, 'The Guerrilla Movement in Guatemala', Part I, p. 33.

5   Turcios Lima, quoted in Montes, 'Una ruptura lógica y necesaria'.

6   Turcios Lima interviewed by Mario Ménendez Rodríguez, *Sucesos*, 18 June 1966, reprinted in *Global Digest* (Hong Kong), VOL. III, NO. 10, October 1966.

7   *Latin America* (Interpress Newsletter), 26 January 1968.

8   *New York Times*, 7 March 1966.

9   *New York Times*, 6 May 1966.

10 *Sucesos* (Mexico City), 18 June 1966.

11 *New York Times*, 18 July 1966.

12 *New York Times*, 18 March 1966.

13 *New York Times*, 26 June 1966.

14 *La Época* (Montevideo), 10 August 1966; reprinted in *Global Digest* (Hong Kong).

15 José Manuel Fortuny, 'Guatemala: the Political Situation and Revolutionary Tactics', *World Marxist Review*, VOL. X, NO. 2, February 1967.

16 *New York Times*, 18 July 1966.

17 *New York Times*, 4 October 1966. Jean Lartéguy's story that Turcios stole the car from outside a restaurant in order to take his girlfriend for a ride, and they crashed into a wall, is equally probable.

18 Lartéguy, 'Les Guérrilleros: portrait d'un maquisard'.

6. César Montes and The Growth of Anti-Communist Organizations

A U.S. professor visiting guerrilla areas last spring [1967] reported that
the school hot-lunch programme was reaching 300,000 kids daily,
'with compliments of the Guatemalan army and "la Alianza del
Presidente Kennedy".' Over 100 water-wells had been drilled,
several kilometres of roads built. The peasants, well aware of
the purpose, were getting what they could out of it. But a peasant in a
non-guerrilla (and hence neglected) zone presented a sad face to the
professor. 'If only,' he said, 'we could get some guerrilleros . . .'
Cedric Belfrage

The natural successor to Turcios was his second-in-command, César
Montes, with whom he had been intimately associated since 1963.
Although Montes was much more closely aligned with the PGT than
Turcios had been, the changeover of leadership was less significant
than appeared. Montes was a member of the Central Committee of the
PGT, and this fact served to postpone rather than to accelerate the
inevitable break between the guerrillas and the orthodox Communists.
More important was the fact that Montes, a civilian, lacked the contacts
that Turcios had always retained in the army. This was to be a major
disadvantage at a time when the army was in the process of launching
a new offensive.

The new leader of the FAR was born in 1942. At the age of 13 he
was expelled from his Catholic school for expressing a hostile attitude
towards the CIA coup that overthrew President Arbenz. At 18 he was

leading student demonstrations, and by the age of 20 he had already taken to the hills. Four years later, barely 24, he was the guerrillas' principal leader. His small stature and baby face earned him the nickname, *El Chiris*, meaning 'small child'. He had some reason to dislike the existing set-up in Guatemala. His brother, who was wholly unpolitical, had been detained earlier by the army and tortured to death.

The death of Turcios in October 1966 had coincided with a new major campaign against the guerrillas, launched by the army. In part this was a measure of the government's desperation, for throughout the period since July 1966 when Méndez Montenegro took office, he had been more in danger of overthrow from the Right than from the Left. Horrified by the fact that their man had not won the elections in March, certain sections of the army began planning a Castillo Armas-style coup. Arms were sent in from Nicaragua, and military training camps were set up in the east of the country and in Honduras. President Méndez had to seek special assurances from the Presidents of Honduras and El Salvador that they would not involve themselves in Guatemalan affairs.

In Guatemala City itself, right-wing groups began a new campaign of violence. Bombs were thrown at newspaper offices, radio stations and public buildings, with a view, as one correspondent put it, to 'trying to create a climate of insecurity that would encourage the army to seize power once again'.[1]

To pacify the army, who suspected him of having Communist sympathies, Méndez was forced to allow them to have a free hand in exterminating the guerrillas—the inevitable result of which was to stir up yet more animosity and hatred within the country. It also appears that he was strongly urged by the United States to liquidate the guerrilla problem once and for all.

Whereas the military dictator Enrique Peralta had refused to involve United States troops in Guatemala, the civilian President Méndez Montenegro had no such scruples. Before long a company of Green Beret 'Special Forces' was installed in the country assisting the anti-insurgency campaign. The United States soon let it be known that it was much happier with Méndez as President than they had been with Peralta.[2] 'The new government,' the *New York Times* reported, 'has found a willing partner in the United States through its local AID mission, which, after three frustrating years of dealing with an inefficient military régime, has suddenly found a group it can talk with and accomplish things with.'[3]

In terms of economic development, this was very little; but as to dealing with guerrillas, the Guatemalan army, with its United States advisers, was to be given an opportunity which had been denied it throughout the period of military dictatorships—the chance of clearing out the guerrillas root and branch.

When Méndez Montenegro came to power, the guerrilla movement was still divided in two, with Turcios and César Montes of the FAR operating in Zacapa province, and Yon Sosa and the MR13 in Izabal. Feeling that the guerrillas were essentially a military problem that had to be dealt with by the army, Méndez appointed one of the tougher colonels, Carlos Araña, to be the military commander of Zacapa.

Colonel Araña soon found that his troops were in an extremely poor state of training and that they had an exceptionally bad reputation with the local civilian population. He therefore set aside July to October 1966 as a period during which intensive training would be carried out. It was during these months that Méndez made his amnesty offers to the guerrillas, knowing that they would be refused. These political moves, however, left the army time to get into better shape.

Together with purely military training, the government organized—on American advice—a 'Pilot Plan for the socio-economic development of the North-East'. This project was put into effect on 1 February 1967 and involved the co-operation of five Ministries, including Defence, Health, Education and Public Works. Its purpose was to provide the peasants in the guerrilla areas with sufficient welfare to coax them out of their friendly attitude towards the guerrillas. César Montes was suitably scathing about the role of the American advisers:

> They operate in a mechanical way. They have read in Mao's works that the guerrilla is to the people what the fish is to the water, and they know that fish die when taken out of water. They really believe that they can do the same thing to us, that

they can isolate us. And perhaps they can deceive part of the people part of the time, but not the whole time. The peasants need land but they don't have any. They need housing, but the government builds homes for military officers. You cannot stop the peasants from helping us when you don't give them the things they need.[4]

At about the same time as 'Plan Piloto' began, Colonel Araña moved into action against the guerrilla forces, using para-military groups as well as regular soldiers. Originally designed as anti-Communist vigilante groups, these para-military brigades very quickly acquired a life of their own. Gradually they coalesced into three major anti-Communist organizations Mano Blanca ('White Hand'), Nueva Organisación Anticomunista (NOA; New Anti-Communist Organization) and the Consejo Anti-comunista de Guatemala (CODEG; Anti-Communist Council of Guatemala). Members of CODEG, according to one of their leaflets, promise under oath 'before the altar of the Fatherland to fight to liquidation the following anti-patriots': the PGT, people associated with the rebels, the Communist Youth wing, the University Students' Association, 'professional people associated with Communism', and 'people named to office by the Deputy Minister of Education, who tries to appoint "Reds".' Finally, the leaflet contains a list of 22 individuals marked down for execution.[5]

In May 1967 ten bodies were found shot dead, bearing the marks of torture, shortly after one of these Fascist organizations had issued a bulletin stating that it intended to kill 'ten leftists for every soldier, policeman, or other anti-Communist' killed by the guerrillas.[6]

Officially the army denied any responsibility for the right-wing terrorist groups. A *New York Times* correspondent gave a different point of view: 'No amount of army denial has been able to shake the conviction, widely held among informed persons here, that most of the rightist, anti-Communist groups are, in fact, a creation of the army and that many of their members are junior army officers. Moreover, there exists a strongly held belief that the government gave at least tacit consent to the underground operations.'[7] Whoever authorized the use of these para-military vigilante groups, they proved to be remarkably successful in slowly eroding the guerrillas' peasant base. This was an area, after all, in which the guerrillas had been active for five years or more. Yet, faced by a systematic military push, and the use of informers, civic action programmes, and indiscriminate methods of attack which led to huge casualties among innocent peasants, the guerrillas soon found themselves very much on the defensive, and forced to adopt a strategy of mobility.

In an interview that César Montes gave to a Uruguyan journalist, Eduardo Galeano, early in 1967, he outlined the new strategy that the FAR was being forced to follow:

> Our columns are extremely mobile. This is why the army can never catch us, despite all the operations they have launched. We have several patrols operating in different parts of the country. They have not been able to capture any of our camps for a simple reason: we never set up fixed camps. Only a few of our food deposits have been discovered, but that is all. It is hard to walk so much, but you soon become used to it. Guerrillas have walked, for instance, from the Izabal Lake to San Agustín Acasaguastlán, which means you have to go across the highest peaks in Guatemala. We have been able to do that in twenty days, without stopping, going from six in the morning until sundown every day, just eating breakfast before leaving and supper before going to sleep.[8]

Although mobility was the order of the day, work among the peasants was not neglected. Whenever possible the guerrillas would continue their by now well-established custom of stopping in villages to explain their activities and their motives. 'The self-definition of the guerrilla would be that he is a teacher,' explained a Maryknoll priest, Father Blase Bonpane, when interviewed in January 1968, shortly after being expelled from Guatemala:

> But he knows from long experience that it is impossible to teach what he wants to without defending himself, so he is armed. The guerrilla is not a tinpot revolutionary. We have hundreds of examples in Latin America of palace revolutions where a small

group moves in, takes over the country, and continues the same corruption as before only under different management.

The guerrilla, however, is working for a development of the thinking of the people, or popular development. The guerrilla in the small village will teach literacy, reading and writing. There will be a sub-machine-gun near by. The people certainly are afraid of him at first because they know he's armed and they have only seen arms in the hands of the military. It sometimes takes a long time to get across the idea that the guerrilla is actually there in the name of the peasant.

Now the guerrilla has not always been successful in this; there have been errors. I don't think we should glorify the movement as something absolutely faultless or perfect. In a certain village a guerrilla asked for something to eat and the peasant refused, so the guerrilla shot him. But I would simply say that such cases are examples of things that the leadership would be opposed to. They want the peasant to be in their favour and they want to develop a popular spirit of community.[9]

The guerrillas also wanted their movement to gather strength without any spirit of sectarianism. 'All these comrades of Indian origin that you see here in the camp,' César Montes told Galeano, 'are Catholic, fervently Catholic.'

The fact that there are some Communists in the FAR does not mean that our movement acts as the military arm of any party. The FAR is not the military arm of the PGT. Ours is a broad patriotic movement, with a very simple programme: we Guatemalans want to run our own affairs without any outside interference, either military, economic or political. We are organizing the people for revolutionary war; the guerrillas are the seed of the great people's army which will eventually be able to offer a power alternative.[10]

Although mistakes of the type described by Father Bonpane were inevitable, it seems that, in general, the guerrillas went to great lengths to ingratiate themselves with the peasantry. With their enemies, however, they were ruthless. César Montes described to Galeano how on one occasion an American named Ronald Hornberger had come to the guerrilla camp, claiming to be a sympathetic journalist:

> He acted very confident; we talked with him in the mountains for a few days. He dropped names and addresses from the capital, but we double-checked within a few days and found that none of the people he had mentioned had ever heard of him. He also lied about the place he had supposedly left his luggage. He seemed to be interested only in the military aspects of our struggle and not at all in our political motivations. All his questions were of a highly specialized military nature. He was an ace in the handling of any weapon. He brought some military equipment that he said was a gift to us.
>
> We tried him and executed him. On his waist under the shirt he wore a fine nylon cord, the kind used by Green Berets for strangling.[11]

It is difficult to calculate the extent of United States interference and how far this played a crucial role in reversing the gains made by the guerrillas in previous years. The FAR itself had concluded that 'sooner or later Guatemala will become another arena of United States intervention. The first military actions in the context of intervention have already been undertaken. And as our struggle grows, this intervention is bound to be extended.'[12]

In September 1967, the Vice President of Guatemala, Clemente Marroquín Rojas, revealed in an interview with an Interpress reporter that sorties were being flown from United States bases in Panama against guerrilla hideouts:

> Marroquín Rojas stated that in recent months a squadron of United States aircraft piloted by U. S. personnel had flown from bases in Panama, delivered loads of napalm on targets suspected of being guerrilla haunts, and flown back to their bases without landing on Guatemalan soil.[13]

This same reporter went on to state that:

> United States Special Forces are carrying out intensive training of local personnel in anti-guerrilla warfare, interrogation of prisoners, and jungle survival. The United States advisers

are also currently accompanying Guatemalan patrols on anti-guerrilla duty. As well as giving training in offensive techniques, the United States forces are co-operating in plans of Civic Action in the countryside, the distribution of foodstuffs such as dried milk and medicines and the execution of simple jobs of public works.

It seems improbable that the Guatemalan army could have dealt with the guerrillas so speedily had it not been for this outside assistance. But the guerrillas also suffered from a malady which is endemic in all clandestine movements—defection and betrayal. Perhaps the greatest blow the guerrillas suffered was the defection of 'El Gallo', a former army sergeant who had joined them after committing a murder.[14]

El Gallo gave himself up to the army and gave invaluable information not only on people and places, but also revealed the operation of the guerrillas' postal system. The communication between town and country was all but destroyed through his betrayal. Treachery is a daily hazard which the guerrilla fighter always has to reckon on. However, its likelihood, and indeed its frequent incidence, must be considered as one of the major difficulties in the way of the fulfilment of guerrilla theory.

Notes

1 *New York Times*, 15 October 1966.

2 Enrique Peralta, like many successful right-wing dictators in Latin America, liked to emphasize his anti-Americanism. According to one source, he restricted the number of Guatemalan officers allowed to go for training to the United States or Panama, refused to allow AID to set up educational television on the grounds that the United States would censor material and put out commercials, and refused to allow his officers to co-operate in providing the United States with intelligence reports on guerrilla activities on the grounds that they already knew 'too much'. See Jon Frappier, 'Guatemala Military Camp under Liberal Command', *Viet Report* (New York), April–May 1968.

3 *New York Times*, 13 October 1966.

4 Galeano, *Guatemala, Clave de Latinoamérica*.

5 *The Times*, 23 May 1967.

6 *New York Times*, 27 May 1967.

7 *New York Times*, 15 July 1967. J. M. Fortuny, a leading Guatemalan Communist, gave the PGT version of the origins of these events in an article in the *World Marxist Review*: 'On 22 May, 1965, after the execution by the revolutionaries of Colonel Ernesto Molina Arreaga, Peralta Azurdia's deputy defence minister and chief liaison agent for the CIA, a secret conference of high-ranking officers proposed to the government that all revolutionary leaders be seized and dealt with summarily in revenge for Arreaga's death. A few hours later this proposal was examined by the Council of Ministers. "After lively discussion" it was agreed that the problem, in view of its importance, should be submitted to the United States State Department for final decision.

'The machine went into motion. The same evening Rafael Escobar Arguello, Minister of Information, left for the U.S.A. "for consultations". Upon his return, he announced that Washington considered the proposal "inexpedient" in as much as its realization would "undermine the prestige of the government and the army" and, moreover, cause serious dissatisfaction among the public. The United States advisers suggested instead that the government, the military and the anti-Communist leaders should form and train special groups who would murder revolutionary leaders "on the quiet".

'The "advice" was accepted down to the last detail. Soon gangs of cut-throats appeared in various parts of the country, and primarily in the areas of guerrilla action. Today it is known that these gangs have special camps of their own and that the army not only turns a blind eye to them but assigns officers to help them.'—J. M. Fortuny, 'Guatemala: the Political Situation and Revolutionary Tactics'.

8 Galeano, *Guatemala, Clave de Latinoamérica*.

9 Interview between Jon Frappier and Father Blase Bonpane on 24 January 1968, in *Viet Report* (New York), April–May 1968.

10 Galeano, *Guatemala, Clave de Latinoamérica*, p. 20.

11 Ibid.

12 Quoted in Fortuny, 'Guatemala: the Political Situation'.

13 *Latin America* (Interpress Newsletter), 15 September 1967.

14 Jean Lartéguy gives this detail.

Faced with these serious military reverses, the guerrillas began a major reappraisal of their political position. This involved the FAR's relationship both with the PGT, and with Yon Sosa and the MR13. Since Castro's attack on Yon Sosa at the Tricontinental, relations between the two movements had been cool, but during 1966 Yon Sosa had divested himself of his Trotskyist support. Hence, in theory, there was little that divided the two groups, and during the course of 1967 there were discussions between Yon Sosa and César Montes about a future common strategy.

The death of Turcios had eased the problem which might have arisen about the leadership of a future united movement. The solution eventually arrived at late in 1967—the death of Che Guevara in October 1967 and the need to close ranks seems to have been an important factor in accelerating the agreement—was for Yon Sosa to join the FAR as its leader, with César Montes as his second-in-command.[1]

The accretion of Yon Sosa and the ex-Trotskyists from the MR13 to the ranks of the FAR would inevitably have led to difficulties with the PGT. But in fact relations between guerrilla movement and parent party had been strained for some considerable time. By the end of 1967 the FAR had little more than a formal link with the Communists. At the Conference of the Organization for Latin American Solidarity (OLAS) in Havana in August 1967, there was some private criticism of this continuing connection, voiced, in particular, by the representative of the Venezuelan Armed Forces of National Liberation (FALN), which had broken with the Venezuelan Communist party the year before.[2] After the

OLAS Conference the Guatemalan delegation, which included Montes, left for Moscow, and many believed that he was going to accept the Russian view, which by this time favoured a strategic retreat on the part of the guerrillas.

Earlier the PGT had been more enthusiastic about guerrilla activity, though always with some reservations. In his article in the *World Marxist Review* written in December 1966, the leading Guatemalan Communist, J. M. Fortuny, wrote:

> Some people feel that the present political situation affords grounds for changing the line of the party, for turning to the peaceful way as the only possible alternative for the present line. Those who think so confuse, at best, the *forms of struggle* and the *overall course of the revolution*, or, at worst, reduce the question of the party line to a purely tactical matter.
>
> The party has already made its stand clear, but it will not be amiss to repeat once again: we hold that defining the course of the revolution is a question of *strategy*, while the choice of the form of struggle is one of *tactics*. The question of recharting the overall course can objectively arise only as a result of radical qualitative changes in the situation which only the victory of the popular, anti-imperialist revolution can bring about. Our party holds that in the present conditions such a revolution can be carried out only by adhering to the strategy of armed action. . . . The form of the struggle is another matter. This is a tactical issue which depends on the arena of struggle and the concrete circumstances, in other words, on transient, non-qualitative factors. . . .
>
> Lenin, as Marx before him, said: '*Never play* with insurrection, but when beginning it realize firmly that you must *go all the way*.' We believe that we are not taking a mechanical approach if we apply this basic rule to the revolutionary people's war (since it is a variant of insurrection) to which the Guatemalan Communists have had recourse because of the specific conditions of the country.[3]

Developing his theme further, Fortuny made it clear that guerrilla warfare was not on any account to be considered the one essential aspect of the anti-imperialist struggle:

The steady development of revolutionary action (in particular, the opening of new guerrilla fronts) in no way detracts from the party's efforts to build alliances or to achieve unity of action with the remainder of the Left and with all groups and organizations having influence among the masses. In particular the party of Labour is determined not to allow the Revolutionary party [Méndez Montenegro's party] to capitalize on our sectarian mistakes to win support among these groups and to isolate the Communists in the Rebel Armed Forces.

The guerrillas themselves had been gradually moving away from this position. Indeed, they had never endorsed it. But it took some time before the inherent incompatibilities between their attitude and that of the PGT became wholly clarified. By the beginning of 1968, however, the guerrillas were ready for a break, and on 10 January, from a camp in the Sierra de las Minas, five of the FAR's most important leaders issued a declaration announcing the separation of the FAR from the PGT.[4]

The declaration rehearsed the major grievances that had arisen between the guerrillas and the Communists in the years since 1965 when the Provisional Centre of Revolutionary Leadership (CPDR) had been set up. From the very beginning, argued the guerrillas, the Communists had insisted that the military leadership thrown up in the course of the struggle should be subordinate to their political directives. Things had come to such a pass, they continued, that 'even Comandante Turcios himself, who had remained in the mountains from November 1963 to February 1965, was forced to come down to the city to fulfil some purely political task'.

The bitterness of the guerrillas against the orthodox Communists is best shown in this phrase: 'After four years of fighting this is the balance sheet: 300 revolutionaries fallen in combat, 3,000 men of the people murdered by Julio César Méndez Montenegro's régime. The PGT (its ruling clique) supplied the ideas and the FAR the dead.'

César Montes was not able to be present at the meeting which produced this document, but ten days later, on 21 January 1968, he too issued a statement supporting the position taken by his guerrilla colleagues. The definitive break, he wrote, that has occurred between the FAR and the PGT 'is by no means an unexpected or fortuitous event'. There was a deep divergence 'between two ideas, two attitudes toward the war, toward the Revolution, toward the people, both determined by deep class roots and a historic moment'.

> On one side there is the revolutionary idea, which sees war as the people's instrument and method for taking power into their own hands so as to liberate themselves and make their revolution: the Socialist revolution. Therefore it is not subject to the fear that this may be a total war, long, bloody and generalized. This is a radical vision, revolutionary, audacious, young, dynamic. On the other side is the pseudo-revolutionary idea, which does not believe in the people's ability to take power into their own hands; which has confidence in the ability of the bourgeoisie to direct a democratic régime of state capitalism progressing peacefully, evolving tranquilly towards Socialism. It is, therefore, a concept that opposes war, is wary of the possibility of winning such a war, prefers a road of successive displacements of the bourgeois factions in power until the arrival at some combination which gives the Left influence, participation in the government. Under the pressure of events and popular feeling, this concept can go so far as to accept a limited, small-scale war, static and indefinite which, in addition, it would try to use as a political argument to make the bourgeoisie recognize its right of participation in government. This is a submissive, opportunist, fainthearted, outmoded, passive vision.

César Montes then went on to support the belief of the other guerrillas that in fact the PGT had never been noticeably active in providing leaders for the fight:

> It is known that no—not a single—military operation in our armed struggle to date has been inspired, guided or led—directly or indirectly—by the leading clique of the PGT, which calls itself a party. Its members never bothered to study the problems of war or its laws; they never made any attempt to analyse the experiences of the combats of the people; on no occasion did they busy themselves even with formulating a strategic plan for the war. How did they presume to lead a revolution whose course, as they themselves have admitted verbally, is that of war?

Montes concluded by announcing his resignation from the PGT:

> Perhaps I should publicly announce my resignation from membership and all the positions to which I was named in the PGT hierarchy. This statement will announce it to the Guatemalan people and comrades and friends from other countries. But I will never resign my position as a Communist, which is earned not through a membership card but through struggle, through combat, through acting ideologically in harmony with the proletariat—that is, serving its interests in every way.[5]

Faced with the withdrawal of the bulk of the guerrillas from the PGT, the Guatemalan Communists hastily had to concoct a scheme which would allow them to continue paying lip-service to the idea of guerrilla warfare without doing very much about it. They hit on the idea of forming their own FAR, and in order to avoid confusion—or perhaps in order to create it—they called it the Fuerzas Armadas Revolucionarias. (Hitherto the initials FAR had, of course, stood for Fuerzas Armadas Rebeldes.)[6] In a statement published on 1 March 1968, the political commission of the PGT described the break with the guerrillas as an internal division that had occurred within the FAR between 'an adventurist minority' and a majority with a 'unitary attitude'. Because of this situation, the 'majority' had decided to form the Fuerzas Armadas Revolucionarias—the Revolutionary Armed Forces.

Exactly what percentage formed the majority is difficult to discover. But according to the guerrillas the split caused 50 per cent of the PGT's Central Committee to resign, and 40 per cent of the party's political commission.[7]

In August 1968 a number of leading figures from the PGT visited Santiago de Chile and in an interview with the *Fidelista* magazine, *Punto Final*, explained the new Communist position. The Guatemalans were asked what were the differences that divided the PGT from the reunited guerrilla movement. They gave the following reply:

> This is a difference which might be called merely tactical, for the different Guatemalan revolutionary organizations have made it abundantly clear that the only road is the armed road, a thesis always upheld by the party. What has happened is that a group of our companions, some of them members of the

Central Committee, do not agree with fomenting a people's revolutionary war—the thesis upheld by the party round which the FAR was formed. In other words, there are no differences of opinion on the road to be followed, for the party began and continues to support the armed road. The differences concern the way of carrying on this armed struggle.

When asked whether the PGT shared the belief of other Communist parties that Che Guevara had pursued a mistaken strategy, they replied that lack of information about the Bolivian experience prevented them from making any categorical judgements. 'What we can assure you,' they concluded, 'is that the Guatemalan Communist party (PGT) and its military arm—the Revolutionary Armed Forces—will turn our already blood-soaked Guatemala into another Vietnam.'[8]

Notes

1 The text of the joint communiqué signed between Yon Sosa and César Montes is printed in *Tricontinental*, March 1968.

2 Ruth Shereff, 'Revolution in the Hemisphere: A Report from OLAS', *Viet Report*, April–May 1968.

3 Fortuny, 'Guatemala: the Political Situation and Revolutionary Tactics'.

4 The text of this declaration is printed in *Pensamiento Crítico* (Havana), NO. 15, April 1968.

5 Compare this with Fidel's remark in his 13 March 1967 speech: 'If in any country those who call themselves Communists do not know how to fulfil their duty, we will support those who, without calling themselves Communists, conduct themselves like the real Communists in action and in struggle.' The César Montes statement is reprinted in *Tricontinental (Bulletin)*, NO. 26, May 1968.

6 During the course of 1968, the American Embassy in Guatemala grew accustomed to differentiating the two by describing one as the 'near FAR' and the other as the 'far FAR'.

7 'La Experiencia Guatemalteca', *Boletín Tricontinental* (Havana), No. 31, October 1968.

8 *Punto Final* (Santiago), NO. 63, 10 September 1968.

8. THE UNITED STATES' ROLE: A DEAD AMBASSADOR AND EXILED PRIESTS

Although Guatemala in 1968 hardly looked like becoming another Vietnam—not even the Vietnam of the late 1950s—it was certainly every day more blood-soaked. Just before Christmas 1967 one of the right-wing gangs, Mano Blanca, assassinated Rogelia Cruz Martínez, a young woman known for her left-wing contacts who had been 'Miss Guatemala' in 1959. In revenge, the FAR shot Colonel John Webber, the head of the United States Military Mission on 16 January 1968, together with the United States naval attaché. In a statement the FAR announced that the American military advisers had been marked for execution because Guatemalan military groups 'created by American orders' had dedicated themselves to sowing terror and death in the country. 'The genocidal work of such bands of assassins,' it added, 'has resulted in the death of nearly 4,000 Guatemalans.'[1]

In March, the Mano Blanca replied by kidnapping the Archbishop of Guatemala, Monsignor Mario Casariego, though it was not clear with what object in view. He was released a few days later. The brains behind the Mano Blanca, Raúl Stuardo Lorenzana, was in turn shot in his motor-car during April.

After the abduction of the Archbishop, the government began to feel that right-wing terrorism had gone far enough, and in a swift move at the end of March, President Méndez Montenegro dismissed three key military officers who were thought to be behind the right-wing groups. These included the Minister of Defence, the Chief of

Police and Colonel Carlos Araña, the officer in charge of the Zacapa base who had been responsible for the major anti-guerrilla campaign of 1967.

To everyone's surprise, the military men went quietly. There was no coup. But there was no end to the violence either. Towards the end of August, Camilo Sánchez, one of César Montes's principal lieutenants, was captured in Guatemala City and held incommunicado. To draw attention to his whereabouts and to avoid his being tortured and shot, the FAR planned the abduction of the American Ambassador, John Gordon Mein. But the plan misfired. The guerrillas forced his car to stop as it was driving along the Avenida Reforma in the middle of the city. The ambassador got out of the car and attempted to resist capture. He was promptly shot. The FAR commented in a statement:

> Today, Thursday, at 15.25, the leading representative in our country of murderous and rapacious imperialism, Amba-ssador Gordon Mein, was executed. He resisted an attempt to kidnap him that had been made for political reasons as a response to the capture of Comandante Camilo Sánchez, of the FAR, on the corner of Fifth Avenue and 18th Street, in Zone 12, on Saturday 24th at 02.50 in a clash between patrols of the government forces of repression and two comrades of the FAR, one of them Comandante Sánchez.
>
> The capture of comrade Camilo so far has been kept from the public. The FAR demands the appearance of Comandante Camilo Sánchez, at present held in the Fifth Sub-post of Zone 11, under the command of the sadist, Noeé Villegas Delgado, head of the Fascist groups in the army, Mano, Cadeg, etc., and ex-head of the Fourth Corps of the National Police, the den of reaction where most of the 6,000 victims of reactionary violence in Guatemala have been tortured and murdered.
>
> The execution of the Yankee ambassador is only the first of a series of measures that will be taken until Comandante Camilo is produced. By making known the capture and dis-

appearance of the Comandante, the FAR repeats its irrevocable decision to fight until, together with the people, it defeats and drives out the greedy and parasitic bourgeoisie.

We shall fight on. Victory or death for Guatemala.

Headquarters of the FAR
Sierra de la Minas
Year of the Guerrillas

The United States Ambassador was, for the guerrillas, a symbol of the force against which they were fighting. But not all Americans in Guatemala were hostile to the guerrillas. Two brothers, Thomas and Arthur Melville, had been sent down from the United States some years previously by the Maryknoll Fathers to work in Guatemala. As with Camilo Torres in Colombia, they found it more in tune with their Christian calling to work with the guerrillas than with the government. They were not alone. There were other priests involved, and it was said that they had made 'successful efforts to win the sons and daughters of wealthy families to their cause'.[2]

The Melville brothers were expelled from Guatemala in December 1967. The American Father Superior of the Maryknoll Order rebuked them for an action which, he said, constituted 'a personal intervention on the part of American citizens in the internal affairs of the country in which they were guests'.

But in an article published in Mexico, after he had left Guatemala, Thomas Melville replied that:

[I]f the American government were not supporting the Guatemalan oligarchy and training the army, the guerrillas might come to an end of their own accord, for the people would immediately expel their oppressors.

Should we stand aside with our arms folded, watching an economic system continually achieving its object of dehumanizing the masses in Guatemala? The fact that the United States is training Latin American armies to maintain a state of exploitation, obliges American citizens to fight to remedy this deplorable situation.

Declaring himself ready to fight to put an end for ever to 'the system of violence organized by the Guatemalan oligarchy', Father Melville concluded by stating that 'if the United States government were not intervening in the conflict, there would be fewer victims and less suffering, and perhaps the two per cent of the population that constitutes the oligarchy would be so frightened that with luck we would have no need to continue the struggle'.

Shortly after leaving Guatemala, Father Melville addressed a letter to Senator William Fulbright in the United States. It admirably sums up what was happening in Guatemala as a result of more than 10 years of American intervention:[3]

Senator J. William Fulbright,   Mexico
U.S. Senate Office Building,   14 February 1968
Washington D.C.

Dear Senator

For the last few weeks, Guatemala has been on the front pages of the world's newspapers due to the acts of violence that have been occurring in that unfortunate nation. The one that attracted the most attention was the killing of two American officials attached to the United States Embassy in Guatemala.

In the past 18 months, more than 2,800 labour leaders, union organizers, students, intellectuals and just plain peasants have been killed by the government secret police, army and right-wing organizations. 'Mano Blanca', one of the right-wing organizations, staffed by policemen, with headquarters in the main police building in Guatemala City, admits that only 'one in 10 is perhaps a Communist'. None of these deaths are publicized in the international press, and few of the bodies are found in a condition that enables them to be identified in the local press. This is all done under the auspices, albeit secret, of the U.S. Military Mission. If the United States wants to know why two of its officials were killed, let it read the quote of one of them printed in *Time Magazine* dated 28 January 1968.[4]

I have been working in Guatemala for over 10 years. I personally started three credit unions, two agricultural co-operatives, one industrial co-operative, two land distribution programmes, the country's only co-operative league, aided in the formation of nearly a dozen other co-operatives and worked as hard as anybody in Guatemala to improve the miserable lot of the peasant. I didn't accomplish much because we forever ran into government indifference at best, and government interference at worst. If any programme showed signs of success, the Alliance for Progress men were right there to offer money in exchange for the right to hang their publicity signs.

I don't write this letter as a complaint. I write it as warning. The masses of Latin America are becoming more and more restless. Their governments do not want any real progress, because it would have to come at the expense of the landed oligarchy, which in turn controls these governments. There is only one solution: Revolution. I would like to think that these revolutions could be peaceful, but I know from personal experience that the two per cent that are bleeding the masses white, will not give up their power peacefully. It must be taken from them. It is they then who are provoking the violence, not the poor.

This insignificant minority maintains itself in power by paying the national armies. The United States sends technical help, money and armaments to modernize these armies. Last year four new troop-carrying helicopters were donated to Guatemala; 2,000 new policemen were added to the force with their salaries, uniforms and latest weapons all paid for from the Alliance for Progress. American experts in anti-guerrilla warfare, with the help of professional torturers of Cuban, Puerto Rican and Dominican nationalities, keep the countryside terrorized. What is the answer?

If the United States government continues with its policy of believing that all national insurrections are manipulated by Moscow or Peking, then it is going to find itself in more than one Vietnam in Latin America.

I was expelled from Guatemala in December along with two other priests and a nun, for the simple fact of having assisted at a reunion where we listened to the guerrilla's point of view. The expulsion was engineered by the United States Embassy. We have given our lives to the Guatemalan poor. Our expulsion does not mean the end of our dedication to them. We intend to do everything necessary to help them get a government 'of the people, for the people and by the people', to quote a great American statesman. I would hate to find myself fighting someday against U.S. servicemen. But if U.S. foreign policy is going to continue to be dictated by men like Paul Warnke, who think that the United States has a moral obligation to step in anywhere at the invitation of the local oligarchy-government to preserve *their* freedom to exploit the masses, then I'm afraid that this is just what is going to happen.

I know that you are very preoccupied with the situation in Vietnam. But it might be well to turn some of your attention to Latin America also. After all, everyone seems to disclaim knowledge as to just how we got involved in that far-off land, and the big difficulty now is how to extricate ourselves 'with honour'. It would be a shame if such an experience should be repeated down here also. But the real shame would be that hundreds of millions of starving human beings would come to realize that their real enemy is the U.S. government and not the local oligarchy. At least they have hopes of toppling the corrupt governments so long as the United States does not interfere. When the United States becomes involved, they are forced to turn to Moscow, to Peking, to anywhere, for help.

May you use your prestige in any circles that are capable of influencing the U.S. foreign policy in Latin America. Hoping that someday I may have the pleasure of meeting you

personally, and asking God that He aid you in maintaining
your courage,

I remain,

Sincerely,

Thomas R. Melville

Melville's letter, while expressing admirable sentiments, almost
certainly over-estimated the possibilities of violent change in
Guatemala. At the end of the 1960s the solution for Guatemala as for
much of the rest of Latin America was certainly revolution, but as the
years passed its realization became increasingly improbable. In some
future history of Guatemala, the names of Yon Sosa and Turcios Lima
and César Montes will feature with honour as the forerunners of a
movement for national independence. But their day is not yet, nor is
the time ripe.

Notes

1 *The Times*, 18 January 1968.

2 *Financial Times*, 23 January 1968.

3 Quoted in 'The Nature of Revolution', *Hearings before the Committee on
   Foreign Relations, United States Senate, Ninetieth Congress, Second Session*,
   26 February 1968, U.S. Government Printing Office, Washington,
   D.C., 1968.

4 'In a way,' wrote *Time*, 'Webber and Munro [the two officers] were the
   victims of Webber's own success in Guatemala. When the tough
   career officer arrived in Guatemala 18 months ago, 200 Communist
   guerrillas were terrorizing the countryside. Webber immediately
   expanded counter-insurgency training within Guatemala's 5,000-
   man army, brought in U.S. jeeps, trucks, communications equipment
   and helicopters to give the army more firepower and mobility, and
   breathed new life into the army's civic-action programme.

   'Towards the end of 1966 the army was able to launch a major drive
   against the guerrilla strongholds in the Sierra de las Minas in north-
   eastern Guatemala. To aid in the drive, the army also hired and
   armed local bands of "civilian collaborators" licensed to kill peasants

whom they considered guerrillas or "potential" guerrillas. There were those who doubted the wisdom of encouraging such measures in violence-prone Guatemala, but Webber was not among them. "That's the way this country is," he said, "The Communists are using everything they have, including terror. And it must be met."'

II
REVOLUTIONARY FAILURE IN VENEZUELA

'The Venezuelans were the first to experience, in the country most
directly colonized by the United States because of its oil and iron,
what the "people's war" has become in post-Cuban conditions.
They paid dearly for their pioneering role.'

Régis Debray
'América Latina: algunos problemas de estrategia revolutionaria' (1965)

1. THE FALL OF PÉREZ JIMÉNEZ

The guerrilla movement in Guatemala in its early years, as has been suggested in the previous chapters, thrived principally on two major elements. Firstly it built on the popular disillusion caused by the overthrow of Jacobo Arbenz and the reversal of his reform programme, and secondly it benefited from widespread discontent within the army. The situation in Venezuela, which permitted a comparable guerrilla movement to flourish, was not dissimilar. In Venezuela, too, it was an unsuccessful military revolt that brought nationalist officers into the ranks of the guerrillas. But whereas in Guatemala the CIA intervention in 1954 had cleared the way for a whole series of conservative military dictators, in Venezuela the crucial event which cast a shadow over the succeeding years was the overthrow of just such a dictator, Pérez Jiménez, early in 1958. But instead of ushering in a new progressive era in Venezuelan history, the popular revolution that got rid of Pérez Jiménez fell into the grasping hands of Rómulo Betancourt and his Acción Democrática party, and was swiftly aborted. The Venezuelan guerrillas derived support largely from those who had misguidedly allowed their hopes to be raised by the 1958 Revolution and subsequently felt betrayed by the reactionary line pursued by Acción Democrática.

After 10 years in power, Marcos Pérez Jiménez was overthrown by a popular uprising in Caracas in January 1958, just one year before Castro's victory in Cuba. In spite of the strong support of President Eisenhower, who in an act of unnecessary solidarity had awarded him a high honour, Pérez Jiménez had been in a shaky position throughout his final year in power. Not without significance was the desertion from his cause of the Church. The Venezuelan Archbishop, Rafael Arias Blanco, delivered a pastoral letter in which he said that 'an immense mass of our people is living in conditions that cannot be regarded as human. Unemployment leads many Venezuelans to despair . . . the excessively low salaries on which a large number of our workers must survive is inexcusable . . . and the situation is worsening.'[1]

Pérez Jiménez tried to legitimize his position by holding a plebiscite in December 1957, in which it was revealed that 85 per cent of the country favoured his continuation in office. Such an obviously fraudulent result only served to heighten enthusiasm for a change, and on 1 January 1958 sections of the military began to take matters into their own hands. There was a revolt at the Maracay air base, some fifty miles west of Caracas. Jet planes flew over the capital, but the uprising, led by a Colonel Jesús Maria Castro León, was speedily suppressed. Nevertheless, under increasing pressure from radical elements within the armed forces, Pérez Jiménez felt obliged to remove the most unpopular members of his immediate entourage—notably the Minister of the Interior and the Chief of the Secret Police.

But this was not sufficient for the students of Caracas University, who had clandestinely been organizing opposition to the dictatorship during the previous year. Several days of rioting began in Caracas on 14 January, and an underground opposition organization called the Patriotic Junta, led by a 29-year-old journalist, Fabricio Ojeda, issued a call for a general strike to be held on 21 January.

According to Ojeda, the idea of forming the Junta had come to him in June 1957 at a time when he was working as a reporter on the paper *El Nacional*. He had secured the support of the opposition parties, both Right and Left (all proscribed under the dictatorship), and became President of the Junta in December 1957.[2] Apart from organizing the co-operation of such diverse political groups as Acción Democrática, the Christian Democrats and the Communists, he had also supervised the formation of factory and student committees dedicated to the overthrow of the Pérez Jiménez regime. Ojeda himself came from

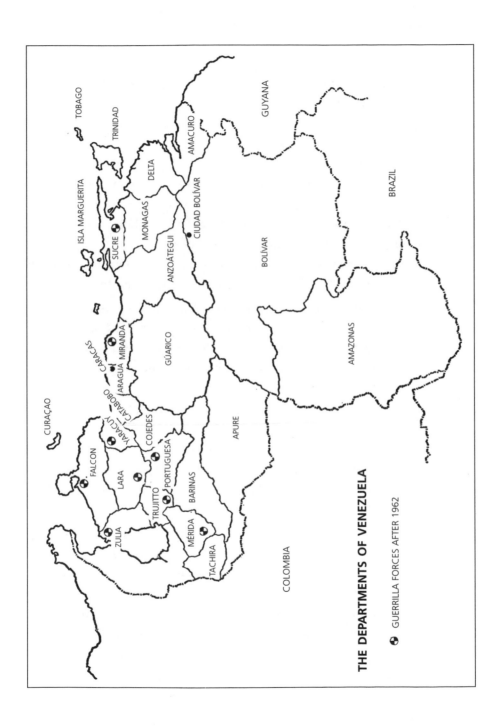

THE DEPARTMENTS OF VENEZUELA

⊕ GUERRILLA FORCES AFTER 1962

the Republican Democratic Union party (URD), which stood marginally to the left of the political spectrum.

Working in close association with the Patriotic Junta was the clandestine Frente Universitario, founded by an Acción Democrática student, Américo Martín, and a Communist student, Germán Lairet. Like the Patriotic Junta, it also worked on an inter-party basis. A further committee existed on which Acción Democrática was represented by Moises Moleiro, which linked the Frente Universitario with other radical youth movements opposed to the regime.[3] All these students who took the lead in overthrowing Pérez Jiménez were later to be involved in organizing guerrilla movements.

The Communists, while working within these popular front organizations, were also making plans of their own. Douglas Bravo, later to become one of the chief guerrilla leaders together with Fabricio Ojeda, described these plans in an interview in June 1967:

> At the end of 1957, when General Marcos Pérez Jiménez was preparing his electoral farce based on fraud, the Communist party set up within the party itself what we could describe as its military apparatus. Some of its leading members were designated to organize it.
>
> In October of the same year the first committee of the military apparatus of the Communist party was formed; it consisted of a union leader, a student leader and a peasant leader. Of course, there were other members. The central nucleus was led by Eloy Torres, Teodoro Petkoff and myself. It formed a shock brigade whose function was to find arms for the fighting which was expected to take place during the 15 December elections.
>
> The first brigades were organized by members of the party and the Communist Youth. Among them I will mention José Gregorio Rodríguez, who was tortured to death by the police and Luben Petkoff, the present second-in-command of the Fuerzas Armadas de Liberación Nacional (FALN).
>
> But it wasn't until January 1958 that these brigades were able to go into action. On 1 January 1958, a military *coup* led by air force officers held the town of Maracay. On 2 January, the

coup was put down, but the government was shaken, and there were spontaneous movements in the army and amongst the people.

On 5 January, in a large-scale demonstration in El Silencio Square, the Communist party shock brigades first used their weapons against the forces of Pérez Jiménez. On 8 January, there was an even bigger demonstration. On 14 January, there was yet another demonstration in Caracas attended by a large number of workers from the lower class districts of the capital. Finally, on 21 January, there was the general strike which overthrew Pérez Jiménez's government; the armed cells of the Communist party took part, weapons in hand.[4]

The Patriotic Junta's strike call was widely observed, and after two days of street fighting Pérez Jiménez left the country for the Dominican Republic in the early hours of the morning of 23 January. Immediately a five-man military junta took over, headed by the Commander-in-Chief of the navy, Rear-Admiral Wolfgang Larrazábal. However, at the request of the Patriotic Junta, Larrazábal dropped two colonels from his team and appointed two civilians instead.[5] His cabinet, announced the same day, was entirely civilian, except for the inclusion of Colonel Castro León, who had sparked off the revolt at Maracay. He was appointed Minister of Defence.

Admiral Larrazábal, then aged 46, had spent three years as a naval attaché in Washington, and he gave routine assurances that Venezuela would maintain its traditional friendship with the United States and would safeguard foreign investment. On 27 January, he promised that elections for a Constituent Assembly and for the Presidency would be held within the year.

Meanwhile in New York, on 23 January, the exiled leaders of Venezuela's three principal political parties had met to sign an agreement to avoid inter-party rivalry until democracy had been fully restored. The agreement was signed by Dr Rómulo Betancourt of Acción Democrática, Dr Rafael Caldera for the Christian Democrats and Dr Jovito Villalba of the Republican Democratic Union.

Already with this declaration the seeds of future conflict were being sown. For there was a great difference between those like

Fabricio Ojeda, who had remained in Venezuela during the dictator-ship and who believed that the downfall of Pérez Jiménez presaged revolutionary changes, and the senior leaders of the various parties who had lived in exile in Mexico or New York and who saw the flight of the dictator merely as an opportunity to take up the political game where they had left off 10 years before.

Acción Democrática was the largest and once the most progressive party in Venezuela, but, like APRA in Peru, it had lost all its youthful enthusiasm for revolution, In exile, Betancourt had established him-self as a leader likely to be looked on favourably by the United States, It was some time, however, before the exiled party could reorganize itself, and its first major mass meeting was not held until 4 July 1958. According to one account, Betancourt took the opportunity to deliver a long and eloquent history of the party's antagonism to international Communism.[6]

Splits within Acción Democrática were almost immediately visible, though not just between those who had been exiled and those who had stayed behind. There was also an important generation gap. The most important of the radicals who were opposed to the 'Old Guard' leadership of Betancourt and his crony Raúl Leoni, were Domingo Alberto Rangel—described by an American observer as 'a brilliant, opinionated, and vociferous controversialist who spewed forth an unending stream of words, both written and spoken'—and Simón Sáez Mérida—'a stubborn partisan of radical solutions, a reader of Marxism, and already a dogmatic admirer of a Cuban guerrilla fight-er named Fidel Castro'.[7] Both were to become important figures in Venezuela's revolutionary struggle.

Sáez Mérida, to whom Betancourt was bitterly opposed, had returned secretly to Venezuela in 1957 as the Secretary-General of Acción Democrática. He had been responsible for the participation of the party in Ojeda's Patriotic Junta, much to the annoyance of the 'Old Guard' in exile. They had no desire to co-operate with the Communists and were unsympathetic to the revolutionary implications of the Patriotic Junta. 'We are not fomenting revolutions,' Betancourt had told a Colombian journalist in 1957.[8]

The radical element, led by Rangel and Sáez Mérida, stayed with the party through 1958 and 1959, but, as they watched it rapidly galloping to the right, it became clear that they could not long remain within it.

By some oversight on the part of contemporary historians, much attention has been devoted to establishing why Latin American countries in the period after Castro's successful revolution in January 1959 did not follow the Cuban pattern, but few people have bothered to inquire why the Venezuelan upheaval, which occurred the year before the Cuban one, failed to develop more revolutionary momentum.

For all Admiral Larrazábal's assurances of friendship, popular feeling in Venezuela against the United States after the fall of the dictator ran extremely high—partly because Pérez Jiménez found a ready refuge there, after a brief sojourn with Trujillo in the Dominican Republic. Consequently, when the then Vice-President of the United States, Richard Nixon, arrived in Caracas on 15 May 1958 at the conclusion of a highly unsuccessful Latin American tour, he was received by a hostile mob armed with stones and sticks. The municipal council of Caracas declared him *persona non grata*, and the car in which he and Mrs Nixon were travelling was smashed up. They narrowly averted being dragged out into the street and beaten up.

Although Admiral Larrazábal went on record as saying that if he had been a student he would have done the same, the chief political leaders—Betancourt, Caldera and Villalba—all criticized the demonstrators for their bad manners, and made no protest when President Eisenhower, in a characteristic gesture, ordered companies of marines and paratroopers to certain Caribbean bases ready to move in—an action foreshadowing the schemes he was later to organize with regard to Cuba.[9]

Internally, too, Venezuela seemed in a progressive mood. In July Colonel Castro León, backed by a number of other military officers, demanded the reintroduction of press censorship and the postponement of elections for three years. Immediately a general strike was called in support of the government, and Admiral Larrazábal promptly secured the resignation of Castro León.[10] Two months later a military uprising by a group of disgruntled officers was swiftly crushed, and again the trade unions called for a strike, both to support the government and to urge that strong measures should be taken against the rebels. It was observed throughout Caracas.

The strong popular militancy seemed to presage a move to the left, and, hoping to benefit from this, Admiral Larrazábal resigned as head of the governing junta on 14 November 1958 in order to stand for the Presidency. Elections, as he had promised earlier, were to be held in December. Although he stood as a non-political candidate, he was supported by the URD and by the Communist party. His opponents were Rómulo Betancourt of Acción Democrática and Rafael Caldera of the Christian Democrats.

Notes

1 John D. Martz, *Acción Democrática: Evolution of a Modern Political Party in Venezuela*, Princeton University Press, 1966, p. 93.

2 *Keesings Contemporary Archives*, 15–22 February 1958.

3 Moises Moleiro, *El MIR de Venezuela*, Guairas, Instituto del Libor, Havana, 1967, p. 106.

4 *Avec Douglas Bravo dans les maquis vénézuéliens*, Dossiers Partisans, François Maspéro, Paris, 1968, p. 40.

5 In his book *El MIR de Venezuela*, Moises Moleiro is extremely critical of the Patriotic Junta's request, pointing out that the two civilians concerned, Eugenio Mendoza and Blas Lamberti, were just as reactionary as the military men. Moleiro obviously considers that the Patriotic Junta was in a position to make much more revolutionary demands than in fact it did. He probably over-estimates its strength. See *El MIR de Venezuela*, pp. 107–8.

6 Martz, *Acción Democrática*, p. 99.

7 Ibid., p. 101.

8 Quoted in Moleiro, *El MIR de Venezuela*, p. 100.

9 The same day, by chance, there were anti-American riots and demonstrations in places as diverse as Algeria, Burma and the Lebanon. To the last country Eisenhower ordered units of the Sixth Fleet. 'Maybe I should be digging out my uniforms,' he told his wife that evening, 'to see whether they still fit.'—Eisenhower, *Waging Peace*, p. 159.

10 General Castro León made another unsuccessful rebellion in April 1960, in the state of Tachira.

2. The Ascendancy of Rómulo Betancourt

Just before the December 1958 elections, the three main parties—Acción Democrática, the Christian Democrats and the Republican Democratic Union—signed a joint declaration of principle, known as the Pact of Punto Fijo, stating that the winner would form 'a government of national unity without partisan hegemonies, in which all national political currents and independent sectors of the community will be represented'. In theory this was designed to perpetuate the political truce that had existed until the elections, but in practice it became a device for crushing opponents who did not share the outlook of Acción Democrática.

Betancourt, having a more efficient party machine, won the election with a clear majority. He secured 1,284,092 votes. Larrazábal received 903,479 and Caldera trailed with 423,262; 93 per cent of the electorate voted.

In Caracas, however, Larrazábal had won by more than five to one, and for two days, on 8 and 9 December, Caracas was once again the scene of serious rioting as his supporters sought to reverse the national result. But Larrazábal himself appealed for calm, and the city soon returned to normal. However, early in the following year, just after he had come to power, Fidel Castro made a triumphant visit to Venezuela, and the inhabitants of Caracas were not slow to tell him what they thought of Betancourt. Years later, Castro recalled the scene:

> Betancourt had a deep grudge against the inhabitants of the
> capital, for he could not forgive their failure to support him,
> nor the way they had affronted him.

In the early stages of the Revolution, visiting our brother country, and speaking in El Silencio square with 300,000 people present, we mentioned Betancourt's name—as we had to, for he was the President-elect—there was a storm of booing from the vast crowd.

As visitors to that country we were put in an embarrassing position. I felt obliged to protest, stating that I didn't mention people's names for them to be jeered at, that it was merely my duty to refer officially to somebody who, after elections, was to take over the government.[1]

As Régis Debray points out in one of his earlier essays, Castro's visit had a lasting effect on Betancourt. It brought home to him just how unpopular he was in his own capital city:

In the 1950s Betancourt could still believe himself to be leading a popular anti-imperialist resistance; after Fidel's lightning visit to Venezuela in 1959, Betancourt knew what his role was to be. In the rabid insults Betancourt shortly afterwards launched against 'Castro-Communism'—an expression which swept the continent—and in his paranoiac unbalance there speaks, in fact, a small and expended politician condemned to an armoured car and solitude, who, one day in 1959, in the Plaza del Silencio in Caracas, allowed his role and accoutrements to be confiscated from him before 500,000 people.[2]

In the first weeks, however, Betancourt seemed to be playing the democratic game. On 11 December he announced that, in accordance with his pre-election promises and with the Pact of Punto Fijo, he would appoint a coalition government from all parties. True to his word, his first Cabinet included only two members of Acción Democrática. URD and the Christian Democrats had three members each, and there were four independents and one soldier.

But from the start he appeared determined to ignore the Communists, who had, after all, been involved in the overthrow of Pérez Jiménez.[3] Taking office on 13 February 1959, he stressed in his inaugural address that 'the philosophy of Communism is not compatible with the development of Venezuela'. He gave a warning that any disrespect for the constituted authorities would be firmly repressed. And on that note he began his four years of power.

Although he survived his term as President, he only did so at the cost of a fierce repression that recalled the worst years of Pérez Jiménez. There is no objective history of the period, and the accounts which the revolutionary guerrillas themselves have left are not unnaturally heavily biased against Betancourt. It is tempting to dismiss many of their stories as mere Communist propaganda, but the fact remains that, although Betancourt began his rule with the formal support of every political group except the Communists, by the end he had antagonized virtually every political movement in the country and had irreparably split the party which he had done so much to build up. And in the beginning the Communist party would have been happy to support him. It was Betancourt himself who declared war on the Left.

One of Betancourt's chief sources of strength was his ability to persuade outsiders that he was a democrat. Nobody was more taken in than President Kennedy. When Betancourt visited Washington in February 1963, Kennedy welcomed him as representing:

> all that we admire in a political leader. Your liberal leadership of your own country, your persistent determination to make a better life for your people, your long fight for democratic leadership not only in your own country but in the entire area of the Caribbean, your companionship with other liberal progressive leaders of this hemisphere, all these have made you, for us, a symbol of what we wish for our own country and for our sister republics.[4]

Yet, in fact, in a few short years, Betancourt had shown that he was second to no military dictator in his ability to smash his political opponents. It was his methods as much as anything that drove his former colleagues to abandon him. In the spring of 1962, he wrote confidently to Kennedy:

> We are hitting both groups, reactionaries and communists, in earnest and in depth, in conformity with the constitution and the law. . . . The impatient ones would like us to go beyond the written law—and even beyond the unwritten but overriding

law of respect for human dignity. I will not, however, deviate from the course laid down for me by the fundamental law of Venezuela and by my own conscience.[5]

There were not those lacking in Venezuela who were to question whether Betancourt, during his four-year rule, had not got beyond 'the overriding law of respect for human dignity'.

Douglas Bravo, in an interview published in Mexico in 1966, explained what occurred during Betancourt's first year in office:

When Rómulo Betancourt took power on 13 February 1959, his message to the country was practically a declaration of war on the people. However, they continued to fight by peaceful means. The reply from Betancourt's government was violent. Thus on 4 August 1959 in Concordia Square, Caracas, a demonstration by 50,000 unemployed was fired on and the first three workers making peaceful claims were killed.

A few days later a group of students demonstrating in the streets of Caracas in support of their claims were also violently attacked. Some of them were killed.

At the same time a group of peasants from the State of Aragua began to take over the land and were violently put down by the National Guard. In the peaceful struggle in support of their claims, the workers tried to hold demonstrations and even peaceful meetings indoors, but they were violently attacked, as occurred in Lagunillas, where the unions and the repressive apparatus of Acción Democrática attacked a meeting of oil workers. Several leaders of the Communist party were wounded.

In Caracas itself, a group of students, together with workers and intellectuals, demonstrated in the streets in favour of the Cuban Revolution, and were violently attacked, with several dead and wounded.

All demonstrations by the people were violently repressed.[6]

In another interview in 1967, Bravo followed up the same points:

It must be recognized that Betancourt drew up a clearly offensive strategy against the revolution and the people. From the beginning he made alliances with the most reactionary circles of the military High Command, the oligarchy and American imperialism. Thanks to these alliances he was able to launch an offensive against the people's movement. But Betancourt did not succeed in destroying the revolutionary movement. The masses had learned their lesson and were determined to continue with the struggle. We should add to that something of paramount importance: in Latin America a patriotic liberation movement led by Fidel Castro had overthrown the dictator Batista, routed his army and taken power. Under this terrible influence, the Venezuelan people swiftly took up their own armed struggle. The influence of the seizure of power by the people of Cuba was important not only for our country but for all the Latin American countries.[7]

Moises Moleiro, a leader of the MIR—a party which split away from Acción Democrática and supported guerrilla warfare—made a similar point when interviewed some years later:

The example of the Cuban Revolution was not only an influence in the birth of the MIR, but also changed the entire political structure of Latin America, at least as far as general ideas are concerned. We saw that while our leaders had been talking about revolution for thirty years, in Cuba the Revolution triumphed in two years of fighting; while Rómulo Betancourt had been talking about agrarian reform for thirty years, and had governed twice without doing a thing about it, in Cuba a far-reaching agrarian reform was taking place; while our leaders had been talking about nationalism and the struggle against imperialism for thirty years, and while each time they came to power they avoided the subject like cowards, in Cuba they were resolutely confronting Yankee pressure, imperialist pressure.[8]

Just how important the Cuban Revolution had become for Latin America became clear at the OAS Foreign Ministers Conference held at San José, Costa Rica, in August 1960. There the United States tried to bully the Latin American countries into accepting a motion hostile to Cuba, and by doing so instantly caused a political crisis in Venezuela. The Venezuelan Foreign Minister, Dr Ignacio Luís Arcaya, together with his Peruvian colleague, laboured to water down the anti-Cuban motion in the hope that the Cubans could be persuaded to sign it. Failing in this objective, Arcaya refused to sign and was promptly recalled and sacked by President Betancourt. This sparked off huge pro-Cuban demonstrations in the streets of Caracas and a grave governmental crisis. Dr Arcaya was one of the leaders of the URD, which at that stage was already beginning to take up a position on some issues considerably to the left of Acción Democrática and the Christian Democrats.

Acción Democrática itself had gone through an important internal crisis earlier in the year. In March 1960, one of the leaders of the Acción Democrática youth wing, Américo Martín, wrote an article about the Peruvian APRA, a sister party of Acción Democrática. In it, he commended the step which had been taken the previous year by the leader of APRA's left wing, Luís de la Puente Uceda, in withdrawing from the party and forming an APRA Rebelde.[9] Although ordered by the party's executive committee to stop writing such articles, Martín continued with attacks on Figueres of Costa Rica and Muñoz Marín of Puerto Rico—soulmates of President Betancourt.

At the same time there was a major disagreement between Domingo Alberto Rangel and the party over oil agreements with foreign companies.[10] Rather than face a showdown, Rangel and Martín decided that the moment was opportune to withdraw from Acción Democrática and to start a new party. On 9 April a youth conference in Maracaibo, meeting in strict defiance of a party order that it should not be held, voted in favour of forming such a party.[11]

The new party was at first called Acción Democrática Izquierdista, though later it was changed to Movimiento de Izquierda Revolucionaria (Movement of the Revolutionary Left, MIR). The first issue of a party journal called *Izquierda* appeared on 13 May 1960. And at a national constituent conference held early in July, the MIR defined itself as a Marxist party.[12]

An American observer points out that 'the impact of the split on Acción Democrática was potentially grave, for the party's youth movement was shattered. Party leaders have agreed that a good 80 per cent of this sector deserted in favour of the MIR.'[13] The *MIRistas* took with them 14 out of 73 Acción Democrática deputies with a sizeable quantity of the rank and file, including such figures as Sáez Mérida and Moises Moleiro.

The government, as might have been expected, reacted harshly against this new body that had been torn from its flesh. On 20 October six members of the MIR were arrested on charges of subversion and of advocating the overthrow of the regime. An investigation was begun into the activities of eight others, including Rangel and Sáez Mérida.

The arrests were followed by several days of street demonstrations mounted in protest. Many of the demonstrators were university students and children from high school. On the night of 24 October, one person was killed in clashes with police which took place in front of the parliament building.

Betancourt promptly ordered all colleges and other places of higher education to be closed. The authorities shut down Caracas University, where students were staging a sit-down strike, and troops were called out. In the following days there were further riots, the demonstrations spreading to the working class areas. By the end of the month at least six people had been killed, 71 injured and an estimated 500 had been arrested.

At a government-organized rally on 1 November, Betancourt told the crowd that Venezuela would not tolerate 'any attempt to establish a dictatorship either of a totalitarian Fascist type or of a totalitarian Communist type'.

> If there is something reprehensible in those who have recently kept Caracas and some other cities in a state of alarm, it is the fact that they have used as tools for their subversive activities high-school students and boys without a trade or employment wandering around the slum areas of Caracas. In the face of these subversive outbursts, proof of which we have in the documents seized by the police, the government adopted an attitude which can be called mild. For three or four days hundreds of youths went about burning motorcars and attacking persons and property. The government chose not to step in for fear of hitting with a bullet some fourteen-year-old boy or girl, but

the time came when a solid and absurd unified front was established by these extreme leftist persons—the leftovers of the dictatorship, and the bums.[14]

After enumerating the government's achievements in the field of agrarian reform, housing construction and housing loans to those with small incomes, Betancourt attempted to refute the allegation made by those whom he described as 'the servile followers of Moscow and Havana', that his government was 'one of capitulation and surrender to foreign capital'. He added that,

> We are anti-imperialist, but we understand anti-imperialism as the defence of Venezuelan interests and of America, not the anti-imperialism which attacks the United States in order to put itself at the service of Soviet expansionist policy. . . . For the same reasons for which we defend the country's interests, we are willing to negotiate with U.S. and European investors who want to deal with a government which is aware of the nation's wealth, and with a working dais that no longer tolerates starvation wages.[15]

The stern measures used against the students, however, caused the end of the governing coalition. Already the URD had been angered by the treatment of Dr Arcaya after the San José Conference and the three URD members of the Cabinet had resigned in protest. On 11 November the Cabinet resigned, and a new one in which the URD had no part was appointed 10 days later. It appears that the URD members of the Cabinet were particularly critical of the United States' role in Latin America and of Venezuela's dependence on foreign capital, particularly in the oil industry. They were broadly favourable to the Cuban Revolution, and disliked the methods used by the United States to oppose it.

But the chief opposition to Betancourt at this juncture came from the MIR. Moises Moleiro, one of the leaders of the MIR at this time, has given the following account of what happened during the last two months of 1960:

> The MIR had defined itself as 'a constitutional alternative', which meant that it had made clear its desire to fight by

peaceful means! But faced by abuses and arbitrary measures, it began to think in terms of replying to these daily attacks. The Venezuelan Communist party, which was receiving the same treatment, came to a similar conclusion.

A month later, in November 1960, a strike was called in the Companía Anónima de Teléfonos de Venezuela. The government hastily declared the strike illegal, on the grounds that the company was a public service. At the same time it tried to crush the strikers by using the National Guard, which raided the premises of the company and intimidated the workers. This brought forth protests from the people. The leadership of the party, making a false estimate of the real correlation of forces, set out to overthrow the government. The MIR called for a mass uprising, though in fact it did not have sufficient means to carry it out. It counted on the crisis that was developing in the Armed Forces and on the rage of the people, who were fighting the police in the streets. It was thought that, given the crisis rocking the government, Betancourt would be unable to resist the onslaught of the forces of the people. The MIR leadership gambled on an insurrection. It was a costly mistake and a heavy blow to the forces of the people. We brought into the insurrection middle and high-level leaders of the URD and the Communist party, as well as rank-and-file members of these parties. A National Liberation Council was set up and called for a general strike. This never took place. This expensive and serious mistake can be explained by the constant abuses of the government and by the power which groups of adventurers held within the leadership of the party. The mistake lay, not in replying to systematic repressive violence with popular violence, but in having illusions about victory in the short term and in not considering the best means to promote the armed struggle.[16]

In spite of the inability of the MIR to capitalize on it, the revolutionary atmosphere continued throughout November 1960. In the final week the police were once again obliged to open fire after teargas had failed to quell the demonstrators. Although an attempt to seize a radio station was unsuccessful, long battles took place near the presidential palace. Students and National Guard units battled it out on the university campus itself.

On 28 November Betancourt again summoned the troops to crush an uprising which, he said, was designed to establish 'a régime similar to that existing in Cuba'. He blamed the MIR and the Communists for organizing the riots and suspended constitutional guarantees throughout the country for an indefinite period. The 'era of leniency', he said, was over. All illegal demonstrations and strikes would be prohibited. The government, he underlined, had no intention of allowing civil war to break out. Constitutional guarantees would only be restored when there was 'a climate of peace and tranquillity'. The military seized the plant where the Communist paper *Tribuna Popular* was printed, and they also moved into the oilfields to prevent sabotage. The MIR weekly, *Izquierda*, was banned. During the ensuing demonstrations, a further eight people were killed and more than 100 wounded.

Betancourt's appeal to the army paid off. Although there were known to be dissident elements within it,[17] the military remained loyal throughout the events of November and December, and the incipient revolution was effectively crushed.

Betancourt's first move, after the suspending of constitutional guarantees, was against Rangel and a leading Communist deputy, Teodoro Petkoff. Although Rangel was cleared of all charges against him, the Congress decided to lift the immunity of Petkoff. He was found guilty of subversion and jailed. Other Communists met a similar fate.

The government's hard line against the Communists was partly responsible for swinging the party round, at its Third Congress in March 1961, to a position increasingly in favour of the armed struggle as the least unsatisfactory way of promoting the revolution. Hitherto the revolutionary pace-setters had been the MIR and not the Communist party.

The Communists had spent anxious years. Illegal under Pérez Jiménez, the party had first supported Betancourt, then passed into opposition, but it had always hoped that it would be able to put pressure on the government coalition to move to the left. In June 1960, for example, after Betancourt had been shot at by one of Trujillo's assassins, the Communist party asked to be allowed an interview with him to express their solidarity. Betancourt, however, refused.[18] But, afraid of being outflanked by the MIR, the party began to adopt a tougher line of more outright opposition, advocating, at the 25th Plenum in September, the defeat of the government's policies rather than a mere change of emphasis in them.

As the repression grew in the aftermath of the events of November 1960, it was logical that the Communist party should begin to look more favourably on the possibility of developing the armed struggle. It was also the moment when the Communists and Castro were drawing closer together. Inevitably some of the Cuban enthusiasm for guerrilla warfare rubbed off on the Old Guard Communists in Caracas.

But the Communist party's drift towards accepting the need for armed opposition to Betancourt was slow. And although the division in Acción Democrática, caused by the formation of the MIR and the abandonment of the governing coalition by the URD in 1960, led them to adopt a more radical position, it was not until Acción Democrática split again late in 1961 that the Communists began to consider that they were perhaps about to assist at the inauguration of a revolutionary situation which would justify the recourse to arms.

This second split in Acción Democrática, led by Raúl Ramos Jiménez, deprived Betancourt of a further 26 deputies, and for the first time his party lost its majority in the Congress. This split, coupled with increased government repression against demonstrations in October and November 1961, made the drift towards open rebellion almost inevitable.[19]

Notes

1   Fidel Castro, speech in the University of Havana, 13 March 1967.

2   Régis Debray, 'América Latina: algunos problemas de estrategia revolucionaria' ['Latin America: Some Problems of Revolutionary Strategy'], *Casa de las Américas*, NO. 31, July–August 1965.

3   One could argue, indeed, that the Venezuelan Communist party had been rather more active in combatting Pérez Jiménez than the Cuban Communists had been in fighting against Batista.

4   Schlesinger Jr, *A Thousand Days*, p. 660.

5 Ibid., p. 658.

6 Mario Menéndez Rodríguez, 'Venezuela empuña las armas', *Sucesos* (Mexico City), 17 December 1966.

7 *Avec Douglas Bravo dans les maquis vénézuéliens*, pp. 41–2.

8 Augusto Velardo, 'Entrevista con el dirigente máximo del MIR Moises Moleiro', *¿Por Que?* (Mexico City), 8 May 1968.

9 See Part IV., the section on Peru.

10 Rangel later told a reporter: 'Betancourt had betrayed all of his principles. At first, his alliance was with the Left, but after San José he turned Right. I could accept even the San José Declaration—if he nationalized the oil and used the money to finance the agrarian reform.'—John Gerassi, 'Latin America—the Next Vietnam', *Viet Report* (New York), January–February 1967.

11 John D. Martz, *Acción Democrática: Evolution of a Modern Political Party in Venezuela*, Princeton University Press, 1966, pp. 180–2; and Moleiro, *El MIR de Venezuela*, pp. 137–43.

12 *El rumbo bacia el socialismo: tesis política del MIR y estatutos del partido*. Summarized in Moleiro, *El MIR de Venezuela*, pp. 147–51. Although the Communist party was later to work with the MIR, it did not at the time greet the split in Acción Democrática with much enthusiasm (p. 146). According to one observer, the Venezuelan Communist party is probably smaller than the MIR. (*Problèmes d' Amerique Latine*, No. 6, p. 8.)

13 Martz, *Acción Democrática*, p. 182.

14 *Keesings Contemporary Archives*, 4–11 March 1961, p. 17966.

15 Ibid.

16 Moleiro, *El MIR de Venezuela*, pp. 154–6.

17 A military revolt on 20 February 1961, led by a former commander of the military school in Caracas, Colonel José Edito Ramírez, was swiftly defeated. However, when a new constitution was introduced on 23 January, the Minister of the Interior declared that the continued suspension of civil rights was necessary, due to a continuing threat of rebellion. The government, he said, had proof of Communist activity within the armed forces, and he alleged that groups of former officers were planning to provoke disorders.

18 Manuel Cabieses Donoso, *¡Venezuela Okey!* Ediciones del Litoral, Santiago, 1963, p. 184.

19 Left-wing demonstrations occurred in Caracas after Venezuela broke off diplomatic relations with Cuba on 11 November 1961.

3. THE BEGINNING OF THE GUERRILLAS

'When we took to the mountains for the first time we were more than
a little taken with the idea that our war was going to be a Cuban-style
war, or very similar to the Cuban guerrilla war. We thought that the
solution to our problems was no more than two or three years away,
and that the guerrillas were going to solve the problems of the
Venezuelan revolution in the short term.'

Luben Petkoff

The year 1962 produced in Venezuela, as in Guatemala, the first outbreaks of guerrilla warfare. The growth of the opposition to the government, especially within the army, coupled with the disintegration
of the governing party, led even the Communists, with their customary reluctance to strike before the iron is hot, to believe that a revolutionary situation was at hand. This had been the only occasion in the
history of guerrilla movements in Latin America that a Communist
party has supported guerrillas in the belief that a revolutionary situation in the Leninist sense justified such an action.

One of the most active young Communists in Venezuela was
Douglas Bravo, the son of a minor landowner in Falcón State. He was
born in March 1933. He had worked in a cement factory, studied law
and been a militant Young Communist. Together with Eloy Torres and
Teodoro Petkoff, he had been one of the leaders of the shock troops
clandestinely organized by the Communist party in October 1957 for
the purpose of assisting in the overthrow of Pérez Jiménez. He had

also been one of the organizers of the ill-fated expedition to the Dominican Republic in June 1959, led by Enrique Jiménez Moya.[1]

He had spent some months in 1961 clandestinely organizing support for a guerrilla movement in the mountains of Turimiquire in the eastern zone of the country, and also in the mountains of the state of Lara in the west between Caracas and Lake Maracaibo. Together with other leaders from the Communist party and the MIR, he decided that the time had come to divert the government's attention away from the cities. Until that moment, the urban movement had borne the full brunt of the government's repressive activities. However, Bravo points out, guerrilla warfare did not break out because the revolutionaries supported the idea of armed struggle for its own sake, but rather because it seemed to be the only possible way forward.[2] It was a logical and inevitable step. But it was not until early in 1962 that the public at large, and in particular the army, became aware that guerrilla bands were forming in a number of different states.

Manuel Cabieses, a Chilean journalist who worked at the time in Venezuela, has described the opening of the guerrilla campaign in his book, *¡Venezuela Okey!*:

> The first signs that guerrilla groups were being organized were found by the army during a reconnaissance operation on 21 January, 1962 in the 'Las Carapas' hacienda, in Sucre State, in the eastern part of the country. Two people were arrested and some training material captured. Three days later, in Turimiquire, in the same area, another training camp was discovered, with firing ranges and a helicopter landing pad. In the raid on this camp nine people found there were arrested.
>
> From that moment on the evidence began to pile up. On 20 February 1962, near Santa Cruz de Bucaral, in Falcón State, a jeep carrying military equipment and supplies was captured. The occupants fled. A week later this led to the capture of nineteen people in the place known as Agualinda; the provisions in the jeep had been meant for them. On 1 March a guerrilla centre was discovered in the Andean region. On

this occasion fourteen people were captured (six students, six peasants, and two workers) two of them wounded in the clash which took place. This happened in La Azulita, in the state of Mérida. On the same day, in another corner of Venezuela, in Portuguesa State, in the El Charal area, the army fired on a jeep going along the road to Biscucuy, killing one of the occupants. Three days later they captured twenty-three people training secretly in Biscucuy. On 24 March, another camp was located in Agua Viva, Trujillo State. Shots were fired and a guerrilla was killed while another five were arrested. On the same day, in Cerro Azul, Yaracuy State there was a clash between the guerrillas and the National Guard and the police.[3] Five guerrillas and a police corporal were killed, seventeen guerrillas captured and a sergeant of the National Guard wounded.

On 1 April 1962 the guerrillas made their first attack. This occurred in another part of the country: Lara State.[4]

A detachment of guerrillas attacked a materials and vehicle store, belonging to the Ministry of Public Works, between the towns of Humocaro Alto and Humocaro Bajo. In the shooting the watchman of the store was killed. Then the guerrillas took the captured vehicles to attack the prefecture of police in Humocaro Alto. One policeman was killed during the attack and the guerrillas withdrew with a large quantity of equipment. The army immediately began a pincer movement in which seven people were killed, five wounded and twenty-one captured: for the most part peasants suspected of helping the guerrillas. The army also captured a generator and a transmitter in one of the abandoned camps.

On 3 April fifteen people were arrested, accused of preparing an attack on the military base at Turiamo. The army stated that they were guerrillas from a group operating in Virigima, Carabobo State.

On 16 April other camps were discovered in El Jobito and Macanillo, Miranda State, where eleven guerrillas were captured, one of them wounded.

In all these operations the army seized two light machine-guns, six sub-machine guns, thirty-seven rifles, sixteen shot-guns, three pistols, twenty-four revolvers, twenty-one grenades, 4,733 rounds of ammunition and 193 sticks of dynamite.

Guerrilla detachments continued to spring up in other parts of the country:

Cerro La Culebra	(Miranda State)
Páramo de La Osa	(Mérida State)
Sierra de Aroa	(Yaracuy State)
Sierra de San Luís	(Falcón State)
Cerro Las Palmas	(between the states of Trujillo and Zulia)

etc.

The tactics followed at first by the guerrillas was to set up bases or centres in different parts of the country in order to oblige the government to scatter its forces. But this idea, which seemed logical, also obliged the guerrilla front to scatter its efforts, arms, provisions and men. This weakened them and complicated the task of supplying them which had to be carried out from the cities until the guerrilla detachments won the confidence of the peasants and were self-sufficient in food. Some detachments, like those in La Azulita and Agua Viva, were destroyed by the army, while others were broken up to reinforce those which had been successful in setting up firm bases in the mountains.[5]

One such stable group was the José Leonardo Chirinos Guerrilla Front, led by Douglas Bravo.[6] Although captured and imprisoned late in 1961, he had managed to escape in March 1962 and had made his way back to Falcón State.

Also in the Chirinos Front were Elías Manuit Camero, who had left the army in June 1962 after the military uprising at Puerto Cabello and who was called 'Emiliano', and Domingo Urbino, an old guerrilla and caudillo of the region, who had escaped from prison[7] and who operated under the name of 'Indio'.

A fourth important member of the Chirinos Front, who joined in July 1962, was Fabricio Ojeda. Before leaving for the mountains, he resigned from the Venezuelan Congress where he had been a deputy for the URD since 1958. Because of his former position as head of the Patriotic Junta which, to all intents and purposes, overthrew the government of Pérez Jiménez, and because of his impeccably respectable antecedents as a member of the far from revolutionary URD, Ojeda was one of the most significant figures ever connected with the Venezuelan guerrillas.

On 12 October 1962, after barely two months in the hills, he was captured with a group of four other guerrillas and condemned to 18 years' imprisonment.[8] From his prison cell he issued the following statement:

I am accused of being Fidel Castro's agent in Venezuela; of being highly paid by the [Cuban] Rebel Army, but my accusers know that these are barefaced lies to confuse the people who on many occasions have given us their affection and trust. As I said in my 'Open letter to Drew Pearson'—a journalist in the pay of colonialism—I am not, nor have I been nor will I ever be more than a soldier of the Venezuelan people in their hard struggle for national independence and liberation. As such I took up arms, left the comforts of the city, left Parliament, left everything, to go to the mountains to fight for the dignity of my country, for its progress and prosperity. I and others are accused of wanting to import into Venezuela all the events of the Cuban Revolution and to make a carbon copy of the history of that country. These people, and amongst them President Betancourt—I mention him because he has been a student of Marxism, and even a distinguished member of the Communist party—know very well that that is absurd, and quite ridiculous. All those who study revolutionary theory, amongst whom I include myself without modesty, know that different situations give rise to different historical processes. They know that Venezuela is not Cuba and that the Venezuelan situation and prospects are different from Cuba's.[9]

And in August 1963, in a 'letter from prison', he made some further observations on the nature of the Venezuelan Revolution:

> This armed struggle, which is the essential part of our chosen path, is not only the product of the wishes and concerns of a generation brought up to sacrifice and hardened by daily combat, but also the result of objective, clear and precise conditions. It is, above all things, the expression of an intolerable situation which nobody, however insensitive, could look upon with indifference. We should all have preferred the fate of Venezuela to have been decided peacefully, by non-military means, because that solution would have avoided the loss of valuable lives and the destruction of tools and resources which could be used for progress and development. But unfortunately the ruling classes have prevented this with all the means in their power. Our people has been left no other means than violence. . . .
>
> Today Venezuela is an erupting volcano. It is a country sown with revolutionary fighters, rocked by a severe crisis which polarizes the struggle into two great currents, two opposed camps: one, those groups upholding progress, liberation and justice; the other, the conservative, colonial and oppressive groups. It is not, as many pretend within and outside our frontiers, a problem inspired by the Communists, which would necessarily limit the solution ideologically; even less is there any question of what has been called an 'importation of the Cuban Revolution' or the transfer to our country of methods, formulas and procedures used by other peoples in accordance with their own historical peculiarities. It is perfectly clear that what Venezuela has in prospect is a national revolution in line with its structure, its economic development and its social life, whose main lines are those of a nation penetrated by American imperialism, which controls and exploits the main sources of wealth and which, by means of this economic domination, prevents the putting into practice of a policy in accordance with the collective desires and feelings of the people. . . .

Venezuela's historical experience, the strength of the enemy that has to be overcome, and the ineffectiveness of so-called 'formal or representative democracy'—well shown in the last five years—have led our people to the conclusion that achievement of the goals set—national freedom, independence and development—can only be reached by means of armed struggle, revolutionary action, which will allow the people to take political power, and will result in a democratic people's policy to get rid of injustice, privilege and serfdom.

Fabricio Odeja

Trujillo Jail, August 1963[10]

After the Chirinos Guerrilla Front in Falcón, the second most important guerrilla group was that of 'El Charal', which operated further south in Portuguesa State. Its leader, Juan Vicente Cabezas, was an engineer known as 'Pablo'. In a letter of 27 August 1962, Cabezas outlined the difficulties facing his troop:

When on 2 March operations began in 'El Charal', we were weaker, there were fewer of us and we had less weapons. We didn't even know the mountains well, nor did we have, as we have today, the confidence of the peasants.

We are not really strong enough to overthrow the government. In comparison with the government's military forces, there are few of us. In comparison with their weapons, we are practically unarmed. Then why does Betancourt want to destroy us? He wants to destroy us not for what we are today, but for what we will be tomorrow.[11]

With Cabezas in the El Charal Front at this time were two other prominent guerrillas, Luben Petkoff and José Manuel Saher, both representative of the type of leader which the guerrilla movement was attracting at this stage. Luben Petkoff, brother of the Communist Teodoro Petkoff, has explained what led him to adopt a revolutionary position:

Who was I up until March 1961? I was a businessman, the owner of a printing works. I had laboriously managed to pay-off a small capital of 65,000 bolivares, which was quite a feat if you consider the disastrous economic situation trade is going through. In spite of this, my work enabled me to live modestly, and until that time I had never failed to meet my obligations with import firms, paper mills, etc. But what happened? In one day, the government took away what had cost me so much work and effort. They made me lose 65,000 bolivares and condemned me to lose any chance of supporting my family. They thought that a person with Communist ideas shouldn't have a printing press, and so they raided it and arrested the workers, who, just because they worked in a company owned by a Communist, spent six months under arrest. . . .[12]

The Petkoff brothers were sons of European immigrants. Their father came from Bulgaria and their mother from Russian Poland, though both had been settled in Venezuela for many years. From his early childhood, Luben had begun to work in his father's printing shop. In 1962, he was not yet 30. The Mexican journalist, Mario Menéndez Rodríguez, has given us the following portrait of him:

His restless, rebellious character, reacting to injustice, led him to take up all sorts of jobs: bus driver, logger in the plains of Venezuela, boxing impresario, breaker-in of wild donkeys— riding them—and farmer. We might say that unsettledness was the prime moving force of Luben Petkoff's youth, but, at the same time, this unsettledness went hand in hand with a spirit of rebellion, unconscious if you like, against the social order which prevailed and still prevails in Venezuela. Besides, this very unsettledness helped him to come into contact with the people, to find the course he now follows out of firm conviction.[13]

José Manuel Saher came from a more oligarchic background than the other guerrilla leaders in the El Charal Front. His father Pablo Saher Pérez, was a prominent member of Acción Democrática and the Governor of Falcón State. He had encouraged his son to go into politics, but when Acción Democrática split in 1960, José Saher chose to follow Domingo Alberto Rangel into the MIR. He joined the guerrillas in 1962, and this caused some stir in Venezuelan society since he prefaced his journey to the mountains with an open exchange of letters with his father, telling the governor that he could no longer live under the same roof as a man responsible for the assassination of the Venezuelan people.

In the autumn of 1962, Comandante Chema, as José Saber was known, was captured. Betancourt suggested to his father that the boy should be allowed to go into exile, but the governor insisted that he be tried by a military tribunal. He was convicted and sentenced to 18 years' imprisonment.[14] From his prison he wrote again to his father:

> Today I occupy a humble position amongst men who are fighting for a new life, without the pressing anguish of perse-cution and poverty. All that I am doing is going on with some-thing which was once part of your life and for which you too were persecuted. At no time have I parted from what you taught me about standing up to dictators. It is true that we are now on different sides, but I am proud to occupy the place you left me. . . . There are thousands of soldiers and policemen who every day commit all sorts of abuses against the people. Do they really need such a large military force to fight 'a small group of lunatics'. You know that the so-called 'Operation Torbes' is on such a large scale that there are even officers from the colonialist army of the United States and members of the CIA taking part, trampling on our national sovereignty and the best bequest of our Liberators. . . . It is understand-able that the truth is not told because you and everybody else knows that many government troops have deserted, and sev-eral soldiers and officers have refused to fight their brothers in arms. It is well known that dozens of members of the Muni-cipal Police have resigned and that there have been serious cases of lack of discipline in bodies like the Digepol. . . . That is why the bombing and strafing from the air has been carried out differently from that ordered by the senior officers. . . .
>
> I really regret your behaviour. Obviously Rómulo Betancourt isn't worried about seeing you go down with him; that's natural, but it hurts me because I am your son. Imagine what I felt and thought when after walking bound and handcuffed for more

than fifteen hours along muddy paths in steady rain, I was brought into your presence in the headquarters of the unit which captured me. Imagine the repulsion I felt when the Military Prosecutor based his charges against me on your evidence. . . . If I am sentenced to eighteen years in prison it is because I was able to understand the urgent need for a nationalist change in Venezuela's status in order to build a really free country.[15]

Another guerrilla group of some importance was that operating in Lara State with the name of 'Simón Bolívar'. This was led by Tirso Pinto and Germán Lairet, a former leader of the Communist Youth Movement. Later, this group was to retire into inaction, following the directives of the party.

Although guerrillas were operating in half the states in the country, on nearly 20 fronts, the absence of any kind of unified command made them exceptionally vulnerable to enemy attacks.[16] In particular, there was little contact between the guerrillas in the countryside and the Tactical Combat Units (Unidades Tácticas de Combate, UTC) which operated as urban guerrillas, chiefly in Caracas.

All those who were involved in this early guerrilla venture have indicated that it was ill-planned, the guerrillas for the most part consisting of enthusiastic students who were in no fit state to bear the rigours of guerrilla warfare. Douglas Bravo commented later:

From the military point of view, our most serious mistake was being too adventurous. Although we talked a lot about a prolonged, long-drawn-out war, at the time we were using shock tactics, as for a *coup*. We wanted to overthrow Betancourt in a few hours, in one or two battles. This resulted in very far-reaching defeats, and prevented us from getting down to building a guerrilla army. We were throwing far too many forces into a hopeless struggle.[17]

Debray criticizes the decision to begin the struggle with a whole series of *focos* in different areas:

It was impossible to supply the arms and other equipment necessary to the guerrillas in such widely separated zones; moreover the centres frequently had no political or military link between them. Many of these attempts, in which students participated almost exclusively, ended tragically through lack of experience, lack of serious military preparation, ignorance of the terrain, and failure to keep military secrets.[18]

Towards the end of 1962, however, after the majority of the guerrilla fronts had been severely beaten, two or three of them began to regroup, solidif, and gradually to acquire some signs of permanence, particularly in the states of Portuguesa and Falcón. The group operating in Humocaros, for example, was defeated, but Argimiro Gabaldón undertook the task of organizing a new movement in Lara. From these new guerrillas and the remnants of the old was formed the National Liberation Army, inspired by its Algerian namesake.

Although the guerrillas had Communists among them, members of the MIR and the URD were also prominent. And most important of all, the guerrillas were joined by progressive-minded members of the armed forces. The year 1962 saw two major military uprisings against the Betancourt government which brought nationalist officers with leftist views into the ranks of the guerrillas.

On May 4 1962 a Venezuelan naval captain, Jesús Teodoro Molina, with the aid of 450 Marines, seized the important Carúpano naval base, situated some 250 miles east of Caracas. He broadcast the following manifesto 'to the armed forces, the people and the nation':

> The command of the garrison of Carúpano informs its comrades-in-arms and the people of Venezuela that at dawn today, 4 May, it decided, together with the popular forces, to assume a responsible and patriotic attitude towards the tragic situation which the country is undergoing, impoverished, divided and bled white, as it is, by the excesses of minority groups who are directly benefiting from the heroic efforts of the democratic sectors and the Armed Forces on the glorious 23rd of January. Our people have been cheated of the democracy won in that memorable battle. . . . We can no longer ignore the numberless abuses, arbitrary actions, murders and tortures to which the people are subjected, which have led to the destruction of peace and harmony amongst Venezuelans. The country is reliving, under Betancourt's reign of terror, the old division of Venezuelans

into two groups; those who have every guarantee and those who have none, the persecuted and the persecuters, prisoners and jailers. A shameless form of discrimination has whittled away rights that should belong to all citizens in a democratic country. Constitutional guarantees only really work for those groups who unconditionally support the anti-democratic bent of this government. The major decisions of the National Congress are ignored. The democratic régime which the people gave themselves as a free expression of its will does not operate. Everybody is aware of these facts. They have been proclaimed many times by all sectors of society. The economic crisis, the wasting of public funds, the irresponsible mortaging of the country, the corruption and inefficiency of the government, all these have led the country to the worst crisis of its history. They affect rich and poor alike. In order to silence the protests and discontent of the people, . . . Betancourt and his minority group are trying to use the Armed Forces as a docile instrument of repression, attempting to re-open the gap between the people and the armed forces which was a characteristic of former régimes. One of the main aims of our movement is to restore the democratic system where the Constitution really holds sway, where the rights of all Venezuelans, and the decisions of the National Congress are respected, so that within this framework of real democratic liberties the country can reconstruct its economy, give work to the hundreds of thousands of unemployed, raise the income of the Venezuelans, carry out a genuine Agrarian Reform and develop the economy on the basis of the higher national interest. In this unyielding decision to restore democracy we are accompanied by the officers, non-commissioned officers and men of the Marine Battalion and the Armed Forces Support Group stationed at this base. . . .

Commander Jésus Teodoro Molina Villegas

Major Pedro Vegas Castejón

Captain Omar Echeverría Sierra

and nine others

Caracas, 4 May 1962[19]

In spite of these brave words and their good intentions, the rebels of Carúpano were not able to survive for long. Within little more than 24 hours after government planes had strafed the radio station and the airfield, Captain Molina Villegas was forced to surrender. The importance of the revolt lay in the fact that it was supported by the Communist party, a party that is usually reluctant to lend its name to military putsches. In a speech to the Venezuelan parliament, the Communist Deputy Guillermo García Ponce explained his party's reasoning:

> The position of our party on the events of Carúpano is in line with the policy our Central Committee has been carrying out up to this date. The programme issued by the officers on 4 May is obviously not a Communist programme, it is obviously not a programme which fits in with all the alignments and positions taken up by our political organization. The programme of the 4 May officers was far-reaching, nationalistic and patriotic, a programme which calls upon all Venezuelans to work for democratic reconstruction. While we do not share each and everyone of the aspects of this programme, we wish to express our complete agreement with it as a whole, we wish to express our support for this programme. We wish to state that the 4 May officers have done Venezuela a great service. They have given Venezuela a programme to unite all Venezuelans. From this stand, in the name of the Central Committee of the Communist party, I wish to declare that our party takes up the 4 May programme. Our party will fight to bring about the democratic programme of the armed forces of the 4 May in Carúpano. The 4 May group of officers is not Castroist, there was no intention of setting up a Castroist government in our country; their declarations show them willing to accept the decisions of the National Congress. We wish to state that here, too, we join the 4 May officers, for our party has never declared its intention of setting up a carbon copy of Fidel Castro's government in Cuba.[20]

Immediately after the short-lived seizure of the naval base at Carúpano, the government began to search the Communist party headquarters in Caracas and to arrest a number of party members. On 10 May a ban was placed on the activities of both the Communist party and the MIR. While uncertain whether the rebellious officers had Communist sympathies, the government was decidedly nervous about the possible repercussions of the Carúpano revolt. And with reason.

A month later, on 3 June, another rebellion broke out 70 miles west of Caracas, at the principal naval base at Puerto Cabello. The leaders of the revolt were the Deputy Commander of the base, Pedro Medina Silva, and Captain Manuel Ponte Rodríguez. After two days' fighting—'the bloodiest and most savage seen in Venezuela for years', according to a *New York Times* correspondent—the rebels were forced to give in, though a number managed to escape to the hills. Unofficial estimates put government losses at more than 200, and the rebels were thought to have had even larger casualties.

Like the guerrilla outbreaks earlier in the year, the military revolts were ill-prepared. Originally, dissident officers had planned for several nationalist garrisons to rebel simultaneously in various parts of the country. According to Debray, this:

> was to serve as a signal for the launching of mass actions in Caracas and in other main towns. The plan was uncovered by the government security services, and the dangerous officers and regiments were either transferred or imprisoned just before the projected date. If Carúpano and Puerto Cabello did revolt in May and June 1962, it was really simply out of despair and to uphold (military) honour; for many had no desire to go and rot in prison for uprisings which had not taken place.[21]

It should not be imagined, however, that these revolts were just a simple case of barrack rebellions. They caused profound repercussions throughout the country. On 6 June 1962 the lower house of the Venezuelan Congress passed a motion stating that the military uprisings were an 'unmistakable sign that the unity of the armed forces is seriously threatened and that within them the growing violence of public life is beginning to find an echo'. The origins of the uprisings lay, the motion continued, in the 'effects of the serious economic, social and political crisis which the country is undergoing, as a result of the failure of this government to solve it, and of its administrative incompetence and its constant and systematic recourse to violent repression and party jobbery in the conduct of public affairs'.[22]

Debray concluded that the military revolt

> accelerated the convergence of left nationalists in the army and civilian militants. . . . But it achieved no more than that, The precondition for achieving even this is that there is already in existence a civilian organization with its own objectives and resources, into which men leaving the army can be integrated; in Venezuela, a guerrilla *foco* already existed in Falcón and Lara before the rising of the marines at Carúpano.[23]

And gradually the soldiers who had been defeated did make their way to the various guerrilla fronts, where they formed an important new element. Rebellious officers who make unsuccessful revolts are natural guerrilla material, Those in Venezuela found, as did Turcios Lima and Yon Sosa in Guatemala, that it is exceptionally difficult to melt back into civilian life. For those with advanced political ideas, the guerrilla camp became the only refuge.

The transition from barracks to guerrilla encampment was not made without some difficulty. And the failure of the armed forces as a whole to respond to the appeal of the nationalist officers involved a certain amount of rethinking on the part of the revolutionaries themselves. Debray explains that:

> the Venezuelan revolutionaries seem to have drawn from this setback the lesson that one cannot confer on the army, even on its most determined and politically conscious elements, too large a role in the revolution because of the resistance to be overcome in many officers and NCOs still dominated by their military formation: for example, their reluctance to keep secrets (military comradeship or caste solidarity often preponderating over political disagreements) or to abandon notions of military honour—in short to acquire revolutionary humility. Thus, the rebels of Carúpano refused to retreat to

the oil fields bordering the Tigre—where they would have been saved from the bombardments—and to dissolve themselves in order to conserve cadres for the future's people's army . . . because this would have been to yield before governmental troops.[24]

Nevertheless a number of valuable men did manage to escape to the guerrillas. One such officer was Elías Manuit Camero, who succeeded in making contact with Douglas Bravo's José Leonardo Chirinos Front in Falcón State. He had been a Captain in the army and was only a month short of being promoted to Major when the failure of the Puerto Cabello revolt put an end to his military career. He immediately became useful to the guerrillas as a source of propaganda to entice other officers to desert. As in Guatemala, the guerrillas made especial efforts not to antagonize the army. From the Sierra of Falcón, Elías Manuit wrote the following letter to his former comrades-in-arms:

> All of you, my eternal brothers, know that the only reason I am here is because of the heart-felt love I have for our country, for I have never sought wealth nor have I stained my hands—nor will I ever—with the blood of the people. Without having been personally affected by the wave of persecution, I decided to leave my wife and children for a while. . . . I had the great good fortune to understand in time that it was the time for sacrifices, the time to leave comforts, for our country demanded it. It was the time to answer the call which our Liberators have been making to us for so long from beyond the grave. The glorious liberating army was created to defend national sovereignty and to secure the happiness of all its children. Are we sovereign? In the concert of nations our country, today ruled by traitors, has no voice of its own, no Venezuelan voice. Its government shamelessly goes on following the dictates of its new master, mortgaging and compromising our sovereignty more and more every day, destroying our most sacred traditions.[25]

Though not himself a former officer, the leader of the El Charal Front in Portuguesa State, Juan Vicente Cabezas, took the same trouble to be friendly towards the army.[26] Hearing, in the middle of August 1962, that troops were planning to advance to his mountain hideout, he sent the following telegram to the commanding officer:

> . . . Our struggle not directed against armed forces whose task is defence democratic institutions and who never place themselves at service of person or party. Since operations began have not fired on regular forces, only replying attacks Digepol, totalitarian creation hated by people. Continuing this policy today have given orders to all guerrilla units in the Sierra Libertadora not to fight regular forces mobilized now thus they can enter the Sierra Libertadora without bloodshed. This voluntarily agreed truce begins at zero hour today Wednesday 19th and should be interpreted as new effort on our part to avoid war between brothers as Betancourt and the Digepol would like. Truce conditional on Digepol not entering Sierra Libertadora.[27]

On this occasion both government troops and the Digepol kept well away from Cabezas' men.

Notes

1 Cabieses *¡Venezuela Okey!*, pp. 221–3. See also, Introduction, p. 11.

2 Mario Menéndez Rodríguez, 'Venezuela: Douglas Bravo', *Sucesos* (Mexico City), 24 December 1966.

3 The Yaracuy Front was commanded by Luben Petkoff, the brother of Teodoro Petkoff—a leading Communist imprisoned in 1961.

4 The Lara Front was under the direction of Lunar Márquez and Argimiro Gabaldón.

5 Cabieses, *¡Venezuela Okey!*, pp. 221–3.

6 José Leonardo Chirinos was the leader of a slave revolt which took place in the same area in 1795.

7   He was imprisoned for being involved in the assassination in 1950 of Lieutenant-Colonel Carlos Delgado Chalbaud, President of the military junta of Pérez Jiménez which had ousted the Acción Democrática President, Rómulo Gallegos, in 1948.

8   A year later, on 15 September 1963, Ojeda made a spectacular escape from the prison at Trujillo, together with Luben Petkoff and Gregorio Lunar Márquez, and they were able to rejoin a guerrilla group.

9   Cabieses, *¡Venezuela Okey!*, p. 229.

10 *La Gazeta* (Bogotá), Year III, NO. 15, July–August 1966, pp. 23–4.

11 Cabieses, *¡Venezuela Okey!*, p. 227.

12 Ibid., pp. 227–8. In addition to this, all known Communists were thrown out of the Acción Democrática trade unions and Betancourt made himself personally responsible for sacking 720 Communist teachers in the public school system. See Richard Armstrong, 'How the Communists Plan to Win Latin America', Saturday Evening Post, 29 June–6 July 1963.

13 Mario Menéndez Rodríguez, 'En Venezuela: unica vía-lucha armada', *Sucesos* (Mexico City), 31 December 1966.

14 Two years later, when Betancourt left office, José Saher was pardoned, and his father sent him to London to finish his economics training. He returned to Venezuela, however, and to the guerrillas. At the beginning of March 1967, he was wounded in a clash with the army in Miranda State, near Caracas, and two weeks later he was killed. His body was given to his father to bury in the family plot in Falcón. See article by Barnard L. Collier, *New York Times*, 26 March 1967.

15 *Clarín* (Caracas), 12 February 1963, quoted in Cabieses, *¡Venezuela Okey!*, pp. 232–3.

16 Régis Debray has made the following comment on this period. 'The number of guerrilla *focos* suddenly increased after 1962; this was an artificial growth that did not correspond to a real growth of the guerrilla movement, nor of its offensive capacity. In fact, this forced growth—cause and effect of the absence of a single command— weakened the guerrillas. This is perhaps one of the reasons for the Venezuelan guerrillas' tardiness in establishing themselves as the political–military vanguard and providing themselves eventually

(1966) with a single command. In any case, that spontaneous and disorderly proliferation of *focos*—manned by untrained personnel, most of whom were wiped out in the first months—demonstrates clearly that the Venezuelan guerrillas did not constitute a unified movement, acting in accordance with a mature plan of action. Among the *focos* that survived the first offensive wave (Falcón, Lara, Trujillo, Oriente), none developed with sufficient speed and strength to be able to catalyse the class struggle around it. Thus, until recently, none of them could act as a substantial counterweight to the scattered centres of power represented by the existing political parties. The lack of a single leadership of the armed struggle, truly authoritative and influential, provokes the dispersion of fronts and this dispersion in turn delays the advent of a single leadership.'— Debray, *Revolution in the Revolution?* p. 79.

17 *Avec Douglas Bravo*, p. 43.

18 Régis Debray, 'Latin America: the Long March', New Left Review (London), NO. 3, October–December 1965.

19 Quoted in a speech to the Venezuelan Senate by the Communist senator, Pompeyo Márquez, and reproduced in *La Batalla de Carúpano: Venezuela en pie de lucha*, Prague, 1963.

20 Reproduced in ibid.

21 Debray, *Revolution in the Revolution?*

22 Quoted in Cabieses, *¡Venezuela Okey!*, p. 242.

23 Debray, 'Le Castrisme: la longue marche de l'Amérique Latine'.

24 Ibid.

25 Cabieses, *¡Venezuela Okey!*, pp. 229–30.

26 Debray makes the following comment: 'Enemy propaganda plays on the theme that the "Castro-Communist" revolution will liquidate the army as such, without of course specifying what "liquidate" means. In Venezuela, this propaganda succeeded in alienating some career soldiers, younger officers of popular origins, who were sympathetic to the revolution. The FALN was accordingly obliged to insist in its clandestine press on the fact that a democratic Venezuela would need its own army, one of a different type, in which anyone of good will would find a place. They explained that there was no question of liquidating physically, one by one, all career officers, nor even of one day retiring them from their posts, but only of destroying the army as a repressive instrument in the service of the ruling class.'—Debray, 'Le Castrisme'.

In Guatemala, the MR13 in its Trotskyist phase had, of course, warned that soldiers guilty of repression would be 'implacably punished'. Ibid., p. 51.

27 Cabises, *¡Venezuela Okey!*, p. 234.

4. THE FUERZAS ARMADAS DE LIBERACIÓN NACIONAL

The setbacks to the Venezuelan revolutionary movement in 1962 were serious. The military revolts had been crushed, the Tactical Combat Units in Caracas had been decimated, and the guerrillas themselves had been wiped out on a number of fronts. Nevertheless, in spite of this, there was still some enthusiasm from an ill-assorted collection of opponents to continue the fight against the Betancourt regime. Support for continuing the armed struggle came firstly from the Communist party, which had been made illegal after the Carúpano uprising. A late convert to the need for violence, it now had little to hope for from the use of legal methods. At the party's Plenum in December 1962, the policy of 'armed struggle' was formally adopted.

The MIR was in a similar position. Illegal like the Communist party, it had nothing to gain by abandoning its earlier decision to organize insurrection.

The third group consisted of army officers and other ranks who had left the army after the unsuccessful revolts in 1962 and had sought security in the ranks of the guerrillas. They had no interest in changing their tactics since, as soldiers, only the guerrilla force could provide them with employment in what they were trained to do.

This strange group of allies—dedicated Communists, utopian radicals and disgruntled officers—had all been involved in some kind of guerrilla action during the course of 1962, and the leaders of the various movements came together in Caracas on 20 February 1963 to set up formally the Fuerzas Armadas de Liberación Nacional (FALN), the Armed Forces of National Liberation. They signed the following document:

> The commanders and duly authorized representatives sign this document in the name of the following groups:

> ‣ 4th of May Movement (Carúpano)

> ‣ 2nd of June Movement (Puerto Cabello)

> ‣ Civilian Military Union (Unión Civico-Militar)

> ‣ 'José Leonardo Chirinos' Guerrilla Front (Falcón)

> Libertador Guerrilla Front (El Charal) and the UTC's and Guerrilla units of Lara, Yaracuy, Anzoátegui, Monagas, Barinas, Carabobo, Zulia, Guárico, the Federal District, etc., represented by the National Guerrilla Command.

> *Whereas*

> ‣ The present government has betrayed the principles underlying its election, placing itself outside democratic doctrine and violating the National Constitution,

> ‣ Official policy has led the country into a severe crisis which is breaking the unity and peace of the Venezuelan family and threatening the very bases of national sovereignty and independence,

> ‣ The violence unleashed threatens to turn into a civil war if the present ruling clique is allowed to keep in power by means of fraudulent elections,

> ‣ It is a bounden duty, set out in the National Constitution and in universally recognized principles, to rise up against arbitrary abuses of power, and especially when, as in our case, they have led to the setting up of a despotic, sectarian and antinational government.[1]

> ‣ It is the duty of the Officer Corps to rescue the armed forces, so that it can play its lofty role of safeguarding national sovereignty and the democratic institutions of the Republic,

Resolve

1) To create the National Liberation armed forces, which shall be known for the present as the Armed Forces of National Liberation (FALN).

2) To approve the statutes and programme of the FALN.

3) To appoint a Supreme Commander, Headquarters and General Staff of the FALN.

4) All the groups who sign this document become part of the FALN, taking over such names as shall be agreed or approved.

Caracas, the twentieth of February nineteen hundred and sixty-three.

▶ *For the 2nd of June Movement*

Commander Manuel Ponte Rodríguez

Captain Pedro Medina Silva

▶ *For the 4th of May Movement*

Captain Jesús Teodoro Molina Villegas

Major Pedro Vegas Castejón

▶ *For the Civilian Military Union*

Lt.-Colonel Juan De Díos Moncada Vidal

Major Manuel Azuaje

▶ *For the José Leonardo Chirinos Guerrilla Front*

Major Douglas Bravo

Captain Elías Manuit Camero

▶ *For the Liberator Guerrilla Front*

Major Dr Juan Vincente Cabezas

▶ *For the National Guerrilla Command*

Pedro Miguel, Executive Secretary[2]

The man appointed the head of the FALN was Captain Manuel Ponte Rodríguez, who had been one of the leaders of the Puerto Cabello uprising. The FALN, from the documents it produced, would appear to have been at this stage an organization very much influenced by its military origins. Its objectives, as outlined at the inaugural meeting on 20 February 1963, were not so very different from those of the Venezuelan armed forces themselves:

Aims of the National Liberation Armed Forces (FALN)

The FALN is an institution at the service of the Country, the People and the Venezuelan Revolution. Democratic and Nationalist, its aims are:

1) To enforce respect for national sovereignty and independence, the freedom and democratic life of the Venezuelan people.

2) To defend the national heritage, its integrity and wealth.

3) To support the authorities set up by the Revolution and to see that the laws made by them in accordance with their powers are carried out.

4) To protect the interest of the people, their property and institutions.

5) To set up a revolutionary, nationalist and democratic government.

The FALN rely on the National Liberation Front and its appointed organs, or organs which are appointed in the course of the revolutionary war, as the expression of the unity and will of the Venezuelan people and of all forces participating in the Revolution.

The FALN receive orders by means of a Supreme Command, the Headquarters and the General Staff of the FALN.[3]

Only a group of revolutionaries deeply imbued with a military tradition could have drawn up the following code of honour:

Code of Honour of the FALN

The operations of the UTC and the guerrilla units of the FALN are the response of the young and the people to the treason and terror restored by the government of Rómulo Betancourt and his accomplices.

The inspiration for these operations comes from the high ideals of serving our country, of fulfilling the nationalist thought of Simón Bolívar and of achieving a democratic and patriotic government.

In view of these principles, operations by units and members of the FALN will be governed by the following code of honour:

1) FALN combatants will only use their weapons in defence of their lives or through an order during operations.

2) No damage will be done nor will operations be carried out against small and medium-sized Venezuelan businessmen, manufacturers, farmers or tradesmen nor to public services which affect the civilian population. The property of large-scale businessmen, manufacturers, farmers or tradesmen who are not accomplices in the government's crimes will also be respected.

3) Combatants will take care to protect by every means possible the property of workers, peasants and members of the middle class, whatever their ideas and even when they are neutral or hostile.

Particular care will be taken to ensure that operations do not affect children, women, old people or invalids.

4) The lives of soldiers, NCOs and officers of the armed forces will be respected, as will those of the municipal police, when they are not engaged in operations against our units.

5) The lives of the children and relatives of soldiers, NCOs and officers, with those of the municipal police will be scrupulously respected, even when these are engaged in operations against the FALN.

6) Prisoners will be respected, will not be ill-treated and their lives will be protected.

This Code of Honour will be scrupulously observed and any breach of it will be dealt with by the relevant organs of the FALN.

HQ of the FALN, 20 February 1963[4]

The Venezuelan revolutionary movement was the first in the continent to use the words *Armed Forces* of National Liberation. Hitherto guerrilla movements had used significant dates in their titles. The movement in Guatemala had been called MR13, to commemorate the uprising of 13 November 1960. Castro had named his movement the

26 July Movement, after the attempt to seize the Moncada barracks in 1953. Elsewhere in the world, in Algeria for example, the revolutionary insurgents referred to themselves as a National Liberation *Front*. But with the Venezuelan emphasis on the armed forces, the way was paved for later movements to call themselves, as they did in Peru, Colombia and Bolivia, the *Army* of National Liberation.[5]

The Venezuelan decision to give themselves a military title was based on history. Conscious, like all Latin American revolutionaries, of the example of the liberation struggle of the nineteenth century, they resolved, like Bolívar, to form their own revolutionary liberation army. They explained their position in their very first appeal to the Venezuelan people:

> Four years of despotic government have brought the country to a catastrophic situation, to an open and criminal division in the Venezuelan family and a split between government and people. . . .
>
> This irreconcilable split and antagonism between a handful of rulers and the majority of the country leaves its overwhelming mark on everything at every level of our society.
>
> A deep crisis can be seen in the most diverse fields. *A national crisis*, because our resources have been mortgaged, our wealth given away, our foreign policy constricted, our interests subordinated to those of a powerful empire. *An economic crisis*, because the country has been impoverished, unemployment is rife, production is going down, independent economic development is at a standstill. *A political crisis*, because police terror has been restored, shameless jobbery is operating and an unprecedented electoral fraud is being prepared. *A government crisis* because the practice of governing for all Venezuelans has been replaced by the improper exercise of power by a clique in favour of a few beneficiaries. *A military crisis*, because the high mission of the armed forces has been debased by putting them at the service of a clique who have a taste for staying in power, undermining their internal unity by favours to unconditional supporters of the régime and to straw men, distorting their role by putting them under

anomalous armed bands to repress the people. *A social crisis*, because the exploitation of the majority by the few has got worse, social inequality has increased and institutions are being debased. *A moral crisis*, because of the appearance of robbery and corruption, embezzlement and crime, the perversion of noble sentiments and the breakdown of values.

The obstinacy and sectarianism of the ruling clique have brought the country to armed violence, to civil war. . . . The clique in power will not abandon its positions peacefully or in an election. Experience tells us this and the present state of national chaos confirms it even more. . . . Such a government can only be defeated by taking up arms.

Without arms, without armed and organized units and without armed forces to interpret the will of the people, it will be possible to overcome neither the terror of the government nor its resources that are based on foreign interests and the selfish calculations of the enemies of the people.

Whether in our country or in others, no group so closely connected with a foreign power and the ruling sectors has ever left the political stage with a good grace or peacefully. That is why the Liberators had to create a Liberating Revolutionary Army to overthrow Spanish domination.

The Venezuelan people again need to create armed forces to make daily replies to the attacks and violence of the ruling group . . . armed forces respected and loved by the people, watchful and ready at all times to defend revolutionary gains, to keep our national birthright and territory intact and crush foreign attacks or intervention.

The embryo of these national liberation armed forces already exists. As a reply to government terror and attacks, guerrilla units have arisen in the mountains and cities of our country. In the last few years, in the very bosom of the national armed forces, honourable and patriotic professionals have been jailed, cashiered, demoted, harassed, brow-beaten and insulted by a clique which besmirches the prestige and distorts the role of the national armed forces by putting them not at the service of the country or of the people, but at the whim of a gang of murdering, corrupt and sticky-fingered politicians.

The heroic risings at Carúpano and Puerto Cabello showed the nation that these officers, like other officers who have risen up, are in the service of the revolutionary cause.

The situation is ripe and there should not be a moment's delay in bringing together all patriots, revindicating the honour of Venezuela, displaying the glory of the armed forces and serving the great nationalist ideals of the Liberators, by creating the belligerent and noble NATIONAL LIBERATION ARMED FORCES, the military arm of the revolution, the power factor that will bring the people to redemption. . . .

> HQ of the FALN, 20 February 1963
> Manuel Ponte Rodríguez, Commander,
> National Commander of the FALN[6]

Some years later, discussing with a journalist the origins of the national liberation movement in Venezuela, Douglas Bravo made the following comments:

> It might seem strange for many people in Latin America and in other parts of the world, that army officers and army units form part of the National Liberation Army of the people when it is precisely the traditional armies who are the mainstay of the oligarchy and imperialism in their repression of the people. But this is one of the peculiarities of the Venezuelan revolution. Each revolution in each country has its own characteristics, its own peculiarities, and one of these peculiarities in the case of Venezuela is the fact that officers have joined the National Liberation Armed Forces.
>
> This did not happen in Cuba, where the whole army, in its entirety with its officers, had to be dismantled to rebuild an army to serve the people. Venezuela's peculiarity is that, as the struggle goes on, these patriotic officers in the army will continue to join the Liberation Movement, some on their own, and others, later, with their own units.[7]

The Venezuelan Communist party only agreed to join in the Armed Forces of National Liberation (FALN) on condition that a Frente de Liberación Nacional (FLN)—National Liberation Front—was set up at the same time to be responsible for the political decisions that would affect the guerrilla movement. In reality, of course, political decisions would have an important effect on the military activities of the guerrillas, influencing tactics as well as general strategy. Although the MIR had some voice in the FLN, it was dominated largely by the Communists—as its equivalent (the FUR) was in Guatemala. The former soldiers in the guerrilla movement were not at this stage an important political force capable of challenging the Communists, and they were kept quiet by the emphasis in the FLN's programme on the value of the military. While there were historic reasons for calling the guerrilla movement the Armed Forces of National Liberation, the name was also adopted to give comfort to former soldiers who could feel that they had never really left the 'armed forces' of the state.

The *Programme of Action* of the FLN, published in 1963, underlines the concern felt for the welfare of these renegade officers:

> The FALN facilitates the conversion of allies and new combatants from the enemy front, accelerates the change of the armed forces, opens up a clear perspective for the officers and soldiers, gives the soldiers a chance to save themselves before the eyes of history, burying the repressive dictatorial tradition at the service of the tyrants and foreign interests, raising justified popular hatred against the corrupt traitors who direct the armed forces. The creation of the FALN provides a way out for every honest, patriotic, nationalist, democratic or revolutionary officer. We are building popular institutions in which we can really put into practice our sublime ideals of patriotism and heroism in service of the Fatherland and the people.[8]

The *Programme of Action* is basically a Communist party document, very much in keeping with the moderate line of the party, though it emphasizes that 'the FLN is not a Communist organization, nor does this programme propose a Communist solution to the country'. It is long—some 24 pages—and it explains the Venezuelan situation in great detail and what needs to be done.

The document begins by describing the practical task that the Venezuelan people have before them, that is:

> to establish a government composed predominantly of progressive forces and capable of leading our country through grave historical changes now impending.

These historical changes become the central objectives of the National Liberation Front (FLN). They are to win national independence, liberty and a democratic life for our nation; to rescue our patrimony, integrity and national riches; to establish a nationalist and popular revolutionary government.

To accomplish these objectives means to shake off the tutelage of North American imperialism; to liquidate the large land-ownership and the semi-feudal survivals in the country; independent industrial development; to guarantee an adequate standard of living for the large majority including the workers of the city and the countryside; to recover our sovereignty in the international arena, elaborating and applying a Venezuean foreign policy, and maintaining close relations with all countries of the world.

To accomplish these objectives it is necessary to unite and organize all forces interested in the independent development of our country—this forms the primary condition for victory—to create our own armed forces capable of defeating the powerful enemy, and to guarantee the fulfilment of the outlined objectives; to manifest the unfaltering decision to be free, to break the colonial administration and the domination of the old traditional ruling classes and exploiters; not to falter before the difficulties and to demonstrate seriousness and firmness in our intentions.

The *Programme of Action* then gives some details about the proposed united front:

> The construction of a united front for national liberation is Venezuela's most urgent task today. To build an instrument that can guide the masses with the slogan: 'To make the country free or die for Venezuela.' This united front shouldn't

exclude any Venezuelan interested in defeating continuism and assuring the independent development of the country. All civilians and military men should strengthen their links in order to realize these objectives.

Workers, farmers, students, white-collar workers, professionals, artists, writers and poets, businessmen with progressive ideas, sincere clergymen; men and women of all ideologies, religious creeds and political party backgrounds; all who desire a Venezuela master of her own destiny and her own riches, belong to this broad united front of liberation. . . .

Our movement is a liberation movement, not the work of adventurers, terrorists or exalted young people. We are not anti-American. We are their friends and we look at the American people, their advances, traditions and struggles with great sympathy. We differentiate with absolute clarity the North American people from the Yankee monopolists and warmongers who exploit and dominate them as well as us.

After calling on workers, students, peasants and soldiers to support the FLN, the document goes on to make an impressive appeal 'to everyone to work among the soldiers, upper classes, officials, national guard and police to neutralize the repressive action. They must understand that they are backing an ignoble and anti-democratic cause. They must be asked not to fire at the people. They must be asked to join in the fight against the government and to be on the side of the people.'

The FLN/FALN during this period, as can be seen from these programmes, was very much under the influence of the Communist party. Although this party, which is one of the most interesting in South America, was later to adopt a position of almost complete hostility to guerrilla movements, at this stage it was wholeheartedly in favour. Potential guerrillas were given training in Cuba, China, and even in the Soviet Union. Revolution seemed just round the corner.

Notes

1   Article 250 of the Constitution of 1961: 'This Constitution shall not become invalid if not observed by act of force or because it is repealed by any other means than those set out within it. In such a case it is the duty of every citizen, invested with authority or not, to collaborate in bringing it back into force.'

2   Cabieses, *¡Venezuela Okey!*, pp. 277–9.

3   Ibid., p. 285.

4   Ibid., pp. 287–8.

5   The short-lived guerrilla movement of Jorge Masetti in 1964 in Argentina called itself the 'People's Guerrilla Army'.

6   Cabieses, *¡Venezuela Okey!*, pp. 282–4.

7   Interview with Douglas Bravo, September 1966, printed in Rodríguez, 'Venezuela empuña las armas'.

     Douglas Bravo tried to explain why this phenomenon was peculiar to Venezuela: 'There is a social reason for this, a historical reason which we must explain: the social composition of the Venezuelan officer corps—not to mention the men, who are mostly working class, workers or peasants. The officers are also from the people; more than 80 per cent of the officers are from the lower middle class, some from the peasantry; and others are from the groups opposed to American imperialism. That is why in Venezuela the army will always produce some patriotic officers who will inevitably join the FALN.' Although it was by no means inevitable that Latin American soldiers would join the guerrillas, it is true—as events in Peru since 1968 appear to indicate—that progressive groups do exist within Latin American armies. The possibility of converting rather than destroying the army has been a course of action that the guerrillas have implicitly rejected. It might have been worth trying.

8   *Programme of Action of the National Liberation Front*. The only version of this that I have been able to find is that published by the 'London Committee of the National Liberation Front of Venezuela', n.d. (? 1964).

Guatemala

1. César Montes, leader of the Fuerzas Armadas Rebeldes (FAR).

2.1. Marco Antonio Yon Sosa, leader of the Movimiento Revolucionario–Noviembre 13 (MR13).

2.2. A girl 'week-end' guerrilla in Guatemala.

Venezuela

3.1. Fabricio Ojeda, leader of the Patriotic Junta in 1958, and president of the National FLN/FALN Command 1965; assassinated 1966.

3.2. Moses Moleiro, a guerrilla leader of the Movimiento de Izquierda Revolucionaria (MIR).

4.1. Elías Manuit Camero, an army captain who joined the guerrillas and became president of the National FLN/FALN Command after the death of Fabricio Ojeda.

4.2. Octavio Acosta Bello (*left*) and Francisco Prada of the FALN.

5.1. Douglas Bravo, leader of the Fuerzas Armadas de Liberacíon Nacional (FALN).

5.2. Luben Petkoff, Bravo's second-in-command.

5.3 Douglas Bravo and Luben Petkoff.

6. Guerrilla group in Falcón.

7. Ciro Trujillo, second-in-command of the Fuerzas Armadas Revolucionarias de Colombia (FARC) and member of the Central Committe of the Colombian Communist Party; killed 1968.

8.1. Camilo Torres (*right*), Fabio Vásquez Casta ño (*left*) and Victor Medina Morón.

8.2. Fabio Vásquez (*centre*) and other leaders of the Ejército de Liberacíon Nacional (ELN).

5. Urban Struggle: Elections and After

In spite of all the setbacks in 1962, the various forces that made up the FALN/FLN had been reasonably active in the months before the agreement to set it up was finally signed on 20 February 1963. Special emphasis was placed on sabotaging American installations. As a reprisal for American pressure on Cuba during the missile crisis of October 1962, four power stations of the US-controlled Creole Petroleum Corporation (an offshoot of Standard Oil) were destroyed by saboteurs on 27 October. A week later four pipelines belonging to Mobil Oil, Texas Oil, and a Venezuelan subsidiary of the Gulf were blown up.

In February 1963, continuing their anti-American activity, revolutionary forces set fire to the vast Sears Roebuck warehouse in Caracas, causing damage estimated at two and a half million dollars, and in June the offices of the United States Military Mission suffered the same fate.

But not all the FALN attacks were against property. During the course of the year they engaged in a number of spectacular exploits, designed principally to draw attention to their existence and to the cause for which they were fighting. Even before the 20 February agreement, they had gone into action to seek publicity. On 16 January they raided an exhibition entitled 'One Hundred Years of French Painting' being held at the Museum of Fine Arts in Caracas. They carried off paintings by Cézanne, Van Gogh, Gauguin, Braque and Picasso, which were returned three days later 'slightly scratched'.

On 11 February the 3,000-ton Venezuelan cargo ship *Anzoátegui*, sailing from the port of Caracas, La Guaira, to New Orleans, was captured at sea by armed stowaways. In a broadcast message, the pirates announced that the ship had been taken over by the FALN and was steaming towards 'friendly territory'. Rather than risk going to Cuba, and thus openly identifying themselves with the Cuban Revolution, they moved along the coast and finally anchored on 17 February in Brazilian territorial waters. Nine people were given asylum in Brazil and the rest were repatriated at their own request to Venezuela.

Six months later, on 24 August, the Argentinian football star, Alfredo di Stefano, who at the time was playing centre-forward for Real Madrid, was kidnapped from his hotel by members of the FALN dressed up as policemen. Released two days later, di Stefano told reporters that his captors had explained to him the aims of their movement, but since he knew nothing of Venezuelan politics, he had no wish to comment.

On 27 November, the deputy head of the United States Military Mission in Venezuela, Colonel James K. Chenault, was captured by the FALN as he was driving in his car to the Mission office in Caracas. He reappeared eight days later, only slightly the worse for wear, having been left blindfolded near the United States Embassy with shoe polish in his hair. Reporters were told that his captors had urged him to read 'books on Communism', some of which had been printed in Czechoslovakia.

The day after the abduction of Colonel Chenault, six teenage students, including a girl, hijacked an airliner on a domestic flight from Ciudad Bolívar, a port on the Orinoco some 270 miles south-east of Caracas. After scattering FALN leaflets over the city, they forced the pilot to fly to Trinidad, where it landed at Port of Spain. The Trinidad authorities refused to grant the students political asylum. They were extradited to Venezuela and arrested on charges of air piracy. A week later, presumably in reprisal, there was a machine-gun attack on the embassy of the Trinidadian Ambassador in Caracas as well as on the British Embassy.

These were publicity stunts organized with the ingenuity and enthusiasm of a student rag. But they took place against a background of growing revolutionary violence and increased repression. The guerrilla groups that had survived the difficulties of 1962 struggled on in the countryside, but for the most part in isolation and with little impact. The main fight went on in the towns. Debray has given an excellent picture of Caracas at this time:

> In the spring and summer of 1963, during the fiercest phase of the urban struggle, not a day went by without simultaneous armed engagements in different *ranchos*. At nightfall the shooting began, to die away only with the dawn. The operations included harassing the forces of repression, ambushes, full-scale battles against the army, and even complete occupation of a neighbourhood which became for a few hours a liberated territory until the concentrations of armed groups in a small area became untenable and they evaporated. The aim was to pin down the military in Caracas, to wear them out, to divide them in order to hasten demoralization and desertion—of which there were numerous cases in the police.[1]

Things took a more a serious turn when there was an attempt on 12 June 1963 to assassinate Betancourt while he was on a visit to Ciudad Bolívar. Immediately, he ordered all Communists and 'pro-Castro extremists' to be rounded up, and a new campaign against leftist elements was begun. Communist and MIR activities had been banned in the previous year, on 10 May 1962, after the Carúpano uprising, but the government now intended to take more positive action.

On 1 October the Venezuelan Congress finally decided to withdraw parliamentary immunity from members of the Communist party and the MIR. Twenty-three Congressmen from these two groups were arrested. Two days later the Supreme Court upheld the decision to suspend the two organizations. By the end of the month several hundred MIR and Communist party members were reported to be under arrest, including the leader of the party, Dr Gustavo Machado.

Elections to choose a successor to Betancourt, whose four-year term of office was drawing to a close, were scheduled to be held in December. On 19 November the FALN called a general strike in an effort to disrupt the elections. Most of the workers were reluctant to support it, but there were two days of demonstrations and rioting in the centre of Caracas. At least 20 people were killed.

Ten days later, on 28 November, the Foreign Minister announced that a large collection of arms coming from Cuba had been captured on the coast of the Paraguaná peninsula. He alleged that the weapons had come from Cuba. The Venezuelan government referred the matter to the OAS, which, in a report of 24 February 1964, upheld the Foreign Minister's claim. Venezuela, stated the report, 'has been the target of a series of actions, sponsored and directed by the government of Cuba, openly intended to subvert Venezuelan institutions and to overthrow the democratic government of Venezuela through terrorism, sabotage, assault, and guerrilla warfare'.

After giving details of the arms that had been found on the Venezuelan coast, the report also described the FALN's plan of operations:

> The policy of aggression on the part of the government of Cuba was confirmed by the discovery on 4 November 1963 by Venezuelan authorities of a plan of operations—the 'Caracas Plan'—prepared for the subversive action of the so-called 'Armed Forces of National Liberation'. This anticipated the use of arms similar in type and numerical proportion to the shipment of arms. The objective of the plan was to capture Caracas, to prevent the holding of elections on 1 December 1963, and to seize the country.[2]

Whether the FALN really had such an ambitious plan at this stage is uncertain. It is possible that the organizers had nothing more serious in mind than the disruption of the elections. And in this they were to be only partially effective.

In spite of a boycott campaign, something like 90 per cent of the registered electorate of 3,300,000 voted on 1 December. (All Venezuelans over the age of 18, regardless of sex or literacy, were theoretically allowed to vote.) Dr Raúl Leoni, the Acción Democrática candidate, secured 32 per cent of the vote, more than any other candidate, and he was consequently proclaimed President. In the Congressional elections, however, which were held at the same time, Acción Democrática's share of the poll dropped by 15 per cent compared with the election of 1958.

Leoni took over on 11 March 1964, announcing in his inaugural speech as a gesture of national reconciliation that if the Communist party were to renounce violence, the ban on its activities would be removed.

The election results, which showed the negative results of the abstention campaign, were a major political defeat for the guerrillas. 'Very objectively,' explained Douglas Bravo later, 'it must be admitted that the triumph of Acción Democrática, supported by the oligarchy and imperialism, was the first great defeat of the popular movement.'[3] The government, wrote Moises Moleiro of the MIR, had won 'a skirmish in the long battle for national liberation'.[4] The elections were a defeat for the popular movement, commented the Communist party's Central Committee, 'and our party and the FLN shared in this defeat'.[5]

Inevitably this political defeat caused all groups engaged in insurrectionary activity to rethink their position. Many of those who were in prison, who had more time for reflection, began to feel that it would be nice to be out of prison, and that an end to the guerrilla struggle might hasten this possibility.

The first group to split on this issue was the MIR. In January 1964, the month after the elections, the Secretary-General of MIR, Domingo Alberto Rangel, came out openly in favour of the peaceful struggle. Experience had shown, he wrote in a letter to the MIR, that Venezuela was not ripe for the armed struggle. Guerrilla warfare had no historical justification in Venezuela. The armed struggle, he argued, had in any case been launched prematurely. It was doomed to failure because, in practice, the Venezuelan peasantry was merely a strategic reserve of imperialism, and not of the revolutionary movement. Rangel also concluded that, since Venezuela was essentially a capitalist and not a feudal society, armed insurrection in the cities remained a more satisfactory course of action than prolonged guerrilla warfare in the countryside.

Rangel's analysis of what was occurring among the Venezuelan peasantry went as follows. The rural population which had been 70 per cent in 1941 had been significantly reduced by 1961. At the beginning of the 1960s, the rural population was only 32 per cent; the bulk of the population lived in the towns. Rangel was convinced that this trend was unlikely to reverse itself. There was little revolutionary potential in the countryside in the future.

Douglas Bravo put a different gloss on the argument:

It is said that today 32 per cent of the population is rural; that the rest are mainly urban. But the issue is not so clear-cut. Firstly . . . the floating population in Caracas cannot be described as urban, because the 300,000 men who live in shanty towns in Caracas bring with them to the city typically peasant habits and customs. Even when they come to a city like Caracas, with nearly two million inhabitants, they still bring these features with them. It has proved impossible to rid them of their peasant, rural mentality. Apart from this, these people are unemployed, don't work, have not yet entered industry and cannot be described as working class; some sociologists have even given them a special term, because they are neither peasants nor working class; they have never worked in a factory and in some cases they are not classified as unemployed. Thus we can say that the characteristics they bring to the city depend on the type of shanty town where they live— without sanitation, sewers or water, etc.[6]

Rangel's letter to the MIR, which was written from prison, caused a grave internal crisis in the movement. He was promptly replaced as Secretary-General by Simón Sáez Mérida, but the change in leadership did not put a stop to the discussion of the issues that he had raised.

The Communists did not at first support Rangel's thesis. In an article published the same month as Rangel's letter to the MIR (January 1964), Pompeyo Márquez, a member of the Political Bureau of the Communist party and the acting Secretary-General of the party during Jesús Faría's imprisonment, explained the party's position:

Within the different ways of carrying on the armed struggle we should put emphasis on the guerrilla struggle; organizing it, preparing it and developing it at the level of present political demands; combining it with the struggle in the cities and with military crises, with mass action and propaganda.[7]

But in the same month, Pompeyo Márquez was captured by the Digepol and imprisoned.[8] Thereafter the Communists began to move gradually into a position of hostility towards the armed struggle. What began in 1964 as a mere criticism of the policy of regarding the guerrillas as the principal means in conducting the political struggle against the regime, was to become, by 1967, outright opposition to the idea of relying on guerrillas at all. In a message to the Venezuelan people published by the Central Committee of the party in May 1964, it was emphasized that an end to the fighting was negotiable. It was something that could be bargained for with the government:

> The situation in which the armed struggle began has not essentially changed. Thousands of Venezuelans are still illegally detained, repression goes on, the persecution of the most clear-thinking patriots continues. There is still discrimination against non-official mass organizations, and policies aimed at a greater surrender to imperialist interests are still in operation. . . .
>
> Since December there has been a pause in the fighting, which apparently our enemies have mistaken for a sign of weakness rather than as a move designed to show our feeling that peaceful channels are not finally closed.
>
> We Communists again say to the country: if an all-embracing amnesty is declared, if public liberties are re-established, if the right to legal action for the banned parties is restored, if officers jailed or exiled because of their nationalist positions are re-admitted into the armed forces with full rights, then political struggles in the country can be directed along peaceful paths.[9]

The decision by the leadership of the Communist party and the MIR to soft-pedal the guerrilla struggle met with little enthusiasm from the guerrillas themselves. Those who had actually been out in the countryside with gun in hand saw things very differently from those who had remained in the town, either in prison or in hiding. Douglas Bravo commented bitterly:

The revolutionary movement then found itself in a severe crisis. The leaders of the Communist party and the MIR who took this line were not in touch with what was going on in Venezuela and were not at the head of military units. In fact many were in prison, and this made them give more weight to their personal problems than to the political problems of the Venezuelan people. And we might say that the defeat of the guerrilla movement, which the government had been unable to obtain by military means, was nearly brought about by the leadership with its policy of giving up.[10]

What had given the guerrillas faith in the future of guerrilla warfare was the fact that, during 1963, when the urban movement had been very severely repressed, they had been able to survive in the countryside without their lifeline to the cities. 'This showed,' Debray has written, 'that the bridges between the FLN and the rural detachments of the FALN could be cut without the latter ceasing to grow and become self-sufficient.'[11] Since the urban leadership had nowhere to escape, he continued, except to the areas where the rural guerrillas had created some small measure of security, 'the fusion of political leadership and military action was now made possible on the basis of the *focos*'. This was of course what happened in Cuba, where it was often safer for a wanted man to be in the Sierra Maestra than in Havana.

Debray, in fact, gives a much more optimistic picture of what had been happening in the Venezuelan countryside in 1963 than that painted by those in the MIR and the Communist party who wanted to see an end to the armed struggle:

Anyone who went to the rural fronts before the elections could testify to the strategy of Douglas Bravo in Falcón, and Urbina and Gabaldón in Lara: guerrilla struggle in depth, taking political more than military forms. The patient creation of support cells among the peasants in each hamlet or village, the daily task of propaganda and contacts, the cultivation of new lands in the jungle, the methodical campaign to achieve literacy among the combatants and peasants, the reinforcement of the organization to maintain contact with villages and towns, the supply and information networks—all this work of political organization culminated in the creation of a fixed revolutionary base with its school, its own jurisdiction and its own radio centre (already established in Falcón).[12]

This state of confidence, which appears to have prevailed in the rural areas was very different from the defeatism in the towns. In July 1964, in the district of Bachiller in the state of Miranda, barely an hour's journey to the east of Caracas, a new guerrilla *foco* went into action. The area, according to Debray, 'had been the object of clandestine action long before the launching of the guerrilla centre.'[13] Subsequently, 'a heavy military offensive, accompanied by raids from B25S, was launched against all the guerrilla zones, after which the government felt able, once again, to announce the liquidation of "bands of armed civilians". But in fact the fronts not only held out but became stronger and more numerous.'

Through personal knowledge and ideological preference, Debray is a somewhat committed witness with regard to Venezuelan events in 1963 and 1964, and his evidence is very similar to that of Adolfo Gilly concerning the situation in the Guatemalan countryside. Both appear to have viewed the revolutionary potential in the rural areas through rose-tinted spectacles. Nevertheless, the fact is that the rural insurrectionaries did appear to have more success in this period than those in the towns, and this factor was important in the prolonged and heated argument about rural versus urban action.

Domingo Alberto Rangel had been in favour of urban action, largely because Caracas was an extremely radicalized city which on many occasions had shown its distaste for Acción Democrática. The countryside, on the other hand, was largely sewn up by the governing party, which had devoted much time and effort to converting the peasantry. At first sight, therefore, urban action seemed more appropriate.

But it had its drawbacks. The American writer, John Gerassi, then a Latin American correspondent of *Time*, believes that FALN tactics in the cities were fundamentally wrong. These tactics, he writes:

were to 'polarize' the population through terrorism; but unfortunately for the FALN, that terrorism was misdirected.

For over a year and a half it was aimed at the cops, 'symbols of oppression'. Yet who *is* a cop? In any country, but especially in an underdeveloped one, a cop is usually a man who cannot find a respectable job. He comes from the lower strata of society and, therefore, he has tight family bonds. Since poor families are big families, a cop in Venezuela is bound to have many brothers and sisters, and perhaps scores of cousins. Once he is made a victim, his brutality and his arrogance are quickly forgotten. He is no longer a symbol for the government. Thus, with a policy of 'kill a cop a day'—a policy that the FALN successfully maintained for over 500 days—it not only gained thousands of enemies in the lower strata of society, but also turned the cop into an underdog. No wonder that when the FALN asked the population to boycott Leoni's election, it suffered a resounding defeat.[14]

Debray, in his detailed, sustained and important criticism of urban guerrilla warfare as practised in Venezuela, concentrates on the military disadvantages:

Operating in a fixed and naturally limited area, the urban guerrilla movement is easily pinned down. In effect, it has neither the choice of time nor of place. The guerrilla is forced to operate at night (the *ranchos* have very weak street lighting) to ensure the safety of the combatants by allowing them to escape identification—although this can be met by switching the groups of neighbouring areas in order to avoid the threat of informers and to ensure the safety of the inhabitants. Streets deliberately deserted cause less innocent victims, although there are always some, since bullets pierce the cardboard or wood walls of the houses. Darkness allows the popular forces to make the most of their advantages such as knowledge of the terrain, mobility, and the enemy's difficulty in using heavy weapons. On the other hand, daylight allows houses to be searched, and cordons to be thrown around whole areas and massive reprisals to be staged. As far as choice of terrain is concerned, it is almost impossible for armed groups to

move in the city, where the large avenues are closely controlled, in order to take a garrison or military detachment by
surprise. Such an operation entails too many risks, because
the lines of retreat are too easily cut off. The guerrilla has
therefore to make the forces of repression fight in the hills
outside their natural terrain. After a certain time the latter
understand the trap and refuse to move, preferring to abandon the *ranchos* to the control of the guerrillas by night rather
than lose a dozen men for each raid. All sorts of stratagems
may be used to try to attract detachments of police and army
into the *ranchos*, among them false alarms: a large bomb
explodes right at the top of the *rancho* where there had been
apparent calm; when the column of soldiers arrives to investigate they are caught in an ambush. But the essential factor is
that the guerrilla is pinned down in the *ranchos*, and the government's tactic is obvious: to station the army and police in
such large numbers in the *ranchos* that it is not worthwhile
attacking them. It is true that in the first stage of the struggle
all police posts had to be evacuated from the working-class
quarters—the enormous apartment blocks of Uraneta, Simón
Rodríguez and January 23rd—as well as the *ranchos*. But the
army and national guard soon established nests of heavy
machine-guns at key-points on roofs, crossroads and on high
ground, and this practically put an end to urban fighting. The
life of a militant is too precious to waste in useless sacrifice,
and happily the revolutionaries have no false sense of honour:
the Venezuelans did not attack.[15]

In describing the problems of urban fighting, Debray was only
voicing the doubts of many militants about its value. It is often asked
why guerrillas have made such a cult of action in the countryside,
seemingly at the expense of the towns. In this passage Debray provides the answer.

With their principal leaders in prison, however, the chief activity
of the Communists during 1964 and 1965 was designed to secure their
release rather than to promote urban terrorism. In June 1964 a
National Committee for the Amnesty of Political Prisoners was

formed, which enjoyed considerable support outside the organized ranks of the party and of the MIR. The following year, in June 1965, a 'European conference for the amnesty of political prisoners and for democratic liberties in Venezuela' was organized under Communist auspices in Rome.

The Italian Communist party at this time was displaying unusual interest in Latin America, causing some observers to suggest that the Soviet Union was using the Italians rather than the Cubans as the main link with the Communist parties of the continent.[16] Perhaps nothing much would have been known about this had not a distinguished Italian Communist, Dr Alessandro Beltramini, accompanied by a lady who was not his wife, been arrested at Caracas airport on 4 April 1965. They were found to be carrying concealed about their persons a sum very close to $300,000. The Venezuelan Minister of the Interior, Gonzalo Barrios, announced that they were acting as couriers of the Italian Communist party and that the money was 'destined to aid the Venezuelan Communist party in a vast conspiracy'.

Curiously, although the money was confiscated, they were never prosecuted, leading some people to believe that their role was in fact not to finance subversion but rather to strengthen those elements in the party who were most favourable to an end to the guerrilla struggle. This would have been in the interests of the government as well.

Whether influenced by Italian money or not, the amnesty campaign made some headway, and the Communist party became increasingly critical of the armed struggle. This affected the FLN, which issued a new *Programme of Action* during this period, emphasizing forms of activity other than military ones.

The struggle, the FLN announced, would be a prolonged one; therefore strategy had to be shaped for long-range objectives. Armed struggle would be centred round the fortification of the *rural* guerrilla fronts, because these offered the best advantages for a long-term defensive struggle and provided liberated areas from which offensive operations could be launched.

In the cities, political work would concentrate on going to the people in the *barrios* and to the workers in the factories to organize them and help them with their immediate transitional demands and needs.

All possible legal and semi-legal means would be used. Political work in urban centres would aim primarily at building support for the guerrilla struggle in the nation's interior.[17]

By the time the 7th Plenum of the party's Central Committee was held in April 1965, the Communists had finally persuaded themselves to give priority in future to legal opposition in preference to urban terrorism or rural guerrillas. The document which the Central Committee produced on this occasion analyses very clearly what had previously gone wrong:

1) There still exist militarist ideas on the way of carrying on and sustaining the revolutionary war. The predominance of military over political considerations makes nonsense of the precept 'politics aims the rifle'. These are positions of military domination and bureaucracy which we must combat severely. They play a part in the sectarian positions adopted during the presentation and development of our armed struggle. . . . So far the revolutionary war has seemed to be a sectarian struggle carried out by a vanguard. Overcoming this failure in the armed revolutionary struggle is essential if we want to turn it into a people's war.

2) The armed struggle has not had a national headquarters, which could act boldly, both in the political and military spheres, which would enjoy the confidence and esteem of the movement, co-ordinate the struggle, centralize plans for operations, and form a link between urban and rural sectors.

3) There is still lack of co-ordination within the FALN ; it has not been possible to bring together the various armed units into a sole body under a single command. Units are still directed and led separately.

4) Many of the difficulties in the development of the armed struggle are related to the lack of qualified cadres at the head of the various units.

5) Attempts to solve the arms and communications problems have been on too small a scale and unproductive. This has prevented a change in the scale of the armed struggle. We are

still facing a strong and well-armed enemy with weak fire-power.

6) There are considerable defects in the urban fighting units. The state of the UTCs and their level of activity have suffered a notable decline. The periods of truce have not been used to create new units, to raise the political and technical level of the combatants, or to assimilate previous experience, etc. All this shows the weakness of our action in the enemy's rearguard.

7) Beside their successes there are still many defects in the guerrilla units: ideological and political weakness in commanders and men, lack of military discipline, the continuing of harassing operations, militarist and personalist tendencies, lack of annihilation operations which would give us arms and equipment and inflict real casualties on the enemy, lack of knowledge and practice in the use of people's weapons.

8) Specialized work is going on in a weak and *ad hoc* way.

9) Training of the party and the youth for the revolutionary war is still slow. Not enough people join in the tasks of war. There is a lack of active co-operation with the guerrilla units. There has been a complete failure to develop paramilitary and militia units as a reserve and as important auxiliary forces for the FALN, etc. After three years of armed fighting, we have failed to make a mark or organize suitably for the armed revolutionary struggle.[18]

Communist parties, of course, are accustomed to go in for a certain amount of self-flagellation, and honesty in admitting past errors can be a rather attractive characteristic. Nevertheless this major indictment of the way in which guerrilla warfare had been conducted in Venezuela clearly went beyond what was necessary. It was calculated to reveal to those who might have been contemplating the armed struggle, not just the inadequacies of those who had actually been fighting and organizing during the previous three years, but the inadequacies of guerrilla warfare as such. It was this aspect of Communist tactics that angered the guerrillas. They could take criticism, but they were not prepared to admit that the whole strategy was wrong.

Notes

1   Debray, 'Latin America: the Long March'.

2   The *New York Times* commented: 'Although it had been believed that other arms shipments might have been received from Cuba, the Paraguaná peninsula cache is the sole confirmed instance of such activity anywhere in the hemisphere. It represents the first case of corroborated evidence on an important scale of Cuban subversive activities in Latin America. The report marks the first time that Cuba has been formally charged with a specific act of aggression by an OAS body.'

3   *Avec Douglas Bravo*, p. 43.

4   Moleiro, *El MIR de Venezuela*, p. 194.

5   Resolution approved by the Sixth Plenum of the Central Committee of the Venezuelan Communist party; quoted in *Punto Final*, NO. 45, 2 January 1968.

6   Rodriguez, 'Venezuela'.

7   Pompeyo Márquez, 'Necesidad de fortalecer la unidad del movimiento revolucionario', quoted in Fabricio Ojeda, *Hacia el poder revolucionario*, Havana, 1967.

8   He did not escape from prison until early in 1967.

9   *Mensaje del Comité Central del Partido Comunista de Venezuela al pueblo venezolano*, May 1964. Quoted in 'Itinerario de una traición', *Punto Final*, NO. 45, 2 January 1968. However, 1964 was a very confused period with genuine divisions in the Communist ranks. Eduardo Gallegos Mancera, for example, a member of the Political Bureau who headed a Central Committee delegation to Peking in August, told the Chinese that 'Armed struggle is the main form of struggle today in Venezuela. Our party has reached a definite decision on this question. We are using revolutionary violence against counter-revolutionary violence. We are determined to gain liberation. The legal ways to liberation have all been blocked, and we have to take up arms and carry on the struggle. Only through the barrel of the gun can we compel U.S. imperialism to give up Venezuela, which it regards as a fat prize.'—'Armed Struggle—the Main Form of Struggle in Venezuelan Revolution', *Peking Review*, 4 September 1964.

10 *Avec Douglas Bravo*, p. 44.

11 Debray, 'Latin America: the Long March'.

12 Debray, 'Algunos problemas de estrategia revolucionaria'.

13 Debray, 'Latin America: the Long March.'

14 Gerassi, 'Latin America: the Next Vietnam'. If the FALN had asked itself 'Who is our true enemy?' Gerassi continues, 'it would have quickly discarded "the cops" as the answer. Venezuela's enemy, by FALN reasoning, cannot even be Betancourt or Leoni, since these men are puppets of American economic domination. The only answer, therefore, had to be the United States. "It took a great deal of debate for us to finally say so out loud," a FALN representative told me in London a few months ago. "We always knew it, but it was difficult for us to accept our own logic. If we said the United States is our real enemy, so we will 'kill an American a day,' and then put it into practice, we were afraid we would lose support from the American radical movement. We know that American radicals are never going to fight our revolutions for us, they can't, but we needed the example of the Vietnamese people to shame us into accepting our own conclusions." '

15 Debray, 'Latin America: the Long March', pp. 46–7.

16 Daniel James, 'Growing Role is Seen for Italian Communists: Moscow's Men in Hemisphere', *Latin American Times*, 19 August 1965.

17 Quoted in James D. Cockroft and Eduardo Vicente, 'Venezuela and the FALN since Leoni', *Monthly Review*, November 1965.

18 Resolutions of the Seventh Plenum of the Central Committee of the Venezuelan Communist party, published in *Principios* (Santiago de Chile), NO. 5, July–August 1965. See also, on the same topic, a document of the FALN entitled 'Our Errors', published in *Studies on the Left*, November 1964.

6. Guerrillas versus Communists

The marked change in the official line of the Communist party during 1964–65 produced an immediate reaction from the guerrilla groups and from those who saw no good reason to abandon the strategy of the armed struggle. Venezuela has never had a pro-Chinese Communist party, but the dispute that went on between guerrillas and Communists during this period bears a superficial resemblance to the debate going on elsewhere in the continent—and indeed in the world—between 'revisionists' and those who favoured a more militant attitude in the face of the imperialist threat.

Already, in October 1964, Douglas Bravo and the regional committee of the Communist party in the mountains of Falcón had elaborated a strategy entitled 'Combined Insurrection' which was in conflict with the official line:

> Combined insurrection [he explained], or combined war, as some people prefer to call it, is a strategic line which, beginning from an objective appreciation of our liberation struggle, recognizes and makes use of short term insurrection factors as well as the constants of the prolonged war which are simultaneously woven together in our country.[1]

This was not the full-blooded strategy of the 'long war' that was to emerge later, but it was already significantly different from the line espoused by the Communist party leadership. And throughout 1965, the contradictions between these two positions became more intense.

Afraid that his arguments were not getting past the Political Bureau of the party to the militants and the rank and file, Douglas Bravo came down from the mountains in the middle of 1965 to work in Caracas. Since the Political Bureau was hostile to his ideas and maintained a tight hold on the party's publications it was difficult for his voice to be heard. Irked by his reception from the party hierarchy, in October 1965 he wrote a long letter to the Central Committee outlining his plans and his grievances:

> I have decided to address our highest organism after thinking coldly and calmly about the problems which the revolutionary movement faces. Most of the things which I shall state have been put to the Political Bureau in the five months I have been here. . . .

He began by criticizing the way in which the FLN worked:

> The FLN does not exist as a true combination of all the political forces which are struggling to liberate our country. That's to say, it does not exist as an organic instrument, either nationally or locally, nor is it the political–military head of the Revolution. It does not exist as a command team nor is it structured amongst the people as a political body. It is true that several attempts have been made. . . . But in most cases the FLN is an amorphous instrument, which does not participate in the tasks of war and most of whose major decisions are connected with parliamentary problems. If we want to bring our war of liberation to a successful conclusion, it is essential to set up this instrument, which will be what conclusively gives our fight the mark of a people's war, a war of liberation, instead of being a war of the vanguard.

He then went on to criticize the political parties that had formerly supported the guerrillas:

> The PCV [Venezuelan Communsit party] and the MIR have not replaced their old structures with new organizational structures. Since they already pay attention to strategic economic areas, they have been forced to emphasize them—for example—the

oil and iron areas, and Caracas. But militarily strategic areas, such as those around the guerrilla fronts, should be given special attention, given the fact that that is where our parties are weakest and that is where we are going to build the most solid People's Army. We should make clear that in making this statement we are not confusing the People's Army with a basically peasant army, as has happened in other countries. In our case the main theatre of war for the formation of our army, and for the destruction of enemy military strength—the rural areas—will be the main zone of operations; but since our rural population is only about 28 per cent of the total, we could hardly describe our liberation struggle as peasant-based, or even as mainly peasant-based.

For this reason the role of the cities and the responsibility they have in the build-up of our people's army through helping the rural guerrillas in every way is of primary importance. The FLN, the parties and the other organizations which take part in it, should undertake legal or illegal tasks, political or military ones, make claims, etc., in the zones where the guerrilla fronts are advancing. . . .

Not content with detailing the errors of the political parties, Douglas Bravo openly attacked the attitude of the Communist party hierarchy:

For you, comrades of the Central Committee, it is no secret that these faults and mistakes can be seen most clearly within our political bureau. The struggle of opinions took place in such a way that Leninist methods of working were not present. We have reached the point where free expression is choked. Fraternity has disappeared. Meetings are held in such a hostile atmosphere that they result in harmful tension which hinders the work of direction. To this must be added the lack of political and organizational co-ordination amongst us, the members of the Political Bureau.

What has to be done now, continued Bravo, is to extend what has been a mere guerrilla struggle into a people's war:

When the masses begin to enter the service of the armed struggle, the revolution takes on a new character; the war of the vanguard makes way for the people's war, in form and content.

Bringing the masses into the armed struggle does not mean abandoning the pressing of claims or other work for the masses. On the contrary, the way to organize and mobilize the people is by means of fighting for their claims, fighting for their interests. In each sector of the population there are problems whose solution will unify these sectors and mobilize them *en masse*. Our role is to find these points of coincidence and to use them politically so that they become the fuse for social problems. For example, many student disturbances, which have begun by making specific claims, have turned into magnificent struggles with a political character.

Many of the 'land seizures' in the time of the previous government also went beyond their original social and economic claims and became good political demonstrations against the government and even against the system. The main thing is to organize and arm the masses ideologically and mobilize them, starting with their own specific interests, all the time raising the political nature of their actions until they get so deeply immersed in this struggle that by making clear the aims of the armed struggle, the masses are finally incorporated directly into it. For, sooner or later, the different sectors realize that our war is a just one. They see how the unarmed roads to economic and political liberation are in practice being closed to them.

Finally Douglas Bravo outlined his conception of insurrectionary action combined with a prolonged war. The cities, he concluded, were ripe for immediate action, but the nature of the struggle against imperialism meant that a long drawn-out war in the countryside was the likely course that national liberation would take:

The insurrectional elements may be summed up as follows:

1) Politically, militarily and economically, the urban areas form the main centre of enemy potential; more than 70 per cent of the total population lives there.

2) In the urban areas the revolutionary movement also has its greatest potential in political and organizational resources, fighting traditions, mass influence, etc.

3) For these reasons the urban area, particularly the capital, is the most sensitive spot for the confrontation of all the contradictions; firstly the enemy's own internal contradictions; secondly those between them and us. The repercussions of our urban actions are still greater in the short term than those of our actions in the countryside. This is a temporarily true fact that we shall overcome as the guerrilla movement has successes and develops. But we should take advantage of it at the present moment by increasing the technical training of our UTCs and preparing the urban revolutionary movement so that it is always ready to take advantage of insurrectional elements that may result in revolutionary outbreaks or in a heightening of the permanent crisis.

Possibilities for long-term success may be summed up as follows:

1) The power resources, the military and economic potential, and the internal and external support which imperialism gives to the enemy, makes him temporarily strategically stronger than we are.

2) Because of our economic potential, the strategic nature of our raw materials, our geographic position and history, the precedent of the Cuban Revolution, the aggressiveness of imperialism towards Liberation Movements—as shown today by the clumsy attacks on Santo Domingo and Vietnam—and the present crisis of unity in the Socialist camp, we are forced to prepare the revolutionary movement for a long-drawn-out war of liberation, for the enemy is not disposed to release his prey without a determined struggle, both economic and military.[2]

Douglas Bravo received his reply the following month, in November 1965. It came in the form of a Central Committee document signed by Pompeyo Márquez, Teodoro Petkoff, Freddy Muñoz, Guillermo García Ponce and the Machado brothers, Gustavo and Eduardo. In this document the Communist leaders went further than they had ever done before in recommending the the guerrillas to wind up:

> Firstly: certain changes have taken place which oblige the revolutionary movement to revise certain aspects of its tactics, especially with regard to the armed struggle.
>
> In broad outline, the situation is as follows: the armed struggle has suffered a series of blows and has been weakened. At the moment the revolutionary movement is not in a position to face its enemies openly and frontally. The armed section of the party has been badly damaged. Bloody and brutal repression is affecting the capacity of the revolutionary movement to organize, unite and mobilize the vast masses and give a suitable answer to the government's policy.
>
> Due to the continual setbacks and reverses suffered, and due to its own weakness—which prevents successful action—appropriate measures must be taken to safeguard its effectiveness if the armed struggle is not to lose the role that it has played up till recently, when it has given the masses some reason to think that revolutionary changes were at hand. In fact, it is no longer playing that role and its future depends on the measures we adopt today.
>
> Feeble armed actions which only repeat similar previous operations without making really significant progress are:
>
> a) Hindering political action and the regrouping of forces against the Betancourist gorillas.
>
> b) Allowing the Betancourist gorilla clique to keep up its alliances.
>
> c) Acting as a break to prevent a swifter decomposition of the 'broad base'.
>
> d) Destroying the conviction and the faith in the right general strategy for the revolutionary movement, the basis for which was set out by the Third Congress of the PCV and subse-

quently enriched by successive plenary sessions of the Central Committee.

Secondly: as a result, the party should retreat on the military front and recommend the suspension of armed action in order to help and rebuild its forces and to get them ready for a new revolutionary stage, which, from the operational point of view, should involve larger numbers than hitherto.

Until there has been a complete recovery, and until there has been some progress in the recruitment of new forces and the regrouping of national sectors, all operations by the FALN should cease.

This military withdrawal should be accompanied by a political offensive to allow us to cover our retreat, reduce repressive pressure and retake the political initiative.

In short, this is not a new truce, but something more basic. It is an attempt temporarily to change the course of the struggle, that is to say, to suspend guerrilla and UTC action, and to bring political moves to the foreground.[3]

It was clear, therefore, by the end of 1965, that there was, and could be, no common ground between Douglas Bravo with the guerrilla commanders and the Communist hierarchy. Consequently, in December, the three members of the general headquarters of the FALN who did not happen to be in prison or in exile organized a meeting of all the guerrilla commanders from the various fronts, with a view to outlining a plan of action for the future. At this meeting which was not attended by the Central Committee in their official capacity, the following decisions were taken:

Firstly, the leadership of the FALN was to be reorganized with Douglas Bravo as the first comandante and with the other guerrilla leaders as members of the directing committee, on the grounds that it was those doing the actual fighting rather than those in the cities who should have a say in the direction of the war.

Secondly, Fabricio Ojeda was nominated as President of the Executive Committee of the FLN, and Américo Martín as its

Secretary-General. These two, together with Douglas Bravo, were to form the joint politico-military leadership.

Thirdly, an FLN/FALN conference was to be held in order to organize the integration within the ranks of the organization of the various groups who wished to associate themselves with it.[4]

Three months later, in March 1966, Douglas Bravo and Elías Manuitt issued from the mountains of Iracara the 'Iracara Manifesto' in the name of the José Leonardo Chirinos Front. It explained in some detail the political situation in the country and the problems facing the revolutionary movement, and concluded with the fresh negotiating programme that the newly formed FLN/FALN was prepared to discuss with the government. It included the following points:

1) General amnesty for all civil and military prisoners.

2) Reinstatement to their ranks of all soldiers who have been removed from the armed forces for political reasons.

3) Legalizing and functioning of all political parties, in accordance with the Constitution.

4) Abolition of Digepol and other repressive bodies.

5) The putting into force of and respect for the Constitution and the law, with equality before it for all citizens.

6) Economic policy to favour the masses.

7) An end to the encirclement of the guerrilla fronts, as these operations are directed against the peasants. Closing of the concentration camps at Cachino, Caburo, El Torcuto, etc.[5]

The important items in the political programme of the new FLN/FALN were outlined by Douglas Bravo in an interview in September 1966:

Industrialization

Industrialization in keeping with the level of development demanded by our society; industrialization to allow our natural resources, especially oil and iron, to be controlled by Venezuelans; industrialization to allow diversification of production and not just monoproduction, as happens now. The fact is that with the production of oil and iron, other forms of production have been greatly weakened, especially agriculture.

Agrarian Reform

The agrarian reform sought by the FLN/FALN, by the liberation movement, is one which will really destroy the feudal structure of the country, give lands to the peasants, give them sufficient credit, medical care and machinery; that will break down the old feudal structure of the country and release forces which will bring about industrialization and open new markets.

We want our agrarian reform to break down the old feudal structure: at present 71.6 per cent of farmers own only 2 per cent of the land, while 1.5 per cent of landowners or heads of farms own 78 per cent. More than 70 per cent of the land in Venezuela is in the hands of a minority, while the great majority of the Venezuelan people owns less than 2.5 per cent of the land. Our agrarian reform intends to make radical and just changes in this structure.

International Policy

These unpatriotic governments that have limited freedom internally, and continually attacked the people, have carried on an international policy wholly subject to American imperialism. They have not been able to make the slightest display of the traditional characteristics of Venezuelan patriotism; they have constantly followed the United States, and have gone so far as to condemn liberation movements in other countries. For many years the government of Venezuela adopted an unjust, unsatisfactory and unpatriotic position on the revolution in Algeria; in the case of the Vietnamese revolution, the Venezuelan government openly supports the United States government; in the case of the independence of British Guiana, the Venezuelan government is taking up a bungling position of surrender to American monopolies. In general, international policy is completely directed from

Washington, from the United States; neither the Foreign Minister of Venezuela nor the President of the Republic are free to give opinions on international politics.[6]

By their action in setting up the new FLN/FALN and publishing the Iracara Manifesto, the guerrilla commanders had thrown down the gauntlet. It only remained for the Communist leaders to pick up the challenge. They were not slow in doing so.

On 18 March 1966 Jesús Faria, Secretary-General of the Communist party, and Domingo Alberto Rangel, former Secretary-General of the MIR, were released from prison where they had been languishing since 1963. They were the two leaders of the campaign within the Left to fold up the guerrillas. At the same time, two other prominent Communists, the brothers Eduardo and Gustavo Machado, were also let out. The amnesty campaign had proved remarkably successful.

Almost immediately they began against Douglas Bravo a bitter campaign of the type which Communists have always been accustomed to wage against heretics within their ranks. According to one account, Germán Lairet, who was in charge of the party's military affairs, actually diverted some of his men to harassing Bravo.[7] Without actually being expelled from the party, Bravo was suspended from his position in the Political Bureau.

Disgruntled with this treatment of his comrades-in-arm, Fabricio Ojeda wrote to the Communist party's Political Bureau towards the end of May 1966:

> The answer from most of the comrades of the Political Bureau to the proposal we put forward—whose sole object is to help to solve some obvious problems in order to give greater force to the line approved by the VIIth Plenum of the Central Committee—is to call one of the people putting forward these measures a 'criminal'. They call him all kinds of names, and include the suggestion that he is an 'agent of imperialism' and other 'fine things'. Is it possible to make such accusations against people who have never shown a moment's weakness in their actions? What sorts of accusations would be suitable for

people who for one reason or another propose suspending the armed struggle and changing tactics.[8]

Guillermo García Ponce replied to Ojeda on behalf of the Political Bureau:

This decision, which is unanimous and irreversible, cannot be misinterpreted: we do not accept comrade Douglas as the head of the Executive Command of the FALN because he represents a fractionalist group. We are prepared to accept unconditionally any decision the Political Bureau of our party makes to defend the unity of our party.

If we were to accept Douglas as first executive comandante of the FALN, we would be lending ourselves to an attack on the unity of the Communist party. And as we believe that there can be no revolution in Venezuela without the Communist party, we are not going to tolerate any attempt to attack the party—at whatever cost.[9]

Fabricio Ojeda angrily replied:

It is we who bear all the weight of the difficulties and carry on our shoulders the main responsibility. We are in the front rank sharing the sacrifice with our selfless guerrillas. And so, in the same way that you do not tolerate comrade Douglas Bravo as first comandante in charge of the FALN, so we can no longer tolerate the existence of leaders who are for the most part in jail or in voluntary exile. We will implement this decision 'whatever the cost'—to borrow an expression of your invention.

As you should know from knowledge of my spirit of unity, I am for the unity of the party, for the unity of the revolutionary movement and for the unity of all Venezuelan patriots, in order to push forward the historic change offered to our country and demanded by our people. But at this moment unity means something different from the unity of 23 January.[10] Now I have a different idea of unity. Perhaps that is why I think I have advanced.

For me unity must have a revolutionary base. It must exist in order to make genuine advances. Unity without armed struggle, without guerrillas, without the solidarity of the working class and peasants, does not fall in with my ideas. A unity without the means of power to defend itself and to develop the changes which it produces is a 23 January type of unity. Unity 'from the Country Club to the Charneca' can only be achieved by concessions and by both tactical and strategic withdrawals. Besides, it is misleading at this moment in time, when Socialism already has one foot firmly set in Latin America.[11]

The existence of Cuba certainly made it difficult for movements that supported the Cuban Revolution to maintain that all they wanted was a bourgeois dominated popular front. Ojeda was one of the first people to point out this illogicality in the Communist position. In a further letter, also written in May 1966, to Teodoro Molina Villegas, Ojeda tried to explain why the guerrillas had different attitudes to the problem from those prevalent in the city:

Filled as I am with a new way of thinking, with my ideas moulded by nearly three years continually in the mountains, where the air you breathe is completely different from the city, perhaps I have got myself into an idealist position. Since there are no differences of opinion of any sort in our guerrilla units, as we have no time for lengthy theorizing and spend most of our time in practical matters, planning ways of extending revolutionary influence to new areas in order to more effectively confront the common enemy, to beat the permanent blockade, etc., etc., I thought that here (in the city) the main problems of the revolutionaries involved concrete matters, necessities. But unfortunately this does not seem to be the case. I have already seen that the main concern is not to discuss objective and realistic plans to face up to and defeat enemy attacks, but rather to smell out any error in the heart of the movement in order to inflate it and make dishonest use of it in petty squabbles. So there is a lot of talk and not much done. Up there we talk less and do more.[12]

And at the end of the month, on 31 May 1966, he wrote in similar vein to Guillermo García Ponce:

I wrote many times, and sent long documents, one of them to you. Other comrades did the same. But our words fell on deaf ears, there was no response. It seems that there is no concern here at the top to solve problems in order to strengthen us, but rather to aggravate them in order to weaken us. It seems that the prospect of a 'swing' and the 'new tactical period' were more important than our sufferings, our growing difficulties. No reply; not a single word, my dear friend. The haste which is now being shown to distort our attitude, was never there when we anxiously looked for efficient, dynamic and consistent leadership.

Finally, in desperation, Ojeda wrote to explain the situation to Fidel Castro:

Dear friend: Here as ever, wrestling as ever against a mountain of temporary difficulties in order to set the struggle on a firmer and more precise base. We have made some progress in this. The main step has been to go to the heart of the leadership problem, of the structure of the national bodies, like the Executive Committee of the FLN and the Executive Command of the FALN. We have begun a general reorganization of the whole structure of the movement, for which purpose we are working hard in order to hold a national FLN/FALN meeting as soon as possible; this conference will have constituent powers in order to study and analyse the situation, to debate strategy, tactics and the political and military line, and to lay down regulations for the appointment of leaders at all levels. . . .

Our determination to direct the struggle towards new bases has led us to bring up certain important questions. The first is the provisional restructuring of the present national bodies of the FLN and FALN. We decided to broaden the present leadership centres. This led to a crisis within the Venezuelan Communist party, with the majority of the

Political Bureau of the party taking sanctions against Douglas Bravo. He has been expelled from the Political Bureau, accused of divisionist anti-party activity.

The second decision is to take every opportunity to bring together all revolutionary forces in order to raise the level of the war of national liberation. This is the only means of advancing towards the seizure of power and the attainment of national independence. . . .

The senior commanders of the guerrilla fronts have joined the general headquarters of the FALN. This decision was arrived at after analysing the present situation of these bodies, since it was considered that the nucleus of three members of the FALN headquarters who were still active was not sufficient to carry on overall military direction, as the other members are either prisoners or abroad. As for the bringing together of the revolutionary forces in order to raise the level of the war of national liberation, a single commission will be set up to study and prepare theoretical material on strategy, tactics and the political and military line of the movement, to be discussed in the next national FLN/FALN conference.

The incorporation of the MIR into the leadership bodies and the preparation of the conference is a very important step, since we can thus begin a period of internal discussion over present differences. . . .

However, there is a new internal split, as a result of the disciplinary measures taken by the majority of the Political Bureau of the Venezuelan Communist party.

Concerning this new problem, I am informed that at the middle and rank-and-file levels, and even in the Central Committee itself, there have been protests against the sanction imposed on comrade Douglas. Documents containing these protests have already begun to circulate. In my opinion, the disciplinary measures taken by the majority of the Political Bureau are due to clearly ideological and political problems, basic issues. These have been partly masked because they have concentrated on attacking the methods and supposed mistakes made by comrade Douglas and others of us who share his view on the strategic and tactical points of our revolutionary process. Two important currents of opinion are being debated within the Venezuelan Communist party.

One, in a minority within the ranks of the party, but stronger amongst the members of the Political Bureau and the Central Committee, is as follows: present conditions allow the revolutionary movement to take the initiative on the political front; however, for this to be successful the FALN will have to order a retreat on the part of the guerrillas and the UTC (Tactical Combat Units). This is not a new truce, but something more fundamental: we are trying to change our way of fighting. That's to say, to open a new tactical phase in which, instead of co-ordinating ways of fighting, guerrilla and UTC action will be suspended. In order that the guerrillas and UTC can withdraw in good order and the revolutionary movement can make changes in its tactics, several conditions are essential, especially the maintenance of unity, internal cohesion, iron discipline and help for the leaders. To achieve these conditions, the party and the youth must act on two fronts: first, by use of persuasion and all kinds of political reasons and arguments in support of new tactical changes, they must discuss them calmly with those who have to be convinced. Secondly, by fighting actively against adventurism and provocation which are what the two documents presented by prominent members of the Political Bureau to this body amount to.

The other, strongly supported in the ranks of the party, though weak within the leadership, is energetically headed by comrade Douglas Bravo. Not only is he opposed to the change of tactics, but he also strongly criticizes the way in which the revolutionary struggle has been conducted.

As you can see, the bone of contention is the armed struggle, which a group of leaders of the Venezuelan Communist party have been opposing since the beginning.

I have no doubt that the sanctions against comrade Douglas are the beginning of the swing, which is aimed at eliminating by disciplinary means whoever opposes the change to a new tactical phase, in which, instead of co-ordinating all forms of fighting, guerrilla action will be suspended.

In a situation like this, our decision to broaden the top bodies, by bringing more consistent and firmer elements into them, is a very important step.

The majority of the Political Bureau has opposed this measure and has publicly tried to discredit us by claiming that the bodies set up are invalid and illegal.

For our part we are standing firm. We have greatly welcomed the appearance of a strong current of favourable opinion, in the guerrilla fronts as well as in the middle and lower sectors of the Venezuelan Communist party, apart from the support found in members of the Central Committee, in other member parties of the FLN, in the urban units of the FALN.

The period for ideological clarification and for defining the revolutionary road is now open. There is a temporarily unfavourable factor in this situation which puts us in a difficult position: this is the problem of funds. The Political Bureau has been running that side of things.

Until now all assistance for the revolutionary movement has been centralized in that body, and used in accordance with its policy, that is to say, the economic strangulation of the guerrilla *focos*. . . .

The morale of our combatants is high and we stand unbreakably firm. We are aware of the present range of difficulties, but we are sure we shall overcome them as soon as possible. Truth will prevail amongst the sceptics, and will bring a blaze of light to our horizon. No going back, not even to gather speed!

Our spokesman can fill in the details and make some things clearer.

We go onwards, towards victory. We shall fight until we overcome. *Un fuerte abrazo* from your friend, Fabricio Ojeda.[13]

Within weeks of writing this letter, Ojeda was dead. In the middle of June he came down from the mountains to Caracas, together with Douglas Bravo, to discuss matters for the last time with the leaders of the Communist party. On 17 June he was captured by military intelligence in a house at La Guaira, outside Caracas. Four days later, on 21 June, according to the government version, he was found hanged in his cell. There is little doubt that he was murdered.

The death of Fabricio Ojeda was a major blow to the guerrilla movement, coming, as it did, at a moment of maximum internal crisis. Ojeda had played an important role in the overthrow of Pérez Jiménez, and since then had been one of the chief proponents of the need for unity in the revolutionary ranks. He was one of the few Venezuelans capable of creating a united revolutionary movement. It had already been disintegrating before he was killed, but his death accelerated the process.

Notes

1 Letter from Douglas Bravo to the Central Committee of the Venezuelan Communist party, October 1965; quoted in Ojeda, *Hacia el poder revolucionario*, p. xiii.

2 Letter from Douglas Bravo, quoted in Ojeda, *Hacia el poder revolucionario*, pp. xii–xxi. A French translation of this letter is reprinted in *Avec Douglas Bravo dans les maquis vénézuéliens*.

3 Document dated 7 November 1965 and quoted in a speech by Fidel Castro, University of Havana, 13 March 1967. He also read out a similar document prepared by Guillermo García Ponce.

4   Further details of this meeting can be found in Ojeda, *Hacia el poder revolucionario*, p. xxii.

5 The full text of the Iracara Manifesto is printed in *Avec Douglas Bravo dans les maquis vénézuéliens*.

6 Interview with Douglas Bravo, September 1966, printed in Rodríguez, 'Venezuela empuña las armas'.

7 Menéndez Rodríguez, 'En Venezuela: desembarco de patriotas', *Sucesos*, 10 December 1966.

8 Ojeda, *Hacia el poder revolucionario*, p. xxiii.

9 Ibid.

10 The date of the overthrow of Pérez Jiménez in 1958 by the Patriotic Junta led by Fabricio Ojeda.

11 Ojeda, *Hacia el poder revolucionario*, p. xxiv. Charneca is a famous left-wing working-class *barrio* in Caracas.

12 Letter of 17 May 1966, quoted in Ojeda, *Hacia el poder revolucionario*, pp. vi and vii.

13 Quoted by Fidel Castro in a speech at the University of Havana, 13 March 1967.

The assassination of Fabricio Ojeda was one of the triumphs of the government's 1966 counter-offensive. Something like 60 per cent of the country's armed forces were involved. In reprisal for the death of Ojeda, the FALN organized an attack in Caracas against Gabriel José Páez, the head of Digepol. Then, in July, it mounted the impressive 'Operation Bolívar'.

On 24 July, the anniversary of the birth of the Liberator, a group of extremely well-trained guerrillas landed on the coast of Falcón State. From the various parts of the world where they had been training, they made their way to Margarita Island, which lies off the coast of Venezuela. From there they launched their attack on the mainland, led by Luben Petkoff, now second-in-command of the FALN.

Later that year, in September, when Luben Petkoff's invading group had succeeded in uniting with Douglas Bravo's José Leonardo Chirinos Front in the mountains of Iracara, Petkoff explained to a visiting journalist his views on the 'Simón Bolívar' landing:

> The aim of the operation was fundamentally military, but there were important political consequences. At that time (July), the Venezuelan revolutionary movement was going through a period of crisis. So it was necessary, indeed imperative, to do something that would not only hurt the enemy, but also reunite our forces and begin a new strategic period in the Venezuelan Revolution.
>
> The success of the landing on the coast of Falcón was a serious military and political setback for the government, the armed forces and American imperialism. Not only did it show

that it is impossible to wipe out the guerrillas, but it also demonstrated that the statements by the oligarchy and its pseudo-revolutionary leaders to the effect that the Venezuelan movement was demoralized and shattered were false.[1]

According to Petkoff, the decision to embark on the Simón Bolívar landing had been taken the previous December at the time when Douglas Bravo and Fabricio Ojeda had assumed the command of the FALN/FLN. Petkoff was given the task of smuggling into Venezuela a number of highly trained guerrilla fighters, all of whom had had some experience of guerrilla tactics in other countries, notably in Vietnam, as well as in Venezuela. Since these men were all known to Venezuelan intelligence, they could not return to the country by the normal clandestine channels. They had made their way to Margarita Island, from whence it was reasonably easy to organize a landing in Venezuela proper, on the shores of Falcón State.

Inevitably the authorities claimed that the landing had been launched from Cuba. Petkoff explains:

> The Venezuelan and pro-imperialist press decided to publish many different stories about our expedition. They said that it had embarked in Cuba, and was made up of Cubans. It was no surprise to us that the press attacked Cuba when it heard about the landing, because this has always happened; they always pick on the vanguard of the Latin American liberation movements in order to try to attack it. It was no surprise to us, because we well know the feelings of the Cuban people; because the imperialists also know them; because Fidel Castro makes no secret of it; because he says it and repeats it in all his speeches to the Cuban people and the whole world; because everybody knows that the Cuban people are prepared to give all forms of help to liberation movements on three continents, not only in the American continent; because the imperialists are aware of Che Guevara's doctrine, which he wrote in a letter to Fidel Castro when he went off to continue the fight, rifle in hand, in another country still under the heel of imperialism.[2] The imperialists have to accuse Cuba, they are obliged to, because it is more difficult to accuse the Soviet Union, or the Socialist camp in general; it is easier and more convenient, bearing in mind the mentality of their Latin American servants and lackeys, to accuse Cuba.

I personally am convinced that the Cuban people are proud to receive these accusations from imperialism and its puppet governments. Everybody can use his imagination. Everyone can believe what they like. For us the main thing is that we got here.

But almost immediately on arrival, the small group of Venezuelan guerrilla fighters were met by the Venezuelan air force—another indication of how exceptionally difficult it is to organize a wholly clandestine landing. The Cubans themselves, it will be recalled, arrived in the *Granma* in December 1956 to be greeted shortly after by a detachment of Batista's forces. Petkoff reveals what happened:

> The day after the landing they began bombing us, every day. Several times a day the hills were bombed, and not only the hills, but also the peasants' fields. For a week they were dropping bombs all over the place, in the morning and the afternoon, and sometimes at night too.
>
> Every day the B 26s and helicopters came along. When we heard the helicopters we knew that strafing and 600-pound bombs would follow. All this was done indiscriminately.
>
> I am in a position to say that bombing is completely ineffective against guerrillas. This is no secret; those who order the bombing know it too. So why do they do it? For several reasons: firstly, as a psychological weapon, to terrorize the peasant, to drive him off his land and destroy his crops, so that he leaves the countryside and cannot help us. This is one of the aims of the bombing; the other is to be able to say to their masters that they have wiped out the guerrillas.
>
> So after a week, when they calculated that they could say they had destroyed the guerrilla group, the bombing stopped.

And the guerrillas managed to make their way from the coast to the mountains, where they were safe from attack.

> With this operation [concluded Petkoff] we showed the broad support our revolutionary movement has amongst the masses. We were able to do this because, in spite of the fact that the government found out about the landing almost on the same day, and the puppet army began hunting us a few hours after we got to the coast, they were unable to surround us or destroy us; they were unable to destroy us. They were unable to do this, not

because of magic, nor because we had become invisible nor for reasons which cannot be stated here. They were unable to, simply because the Venezuelan people protected us, helped us and made it possible for us to carry on the struggle.

We do not see the liberation of Venezuela as the liberation of our country, as the liberation of the land where we were born. No, when we talk of the liberation of Venezuela, we mean the liberation of all of Latin America. We do not recognize geographical frontiers within Latin America. Our frontiers are ideological. We interpret international solidarity in a truly revolutionary way, and that is why we are ready to fight against imperialism until it ceases to exist.

The Venezuelan people can rest assured that we, the true Venezuelan revolutionaries . . . are ready to give everything, even our lives if need be; we are ready to use any means available to us to liberate our country. We are not prepared to lay down our weapons until Venezuela is free and sovereign.

We are full of confidence in what we are doing, our battles will be the most effective way of supporting those who are helping us today. We see international solidarity as two-way, we consider that when some friendly country gives us material or moral help, when a people helps us, we are also helping them when we use this aid effectively. When we attack the enemy, when we attack the puppet army, we are backing up our helpers, the national liberation movements, not only in Latin America, but on three continents. We are sure that we are helping to bring about the victory of the peoples of the world over American imperialism and all other forms of imperialism.

By the end of 1966 the only important guerrilla movement operating in Venezuela was that of Douglas Bravo and Luben Petkoff. Although the Communist party maintained the pretence of keeping up guerrilla fronts, in reality these were totally inactive and the party had no intention of reactivating them. In an interview, Douglas Bravo explained firstly the composition of the new FALN, then its importance in the revolutionary history of Venezuela, and finally he briefly outlined its programme:

It has been said many times that the FALN is made up exclusively of Communists; other people say that there are only members of the MIR. These people are mistaken. The FALN is made up of Communists, members of MIR, of URD, of patriots from all sectors. Indeed I am going to tell you something which will probably surprise you; in the FALN, right here, amongst the guerrillas, you can find men from Acción Democrática, from the Christian Democrats, from URD and from the other groups who are in power, or who have been in power in the last seven years.[3]

Bravo then reviewed the entire history of the previous eight years, concluding that the great failure of the Patriotic Junta had lain in its inability to form its own army:

It is essential for the peoples of the world who are fighting for their freedom, essential, I say, to build an armed unit.

There are two examples of recent liberation movements which can illustrate this fact, and whose experience was useful in the setting up of the FALN in Venezuela. Early on the morning of 23 January 1958, a combined movement of the people and patriotic army officers overthrew the dictatorial government of Pérez Jiménez. The people came out on the streets. Eight hundred thousand people in Caracas took over the streets. The people recovered their freedom. The trade unions surged ahead; an unprecedented mass movement spread over the whole country. The people then held in its hands the mass media; it had the press, the radios, it was out in the street, it unquestionably won great victories. But the power of American imperialism, and the power of the conservative local oligarchy, kept the army—their instrument of repression—intact. And since the movement which arose on 23 January was a civilian movement called the Patriotic Junta which did not build up its own liberation army, little by little American imperialism and the local oligarchy moved from the defensive to the offensive, and gradually made up lost ground, until finally they were able to put Betancourt in power.

The Patriotic Junta movement, the movement of rebellion which overthrew Pérez Jiménez in 1958, suffered from the lack of armed units. This did not happen in Cuba. In Cuba, on 1 January 1959, Fidel Castro came to power with the rebel army; they destroyed the enemy army. Yet the press, the radio and the ministries themselves were in the hands of sectors which opposed the revolutionary movement. Key figures of the Cuban oligarchy and American imperialism held important posts in the revolutionary government.

But as the revolutionary army became a people's army, and as the revolutionary army had destroyed the enemy army, the liberation movement led by Fidel Castro was able to expel the oligarchs and the imperialists from the positions they still occupied, above all because they could rely on a strong armed movement, a people's army, made up of workers, peasants, students and progressive intellectuals.

This was the base the Cuban government relied on to carry out great changes, unlike us in Venezuela. On 23 January we had a great mass movement, a great union movement, a great student movement, but we had no people's army.[4]

The emphasis on destroying the old army is central to the guerrilla thesis throughout Latin America. Debray in his writings gives it especial importance. During most of the 1960s, it seemed sensible enough. The armies were repressive, and indoctrination of the officer corps in Panama and elsewhere seemed to ensure that a decreasing number of officers held the advanced Left nationalist views of men like Turcios Lima or Elías Manuit Camero. Nevertheless there is a flaw in the argument. In practice revolutionary regimes, whether in Cuba or in China, have had to rely to an ever greater extent on the organization and discipline of an army. Indeed, it could be argued that certain traditional military virtues—discipline and obedience, for example—play a major role in the development process. While, given the reactionary nature of Latin American armies in the early 1960s, it was natural to believe that only their physical destruction would enable a true revolution to take place, towards the end of the decade the anti-American nationalism of certain Latin American armies seemed to suggest that it might be possible to subvert them from within.

Notes

1 Rodríguez, 'En Venezuela: desembarco de patriotas'.

2 Guevara wrote to Fidel as follows: 'Other nations are calling for the aid of my modest efforts. I can do what you are unable to do because of your responsibility as Cuban leader. The time has come for our separation.'— Fidel Castro in speech on 3 October 1965.

3 Rodríguez, 'Venezuela empuña las armas'.

4 Interview with Douglas Bravo, September 1966, printed in Rodríguez, 'Venezuela empuña las armas'.

8. Communists versus Fidel

Early in 1967 an event occurred in Caracas which was to bring the latent quarrel between the guerrillas and the Communist party out into the open. On 1 March Dr Julio Iribarren Borges, the brother of the Foreign Minister and the former Director of the Social Security System, was kidnapped in Caracas. Two days later his dead body was found some 20 miles outside the city with three bullets in it. Near the body, according to a police report, were FALN leaflets which stated bluntly: 'We have three other political leaders on the list.'

Apart from these leaflets, which may or may not have been the work of the FALN, there was little further evidence of who was responsible for the murder. According to one journalist, Iribarren was 'the most hated man in Venezuela at the moment'. He was responsible for raising the social security tax without at the same time doing anything to improve social services. There was also a story which maintained that Iribarren had been responsible for betraying the existence of a right-wing conspiracy against the government. Consequently he had enemies on the Right as well as on the Left.

The day after his murder, the Communist party hastened to assert its respectability and non-involvement in the affair. A Central Committee member and Caracas University professor, Héctor Mujica, announced that the party categorically and unequivocally denounced this form of activity since it had nothing to do with the revolution. He said that he had sent that morning, in the name of himself and his family, a telegram of condolence to the brother of the murdered man, the Foreign Minister.

On 5 March three Communist leaders who had managed to escape from prison the previous February, Pompeyo Márquez, Guillermo García Ponce and Teodoro Petkoff, issued an official statement in which they maintained that attacks on individuals and anarchist or terrorist methods were not only not revolutionary acts, but were harmful to the cause, and for that reason should be repudiated.

The following day, however, in Havana, the newspaper *Granma* appeared with a statement signed by Elías Manuit Camero, President of the National Command of the FLN/FALN since the death of Fabricio Ojeda, He had happened to be in Cuba at the time:

> In a new display of growing weakness and fear of the revolutionary forces' heavy blows, Raúl Leoni's government has just issued a new decree suspending constitutional guarantees, with the pretext of the recent execution of Julio Iribarren Borges.
>
> Recently . . . the National FLN/FALN Command in Venezuela issued a communiqué stating that for every revolutionary fighter murdered by the government, the patriotic forces would reply with revolutionary justice, passed on three people from the government responsible for the repression and poverty existing in our country, which is governed by traitors in the service of the Americans.
>
> In the case of the revolutionary leaders who have disappeared, and as was later discovered had been murdered by the government, appeals to the courts, requests for information on whereabouts, and statements to the press by their mothers or wives, all have been useless.
>
> As we declared in the handbills which circulated in Caracas, this was the reason why our movement decided to bring to revolutionary justice Julio Iribarren Borges. . . .
>
> The war to the knife will go on against the enemies of our people, those who are directly or indirectly involved in Venezuela's present situation. . . . The Venezuelan people is no longer helpless, it now has an armed and determined vanguard, which will protect it at all times, will avenge its dead and lead it to final victory, its ultimate and total independence.

The fight goes on until victory or death.

Commander Elías Manuit
President of the National FLN/FALN Command
Havana, 4 March 1967[1]

The Venezuelan Communist party's spokesman for this affair, Héctor Mujica, promptly replied: 'Manuit's statements have caused as much amazement as this dreadful crime, and it is regrettable that a newspaper, *Granma*, belonging to a brother party, should give space to such excesses. . . . ' His statement emphasized the 'unqualified rejection of the crime carried out against the brother of the Venezuelan Foreign Minister and the insane statement made by an ex-member who was publicly expelled from the Communist party for attempting to divide it and taking a different line, like Douglas Bravo, Lunar Márquez, Freddy Carqués, Francisco Prada and others who use the name of the National Liberation Movement'. The statement concluded by exhorting 'the democratic movement not to be confused and dragged into imperialist provocation of Cuba, as part of the new attack being launched against that country by fractionalists and adventurers expelled from the Communist party'.[2]

In the meantime, other Communist leaders were preparing themselves to do battle with the guerrillas. According to cables from Caracas, the former naval lieutenant and guerrilla commander, Pedro Medina Silva, stated in a document circulating clandestinely that revolutionary justice would be applied to the murderers of Dr Iribarren Borges. The document, which was also signed by the former guerrilla leaders Germán Lairet, Tirso Pinto and Pedro Vega Castejón, stated that 'those who usurp the name of the fighting organization which we lead, become *agents-provocateurs* and accomplices of the enemies of the people'.

This open attack by the Communists on the guerrillas who had broken away from the party could hardly be left without a reply. It was true that Germán Lairet and the others were still titular chiefs of a guerrilla organization, for while the party had moved into a position of opposition to the idea of guerrilla warfare, it had never formally wound up those guerrilla fronts which it controlled. But they existed in embryonic form and did not go into action. Germán Lairet and the others had no claim to represent a 'fighting' organization.

For the first time in the dispute between Communists and guerrillas, Fidel Castro decided to take a hand. He had received Fabricio Ojeda's letter the previous year, and had watched with growing concern the alienation of the party from the guerrillas. The attack on *Granma* had to be answered. For the occasion, he chose his annual speech to the students of the University of Havana—the 10th anniversary of the attack on the Cuban Presidential Palace in 1957.

With regard to the death of Iribarren, Fidel explained that he knew nothing of the antecedents of this man, nor who was responsible for killing him. He made it clear, however, that he was not enthusiastic about this method of revolutionary action:

> It is our opinion that revolutionaries should avoid doing things which play into the enemy's hands; kidnapping someone who is later found dead. We never did that, however indignant we were about the enemy's ferocity. We also respected prisoners taken during the fighting.
>
> Revolutionaries should avoid actions similar to those of the repressive police. We know nothing about how this death occurred, nothing about who did it, nothing about whether it was accidental or deliberate, or if it was done by the revolutionaries or not. Our honest opinion—and it is the right of all revolutionaries to express it—is that if it was the revolutionaries, we consider that it was a mistake to do it, for the enemy will use it against you and the people will not be able to distinguish between you and the enemy.

But having criticized those who did the deed, Fidel then launched into a massive attack against the Venezuelan Communist party, accusing its leaders of having betrayed the guerrillas.

The Venezuelan Communists counter-attacked in equally intemperate vein, accusing Fidel of wishing to set himself up as the Latin American Pope. 'The anti-party faction of Douglas Bravo' was in the process of being defeated. And the Communists made it clear that nothing was going to deflect them from their plan to contest the next elections.

In April 1967 the Communist party's Central Committee met in its Eighth Plenum since the Third Congress in 1961 to discuss the serious situation which had arisen after the decision of Douglas Bravo to organize a joint FLN/FALN in the mountains—beyond the control of the party. The meeting was held inside the University of Caracas—traditionally a left-wing stronghold in an increasingly hostile environment.

The main business of the Plenum was to ratify the decision of the party to abandon the armed struggle and to contest the elections, and, by appealing for unity, to ensure that the majority of the party did not side with Douglas Bravo. As an orthodox Communist explained: 'The attempts by the ultra-Left group to push the party into the background, to divide and destroy it, was one of the most severe tests to which the unity and the very existence of our party have been subjected.'[3]

A resolution passed by the Central Committee concluded that the errors committed in the recent period had led to a dangerous situation, a situation in which the Leninist principles of organization and leadership were frequently violated, norms of democratic centralism were not observed and the higher committees were ignored.[4]

The resolutions dealing with the armed struggle were worded in such a way that it was possible to conclude that the party was in favour of both the armed struggle and the peaceful road. Thus one resolution confirmed 'the correctness of the decision to take the way of armed struggle and to define the non-peaceful revolutionary path as the axis of the Venezuelan people's strategy of struggle for national and social liberation, for Socialism'. However, this was merely emphasizing the correctness of the party's previous decision. The Plenum agreed that, in 1962, a revolutionary situation had matured in the country, but pointed out that 'beginning with 1963 the political and economic pattern of the struggle began to change. The economy was gradually put on its feet.' After the 1963 elections, 'the change in the correlation of forces became evident and the conditions for insurrection . . . became even more unfavourable, ending ultimately in the situation confronting us now'.

Today, one resolution concluded, the political and social situation 'is characterized by an unfavourable change in the balance of forces and also in the conditions for armed struggle, a weakening of the democratic movement, the isolation of the revolutionary forces and their disunity, and by the influence exerted on the country's political life by the preparations for the 1968 general election'. Only by using the election campaign would it be possible to restore unity in the popular forces.

The Plenum was particularly sad about the way the party had failed to make the maximum use of the election campaign in 1963.

> We should have taken part in the elections—temporarily suspending the armed operations—and put the accent on a policy of a broad alliance with a view to regrouping the democratic opposition; this would have made it possible to defeat Betancourtism at the polls and, at any rate, to create a broad Left mass movement.

A participant in the Plenum wrote subsequently:

> While not rejecting the experience of guerrilla warfare as a specific form of armed struggle, and while not taking the view that it has outlived its purpose in our country ('the party holds that guerrilla warfare in our country, waged in keeping with the specific features of our revolution, will play a significant role'), the Central Committee meeting noted at the same time that in the present conditions to regard guerrilla warfare in the rural areas as the *main* form of revolutionary struggle would be to mechanically transfer an experience which, while successful in other countries, does not correspond to the peculiarities of national reality.
>
> We proceed from the fact that nearly three-quarters of our population are urbanized, that the radicalized masses and the main motive forces of the revolution are concentrated in the towns. We also proceed from the fact that the foreign monopolies—which dominate our economy—and native capital have their principal industrial centres in the towns and in the adjacent areas. Furthermore, Venezuela's history since the turn of the century shows that, as a rule, it was in the cities and towns that the main political conflicts erupted and were resolved. Revolutionary armed actions were therefore mostly in the form of *urban insurrections* in which patriotic military men par-

ticipated with civilians. This was particularly the case after the events of January 1958.

In other words, the Central Committee meeting held that the guerrilla movement is an auxiliary form of struggle in Venezuela and for Venezuela. The concrete conditions of our life and the course of events completely disprove the view that the guerrilla unit is 'the embryo of a real Communist party', which is counter-posed to the existing Communist party, disprove the claim that the guerrilla movement is the decisive strategic force of *any* national-revolutionary struggle.

Critical discussion of this problem helps the collective thinking which aims at defining the party's strategic line, and contrasts sharply with the attitude of the factionalists who persist in the old errors. As the Central Committee meeting noted, 'the deviationists, by exaggerating the importance and possibilities of the guerrilla movement, are steering it towards defeats, which we are witnessing today.' Furthermore, this deviation with its 'underestimation of work in the towns, weakens revolutionary activity in general'.[5]

Finally, the Party Plenum decided that Douglas Bravo should be formally expelled. As Pompeyo Márquez, the new Secretary-General, was later at some pains to point out (Jesús Faria was in exile in Europe):

Bravo was not expelled for leading a guerrilla movement, for there are members of the Central Committee who remain at the head of guerrilla fronts, notably Tirso Pinto and Alfredo Maneiro, of the Simón Bolívar and Manuel Ponte Rodríguez Fronts. Bravo was expelled for rebelling against party discipline, for setting up a parallel apparatus and for fractionalism, dividing the party. His punishment is due to his attempts to destroy the Venezuelan Communist party and to replace it with an unstructured and non Marxist–Leninist body.[6]

Castro returned to the attack against the Venezuelan Communists in a major speech to the OLAS Conference in Havana in August 1967. The Communists, he charged, had 'almost achieved what neither imperialism nor the repressive forces of the régime could achieve'. He went on to accuse the right-wing leadership of the party of treachery. Part of the reason for Castro's anger can be sought among his internal problems, and rightly belong in a history of the development of the Cuban Revolution rather than here. Castro's problem with his own 'microfaction' of right-wingers within the Cuban Communist party came to a head later in the year and resulted in the imprisonment of an 'old guard' Communist, Anibal Escalante, in January 1968. But Castro was very clearly disgusted with the behaviour of the Venezuelan Communists. It should be borne in mind that this important polemic between 'Castroites' and Communists was taking place at the very moment when Ernesto Guevara was leading a guerrilla movement in Bolivia with almost total absence of support from the local Communist party.[7]

Notes

1   Text in *Granma*, 6 March 1967.

2   Quoted in Fidel Castro's speech of 13 March 1967.

3   Rodríguez, 'The New in the Political Line of the Communist Party of Venezuela'.

4   Quoted in ibid.

5   Ibid.

6   Letter from Pompeyo Márquez to *El Nacional* (Caracas), May 1967.

7   See Part Five.

9. A COMMUNIST CONCLUSION?

Since 1967, the guerrillas in Venezuela have remained in action, but without any striking successes. In May of that year, as though to indicate in a more dramatic form their rejection of the theses put forward by the Venezuelan Communist party, the Cubans involved themselves directly with the Venezuelan guerrillas. On 8 May a small boat from Cuba landed on the coast of Miranda State. In it were four Cubans and a group of Venezuelans trained in Cuba who had planned to join the guerrillas fighting in the region of El Bachiller, where Américo Martín and the MIR had a guerrilla front. But the Venezuelan armed forces were waiting for the little band, and in the ensuing fight one of the Cubans, called Pico, was drowned. The leader of the expedition, a Cuban called Antonio Briones, was shot, and two others were captured. One of them was subsequently found hanged in his cell.

The Secretary of the Cuban Communist party admitted that Cubans had participated in the landing, but he denied that they had been members of the Cuban armed forces. A Cuban statement of 18 May declared that 'our party stands in profound solidarity with the altruistic, revolutionary, internationalist and heroic gesture of Antonio Briones, who died in assisting the Venezuelan revolutionaries.'

Two months later Américo Martín was himself captured while trying to leave Venezuela in order to attend the OLAS conference in Havana. Since then, both the guerrillas of the MIR and of Douglas Bravo have been in a state of decline. There are those who criticize Fidel Castro for having given too little aid too late to the revolutionaries. If

Cuban aid had been flowing to the guerrillas in 1962 and 1963 when there really did seem to be the possibility of a successful insurrection, it might have proved decisive. But this is to be wise after the event. Perhaps the best summary of what went wrong in Venezuela during these years comes from Teodoro Petkoff, one of the most intelligent and least dogmatic members of the Central Committee of the Communist party. Once a supporter of the guerrillas, he joined the Communists in turning against them. But his brother Luben continued the fight, and this family connection with the guerrillas who remained in the field gives Teodoro Petkoff a more sympathetic insight into the issues involved.

The following is taken from an interview with Teodoro Petkoff, summing up the guerrilla experience in Venezuela, which was printed in the *World Marxist Review* in January 1968:

> What we have today is not armed struggle in the proper sense of the word, but merely armed units: two under Communist leadership which, by a decision of the party, are not engaged in military action at the moment; then there is one headed by Douglas Bravo, which engages only in sporadic action, and there are two of the MIR, which are in much the same position. But that applies to the countryside. The situation in the towns is worse. That part of the urban apparatus which joined Douglas Bravo has been almost entirely wiped out in government reprisals. The MIR is in much the same position. The surviving urban forces are extremely weak and inactive.

Asked to explain the continued existence of the guerrilla units, Teodoro Petkoff replied as follows:

> To begin with, the composition of the units has changed drastically. At first, they were made up almost entirely of people from the towns (mostly students and some workers), with some peasants joining later. Now, the Communist-led units and the Douglas Bravo column consists mostly of peasants, though I cannot tell whether this applies equally to the MIR people.
>
> That the guerrillas are chiefly peasants explains why they can survive more easily than before, for they are native to the

areas in which they operate and have contact with the local people; also, they are accustomed to the adversities of rural life and are better equipped to obtain food, contact friends in the villages and find shelter.

That they are able to survive is also due to their political work among the peasants. Someone compared a guerrilla unit that does not fight to an aircraft whose engines go dead in flight and which is therefore doomed. But our experience disproves this. The periods of fighting add up to much less than those of no fighting. But the latter are profitably employed for work with the people, expanding the social base, recruiting and building up defences. Both our good and bad experiences are therefore of considerable interest. Take the Simón Bolívar Front in the state of Lara, the most important guerrilla centre with considerable combat experience, which dealt some hard blows at the enemy. Crushed at the beginning of 1963, it managed to reorganize, but fought no battles until mid-1965. In the two-year interim our guerrillas did important political work, boosting the influence of the Communist party and revolutionary movement in the villages of Lara, Portuguesa and Trujillo with a population of some 100,000.

The work with peasants was conducted in relatively peaceful periods, though we kept our rifles slung over the shoulder. Guerrilla influence spread to a fairly extensive zone of about 125 villages, some quite large. Our big mistake was that we worked in the open, founding National Liberation Front (FLN) committees in the villages, the units moving about freely in the large mountain area, under the illusion that we were in full control. However, when the army mounted an offensive, informers promptly supplied it with lists of our people and their helpers, and nearly 200 people were executed and most of our political organizations were crushed.

But I want to make it clear that our propaganda work had by then produced a social base which functioned effectively despite the army offensive and our mistake of working in the open, because we also had an underground organization which helped our guerrillas to escape annihilation, so that they renewed operations against the army with appreciable success in 1965–66. When I say success, I mean military success, not any gain in political influence. We fought several highly effective engagements and hit the army effectively, ambushing troops and learning to use explosives as a kind of guerrilla heavy artillery. To sum up, we owe our guerrilla success in the state of Lara to the unit's work with the people during the two years of no fighting.

As you see, the inference that a militarily inactive guerrilla unit is like a plane with dead engines does not apply in our case. Our experience speaks of the contrary. Now, too, when our guerrillas do not engage in fighting, they are anything but like a falling plane, because they are in the mountains and hard at work extending their political ties with the peasants.

Teodoro Petkoff was then asked about Douglas Bravo and his group:

At present, the Bravo group exists chiefly in foreign propaganda reports, though it started as a fairly large force. When Bravo broke with the party, he took over the bulk of our urban military apparatus and the José Leonardo Chirinos guerrilla front in the state of Falcón, also 19 men of the Simón Bolívar Front in Lara, Portuguesa and Trujillo. That made a considerable force, the largest in numbers and the best armed, with a strong urban military apparatus.

Bravo's tactic was to mount what he called an armed offensive. Predictably, however, his offensive ended in disaster. If the army and police succeeded in crippling a military apparatus like ours, this applied doubly to Douglas Bravo's, for it had no political shield since Bravo had no party to back him, no political links and no influence among the people. His unit buckled in face of the police reprisals, and his urban force was, in effect, almost entirely wiped out in three large police actions in the first six months of 1967. Not only the original members of Bravo's urban apparatus, but also guerrillas sent from the mountains 'to reinforce the town' were arrested, with the result that the strength of his guerrilla column was considerably reduced.

This was when differences broke out among his colleagues. A split developed, and some of them are now abroad. So there are grounds to think that the Bravo group is breaking up. I am trying to be as impartial as I can, because when factional difference arise, each side usually tends to say the worst about the other. But I may be more objective, because my brother is on the other side and I am deeply attached to him and feel badly about his defeat. Besides, some splendid people are on the other side, too, with whom our spiritual bonds are still alive because only recently they had been our comrades and we know that they are not counter-revolutionaries despite their unfortunate choice. They are men frustrated by years of armed struggle with no tangible results, men somewhat like the old Anarchists who thought a declining movement could be revived by plots or acts of terror. But they are good people all the same, fired with revolutionary ardour, and their defeat is not just their own, being to some extent also a setback for our entire revolutionary movement, affecting the movement as a whole because it is difficult for the people to distinguish between the various groups. What the people see is an armed movement suffering setbacks—the sad picture of a movement with no real victories, while the newspapers report the numbers killed and the number captured, and that there are informers in their ranks. This naturally reflects adversely on the armed struggle and the revolutionary movement.

In conclusion, it would be interesting to examine the following facts: Douglas Bravo declared that once his group had got rid of the restraints of the 'Rightist' Political Bureau of the Communist party, the war in Venezuela would expand rapidly. Yet, for two years now, Douglas Bravo has been on his own, but far from expanding, the war has subsided and the hopes Bravo placed in his guerrilla column, expecting it to fight day in and day out, to set the country ablaze, overthrow the government and establish revolutionary power—all these hopes have vanished, even among the leaders of his group.

Militarily, our situation is grave. The Communist-led guerrilla units are operating on two fronts—in the west and the east. They are a larger force than Bravo's and larger, too, than that of the MIR, which also has two fronts. We are reorganizing: that is part of our general line, which lays the accent on a political offensive while temporarily discontinuing armed action. We want to improve our organizational work, because our position has not changed. For us, armed action is still the main way, for no revolutionary or democratic change can be attained without it. Our experience in Venezuela teaches us that no revolutionary movement can be victorious without armed struggle. We must therefore remodel and reinforce our apparatus, in order to operate more effectively than before at those critical moments when the objective evolution, our political work and renewed links with the masses create a revolutionary situation.

Asked for a final word on the current position of the guerrilla fighting, Teodoro Petkoff replied:

I would put it like this: there is a sincere and realistic reassessment of the guerrilla movement. In substance, guerrilla warfare has never been in the forefront of our political struggle, nor has it been the most important component of our armed struggle. The decisive battles—those that could have yielded victory, or in which we suffered defeat—were fought in the towns. In my opinion, we could have won if in 1962 we had properly combined the armed struggle in the towns with risings by army patriots and revolutionaries. In January 1962 we were close to victory: the transport strike in the state of Tachira grew in a matter of days into a national strike of transport workers and merged with a popular rising in Caracas. By that time we had an effective apparatus in the armed forces, which, if we had activated it, would have made a revolutionary victory very likely.

The later army risings (though they were the first truly revolutionary insurrections in Venezuela in this century) had little chance of victory. No specific situation existed at the time of the Carúpano rising, no popular ferment that could have helped it to spread. Therefore it fell far short of being the spark that could have inflamed the people. The fighting in Carúpano was relatively brief, the people were not given arms, and none of the other garrisons joined in. Things were different at Puerto Cabello, the chief naval base, where a three-day battle developed into a popular uprising claiming a toll of 500 lives. There, arms were distributed to guerrillas released from the fortress-prison and to the townsmen.

The people and some military units fought fiercely against the government troops. The air force bombed Puerto Cabello as though it were an enemy city. The government did not hesitate to use rocket missiles and heavy artillery. But the Carúpano rising and the government's counter-measures had so weakened our apparatus by then that we could not secure the support of other garrisons to back up Puerto Cabello. Neither could the people of Caracas and the other cities, who were taken unawares by the events.

Speaking of the armed struggle in towns, I should like to say that our experience, especially in Caracas, is of considerable interest. The National Liberation Front had five units there, each consisting of 101 men. Each unit had what is called a rear-line base—a system of secret hiding places, a medical and legal service, transports of all kinds and caches of arms and ammunition. Extensive contacts made the units highly mobile; they could disappear when necessary, had considerable resources and were backed by the people. Many of the unit members were students from the petty bourgeoisie, from the propertied classes, so that wealthy homes, too, were a source of help.

In action, the units were highly effective. Their planning was so detailed and precise that at times it appeared excessive. For example, the raid on the U.S. military mission in Caracas was thoroughly prepared, especially as regards reconnaissance, and was therefore successful.

The units engaged not only in group operations. They led full-scale battles between the people of an entire city quarter and the police and the army. The fearlessness and tenacity shown by our comrades in the street fighting were little short of miraculous. The hills of Caracas became fortresses and were a nightmare for police and troops. After any large-scale operation, with the city quarter blocked off, the police searches usually yielded next to nothing (fighters and arms 'vanishing' inexplicably), because the vanguard was closely linked with the people in the area. We treasure this experience, which will surely yield fruit in the none-too-distant future.

To sum up, our analysis of past activity shows that, though guerrilla warfare is something we cannot abandon, it is not the chief form of armed struggle. In our country, guerrilla action depends on developments in the town; guerrilla units may survive without help from the towns, but they cannot develop without it.[1]

This final conclusion of Teodoro Petkoff is important. Earlier the rural guerrillas had discovered to their amazement that they could survive without urban assistance. But to be politically effective they needed to be able to do more than merely assure their survival. The Venezuelan guerrillas have proved that prolonged existence in inhospitable terrain is perfectly possible: it has yet to be proved that they can go on from this to make a major political impact.

Notes

1   'Pre-election climate in Venezuela: an interview with Comrade Teodoro Petkoff' *World Marxist Review*, April 1968.

III
Violence in Columbia

'The armed struggle has been going on in Colombia, in its peasant guerrilla form, even before there could be said to be a revolutionary situation in the country.'

Tenth Congress, 1966, Colombian Communist Party

1. *LA VIOLENCIA* AND ITS LEGACY

'During the bloody civil war of 1948–53, a group of bandits burned the home of a wealthy Conservative landowner, killed his foreman and two sons, ravished his daughter, and left the owner wandering dazedly before his flaming hacienda. In shocked horror, the man mumbled over and over, "*¿Por qué?*"—"But why, why?" 'And the scornful answer was: "*Porque usted es rico y blanco*"—"Because you are rich and white." '

Vernon Lee Fluharty, *Dance of the Millions: Military Rule and Social Revolution in Colombia, 1930–1956* (1957)

In the middle of the 1960s there were two left-inspired guerrilla groups operating in Colombia. One of them, the Fuerzas Armadas Revolucionarias de Colombia (FARC), was run by the Moscow Communists and had roots stretching back for almost 20 years. The other, the Ejército de Liberación Nacional (ELN), had *Fidelista* leanings whose inspiration was of more recent origin. It was to this latter group that Father Camilo Torres belonged—the most charismatic figure in Colombian history since Gaitán, and in death second only to Che Guevara as a continental martyr.

The conditions that permit a revolutionary guerrilla movement to spring up are the same in Colombia as elsewhere in Latin America, but it is important to isolate two which are specifically Colombian. That something is very seriously wrong with the country's political processes can be gleaned from the fact that when President Carlos Lleras Restrepo was elected in 1966, he secured only 20 per cent of the votes cast. Sixty-five per cent of those entitled to vote did not do so at all. The frustration caused by an electoral agreement which permits only two indistinguishable parties to compete is one cogent reason why revolutionaries feel impelled to destroy the existing system by force.

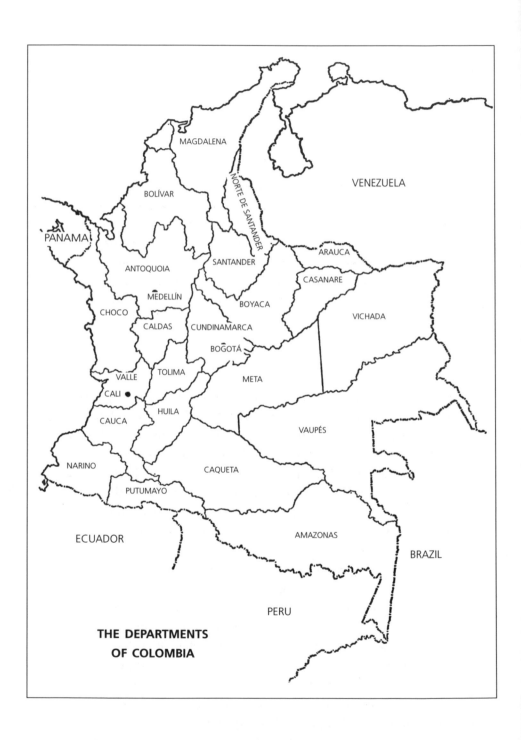

**THE DEPARTMENTS
OF COLOMBIA**

A more crucial factor, however, is the background of violence and civil war which makes Colombia unique among Latin American countries. An American political scientist, Richard S. Weinert, has admirably summarized the events of the late 1940s and early 1950s which so convulsed Colombian society:

> From 1946 to 1953, rural violence ranging from physical assault to brutal inhumanity engulfed most of Colombia, and touched every social institution from the family to the Church. It was so widespread and pervasive that the most appropriate name Colombians found for it was generic: the Violence. Though it varied in intensity among regions, violence was present in all of interior Colombia; only regions near Colombia's borders with the Atlantic, the Pacific, Venezuela, Ecuador and Peru were exempt. The destruction and disruption of life caused by the violence is difficult to overstate. Careful estimates indicate 135,000 deaths from the violence between 1949 and 1958.[1] In a town in Tolima to which many fled to escape the violence, investigators found that 503 of 509 families had suffered the loss of some close relative, that one third of immigrant families had been landowners, and that violence in the town itself around 1950 had destroyed its four coffee-mills and five iron foundries. Doubtless similar conditions prevailed in scores of other towns.
>
> The violence existed for the entire 1946–53 period. It began on a small scale in 1946–47, shortly after a Conservative assumed the Presidency after 30 years of Liberal rule. In April 1947, the Liberal leader, Jorge Eliécer Gaitán, presented a memorandum protesting acts of violence in 56 towns in 11 of 15 states. In February 1948 he made an 'Oration for Peace' at a large Bogotá rally asking for public order. Violence increased following the *Bogotazo* in April 1948, and reached a peak in 1949–53 during the presidential period of Laureano Gómez.[2]

More remarkable, perhaps, than the scale on which the *violencia* took place was the astonishing savagery that accompanied it. Another American political scientist, Norman A. Bailey, writes:

> Yet all of this could have happened, and yet still not have been given the name of 'The Violence', perhaps, had it not been for

the almost incredible ferocity with which most of the killings, maimings and dismemberings were done. Certain techniques of death and torture became so common and widespread that they were given names, such as '*picar para tamal*', which consisted of cutting up the body of the living victim into small pieces, bit by bit. Or '*bocachiquiar*', a process which involved making hundreds of small body punctures from which the victim slowly bled to death. Ingenious forms of quartering and beheading were invented and given such names as the '*corte de mica*', '*corte de franela*', '*corte de corbata*', and so on. Crucifixions and hangings were commonplace, political 'prisoners' were thrown from airplanes in flight, infants were bayoneted, school-children, some as young as eight years old, were raped *en masse*, unborn infants were removed by crude Caesarian section and replaced by roosters, ears were cut off, scalps removed, and so on. The purpose of this recital is to indicate that we are dealing here with a phenomenon of unparalleled ferocity in modern times, in so far as movements at least to some extent spontaneous are concerned.[3]

Although the *violencia* began on a small scale after the election of a Conservative President in 1946, it really got into its stride after the assassination of the Liberal leader, Gaitán, in 1948.

Just as the overthrow of President Arbenz in 1954 coloured the whole subsequent history of Guatemala, so the cardinal event in recent Colombian history was the *Bogotazo* of 1948—a three-day popular uprising after the assassination of Gaitán that left the capital city in ruins. For the looting of Bogotá and the subsequent violence in the countryside indicated what tremendous reserves of popular emotion resided in the Colombian people. Had Gaitán—a political figure with immense skill and appeal—lived to canalize this immense dynamic force into constructive channels, Colombia's 20 years of violence, backwardness and frustration might have been very different. The British historian, Eric Hobsbawm (writing in 1963), maintains that:

> The history of Colombia in the past fifteen years can be understood only in terms of the failure, or rather the abortion, of a classic social revolution. From at least 1930 onwards, by a coherent historic evolution, a social revolution was in

preparation in Colombia which ought logically to have produced something analogous to *Fidelism*, a populist left-wing régime working closely with the Communists. In fact, this movement reached its climax, a plainly insurrectionary situation, at a moment when the taking of power was feasible. More than this: insurrection actually broke out spontaneously in April 1948 and was freely supported by the police of Bogotá. But there was no one to direct and organize it. The populist movement of Jorge Eliécer Gaitán, being entirely unorganized, was decapitated by the assassination of its leader; the Communists did not recognize what was happening until it was too late. In consequence the country subsided into the state of disorganization, civil war, and local anarchy which has obtained during the last fifteen years.[4]

By a curious historical chance, while Ernesto Guevara had been present in Guatemala during the last days of Arbenz, so Fidel Castro was in Bogotá at the time of the assassination of Gaitán, and witnessed the insurrection that followed.[5] He arrived as part of a delegation to an anti-imperialist student congress being held there to coincide with the Ninth Pan-American Conference which opened on 30 March 1948. It was at the very beginning of the cold war, and the United States Secretary of State George Marshall, fresh from his European triumphs, had come to this important inter-American conference to tell his southern neighbours that although United States money could only be made available to Europe, 'the problem of foreign-inspired subversive activities directed against the institutions, peace and security of the American republics' was of considerable concern to Mr Truman's government. Expressing equal concern with him were Mr Averell Harriman and General Matthew Ridgway.

Among the items on the conference agenda were the colonies of the European powers that still remained in Latin America. The Argentine government, then in the hands of Juan Perón, was in the middle of a campaign to assert the rights of Argentina over the Falkland Islands and British Antarctica and in consequence the Argentine representative at the conference, together with some of his colleagues, was not at all averse to the anti-colonialist propaganda being put out by Castro's student congress.

On 9 April Castro and the other student delegates were scheduled to have an interview with Gaitán at midday in the offices of the Liberal newspaper *El Tiempo*. Gaitán had spent the early part of the morning at his office near the Capitol where the Pan-American Conference was meeting, but while walking from there to the newspaper building, he was shot down by an unknown assassin who was immediately lynched by the crowd.[6]

> Within a few minutes of the attack on Senor Gaitán, armed mobs began looting and setting fire to public buildings and stores in the centre of the city, the United States Embassy being the object of a fierce attack which was, however, beaten off by members of the Embassy staff, who fought fires in the buildings for many hours. . . . The Capitol which housed the Pan-American Conference was also devastated and a great quantity of the equipment of the Conference, together with its records, destroyed or looted. Although all the members of the foreign diplomatic missions and of the Conference delegations, which had taken refuge in various parts of the city, escaped unhurt, they suffered considerable hardships due to the interruption in food supplies, power and light services, and other amenities in Bogotá where fires raged for several days.[7]

On 12 April, when the insurrection had died away after the leaderless Liberals had agreed to rejoin the Conservative Cabinet, Secretary of State Marshall accused 'international Communism' of inspiring the revolt. He described it as the first major Communist attempt in the Western Hemisphere since the end of the war. He warned that 'in the actions we take here in regard to the present situation we must have clearly in mind that this is a world affair, and not merely Colombian or Latin American'. Not to be outdone, the British Ambassador, Gilbert Mackereth, also declared that the revolt had borne all the marks of Communist inspiration and direction.

In fact, the Communists appear to have been caught unawares, and displayed their customary lack of enthusiasm for promoting revolution. The historian of Latin American Communism, Robert J. Alexander, believes that:

> Had the Communists been behind the *Bogotazo* the result of these events would have been much different. The mob was in control of the city for forty-eight hours, and with determined

leadership could have overthrown President Ospina Pérez. One of the notable things about the Bogota insurrection was the fact that the government did not fall. Instead, the President maintained his position, and the formation of a new coalition government of Conservatives and Liberals was the only immediate political consequence of the revolt.

The Communist leaders were nowhere to be seen during most of the *Bogotazo*. It is widely believed that Gilberto Vieira spent most of the time hiding in the offices of *El Tiempo*, the Liberal newspaper, which naturally was immune from attack.[8]

After the *Bogotazo*, Colombia degenerated into violence and anarchy. The Liberals refused to participate in the presidential elections of 1949, and Dr Laureano Gómez of the Conservative party was elected unopposed.[9]

Notes

1 This figure comes from Guzmán Campos, *La Violencia en Colombia*, 1962, p. 292. Guzmán gives the following breakdown:

Murdered peasants	85,144
Other civilians	39,856
Army	6,200
Police and state functionaries	3,620
	134,820

He brings this figure up to 180,000 to include those who died from their wounds, and considers 200,000 a correct figure for the period 1949–62.

2 Richard S. Weinert, 'Violence in Pre-modern Societies: Rural Colombia', *American Political Science Review*, June 1966. See also, Ronald H. McDonald, 'Political Protest and Alienation in Voting: the Case of Colombia', *Interamerican Economic Affairs*, VOL. xxi, NO. 2, Autumn, 1967: '*La Violencia* left an imprint on the political culture of Colombia which is best characterized as political alienation, resignation and fear.'

3 Norman A. Bailey, '*La Violencia* in Colombia', *Journal of Inter-American Studies*, October 1967.

4   Eric Hobsbawm, 'The Revolutionary Situation in Colombia', *The World Today*, VOL. xix, June 1963. The Colombian ruling party, the Liberals, split in 1946 between its left-wing, led by Gaitán, and the right-wing, led by Gabriel Turbay. This led to the election of a Conservative President, Señor Ospina Pérez. The Liberals were represented in his government, but after Gaitán gained complete control of his party, he began to undermine the bipartisanship that had existed. Shortly before the Pan-American Conference held in Bogotá in March and April 1948, he withdrew all the Liberals from the Cabinet. There seems little doubt that, had he lived, he would have been elected President in 1949, thereby inaugurating a totally new era in Colombian history. 'In one sense Jorge Gaitán could have been the Fidel Castro of Colombia. His death deprived the Colombian Left of a genuinely popular leader of high class.'—Marcel Niedergang, *Le Monde*, 8 February 1966.

5   An account of Fidel's activities during the *Bogotazo* is included in Jules Dubois, *Fidel Castro: ¿rebelde, libertador o dictador?* Editorial Grijalbo Argentina, Buenos Aires 1959, pp. 18–23, and Herbert L. Matthews, *The Cuban Story*, New York, George Braziller, Inc., 1961, pp. 140–4.

6   'As Gaitán slumped to the sidewalk, a vendor of lottery tickets made a rush for the assassin. Another man ran from a near-by café and smashed a chair over the killer's head. In an instant a mob had gathered around the assassin, and quite literally they kicked him to death, disfiguring him so badly that his features were unrecognizable and identification had to be made from documents on his person.'—Fluharty, *Dance of the Millions*, University of Pittsburgh Press, Pittsburgh, 1957, p. 100. This is the best single book on modern Colombia; it is one of the great classics of Latin American history.

7   *Keesings Contemporary Archives*, p. 9236.

8   Robert J. Alexander, *Communism in Latin America*, Rutgers University Press, New Brunswick, 1957, pp. 250–1. What was lacking, of course, was 'determined leadership'. Even if the Communists had decided to lead, organize, control or 'get behind' the *Bogotazo*, it is doubtful whether they really had the leaders to bring it to a successful, revolutionary, conclusion. (Gilberto Vieira was the leader of the Colombian Communist party.)

9   The Liberal boycott was almost complete, as the following figures for Bogotá show:

	Conservative	Liberal
Parliamentary elections, June 1949	20,000	63,000
Presidential elections, November 1949	20,181	27

2. COMMUNISTS AND INDEPENDENT REPUBLICS

Throughout the late 1940s and early 1950s, guerrilla bands carrying the Liberal or Conservative label wrought havoc in the Colombian countryside. According to Richard Weinert,

> Considerable documentary evidence supports the suggestion that traditional party loyalties and not class hostilities underlay the violence. A chief of one band of antagonists in Antioquia wrote in July 1953 of having seen a man's tongue removed by police, who explained to their victim, 'We're cutting it out so you won't ever again shout *vivas* to the Liberal Party.'[1]

However, although the bulk of the assassinations and atrocities committed during the period of the *violencia* was the work of Liberals or Conservatives, the Colombian Communist party took advantage of the anarchic situation to organize its own little guerrilla band of peasants.

Since the early 1940s, the Colombian Communist party had been in a state of decline, largely due to the upsurge of *Gaitanism*. Gaitán, rather than any Communist leader, attracted the support of great numbers of poor Colombians. The Communists misjudged badly when, during the presidential elections of 1945, they told their members to vote for Gabriel Turbay, a right-wing Liberal and former Communist, rather than Gaitán. The result of a split Liberal vote was victory for the Conservatives. Although the Communists had called Gaitán a 'Fascist' during the election campaign, they swung round to support him after his defeat.[2] But when Gaitán was assassinated, the Communists did not know what to do. As one story puts it,

> the entire central committee presented itself in the office of the national direction of the Liberal party, to await orders on what attitude it should adopt. The people died in street fighting, without any political direction.[3]

With each vacillating step that the party took, its most active members broke away. In the late 1940s little more than a rump remained. And it was this group that began enrolling peasants, mostly Liberals, for its own purposes.

The Communists were not without experience of peasant organization. In the early 1930s, taking advantage of the peasant disturbances that had occurred between 1928 and 1930 in the region of Tequendama, the newly formed Communist party persuaded the peasants in an area called Viotá to keep the lands that they had seized. Cadres from Bogotá went out to help them.

> Powerless to crush the movement by force in its early years, the landowning class chose to isolate the Viotá areas as far as possible and to keep quiet about what had happened. The extreme contempt of the government for the people fostered the illusion that this popular experiment would fail, and they decided to wait for it to blow over. But agriculture in Viotá very soon became competitive. A network of economic interests began to appear around the area. Neighbouring businessmen and even landowners came to terms with the peasants attracted by the businesslike and prosperous way they carried on their affairs. Thus the blockade failed.[4]

The peasants of Viotá had their own armed forces, their own judiciary, and to all intents and purposes they were self-ruled. During the anti-guerrilla campaigns in the late 1940s the Colombian army left them well alone.[5]

With this practical experience of peasant organization over nearly two decades, the Communists were well placed to use the situation of near anarchy which prevailed in the years after Gaitán's death.[6] In

November 1949, at the time of the presidential elections which were won without opposition by the Conservative candidate Gómez, the Communist party adopted a policy known rather inelegantly as 'the self-defence of the masses'. With the slogan 'To reactionary violence must be opposed the organized violence of the masses', Communist cadres began to gather together survivors of the *violencia* into areas where they could defend themselves. In an article in the *World Marxist Review* of April 1967, a Colombian Communist, Alberto Gómez, describes what happened:

> In the early 1950s more than 1,000 peasant families from other areas gathered in the district of 'El Davis', Tolima Department, in the central cordillera. The adults were organized in the party, the young people in the Communist Youth organization, the children in the so-called Sucre Battalion and the women in their own committee. This was the first closely knit armed group to embark on guerrilla action. Soon the entire southern part of Tolima Department was gripped by guerrilla warfare. Many outstanding fighters, such as Manuel Marulanda, Ciro Trujillo, Isauro Yosa, Alfonso Castañeda (Richard), Jacobo Frías Alape (Charro Negro) and Isaias Pardo, got their baptism of fire in 'El Davis'. This was the first major centre of guerrilla struggle in Latin America led by the party of the proletariat. The present guerrilla is carrying on in the traditions of these fighters.

> However, the first stage of the armed peasant movement (1949–53) also had features which retarded the all-round development of the struggle. The movement had neither a united military–political leadership nor a clear-cut programme aimed at winning power. It was rather a conglomeration of groups which had considerable manpower resources but were politically disunited, joint planning of the struggle was out of the question. The Liberals, Conservatives and Communists each led their own movements, pursuing, moreover, entirely different aims. For the Liberal bourgeoisie the guerrilla move-

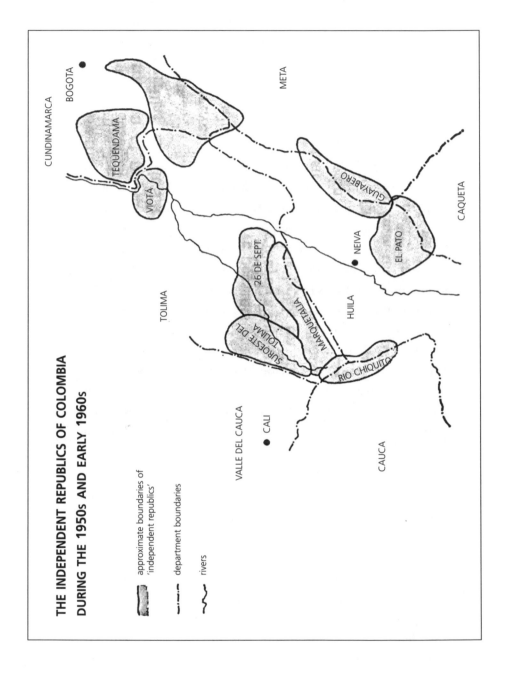

THE INDEPENDENT REPUBLICS OF COLOMBIA DURING THE 1950s AND EARLY 1960s

approximate boundaries of 'independent republics'

department boundaries

rivers

ment was a means of stepping up inter-party struggle which fostered the illusion that only a military takeover could solve the problems at issue. The Conservatives mainly sought to use their combat detachments to maintain the dictatorship. The Communists worked to unite the diverse groups, and in the Boyaca Department they managed to convene a conference of guerrillas but were not able to achieve their aims on a national scale.[7]

This conference, known as the Conference of Boyaca, was organized by the Communist party with a view to giving the guerrilla groups a more revolutionary orientation. It was held at the beginning of 1952. According to an account by the Communist leader, Gilberto Vieira, 'the national conference of guerrillas declared itself in favour of the struggle for power through the formation of popular governing councils in the areas dominated by the guerrillas, and it sketched out an anti-imperialist and anti-latifundist programme'.[8]

However, it would be a mistake to overestimate the role of the Communists during the *violencia*. Basically it was a civil war in which Liberal peasants fought Conservative peasants who were egged on by the government. The Communists merely played a supporting role.[9]

Germán Guzmán, in his book on the *violencia*, gives something of the flavour of the situation in the Communist areas when he describes the atmosphere in the peasant-held region of 'Gaitania':

Conservatives, Liberals, Communists, Catholics, Protestants, all arrived at Gaitania to escape from the persecution; the revolutionary organization gave them land, medicaments, and protected them; the only condition it demanded from the new arrivals was that they should not bear a grudge against those with different political or religious views. None of them renounced their former political or religious attitudes: they merely added a new one—Communist![10]

Gaitania, which later became famous as the independent republic of Marquetalia, was originally founded in 1949 by Fermín Charry

Rincón. 'Charro Negro', as he was called, was a peasant leader and one of the great figures of the early period of the *violencia*. He was a member of the Communist party's Central Committee appearing in their publications under the name of Jacobo Frías Alape.

Marquetalia was situated on the borders of the provinces of Tolima and Huila, and at one stage appears to have included about 4,000 peasants within its boundaries. It covered an area of nearly 2,000 square miles and was named after a prison colony that had existed there in 1915. No roads connected it with the rest of the country. In the 'republic' the government's writ did not run, and on many occasions local government officials had to ask the guerrilla chiefs to co-operate in the capture of criminals fleeing from justice.[11]

'Charro Negro' was killed in January 1960, allegedly by a rival band, and he was succeeded by an even more legendary figure, Manuel Marulanda Vélez. Marulanda, who was also called Pedro Antonio Marín, enjoyed the nickname of 'Tirofijo'—or 'Sure Shot'. Like 'Charro Negro', he was a member of the Central Committee of the Communist party. Later he was to lead one of the country's most important guerrilla movements.

Other independent republics supervised by the Communist party were Río Chiquito, Sumapaz, Agriari and Guayabero. In Río Chiquito, on the borders of Huila, Tolima and Cauca, about 400 men had arms. They were led by Ciro Trujillo Castaño sometimes known as 'Mayor Ciro'. Here too the national government had no control. There was an agreement between Castaño and the local authorities whereby they recognized the autonomy of the territory under his control. If the agreement was violated, the guerrilla chief reacted quickly. In 1962, after government troops had entered his territory, Trujillo sent a stiff letter to the President of the Republic:

> As it is well known that, for more than five years, there have
> been no disturbances nor attacks of any sort against anybody
> in this territory of Eastern Cauca, either from us or from the
> municipal authorities, it is clear that we were living in peace and
> quiet, apart from small problems which might have disturbed

the peace, but in fact were easily settled. Since 23 February, however, two peasant homes here have been brutally attacked, not in a private quarrel, but by the armed forces. . . . [12]

Perhaps the most famous figure to emerge during this period was the guerrilla chief, Juan de la Cruz Varela. Born in Boyacá at the turn of the century, he had for long been a staunch Gaitanista. From 1950 onwards he was head of the 'independent republic' of Sumapaz, situated in the south of Cundinamarca. In the 1960s he abandoned the guerrilla struggle and was elected to the House of Representatives. In an article that he wrote for the Cuban magazine *Bohemia* in 1960, he goes some way to explaining why it was that these strongholds of armed peasants in Colombia were never able to make the impact at a national level which had enabled Fidel Castro to come to power in Cuba:

We had as many as 25,000 armed men, although we must confess that the quality of the weapons was not good. We had an additional problem in that, as we were in the interior of the country, we had no access to a port. Thus we were unable to receive arms shipments. We were practically surrounded by government troops, and had no support in the cities. That's to say, contrary to what happened in Cuba, we could not count on action and sabotage groups in the big cities to help us to undermine the morale of the tyranny's lackeys.[13]

In Colombia the *violencia* was almost entirely confined to the countryside. Bogotá never knew the terrorism and brutality that became a commonplace in Caracas and Guatemala City. Had the urban guerrillas of Venezuela been able to operate accompanied by peasant violence on the scale that existed in Colombia, the Venezuelan revolution might not have been such an aborted affair. Similarly, had the Colombian peasants been able to count on an efficient urban organization, they might have had more success in spreading out beyond the confines of their 'independent republics'.

In Bogotá the opposition to the government of the day preferred the easier task of electoral manoeuvre or military coup.

In June 1953, the Conservative President, Laureano Gómez, was deposed in a military coup led by General Gustavo Rojas Pinilla. Immediately all military operations against the guerrillas were suspended. The new President announced a total amnesty. Material aid, he said, would be forthcoming to those willing to give themselves up. A very large number took advantage of this offer.[14]

Many of the Communists, however, grouped in their embryonic peasant republics, ignored the amnesty. But it was hard for guerrillas to prosper when everyone was laying down their arms on all sides. The country was tired of war. Alberto Gómez has explained the situation from his party's point of view:

> The year 1953 was one of painful experiences. More than 5,000 guerrilla followers of the Liberal party who had been operating in the eastern plains surrendered to the dictatorship of Rojas Pinilla. Later, other Liberal detachments followed suit. The Communists, although fewer in number and forced to retreat to Southern Tolima, continued the struggle. 'Charro Negro', Isauro Yosa, and Manuel Marulanda launched operations in the zone that later came to be called Marquetalia. Ciro Trujillo moved into the Cauca Department, an area inhabited by Indians with traditions of peasant struggle. The latter zone was later named Riochiquito.
>
> The Communist party led the guerrilla war at its second stage (1954–57). For more than six months, positional warfare was waged in Villarica and Conday against the numerically superior troops of the enemy. Bitter fighting went on for every metre of terrain. When further resistance became impossible, many of the peasants moved to the south, to the Tolima and Huila Departments. Subsequently the guerrillas were redeployed in Meta and Caqueta Departments. The march was effected by mobile groups which fought the enemy through 1955–57. A column under the command of Alfonso Castañeda moved into the El Pato and Guayabero districts.[15]

At first the dictatorship of Rojas Pinilla was welcomed by the Liberals, who were glad to see their great rivals, the Conservatives, overthrown at last. Initially, too, it did seem that his coup would dampen down the spasms of violence that had overtaken the country. But the civil war encouraged under Gómez had left deep scars. The original reasons for fighting were forgotten; the war entered a new phase as embittered relatives of murdered men sought to obtain their revenge.

Rojas Pinillo, in short, proved incapable of putting an end to the *violencia*. In addition, he gave every sign of wishing to prolong his stay in power, and as many a *caudillo* before him, he did not lack a certain popularity among the poorer sections of society. He had distinct leftist leanings and, as these became increasingly apparent, both Liberals and Conservatives became alarmed. It was reasonable to call on a military man to restore law and order, but neither of the two parties of the oligarchy were keen to see their power usurped permanently.

Consequently, in July 1956, the Liberal leader, Alberto Lleras Camargo, travelled to Spain to confer with the Conservative, former President Gómez. Together they planned to form a united front against Rojas.

In April 1957 a coalition of Liberal and Conservative leaders announced that they would support Guillermo León Valencia as a candidate in opposition to Rojas in the presidential elections scheduled for 1958. While Valencia was campaigning in Cali, Rojas tried to have him arrested. With the support of the Catholic Church, however, Valencia succeeded in outmanoeuvring Rojas, and the troops sent to keep him under house arrest were withdrawn. On 10 May a group of senior officers told Rojas that he must resign.

Alberto Lleras flew once again to Spain to consult Gómez. They arrived at an agreement—ratified by plebiscite in December—whereby all elective and political posts in the country would be divided between the two parties for a period of 12 years beginning in 1958. Informally it was agreed that the two parties would suppport a single candidate for the Presidency. Subsequently the National Front—as it came to be known—was subjected to a constitutional amendment. The arrangement was extended to 16 years, and it was agreed that the Presidency should alternate between the two parties. Thus began one of the most cynical electoral carve-ups in Latin American history.

In May 1958 Alberto Lleras Camargo was elected President with 2,500,000 votes. His only rival, a dissident Conservative, Jorge Leyva, hostile to the National Front, secured only 615,000 votes.

Though many people welcomed the end of Rojas Pinilla's rule, enthusiasm for what took his place was strictly limited. The entire Gaitanist wing of the Liberal party was hostile to the National Front. Groups further Left saw little possibility of the country's basic problems being resolved by a government which, although a coalition, only represented two sections of the oligarchy.

Notes

1 Weinert, 'Violence in Pre-modern Societies'.

2 Alexander, *Communism in Latin America*, p. 249.

3 Rafael H. Gaviría and Calarca Moeschamp, 'La lutte en Colombie', *Partisans* (Paris), April–June 1967.

4 Santiago Solarte, 'L'Armée colombienne tente de réduire les républiques paysannes indépendentes', *Le Monde*, 31 January/1 February 1965. (Solarte was a member of the Colombian delegation at the Tricontinental Conference at Havana in January 1966.) Viotá, however, was not a Communist paradise. Adolfo Gilly writes: 'Viotá could not be broken from the outside. However, it became more bourgeois from within, paralleling the rightward turn of the Communist party in the Popular Front era. Instead of being inspired by the leadership of the party to extend their movement, the peasants who took the land were encouraged to prosper, many of them becoming rich, thus reducing "Red Viotá" to a memory and the real Viotá to a base for careerism and bureaucratic control.'—Adolfo Gilly, 'Guerrillas and "Peasant Republics" in Colombia', *Monthly Review*, October 1965. Gilly, it must be recalled, writes from a Trotskyist viewpoint and is thus not overly sympathetic to orthodox Communist activities.

5 Alexander, *Communism in Latin America*, footnote p. 252.

6 According to one writer, although the Communist party's 'small cadres were striving to penetrate the guerrilla movement, the Liberal party's democratic and Christian orientation and the Communists' weak leadership prevented widespread acceptance of Communist assistance. The Communists donated literature and organizational procedures to such an extent that the guerrilla movement was organized along classic lines developed by Mao Tse-tung. But the leaders were unquestionably idealistic and vigorous young Liberals. The Communist party attempted to capitalize on the social division existing in Colombia and turn the war into a class struggle. But, to its dismay, much of the fighting consisted of traditional Liberal–Conservative mob battles and outright banditry.'—Russell W. Ramsey, 'The Colombian Battalion in Korea and Suez', *Journal of Inter-American Studies*, October 1967.

7 Alberto Gómez, 'The Revolutionary Armed Forces of Colombia and Their Perspectives', *World Marxist Review*, April 1967. The Communists in Latin America have always liked to cite the Colombian example to left-wing critics who accuse them of failing to support guerrilla warfare. Hence the emphasis on the fact that 'El Davis' was the 'first major centre of guerrilla struggle' led by the Communists, i.e. long before the Cuban Revolution took place and made guerrilla warfare a thoroughly ordinary strategy.

8 Gilberto Vieira, 'La Colombie à l'heure de Marquetalia', *Démocratie Nouvelle* (issue entitled *Où va Mister Johnson?*), July–August 1965.

9 One writer on the *violencia* has produced for 1960 a breakdown of deaths as a result of political violence, according to the political affiliation of the victims: Liberals, 611; Conservatives, 646; Communists, 6; political affiliation unknown, 1,468, total, 2,731—Alonso Moncado Abello, *Un aspecto de la violencia*, Bogotá, 1963, p. 9. This book is dedicated to uncovering the role of the Communists in the *violencia*, but the author has to admit that he cannot pin all the blame on them—hence the title.

10 Guzmán Campos, *La Violencia en Colombia*, pp. 161–2.

11 Moncado Abello, *Un aspecto de la violencia*, p. 354. The term 'independent republic' appears to have been popularized by Gómez's son, Alvaro Gómez Hurtado. It was not used by the guerrillas themselves.

12 Ibid., p. 366. Trujillo Castaño was killed in 1968.

13 Juan de la Cruz Varela, 'Mi montaña, mi rifle y yo', *Bohemia* (Havana), 7 August 1960; quoted in Moncado Abello, *Un aspecto de la violencia*, p. 227.

14 Eric Hobsbawm gives as 'a fact' that 'during a mere five days of 1953 at the end of the civil war, 6,500 rebels laid down their arms; this is a considerable figure for irregular forces.'—'The Revolutionary Situation in Colombia', *World Today*, VOL. xix, June 1963.

15 Gómez, 'The Revolutionary Armed Forces of Colombia'.

9. Manuel Marulanda (*seated*), otherwise 'Tiro-Fijo', leader of the FARC.

10. Victor Medina Morón (*left*), with guerrilla detachment in Santander.

Peru

11.1. Luís de Puente Uceda (*left*), photographed when leader of Apra Rebelde, and Gonzalo Fernández Gasco.

11.2. Luís de Puente Uceda (*left*), when leader of the guerrillas of the Movimiento de Izquierda Revolucionaria (MIR); killed 1965.

12. Héctor Béjar, leader of the 'Javier Heraud' detachment of the Ejército de Liberacíon Nacional (ELN); captured 1966.

13. Albino Guzmán, guerrilla in Luís de la Puente's detachment.

14.1. Hugo Blanco (*left*); Trotskyist peasant organizer; captured in 1963 and imprisoned in El Frontón.

14.2. Bridge at Comas dynamited in June 1965 by guerrillas under the command of Guillermo Lobatón.

Bolivia

15.1. Roberto 'Coco' Peredo, leader of the Ejército de Liberacíon Nacional (ELN); killed 1967.

15.2. Jorge Masetti, leader of the Argentinian Ejército Guerrillero del Pueblo; killed 1964.

16.1. Tamara Bunke, known as 'Tania'; killed 1967.

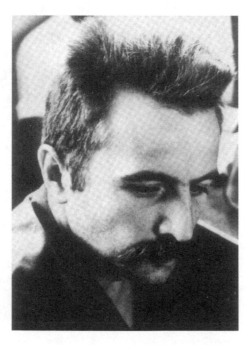

16.2. Régis Debray, sentenced by a military court in Camiri to thirty years' imprisonment for his part in the Bolivian guerrilla campaign.

3. MOEC AND FUAR

'In Colombia, where everybody talks so naturally about representative
democracy and where there are only two parties who share power half and
half for years, the oligarchy has attained what we might call the peak of
democracy. They are divided into Liberals and Conservatives, and
Conservatives and Liberals: four years of one and four years of the other.
Nothing changes. These are the electoral democracies.'

Ernesto Che Guevera, speech at the United Nations, December 1964

The farce of the National Front, which kept Colombian politics tightly in
the grasp of the leaders of the Liberal and Conservative parties, had
barely been in operation for more than six months when Fidel Castro
came to power in Cuba in January 1959. The impact of this event was
as great in Colombia as elsewhere in the continent. Colombians who
had watched the fall of Pérez Jiménez and of Batista—the dictators
who appeared to symbolize so much of what was wrong with Latin
America—and had seen great popular manifestations in the streets of
Caracas and Havana, wondered why they had been so short-changed
after the fall of Rojas Pinilla, who to many (though by no means all)
was cast in a similar mould to the tyrants of Cuba and Venezuela. What
could Albert Lleras Camargo offer compared to a Castro who could
hold the multitudes of Havana and Caracas spellbound?

It was not just the promise of Castro that seemed to fascinate.
Colombians, with 10 years of guerrilla warfare behind them, could not
help being interested in a country where guerrillas had taken over the
government within 25 months of launching their campaign. The circumstances were different, but the word 'guerrilla' was one to which

the Colombians were bound to have a reaction. In consequence a whole series of political groupings arose in Colombia, opposed to the National Front and deeply sympathetic to the Cuban Revolution. It has to be emphasized, however, that these groupings were a distinctly minor element in the political life of the country. Unlike Caracas, Bogotá could never produce great left-wing demonstrations. It is an essentially conservative town. Even the students were less active politically than their Venezuelan counterparts.

The most important semi-revolutionary organization was the Movimiento de Obreros, Estudiantes y Campesinos (MOEC)—the Workers', Students' and Peasants' Movement. This was founded in January 1960 by a student called Antonio Larotta. The event that originally called it into being was a rise in Bogotá bus fares, but from such a trivial beginning sprang Colombia's first *Fidelista* political movement. It attempted to do some political organizing in the Department of Valle de Cauca, but the movement lost its dynamism after Larotta was killed on 6 May 1961. Another student, Federico Arango, tried to keep it going, until he too was killed.

It was not in any sense a Communist movement, being in favour of electoral abstentionism and opposed to the 'pacific' and parliamentary line of the Colombian Communist party. One account of its activities states that it 'succeeded in unmasking the reformist, pacifist and opportunist theses of the "aristocratic" Secretary-General, Gilberto Vieira White, and his group, long before the Sino-Soviet dispute broke out'.[1]

Another group founded at much the same time as MOEC was the Frente Unido de Acción Revolucionaria (FUAR)—the United Front of Revolutionary Action. This was led by Gaitán's daughter, Gloria Gaitán, and her husband Luís Emiro Valencia. This was a movement chiefly composed of intellectuals who hoped to revive Gaitanism.

More orthodox than either of these two was the Movimiento Revolucionario Liberal (MRL)—the Revolutionary Liberal Movement—which constituted the left wing of the Liberal party. It secured 20 per cent of the Liberal vote in 1960 and 36 per cent in 1962 but, unlike the leftist parties in Venezuela, most of its support came from the countryside and the provinces. In Bogotá it made no impact. Its leader, Alfonso López Michelsen, was the son of a former Liberal President. The MRL did not openly encourage guerrilla activities, though it accommodated a number of ex-guerrilla leaders, notably Juan de la Cruz Varela.

The guerrilla groups that sprang up in the early 1960s were for the most part organized by students and intellectuals associated with FUAR or MOEC. Their ideas on how the armed struggle could be used to promote the revolution were decidedly clear. All that was necessary was to go out to the country and reorganize the old guerrilla groups that had existed during the *violencia*. In a short time this rural agitation, with political leadership of a more determined kind than had ever existed before, would spread to the cities and the Colombian revolution would be achieved, much as the Cuban one had been. The only snag to this admirable scheme was that the MOEC showed a remarkable lack of leadership and, in addition was quite unable to agree on a political programme.

The Communists were of course opposed to the activities of these youthful revolutionaries which they regarded at best as romantic, at worst as simply adventurist. A Colombian Communist, Ramón López, has explained the party's attitude at this stage:

Some revolutionary groups, mostly consisting of young people carried away by romantic ideas about armed struggle, embarked on armed action without the active support of the *local* peasants and at a time when the government had not been sufficiently discredited on a *national* scale and when a number of other factors facilitating armed action were lacking.

The Communists wanted all groups of revolutionaries eager to take guerrilla action to have a clear idea of the enemy and to prepare accordingly. Revolutionaries have no right deliberately to commit suicide, for the defeat of any group— because of either improper preparation for the conduct of hostilities or a wrong approach to the masses—can only demoralize the people and strengthen the adversary.

The enemy, on the contrary, wanted the 'theory of armed struggle at any price' evolved by romantic revolutionaries to induce honest and dedicated but not sufficiently prepared revolutionary fighters to take premature armed action. For this would enable the reactionaries to destroy such combat groups and thereby undermine the faith of the masses in the efficacy of armed struggle. And this did indeed happen in six instances.

Special mention should be made of the guerrilla detachment in Vichada near the Venezuelan frontier. This group consisting of nearly a hundred members successfully carried out a brief offensive operation. But it was unable to keep up the pressure over any length of time and had to fall back on the defensive, which, as a result of the group's isolation, led to its complete defeat. The same happened in Puerto Boyacá, in the central part of the country, where an armed group was surprised by superior enemy forces and destroyed. Generally, the young revolutionaries suffered at the hands of the reactionaries.[2]

López is, of course, writing several years later, with the advantage of hindsight. Looking back, the early efforts of MOEC did seem somewhat utopian. The guerrilla detachment in the department of Vichada, for example, which López mentions, had more of the characteristics of a comic opera than a serious political movement. It was supported by MOEC and FUAR, and led by Dr Tulio Bayer. His second-in-command was Rosendo Colmenares. They recruited somewhere between 100 and 200 men, mostly intellectuals and ex-guerrillas. Vichada is in the Llanos Orientales, the vast plains in the east of Colombia that spill over into the south of Venezuela. It had been an important Liberal guerrilla area during the *violencia*, and at no stage did the central government have much control over it.

Bayer gave an account of his curious history in an article published in Caracas in 1963:

> I had been persecuted since 1959, when I produced a well-documented report on the poor quality of the drugs made by a Colombian laboratory. . . .
>
> A terrible organization called the 'Black Hand' began to harass me and I took refuge in Venezuela. I worked as a doctor in the hospital at Puerto Ayacucho and later as an Indian doctor for the Ministry of Justice and as honorary Colombian consul.
>
> I resigned after reporting to the Colombian Foreign Office and to Ambassador Francisco José Chaux that the Public Health and Education budget for Vichada was being stolen by the commissioner and the Montfortian Fathers Mission which operates in Puerto Carreño.
>
> When this commissioner began persecuting the settlers in Vichada, who were mostly members of the Liberal Revolutionary Movement (MRL), I went to lend my services to them for nothing.[3]

Hence Bayer was able to plead when he was captured that he had only acted as a doctor. There was no proof that he had been a guerrilla, and the trial lapsed.

The most notable triumph of this group was to capture a squad of 40 Colombian soldiers. Bayer then telephoned the central government and asked for a civil plane to be sent to take the soldiers away, as he did not know what to do with them.

Of some importance is the interest that the Cubans took in this sporadic activity in the Colombian *llanos*. On one occasion, the army, under Colonel Alvaro Valencia Tobar, captured a letter written by one of the intellectuals in Bayer's group, Ramón La Rotta, to Che Guevara:

Somewhere in los Llanos. 7 December 1961
Comandante Ernesto Guevara,
La Habana,
Cuba

Dear Comrade,

I trust that the great Cuban Revolution is making progress every day, for every triumph of the Cuban people brings encouragement to our people and to the other oppressed peoples of the world to win their own freedom in all fields and to construct the Socialist society we so long for.

Comrade Alfredo Marín will give you details of the first actions and the aims of our Revolution. He will show you some of our basic documents, for example: The Revolutionary Code, Minimal Programme and others.

The various left-wing movements here are becoming more and more united around the National Guerrilla Command, made up of representatives of the armed groups and of the left-wing movements. Of the latter, the Gaitanist Movement and the MOEC are making the greatest efforts to secure this great unity of the Revolutionary Forces. Comrade Alfred, who brings you this letter, is a member of this Command. We are aware that unity is absolutely fundamental if the Revolution is to triumph, as comrade Fidel has insisted, and even demanded if the Cuban Revolution is to declare its solidarity with ours. . . .

Our first actions in different parts of the country have made an insufficient impact on the masses, partly because of the censorship and the nationwide state of siege, and partly because of the lack of equipment on the part of the revolutionary forces.

Within the guerrillas' radius of action the peasants help us in many ways. Many of them want to join our forces. But because of our lack of equipment for these future guerrillas we are unable to accept them.

Until I have the pleasure of returning to your free country, accept *un fuerte abrazo revolucionario* from your comrade,

Ramón La Rotta S.[4]

However, assuming this letter to be true—there seems no reason why it should not be—it does not indicate anything more than a friendly interest on the part of the Cubans. Indeed, Tulio Bayer himself has gone on record to indicate that Che Guevara was not particularly interested in the Colombian experiment at this time. In an interview in 1968, he told a French journalist the following story:

I had an interview with Che Guevara when he was still in Cuba that lasted six or seven hours. It took place in his office at the Ministry of Industries. I talked to him for a long time about the *maquis* of Colombia and of other countries in Latin America. I talked of total war and of the need for a change in strategy and a modification of the Cuban model in favour of something more effective. But he replied with the same arguments that the Czech Communists were to use against him after the publication of his famous letter 'To create two, three, many Vietnams'. He thought the idea somewhat Fascist, or Trotskyist.

Later, when he had returned to the guerrilla, he was to write quite the opposite.[5]

Notes

1 Gaviría and Moeschamp, 'La lutte en Colombie'.

2 Ramón López, 'New Stage in Guerrilla Struggle in Colombia', *World Marxist Review*, February 1967.

3 *Clarín* (Caracas), 19 March 1963; quoted in Moncado, *Un aspecto de la violencia*, p. 430

4 Moncado, *Un aspecto de la violencia*, pp. 407–8.

5 Georges Dupoy, 'Au-delà de Che Guevara, la guérilla . . .', *Le Figaro*, 1 February 1968.

The proliferation of leftist political groups, largely inspired by the Cuban Revolution, and the fact that many of them were taking advantage of the disturbed situation in the countryside to begin guerrilla movements of their own, forced the government—doubtless under United States pressure—to consider the task of 'cleaning up' the independent Communist republics.[1] Had the political rebellion against the National Front ever reached the dimensions of Castro's fight against Batista, the peasant-held areas of Marquetalia, Sumapaz and El Pato would have provided an indispensable refuge from which major guerrilla campaigns could have been planned and launched.

From the very beginning the National Front had made efforts to improve conditions in the areas that had been most subject to the *violencia*. The Communist writer, Alberto Gómez, has explained the technique:

> The Lleras Camargo government (1958–62) pursued a dual policy towards the guerrilla areas. On the one hand, measures were taken towards what was called rehabilitation of the 'zones affected by the violence'. The key elements of this policy were infiltration of the peasant areas by means of credits for promoting production and housing, and a lavish dispensation of promises. Rehabilitation was selective and aimed at winning the political support of sections of the peasantry, especially the ex-guerrillas and their leaders, or at least neutralizing them. On the other hand, districts whose population continued to regard the government with distrust were denied economic aid. The local organizations in these areas were persecuted as

before and many of their leaders, especially ex-guerrillas, were murdered.[2]

However, as a *New York Times* correspondent put it, 'the apathy lends to the government's efforts to mount an anti-violence campaign something of the effect of an egg-beater working without an egg'.[3]

During the course of 1961, the government uttered violent verbal threats against the independent republics and, at the beginning of 1961, the army's Sixth Brigade was given orders to attack Marquetalia. According to the account by the veteran Communist leader, Gilberto Vieira, the operation was mounted with 5,154 soldiers, 1,154 NCOs and 189 officers. The units had all had special training in anti-guerrilla warfare.[4]

This initial attack was not very successful. The peasants chalked up a number of victories and captured quantities of ammunition. At the same time, in the cities, the Communist party and the MRL organized a solidarity campaign with the peasants of Marquetalia which forced Lleras Camargo—now at the end of his period in office—to withdraw the troops. For a brief moment Marquetalia appeared to be safe.

Nevertheless during 1963 the army made probing movements into the peasant-held areas and, on 1 January 1964, Lleras's successor, León Valencia, announced that the government had decided to destroy the republics before the end of the year. 'Operation Marquetalia' began on 1 May, and involved some 16,000 soldiers—almost a third of the Colombian army.

Colombia was the first country in Latin America where the United States began to put into action the new anti-guerrilla strategies that had been evolved during the first years of the Kennedy administrations. Gilberto Vieira has left an account of the stages into which the strategy was divided:

Phase one: *preparation and organization*: Once the troops have been trained in anti-guerrilla action, spies are sent into the area and informers recruited. For this purpose, 'civil–military action' is organized, in which the army appears under the guise of a benefactor, bringing presents to the peasants (clothes, medical supplies, American food from Care and Caritas), medical and dental services, bridge-building, roads and schools.

Phase two: A larger-scale programme of psychological action is then put into operation, using the factor of surprise. Measures are taken to control the civil population. This is the first stage in setting up a blockade of the area.

Phase three: The next operations try to isolate the armed rebel groups in order to destroy them.

Phase four: The armed rebel movement is systematically divided, using psychological techniques. Advantage is taken of internal splits, resulting from political differences, the ambitions of the leaders, human weaknesses or mistakes by the guerrilla command. This is an attempt to win over those who would be likely to carry on the guerrilla struggle.

Phase five: The final stage is the economic, political and social 'reconstruction' of the zone of operations, using the American aid that was previously used to destroy the area.

The first stage of 'Operation Marquetalia'—civil–military action—was an encircling and reconnaissance movement. But hostilities broke out. The army tried to close off a vast circle, and what had been a self-defence movement immediately turned into guerrilla warfare.

After a series of clashes, the Colombian and Yankee strategists perfected what they thought were shock tactics. They thought they were so effective that they invited Colombian and foreign war correspondents to come and watch.[5] A large-scale airborne operation was mounted using a lot of helicopters. The object was to cut off the guerrilla command's retreat and to destroy it. An entire army was transported by helicopter at tree-top height to a place close to two peasant huts where the guerrilla commanders Marulanda and Yosa lived with their families.

Naturally the place was guarded and the guerrillas suffered no losses. They retired as planned into the mountains. The government, the general staff of the army, the Colombian bourgeois press and Yankee publications like *Life* made a great deal of this, calling it 'A Defeat for the Reds in the Andes' and 'The Final Occupation of Marquetalia'. But the struggle was only just beginning.

The guerrillas fortified their impressive mountain stronghold and the army began to count its dead.[6]

Another Communist, Alberto Gómez, has tried to explain—with some difficulty—why the fall of Marquetalia was a victory and not a defeat:

> We never expected the self-defence zones to be impregnable from the military standpoint. On the contrary, the possibility was foreseen that they might fall into enemy hands. At the same time, however, we regarded them as a base for a future movement, centres of a popular armed movement. . . .
>
> The test of a policy is practice. Marquetalia was a test which proved the correctness of our policy. The army threw the full weight of modern weaponry and its experience in anti-guerrilla warfare against it. But Marquetalia, too, had prepared for guerrilla warfare. It was not simply a matter of resorting to arms on the spur of the moment, for the leaders of the area were well acquainted with past experience, had made a study of the success scored by the enemy, and from the outset were guided by a clear-cut concept of guerrilla war.
>
> Before the aggression, Marquetalia itself had not been a zone of military action. But the work done earlier by its leaders in *peripheral* areas had laid the groundwork for the subsequent operations. . . .
>
> The peasant population of Marquetalia was not left to the mercy of fate either before or after the invasion. At no time, however, was it proposed to have the women and children accompany the guerrilla detachments, or to burden these detachments with the peasants' livestock and personal belongings. The evacuation of the families was planned in advance so as to leave in the zone only those able to bear arms. The families were taken to neighbouring areas where they played an important role in rallying support for the fighting men. . . .
>
> A plan of hostilities was worked out in advance. The army found itself facing detachments subdivided into groups operating both inside and outside the traps laid by troops. The guerrillas engaged the government forces the moment they entered the zone. Although the army eventually occupied Marquetalia, it encountered minefields and ambushes everywhere, suffering telling losses under constant harassment. The guerrillas soon moved into mountainous and jungle

country. The government forces now lost contact with them, while the guerrillas had the enemy's every move under observation. Although the army occupied the central part of Marquetalia, it could not cordon off the entire 5,000 sq. km. area, and the initiative in the choice of the battlefield passed over to the guerrillas.[7]

Nevertheless, in spite of the Communist ability to see a new victory in every major defeat, the fall of Marquetalia must be accounted a major loss to the revolution. And it was not just Marquetalia. Once this stronghold had been reduced, the government proceeded without much difficulty to wipe up the other zones where peasant leaders had held sway for so many years. Río Chiquito and Guayabero fell, and finally, in March 1965, the *New York Times* announced that government troops had 'smashed the thirteen-year-old Communist Independent Republic of El Pato. . . . Warplanes and helicopters airlifted several battalions of infantry and national police detachments into the region to seize strategic spots and mopping-up operations are now in progress.' With the fall of El Pato, the 'independent republics' were no more than a memory.

They were probably doomed to failure in any case. As with Viotá, they would have grown fat and comfortable with the passage of time. Their prospects of growth were strictly limited. But once the army had flushed the peasants out of their homes, they became more of a menace to the stability of the state. Uprooted, they had nothing to do except to pursue the guerrilla road, and in the process their demands became more revolutionary.

The Colombian Communist party, more by accident than by design, now had a real guerrilla movement on its hands. Over a number of years they had encouraged hundreds of peasants to believe in the infallibility of the party. Yet these same peasants had been chased from their homes as a result of following the party's directives, and the party leaders had to do some quick thinking to explain to the faithful what had gone wrong. First they blamed the ultra-leftists of the MOEC for having created the illusion that the army could be defeated:

> From the beginning of the struggle in 1964, the guerrillas were aware that the enemy was now stronger and had practically unlimited resources. . . . The party pointed to the need

to renounce the old views concerning popular armed struggle and to put an end to braggadocio and shortsightedness which had cost us needless sacrifices. These warnings were correctly understood by the armed peasants.

There were, however, revolutionaries who argued (and some still do) that the Communists were overestimating the enemy's strength, exaggerating his possibilities, which they claimed made for passivity on the part of the masses. But experience has shown who was right.[8]

Then, more logically, the displeasure of the Communist hierarchy fell on the government itself. Alvaro Delgado, a member of the Central Committee, in the course of an article lauding the anniversary of the Russian Revolution, pointed out that:

> The armed struggle now being fought by our people is not of our making. The possibilities for legal struggle were not exhausted when the peasants were forced to take to arms. It was the anti-national government that, alarmed by the vigour of the independent peasant movement, mounted an offensive against them. The armed struggle was forced on us by the enemy, and the peasants under our leadership responded to the challenge without hesitation. It is the class enemy who is blocking the way to legal, democratic political struggle. We are fighting for democratic rights because the régime is constantly whittling them down. We do not tell the masses to make the supreme sacrifice in all circumstances. We tell them that they must organize and fight for power, that the fight will be long and arduous, and that at one stage or another it is likely to entail armed struggle.
>
> It is a not a question of our wanting or not wanting armed struggle. The facts are that we have to fight. We cannot choose or decree the form of struggle. The Colombian Communists are not committed to the existing state of affairs any more than they are committed to any specific form of struggle. We employ a variety of forms, not because we like variety, but because the practical battle of the masses and the people's unity are developing on this basis.[9]

On 20 July 1964, after nearly three months of fighting, the peasants who had retreated from Marquetalia under the leadership of Marulanda found time to pause to draw breath. They convened a guerrilla assembly and drew up a far-reaching agrarian reform, calling for the confiscation of the large estates and the free distribution of land to the peasants.

As a Central Committee member, Diego Montaña Cuellar, a somewhat maverick figure within the Columbian Communist party, later explained:

> Such a proclamation did not spring from an isolated group of purely local significance, but from the most advanced organizations of the Communist party. It was the fruit of long and patient indoctrination of peasants who had been violently dispossessed, and who found political expression in these organizations. This historic event marked a qualitative leap forward in the revolutionary process: the passive concept of mere self-defence was left behind.[10]

At the end of September 1964, a further conference was held bringing together all the guerrillas and self-defence detachments operating in southern Colombia who had been expelled from their independent republics by the army. This conference established the Guerrilla Block of the South—a loosely united movement of dispossessed peasants carefully watched over by the Communist party.

This conference, in its resolutions, declared that 'five months after the first stage of the offensive against Marquetalia, the mobile guerrilla units achieved complete victory over the government's anti-guerrilla tactics'. And it added, optimistically, that 'the revolutionary armed action movement, which has adopted tactics based on mobile guerrilla operations, is an invincible movement capable of standing up to the far superior forces of the enemy, witness the situation in Marquetalia where the peasant detachments are fighting 16,000 government troops'.[11]

But even though the peasant guerrillas had 'sprung from' the Communist party, this did not provide them with much advice on how to conduct a guerrilla war. Throughout 1965, the guerrillas of Marulanda and the other survivors of the independent republics were notably quiescent, with the result that Debray, writing later in the year, was outspokenly scornful of the Colombian Communist party's revolutionary achievements in recent years:

> Today, self-defence as a system and as a reality has been liquidated by the march of events.
>
> Colombia, with its zones of peasant self-defence, and Bolivia, with its zones of worker self-defence, constituted the two countries in which this conception acquired the strength of a line. These two 'nuclei of subversion' were, within a few months of each other, liquidated by the army: Marquetalia, in southern Colombia, occupied in May 1964, and the Bolivian mines invaded in May and September 1965, after tragic battles. This double defeat signifies the end of an epoch and attests to the death of a certain ideology. It is necessary that the revolutionary movement should once and for all accept this demise.[12]

Diego Montaña Cuellar replied:

> The sweeping statement that the occupation of Marquetalia by the regular army means the defeat and death of the armed struggle in Colombia is a false appreciation of the different stages of 'self-defence' and a wrong appreciation of the time factor. At the very moment that the essay *Revolution in the Revolution?* was published (in January 1966), comrade Marulanda's forces had changed over to mobile guerrilla tactics and were striking the heaviest blows ever received by the Colombian army. The passive concept of 'self-defence' could be criticized *up to 1964*. After the organization said 'Now we are guerrillas', there surely does not exist in the whole of Latin America such a firm, serious and experienced guerrilla force.[13]

Later, in 1967, Diego Montaña Cuellar was to resign from the Communist party on the grounds that it did not give enough emphasis to the guerrillas but, as the conclusions from the Tenth Congress of the Colombian Communist party, held in January 1966, seem to show, the Colombian Communists' position was in some respects more favourable towards guerrillas than, say, that of the Venezuelan party. But although the form of words was different, enthusiasm for the armed struggle among Colombian Communists was in fact hardly more developed than among the Venezuelans.[14]

The 10th Congress emphasized that the guerrilla struggle in Colombia had preceded the development of a revolutionary situation. The Communist party had felt that it could not 'stand by and watch' while 'waiting for a revolutionary situation to mature'. 'Armed aggression' had to be met by 'guerrilla resistance'.

Nevertheless guerrilla resistance was not the most important factor in the revolutionary process. 'Mass struggle' was more crucial in the eyes of the orthodox Communists.

With the blessing of the Tenth Congress, the guerrilla bloc of the south held a further conference in April 1966 and decided to set up the Fuerzas Armadas Revolucionarias Colombia (FARC)—the Revolutionary Armed Forces of Colombia. The reason for giving what had been an armed peasant movement a name which turned it into a guerrilla movement arose from the need of the Communist party to appear more revolutionary than it really was in the face of opposition from other left-wing groups. In an article by an orthodox Communist discussing the foundation of the FARC, one can detect an almost frantic concern to appear revolutionary and to prove that the Communist party dominates the revolutionary scene in Colombia:

> Colombia is the scene of a life-and-death struggle. In the centre of this struggle is the guerrilla movement headed by FARC and its headquarters. The united military–political leadership of FARC follows the line of the Communist party as set forth in the decisions of its central bodies. To meet the requirements of the revolutionary process in our country, the Tenth Congress of our party centralized the leadership of armed action in the rural localities. The leading positions in the headquarters of FARC are held by such tried and tested fighters as Manuel Marulanda Vélez, Ciro Trujillo, Jacobo Arenas and Isauro Yosa, all members of the Central Committee of our party. Our combat planning, based on the decisions of the inaugural conference of FARC, takes cognisance of both the concrete situation and the general situation in our country. It is not by chance that 48 per cent of the delegates to the Tenth Congress were peasants, some of whom have been waging armed struggle since 1950. It can be said that the revolutionary armed struggle in our country is largely the result of the work done by the Communists.[15]

But when interviewed by *L'Humanité* in June 1966, the Secretary-General of the Colombian party, Gilberto Vieira, maintained:

> Our party . . . nevertheless considers that there is no revolutionary situation in Colombia as yet. It does not consider armed struggle in cities because such a struggle can be little more than a series of isolated events accomplished by little groups. . . . The guerrilla struggle is not actually the principal form of battle.[16]

Notes

1 According to the Communists, a CIA report in 1960 'listed these districts and stressed that it was up to the government to abolish them with utmost speed.'—López, 'New Stage in Guerrilla Struggle in Colombia'.

2 Gómez, 'The Revolutionary Armed Forces of Colombia'.

3 *New York Times*, 9 January 1963.

4 Vieira, 'La Colombie à l'heure de Marquetalia'.

5 A rare occurrence. In Peru in 1965 no correspondents were allowed into the battle zones and in Bolivia, in 1967, military details of the anti-guerrilla campaign were hard to come by until the final weeks.

6 Vieira, 'La Colombie à l'heure de Marquetalia'.

7 Gómez, 'The Revolutionary Armed Forces of Colombia'.

8 López, 'New Stage in the Guerrilla Struggle in Colombia'.

9 Alvaro Delgado, 'The Working Class and Labour Movement in Colombia', *World Marxist Review*, September 1967.

10 Diego Montaña Cuellar, 'Los problemas estratégicos y tácticos de la revolución en Colombia' (political thesis submitted to the Colombian Communist party), *Punto Final*, NO. 47, 30 January 1968.

11 Quoted in Gómez, 'The Revolutionary Armed Forces of Colombia'.

12 Debray, *Revolution in the Revolution?*

13 Cuellar, 'Los problemas estratégicos y tácticos de la revolución en Colombia'.

14 For a chapter from the central report approved by the Tenth Congress.

15 Gómez, 'The Revolutionary Armed Forces of Colombia'.

16 *L'Humanité*, 3 June 1966.

5. THE NATIONAL LIBERATION ARMY

'For the first time in our country, after many unsuccessful attempts, a
revolutionary guerrilla movement comparable to that in the Sierra Maestra,
led by political cadres from the cities, has managed to triumph, consolidate
and get popular support, under the name of the National Liberation Army
(ELN). The fact that for many years the army has had to concentrate
the mass of its forces against the self-defence zones . . .
was a great help in the creation of the ELN.'

From the diary of a Colombian guerrilla

At the same time that the Colombian army launched its attack against
Marquetalia and provoked Tirofijo into organizing his peasant followers into a mobile revolutionary movement, a group of students led by
Fabio Vásquez Castaño was examining the possibilities of starting a
guerrilla *foco* in the department of Santander. Vásquez, unlike Tirofijo,
was neither a peasant nor a member of the Communist party. His ideological origins lay with the revolutionary MOEC rather than with the
more sedate Communist party. He was born in about 1937, and his
father was a Liberal farmer, who was killed during the *violencia*. His social
origins appear to be very similar to those of Douglas Bravo in Venezuela.

The details of how he set about forming his Ejército de Liberación
Nacional (ELN)—National Liberation Army—are somewhat obscure,
though some information can be gleaned from an interview that he gave
to the Mexican editor, Mario Menéndez Rodríguez, in the middle of 1967.

A group of students, it seems, after some preliminary investigation,
met with a number of peasants in the hut of a peasant called Parmenio:

Like most of our country the area was very suitable for an uprising.

The peasants were tired of promises and fed up with deceit, and with waiting peacefully for elections to better their ever worsening position. Their grandfathers had died as serfs, so had their fathers, and if things went on like this, a similar future would await their sons. There is no other solution: they are ready to support the armed struggle. It was absolutely essential to create guerrilla forces. 'There are no arms,' said one. 'The enemy has them,' we answered. We toured the area bringing together those with the most determination. These first steps required extreme security measures, great secrecy; any slip could have had dire consequences.

The repressive forces of the government were on the alert, they had had many years' experience of reactionary violence. We selected the guerrilla nucleus: eighteen peasants in all. Deeply convinced of the justice of our cause, we began the difficult life of a guerrilla. That was on 4 July 1964. The first stage of guerrilla life involved the following points: firstly, survival in hiding; secondly, reconnaissance of the terrain; thirdly, the political and military training of the men; fourthly, the creation of a basis of revolutionary support amongst the peasants; fifthly, the setting up of an information and liaison network. What did we possess to do all this? Naturally we had previously studied at length the real situation of our country. This showed us that the road we were taking so firmly and decidedly was the just one and the only one. But apart from these objectively analysed factors, we had the support of the peasants. They gave us supplies and the first shotguns, with which we made our entry into Simacota to end the first stage of clandestinity.[1]

Simacota, near San Vicente, was the scene of the Liberation Army's first public appearance on 7 January 1965, the sixth anniversary of the foundation of the MOEC. Twenty-seven men and one woman, dressed in olive green and equipped only with hunting rifles, entered the town at dawn and held it for two hours. According to a correspondent of *The Economist*, they robbed a government lending agency of about $4,000 and a beer distributor and a private home of another $1,000. The raiders . . . cut the town's external communication lines and, before departing in the direction of San Vicente, made speeches proclaiming a war against imperialism and oligarchy and announced that they had come 'to attack the government and not the people'.[2]

The guerrillas, who belonged to the José Antonio Galán detachment of the ELN, left behind a manifesto:

The Simacota Manifesto

The reactionary violence unleashed by the various oligarchic governments and continued by the corrupt Valencia-Ruíz Novoa-Lleras régime, has been a powerful weapon used to crush the revolutionary peasant movement. It has been a powerful weapon of domination in the last fifteen years.

Education is in the hands of businessmen who get rich as a result of the ignorance in which they keep our people.

The land is worked by peasants who are miserably poor. They use up their energy and that of their families to benefit oligarchs who live like kings in the cities.

Workers get starvation wages. They are ground down into poverty and humiliation by big foreign and national companies.

Young democratic intellectuals and professionals find themselves harassed. They are forced either to serve the ruling class or die.

Small and medium-sized producers, both in the countryside and in the towns, are ruined by the ferocious competition and the monopoly of credit by foreign capital and its anti-patriotic followers within the country.

The wealth belonging to the whole Colombian people is looted by American imperialists.

But our people, who have felt the lash of exploitation, poverty and reactionary violence, is rising up and is ready for war. Revolutionary struggle is the only way for the whole people to overthrow the present rule of deceit and violence.

We, who form part of the National Liberation Army, are in the fight for the national liberation of Colombia.

Whether Liberals or Conservatives, the people will join together to overthrow the oligarchy of both parties.

Long live the unity of the peasants, workers, students, professionals and honest men who wish to make Colombia a country fit for honest Colombians!

Liberation or Death

National Liberation Army

'José Antonio Galán' Front

Carlos Villareal	Andrés Sierra
(Fabio Vásquez Castaño)	(Víctor Medina Morón)

'This,' continued Vásquez in his interview with the Mexican journalist:

> was the public announcement of our rebellion against the bourgeois and pro-imperialist laws which govern our people. It was our way of letting them know that there was now an armed vanguard fighting for their interests. Above all, the essential point of the taking of Simacota was to show the people a revolutionary line: armed struggle as the only effective way of taking power.
>
> The political and military aims of the ELN are the seizure of power for the lower classes. The principal form of struggle is the insurrection. According to our conception of a people's war—a people's war being one carried on by the immense majority of the exploited—we consider that when all purely political means of fighting have been exhausted, the vast masses must provide the armed vanguard to ensure that the struggle for political power continues. Besides, given the unlimited greed and cruelty of the reactionary oligarchy—linked to American imperialism—we are sure that they would not allow the people to rise to power by peaceful means. We are convinced that concentrating on these means is playing the reactionaries' game. . . .
>
> It is hard to recognize the armed way as the only solution to our national problems, because of the difficulties and grief that lie in store for our beloved peoples of Latin America. But to deny it would be dishonest. . . . Our generation, our Latin American youth, must recognize this reality and get ready for the revolutionary war. . . . Thus it is absolutely essential to develop guerrilla forces in order to form a National Liberation Army that will be able to fight for power with the oligarchy and

American imperialism, and that will be able to take power and form a democratic and revolutionary government to carry out in our Colombia a programme in favour of the people. . . .

The programme of the ELN, of which Vásquez spoke, was first made public at the time of the Simacota attack.

Like other guerrilla movements in Latin America, the National Liberation Army of Colombia had no military ranks. The only two exceptions were posthumous—'Captain' Parmenio, the 23-year-old peasant in whose hut the Liberation Army was founded, and 'Comandante' Camilo Torres.

Fabio Vásquez, too, had very strong views about the role of the guerrilla chief, similar to those of Che Guevara :

He is not allowed to leave his battle position, nor may he go down to the city. His mission is at the front with his men. His only excuse for a return to urban surroundings is to capture an enemy position.

The ELN was in the planning stage just at the time when the Colombian army began moving against Marquetalia in the middle of 1964. But the attack on Simacota in January 1965 somewhat relieved the pressure on Marulanda and his group by diverting some units of the Colombian army away from the Marquetalia area, north to the region of Santander. Nevertheless relations between Vásquez's independent guerrillas, and those of Marulanda, which were controlled by the Communist party, were never good.

Early in 1965 the ELN asked for an interview with a member of the leadership of the Communist party. A man came on 15 May 1965, and they discussed their experiences, though nothing concrete emerged from the discussions. A month later an envoy from Marulanda's 'Guerrilla Bloc of the South' came to Santander. Again nothing definite was decided.

To re-establish contact the ELN sent a message of greeting to Marulanda on the occasion of the 10th Congress of the party in January 1966.

We understood [said Fabio Vásquez later] that the guerrillas took the initiative at this Conference to reinforce unity with the ELN and to discover how a national guerrilla conference could be held with us taking part. We replied immediately, asking whether we could send a delegation to talk to comrade

Marulanda to study the political and military experience of both our movements. We always got the same answer to all these approaches: let's see if we can do it next month.

In April 1966 the second conference of the Guerrilla Bloc of the South was held—in which the FARC was formally founded—and it concluded that the next stage of the struggle should be in concert with all revolutionaries. The ELN thought that this sounded optimistic, but by August 1966 they had still not received a reply from Marulanda to the greetings sent in January. In August, therefore, the ELN sent a further letter to the Central Committee of the Communist party, reaffirming its desire—and indeed the necessity—of working together:

> Considering that the ELN is an organization operating completely outside the law, openly fighting the instruments of oppression, exploitation and repression of the Colombian oligarchy, allied with American imperialism, it is easy to understand why revolutionary solidarity as far as we are concerned is basically the fighting carried on by the guerrilla bloc of the south (politically orientated by the Colombian Communist party)—by the heroic guerrillas commanded by comrade Marulanda. All efforts that make towards collaboration, knowledge, co-ordination and unity with other guerrilla forces, however recently formed, are playing a great part in the development of the struggle for national liberation.

The Communist party's reply was brief:

> Comrade Marulanda has been informed by our party of your activities, which have not pleased the party. The party, the general staff of the PARC, and Comandante Marulanda Vélez himself, consider that such relations as you suggest will not be possible unless you accept the policy of the Communist party.

The ELN's experience with the Colombian Communist party was, of course, very similar to that of Douglas Bravo and the Venezuelan Communist party, though in Venezuela the Communists carried their desire to wind up the guerrillas to greater lengths than in Colombia. Vásquez explained the situation:

> Much has been said about the conditions for the struggle in Venezuela; truces and a return to peaceful methods have been mentioned. But all these are words hiding the truth: deser-

tion. There are always men with faith in the people, however, with confidence in the triumph of the revolution. There are men who remain faithful to the slogan 'Free your country or die for Venezuela'—men like Douglas Bravo and his companions who have undergone great hardships and have not betrayed the people.

The revolutionary process is bringing forward the true and worthy leaders of the people. The people can be confused, tricked in its choice of leaders, but the process unmasks the unworthy and raises up the worthy and those who do not lose faith, those who are not opportunists and who do not put secondary considerations, personal considerations, above the struggle; those who are genuine revolutionaries, who do not join a movement merely to destroy it.

This is a scarcely veiled attack on the orthodox pro-Moscow Communists, and Vásquez becomes explicit when he discusses the question of international solidarity. Here he is almost repeating the exact words of Guevara's message to the Tricontinental:

It is not just a question of choice, it is a responsibility and an obligation which all revolutionaries of the world should take up. It is a very serious contract with the people, and this contract is even greater for those parties that are in power.

At a time when the Yankee imperialists are every day landing marines in Vietnam and indiscriminately bombing villages and civilian settlements in the South and in the Democratic Republic of North Vietnam, this engagement becomes more glorious; this is when we revolutionaries should be more united in a clear, resolute, firm, and unconditional solidarity for those who need it. We think that all the free peoples of the world should get together, not to discuss who is right, nor which country is going to lead the international movement, but to underline that it is Vietnam which is right and is bleeding, that while revolutionaries argue, American imperialism is acting mercilessly against peoples it believes to be weak. That is where real international solidarity is most needed. There should be solidarity with Cuba, the glorious island which became a shield against which the shameful lances of American imperialism have more than once been broken.

As for Latin America, we believe, essentially, that there should be solidarity between organizations engaged in the armed struggle for national liberation, with closer relations, the exchange of experience to correct errors, and where possible the use of other peoples' successes, with the intention of co-ordinating the Latin American insurrection; we consider that this should be the main purpose of the Organization for Latin American Solidarity (OLAS).

We consider that the best and surest solidarity which we can offer to Vietnam and Cuba is to begin the armed fight for national liberation in our own countries.

Victor Medina Morón, the second-in-command of Vásquez, goes further:

One question above all bothers us. In our country there is no shortage of people and movements calling themselves revolutionary and using phrases and propaganda setting out the problem of armed struggle. We have our own ideas about this. The triumph of the Cuban Revolution caused a tremendous stir amongst revolutionaries in our country, and especially amongst the masses. Since 1948 the Colombian countryside has been ravaged by political violence which began with official repression and resulted in a large-scale guerrilla movement led and guided by the peasants against the repressive government. However, it stopped short of a victorious revolutionary war, precisely because of being betrayed by the intellectual leaders of the Liberal party, which is controlled and led by the Colombian oligarchy. However, after the triumph of the Cuban Revolution, there arose groups, movements, personalities who used newspapers, speeches and leaflets from all sides to express themselves in favour of an armed revolutionary struggle to take power and carry out the Colombian Revolution.

However, the Cuban Revolution coincided in our country with the fall of Rojas Pinilla's dictatorship, and a return to traditional representative democracy with Liberal and Conservative politicians. This brought about conflict between those who supported stepping up the electoral struggle and forming electoral movements, and those who advocated the insurrectional war. After the fall of Rojas Pinilla, the only movement with revolutionary ideas was the Communist party. But at the same time they proposed forming broad political fronts with so-called progressive sectors within the Liberal party, for example, the Liberal Revolutionary Movement (MRL) which was headed by Dr Alfonso López Michelsen. Meanwhile those who followed the pattern of the Cuban Revolution looked for armed solutions. They had a decisive clash with the directives, tactics and strategy of the Communist party and the MRL, which at that time was the most representative left-wing movement in Colombia. This was when the Workers–Peasants–Students Movement (MOEC) appeared, headed by Antonio Larrota, a student leader, who proposed armed struggle. From the beginning the MOEC had major difficulties and clashes with the official leadership of the Communist party, which was concentrating its efforts on helping to form the MRL in order to take part in the elections which were beginning to take place after the fall of the dictatorship. We consider that the MOEC was not wrong in its idea of the armed struggle; but their working methods, their style, their practical ideas of how to carry out the armed struggle, link up with the peasants, etc., were wrong, as was shown in practice. The MOEC failed in several attempts to get the armed struggle going in the countryside. The death of their main leader when he was working to create armed groups in northern Cauca may be said to have been the decisive blow in the decline of the movement.

There also appeared at that time several local or regional left-wing movements whose aims were not electoral but military. This was how a national congress of several of these organizations set up by the United Revolutionary Action Front (FUAR), controlled by Gloria Gaitán, daughter of the great popular leader, Jorge Eliécer Gaitán and by her husband, Luis Emiro Valencia. However this movement was not even capable of remaining organized for any length of time, as the leaders stayed in Bogotá.

There was also the Vichada movement, in which Tulio Bayer was involved, and which was easily crushed by the army because of the way it was organized. In fact the FUAR did not last very long.

All these people published a lot of pamphlets, made a lot of speeches, but failed completely to organize a revolutionary guerrilla force.

Besides, in the last few years, and particularly in the immediate past, there arose in our country a group of people who broke away from the Communist party and created the so-called Marxist–Leninist Communist party, that is a fraction which follows the Chinese line in the world Communist movement. This group also put out a lot of propaganda, and called for the armed struggle; it is in favour of revolutionary war. It seems that these gentlemen also failed when it came to doing anything. We have quite detailed information of the failure of various attempts by this group in different parts of the country. . . .

We believe that many of these people had opportunist aims and objectives: some sought to make use of the mass feeling in favour of the armed struggle; while others sought to try to take up revolutionary positions and to win prestige within revolutionary circles, displacing those who took up frank revolutionary stands, many of whom were to die trying to put their ideas into practice. We can say quite simply that within the Colombian revolutionary movement there are a good number of charlatans, wheeler-dealers, mercenaries, and people who have made the correct theses of armed revolutionary struggle into a way of life, a way of disguising and partly solving their personal problems.

At the moment there is one question which especially bothers us, and that concerns the Revolutionary Armed Forces of Colombia (FARC). In fact at present the ELN and the FARC are the only organizations which have guerrillas and are carrying on increasing military activity.

It is well known—the documents, the public statements say so—that the leaders of the Colombian Communist party had a part in the setting up of the FARC. This bothers us because we have a clear idea of the revolutionary war. We believe that the heroic efforts of all guerrilla fighters should be channelled seriously and clearly towards revolutionary war objectives, towards objectives defined by a political line decided by the clash with the oligarchy and imperialism. The leaders of the Communist party have taken a clear stand on revolutionary war. Even though they are aware of the importance and the existence of guerrilla warfare, their political position is not aligned with the needs of the movement of insurrection. It is at variance with the basic assumptions of insurrectional war. Its political position is too abstract. It leads to confusion by putting too much emphasis on traditional democratic and peaceful solutions, like expanding mass activity, and legality within the bourgeois system. We believe that to make possible the development of revolutionary war in Colombia, the Communist party should take up a clearer position, a better defined stand on our people's revolutionary future.

When the Communists did choose to define their position, however, it was not much to the liking of the National Liberation Army. In an article published early in 1968, the Communists revealed just how far they were from co-operating with the ELN:

The building of the Patriotic Liberation Front is not an easy matter. Certain ideological questions facing the movement await clarification. Besides FARC, there is the National Liberation Army (ELN), an independent organization formed in 1965. The party is eager to work with this organization, but its tendency to deny the role of our party, recently reflected in open attacks against us, is making it difficult to achieve unity.

The October (1967) meeting of the FARC staff discussed this question and called on ELN to join forces on the basis of mutual respect. The meeting stated: 'We reaffirm our policy of seeking unity with the ELN and with any groups that might arise in the future, for we realize that, without unity and fraternal co-operation, it will not be possible to ensure any serious advance of the revolutionary movement. We are fighting in a war that has been unleashed against our people by imperialism and its local agents. We therefore call on the aforementioned groups to cease their attacks on the Communist party, for these attacks can only benefit those who have the power, the money and the means with which to strike at the revolutionary movement.'

This statement is a cogent reply to the thesis that seeks to deny the role of the Communist party and artificially opposes the guerrilla movement to the party. This thesis separates work in the town from work in the countryside, political work from military, legal work from illegal, the fighter in the hills from the fighter in the towns. The advocates of this thesis declare that the policy of combining all forms of struggle is 'no good', that the guerrilla movement gives 'birth' to the party. In Colombia, the course of development is proof of the fallacy of this concept. The armed struggle is developing on the background of the extensive work by the party among the masses and is, in effect, an expression of revolutionary political activity.

These issues are being ironed out in the interests of unity in the course of the ideological struggle, in practice. The FARC message to the National Liberation Army says: 'The purpose of the war waged by imperialism and its local agents against our people is to halt the revolutionary process. We revolutionaries must unite, and we do not believe that unification signifies the subordination of one to another.' Saluting the Communist party, FARC declares that 'the first meeting of the staff of the Revolutionary Armed Forces (FARC) salutes all members of the Communist party, party committees and the Central Committee. In our policy we are guided by the policy of the party, expressed in the decisions of its Tenth Congress and meetings of its Central Committee.'[3]

Faced with this undying loyalty to the orthodox Communist party on the part of Marulanda's guerrillas, the National Liberation Army of Fabio Vásquez had no alternative except to proceed alone.

Notes

1 Mario Menéndez Rodríguez, 'Colombia (II): ni un paso atrás', *Sucesos* (Mexico City), 1 July 1967.

2 *The Economist*, 28 August 1965.

3 Jaime González, 'The Armed Forces of the Revolution in Colombia', *World Marxist Review*, February 1968.

6. Camilo Torres and the Church

Although the Colombian oligarchy and its National Front had the military capacity to put an end to Marquetalia and the other 'independent republics', they clearly did not have the political will or ability to solve the more fundamental problems of Colombian society. They had mistaken the symptom for the disease. The *violencia* had arisen as a result of Colombia's peculiar economic and social system. 'Pacifying' large tracts of country could not bring about change and development unless the system itself was changed.

One of the more unnerving factors in the situation from the government's point of view was the listlessness and apathy with which the population as a whole greeted its every move. The *violencia*, coupled with years of irrelevant political activity, had made the Colombians largely immune to the blandishments of politicians. The National Front, an agreement between two rival groups in the oligarchy to share the fruits of power, was a farce—and the great majority of Colombians had no difficulty in recognizing it as such. In 1962, when called upon to register their votes for the National Front presidential candidate, an old Conservative called Guillermo León Valencia, 70 per cent abstained.

It was easy to conclude that this high rate of abstention, reiterated at subsequent elections, was a protest against the National Front. But was it also right to deduce that there must be within the Colombian body politic a large group of 'non-aligned' who, without party affiliation, could be won over to support some new kind of politics? Father Camilo

Torres, the most charismatic figure to arise in Colombian politics after
the assassination of Gaitán, believed that it was. He was obsessed by
the thought of this vast mass of Colombians who remained outside the
system, disenfranchised. The only worthwhile political activity, he concluded, was to organize these 'non-aligned' into an effective conscious
force. He wrote in October 1965:

> The organization of this sector will be one of the most impor-
> tant steps towards the formation of a revolutionary move-
> ment, and the seizure of power. When it is achieved, Colombia
> will see the great mass movement necessary to carry out the
> revolutionary change that was thwarted by the murder of
> Gaitán, by the advent of political violence and by the dialecti-
> cally genuine inadequacy of other political movements. When
> it finally comes about, the conditions—the historical basis—
> which have permitted and even encouraged the long domi-
> nation of the Colombian people by the oligarchy will be swept
> away.[1]

Camilo Torres was no orthodox politician. Nor was he a particularly competent one. Had he not taken to the hills and been killed
fighting with the guerrillas, he would have been remembered merely
as a sociologist and a rebellious priest. But his heroic death ranks him
with Che Guevara in the pantheon of the Latin American Left.

He was born in Bogotá on 3 February 1929 of extremely respectable upper-middle-class parents. Although he journeyed to Europe
with his parents as a small child, most of his schooling was in Bogotá.
He spent a semester at the National University, reading law, but rejecting this subject, he decided to become a priest. He entered a
Dominican seminary. From there he went to the famous university of
Louvain in Belgium, where he spent a year studying sociology.

On his return to Bogotá he became the chaplain of the National
University and one of the founders of the sociology faculty. Quarrel-
ling with the authorities for defending two students who had been
unjustly expelled, he was deprived of his job as chaplain. Subsequently
he became Dean of the Escuela Superior de Administración Publica
(Advanced School of Public Administration—ESAP) working on the

problems of co-operatives. Within ESAP he helped to found an Institute of Social Administration, and he was also appointed as the Cardinal's representative on the governing board of the Colombian Agrarian Reform Institute (INCORA). These two tasks gave him many opportunities for travel through the country, lecturing and organizing courses on agrarian reform, about which he developed strong views:

> I find that the main thing wrong with INCORA is that it has not concerned itself enough with educating the peasants. Not so much education in the formal sense, since schools and some co-operatives have been set up, but in the informal sense of creating awareness in the peasants so that in the future they can form a large pressure group, capable of turning this pseudo agrarian reform into a real reform carried out by the peasants.[2]

This was the great interest of Camilo Torres, as indeed it was of many young Latin Americans concerned with securing basic structural change. How may the vast mass of the people, in the country or in the shanty towns that surround the great cities, be brought to a position where they make political demands, rather than have their imagined wishes satisfied by a government in which they do not participate? This was the basic concern of a group of sociologists with whom Camilo worked in close co-operation in the early 1960s.

His interest in the future of Colombia had first been awakened in Louvain, where, in 1954, he was the leading light in organizing a 'Colombian socio-economic research group', constituted from a number of Colombian students studying at the university there. When he returned to Bogotá, he became involved in various communal action schemes, some of which were more or less openly favoured by the government. One of the reasons why Camilo created such an impact was that he had a foot in both camps. On the one hand he was an oligarch, a cleric, an academic inquirer into the causes of present misery; on the other he was a man who was perfectly content to abandon this upper class background and to go out into the shanty towns and into the most abandoned parts of the country to talk to people and to discover for himself the reality of Colombia. As a cleric, he could stand somewhat apart from party politics and, in consequence, when the long inquest on the failure of the left began to be held in the 1960s Camilo was a figure to whom people listened with some respect.

The fundamental problem in Colombia was not disimilar from that in Guatemala or Venezuela. In Guatemala the left had to ask itself why the reformist regime of Arbenz had fallen so easily, and why the military had ruled almost without problems ever since. The CIA and American aid had, of course, played their role, but was there not also something basic in the organization of Guatemalan society that was preventing the emergence of a popular regime that could maintain itself in power?

In Venezuela the problem was to discover why the popular revolt that had overthrown Pérez Jiménez collapsed under the Betancourt–Leoni regime. And how had a regime which had no intention of making the socio-economic changes that might have led to development been able to preserve itself in power when a superficial analysis of the situation might have concluded that the country was on the verge of a major revolt?

In Colombia the problem was the same. Why had a regime which had shown itself incapable of resolving the contradictions in which the country found itself been greeted not with popular fury but, rather, with apathy? When the army moved into Marquetalia, hardly a finger moved to save it.

Among the sociologists at the National University, the idea gradually emerged that Colombian society was not a fragile fabric that could be easily pushed into a revolutionary direction. On the contrary, it was obviously extremely tough and resilient. Far greater understanding of it was necessary before any potential revolutionary could hope to take advantage of the crisis situation which undoubtedly existed.

The Left did not even really know what it wanted; it certainly did not know what was the common denominator that united those hostile to the National Front. And so, towards the end of 1964, Camilo took it upon himself to elaborate a minimum programme. It was made public at a meeting in Medellín on 17 March 1965, and subsequently published under the title, 'Platform for a Movement of Popular Unity'.

The publication of Camilo's 'Platform' stirred all Colombia, and sparked off one of those great ecclesiastical controversies with which the history of the Catholic Church is littered. The Catholic hierarchy is such an integral part of the Colombian oligarchy that the curbing of a turbulent priest could only be a matter of time. Camilo himself has explained what happened:

> When I began to publicize the 'Platform', I went to my hierarchical superior the bishop and told him what I was doing. He didn't even ask me for a copy. However, at the same meeting (I knew that the Curia was already aware of my 'Platform'), I was told to immediately leave the post of Dean of the Higher School of Public Administration (ESAP) which I held.[3]

Having deprived him of his job in the university, the Church offered him work at a very low salary in their own statistics department to do some research on the city of Bogotá. The salary, however, was insufficient to provide for both Camilo and his mother, who had become largely dependent upon him financially. He asked to be allowed at least to continue his classes at the university. This too was refused. The possibility was raised, however, of sending him back to Louvain to finish his doctoral thesis in sociology. He had always looked forward to this possibility and, from the viewpoint of the hierarchy, such a solution would have conveniently removed him from the country at a moment when his fame was rapidly growing.

On 22 May at the invitation of the National University Federation, he spoke in Bogotá about the 'Platform' that he had elaborated. This meeting, in the capital city, created even more of a stir than had the earlier one in Medellín.

A few days later, without warning Camilo, the Colombian Cardinal, Luis Concha Córdoba, issued a press statement declaring that the plan to send Camilo to Louvain was not the result of pressure from the eclesiastical authorities. He added that in the 'Platform' of Father Torres, there were various points that were 'irreconcilable with the doctrine of the Church'.

Camilo immediately asked the cardinal to specify the points in his 'Platform' that were at odds with the Church's teaching, but the cardinal replied that since Father Torres was perfectly familiar with this there was no need to go into detail.

The break between Camilo and the Church was not very far off. Already, on 20 March, three days after the meeting at Medellín in which he had launched his 'Platform', Camilo had written to the cardinal asking that he should be allowed to abandon the priesthood:

> When I chose to join the clergy I did so mainly because I thought that it would be the best way of serving the Church and Colombians. After more than ten years of being a priest I realize that, given the particular historical circumstances of the Church, Colombia and myself, I can best realize these aims as a layman. Indeed, I believe that these circumstances force me to take up positions in the temporal field which I cannot draw back from without jeopardizing my loyalty to Christ, the Church and Colombia.

Things might still have been patched up had not Camilo begun a wholesale campaign against the Catholic hierarchy, including an attack on the Church's wealth. In an interview published in the middle of June, he explained that:

> The greatest obstacle for the Colombian Church is having both property and political power, which leads it to take into account 'the wisdom of men rather than the wisdom of God' as St Paul put it. The property and political power I refer to are the result of the attitude of the leaders who have surrounded it with economic and legal guarantees. That is why the Church is an economic and political force.
>
> This has happened in spite of the fact that Christ says: 'it is impossible to serve two masters: God and mammon'. The Colombian clergy is the most backward in the world. Even more so than in Spain. It is clear that the only progressive churches in the world are the poor ones.

And on 20 June, in a radio broadcast, Camilo declared: 'I am in favour of expropriating the property of the Church, even if there is no revolution.'

But the cardinal had already had enough. Two days earlier he had issued a declaration warning faithful Catholics of the dangers of associating with this dangerous priest:

The Cardinal Archbishop of Bogotá believes it a duty of conscience to tell Catholics that Father Camilo Torres has consciously strayed away from the doctrines and directives of the Catholic Church.

It is sufficient to open the Papal Encyclicals to realize this lamentable truth. It is even more lamentable since Father Torres goes so far as to advocate violent revolution and the seizure of power at a time when the country is undergoing a crisis caused mainly by the violence which is being combatted at great cost.

Father Camilo Torres's activities are incompatible with his position as a priest and with the ecclesiastical habit he wears. It is possible that these two facets may lead some Catholics to follow the doctrines which Father Torres proposes in his programme. They are mistaken and pernicious.

On 22 June, Camilo went to see the cardinal:

'How was your interview?' asked a friend.

'Well,' Camilo answered, 'it was like this. We greeted one another. I told him I wanted him to tell me which points of mine were mistaken and which ones went against Church doctrine.'

The cardinal replied, 'My answer is given in my statement of 18 June.'

'But what I should like,' Camilo argued, 'to calm my conscience, is for your Eminence to point out where my mistake lies.'

'Pay attention to my statement,' said the cardinal. 'The clergy should not meddle in politics.'

'I believed, your Eminence, that as a priest and as a Christian, I could seek a dialogue.'

'No. I have nothing to add. It's all there in the statement.'[4]

On 24 June Camilo asked the cardinal if he could be exempted from performing the external duties of a priest. Two days later it was agreed that he should return to the ranks of the laity.

Notes

1   *Frente Unido*, 28 October 1965, quoted in Germán Guzmán Campos, *Camilo: Presencia y Destino*, Servicios Especiales de Prensa, Bogotá, May 1967, p. 149. (This book was subsequently published by Siglo XXI, Mexico City.)

2   Speech on agrarian reform, 20 June 1965, quoted in Guzmán Campos, *Camilo*, p. 36.

3   Interview with Otto Boye Soto, published in *La Nación* (Chile), 14 September 1965, and reprinted in Norberto Habegger, *Camilo Torres: el cura guerrillero*, Editorial A. Peña Lillo, Buenos Aires, 1967, p. 141.

4   Guzmán Campos, *Camilo*, pp. 19–20.

Once outside the Church, Camilo was able to devote all his time and energies to political campaigning, in particular to organizing the United Front of Popular Movements of which he had originally talked in his 'Platform' speech at Medellín. The first thing he did was to make contact with the National Liberation Army. On 6 and 7 July he had long discussions with Fabio Vásquez and the leadership of the ELN. The guerrillas of the ELN had by that time been operating for more than six months with a number of military successes to their credit. But they lacked a large urban organization, and unless they could create one in harmony with their views, they would be destined to remain in the jungle without further impact on the towns. Hence their interest in Camilo's 'United Front' which, had it materialized, might well have proved to be exactly the type of non-sectarian revolutionary grouping that had proved so successful in Cuba.

Later that month, Camilo wrote to Fabio Vásquez to tell him of his activities:

22 July 1965.

Dear brother and comrade Helio,

The revolution is going on tremendously well. Popular feeling seems unanimous: Cúcuta, Ocaña, Convención, Río de Oro, Bucaramanga. Everywhere I have tried to explain what is happening and to forecast the future. Everywhere (although not in Bucaramanga) co-ordinating committees of the United Front have been set up with members of existing political groups in a minority. There have been difficulties with 'the comrades'[1] from the beginning because they want to control what is going on, but they seem to be understanding little by little. They have helped us a lot. I have continued to insist on the need to form local committees, first of all to discuss and spread the platform and to distribute the newspaper, and then to set up regional committees and a national committee.

The national committee will give instructions to the United Front to take power. I have tried to explain the problem of taking power, showing them that, for example, during a state of emergency as we have at present we can't take over a post, or a town with a mere demonstration. Power will be won when the peasants can control a farm, a large estate, an entire area, a road, a factory, a town. As you can see, all this leads one to think that making trouble is necessary. You will also understand that I wouldn't be telling you all this if I didn't know what you were doing. My experience with you in the hills has been a continual encouragement, example and a point of support for me in this agitation campaign.

I have also left one or two people in each town to work clandestinely as we discussed. Of course they have to be tested, but something is something.

I will be the editor of the newspaper. Manager, Israel Arjona; assistant editor, Julio Cortés; technical director, a member of the printers' union.

It would be very nice to have an ELN bodyguard. I am very grateful to you and the ELN for your magnificent collaboration and efficiency in Bucaramanga and the tour around Santander. . . .

I hope you are looking after yourself. Your comrade and brother,

Alfredo[2]

Two weeks later he wrote again:

7 August 1965.

Dear Helio,

Thank you very much for your letter of the 7/8. Since I last wrote to you we made a trip through El Valle, a good part of the Coast and finally through Medellín. We have set up well, and what is much more important, we have always found somebody for what we want: the fight to support the guerrillas and fight with them. My personal ideas on electoral abstention, which the enemy has already taken as a United Front position, has been greeted with enthusiasm by the rank and file and has brought up the first enemies amongst the government opposition (López and ANAPO). I didn't even try to neutralize the clergy as there are so many, but I had a long talk with Rojas, and now his opposition is not so radical. We should try him of course . . . he knows nearly all of them personally, which is also important for later. . . .

Alfredo

The ELN was the only *Fidelista* guerrilla movement in Latin America which took seriously the need to form a mass urban movement that would unite a variety of different political sectors, as the Cuban 26 July Movement had done. Camilo discussed some of the problems of such a movement in an article written for *Frente Unido* in October 1965:

The People's United Front is the result of several years of experience and reflexion. There were two main problems in trying to bring together opposition political groups and other discontented Colombians:

Firstly, the lack of a sufficiently broad-base; secondly, the lack of clear aims. The broad-base might have been affected by religious reasons, traditional political thinking, group feelings or loyalty to leaders. Union had to be put forward based on concrete aims to unite all Colombians without distinction of religious beliefs, political, group or personal ties. The fighting platform of the People's United Front, can only be carried out after it takes power. The only new thing about it is that it seeks common revolutionary points, without going into party or religious differences. It can be accepted by Catholics or non-Catholics, by poor Liberals and poor Conservatives, by revolutionary members of the MRL (Liberal Revolutionary Movement), the Communist party, ANAPO (National People's Alliance-Rojas Pinilla), the Christian Democrats, etc., and especially by revolutionaries outside these groups. However, we should make clear that this platform will lead to the setting up of a Socialist state, with the proviso that we understand Socialism in a purely technical and positive sense, with no ideological overtones. It will be practical not theoretical Socialism.

You get plenty of support by talking about a revolutionary platform. However, many people back out when you say that the revolution involves a basic reorganization of the State using science and technology to achieve reforms to help the masses.

As supporters of the platform, who consider that seizing power is the only way to put it into practice, we have to make a tactical decision: fighting to the last and by any means which the oligarchy leaves to us to take power.

This does not have serious ideological consequences because the Church itself has laid down conditions for a just war. However, as a matter of fact, many 'revolutionaries' do not want to fight to the end.

A platform putting forward a Socialist state and the freeing of Colombia from American imperialism cannot ignore movements which are also working towards Socialism and freedom from imperialism. Although these movements have ideological differences, from a scientific, positive and practical point of view they are nearest to us. This solidarity actually keeps away many timid 'revolutionaries', who prefer ideology to revolution.

There is something clear about the United Front movement and that is that it is the quickest mass movement to have got going. There are a lot of recent recruits who have joined for different reasons. Some came for the pickings and went away disappointed. Others thought it was a new party and left in the same way they came; very quickly. As the revolutionary line of the United Front becomes more decided and clear-cut, the revolution's camp followers will drop off and return to where they started from, or they will wait for us to start the revolution and then join it.

The main thing is for the Colombian people to go on without faltering, despite desertion, false rumours, and betrayal. The decisive factor will be the poor who don't want their children to accuse them in the future of betraying their historical and revolutionary mission. They should know that I will fight to the end and that, even if I am left with a handful of resolute men, I will continue the fight with them.

Although this will be a long fight, the important thing is for everybody who joins to decide to stick it to the end.[3]

In spite of Camilo's enthusiasm for Socialism, his views could hardly be described as extremist. His ideas on foreign policy were as moderate as those on domestic affairs:

Given its basis of unity, the United Front does not wish to introduce discord over its international policy. Its stand against colonialism and neo-colonialism is based on its wish that Colombia should enjoy full economic, political, diplomatic and cultural sovereignty. It defends any movement which in its own way works for this, whether in Latin America or the Third World. While it may not fully identify with it, the Front considers its activities to be positive against any expansionist and warlike policy. Thus we have shown our sympathy for Frei in Chile, without making theoretical compromises, and for Goulart in Brazil, even as we also consider some acts by the Mexican government to be praiseworthy.

We also think that any attack on Cuba is a problem not only for the country of Martí, but involves the whole of Latin America. We do not agree with those who oversimplify. As a complex phenomenon, Cuba is today the first experiment in Socialism in the Western Hemisphere and was the sign of the awakening of the mass of Indians, Negroes and mestizos in our poor and underdeveloped continent. We also energetically protest against American intervention in the Dominican Republic.

The case of Egypt is important as an example of nationalism, even though its foreign policy cannot altogether be seen in the same light. The behaviour of the socialist camp towards developing countries is not only positive, but decisive. Today one cannot turn one's back on facts like this, which have even sparked off a campaign by certain capitalist groups in favour of tied aid.

Apart from this, our neutrality takes the course of friendship with all peoples and actively supports the Third World in its struggle for decolonization.[4]

Camilo's work during the second half of 1965 lay chiefly in travelling round the country addressing political meetings and in writing for his movement's journal *Frente Unido*. The first edition of this appeared on 26 August. It was a weekly costing one peso—about twice the price of a normal newspaper. It had eight pages, and almost immediately 50,000 copies were sold, an event unprecedented in the history of Colombian journalism.

Camilo was indefatigable. Between August and December 1965 he wrote no less than 12 major 'messages' to various groups in Colombian society, relating the programme of the 'United Front' to their special interests.

Initially, support for the United Front was quite impressive: the Christian Democrats were enthusiastic; on 20 July 1965 the Social Christian Democrat party announced that:

we consider it a duty to express our identification and solidarity with the objectives pursued by Father Camilo Torres in his platform and recent campaigns. In essential things they coincide with the ideas of the Christian Democrats.

The MRL at no stage committed itself formally to the Frente Unido. But its leader, Alfonso López Michelsen, on one occasion told Camilo 'we agree with you. We would have no objections to subscribing to your platform, although we would have one or two reservations.' But in fact the MRL was always deeply committed to the electoral process, and was in favour neither of abstention nor of taking to the hills.

Various small leftist groups like the FUAR and the pro-Chinese Communist party began by supporting Camilo, but withdrew after they had come to regard him as being too compromised with the more conservative groups.

The Communists, too, supported him to begin with. He was exceptionally kind to them in one of his 'messages', printed in *Frente Unido* on 2 September:

> I have said that as a Colombian, as a sociologist, as a Christian, as a priest, I am a revolutionary. I consider that the Communist party has genuinely revolutionary elements, and thus as a Colombian, as a sociologist, as a Christian and as a priest I cannot be anti-Communist.
>
> As a Colombian I am not anti-Communist, because anti-Communism persecutes my fellow-countrymen who protest, whether Communists or not, and most of these are poor people.
>
> As a sociologist I am not anti-Communist, because the Communists' approach to the problems of poverty, hunger, illiteracy, the shortage of housing, the lack of essential services for the people, provide efficient and scientific answers.
>
> As a Christian I am not anti-Communist, because I believe that anti-Communism involves a total condemnation of all that Communists stand for, and amongst these things some are just and some are unjust. Condemning them *en bloc* means condemning things which are just and things which are unjust, and this is anti-Christian.
>
> As a priest I am not anti-Communist, because although they may not know it, many of them are true Christians.
>
> The Communists should be well aware that I will not join their party, that I am not nor will I become a Communist, neither as a Colombian, nor as a sociologist, nor as a Christian, nor as a priest.

However, I am ready to fight with them for common aims: against the oligarchy and the domination of the United States, to seize power for the people. . . .

Camilo's intention was to be as non-sectarian as possible with a view to including the maximum number of those in opposition to the existing set-up with the United Front. Having addressed himself to the Communists, he then turned to other sectors in society. First to Christians:

The basic thing in Catholicism is loving one's neighbour. For this love to be true, it has to be effective. If welfare work, alms, a few free schools, a few housing plans, what is called charity, doesn't give most of the hungry enough to eat, nor clothes to most of the naked, nor knowledge to those who are ignorant, then we must find more effective means of bringing welfare to the masses.

These means will not be sought by the privileged minorities who hold power, because generally these means will force the minorities to give up their privileges.

We must therefore take power from the privileged minorities in order to give it to the poor majority. This is what a revolution is all about, if done properly. The Revolution can be peaceful if the minorities do not offer violent resistance. The Revolution is the way to achieve a government which gives food to the hungry, clothes to the naked, education to the ignorant, which carries out works of charity, which loves its neighbour, not only by chance and randomly, for the benefit of a few, but for the majority of our fellow human beings. That is why Revolution is not only allowed to Christians but is obligatory for those who see in it the only effective and large-scale way of carrying out works of love for everybody. . . .

Later in the month he wrote a message to trade unionists, criticizing those who believed that Latin American unions were too bound up with the defence of their own narrow interests:

Few groups in Colombia have such a tradition of fighting to organize as the urban workers. . . .

People have said that the trade unionists are the oligarchs of the working class. I do not agree. Because of exploitation by the oligarchy, even those workers who work in monopolies and thus have a part in the privileges they enjoy, have taken up, or at least many of them have taken up, an openly revolutionary stand.

At this crucial point in our history, the Colombian working class must make every effort toward unity and the organization of the people to take power.

In every small-scale struggle for immediate gains, never lose sight of the fact that the realization of the claims of the working class can only come about as a result of the majority, the Colombian people, taking power.

Like all supporters of revolutionary armed struggle in Latin America, Camilo was very conscious of the importance of trying to convert sections of the army to the revolutionary cause. A 'message to the military' was essential:

> On several occasions I have seen uniformed peasants and workers, amongst whom I have never seen members of the ruling class, beat up and attack peasants, workers and students, who make up the majority of Colombians. With very few exceptions, I have never found members of the oligarchy amongst the NCOs nor amongst the officers. Anyone who looks at the contrast between the Colombian masses clamouring for Revolution and a small military minority repressing the people to protect a few privileged families, has to ask himself how can these people who emerge from the masses persecute their fellows.

After explaining why he thinks that the military supports the oligarchy, Camilo concludes that they would in fact be better off after the Revolution:

> Soldiers: the United Front promises to unify the people and organize them to take power. Do not miss the rendezvous on the battlefield where we will strike the mortal blow against this oligarchy which oppresses all Colombians, you as well as us.

Lastly Camilo wrote 'messages' for the two groups in society that were likely to give him the most support, the peasants and the students:

According to the censuses the peasant population has gone down. However, they consider that people living in towns of over 1,500 inhabitants are urban. This is not true. We can say that the majority of Colombians live in the country.

Apart from their numbers, the most important thing is that the peasants make the biggest contribution to national income. Ninety per cent of exports are agricultural produce (coffee, bananas, tobacco, sugar). Without agriculture we would have no way of importing machinery or the food we need. Unfortunately the work of the peasants only goes to help a few, like everything in this system. Those who run the federations (of coffee growers, cotton growers, United Fruit, banana growers, tobacco planters, etc.) and those who run the banks (especially the Bank of the Republic) keep all the profits. The profits the government gets are used in what they call running costs, that is to say paying civil servants (who have been doubled to keep parity), and to buy second-hand weapons to kill the peasants who have given the money to buy them.

The contrast between the economic and social importance of the peasants and the treatment they get from the present system is a crying scandal.

Our peasants already know what to do. They know what they are getting ready for. They are not rushing in blindly, nor are they refusing to fight. The oligarchy has already removed the people from public squares by imposing a state of emergency. They are already machine-gunning crowds, as in Medellín. When life becomes impossible for us in the towns, we must go to the countryside. We cannot jump from there into the sea, we have to stand and fight. That is why the peasants must be ready, organizing United Front commandos of five or ten men; clearing the area of traitors to the people; preparing stocks of food and clothes; getting ready for the long struggle; not letting themselves be provoked, nor resisting when conditions are unfavourable for the people.

The oligarchy will go on confirming the people in their conviction that they must support the revolutionary forces. Why haven't the Simacota guerrillas been wiped out? Simply because of peasant support.

When the oligarchy leaves us no choice, the peasants will have to give shelter to the revolutionaries from the towns, the workers and the students.

For the time being they should unite and get organized, so as to be ready for us and begin the long final struggle.

In his 'message to students', Camilo warned them that they had certain obligations to society:

Students are a privileged group in an underdeveloped country. Poor nations keep a few graduates at very great cost. In Colombia especially, given the large number of private schools and universities, money has become the decisive factor in education. In a country with 60 per cent functional illiterates, 8 per cent of secondary school graduates and 1 per cent of professionals, the students are one of the few groups who are able to analyse the Colombian situation, compare it with other situations and think out possible solutions. . . .

I don't want to be dogmatic about the revolutionary crisis we are undergoing. All I want to do is to encourage students to come into contact with first-hand sources of information, to consider the moment, their responsibility and what must be done. Personally, I believe that we are getting closer and closer to the beginning of the Colombian Revolution. But the only people who can say this with any authority are the workers and peasants. If they take over the leadership of the people, without any paternalism, wanting to learn rather than teach, they can make an objective judgement of the right moment. . . .

In spite of the initial impact of Camilo's tours round the country, it was not long before the lack of definition in the political programme of the United Front began to be felt. But as soon as Camilo or the editors of *Frente Unido* began to define policy more exactly, they caused disgruntlement among the Front's component parts. The first to withdraw their support were the Christian Democrats.

The occasion was the Solidarity with Workers', Students' and Peasants' Congress held at Medellín from 17 to 19 September. The arguments at the Congress ranged around the question of the armed struggle, the attitude to be adopted towards Cuba, the declaration against imperialism and the problem of electoral abstention.

The Christian Democrats present took exception to most of the ideas put forward by Camilo, and they were particularly perturbed by what seemed to them the Communist domination of *Frente Unido*. Camilo invariably found himself to the Left of the Christian Democrats, and immediately fell out with the more conservative representatives of CLASC, the Christian trade union organization.

In the aftermath of the Medellín meeting, the Executive Committee of the Christian Democrats in the department of Santander issued the following declaration:

1) Considering that Camilo Torres took the part of the Marxists at the Workers–Students–Peasants Conference in Medellín, ignoring Heliodoro Agudelo Rivera, the Christian leader of CLASC, to whom his United Front owed most and with whom he should have identified himself as the Christian he claims to be;

2) Considering the Marxist–Leninist twist his misnamed weekly *Frente Unido* has taken, and the ignoring of the Christian Social Democrats in all the meetings of the Front;

3) Considering that we have more advanced platforms than that of the 'Platform for a Movement of Popular Unity';

We declare:

1) That we withdraw our support from Camilo Torres' movement and state that as Christians we cannot play the game of the Marxists, of whose electoral strength we are ignorant;

2) We denounce to the people of Santander and Colombia the trick they are trying to play, by using Camilo Torres to make a movement look Christian that is actually led by Marxist–Leninists like Julio César Cortés and Jaime Arenas;

3) We state that the Christian Social Democrat party of Colombia needs nobody's permission to be revolutionary, and that the

revolution in liberty which we are putting forward with the same enthusiasm as ever is the only salvation for Colombia, to free it from imperialists of all kinds, who wish to exploit it through their capitalist or Communist lackeys.

4) That we forbid Social Christian Democrats in Santander to join committees of the United Front, either individually or as a party, and that we hereby inform the general public that the Christian Social Democrats no longer form part of the United Front led by Camilo Torres and his comrades;

5) We invite the people of Santander to fight under the banner of Christian Social Democracy in order to form a single people's force, capable of carrying out the revolution in liberty which we are putting forward.[5]

With the first signs of disintegration, others immediately began thinking of doing the same. The MOEC, a rather more dogmatic organization than in its earlier days, issued an explanation of its disillusion with the United Front:

A real United Front should be based on a fighting alliance of poor and medium workers and peasants; it is not enough to get a number of figures from the left-wing opposition interested, or simply to agitate the masses, or to canalize this agitation through some sort of organization. Camilo Torres put out the idea of the United Front, whipped up the dispossessed masses, but got no further than suggesting the need to organize them. A United Front cannot be set up by making flimsy alliances between the discredited heads of factions with revolutionary aspirations, nor by means of simply stirring up the masses, nor by defining as the masses sectors other than poor workers and peasants who attract other sectors by their seriousness and numbers. Working for alliances between individuals and not making a serious attempt to organize an alliance of the exploited classes which is the essence of the United Front will only stimulate the ambitions and pretensions of many of the present unscrupulous and opportunist leaders of left-wing factions. This does not mean that the MOEC does not empha-

size the need to form a United Front which the people's revolution demands.

There has been a visible lack of a Leninist vanguard
organization to canalize and bring together the struggle of
the masses which the United Front managed to bring together. Several groups fought bitterly and slyly for leadership
which was by no means united, partly because of too much lib-
eralism on Father Torres' part, for he was determined that the
union should be broader than was wise and that nobody
should be excluded. The result was the entry of revisionists
and all sorts of opportunists and even elements like the
Nationalist Vanguard, well known to be enemy agents.[6]

Some took exception to Camilo's political views, others objected
to his lack of enthusiasm both for existing political parties and for
elections. Camilo believed that the elections should be boycotted, and
he also believed that there was a majority of Colombians (70 per cent)
who had abstained at the last elections who could be counted on to
join the ranks of the United Front. Neither of these two ideas was
widely accepted by the leaders of groups that subscribed to the basic
platform of the Front. Some wanted to fight elections in order to prove
the viability of their own group, few believed that the 'non-aligned'
could simply be brought over to support the United Front.

In his 'message to the non-aligned' of 16 September, Camilo had
gone very close to advocating the formation of a new party out of the
Frente Unido:

In the recent elections the oligarchy still did not need to
invent votes (if we allow the next elections to be held they will
have to invent a lot of votes).

The abstainers proved to be the vast majority of the electorate. Seventy per cent of Colombians did not vote. Anybody
who has any idea of the Colombian people, anyone who, like
me, has attended mass gatherings, must have come to the
conclusion that the non-voters are opposed to the National
Front and the oligarchy.

The non-voters are generally those revolutionaries who
are not organized in political groups. Although the revolu-

tionary and anti-sectarian spirit shown by political groups which have entered the Frente Unido has allowed them to get more members, the majority of Colombians have joined the Frente Unido without previously joining one of the existing political groups. These groups should understand that the main activity of the Frente Unido must be to organize the non-aligned. . . .

The organization of the non-aligned should be formed from the base upwards, with its own leaders and rigid discipline, but without excessive dependence on leaders. At present the main link between them is the Platform of the People's United Front which I have put to the Colombian people. Perhaps too much will be made of my name at the beginning, but so long as it serves to foment agitation and organize for the revolution, it will be quite useful. However, it would be childish to make the same mistakes which have made other revolutionary movements fail. We all saw how the oligarchy murdered Jorge Eliécer Gaitán. We all saw that the reaction of the people was not to unite around revolutionary leaders, but to go to the leaders of the oligarchy who came to the presidential palace on the shoulders of the people to sell the revolutionary movement. We all saw how the people, without organization, tried to fight in the cities, where the enemy is stronger. We all saw how the people went about aimlessly burning and looting instead of falling back on the countryside, where the enemy is weaker and the revolutionaries have greater strength.

We are gambling on a race with the oligarchy. They may kill us before we set up a strong organization of the non-aligned. I think it would be too clumsy to jail me or try me. That is why I am inclined to think of murder. The main thing is that the Colombian people should have precise instructions if that should happen.

The first thing is to fall back on the countryside and not to fight in the towns. The second is not to wage an offensive until the organization in the countryside is capable of supporting it. . . .

Mass demonstrations, revolutionary enthusiasm and agitation are useful in as much as they are immediately turned into grass-roots organizations.

Every rank and file peasant, every rank and file worker, every revolutionary must feel obliged to form a United Front command with a few companions and friends, without waiting for instructions or orders.

They should meet:

1) To discuss and publicize the platform of the United Front;

2) To distribute and finance the newspaper *Frente Unido*;

3) Carry out instructions for immediate action;

4) Link up with other commands to form commands in streets, districts, factories, schools and universities, in towns, areas and departments;

5) Appoint delegates to the great national convention of the people on 11 or 12 December 1965.

Abstaining from elections is not by itself a revolutionary weapon; it has to go hand in hand with vigorous and active organization and discipline. The non-aligned, the revolutionaries outside the parties, will have to change from a shapeless and weak mass to a battering-ram never ceasing to strike the system until it collapses.

Such a programme hardly appealed to the various political parties working within the framework of the United Front. They themselves wanted to exploit the non-aligned for their own benefit. The matter was made worse by an editorial in *Frente Unido* in September, not actually written by Camilo, but carrying his argument a stage further—further probably than he would have wished, for Camilo never openly came out in favour of the formation of a political party. The crucial paragraph in the *Frente Unido* article was as follows:

There can be no question of a split or a compromise between the 70 per cent of non-voters and the belligerent and militant sector of the non-aligned, for I am sure they include the same people. Both come into the broad revolutionary people's union which, by means of the United Front, will undertake the tasks necessary to turn this movement into the true party of the Colombian revolution.[7]

The response to this was immediate. The existing revolutionary groups within the United Front were horrified. One group complained with the following statement:

The Co-ordinating Committee of the United Front of the Cauca Valley in a session on the 22nd of this month, attended by representatives of the Communist party, the hard-line MRL, People's Nationalist Vanguard, Fedetav, Independent Union Block, Association of Democratic Women, National Housing Centre, the non-aligned and students passed the following motions:

1) In the fourth number of the newspaper you edit, the United Front is described as a new party which will bring together the great mass of non-voters, who are theoretically held to belong to the non-aligned.

This viewpoint is expressed vaguely in your 'Message to the Non-aligned', and openly and directly in articles by Julio César Cortés and Ricardo Valencia. The latter states that the United Front will be the 'true party of the Colombian revolution', and that the sector of the non-aligned will be 'the basic support'.

This new approach implies a basic change in the concept of a 'united front' with all its political consequences. It is now clear that the United Front is not a unified movement trying to bring together all the revolutionary forces on the basis of a limited programme; it is not an alliance of parties and other organizations; but rather a new party made up of the non-aligned.

If this idea were to be accepted, the first and most serious result would be that we revolutionaries who are members of different political parties would be faced by a dilemma: either we leave our parties to join the non-aligned, or we stay in our parties and are unable to join the United Front.

It will not escape you that this idea of the United Front as the party of the non-aligned is divisionist and sectarian, and thus contrary to the spirit which you displayed at the beginning and which won you the support of the masses.

We naturally do not share this point of view, and are ready to carry on the fight for a United Front without any conditions or orders of precedence, prepared to face any attempt at division. Obviously we do not object to the sector of the non-aligned becoming a revolutionary party. On the contrary, we consider that this would be a step forward in the Colombian revolutionary process. But it would not be just for this party to be formed against the other revolutionary organizations, nor to be identified with the United Front.

2) The articles by Julio César Cortés and Ricardo Valencia contain irresponsible slanders on parties which at present form part of the movement for unity which you are in. Sr Cortés speaks of 'small revolutionary groups' or simply the 'opposition' when he refers to members of the United Front other than the non-aligned. Ricardo Valencia goes further in his lofty contempt, for he states that these 'groups' have been rejected by their people because of their incapacity to carry out the Colombian revolution.

We do not know what vast masses follow these columnists, nor do we know of their efficient revolutionary work, but we consider that however many people follow them and however meritorious their services to the revolution they have no right to use such expressions.

We thus reject these and other slanderous expressions with which these articles abound, and consider that they are a real danger to popular unity, and that there should be more revolutionary vigilance in the ranks of the United Front.

We would like these points to be published in our newspaper, *Frente Unido*.[8]

In an editorial in *Frente Unido* on 7 October 1965, Camilo wrote pleading for calm:

For the moment let us respect each other, and instead of asking for honours and preferment in the revolutionary hierarchy, let us get on with the Revolution. Let us get on with organizing those who are not organized. Let us call them whatever they want to be called. 'Non-aligned', 'aligned with the United Front', 'revolutionaries'. I do not agree with the idea of having leaders above the organization, but if they are bound to the ideal of the organization we can accept them for the moment. If the people want to call themselves 'Camilists', let them, provided they organize. It is not a new party, nor a new movement. It is a new organization of those who were not organized, so that they will come into the United Front and the Revolution, but not so that they have to accept new names if they don't want to.

Obviously at a 'high level' there will be differences. Let us not exaggerate them, but rather get on with the Revolution. The people will decide on a name for the non-aligned. They will decide if a new party will be formed. . . .

But differences which ran very deep could not easily be bridged, and the United Front, which had been built up so rapidly in such a short space of time, vanished almost as rapidly as it had arisen. Its brief history illustrates the enormous difficulty of persuading the Latin American Left to unite. Fidel managed to dominate Cuba with his 26 July Movement, but no other leader anywhere else has succeeded in imitating him. The failure of guerrilla movements, notably in Bolivia, can often be ascribed to the failure of the *foco* to unite the Left in its support. The experience of Camilo Torres in Colombia shows what a near impossible task this is.

Notes

1 A reference to members of the Colombian Communist party.

2 Quoted in *Camilo Torres: Liberación o Muerte*, Instituto del Libro, Havana, 1967.

3 *Frente Unido*, 14 October 1965, quoted in Guzmán Campos, *Camilo*, pp. 86–7.

4   Editorial in *Frente Unido*, 23 September 1965, quoted in Guzmán Campos, *Camilo*, p. 145.

5   Quoted in Guzmán Campos, *Camilo*, p. 144. The Christian Democrat students were not quite so harsh. They only moved into opposition against Camilo when he began to advocate the armed struggle: 'As for the Student Social Democrat Movement, it backed up Father Camilo Torres as the leader of the Colombian Revolution until he made the strategic decision to use guerrilla warfare to take power. This is because we believe that in the present international situation, particularly in Latin America, guerrilla warfare is not a revolutionary solution. We must point out here to student opinion and to the country generally, that our movement did not withdraw support from Father Camilo Torres at the time of the Workers', Students' and Peasants' Solidarity Conference held in Medellín last September, as many people have stated, although relations were strained because of some confusion over ideology, but not doctrine, on his part and also on ours'.—PSDC student movement document written after the death of Camilo, quoted in ibid., pp. 144–5.

6   Movimiento Obrero Estudiantil, 7 January, Third Congress (n.d.), a pamphlet published in Bogotá in 1966, quoted in ibid., pp. 147–8.

7   Ricardo Valencia, 'Los No-Alineados: el por qué del repudio a los partidos', *Frente Unido*, 16 September 1965, quoted in Guzmán Campos, *Camilo*, p. 135.

8   *Frente Unido*, 7 October 1965, quoted in Guzmán Campos, *Camilo*, pp. 135–6.

8. CAMILO TORRES AND THE GUERRILLAS

Exhausted and disillusioned by his efforts to secure unity among the various elements of the Colombian opposition, Camilo Torres joined the guerrilla force of the National Liberation Army. In December 1965 he abandoned the public platforms which he had frequented during that hectic year and retreated into the clandestinity of the mountains. In January he issued a statement explaining his reasons:

From the Mountains, January 1966

Colombians,

For many years the poor of our country have waited for the battle-cry to begin the final struggle against the oligarchy.

When the desperation of the people has reached a peak, the ruling class has always found a way of deceiving the people, distracting and calming them with new words which always come down to the same thing: suffering for the people and well-being for the privileged class.

When the people called for a leader and found him in Jorge Eliécer Gaitán, the oligarchy killed him. When the people called for peace, the oligarchy spread violence up and down the country. When the people could take no more violence and organized wars to take power, the oligarchy invented a military *coup* to fool the guerrillas into giving in. When the people called for democracy, they were deceived again with a plebiscite and a National Front which brought the dictatorship of the oligarchy.

The people will believe them no more. The people do not believe in elections. The people know that legal resources are exhausted. The people know that armed force is the only way. The people are desperate and ready to risk their lives so that the next generation of Colombians are not slaves, so that the sons of those now willing to give their lives have education, houses, food, clothes and, above all, DIGNITY; so that in the future Colombians can have their own country, independent from American power.

All sincere revolutionaries have to recognize that the armed way is the only one left. But the people are waiting for the leaders to give an example and be present, and give the battle-cry. I want to tell the Colombian people that this is the moment. I have not betrayed them. I have travelled through the towns and the cities working to unify and organize the people to take power. I have asked that we should all give ourselves over to these aims until death.

Everything is ready now. The oligarchy wants to organize another electoral farce; candidates who resign and then accept again; two-party committees; renovation movements based on ideas and people who are not only old themselves but have betrayed the people. What else could we expect?

I have joined the armed struggle. I intend to go on fighting in the mountains of Colombia until power is won for the people. I have joined the National Liberation Army because I found there the same ideals as in the United Front. I found the wish for and the existence of unity from the bottom, amongst the peasants, without religious or traditional party differences. Here there is no desire to fight revolutionaries from other sectors, movements or parties. There are no personalist leaders. They are seeking to liberate the people from the oligarchy and imperialism. They will not lay down their arms until the people enjoy full power. They accept the aims of the platform of the United Front.

All Colombian patriots should be mobilized for war. Experienced guerrilla leaders will begin to rise in all the corners of the country. Meanwhile we must be alert, we must collect arms and ammunition, get guerrilla training, talk to the experts, recruit troops, gather supplies and drugs to prepare for a long struggle.

Let us carry out small operations against the enemy where victory is certain. Let us test those who claim to be revolutionaries, and eliminate traitors. We must act, but not hastily. In a long war everybody will have to act some time. The important thing is that at that moment the revolution should find us ready and prepared. Everybody need not do everything, we should split the work. The soldiers of the United Front are already at the head of initiative and action. Let us have patience to wait and confidence in final victory.

The struggle of the people should become a national struggle. We have begun, but the task is long.

Colombians: let us answer the call of the people and the revolution.

Soldiers of the United Front: let us carry out our orders.

For the unity of the people, till death.

For the organization of the people, till death.

For the seizure of power by the people, till death.

Until death, because we have decided to fight till the end.

On to victory, for a people who decide to go on till the end always achieve victory.

On to final victory, with the watchword of the National Liberation Army.

No faltering. . . . Liberation or death! . . .

Camilo Torres

The news that Camilo Torres had joined the guerrillas caught all Colombia by surprise, and the impact of his decision was felt even outside the country. The *New York Times*, in an editorial, commented that the news added 'a colourful note to a spectacular career'. Camilo Torres, it concluded, had chosen the wrong moment for his gesture:

His chances of achieving his aims are now minimal, because the economic and political situation in Colombia has taken a dramatic turn for the better in recent months. The first half of 1965 was almost disastrous for the country. Inflation, a serious decline in the peso, a flight of capital, unemployment, a minimum of foreign and domestic investments, an apparently hopeless contest between the legislature and President Valencia, and the withdrawal by Carlos Lleras Restrepo, the chosen Liberal candidate for this year's presidential elections, all added up to a dismal and dangerous picture. The 'Violence'—a long-

standing mixture of criminal and political banditry, kidnapping and terrorism—while reduced, was still disturbing.

The situation today has been reversed in almost every respect.
Inflation was cut from 80 to 45 per cent in 1965. A package
loan of about $322 million was pledged in November by the
United States and the international agencies. Income taxes
were raised. Carlos Lleras changed his mind and agreed to
run for the presidency. This will most likely assure a continu-
ance of Colombia's 16-year political plan of alternating
Conservative and Liberal presidents. Dr Valencia is now virtually certain to complete his term of office.

Although dark patches remain, Father Torres has chosen a
poor time to make his sensational move—and a poor method.
Colombia, like other Latin American countries, needs evolution, not revolution.[1]

On 17 January 1966 the following analysis of the guerrilla campaign appeared in the press:

The Armed Forces recently decided to attack the so-called
National Liberation Army which has been operating in an
area in eastern Colombia and which was joined a few days ago
by the ex-priest Camilo Torres.

It was officially revealed that senior officers and army
brigade commanders met in the last week of December to
make a careful analysis of the situation caused by this new
extremist group.

The appearance of the ELN reaffirms what was revealed
on 5 November by the National Defence Ministry, that a new
sort of violence had appeared in the country, with definite
Communist orientation.

At the meeting of the military commanders, and after the
report of Colonel Alvaro Valencia Tobar, commander of the
Fifth Brigade, based in Bucaramanga, it was concluded that
the so-called National Liberation Army does not represent
any serious threat to the stability of the country.

It was deduced that this organization is led by extremist
elements with definite aims like imposing a Communist revolution by force.

It emerged from the meeting that special measures had been taken to prevent extremist elements from breaking out into other parts of the country. It was decided to blockade a large area between the towns of Gamarra (Magdalena) and San Vicente de Chucuri (Santander).

The military spokesman said that civic–military action would be stepped up in the area and that the armed forces would be on the alert to prevent new raids by the ELN.[2]

A month later, on 15 February 1966, Camilo Torres was killed in action. The following version of the circumstances surrounding his death is the most reliable that his biographer could unearth:

For some days the guerrillas had been following the patrol. The ambush [by the military] was prepared in good time, based on knowledge of the ground and strategic advantages. The military unit was split into two groups. The lieutenant was in the second group, some yards from the leading group. When this group entered the area, the guerrilla leader fired his Madsen and four soldiers fell. The others scattered as the fight warmed up. Camilo tried to pick up a rifle from a soldier shot some five feet away. He was wounded at his first attempt. The leader asked him if he was wounded and Camilo answered: 'They hit me, but I can still make it.' The leader shouted to him: 'Get back!' but Camilo tried to get the weapon again, showed himself and was mortally wounded. A guerrilla tried to rescue the body and was shot. He was a young peasant who managed to get into the firing line where Camilo lay.

Two more guerrillas were killed in the clash. The damage was done by a sergeant, a veteran in anti-guerrilla warfare, who got into a very good position.

Meanwhile, the lieutenant had begun an encircling operation, but he was stopped by a guerrilla support group. He fell wounded a long way from Camilo. A guerrilla who carried a grenade was ordered several times to throw it to eliminate the sergeant, but for some unknown reason he didn't. He deserted the same night. Was this due to treason, fear or confusion?

When they realized there was a danger of being surrounded and that it was impossible to rescue the bodies, the remaining guerrillas crossed the Río Sucio and withdrew to their bases.[3]

At the end of the month the National Liberation Army issued a statement on the death of Camilo Torres:

> It is with deep sorrow and bitter hatred of the oligarchy that the National Liberation Army informs the Colombian people and revolutionaries of the world of the death of the great revolutionary leader, Father Camilo Torres Restrepo, which occurred on 15 February this year in an encounter between our forces and a punitive expedition from the anti-patriotic army of the 'National Front'. In this clash our heroic soldiers valiantly faced the enemy forces, inflicting heavy casualties on them, capturing several long-range weapons and assorted military equipment and again thwarting the army's attempts to wipe us out. However, we suffered the irreparable loss of five courageous patriots, among them the irreplaceable Camilo, shot down by the reactionaries together with other hardened companions who tried to rescue him from danger.
>
> This new crime committed by official violence is the result of punitive action against the noble efforts of our people to shake off the odious yoke of oligarchy and American imperialism, obliging them to offer the blood of our best sons on the altar of the interests of the country.
>
> Camilo died heroically, knowing that leaders must set an example. He would never agree to being put out of danger. He knew the risks of war and accepted them in the conviction that eventually his death would be the spark, perhaps the decisive one, which would light the fire laid by the Colombian people with hatred and resolution against the government forces who support a system of injustice and dishonour. . . .
>
> But this thought springs up with his martyrdom. His ideas are being taken up by the workers. As a tribute to his memory, we will strive to bring about the popular unity which he put so much stress on. Thousands of peasants, workers, students professionals and honest people will physically and spiritually fill the post which the fighting hero left in the ranks of the ELN. Our strength will increase, firmly guided by Camilo's example. His memory has filled our hearts with fighting spirit and hatred for the lackeys of the oligarchy. Our people will make those responsible for the death of our great leader bite

the dust. We will redouble our determination to fight to the end, because, as Camilo taught us, 'a people who fights to the death always achieves victory'.

Peasants: We will achieve grass roots unity, peasant unity, without religious or traditional party differences, by strengthening the fighting units of the ELN.

Students and Intellectuals: Your struggles will no longer be fruitless when they are closely linked to the efforts of the guerrilla fighters.

Workers: The final decision on the liberation struggle going on in the country rests in your hands and your class organization.

Officers, NCOs and men: Stop your repressive action. Do not act as the murdering instrument of the oligarchy and its unpatriotic government. Do not stain your hands with the blood of those who, like Camilo, are only seeking dignity: for their country.

Priests: Take the martyrdom of Camilo as a sublime example of love for one's neighbour which gives everything and demands nothing. Take the side of the people in the struggle against their oppressors.

Finally, we call on all the peoples' organizations to make active demands for the body of our beloved leader, to rescue it from the claws of his murderers. Let us make a National Monument of his tomb.

For the unity of the people, till death!

For the organization of the people, till death!

For the seizure of power by the people, till death!

No faltering . . . liberation or death!

From the Mountains, February 1966,
National Liberation Army
Fabio Vásquez Castaño, Victor Medina Morón[4]

Although it was not obvious at the time, the death of Camilo Torres was also the beginning of the decline of the ELN. But, as with Che Guevara, Camilo Torres in death was a more potent symbol than he had been when alive, especially outside his own country. Revolutionaries both, the exact nature of their doctrines has been forgotten; their example lives on.[5]

Notes

1 *New York Times*, 22 January 1966.

2 *El Siglo*, 17 January 1966, quoted in Guzmán Campos, *Camilo*, pp. 195–6.

3 Ibid., p. 203. (Guzmán does not give his source, but suggests that this version is closest to the truth.)

4 *Insurrección* (número especial), 1 March 1966, quoted in Guzmán Campos, *Camilo*, pp. 204–5.

5 In February 1968, in Montevideo, more than 50 'revolutionary Christians', both cleric and lay, from Argentina, Chile, Colombia and Uruguay, met to discuss preparations for a 'Camilo Torres Meeting' to be held in Bogotá in March 1969. The Uruguyan police allowed it to take place, but refused permission for Mgr Germán Guzmán to enter the country.

   The conference was organized by Juan García Elorrio, an Argentinian priest who leads the 'Comando Camilo Torres' in Argentina. On 1 May 1967, during a mass in Buenos Aires attended by General Onganía, García Elorrio read out a revolutionary manifesto—to the consternation of the congregation. He managed to escape, but has subsequently had to live in exile.

   Another participant in the Conference was the Uruguayan worker-priest Juan Carlos Zaffaroni who, together with Mgr Guzmán, a Belgian, R. P. Paul Blanquart and a Mexican priest, Pedro de Euzcardia, had written a manifesto in Havana affirming that 'Marxism gives the most scientific analysis of imperialism and the most effective stimulation for revolutionary action by the masses'—a phrase that Fidel included in his closing speech to the Cultural Congress held in Havana in January 1968.

   The Conference made two appeals: one, to Christians of all faiths to enrol themselves in the revolutionary struggle; two, a denunciation of American intervention in Vietnam which it described as genocide. 'Christians must assume their responsibilities in the face of this war because Latin America will be the Vietnam of 1970.'

   In addition the Conference sent a letter to Pope Paul, asking him not to make his planned journey to Colombia, Brazil, and Argentina. (See the article by Carlos María Gutierrez in *Le Monde*, 6 March 1968.)

9. The People's Liberation Army

In January 1968 a new guerrilla movement began in Colombia, unique in Latin America. Its inspiration came neither from Havana nor from Moscow, but from Peking. It was called the Ejército Popular de Liberación (EPL)—the People's Liberation Army—a somewhat grandiose title derived from Mao Zedong. In an article announcing the start of this new guerrilla venture, published in the Chilean pro-Chinese magazine, *Causa Marxista–Leninista* the author explains the background to the movement:

> The struggle against the revisionist leadership of Gilberto Vieira, who has followed the line of elections and of abandoning the armed struggle in Colombia, goes back to 1959 when the Bogotá Regional Committee rebelled; this led to the setting up of a group in favour of a guerrilla nucleus. Later, in a conference held in 1962, the Magdalena Regional Committee rebelled, and proposed the reconstruction of the Communist party on Marxist–Leninist lines. As a result of this recovery of revolutionary principles, a National Conference was held in March 1964. Finally, in July 1965, after intense ideological discussion, a National Congress was held which expelled Vieira and his revisionist clique. The Communist party of Colombia (Marxist–Leninist), purged of opportunists, is beginning to organize the people's war.[1]

This Conference, which the pro-Chinese elements described as the 10th Congress of the Communist party, adopted a new programme and constitution. In a political resolution, the new party put forward ideas that were indistinguishable from the ideological line that the Chinese Communist party was following at the time:

> Wars of liberation are just, necessary and inevitable. Revolutionary violence is the midwife of history. The existing political situation in the world shows that peaceful transition from capitalism to Socialism is impossible.[2]

But even more important than wars of liberation, was the fight against revisionism:

> It is the biggest hurdle in the way of revolutionary struggle. . . . The anti-revisionist struggle is a matter of life and death for the Communist parties. It must be carried through till victory is won.

The resolution went on to denounce the favourite enemies of the Chinese:

> Yugoslavia is a most outstanding case in point, where the people have been robbed of the fruits of their revolution and subjected again to capitalist exploitation. . . . The case of Yugoslavia proves to the hilt the pressing need to cope with revisionism with every means at our disposal. We shall not speak about the Eastern European countries here, but in the Soviet Union certain features of capitalism have already begun to appear as a result of modern revisionism. The danger of the restoration of capitalism exists as long as there is imperialism in the world.

Specifically referring to the situation in Latin America, the resolution concluded:

> In our countries, a civil war against the oligarchical forces can speedily develop into an out-and-out national liberation war against U.S. troops. Our struggle will be hard and protracted. In the present conditions on our continent, the village is the natural battleground for a people's war.

The only thing lacking hitherto, the resolution insinuated, was a vanguard party to channel the latent revolutionary fervour of the people:

It is the great historical mission of our party at the present stage to enable the partial political consciousness of the discontented masses of Colombia to develop into full political consciousness and lead them to seize power through armed struggle.

With these ideological flourishes the new pro-Chinese Communist party of Colombia was launched, one of the few such parties in the continent that enjoyed recognition by Peking—though there is no evidence that the Chinese government ever took much interest in it.

The pro-Russian Communists in Colombia must have been glad to see their erstwhile comrades depart. One party member wrote:

No little difficulties have been caused in this field [of unity] by the leaders of the Communist party of China, who are seeking to interfere with the work of our party and cause confusion by the same methods they are employing in the entire world Communist movement. Patronizing the small groups of 'ultra-revolutionaries' embodying the most negative petty-bourgeois trends, they encourage anarchic subjectivism which tragically persists in artificially and even forcibly pushing the people into battles the meaning of which they do not yet understand, and are not yet prepared to wage.[3]

There is no estimate of the size of the group that left the pro-Soviet party, but there is some evidence to suggest that some of Marulanda's guerrillas left him to help to organize the 'Marxist–Leninist' guerrillas who later formed the People's Liberation Army.[4]

These new pro-Chinese guerrillas went into action on 6 January 1968 in the area of Alto Sinu in the province of Córdoba. They had been working in the region for two years previously, organizing and arming the peasants into what were called 'Regional Patriotic Juntas'. Their first major pronouncement, with its obligatory reference to the thought of Mao Zedong, came in February. The new movement emphasized that it was not a *foco*; it had grown 'from the very heart of the people'.

According to one source, the US Major, Ralph 'Pappy' Shelton (who had trained the Bolivian Rangers who captured Che Guevara) was subsequently sent to Colombia to deal with the new guerrilla outbreak in Colombia. The CIA prepared for him the following comments on the EPL:

> The People's Liberation Army, which is operating in northeast Colombia, is not one of the typical guerrilla forces backed by Havana, for the EPL does not recognize and even rejects directions from there. They have real peasant support based on previous effective indoctrination work. Their leaders, who are armed and live in the area, have shown that they have assimilated other people's experience and learnt from their own mistakes, and are conducting a type of struggle new to Latin America. It is not easy to discover their urban links.[5]

Although the EPL received very severe blows from the Colombian army, it managed to maintain its organization intact. By the beginning of 1969 Colombia presented a rare picture in Latin America, boasting three guerrilla movements in operation, all of which owed their foreign ideological inspiration to different poles within the Communist world. It cannot be said that this ideological disunity did much to assist their cause.

Notes

1 'La Guerra Popular de Liberación en Colombia', *Causa Marxista–Leninista* (Santiago, Chile), NO. 1, May–June 1968.

2 Political Resolution of the 10th Congress of the Colombian Communist party, *Peking Review*, 20 August 1965.

3 José Cardona Hoyos, 'Colombian Communists Building Popular Unity', *Information Bulletin of the World Marxist Review*, NO. 30, p. 52, quoted in Norman A. Bailey, *Latin America in World Politics*, Walker, New York, p. 105.

4 See *La República* (Bogotá), 30 June 1965, and also 'Guerrillas: estrategias de chinos y soviéticos en América Latina', *Informes de China* (Buenos Aires), November–December 1966.

5 'La Guerra Popular en Colombia', *Causa Marxista–Leninista* (Santiago, Chile), NO. 4, November–December 1968.

IV

DISASTER IN PERU

'The strength of revolutionaries does not lie in their philosophy;
it is in their faith, their passion, their will.
Theirs is a religious, mystical and spiritual strength.'

José Carlos Mariategui

1. THE PERUVIAN BACKGROUND

It is difficult to understand the two revolutionary movements that sprang up in Peru in the 1960s without some regard for the political and social background. For both the leaders of the two movements—Hugo Blanco, a militant Trotskyist, and Luís de la Puente Uceda, a dissident member of a bourgeois reformist party—were concerned essentially with the condition of the Peruvian peasant. Under the existing system he has no political rights, because he is illiterate. And he is illiterate because he speaks Quechua or Aymará. No school will teach him to read or write it, yet Spanish is of little use to him.[1] The 1940 census showed that 88 per cent of the Indian population of Peru between the ages of 6 and 14 received no education at all.[2] Nothing has happened in the last 30 years to suggest that these figures have changed significantly. In the 1961 census it was revealed that 39.8 per cent of the entire population over 17 was illiterate. And according to figures released by the Ministry of Education in 1962, 40 per cent of the children of school age could not go to school at all, largely as a result of a lack of schools and teachers.[3] Most of these underprivileged children are Indian. For the Indian forms the largest single element in the population of the country.[4] And while he continues effectively on the margin of national life, the old corrupt oligarchy will remain in control.

If the Indian peasant had education and the vote, the first thing he would demand from his elected representatives would be land. At present he has none. He works for free for somebody else. The figures speak for themselves: there are nine million hectares of cultivable land

and natural pasture available at present in Peru; 3 per cent of the owners possess 83 per cent of the land; 97 per cent of the owners possess the 17 per cent that remains.[5] Lack of land, lack of schooling, and lack of political influence ensure that the Peruvian Indian lacks everything else as well. While Lima has a doctor for every 2,000 inhabitants, the department of Cuzco—the principal centre of revolutionary activity—has only one for every 40,000. For the department of Puno, the figure is even worse: one for every 58,000.[6]

The examples of the deprived and unsatisfactory conditions in which these Indians live could be multiplied 100-fold. But the key to their fate is land. Hugo Blanco put their demand into a slogan, 'Land or Death', culled partly from Fidel Castro and partly from the Mexican revolutionary Emiliano Zapata. Luís de la Puente, who had written his university thesis on the subject of the Peruvian agrarian situation, made land reform the central plank of his guerrilla movement's political programme.[7]

Land also lies at the root of the problem of the big cities. Ten per cent of Peru's population live in the foul slum shanty towns, or *barriadas*, that surround Lima and the other large towns. The CIDA Report on Peru, published in 1966, makes the following comment:

> The low economic capacity of the majority of the population due to the lack of well-paid employment, is perhaps the determining factor of the *barriadas*. But without doubt the deepest cause, the origin of the phenomenon, must be found in the lack of attention to the problem of the land in its two aspects: agrarian reform and the expansion of the land surface dedicated to agriculture.[8]

Like some other Latin American countries, Peru has geographical features which elsewhere would need to be encompassed by a continent. Luís de la Puente himself, a man profoundly interested in the formation of his country and fully aware of the impact of geography on politics, has left an impressive picture of Peru's diversity:

> The Andes range overlies our country as a sort of backbone separating it into two parts. On the West there is a kind of shelf by the sea, a region called the Coast; and to the East an immense territory, slowly descending and merging into the

Amazon basin. The coast is a long strip of land by the sea, 95 per cent uninhabited owing to a lack of rainfall. The dryness of the climate as well as its temperateness, despite geographic location in the torrid zone, is caused by the Humboldt cold current which washes the coastline. Small valleys formed by the rivers that gather the rain waters from the western slopes of the Andes traverse this deserted strip and determine the sites of the towns. The main cities of the country are on the coast. The fertile coastal lands are in the hands of monopolies (as in the rest of the country), and are mainly devoted to the production of cotton, sugar cane, and some other foodstuffs. Peruvian industry is chiefly located in this region, and about 80 per cent of it is concentrated in Lima. Nearly four million people live within the coastal zone: it might be considered the capitalist zone of Peru.

The mountainous region known as the Sierra is a lofty labyrinth with snowcapped peaks and deep valleys; with huge plains called *punas* or *jaleas*; with zones of meagre vegetation near the summits and impenetrable wooded fields in the valleys, most of which extend toward Amazonian jungle; and with cold and dry or moderate and tropical climates, depending on altitudes and topographical features. The sierra is the largest and most densely populated region in the country. The *latifundio* system, with its feudal or semi-feudal relations, prevails there. The indigenous communities, the primitive *Ayllus* of the Incas, survive in a permanent struggle against *gamonalist* usurpation and against the individualistic influences within themselves. Inside the communities, and among the peasantry in general, collectivist methods of work and feelings of mutual aid and help still prevail. This is a region of extreme backwardness. Most of the land is devoted to food production and cattle raising. The most important mining centres are also in this region and provide jobs, mainly temporary, for some 200,000 workers who come from the countryside. The sierra has a population of about seven million people, principally Indians and *mestizos*. The sierra expresses the real Peru, the feudal Peru, the Indian Peru.

The *Selva* (jungle) is a vast, largely uninhabited region, where the rivers provide the only gateway and where vegetation is luxuriant. Its population is barely 300,000 including whites, *mestizos*, and savages. The highlands, known as the Jungle's Eyebrow (*Ceja de la Selva*), on the escarpments of the Andes, have a large potential for short-term development due to the fertility of the land, its topography and climate; they are chiefly devoted to tropical fruit production and livestock. The lowlands, flooded during most of the year, contain huge forest resources, and are uninhabited and inhospitable. Little towns are scattered along the rivers and earn their living from the sale of wood, medicinal herbs, wild animals, furs, etc. The best lands have been monopolized by native or foreign enterprises under cover of supposed colonization plans, a good example being the American-owned Leturneau which controls over 40,000 hectares.[9]

The political background can be briefly told. One party and one leader in Peru for 30 years monopolized the energies of those who felt reformist or even revolutionary minded. This was the American Popular Revolutionary Alliance (APRA), founded in 1924 and led from the beginning by Victor Raúl Haya de la Torre.[10] Whenever APRA looked like winning an election, the military moved in to prevent it [from] taking power. But after 30 years, and even before, APRA ran out of revolutionary steam. It began to think that the United States provided most of the answers to the problems of the country. Although the military continued to intervene against APRA electoral successes, it did so more as a reflex action than to ensure that APRA did not upset the Peruvian upper classes. This latter group have been living in extremes of luxury for several centuries and have no plans to legislate themselves out of existence.

During the eight years from 1948 to 1956—known as the *ochenio*—Peru was ruled by a military dictator, General Manuel Odría. Though he legalized his coup in the usual fashion by having himself elected President in 1950, he remained a military dictator. Throughout the period, APRA and the Communist party were banned.

In 1956, he was succeeded by ex-President Manuel Prado (who had been President, from 1939 to 1945), a reactionary who devoted his time, in the manner of the Peruvian ruling classes, to enriching himself at the expense of his country. His period of rule, known as the *convivencia*, or co-existence, was characterized by the support he obtained from APRA in exchange for granting them a legal status.

Fresh elections for President were held in June 1962. The three most important candidates were Haya de la Torre, Fernando Belaúnde Terry, representing his Popular Action party, and General Odría. Belaúnde and de la Torre, both received slightly more than half a million votes, with the APRA man just ahead. General Odría polled slightly less than half a million.[11]

With the prospect of Haya de la Torre as President, in spite of (or perhaps because of) the fact that his views were barely distinguishable from those of ex-President Prado who had so admirably upheld the traditions of the Peruvian ruling elite, the army could hardly wait to intervene. On 18 July 1962 a military junta seized power, announcing that new elections would take place the following June. The head of the junta, General Nicolás Lindley López, was an enthusiastic supporter of the Moral Rearmament Movement.

The United States, which was still then in its liberal hey-day under President Kennedy, promptly suspended diplomatic relations and cut off military aid. But needless to say, this policy did not last long. The military junta promised that the next elections would be free and that they would not intervene again. United States business interests accepted the new regime.[12] So the United States government, impressed by the military men's sense of liberal decorum, resumed diplomatic relations on 17 August. Military aid began again in October.

And in the elections the following June, Belaúnde, to no one's surprise, managed to secure nearly 100,000 more votes than Haya de la Torre.[13] The army kept their promise, and Belaúnde was allowed to become President.

The nature of Peruvian society and its political system has been studied exhaustively by a large number of Peruvian and foreign academics.[14] There is no consensus of opinion, and it is not my intention here to try and act as umpire between the contending arguments. I am not concerned with whether Peruvian society is in fact feudal or capitalist: my concern is with what the guerrillas themselves thought about it.[15] Luís de la Puente in an important speech made in the Plaza San Martín, on 7 February 1964, made an interesting analysis of the Peruvian situation, and at the same time explained why the Peruvian

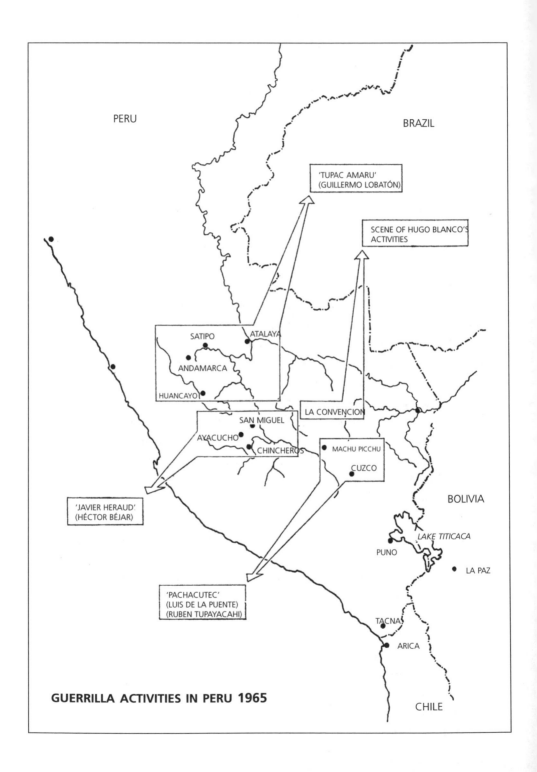

PERU

BRAZIL

'TUPAC AMARU'
(GUILLERMO LOBATÓN)

SCENE OF HUGO BLANCO'S
ACTIVITIES

SATIPO   ATALAYA

ANDAMARCA

HUANCAYO

LA CONVENCION

SAN MIGUEL

AYACUCHO

CHINCHEROS

MACHU PICCHU

CUZCO

'JAVIER HERAUD'
(HÉCTOR BÉJAR)

BOLIVIA

LAKE TITICACA

PUNO

LA PAZ

'PACHACUTEC'
(LUIS DE LA PUENTE)
(RUBEN TUPAYACAHI)

TACNA

ARICA

GUERRILLA ACTIVITIES IN PERU 1965

CHILE

revolutionaries rejected the electoral road and why they felt that the Peruvian Revolution was inevitable.

He tells a story of oligarchic rule, electoral fraud, and military intervention, and it is against this background that there took place the short-lived but momentous revolutionary movements, led first, in the period 1959–63, by Hugo Blanco, and then, in 1965, by de la Puente himself. Although they both chiefly took place in the region of the Valley of La Convención, tragically they failed to overlap in time. For Hugo Blanco's movement essentially consisted of organized peasants in desperate need of guerrilla support, while de la Puente's guerrilla movement failed largely through lack of support from the organized peasantry. Hugo Blanco's peasants seized the land, but had no guns to defend their gains. De la Puente's well-armed guerrillas had no peasants to defend.

The reason was simple. In the years between 1963 and 1965— between the fall of Blanco and the rise of de la Puente—the government enacted a land reform. Though hopelessly inadequate, it gave the peasant just sufficient hope for the future to dampen his revolutionary zeal.[16] And, more importantly, the army descended on the area of Hugo Blanco's triumphs and, with bloody repression, ensured that no peasant who valued his family's life would again look to a revolutionary and bearded saviour.

Notes

1 According to a Communist writer, 'there are two million peasants who speak the language of the Quechua only, half a million who speak nothing but Aymará. Yet there is not a single school in the country where the peasants are taught in their native tongue.'— César Levano, 'Lessons of the Guerrilla Struggle in Peru', *World Marxist Review*, VOL. ix, NO. 9, September 1966.

2 R. J. Owens, *Peru*, Oxford University Press, Royal Institute of International Affairs, 1966, pp. 93–4.

3 *La Prensa* (Lima), 6 March 1963.

4 According to the census of July 1961, the population of Peru is 10,420,357. The rural population is approximately 53 per cent and the urban 47 per cent. About 50 per cent is Indian, 10 per cent white, yellow or Negro and 40 per cent *mestizo*.

5   Ricardo Letts Colmenares, 'Breve reseña contemporánea de la lucha por la reforma agraria', *Economía y Agricultura* (Lima), February 1964.

6   Owens, *Peru*, p. 93.

7   Thesis by Luís de la Puente Uceda, published as *La Reforma del Agro Peruana*, Ediciones Ensayos Sociales, Lima, 1966.

8   *Tenencia de la tierra y desarrollo socio-económico del sector agrícola: Perú*, produced by the Comité Interamericano de Desarrollo Agricola, and published by the Panamerican Union, Washington, D.C., 1966, p. 259.

9   Luís de la Puente Uceda, 'The Peruvian Revolution: Concepts and Perspectives', *Monthly Review*, VOL. xvii, NO. 6, November 1965.

10 Technically APRA was an international party. The Peruvian branch was called the Partido Aprista Perusano. See Harry Kantor, *The Ideology and Programme of the Peruvian Aprista Movement*, University of California Press, Berkeley, 1953. Debray calls it 'a kind of Latin American Kuomintang'.

11 It is interesting to note, however, that Odría secured more votes than the other candidates both in Lima and in Callao, Lima's port. The three left-wing candidates barely secured 10 per cent of the votes between them.

12 Owens, *Peru*, p. 185.

13 See Richard W. Patch, 'The Peruvian Elections of 1963', *American Universities Field Staff Report*, July 1963.

14 See, in particular, François Bourricaud, *Poder y sociedad en el Perú contemporáneo*, Paidos, Buenos Aires, 1967; and Aníbal Quijano, 'Naturaleza, situación y tendencia de la sociedad peruana contemporánea', *Pensamiento Crítico* (Havana), NO. 16, May 1968.

15 The editors of *Monthly Review*, in particular, took de la Puente to task for describing Peruvian society as being in part 'feudal' or 'semi-feudal'. I was brought up to believe that the feudal system in Europe barely lasted two generations except in an extremely adulterated form; it is difficult to understand how it can be considered to be surviving in Latin America. Clearly there are land tenure systems reminiscent of feudalism—it is also a conveniently pejorative adjective to apply to what is an extremely unsavoury situation—but basically Latin America is a victim of capitalism—and imperialism—rather than feudalism.

16 Of special importance in this respect was Decree Law 1444 of the Agrarian Reform which applied particularly to La Convención. It was enacted by the military junta on 28 March 1963.

2. HUGO BLANCO AND THE VALLEY OF LA CONVENCIÓN

'Hugo Blanco is the head of one of the guerrilla movements in Peru.
He struggled stubbornly but the repression was strong. I don't know
what his tactics were, but his fall does not signify the end of the
movement. It is only a man that has fallen, but the movement
continues. One time, when we were preparing to make our landing
from the Granma, and when there was a great risk that all of us
would be killed, Fidel said: "What is more important than us is the
example we set." It's the same thing. Hugo Blanco has set
an example, a good example, and he struggled as much as
he could. But he suffered a defeat, the popular forces
suffered a defeat. It's only a passing stage.'

Ernesto Che Guevara, Algiers, July 1963

Hugo Blanco Galdós was born in Cuzco in about the year 1933.[1] He
was the son of a lawyer, though his mother was of peasant origin. He
studied at the Colegio Nacional de Ciencias in Cuzco but, apart from
an obligatory performance in a student strike to throw out the director, he showed few revolutionary leanings. Cuzco itself, however, is a
radical town. It nurses its memories of the great Túpac Amaru who
rose up against the Spaniards in the late eighteenth century. In more
recent years it was a Communist stronghold, at a time when the orthodox Communist party was still a revolutionary force in the land. The
party had a radical influence both in the town and in the surrounding
countryside.

After leaving the college in Cuzco, Hugo Blanco travelled to Argentina to enrol in the school of agronomy at the University of La Plata. Although his father could easily have financed him, Blanco preferred to pay his way through university by earning money as a labourer. He very soon became active in left-wing politics, but chose to join the Trotskyists rather than the orthodox Communist party. At that time the Argentinian Communists were vigorously opposed to Perón, whose government, for all its faults, was devoutedly anti-imperialist and anti-American—and consequently enjoyed the support of a sizeable percentage of the working class.

Blanco was active in a Trotskyist group, Palabra Obrera, run by Hugo Bressano, a professor from the University of La Plata. Bressano, who operated under the pseudonym of Nahuel Moreno, was later to have much to do with revolutionary developments in Peru.

At the end of 1956, Blanco returned from Argentina to Peru, where he immediately joined the Partido Obrero Revolucionario (POR), 'the Revolutionary Workers' party', a Trotskyist party which was the equivalent in ideological outlook to Palabra Obrera. Víctor Villanueva, who has written the only book on Hugo Blanco, suggests that already at this time he was thinking in terms of returning to the Cuzco area in order to begin a trade union campaign among the peasants that would become the base for future revolutionary activities.[2] But in fact he did not return permanently to Cuzco until 1958. As in Argentina, he sought to identify himself with the class that he was anxious to help. He began to live with *campesinos*, dressing like them, sharing their work, and speaking their language—Quechua.[3]

Hugo Blanco was primarily a peasant organizer—one of many. Because Cuzco was a Communist town, the surrounding area had been subjected for some time to the blandishments of Communist organizers. But there was by no means a superfluity. The task of organizing the peasants into unions was endless. The chief problem of these organizers and embryonic revolutionaries was that they were divided among themselves. And few ideological splits are more profound than that between Communists and Trotskyists. Thus, as well as fighting the landlords, Hugo Blanco found himself perpetually feuding with the entrenched interests of the local Communist party.

Peru, together with Guatemala and Brazil, are the three countries in Latin America where the Trotskyists have been most active. But Peru is the only country where they found an indigenous leader who was himself a convinced apostle of the faith. After so much emphasis placed by the guerrilla movements discussed in this book on Marxism-Leninism, it is a slight relief to find a peasant leader often operating 10,000 feet up in the Andes extolling the virtues of Trotskyism-Leninism. The following document was written late in 1962 when Hugo Blanco was already declining in influence. It is a letter he wrote to the comrades of the Valley of La Convención where he had been working. It expresses clearly the Trotskyist bent of his ideological outlook:

Comrades of the Valley of La Convención and Lares

I am writing to you with the happiness the combatant feels as he sees that triumph in the war is near after fighting in a hundred battles. I am also full of satisfaction because you can see that the line we have followed and are still following, our methods, and our policy, are the correct ones.

Now I feel even more deeply grateful to the memory of Comrade Leon Trotsky, who foresightedly indicated this method in 1905. Following his method of 'Permanent Revolution' we are reaching victory, comrades. That is why it is vital now to bear in mind some of the general principles of our Trotskyist–Leninist doctrine:

The working classes will achieve the recognition of their rights by violence, and not by legal forms.

We are experiencing this, comrades, we are reaching victory by means of stoppages, strikes, meetings, division of land contrary to bourgeois law, and the confiscation of haciendas that is also contrary to bourgeois law.

Opportunist methods, 'Pockochunracc' methods, have proved to be a failure. We have seen the uselessness of court cases, memoranda, delegations to the government, sending telegrams, elections, candidates, etc.

Looking at this, we can see that to gain our triumphs, we have not waited for the bourgeois legalist government. Instead we have broken and smashed the power of that government in our area, setting up our own workers' and peasants' government, with its own institutions, own ways and own laws. That is, we are carrying out a revolution, and not waiting for reforms or half-measures within the bourgeois régime.

Only a government of workers and peasants will solve the country's pressing problems.

The masses of Convención and Lares are peasants and we, their leaders, have a Socialist, working class doctrine.

As the peasants begin to work in the fields or factories of their co-operative they are beginning to be Socialist workers.

All over Peru we workers and peasants will have to take power, destroying the bourgeois régime (as we have already done in some areas), in order to solve the main national problem: Agrarian Reform (or rather Agrarian Revolution), the expulsion of imperialism, and industrialization. Only a government of workers and peasants, taking power in a revolution by destroying the bourgeois state, will be capable of carrying out these tasks, and not a 'People's Democracy' or a 'Democratic Coalition' nor any other abortion resulting from bourgeois elections.

The triumph of the movement depends on it spreading. Any gain, any triumph, by the workers in one place; any fight, either a strike, a stoppage, occupation of land, confiscation of estates, etc., should be extended before it is deepened.

Russia has not reached Socialism nor will it do so until revolution is victorious in the world. Chaupimayo will not make progress in its Agrarian Revolution until it is extended to the whole valley, and the valley will not make progress until it is carried all over the country.

The isolationist and anti-revolutionary spirit of the Stalinist theory of 'Socialism in One Country' is dangerous and suicidal. That is why comrade Trotsky fought this theoretical aberration, and that is why he was murdered. We must concern ourselves with spreading the movement rather than deepening it.

Let us confiscate all the estates in the valley as was done at 'Paltaijbamba'. If the landowners join the union and obey its decisions, they will then get suitable housing and be informed of the improvements that will have to be made.

Peru is a backward, semi-colonial, capitalist country, with some feudal characteristics; that is why its revolution must be a mixture of bourgeois democracy and Socialism.

Peru is not a feudal country, it is an integral part of the imperialist system; it is a backward producer of raw materials, which the imperialist countries with their highly developed industries turn into products which they sell to us at exorbitant prices. Our country is not feudal because it neither produces solely for internal consumption nor is it self-sufficient; I repeat, it is an integral part of the imperialist body and imperialism is the last stage of capitalism.

With this in mind our revolution is bourgeois-democratic and Socialist. Bourgeois-democratic in the case of feudal and pre-capitalist aspects: the dividing up of land is a bourgeois-democratic measure. Socialist in the case of capitalist aspects: factories, mines, foreign trade, industrialized plantations, etc. Besides, our revolution is taking Socialist steps even in the backward estates of our area: the goods of the landlords, crops, livestock, etc., are becoming the Socialist property of the union.

This aspect of our revolution is the most striking reaffirmation of Trotsky's theory of 'Permanent Revolution'.

The Peruvian revolutionary process is marking the end of the Stalinist theory of 'Revolution by Stages', which wrongly states that our revolution can only be bourgeois-democratic, and that the local capitalists, whom they call 'progressive bourgeois', will join us in our fight against land-lordism and imperialism. All this is a lie as we are proving, another opportunists' tale.

Land or Death

We shall overcome[4]

This letter was written when Hugo Blanco was beginning to feel the full weight of the Communist attack against him. Four years earlier, in 1958, when he first went to the Valley of La Convención, things had been easier.

A tenant farmer had granted him part of his own parcel of land in the area of Chaupimayo in the valley.[5] Hugo Blanco thus began his life as a union organizer from a base as a sub-tenant farmer. Víctor Villanueva writes:

And so began his union campaign to organize the peasants, creating class consciousness, instructing them in unionism as well as in questions of hygiene, clarifying the problems of the area itself, inculcating in them a knowledge of their own rights, organizing cultural work—with the creation of schools—and sanitary work, and arranging for medical assistance posts to be set up. In short, making an enormous effort for the benefit of the peasantry.[6]

In his educational activity he even succeeded in suppressing the widespread use of coca and of alcohol.

When he first arrived in the Valley of La Convención, there were only six unions. They were almost entirely preoccupied with legal matters, and according to Adolfo Gilly, they were of more use for prestige purposes to leftist lawyers in Cuzco than they were to the peasants themselves.[7] Yet within three years Hugo Blanco had created 148 unions in La Convención alone.[8] He himself was the delegate of his union, of Chaupimayo, to the Provincial Peasants' Federation of La Convención and Lares. Later he was the delegate from this organization to the Departmental Peasants' Federation of Cuzco, where he acted as the Secretary in charge of agrarian reform problems.

This activity was of course directly in line with what the Trotskyist theory demanded. In one sense, Hugo Blanco was just another union organizer, although he happened to be exceptionally well-qualified for the task. He wrote:

The new instrument that has been given to the peasantry in their struggle for agrarian reform is the peasants' union. . . . This will be the basis of the future government of the Peruvian people, of the revolutionary government.[9]

Hardly had he got the first unions organized, than he set about organizing strikes—chiefly for better treatment and better conditions of work. Thus, already in 1959, there were strikes in the haciendas of Paccha Grande, Chaucamayo and Chaupimayo. The strikes were immediately labelled illegal, the authorities claiming that, since the unions were illegal, the strikes must be too.

Villanueva explains the situation:

What does a strike by tenants involve? Nothing more than a stoppage of work. That's to say, a refusal to pay the *patrón* the rent for the land that is paid for with work. During the strike the boss loses the free labour to which he is entitled, and this loss in harvest time can be extremely grave. The tenant has an additional advantage. Since he is not working for the *patrón*, he has more time at his disposal for his own parcel of land. The strikes were a success in spite of their own parcel of land. The bosses were forced to give in; the peasants won. Consequently the unions spread over the valley like wildfire.[10]

Apart from the efforts made by Hugo Blanco, other Trotskyist organizers, members of POR, had been active elsewhere, notably in Puno and Arequipa.

So optimistic were they about the effects of unionizing peasants that, in November 1960, a POR Congress was held in Arequipa and an insurrectional programme was outlined. The form of insurrection was to be guerrilla warfare. The decision to embark on this was taken unanimously. Villanueva suggests that many of the delegates can hardly have realized what they had put their names to:

> It is probable that the various factors taken into account were only studied very superficially, with a great deal of optimism, and that they overestimated some of the subjective conditions. But the fact is that the voting was unanimous.
>
> It could also be that the inner voice of conscience of each delegate thought that the conclusions at which they have arrived were so utopian that it did not cost much to approve the 'insurrectional line' which, it could be safely assumed, would never be put into practice.[11]

Nevertheless the Congress was obviously aware of the weaknesses of the POR acting on its own. One of the proposals emanating from it was for the formation of a 'Revolutionary Front' that would unite the Peruvian Left around a single revolutionary programme. The Congress also appealed for advice and assistance to the Bureau of the Fourth (Trotskyist) International in Buenos Aires, known as SLATO (Secretariado Latinoamericano de Trotskismo Ortodoxo).

SLATO, aware of the activity occurring among the Peruvian peasantry, had already had a meeting of its leaders in August 1960 in Santiago de Chile to discuss the situation. Now, answering the appeal from the Peruvian POR, it organized a further meeting in Buenos Aires in April 1961, attended by delegates from Peru, Chile, Argentina, Bolivia, Uruguay and Venezuela. At this meeting the

Peruvian thesis—as outlined at the Arequipa Congress of POR—was accepted, and it was agreed to send money and trained cadres to Peru. At the same time the hope was expressed that it would be possible to step up insurrectional activity in other countries in Latin America— notably Brazil, Venezuela and Colombia—with a view to accelerating the continental revolution. The Buenos Aires meeting envisaged the possibility of developing processes similar to those in Peru, in Brazil among the peasant organizations of Francisco Julião and in Guate- mala among those of Yon Sosa.

As far as providing cadres went, SLATO was quick to fulfil its promise. In June 1961 the Argentine Trotskyist, Arturo 'Che' Pereyra, arrived in Lima, and he was followed in October by R. Creuss and a Spaniard, José Martorell, who had worked in the French Resistance during the war. All three were members of the Argentine branch of SLATO and had long revolutionary pasts.

They worked quickly and efficiently. They made sure that the paper POR appeared regularly. They formed new party cells, and they estab- lished contact with various minor organizations. The paper POR prop- agated the ideas of the Arequipa Conference, namely the need for the formation of a 'single party of the Peruvian revolution' that would unite all the groups of the revolutionary left around a single programme.

In Cuzco in June, a Revolutionary Front was created, and in December the Frente de Izquierda Revolucionaria (FIR)—the Left Revolutionary Front—was formed from a union of POR and a number of independent groups which had been gathered together within the Agrupación pro-Unificación de Izquierdas Revolucionarias (APUIR).

Ricardo Letts Colmenares has explained some of the problems confronted by FIR:

> In Lima, the FIR had got together a theoretical team of rea- sonable quality and had set up a military organization, albeit only urban, with about sixty members. Basing themselves on a somewhat exaggeratedly orthodox internationalism, the international Trotskyist organization had moved its best men to Peru. Foreign Trotskyist groups appeared in Lima and worked actively, scrupulously carrying out their party's instructions. From time to time there were visits from the top leaders of the international organization, who normally lived

abroad. All this was something completely new in the country and soon became too much for the politically underdeveloped conditions to which the Peruvian left-wing organizations had long been used to. The whole political apparatus was oddly and mistakenly mixed up with the relatively strong military apparatus. Yet neither of them was at all strongly connected with the other end of this revolutionary axis, the peasant end, the Cuzco and Convención leaders. . . .[12]

Immediately on arrival in Lima, Martorell sent Pereyra to Cuzco to work with Hugo Blanco. Pereyra was to prepare and organize guerrilla groups, while Blanco was to turn the existing peasant movement into a more solid, cohesive force.

Some time later Hugo Bressano himself, Hugo Blanco's old political mentor and the head of SLATO, arrived in Peru from Argentina. Immediately he began discussions with leaders of various leftist factions. Soon, however, it became clear that there were serious seeds of discord between the group operating out of Cuzco which was thinking in terms of organizing a guerrilla movement, and that of Bressano in Lima which had no intention of supporting anything further than the seizure of land by the peasants and the formation of peasant militias to protect their gains.

The disagreement took the form in the first instance of a refusal by the Cuzco group to consider meeting with the other organizers in Lima. Cuzco, they felt, was the obvious site. The matter was smoothed over by convincing the *Cuzqueños* that it would be worth going to Lima, and eventually Pereyra was sent down to the meetings held in Lima in February 1962.

The first major problem to be solved—indeed the fundamental problem in the whole effort—was that of raising money. In December 1961, one of the branches of the Banco Popular was 'expropriated', but all they could secure was 105,000 soles (about $4,000), nearly half of which was in new notes that could not be used since the police knew the numbers.

SLATO had originally offered a subsidy of eight or nine million Argentine pesos (about $120,000), but Villanueva doubts whether anyone took such a large offer very seriously.[13] However, some time after his arrival in Lima, Hugo Bressano announced his intention of returning to Buenos Aires with a view to winding up the accounts of his organization's branch in Argentina and handing over half a million soles (about $20,000) to the Peruvian branch as a loan. Bressano arranged that half of this should be turned over in February 1962, and the rest not later than 15 March.

Hugo Blanco's need of the money was becoming increasingly urgent since there were two congresses planned, one of the peasants of La Convención and Lares, and the other a peasant congress of the department of Cuzco. In both of these there was bound to be a serious clash between the FIR and the Communists. The latter were already planning to expel Hugo Blanco from the Peasants' Federation.

But when it came to the point, no money was forthcoming from Bressano. On 11 March 1962, Arturo Pereyra had to be sent down from Cuzco to Lima to secure the necessary funds from the National Directorate of FIR. The latter, aware that Bressano had no intention of fulfilling his promise, had already embarked on planning a second 'expropriation'—this time the branch of the Banco de Crédito in Miraflores, one of Lima's most luxurious suburbs. But the plans for this were not yet ready and in the meantime the organizers in the Cuzco area were getting desperate. At the end of March, the Departmental Directorate of FIR in Cuzco sent an ultimatum to Lima calling for a National Congress to be held in Cuzco not later than 5 April. If this was rejected, the Cuzco leadership threatened to take over the National Directorate.

But when this ultimatum reached Lima, it so happened that Bressano had just returned from Buenos Aires. Immediately he accused the Cuzco organizers of lack of discipline, and he ordered that they be expelled from their positions, Hugo Blanco among them.

Meanwhile, on 1 April, FIR's urban group in Lima had at last got hold of the car they planned to use in the attack on the Banco de Crédito, and on 12 April the operation took place. It was a complete success, and the total secured was nearly three million soles (about $120,000).

It was decided that half a million soles should be taken to Cuzco straight away. Three hundred thousand soles were to be handed over to Bressano, and the rest were left with a Peruvian in Lima to buy arms.

Apart from the money, a number of important leaders, including Pereyra, Martorell and others, were also scheduled to go to Cuzco. The problem was how to get them and the money safely there. After the assault on the bank in Miraflores, all the roads out of Lima had been closely guarded, and the authorities were in such a flap about rumoured uprisings in the Cuzco area that it was practically impossible to get into Cuzco itself without being searched. The obvious solution would have been to send them off in ones and twos by different routes, but instead of this, Bressano decided that they should all go hidden in a lorry.

The Cuzco organizers were firmly opposed to such a mad scheme, and suggested that the lorry should at least go straight to the valley of La Convención rather than risk entering Cuzco. And they were extremely hostile to the idea of the money accompanying the men. But the SLATO leaders in Lima were equally firm. Men and money would travel in one lorry to Cuzco. Villanueva comments caustically:

> It appears really as though the leadership of SLATO rather than finding solutions to problems, took delight in putting the nerves of militants and leaders to the test, playing unnecessarily with fire by placing the entire organization in danger and, what is even worse, jeopardizing the possibilities of the insurrection itself.[14]

The words do not seem to be too strong for what subsequently occurred. On the night of 24 April 1962, a hired lorry set out from Lima with a hidden compartment holding nine men. Three days and 15 police posts later they arrived at Limatambo, within 30 kilometres of Cuzco.

Awaiting them there were a number of the members of the Departmental Directorate from Cuzco. They proposed a change of plan. Instead of driving on into the city, the lorry should stop a couple of kilometres outside and the men should make their way by separate routes, moving at different hours. But the chief of the group from Lima refused and the lorry continued its journey, arriving in Cuzco at two o'clock in the morning.

Hardly was there time for four of the nine men hidden inside to disembark before a police patrol suddenly appeared. Pereyra managed to open fire and he wounded a guard, but he and another were soon captured. The others managed to get away, but the police found on Pereyra the sum of 438,000 soles (about $17,600).

That same night, 28 April, a few hours after the capture of the lorry, the surviving leaders from Lima had a meeting with those from Cuzco to discuss how matters should proceed. Martorell took over from Pereyra, but since Hugo Blanco and two of his principal assistants had been earlier demoted by Bressano, another man had to be sent from Lima to take over FIR's Departmental Directorate in Cuzco.

The night before the lorry had left Lima, Bressano, in an emotional farewell, said that he would be flying to Cuzco the next day to take part in the SLATO National Congress that was to take place there. The next day, however, saw Bressano on a plane to Buenos Aires.

And on 4 May, Hernán Boggio gave himself up voluntarily to the police. Not only had he been the chief recipient of the money, but was also a member of the Central Committee of FIR and one of the Peruvian representatives in SLATO.

Thus ended Hugo Blanco's connection with the international Trotskyist movement.[15] It had proved disastrous, but, as with Yon Sosa in Guatemala, lack of a national organization to provide him with adequate support had given him little choice. Víctor Villanueva, from whom this account is taken, perhaps paints Bressano in too villainous tones. Nevertheless, it was a sorry episode. Ricardo Letts has summed up briefly what happened:

> In Lima, the organization had begun to act. Two banks were successfully 'expropriated' by commando operations to provide funds for the revolutionary struggle. After these operations, the majority of the group was to have gone to Cuzco to make contact with the organization working in the countryside. They would have then gone on to develop tactics to coordinate the peasant 'mobilizations' for land, together with the sort of flimsy *ad hoc* union organization based around a leader and some very elementary slogans, and finally the guerrilla force which was about to be set up. . . .

> There were serious differences in Lima amongst members of the political leadership and even worse ones between them and the military unit. To cap it all, relations between all these and the international leadership were at breaking point. Two

factors were especially important in this situation: One of them was the question of what was to be used, distributed, accounted for and kept; this was the main point which provoked difficulties with the international leadership. The other was the question of the chain of command and the complete and profound lack of knowledge of the tactical line to be taken. This was what caused difficulties between the political bureau and the military organization. When the time to act was close, the need for having a political leadership at all was discussed, and if so, whether it should be above the military leadership.[16]

Left to his own devices, Hugo Blanco could do little else but continue to create peasant unions. But together with this work, he moved on to a new stage: that of encouraging the peasants actually to occupy the land, under the slogan '*Tierra o Muerte*'.[17] In his capacity as Secretary of the Agrarian Reform of the Peasants' Federation of La Convención, he issued the following decree:

1) The General Assembly of each union shall nominate an 'agrarian reform commission' from within itself.

2) The tenants (*arrendires*) and the sub-tenants (*allegados*) are automatically converted into the owners of the land they work.

3) Uncultivated land is to be distributed in plots, beginning with the poorest peasants.

4) Lands in which plantations have been planted for the owner shall remain in his power, provided that his attitude has not been characterized by a human outrage. If it has, these cultivations, and possibly the hacienda house, shall pass collectively into the power of the union to be used as a school, etc.

5) The authorities in the service of the bosses may not intervene, for the only people who understand agrarian reality properly are the peasants themselves.[18]

But deserted by the Trotskyists and under continued continental attack from the Communists, Hugo Blanco became increasingly isolated. And bearing in mind the isolation of the La Convención Valley itself— it is only connected with the outside world by a narrow gauge, single-line railway used chiefly for bringing tourists from Cuzco to Machu Picchu—there was little hope of his revolutionary ideas spreading far.

The seizures of land that he helped to organize were soon put down brutally by the police and the army, which moved into the valley towards the end of 1962. In the meantime Hugo Blanco got himself into more serious trouble.

A rich and powerful landowner in the valley had raped the wife and one of the younger daughters of a peasant named Tiburcio Bolaños. The landowner, as was normal, then accused the peasant of threatening him and demanded that he should appear at the post of the Civil Guard to explain his action. When a police sergeant arrived to tell the unfortunate peasant that he should report to the office of the Civil Guard, Bolaños replied that nothing would induce him to do anything of the kind. The sergeant then sent two policemen to capture the recalcitrant peasant. However, on the way they fell in with the landowner and a number of others, and by the time they got within striking distance of Bolaños's hut, they were all drunk. So they sent a boy ahead to tell Bolaños that he should appear immediately before the Civil Guard. The boy returned, saying that Bolaños had promised to turn up at the police post the following day. Whereupon the inebriated and infuriated landowner got down off his horse and loosed off with his revolver, wounding the boy in the left arm.

When the boy's mother eventually found him, she immediately complained to the Secretary-General of the peasants' union of Ocayara—Tiburcio Bolaños. He immediately wanted to set off for the town of Quillabamba to denounce the crime before a judge, but another peasant advised him to discuss his complaint first with Hugo Blanco.

Blanco called a meeting of the union, listened to Bolaños' story, and then organized a group to go with him the following day to the town of Pucyura. Knowing how dangerous the landowner and his men were likely to be, and being after all a revolutionary, Hugo Blanco planned to get arms from the police post in Pucyura.

At five o'clock in the afternoon of 13 November 1962, Blanco left his group outside the police post and went in alone. He found a guard, one of the soldiers who had been sent the previous day to capture Bolaños, and he explained to him that as the landowner's men were armed, his men needed to be armed too. Blanco then asked the police guard to hand over all the arms in the police post. The man refused, and Blanco threatened him with his revolver. The policeman tried to fire, but Blanco fired first. After an exchange of fire, the policemen fell wounded. Later he died.

But the attack on the post had not proved of much value. Blanco and his men only managed to secure three rifles, a revolver and some ammunition and equipment. And instead of being a group that had come to investigate the crimes of the landowner, they had turned into fugitives from justice for having killed a policeman.

From then on, Hugo Blanco was on the run. Under severe repression the peasants often turned against him. The Communists too made propaganda against him. Ricardo Letts comments:

> Instead of guiding, hardening and strengthening the peasant masses who had followed him throughout the whole process of agitation and strikes, this development made them fall back even further than they had been before, largely because of police repression. Faced with this, Blanco felt abandoned not only by his own organization, the FIR, which had been destroyed by the police in Lima and then in Cuzco, but now by the peasants as well. With no political or theoretical training, and with no real experience of armed insurrection, they relapsed into apathy without really understanding what had been going on.

Hugo Blanco was captured on 29 May 1963. He was imprisoned, later tried, and sentenced to 20 years' imprisonment. He sits in an island jail off the coast of Callao, writing and occasionally receiving visiting journalists.

Notes

1   The following account is taken directly from Villanueva, *Hugo Blanco*.

2   Ibid., p. 75.

3   Inadequately, I am told.

4   Written from Chaupimayo, c. October 1962; quoted in Marío A. Malpica, *Biografía de la revolución*: *historia y antología del pensamiento socialista*, Ediciones Ensayos Sociales, Lima, 1967, pp. 468–71.

5   The situation of the peasants in La Convención is ably dealt with in the CIDA Report on Peru, pp. 206–9.

6   Villanueva, *Hugo Blanco*, p. 75.

7   Adolfo Gilly, 'Los sindicatos guerrilleros del Perú', *Marcha*, Montevideo, August 1963. The reader must once again be reminded of Gilly's Trotskyist sympathies, which make him hostile to orthodox Communist activities.

8   Wesley W. Craig Jr, in his paper paper presented to the seminar on peasant movements in Latin America, Cornell University (December 1966) 'The Peasant Movement of La Convención, Peru: Dynamics of Rural Labour Organization', says that there were 'over sixty'. He also calculates that there were between 10,000 and 11,000 tenant farmers in the valley.

9   Hugo Blanco, *El camino de nuestra revolución*, Ediciones Revolución Peruana, Lima, 1964.

10 Villanueva, *Hugo Blanco*, p. 77.

11 Villanueva, *Hugo Blanco*, p. 79.

12 Ricardo Letts Colmenares, 'Perú: revolución, insurrección, guerrillas', *Partisans* (Paris), quoted in Malpica, *Biografía de la revolución*, pp. 476–8. The same article is published, under the pseudonym 'Americo Pumaruna', in *Pensamiento Crítico* (Havana), NO. 1. It was first published in *Cuadernos de Ruedo Ibérico*, NO. 6, April–May 1966.

13 Villanueva, *Hugo Blanco*, p. 93.

14 Ibid., p. 120.

15 See also Gonzalo Añi Castillo, *Historia Secreta de las Guerrillas*, Ediciones 'Mas Alla', Lima, 1967, which contains an account of the trial of FIR members involved in bank robberies.

16 Ricardo Letts, 'Perú': revolución, insurreción, guerrillas.

17 'Land or Death'; a mixture of Zapata's post-1916 cry '*Tierra y Libertad*', and Fidel Castro's slogan '*Patria o Muerte*'.

18 Villanueva, *Hugo Blanco*, pp. 127–8.

Bolivia

17. Régis Debray, during his trial at Camiri, with Captain Hurtado of the Bolivian Navy.

18. The grave of Tania at Vallegrande.

19.1. Poster on the streets of Camiri attacking Debray: 'He who lives by the sword shall die by the sword'.

19.2. Che Guevara at the camp at Nancahuazú.

20.1–24. The following nine photographs were probably taken by Che Guevara himself during the course of the Bolivian campaign. They come from the roll of film that was found in his rucksack.

20.2.

21.1.

21.2.

22.1.

22.2.

23.1.

23.2.

24.

In the very month that Hugo Blanco was captured, May 1963, help was on its way. A group of young Peruvian intellectuals, returning to the country from Cuba, planned to bring him armed assistance. Among them was a young 21-year-old poet, Javier Heraud. A typical product of the Peruvian upper classes, he had been educated at Markham, the English public school in Lima, and at the Catholic University. But, turning against his upbringing, he became an extremely short-lived revolutionary. Perhaps because of his aristocratic antecedents, or because of his promise as a poet, his death caused a great commotion in Peru. Later, when guerrillas sprang up again in 1965, one of the various fronts took the name of Javier Heraud.

The Peruvian military have given the following account of the action that led to his death.[1] On 2 May 1963, two boats moored in the Rio Manuripe near a hacienda called 'Tres Barrancas' on the Bolivian side of the Peruvian frontier. About 40 men disembarked. There they made contact with two Bolivian Communists, Roberto Soria and Abelardo Murakami Baca. Murakami, who was married to a Peruvian, was responsible for taking them across the frontier into Peru. He set off on 6 May with about 15 men, travelling through the jungle. First they went to a Peruvian hacienda called Santa Maria, and then they moved towards Ahiringayoc and Puerto Maldonado—the largest town in the area.

On 14 May a police sergeant in Puerto Maldonado was told that there was a suspicious group of men staying in a hotel. There were six of them, including Javier Heraud, and after their papers had been examined they were taken to the local police post. But hardly had they left their hotel before they turned on the three policemen who were supposed to be guarding them. One was killed. The six guerrillas managed to escape, but they were unable to get very far. Three of them were captured that night, and the following day, 15 May, there was a clash at a spot called La Cachuela, and Javier Heraud was killed. The two who were left were also captured in the next few days, one of them across the frontier at Aposento, in Bolivia.

A more sympathetic chronicler, Ricardo Letts, has given a different story:

> The revolutionary group consisted of about thirty-five men trained in guerrilla warfare and with some background in Marxist politics. A number of them had been members of Peruvian left-wing parties, which they had left for reasons which were often related to the need to take armed action. . . .
>
> The strategic and tactical plan was to enter Peru armed, cross the two hundred miles of jungle between the frontier and the valleys where the peasants led by Hugo Blanco were operating, and lend them military aid, which they obviously needed. The group would consist of a nucleus which by co-ordinating action with the peasant masses in the area would work towards the taking of power. The members of the group, all of great valour and courage, were mainly from the middle class; a few were from working class and even peasant families. Almost all were university students. . . .
>
> The events of 15 May 1963 were as follows: there was a skirmish in the streets of Puerto Maldonado between the spearhead of the group and the local police who appeared on the scene to arrest them. The next thing was the pursuit of the revolutionaries by the armed forces and local landowners with hunting weapons. These groups had been on the alert for some days, as the presence of guerrillas in a jungle area near Puerto Maldonado had given them away. The manhunt lasted some days, and cost the life of the young prize-winning poet and fighter for the revolution, Javier Heraud, a member of the advance guard. . . .[2]

A letter to the Peruvian press, written in July 1963 (but not published until 1967), gives more detail as to what actually happened, but is non-communicative about what the group was doing in Puerto Maldonado and what it planned to do. It was written by the survivors of this ill-fated *foco*:

After walking across four hundred miles of jungle, we reached Puerto Maldonado tired, hungry and sick in the early hours of the night of 14 May. We had crossed the frontier with Bolivia three days before and we imagined that from this city—which is part of Peruvian territory—we could travel on legally to our homes; a right which we were arbitrarily refused.

We remembered perfectly that as we entered Puerto Maldonado we could hear Belaúnde's election speeches. Loudspeakers filled the air with expressions like 'Peru for the Peruvians, renovation and revolution'.

However, when we were registering at a hotel we were rudely interrupted by a group of policemen and a member of the PIP [the Peruvian criminal investigation police] who asked for our documents. Despite the fact that these were in order, we were forced to go, guarded, to the police station. When we protested about this arbitrary and unjustified action we were told we might be smugglers. So we asked them to search our luggage, which they refused to do, insisting arrogantly on arresting us. During this short journey we continued to protest since there was no reason for such treatment. With half a block to go we refused to follow the squad.

Most of us were returning from Cuba, a beautiful country where we had been studying and finding out what the creative advance of national liberation can achieve.

As the Peruvian government, breaking the Constitution, prevented citizens who went to Socialist countries from returning freely, we tried to get in secretly. Faced with the prospect of being arrested and exiled if we tried to return the normal way, we met in La Paz and decided to enter through the jungle of Madre de Dios.

When the police surrounded us at the door of the Hotel Chávez, we remembered the hundreds of Peruvians imprisoned without trial and shut up in prison; the hellish settlement of 'El Sepa' and the all too famous 'Frontón'. It was natural that we should all decide, without any previous plan, that the only solution was to run for it. But somebody had to make the first move, and it was the police themselves. As we protested, the officer in charge of the squad threatened us and gave a command which we didn't understand but which made the police move to their pistols.

It has been impossible to find out who fired first, although they say, without sufficient details, that it was one of us. Anyway, there was an exchange of fire as we ran in several directions. It has also been impossible to find out who fired the shot which mortally wounded Sgt Sam Jara, or who wounded our companion Nelson Rodríguez in the base of the skull, failing to kill him by a fraction of an inch.

Two of us were captured that night (as we didn't know the town we got trapped in a blind alley), and the rest were fiercely hunted down, with the distinguished Peruvian poet Javier Heraud Pérez being killed . . . .

The next day in the afternoon, Heraud and Elías were surprised trying to get across the Madre de Dios river. Hundreds of people witnessed the butchery they were subjected to. The evidence of the owner of the canoe who came to pick them up from the waters of the river indicates that without any warning the police opened fire with rifles and machine-guns. We will let the heartfelt words of Dr Jorge Heraud, Javier's father, tell us the story:

. . . 'In the middle of the Madre de Dios river, drifting, without oars, my son could have been captured without any need for shooting, especially as his companion had hoisted a white flag. Despite this, the police and the civilians whom they encouraged, fired at them pointblank for an hour and a half, and even used bullets used for hunting animals. When my son's companion shouted: "Stop shooting" (they were near the bank where they were shooting from, according to what I was told by the inhabitants), a captain shouted: "Fire, we must finish them off." A lieutenant, more humane and more respectful of the laws of war which forbid firing on an unarmed and wounded enemy, stopped the shooting, but it was too late. An explosive bullet had made a huge hole in my unfortunate son's stomach and his body had been struck by many more bullets. Thus ended the physical life of my son, who with his twenty-one years and his illusions, had tried to begin the process of ending the ills, which he said should be banished from our country. . . .'[3]

Javier Heraud, winner of the 'Young Poet of Peru' prize with a book whose title is strangely related to his dramatic death, *The River*, was already internationally recognized as one of the leading young poets of Latin America. One of his poems appears in a world anthology published in France.

Together with Heraud, Roberto Vásquez was also killed by the police: he was a poor peasant who was in the canoe which approached Heraud and Elías before the shooting began. Surprised by the shooting, all Vásquez managed to do was to jump overboard and hang on to the stern, as he didn't know how to swim, shouting to them not to hurt him. A bullet in the skull, fired from the bank, silenced him for ever.

The ferocity of the manhunt, the huge reinforcements sent from the capital, as well as the 'impressive' interrogation we were given, when they asked us about 'Hugo Blanco' and another forty imaginary friends of ours who were supposed to be coming with sub-machine-guns, show that the police acted out of fear, fear out of all proportion to the real danger offered by six exhausted students, only armed with pistols with a maximum range of fifty yards, who were trying to pass peacefully through the area.

Those of the original group who had not penetrated as far as Puerto Maldonado heard the news of the clash on the radio. Judging discretion to be the better part of valour, they withdrew again to Bolivia, and spent an anxious time trying to avoid falling into the hands of the Bolivian police. For two years they disappeared from public view, though during this time they formed the '15 May Movement'—to commemorate the clash at Puerto Maldonado. This group, led by Héctor Béjar, began to work among the peasants in the province of Huanta, in the department of Ayacucho. Later it formed the nucleus of the Ejército de Liberación Nacional (ELN)—the National Liberation Army.

Later still, after the death of Che Guevara in 1967, the pro-Chinese Communists in Bolivia were to cite the Puerto Maldonado episode as yet another example of the perfidy of the pro-Russian Communists in Bolivia:

Puerto Maldonado, Peru, a town on the frontier with Bolivia, scene of the first betrayal by Monje's revisionists.[4] The Peruvian guerrilla group, on your instructions,[5] stayed in Bolivia under the safe-keeping and directions of Monje and his clique. The Bolivian political police, led by San Román,[6] were informed personally of the presence of these guerrillas by the Monje brothers themselves. It has been fully proved that Monje is linked to San Román. The Peruvian government found out about the guerrillas and the fact that they were going to enter Peruvian territory, with the result that several of them were murdered soon after they crossed the frontier. The grave of the revolutionary poet, Javier Heraud, is a monument to revisionist betrayal. The guerrillas who managed to return to Bolivian territory were released as refugees and went to live in the houses of the Bolivian Marxist–Leninists,[7] thus showing their repudiation of the betrayal by Monje and his clique. There are witnesses of what happened at Puerto Maldonado who can establish the historical truth on these two points: Who put them in the hands of revisionists? What was the role of the revisionists?[8]

The exact story of what happened at Puerto Maldonado will remain obscure for some time to come. In his book on the Peruvian guerrillas of 1964, Héctor Béjar writes that there were a series of occurrences which it is not yet timely to explain.[9]

Notes

1   *Las Guerrillas en el Perú y su represión*, Ministerio de Guerra, Lima, 1966, p. 29.

2   Colmenares, 'Perú: revolución, insurreción, guerrillas'.

3   Rogger Mercado, *Las Guerrillas del Perú, el MIR: de la prédica ideológica a la acción armada*, Fondo de Cultura Popular, Lima, 1967, pp. 55–60.

4   Marío Monje, Secretary-General of the Bolivian Communist party.

5   Fidel Castro's.

6   According to Antonio Arguedas, San Román, who was head of Paz Estenssoro's political police, had been trained by the FBI.

7   The pro-Chinese elements within the Bolivian Communist party.

8   Quoted in a letter from Oscár Zamora, leader of the pro-Chinese Bolivian Communist party, to Fidel Castro, July 1968, printed in *Los Tiempos* (Cochabamba), 14 July 1968.

9   Héctor Béjar, *Perú 1965: apuntes sobre una experiéncia guerrillera*, Casa de las Americas, Havana, 1969.

At the time when Hugo Blanco was effectively in decline—towards the end of 1962—another revolutionary figure came up to Quillabamba to meet him. Although Luís de la Puente Uceda had not at that stage attained the fame accorded to Hugo Blanco, he had received a certain notoriety in political circles as the man who had led an important group of radicals out of APRA in 1959 to form APRA Rebelde.

De la Puente was the most important guerrilla leader produced by Peru, and he ranks with Che Guevara and Camilo Torres as among the most impressive intellectuals of the Latin American Revolution. (Hugo Blanco was a peasant organizer rather than a guerrilla chief.) He was born in 1926, the son of a landowner. He was distantly related to the APRA leader, Haya de la Torre, and from his childhood he had been an APRA supporter. At the time of the 1948 *coup d'état* by Manuel Odría, when APRA was declared illegal, de la Puente, together with other *Apristas*, was imprisoned and subsequently exiled. For some years he lived in Mexico where he made contact with many other Latin American leftists in a similar position to his own, debarred from returning to their countries.

In 1954 he entered Peru secretly with a view to preparing an insurrection against Odría's dictatorship. Various *Apristas* were involved in the scheme, though not the leadership. Before their plans had matured, however, de la Puente and his friends were betrayed and captured. Once again he found himself in prison. From the little that is known of the plans of his group, it appears that they were trying to repeat the experience of the Bolivian Revolution of 1952, which, in a country not dissimilar from Peru, had succeeded in bringing about enormous changes within a very short period of time. There is no evidence that they were planning to launch a guerrilla movement.

Some months before the 1956 elections, de la Puente, together with a number of other political prisoners, was released. He returned to the University of Trujillo to continue his law studies. His chief interest was in the land problem, and in 1957 he completed his thesis under the title, *Towards the Agrarian Reform in Peru* (published at the end of 1966 as *La Reforma del Agro Peruano*).

At that time he was a fervent Catholic, and he shared APRA's generally anti-Communist outlook. In his thesis he described how:

America and the world have before them, on the one hand, divine paths of justice, peace, and love, shown by the Divine Redemptor, which unfortunately have not until now been brought into the socio-economic plane, and on the other, imminent danger of a very bloody awakening of the Indian peasantry which could well be used as a platform by international Communism.

Like many Latin American leftists, de la Puente's principal motivating force was nationalism, and it was not surprising that, in the company of many other young hopefuls stirred by events in the Caribbean, he should have found himself in Cuba in July 1959, barely six months after the success of the Revolution.

The occasion was the First National Agrarian Reform Forum, held in Havana. There were many delegates present from all over the continent. They had come to exchange opinions, and to discuss the possibilities for land reform in their own countries in the light of the Cuban experience. Within no time at all, de la Puente was arguing heatedly with the Cuban President Dorticós about the 'capitalist' nature of the Cuban reform: 'It is essential to decide whether we are talking about an agrarian reform based on capitalism, that is to say, a reform which distinguishes between capitalists and Socialists.' De la Puente added that the Cuban reform law must be capitalist 'because it recognizes and respects property'. He then asked Dorticós if the agrarian reform law was really so. Dorticós replied:

'As far as your definition goes, I would change the terms a little. The agrarian reform law is not Socialist, but neither do I think it could be described as a capitalist law, if we consider what capitalism is today, as it does not recognize the existence of large land holdings. . . . Thus I would not accept that definition literally.'

'I am making this distinction,' argued de la Puente, 'in the light of modern agrarian thinking, which considers a capitalist agrarian reform to be one where property is respected. . . .'

At this point a delegate from the Cuban 26 July Movement interrupted: 'I don't really know what legal system has given you the experience to define an agrarian reform as capitalist or non-capitalist.' De la Puente, who was described at the forum as 'the APRA delegate', answered as follows:

We Peruvian delegates are here to represent Aprismo and it is this party which for the last thirty years in Latin America has been calling for what the 26 July Movement is now carrying out, for let it be said that we have tried to do it but have never been able to bring it to fruition. We are the staunchest defenders of Cuba's great experience and this agrarian reform, and we shall have to borrow many points from it to include in our own party's outlook on agrarian matters; but that does not mean that we are frightened of terms.

He then returned to the attack, asking the Cuban delegates for a definition, and citing the cases of the Bolivian, Guatemalan and Chinese agrarian reforms which, he claimed, 'we cannot call Socialist reforms'. 'The capitalism proposed by the 26 July Movement,' he added, 'is capitalism, as Dr Fidel Castro has said, with justice and freedom.'

The Cuban delegate spoke again to ask the Peruvian whether:

when he describes the 26 July Movement in terms determined by the process of historical transformation which it is carrying out, he should not use adjectives which the 26 July Movement

does not use to describe itself. 'We use the word humanism,'—
he added—'which is an essential part of us. . . .'[1]

The enthusiasm for the Cuban Revolution among numerous
young *Apristas* was not shared by the leadership of APRA. Already, a
sizeable group within APRA, especially among the youth sections, had
become seriously disillusioned with the policies of the leadership,
which were characterized by a willingness to seek a share in power at
the sacrifice of virtually every political principle that the party had
held during 30 years of revolutionary struggle. Consequently, in
October 1959, when the Fourth Convention of APRA was held, de la
Puente and others presented a motion that was critical both of Manuel
Prado's government and of the APRA leadership which was supporting that government. As a result, they were suspended from the party,
and on 12 October they formed a committee within APRA called the
'Comité Aprista de Defensa de los Principios y de la Democracia
Interna'. The objective of this committee was to remind the party of
the principles for which it was supposed to stand.

This group subsequently became the 'Comité Aprista Rebelde',
and finally, a year later, in November 1960, cutting their ties with the
parent party, the name was reduced to simple 'APRA Rebelde'.

That month APRA Rebelde produced its first considered policy
document, the 'Manifesto of Chiclayo'. This was largely the work of
Héctor Cordero, a former *Aprista* who had left the party long before
the 1959 Fourth Convention, and who had subsequently studied
Marxism in Argentina. It largely consisted of an analysis of the internal situation in Peru, and it was incomparably more radical than anything that APRA itself had produced for many years.

Much of APRA Rebelde's political work consisted in agitating on
behalf of a radical land reform. In November 1961, just a year after
they had set themselves up in independence from APRA proper,
APRA Rebelde presented a draft Agrarian Reform Law to Congress.
After circulating for a while in a mimeographed form, the draft law
was eventually printed in Carlos Malpica's book, *Guerra o muerte al latifundio*, at the end of 1963. In the inside cover of the book, under the
title: 'The MIR's agrarian reform: challenge to the oligarchy', Luís de
la Puente wrote the following lines:

Fulfilling the historic mandate of the blood spilt by the thugs of the *Ochenio* and the period of the *Convivencia*, the First National Assembly of *APRA Rebelde* named a committee to draw up an overview of the Peruvian agrarian situation to serve as a banner to lead peasant struggles in the country.

During 1960 and 1961 several committees combined to bring together the Agrarian Reform Law presented to Parliament by the national deputy, Carlos Malpica Silva Santistebán, on 6 November 1961.

The various committees consisted of comrades Carlos de la Puente, Dr Luís de la Puente, Dr Gonzalo Fernández Gasco, Máximo Velezmorro, Dr Luís Ibérico Mas, Dr Luís Pérez Malpica and many other comrades, peasants, workers and students, who contributed in one way or another to the drawing up and polishing of this instrument of struggle for the Peruvian people.

It is worth noting that one of the martyrs of the Colombian and Latin America Revolutions, Antonio Larrota,[2] founder-leader of the 'Workers', Students' and Peasants' Movement' (MOEC) in Colombia, took part in the discussion of the draft project, as did Dr Juan Gualberto Caballero and Fernando Aguiar, of the Cuban 26 July Movement, and the Argentine comrades Jorge Hammar and Olga Martín.

The draft law we are talking about does not contain a SOCIALIST exposition of Peruvian agrarian problems. It is rather an instrument of struggle in certain defined conditions aimed mainly at beginning the process of transforming the countryside.

Turning this study into a draft law and putting it before Parliament was meant to show that our movement, in spite of being only two years old, was in a position to contribute worthwhile solutions and serious expositions of problems, and had got over the outworn tendency of getting bogged down in vaporous generalities.

We knew perfectly well that a draft law like ours, in spite of being consciously moulded to the political, economic and social conditions of the country, was condemned to be filed and forgotten, because it contained precise and weighty proposals aimed at the large estates, which, together with American imperialism, are the main reasons for the poverty and backwardness of our country.

It was a challenge to the oligarchy and the national bourgeoisie, represented by the followers of Prado and Odría, APRA, Acción Popular and the Christian Democrats. It provided the proof that the people needed to fully understand that these groups, whatever the demagogic mask they put on, are prevented by their own nature from undertaking the transformation of the country. What we are witnessing in this government with the farce of the 'Agrarian Reform' is the final proof that they are incapable of even beginning the process.

We had been very realistic when we drew up the plan. We were fully aware that *ad hoc* radical measures lead nowhere. We were convinced that the struggle against imperialism and feudalism demands the unity of the exploited or neglected sectors in the country and in the towns. It was essential to set up a united front of those exploiting land in common, serfs, settlers, sharecroppers of various kinds, tenant farmers, temporary and seasonal labourers, and small and medium farmers, who together with progressive workers, craftsmen, students, professionals and technicians, could destroy the common enemy: the large estate.

The Indian community is the corner-stone of the draft law we are discussing. We start with the community and hope to come to the modern Socialist community. We bring in the traditional Indian forms of organization in order to provide sound foundations for the future.

Because we have faith in the people and in the revolution and because we are sustained by a well-defined ideology, because we know that the path is made by advancing, we do not spend time on maximalist theorizing. We intend to begin the process. We are getting ready to begin the Long March.[3]

In June 1962, when the leaders of APRA Rebelde felt that any connection with APRA was a liability, they decided to change the name again, emerging this time as the Movimiento de Izquierda Revolucionaria (MIR)—Movement of the Revolutionary Left—adopting the same name that had been taken by the dissidents from Rómulo Betancourt's Acción Democrática in Venezuela. The Secretary-General of the metamorphosed organization was de la Puente.

According to one story, de la Puente was responsible for killing in a fight during the course of 1961 a member of APRA called Francisco Sarmiento. He was sent to prison for a year. During this period he became increasingly convinced of the need to provide radical peasants with armed backing. Although he and many other members of the Peruvian MIR had travelled to Cuba, there was no question of their adopting a blind acceptance of the Cuban road to revolution. Nor was there unanimity in the ranks of the MIR about the need to embark on a guerrilla struggle. Some felt that the political conditions were not right, and that the revolutionary potential of the peasants had been exaggerated.

But de la Puente had a reasonably clear idea of what it was necessary to do, and in October 1962 he journeyed to Quillabamba to interview Hugo Blanco, whose ideas about the development of the peasant struggle seemed to be moving along similar lines.

The meeting between Hugo Blanco and Luís de la Puente in October 1962 should have been of historic importance, but in practice it added up to little more than a historic footnote. There is no direct record of what happened, though it emerged afterwards that the two leaders had agreed to disagree. The differences between them outweighed the points of common interest. Hugo Blanco had by this time argued himself around to the need for peasant militias, but he had nowhere near reached the position of de la Puente who was firmly convinced that nothing short of a full-scale guerrilla campaign, with a fixed base in the mountains, could provide the peasants with the defence that they needed.

Apart from these tactical–military problems, they were miles apart ideologically. Although de la Puente had been brought up as a Catholic and an APRA militant, he was now a 'Marxist–Leninist' of the

Cuban brand. And at that stage this ideology was still at daggers drawn with the 'Marxism–Trotskyism' of Hugo Blanco and SLATO. As Víctor Villanueva has pointed out, even if the two revolutionaries had managed to come to some kind of personal accord, neither of them was a free agent.[4] Both had organizations behind them that they could not afford to ignore. To have reached a lasting agreement, de la Puente, in his capacity as the Secretary-General of MIR, would have been better advised to have approached the political directorate of SLATO. Immediately the idea becomes absurd. SLATO had sufficient problems with Hugo Blanco. They could hardly have taken on de la Puente as well.

Conceivably several years later their paths might have converged more closely. In 1962 Fidel Castro had not yet moved to the independent position vis-à-vis Moscow and Peking that was to characterize the Castroite movements in the continent by 1967, by which time Hugo Blanco had become 'a popular Latin American hero' in the Cuban pantheon.[5] In later years, Hugo Blanco might have disengaged himself from the dogmatism of SLATO and have looked with more favour on the guerrilla thesis of de la Puente. But this is pure speculation. De la Puente is dead; Hugo Blanco is serving a 20-year prison sentence.

Nevertheless the question why Cuban support was forthcoming for the MIR and not for the FIR is an intriguing one. Villanueva thinks that it was due less to Hugo Blanco's position as a Trotskyist than to the fact that Fidel knew and approved of de la Puente—whose ideas on guerrilla warfare were not dissimilar from his own—while he was unfamiliar personally with Hugo Blanco and, perhaps more importantly, with the leadership of SLATO.

A spokesman for another Peruvian leftist group, Vanguardia Revolucionaria, writing in 1966 under the pseudonym of 'Silvestre Condoruna', explains the situation as follows:

> The Trotskyist position of Blanco and the definite Socialist
> character of his movement together with the probable distrust
> of the flexibility of tactical and strategic schemes derived from
> a system of highly rationalized ideas which had been marginal,
> if not in opposition, to the development of the victorious
> Cuban guerrilla and of 'Castroism' as a politico-ideological

tendency, were, it appears the most important factors in the aid given to the MIR, and to the abandonment of Blanco.

It was a curious decision if one takes into account the fact that a guerrilla war cannot prosper without definite support from the organized peasantry; and the group most rooted among the peasantry and with the greatest prestige among their movement was, precisely, the FIR, and Blanco was the most respected and obeyed leader. The MIR, on the other hand, at that stage, took no effective part in the development of the peasant movement.[6]

All that remains of the meeting of the two revolutionaries is the memory of a missed opportunity and, apparently, a film of the joint demonstration that they held in Quillabamba, where they both addressed the crowd. The film was subsequently shown in Havana.[7]

In 1964 the MIR began to define its position more closely. In the long speech quoted earlier, made by de la Puente in Lima's Plaza San Martín on 7 February 1964, some of the main planks of policy were outlined. Some months later, in July 1964, the MIR published its major policy document, *Nuestra posición frente a la revolución mundial* (*Our Position in the Light of the World Revolution*). This was basically the work of Héctor Cordero, Ricardo Napurí and Guillermo Lobatón, but it drew on many of the ideas that had been outlined by de la Puente in his speech in February.

While not endorsing the Chinese position, the MIR document is devoted to a very serious criticism of the Russian policy of peaceful co-existence. It admits that imperialism is quite capable of unleashing a nuclear Third World War, and that the decision of the Socialist countries to opt for peaceful co-existence is therefore quite understandable. But it points out that, although there can be peaceful co-existence between equal and sovereign states, it is unthinkable between colonies and the metropolis. Colonized peoples and exploited classes must engage in an intransigent struggle which, in the last resort, may involve revolutionary war.

Such a struggle, the MIR document argues, is in fact a contribution to peaceful co-existence, for, by fighting for their liberation, those countries that are at present in a state of dependence are helping to weaken imperialism's strongest supports. This is the best way of avoiding a Third World War, for even if the imperialists do eventually unleash a war, they will do so in less favourable conditions. An indefinite postponement of national liberation revolutions will not contribute to peaceful co-existence, nor will it diminish the danger of the destruction of the human race by nuclear weapons. Since imperialism has never renounced its war plans, such a policy would leave it with its hands free.

One cannot assume either that the economic victory of the Socialist over the capitalist camp, after long peaceful competition, will gain new countries for the Socialist cause. The revolution can only be advanced by the efforts of each individual country, and, in the colonial and semi-colonial countries at least, the road followed will be violent.

The principal contradiction of our time, the MIR document continues, is between the colonial and semi-colonial countries and the imperialist metropolis. In their state of exploitation, the peoples of these countries cannot stay quiet in the name of an uncertain world peace, nor in the hope of liberation from outside. Already they have put themselves in the vanguard of the world revolution.

History shows that the revolutionary road runs through the underdeveloped countries. Except for Czechoslovakia and East Germany, all countries that have become Socialist were underdeveloped. The conditions of the exploited classes within the metropolis countries have improved immeasurably compared with the last century, and so naturally the vanguard is now composed of those who more urgently feel the need for revolution. By struggling for their own liberation, they are also contributing to the liberation of the working classes of the imperial powers and to the consolidation of the Socialist camp.

In Latin America, the MIR policy document continues, 'the most important semi-colony of the most powerful empire in the world and in history: yankee imperialism'—the revolution will be a single one. No revolution in the continent will be safe while 'the great monster of the north' survives. The beginning of the Latin American Revolution was marked by the Cuban Revolution. This was the triumphant beginning of the second great effort for the emancipation of Latin America. But it would be difficult for an authentic revolution to take place, as it did in

Cuba, in isolation. In all probability the Latin American Revolution will be played out in one great single war of all the oppressed peoples of the continent against the imperialist monster.

Only a Socialist revolution, states the document, can lead the way out of underdevelopment. And it must be a revolution with arms in the hands of the people. Failure to arm the people explains the breakdown of the Guatemalan Revolution and the backward steps taken by the revolution in Bolivia.

The revolutionary road, says the document—echoing the Chinese—runs through the countryside.

> The peasantry in these countries is not only the most numerous class but also the most exploited. The problem of land is the key problem. It is an insoluble problem, faced with which all efforts at reform have failed. The countryside, therefore, is the weakest part of the whole system.

It is also the most vulnerable because the power of the state is essentially concentrated in the cities. There the feudal oligarchy and the bourgeoisie have constructed impregnable fortresses which smash the revolutionary impetus of the working class, which needs the assistance of the peasantry to help to destroy it.

Peru is living through a pre-revolutionary stage of unprecedented depth and continuity. 'If the revolution has been checked and the revolutionary parties have failed, it is not because conditions have not existed—conditions have existed for a long time, even better than those in Cuba—but because the right road has not been found.' The tendency has been, continues the MIR document, to follow the pattern of bourgeois revolutions, struggling in the cities and making the urban proletariat the pivot of the revolution.

This erroneous view failed to take into account the special circumstances (the First World War) surrounding the Russian Revolution, and the fact that when the bourgeoisie took power, it had already got a substantial share in it, and could take over with a lightning stroke. The proletariat, on the other hand, has never had any share in power.

The document concludes with a note of optimism. If some conditions are lacking, it states, they will be created. The revolution should begin now. 'The masses will respond to the call of a revolution, which is able, with its first successes, to show them a new form of struggle.'[8]

Shortly after this major policy statement was published, in July 1964, the principal leaders of the MIR retired from public view and retreated into clandestinity to begin organizing the guerrilla struggle. Their first guerrilla hideouts were to be up in the mountains. 'We envisage,' wrote de la Puente, 'a people's war pushing outward from the Andes to the coast, from the countryside to the cities, from the provinces to the capital.' He has left a very full account—perhaps the most comprehensive of any Latin American guerrilla leader—of what he considered would be the effect of his planned guerrilla war.[9] First, he deals with the peasants:

> We think our insurrectional process will assume new forms characteristic of a real agrarian revolution, and the peasant mass actions will start with the invasion of the *latifundios* usurped from the communities and peasant groups, under the leadership of clandestine cells and committees of the revolutionary party and supported by guerrilla groups. Peasants will organize their own defensive militias and, according to their ideological level and enthusiasm, will be incorporated into the guerrilla bands or the rebel army ranks.

Secondly, de la Puente explains how the guerrilla action in the peasant areas would be capable of making the leap to the towns:

> The working class continues its process of radicalization, beginning with the miners and farm labourers. Further, the unemployed and underemployed people in the shanty towns, suffering from alienation and misery, are in a position to understand the social and economic differences prevailing in the country owing to their living in the cities as servants of the oligarchs, as exploited labourers, as itinerant salesmen, or as mere witnesses of the ostentation of the oligarchs, of their luxurious dwellings and their insensibility and contempt for the people. These victims of the system can easily become an uncontrollable avalanche in a certain stage of the revolutionary process.

Within this conception of a people's war, guerrillas act as catalysts of the social outburst, seed for the rebel army, instruments of propaganda and organization, as well as ideological and military schools.

Thirdly, he considers the effect of the guerrilla struggle on the creation of an adequate political organization:

The unity of the Left is another important aspect of this outlook. We see such unity as indispensable for developing the struggle and bringing it to a climax. We believe that this unity will be born during the process of the struggle. . . .

We believe that the party of the Peruvian revolution will shape itself within the insurrectional process, and that its cadres and leaders will emerge from the struggle itself. We do not use a party label; we call ourselves what we really are, a movement which aspires to be a promoter of the party of the Peruvian revolution.

We think that, starting from certain minimum levels of party organization and prestige among the masses, we must devote ourselves to the work of insurrection convinced that during the preparatory stage in the guerrilla zones, and more intensively after the beginning of action, it will be possible to build the party and mobilize, organize, give consciousness to, and incorporate the masses into the armed struggle. This involves starting from the highest level of popular struggle, armed struggle, through which we shall be able to build a true revolutionary party and win over the masses.

Fourthly, de la Puente explains his belief that the objective conditions for revolution were present in Peru and that the subjective conditions could be created:

It is unnecessary to speak about the objective conditions because they are not only ripe now but have always been. I think there is not a country in America where infra- and super-structural conditions are so unjust, so rotten, so archaic as in ours.

As to the subjective conditions, we start from the idea that they are not fully ripe, but that the beginning of the insurrectional process will be the triggering factor leading to their development in ways which no one can foresee. Moreover, it must be stressed that if such subjective conditions have not attained their necessary ripeness, this is partly due to the inability of the leftist parties and groups to foster and cultivate the ground.

Fifthly, and this was written long before Che Guevara enunciated his views about the desirability of United States intervention for provoking a nationalist reaction, de la Puente affirmed that the United States would have to intervene. Such intervention, however, would have its positive aspects, from the point of view of the development of the revolutionary struggle:

We think that American imperialism will desperately call on its huge resources in order to choke the continental war of emancipation. We feel sure that American armed intervention in our country will come more quickly than in other nations, because the Pentagon is perfectly aware of the importance of a triumphant or developing insurrection in the very heart of Latin America. In any case, we hope that the national liberation war in our country will be a positive factor in mobilizing and stiffening popular consciousness against the foreign exploiter and interventionist. . . .

Our national revolutionary struggle will become, sooner or later, a continental revolutionary struggle, because all our peoples feel the same eagerness for liberation, and the process in one country will help to radicalize the others and make them join the struggle through methods and forms suited to their own realities.

Lastly, de la Puente explains that the MIR's insurrectional scheme is based on the following principles:

1) The objective and subjective conditions are present, and the latter, even if they are not fully ripe, will mature in the process of the struggle.

2) The exploited masses must immediately propose the seizure of power through armed struggle.

3) The strategy and tactics must in the first stage be those of guerrilla war, and later those of manoeuvre, or even positional warfare.

4) Given our condition as a mainly peasant country, and our geographic features, insurrection must start in the sierra or in the eastern Andean escarpments.

5) Given the size of our country and its lack of geographical integration and transportation systems, its multiplicity of languages, races, and culture, it is advisable to organize several guerrilla centres to initiate and develop the struggle.

6) The impact of guerrilla actions will serve to build and develop the party and to start mobilizing the masses, stimulating their consciousness, and incorporating them in the struggle, both in the countryside and in the city.

7) Due to our condition as an underdeveloped country suffering from the combined oppression of *latifundists*, big bourgeoisie, and imperialists, it is essential to unite the exploited sectors: peasants, workers, petty bourgeoisie, within a united front led by the worker–peasant alliance represented by the revolutionary Marxist–Leninist party.

8) The Peruvian revolution is part of the continental and world process, which demands progressive forms of integration in every aspect and stage, in order to defeat the oligarchic and imperialist forces which are working together all over the continent.

With these principles, de la Puente began organizing a number of insurrectionary *focos* in the Andes that would be ready at a given moment to precipitate the Peruvian Revolution.

The moment seemed propitious. The years 1963 and 1964 saw the most amazing wave of peasant agitation in the whole of the recent history of Peru. Whether stirred up by the activity of Hugo Blanco and those like him, or whether the result of the immense political propaganda in favour of a land reform that was never likely to see the light of day, the peasant invasions that took place in those years in the Andean valleys and plateaux were without precedent and largely without explanation.[10]

Notes

1 First National Forum on Agrarian Reform, Havana, Cuba; quoted in Malpica, *Biografía de la Revolución*, pp. 501–4.

2 See section on Colombia, p. 183.

3 Quoted in Malpica, *Biografía de la Revolución*, pp. 506–9.

4 Villanueva, *Hugo Blanco*, p. 131.

5 David Alexander, 'Un nouvelle internationalisme révolutionnaire', *Les Temps modernes* (Paris), March 1967.

6 Silvestre Condoruna, *Las experiencias de la última etapa de las luchas revolucionarias en el Perú*, Ediciones Vanguardia Revolucionaria, Lima, 1966; *Estrategia*, NO. 3 (Santiago), 1966

7 Villanueva, *Hugo Blanco*, p. 131.

8 *Nustra Posición*, Ediciones Voz Rebelde, Lima, 1964. There was in fact an earlier policy document, published in February 1963, entitled *MIR: Bases Doctrinarias y Programáticas*, published by Ediciones Voz Rebelde. I have been unable to secure a copy, but it is referred to extensively by Américo Pomaruna in 'Perú: revolución, insurrección, guerrillas'.

9 Uceda, 'The Peruvian Revolution'.

10 See especially the writings of Gerrit Huizer (1965, 1967), Hugo Neira (1964, 1968), Ricardo Letts (1964, 1967), and the chapters on peasant unrest in the CIDA report on Peru.

5. 'Túpac Amaru' and Guillermo Lobatón

Towards the end of May 1965 the chiefs of the various *focos* met at de la Puente's headquarters, Camp No. 6, situated on the Mesa Pelada above the village of Maranura, which itself is on the Río Urubamba some way downstream from the great Inca town of Machu Picchu. Among those present were Guillermo Lobatón, Maxímo Velando, Gonzalo Fernández Gasco, Elio Portocarrero Ríos, and Ruben Tupayachi.

According to the Ministry of War's account, the guerrillas' original scheme was to start operations in the Satipo area where the Túpac Amaru group under Lobatón and Velando Gálvez were quietly preparing. Subsequently, when the army's forces had been enticed into the area, guerrilla activity would break out in other regions—in the north where Fernández Gasco was organizing a *foco* close to the Ecuadorean border, and in the country around Ayacucho. Finally the Pachacutec group, based in the Mesa Pelada and led by Tupayachi and de la Puente himself, would come into action. At the same time a political campaign to support the guerrillas would be launched in all the major cities of Peru.

It is doubtful whether the MIR really had things quite as well organized as the army would like to imagine. In particular, there seems to be no evidence that the group which operated to the east of Ayacucho, led by Héctor Béjar of the National Liberation Army, was privy to the detailed plans of the MIR before June 1965.

Once the guerrilla groups were fully organized and prepared, and had settled into their respective zones, the leaders met together at de la Puente's encampment and drew up a long 'Revolutionary Proclamation'. This was widely dispersed throughout the country, and appears to have been the first inkling that the Peruvian authorities had of a planned guerrilla outbreak.

It is a long document of some 15 pages. Here it should be sufficient to quote the demands the guerrillas made of the government:

> With the arms in hand, and in the knowledge that it interprets correctly the feelings of the people, the MIR makes the following demands:
>
> Firstly: IMMEDIATE DISSOLUTION OF THE CONGRESS which, with few exceptions, is a den of big landowners, the *haute bourgeoisie* and the lackeys of imperialism. It is the great obstacle in the way of all attempts to change the unjust structures of the country. It is a burden on the Exchequer and thus on the economy of the people. It has demonstrated not only that it is useless, but also that it is damaging to the interests of the country and the people.
>
> Secondly: A GENERAL AMNESTY and freedom for all those who have been imprisoned, persecuted and tried for political and social crimes. Severe and immediate punishment will be meted out to all those, either civilian or military, who have been guilty of the recent massacres of the people.
>
> Thirdly: A GENUINE AGRARIAN REFORM, which means,
>
> ▸ the complete and final destruction of the large estates, with ownership being given to the peasants who work it, immediately and in their entirety.
>
> ▸ Immediate return of all land stolen from Indian communities, and payment of indemnities for damage and illegal profits.
>
> ▸ Immediate abolition of all pre-capitalist work contracts, and payment of indemnities to peasants who have suffered servitude, based on different forms of sharecropping.
>
> ▸ Seizure of the big estates and large-scale capitalist agricultural companies on the coast, in the mountains and in the jungle, and inclusion in the land to be shared out or given to the appropriate group of peasants of territory in the hands of

large landowners, as far as the limits of medium-sized property.

▸ Exclusion from this process of small and medium owners who work their land and increase production, by protecting their interests and helping them to increase the productivity of their land and their work.

▸ Preferential treatment from State bodies for all aspects of peasant life and work, to complete the process of transforming agriculture.

Fourthly: A LIVING WAGE FOR THE FAMILY adjustable in accordance with the cost of living, for workers, public and private employees, professionals and technicians.

Fifthly: AN URBAN REFORM to put a stop to landlordism and the profits from it, making present tenants the owners, except for small and medium house-owners who will get special treatment.

Sixthly: IMMEDIATE RECOVERY OF THE PERUVIAN OIL, demanding the payment of damages and the profits illegally made by the IPC, and ending of contracts with imperialist companies over our natural resources, like the Marcona, Toquepala and Letourneau companies, etc.

Seventhly: RECOVERY OF FULL NATIONAL SOVEREIGNTY, throwing off all the yokes of imperialism; expulsion of all 'advisers' and agents of imperialism, whether civilian or military; ending of treaties or contracts which compromise our national independence and sovereignty; and the re-establishment of diplomatic, cultural and trade relations with all countries in the world.[1]

Rogger Mercado, the biographer of the Peruvian guerrillas, is somewhat critical of the tactic employed by de la Puente of announcing the existence of the guerrillas before going into action. Were the guerrillas really wise to publicize their presence before they had actually begun to fight? It was presumably done in order to stir up the peasantry, to make them realize that this was not, as the government soon attempted to say, merely a question of a few cattle-thieves. But it was also designed to stir up the Peruvian Left to take a more determined

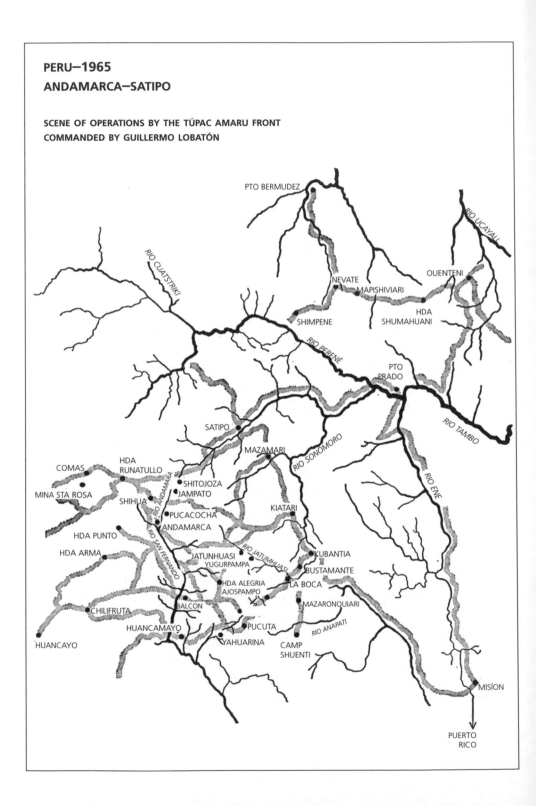

PERU—1965
ANDAMARCA—SATIPO

SCENE OF OPERATIONS BY THE TÚPAC AMARU FRONT
COMMANDED BY GUILLERMO LOBATÓN

stand. The Revolutionary Proclamation included a fervent appeal for unity on the Left.

Without further ado, the guerrillas of the MIR moved into action. The first to begin the struggle was the Túpac Amaru group in the centre of the country, led by Guillermo Lobatón. They began in June 1965.

They were based near the village of Andamarca, by the river of the same name. The country around is extremely mountainous. The Ministry of War's account details the following events: On 7 June the guerrillas captured two civil guards in the neighbourhood of Jampata in the upper reaches of the Andamarca. They had been sent to investigate rumours of guerrilla activity, but since the guerrilla movement was about to go into action, they were released two days later without weapons or equipment.

On 9 June the campaign began with an attack by the guerrillas on the powder magazine of the Santa Rosa mine. They escaped with a large quantity of dynamite, and with this they blew up a bridge on the Río Maraniyoc. They also sacked the Runatullo hacienda. Having achieved this, they retired to the area of Pucacocha, between Andamarca and Jampata.

At the same time, a second group attacked the civil guard post in Andamarca and captured the arms, munitions and equipment that they found inside. Ten days later, on 18 June, the guerrillas made attacks in three different places: they dynamited another bridge at Comas, sacked the electric plant at the Punto hacienda, and removed cattle from the Armas hacienda.[2]

Meanwhile, on 14 July, a police detachment set out from Andamarca to make a journey through the zone in order to see what was really happening. They reached Jampata that night, and ran into a minor ambush near Shitojasa the following day. The ambush was a failure from the point of the view of the guerrillas since one of the band allowed himself to fire his rifle before the signal was given.

It will be appreciated that the above is the official account provided by the army of the first events of the guerrilla campaign. Obviously it was in their interests to present a picture of a group of bandits with little aim except the wanton destruction of property. The guerrilla side of the story comes in a letter written, probably to de la Puente, by Guillermo Lobatón on 20 June:

Inti Yalhamuy

20 June 1965

Dear Comrades,

I am taking advantage of a halt in our march to send you this letter and to make contact again with our organization. I am writing things as they come into my mind. There is a lot to say. . . .

Our first action went as planned. We had practically finished all the preparatory tasks which the situation of the country demanded. . . . Since we had carried out all the first-stage tasks, we had to take up the armed struggle. We believe that events have justified our estimate of the situation. Indeed we believe that they have gone further than we could have hoped. The press and the radio have reported our first operation, though naturally in a somewhat distorted fashion. Essentially it consisted of raiding a mine and blowing up a bridge on the road to Satipo, just in front of the Runatullo hacienda. There was also an attack on this hacienda by one group and an attack on the police station at Andamarca by another group, all on the same day. The day before we had had to arrest two policemen from the same district who had entered our zone of influence for the very purpose of investigating rumours about us being there. We ran into them as we were heading for our objectives. After the attacks, we let them go, guaranteeing their safety.

The two operations were very successful. We carried out armed propaganda everywhere: at the mine, at the hacienda, at the bridge, in the town. We held meetings and gave out food from the stores, all along the road, from the lorry which we captured and returned undamaged. All the next day we were masters of our zone of influence, which is very large and covers several districts and many communities. We spent the night of the ninth, the day of the operation, in—and the next day shared out all the possessions of our deadly enemy, Julio Dávila, who although only a small farmer nevertheless abused and exploited the peasant. He was also a crooked lawyer.

The next day, the 11th, we accounted for the Alegria hacienda, which belonged to one of our worst enemies and a scourge of the poor, Raúl Ribeck. The police were already in Andamarca, one day away from the hacienda. We turned it into a commune and the goods (animals and produce) were shared out among the peasants. The same day we set out to begin harassing the enemy along the most dangerous road and to observe his movements along the others. We took up positions. We waited until midday on the 15th. The enemy arrived about then. While we were waiting, the support given by the peasants was unbelievable: supplies, information, new members. The details would fill a book or a very long conversation. Everything was going very very well. The time for our first encounter with the enemy had arrived. At that moment we remembered those helpless and unarmed people who were massacred at Ongoy, at Chaullay, at Anta, at Urcos, at Sicuani, at Cerro de Pasco, at La Oroya, in the National Stadium, so many unpunished crimes.

There were about fifty or sixty of them, well armed, most of them with sub-machine-guns. But at the height of the suspense, one comrade let off a shot and spoiled all our work. From then on we began to fall back for two or three days, changing positions, but not without continuing to harass the enemy. Now we are all together for the first time and learning from our mistakes. I reassure them saying that we have had no losses.

Three or four peasants have been shot down who were not involved in the fighting, possibly after torture. Others are in jail in the worst possible conditions. The police are spreading terror, and burning the peasants' huts. Many of them are living in caves with all their families. But our peasants are extraordinary, they are still with us. The security of both groups has obliged us to keep away from the masses, yet we have already taken measures to keep in contact with them and lead them.

Other measures have been taken to make new forays, get new help and prepare to continue the fight. The experience has been extremely valuable. Nobody has been out of danger and the reactions have been various. The balance is extremely positive; good possibilities of extending the fight and proof that the masses and our comrades are staunch revolutionaries even under fire.

I don't think I have left anything important out, although I would like to give you lots more details. There are falls, sweat and curses all along the way, but never have we been more optimistic or confident. We feel proud of having got to our second moment, beginning the armed struggle.

Guerrilla greetings to all our comrades,

Confident in our victory, I will see you soon, brothers,

Guillermo Lobatón

P. S. The comrade who fired the shot is one of the leaders. He has returned to the rank and file.[3]

On the same day that Lobatón wrote this letter, 20 June, a group of 29 soldiers was sent from Huancavelica to Huancamayo to prevent the guerrillas moving southwards out of the zone in which they were in. Informed that there were guerrillas in the region of Pucutá, the major in charge of the detachment decided to move in that direction. But on 27 June, near Yahuarina, he and his men fell into ambush under Lobatón's second-in-command, Maxímo Velando Gálvez. Seven soldiers were killed, and later the army accused the guerrillas of capturing two members of the patrol's vanguard and torturing them to death. The guerrillas' account of the ambush at Yahuarina was published later in *Voz Rebelde*:

At Yahuarina, seventeen guerrillas helped by the peasants faced an enemy force nearly twice the size, well armed with sub-machine-guns, light and heavy machine-guns and grenades. The guerrillas had much less effective weapons, home-made grenades and their courage. This battle was led by Comandante Maxímo Velando. The guerrillas inflicted casualties of nine dead, several wounded and twelve prisoners, among them an officer, who were freed without being ill-treated.

On the basis of detailed information on the engagement at Yahuarina, . . . we state categorically that the reports by the Ministry of War and the oligarchic newspapers that the policemen Diógenes Valderrama and Eusebio Gálvez Silvera were captured at Yahuarina, tortured and then murdered by the guerrillas, are absolutely false.

The policemen mentioned were the vanguard of the detachment led by the well-known murderer of workers and peasants, the civil guard major Horacio Patiño. They were advancing towards Inti Yalmahuy, dangerously close to the 'Túpac Amaru' guerrilla force's security zone. Comandante Velando, in charge of this sector, decided to cut off their advance; to do this successfully, he had to ambush them after letting through the vanguard the two policemen already mentioned. When the column was destroyed, the vanguard, despite being cut off, opened fire on the guerrillas, who were retiring after the engagement. They were obliged to beat off the attack, killing the two policemen. After this the area was cut off. Some days later the forces of repression returned to the place, found the bodies and spread the story that they had been killed out of the fighting after being barbarously tortured. All this, as is obvious, is completely untrue. . . .

The guerrillas have always respected prisoners and always will. Let us take one example. In this same engagement at Yahuarina, Comandante Velando took prisoner twelve members of the civil guard, among them an officer: this fact cannot be denied even by the lackeys of the oligarchy. When the leader of the people's guerrilla force accepted the surrender of these men, he told them not to be afraid, that their lives would be respected. He also pointed out that the guerrillas would always do this, although he knew that a very different fate awaited any of the guerrillas if they were captured. He then had the five wounded men from the detachment treated, as well as the limited supplies and knowledge available permitted, and finally bid them farewell, saying that he was sorry he could do no more for them because of the danger this would mean for his group.[4]

The ambush at Yahuarina was serious enough to make the army realize that they were dealing with more than a gang of rustlers. Consequently far-ranging counter-measures were planned in late June and July. The nearest important airbase to the guerrilla zone at Jauja became a crucial centre for troop transports, and planes were used for guerrilla-spotting. The navy's river force, based in Iquitos, was told to intensify its control of the upper Ucayali, and it co-operated with the army in patrolling the Tambo, the Perene, and the Ene.

The Ministry of War's account continues:

> Together with these preparations, the armed forces carried out an intensive information and warning campaign, giving out messages in the native language through loudspeakers in aeroplanes and helicopters, and dropping thousands of leaflets so that both the literate and illiterate peasants of the area would not co-operate with the guerrillas through ignorance or fear.
>
> To facilitate the task of cleaning up and re-establishing order in the area between the San Fernando, Mantaro, Ene and Sonomoro rivers, the inhabitants were recommended to avoid any sort of contact with strange or suspicious people whom they should attempt to arrest and hand over to the authorities. They were made to understand that resisting the forces of order whose function was to defend national sovereignty helped subversive acts. They were warned that it was an offence to possess arms or explosives without due authority from the Ministry of Government, as was concealing spies or agents, whether Peruvian or foreign.
>
> Knowing that the extremists' tactics, when they retreat, is to use local inhabitants as guides or hostages, they were

warned that those who collaborated would be captured and punished as accomplices.

Finally, to avoid having innocent victims in the trouble areas, women and children were told to keep clear of anything suspicious.[5]

Since there were no made-up roads in the guerrilla zone, the troops could only be sent by truck to the outskirts. On 19 July, two companies advanced as far as the road would go, in the north to Shihua and in the south to Chilifruta.[6] In Chilifruta they built a heliport, which eventually provided a base for two helicopters. The Chilifruta group then marched east to its forward base at Huancamayo, while the company in Shihua marched south down the valley of the San Fernando to Balcón.

During their march they captured peasants who had had contacts with the guerrillas, and received confirmation of the fact that there were guerrilla encampments in Pucutá, Inti Yalhamuy, Ajospampa, Jatunhuasi and Yugurpampa. From Balcón, one group began to move towards Inti Yalhamuy, and on 30 July there was a clash with the guerrillas. Rather than continue on to Inti Yalhamuy, this group then turned south to join up with the other group proceeding from Huancamayo which was advancing on Pucutá. The combined two companies succeeded in taking Pucutá on 2 August, after the area had been thoroughly softened up by machine-gunning and bombing from the air by two planes of the Peruvian air force.[7]

The following day, 3 August, the troops began to move towards Inti Yalhamuy. There was a further clash on the way, and when they arrived at their destination, they found that the guerrillas had already left. Leaving sufficient soldiers to guard Pucutá and Inti Yalhamuy, the main body of troops moved on to take over the guerrilla encampments at Ajospampa, Yugurpampa and Jatunhuasi. Apart from a minor skirmish near Yugurpampa, these places were captured without further incident.

Within two or three weeks, therefore, of having taken the offensive, the army could congratulate itself on having cleared the mountainous area which the guerrillas had chosen as their base of subversive elements. The forces of Lobatón and Velando, following classic guerrilla tactics, had withdrawn rather than face a major engagement with the enemy. Thus, the army, having placed 40 men in both Jatunhuasi and Kubantia, could afford to allow the rest to move around in small mobile groups to make sure that the guerrillas had genuinely left the zone. Their job was essentially to show by their presence that they, and not the guerrillas, were now the dominating force.

The guerrillas, however, had not moved away very far. A police patrol, moving between Kiatari and Kubantia, was ambushed on 9 August and this confirmed to the army the fact that the guerrillas were now choosing to operate in the forest areas bordering on the Río Sonomoro. Their base was at Bustamante, between Kubantia and the junction of the Jatunhuasi with the Sonomoro river. This area was largely inhabited by Campa Indians, a semi-aboriginal tribe known for their fierceness. The Ministry of War's account states that the Campas sided with the guerrillas and rarely co-operated with the army. Unfortunately we have no guerrilla account that describes the preliminary work done among the Campas before the guerrilla fighting broke out. An American journalist, Norman Gall, who travelled through the area, is somewhat critical. 'Lobatón,' he writes, 'was apparently attempting to work with the warlike Campas the way General Vo Nguyen Giap worked with the mountain tribes of north-eastern Vietnam during the Second World War. The difference, however, is that Giap worked *politically* with his tribesmen for two years before entering into combat; the Peruvian guerrillas worked with the Campas for less than six months in a very desultory fashion. . . .'[8] The fact remains, however, that the Campas were, by and large, loyal to the guerrillas. And they paid for their loyalty. Norman Gall writes that the repression by the Peruvian army:

> led to the death of hundreds of Campas. American missionaries working in the zone reported that the Peruvian air force had bombed a number of Campa villages.[9] While the guerrilla insurgency was still alive, however, a special school was set up under AID auspices in the area to train the Peruvian rural police in counter-insurgency operations.

The ambush on 9 August, coupled with rumours that bearded men had been seen further north in the Satipo area, seems to have made the army realize that they did not have sufficient troops available. Consequently a fresh contingent were flown in to Satipo, from where they marched for two days until they reached Kubantia. A further group of 80 soldiers were brought up from the south to Misión, on the upper waters of the Río Ene. With these reinforcements an advance was made on the guerrilla camp at Bustamante. But there was no sign of the guerrillas, and two Campas who were captured revealed that they had moved south towards Mazaronquiari.

For more than a month there was no contact between the guerrillas and the army. Then, on the night of 22 September, the guerrillas launched an attack on Pucutá, which was guarded by only 30 soldiers.

According to the army, this was a desperate move on the part of the guerrillas and the attack was repulsed. The guerrilla account was more optimistic:

> At Pucutá, in an engagement led personally by Comandante Guillermo Lobatón, the guerrillas defeated a specially chosen detachment of Rangers in their own camp, capturing a large quantity of food and weapons and causing them heavy casualties, both dead and wounded. Again it was proved that the people can defeat any repressive force however strong, that no enemy is invincible, if only the revolutionary organization manages to lead the masses and put them on the right path of guerrilla warfare.[10]

Together with the clash at Yahuarina, the taking of Pucutá was chalked up by the guerrillas as one of their most important and successful engagements and, when it was over, they retired south to the base beyond Bustamante at Shuenti.

Shortly after, the army was on their trail again, moving both from the north and from the south upon the camp of Shuenti. The southernmost group had the advantage of surprise and, on 2 October, there was a major clash at Shuenti in which the guerrillas appear to have come off the worse. According to the army's figures, 11 guerrillas were killed and 17 captured, while the rest, including Lobatón, and Velando, who had not been at Shuenti, moved north again to the lower reaches of the Sonomosa, near Mazanari.[11]

It was here that the United States 'advisers' had made their head-quarters. At the beginning of November, the army received word that the guerrillas were planning to make a break northwards across the Río Perene. Velando Gálvez had been sent ahead to Puerto Bermudo, presumably to check the route, but he was betrayed by a Campa to the garrison there. Once captured he was transferred to Satipo, where, according to the army account, he tried to commit suicide.[12] This caused injuries from which he did not recover, and he died on 7 December while being transferred by air to Huancayo. The guerrilla account on the same incident is rather more sinister:

> Not only have defenceless prisoners been murdered in cold blood, but this has also happened after they have been cruelly tortured, as in the case of the heroic Comandante Maxímo Velando, who was taken prisoner together with the Satipo peasant leader, comrade Paucarcaja, who was also murdered. The victor of Yahuarina was tortured and left unconscious for several days. They wanted to know the whereabouts of the unit commanded by Comandante Guillermo Lobatón, but the mercenaries did not find out. As it was impossible to make his death look natural, he was put in a helicopter and thrown out, while still alive, but unconscious, into a ravine in the Andes. We state this on the basis of information from a wholly reliable source.[13]

At the end of November the guerrillas were moving from Mapishiviari to Oventeni, via the hacienda Shumahuani. Then, at the beginning of December, they doubled back to Nevate, where the army was waiting for them. The guerrillas lost eight men, and the rest moved south, back towards the Río Perene. There was a minor clash at Shimpene on 14 December, and then, on 22 December, one of the leaders, Florian Herrera Mendoza (Jaime Martínez) was killed near the Río Kuatsiriqui. A fortnight later, the army tightened the circle around Lobatón and his remaining group. They were killed near the Río Sotziqui on 7 January 1966.[14]

There are, however, some doubts as to what really happened to Lobatón. His death was first listed as occurring in the clash at Shimpene in mid-December, though this was subsequently denied.

The Lima papers of 6 January announced again that he had been killed—in a clash the previous day—and they quoted General Alejandro Sierralta as their source.[15] Subsequently this general appears to have denied saying anything, and in a communiqué dated 18 January the MIR maintained that the news about Lobatón was completely false. They pointed out that no army communiqué had been issued, as had been the case after the death of de la Puente in October.

The Lima paper *El Comercio* published an official army communiqué on 7 January stating that Lobatón 'has not been captured and therefore cannot be in detention. The group that he led has been disbanded and is in flight.'[16]

Whatever the exact story—and capture, torture and disposal would seem to be the most likely—the Latin Left and his French wife still believe that he may be alive.[17]

Notes

1 *Proclamación Revolucionaria al Pueblo Peruano*, quoted in Mercado, *Las guerrillas del Perú, el MIR*, pp. 120–35.

2 *Las guerrillas en el Perú y su represión*, p. 47.

3 Mercado, *Las guerrillas del Perú, el MIR*, pp. 153–6.

4 *Voz Rebelde*, NO. 46, quoted in Mercado, *Las guerrillas del Perú, el MIR*, pp. 157–8.

5 *Las guerrillas en el Perú y su represión*, p. 55.

6 Ibid., p. 57.

7 Ibid.

8 Gall, 'The Legacy of Che Guevara'.

9 'It is a national duty to denounce by every means to the entire world the useless, massive and odious massacres of unarmed peasants undertaken by the repressive forces in Andamarca, Pucutá, Balcón, Ajospampa, and in the Campa settlements of Bustamante and Satipo . . .'—Summary of the Central Committee meeting of MIR, quoted in Mercado, *Las guerrillas del Perú, el MIR*, p. 161.

10 Summary of Central Committee MIR meeting, quoted in Mercado, *Las guerrillas del Perú, el MIR*, p. 16.

11 I have purposely not quoted many casualty figures in this section, since, although the army account appears reasonably accurate as far as it goes, obviously much is missing. The attack on Shuenti may have caused the death of eleven guerrillas; the dead may equally well have been simple peasants.

12 *Las guerrillas en el Perú y su represión*, p. 64.

13 Summary of the MIR Central Committee meeting, quoted in Mercado, *Las guerrillas en el Perú, el MIR*, pp. 159–60.

14 ,*Las guerrillas en el Perú y su represión*, p. 64.

15 *Le Monde*, 12 January 1966.

16 'Guillermo Lobatón a-t-il été réellement tué?', *Le Monde*, January 1966.

17 Jacqueline Eluau de Lobatón, 'Tras las huellas de Lobatón', *Punto Final*.

6. 'PACHACUTEC' AND LUÍS DE LA PUENTE

The 'Túpac Amaru' guerrilla front commanded by Guillermo Lobatón had managed to survive for six months. Luís de la Puente and the 'Pachacutec' Front, led by Ruben Tupayachi, were less fortunate. From the very start the army knew roughly where they were, and it was able to saturate the zone with troops before the guerrillas had taken their first offensive action. The area, too, was singularly inhospitable. The Pachacutec Front was scheduled to operate in the valley of La Convención, which had once been the scene of Hugo Blanco's activities. But de la Puente's headquarters were higher up on the Mesa Pelada. The Peruvian army's book on the guerrillas gives a good description of the zone:

> Mesa Pelada is a plateau on the spurs of the 'eyebrow of the jungle' in the Eastern range of the Andes (near La Convención in the department of Cuzco). It is about 40 miles long and some 12 wide. Its average height above sea level is 12,000 feet, while the four valleys that surround it are about 3,000 feet. The reader can thus get some idea of what a difference of 9,000 feet between the surrounding valleys and the highest point of the plateau means. Add to this very broken ground, completely covered with tall thick jungle at the bottom and to half-way up, topped by thick high 'ichu' grass at the summit; heavy rain throughout the year and thick mist in the early morning. The reader should also bear in mind the temperatures, which at the bottom have an annual average of 75F while at the top it is often at freezing-point; adding

together all these things, the reader will have a good idea of what Mesa Pelada is like.[1]

The army moved into the area at the end of August 1965, after Lobatón's group had gone into action but before de la Puente had gone over to the offensive. The MIR leader issued a communiqé to celebrate the event:

1) The insurrection is following its planned course of expansion, mobilization and growth, not only in the departments of the centre, but also in the south, in Apurimac, Cuzco and Arequipa and in the north, in La Libertad, Cajamarca and Piura.

Official communiqués are contradictory, for while on the one hand they talk of small, indeed tiny, groups of extremists and criminals, on the other they report the death or capture of tens and hundreds of guerrillas. What does it mean? Are they a small group, or are the dead they report not guerrillas but defenceless peasants who have been murdered in order to show off victims and quench the thirst for blood of the leaders and their oligarchic and imperialist masters?

In the newspapers and on the radio, the forces of repression and the oligarchy and their hacks speak of cowardice, because the guerrillas do not face up to the enemy and because they withdraw, attack by surprise and spring ambushes. For their information, these are the tactics of guerrilla warfare. The moment will come when we enter the stage of fighting a war of manoeuvre or positions, and then the rebel army will fight great battles against the mercenary forces, on an equal footing. Cowardice is better applied to those who dance to the tune of those in power and share out the rewards. There will be a chance to hear and read them when the balance of forces changes and victory is near. Then we shall remember these parrots and pen-pushers.

2) The oligarch's Congress—with the honourable exception of eight members—passed a law changing some articles of the Penal Code and the Code of Military Justice, establishing the death penalty, loss of nationality, etc., for those who attack the established order. This law is unconstitutional, and only

expresses the panic of the oligarchy and their servants in the Congress. . . .

In the name of the people we shall condemn to death all mass murderers, all traitors, all spies, all the oligarchs who play a part in sucking the blood of our people, all millionaire thieves, all those using public office to carry out deals and corruption, and these decisions will be carried into effect in town and country, during the struggle and after victory. So let us be prepared. Let us warn the oligarchs and their servants that we are not afraid of their blustering and that we are ready for anything to save our country from poverty, exploitation, ignorance, injustice, under-development, dependence, administrative corruption, immorality, complete crisis and bankruptcy.

3) Pedro Beltrán has been the first to buy bonds for National Defence and Democracy. The bankers will contribute a third of the internal credit. They will be followed by the big industrialists, the big exporters, the big importers, the big mines, etc. All this is natural. Those who haggle over a sol on workers' wages, or an ounce of salt in labourers' food, or a cent on the price of our products, hand over millions to defend their own interests. They are paying the armed forces to defend the established order, that is to say their interests, their privileges and their fortunes, amassed with the sweat, health and blood of our people. The police and soldiers are mercenaries fighting against their class brothers, defending the great exploiters, the millionaires, the sole cause of the ills of the country. Anti-Communism is a pretext to defend base and anti-patriotic interests. The country which they talk about is their estates, their mines, their banks, their millions, their deals, their privileges, their profits. *That* is the country which they say is in danger.

4) The MIR's guerrilla actions are generally being written off as 'Communist'. Anti-Communism is a well-known ploy of the oligarchy and its servants. We must make it clear, however, that the guerrillas in the centre, the south and the north belong to the MIR. Indeed, the two factions of the Communist party have made statements against us, although

they don't have the full support of their membership, especially of the youth. The MIR does not belong to the Communist party, to either of its factions. Nor does the MIR belong to any of the Trotskyite groups. The MIR is a completely autonomous movement, ideologically, politically and organizationally. The MIR supports the unity of the Left, but considers that it will be achieved in the struggle and not round a café table. . . .

The MIR supports the unity of all progressive and patriotic sectors of the country who are not compromised with the imperialists, the bourgeoisie or the great landowners, in a great NATIONAL UNITED ANTI-OLIGARCHICAL AND ANTI-IMPERIAL-IST FRONT, without sectarianism, without reservations, without discrimination. That is why we are calling on all honest men and true patriots, civilian or military, professionals, intellectuals, technicians, office workers, peasants, small and medium landowners, businessmen, industrialists, transport workers, miners, etc., artisans, craftsmen, soldiers, both officers and men, etc.

5) Our battle platform is already clearly set out in our revolutionary call to the Peruvian people. . . .

6) It is now up to all true patriots. We have spoken and backed up our words with actions. Civil war threatens the whole country. We are not responsible for this violence. We are answering reactionary violence against workers and peasants with revolutionary violence by means of guerrilla warfare. Nobody and nothing can stop our movement. The Revolution is in progress and leads to victory against the enemies of the people. Our platform is perfectly clear and nobody can deny that it interprets the feelings of the majority of our people.

7) We reject all the conditions of the pseudo-Christians and the Archbishop and Primate of the Peruvian Church, who is justifying the death penalty and putting the Church at the service of the oligarchy and its lackeys. Those who said nothing when workers and peasants were massacred in this country, those who did nothing about hunger, poverty, unemployment, injustice and the exploitation of the humble, those who forget

Christian principles, are condemning themselves and showing themselves to be servants of the exploiters, the sole cause
of the ills which beset the country.

8) The armed MIR calls on all sectors of the people to fight.
Victory is ours. The guerrillas are spreading. Armed fighting
is sweeping the country. Liberation is at hand. What today is
a spark, tomorrow will be a fire, which will consume all false
patriots, all liars, all hired thugs, all the torturers, all the hyp-
ocrites, all those who are behind the crimes and abuses our
people have suffered.

> Long live the Peruvian Revolution! Long live the guerrillas!
> Long live the MIR!
> Long live the unity of all the people!
> Down with the Oligarchy, imperialism and their servants!

The Cordillera of the Andes,\
30 August 1965\
Luís de la Puente Uceda,\
Head of the National Revolutionary\
Command of the MIR[2]

But proclamations of revolutionary intent could not stave off the
Peruvian army. Almost immediately after its arrival in the area at the
end of August, the army began to make its presence felt among the
peasantry. The first clash with the guerrillas occurred on 9 September.
At least one United States army counter-insurgency expert was said to
have helped plan and direct the attack.[3] On 20 September, five army
detachments began moving on the summit of Mesa Pelada, capturing
guerrilla Camp No. 6 on the same day. As an example of the climatic
conditions, it is worth noting that three soldiers died of the cold at this
stage of the expedition.[4] Four days later, the army captured Camp Nos
3 and 4 and, although the guerrillas made a gallant effort to recapture
Camp No. 4 on the afternoon of 25 September, they were unsuccessful.

The Ministry of War's account goes on:

> Operations continued at an intensive level to prevent the
> guerrillas from regrouping and to facilitate the capture and
> destruction of the bases they still held. At the same time the

air force made some daylight bombing raids to neutralize and confuse the rebels. Heavy 120-mm mortars provided harassing fire at night to oblige them to stay on the alert and ready for anything. These operations were possible owing to the fact that the higher parts of Mesa Pelada are uninhabited.

The guerrillas, however, gave a different picture: 'Saturation bombing with napalm and high explosive burnt up the plateau, ruining and massacring peasants.'[5] And the *New York Times* correspondent, writing in October, stated that 'every day air force planes plaster the suspected guerrilla concentrations with napalm bombs and machine-gun fire'.[6]

In these circumstances, de la Puente's guerrillas had little hope of surviving on the inhospitable slopes of Mesa Pelada. Yet they were surrounded and escape was impossible. One member of his band, Albino Guzmán, found the strain too great. He left the guerrillas, gave himself up to the police, and explained exactly where the hiding places of the guerrillas were located. With treachery within their own ranks, the guerrillas' days were numbered.

In a desperate effort to break out of the circle which the army was gradually tightening around them, a guerrilla column, led by de la Puente himself and by Ruben Tupayachi, clashed with the army near Amaybamba on 23 October. The guerrillas were either captured or killed. There is some doubt as to what happened to de la Puente and Tupayachi, but it seems probable that they were captured and shot in captivity two days later. The group had barely seen a month's action.

Notes

1   *Las Guerrillas en el Perú y su represión*, p. 31.

2   Quoted in Mercado, *Las Guerrillas del Perú, el MIR*, pp. 193–8.

3   *New York Times*, 12 September 1965.

4   *Las Guerrillas en el Perú y su represión*, p. 66. The guerrillas maintained that the soldiers that the army claimed had frozen to death had really been killed in ambushes (Mercado, *Las Guerrillas del Perú, el MIR*, p. 184).

5   Mercado, *Las Guerrillas del Perú, el MIR*, p. 186.

6   *New York Times*, 8 October 1965.

7. Héctor Béjar and 'Javier Heraud'

The Peruvian army appears to have been quite taken by surprise when the ELN moved into action on 25 September in an area between that dominated by Lobatón and de la Puente. The ELN, led by Héctor Béjar, was the revolutionary group dating back to 1962 which had been responsible for the guerrilla episode at Puerto Maldonado in May 1963 when Javier Heraud had been killed. It had been preparing itself for the guerrilla struggle for a long time, but when Lobatón's group went into action in June 1965, it did not regard itself as wholly ready to start full-scale revolutionary activites. However, bearing de la Puente's solidarity appeal in mind, it decided that it had no alternative except to launch itself into the guerrilla struggle. On 9 September representatives of the ELN and the MIR signed a joint communiqué in Lima, pledging each other their support:

> The armed process of the Peruvian Revolution has made a start and this fact has the characteristics of an irreversible historical change. Now that the guerrillas have begun, the national and social liberation of the Peruvian people must follow from the armed struggle.
>
> This situation demands the unity of revolutionary groups—a process which is made, developed and consolidated in action. Knowing this, the Movement of the Revolutionary Left (MIR) and the National Liberation Army

(ELN) have agreed to improve relations at the level of co-ordination in order to face together the different tasks involved in liberating our country, beginning with the setting up of a National Co-ordination Command.

The aim of the struggle is to carry out the National, Anti-imperialist, Democratic People's Revolution, an essential stage in the construction of a social system which will put an end to man's exploitation of man, and will fully recover national sovereignty, and achieve our destiny as a Nation, in our country, in the continent and the whole world.

Reaching these goals can only be the result of the struggle of the people led by the alliance of workers and peasants, with the support of students, of progressive intellectuals, of the exploited middle classes, of the lower middle class and all patriotic sectors in the country who oppose landlordism, the monopolistic bourgeoisie and imperialism; that is to say, the vast majority of the Peruvian people who make up our most glorious traditions, handed down to us by the Incas, and those who gave up their lives for their country, like Manco Inca, Juan Santos, Túpac Amaru, Pumacahua, the heroes of the Wars of Independence and the struggles for the Republic and all those who throughout the last few decades have given up their lives to liberate the people, among others Sub-Lieutenant Vallejos, the peasant Mayta, and the poet Javier Heraud.[1] This agreement is not exclusive and remains open to any other organization which fully identifies itself with the aims of the struggle and its demands.

The MIR and the ELN are fully aware that the present struggle for national liberation will give rise to the powerful United Party of the Peruvian Revolution, an essential historical instrument to carry out the process, and of which the two organizations feel themselves to be founder members.

OUR COUNTRY OR DEATH! WE SHALL OVERCOME!

Lima, 9 September 1965[2]

In October, shortly after its first major action, the ELN issued a manifesto outlining its specific point of view:

Since Belaúnde became President of the Republic, there have been no fundamental changes in the desperate situation of our country and our people.

Forgetting his election promises, giving in more and more to oligarchic pressure, Belaúnde unscrupulously goes the way of his predecessors; in exchange for their allowing him to stay in power, he lets International Petroleum, Cerro de Pasco and other American monopolies plunder our oil, copper, iron, lead and zinc; he traffics in the poverty of the peasants with a farcical agrarian reform which does not affect the large estates and crushes the people violently with the armed forces.

We are going through the biggest crisis in our history, the ruling classes have decided on total violence. Under the control of parties known for their ferocity against the people, Belaúnde has betrayed our national sovereignty and independence by taking refuge under the brutal claws of the State Department.

The merciless plunder and exploitation of our country does not stop. It goes on. The people are calling for an end to it.

Following the revolutionary traditions handed down to us by Túpac Amaru, Pumacahua and other leaders in the struggle against colonialism, we take on the cry of National Liberation and the need to create armed units.

In 1962 political leaders from the workers, peasants and students decided to create the National Liberation Army (ELN) with two main methods: the Armed Struggle and a Policy of Unity, the dialectical complement of one another.

The armed struggle will make the people trust more and more in their own strength, but they cannot be successful unless they are broadly based on popular unity. Only a united and organized people will be able to defeat the powerful forces of the oligarchy. Divisionism has always been the oppressors' most effective weapon. The enemy always tries to create

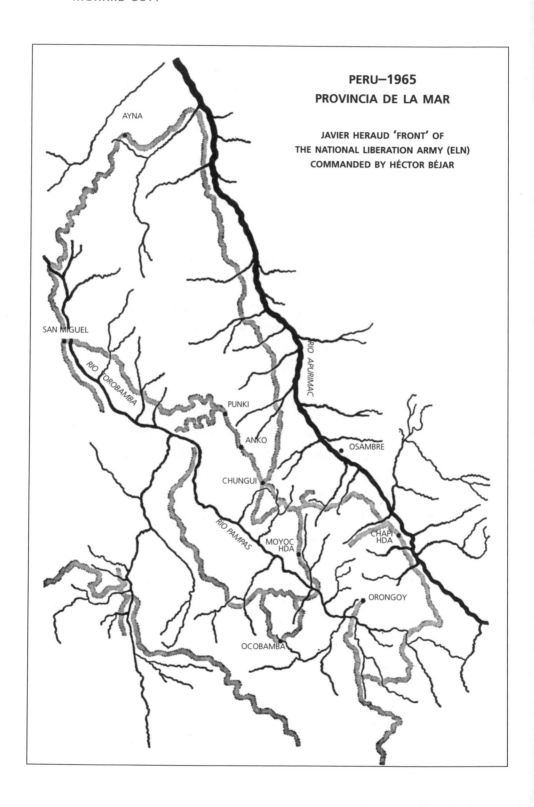

PERU—1965
PROVINCIA DE LA MAR

JAVIER HERAUD 'FRONT' OF
THE NATIONAL LIBERATION ARMY (ELN)
COMMANDED BY HÉCTOR BÉJAR

splits amongst the revolutionaries, because they know that a people divided internally is easily dominated.

That is why sectarians and divisionists are dangerous allies of the enemy within the ranks of the people.

Only armed struggle will allow the creation of really popular unity. We do not believe in violence for violence's sake. But we cannot deceive ourselves nor deceive the people by advocating peaceful means in a country exploited by an economically and militarily powerful oligarchy, used to tyranny and *coups*.

We believe that we must reply to the criminal violence of the oligarchy with a Peoples' War aimed at taking power.

The experience of liberation movements in the last few decades shows that the people can successfully face a large and well-armed army by means of guerrilla warfare. This is the lesson of Algeria, Cuba, Vietnam, and of all the people who have defeated imperialism or who are fighting against it successfully.

The aim of a military force is to build up a powerful National Liberation Army to carry out guerrilla warfare throughout the country, and finally to defeat imperialism and the oligarchy. . . .

The immediate aim of our policy of unity is to form a broad front bringing in all the people.

The front will not be the result of long-winded haggling behind the backs of the masses; it will be the culmination of a stage in the armed struggle by the people in which action brings together all popular forces.

Nobody can lay claim to the leadership of the masses, unless he has shown in practice that he is at the head of the masses and is able to lead them to victory. Leading the people is not a privilege, but a serious responsibility conferred by popular support.

The opening of guerrilla fronts in Junín and Cuzco, with the glorious units 'Túpac Amaru', 'Pachacutec' and 'Pumacahua', belonging to the MIR have shown with their revolutionary example that the Peoples' War has begun.

The National Liberation Army (ELN) informs the people that a guerrilla front has been opened in the department of Ayacucho.

The ELN, with the 'Javier Heraud' guerrilla unit commanded by comrade Héctor Béjar a shining example of revolutionary selflessness, has begun the first armed propaganda operation.

In the Chapi hacienda, owned by the bloodthirsty Carrillo brothers, 2,000 peasants were exploited, working nine months of the year without any payment, From the age of nine the children did a pitiless day's work; if any animal in their care was lost, they had to make up for it with more work. The wives and daughters of the peasants were raped and taken into the service of this ferocious landowner. Nobody was ever paid.

In 1962 some peasants protested to the Carrillo brothers about this inhuman treatment. They were murdered in cold blood.

In 1963 the peasants could put up with it no longer and arrested the Carrillos. They went to the authorities who were responsible for dispensing justice, but they themselves were arrested and accused of stealing cattle and crops.

Referring to these events, naturally rather euphemistically, the oligarchic and McCarthyite newspaper *La Prensa*, belonging to Pedro Beltrán, gives the following report on 4 October this year, page 6: 'The police also remember that the tenants have always been aggressive towards the Carrillo brothers. A year ago they took one of them to Ayacucho, barefoot and gagged, accusing him of grave irregularities. The police had to act severely to prevent a crime from being committed.' That was the report in *La Prensa*.

In September 1965, in the Chapi hacienda, at a people's meeting held by the peasants and backed up by the arms of the ELN, sentence was passed and revolutionary justice carried out: the Carrillo brothers and their lackeys have paid for their crimes.

Long live the guerrillas of Junín, Ayacucho and Cuzco!

Long live the peasants and their unity with the guerrillas!

Down with the brutal murderers of defenceless peasants!

Down with imperialism and the oligarchy!

Long live the National Liberation Army![3]

The ELN had therefore begun its military operations on 25 September, capturing the Chapi hacienda and shooting the Carrillo brothers who owned it. The reasons for this apparently brutal opening were not far to seek. The guerrillas explained it as follows:

The execution of the murderers Gonzalo and Miguel Carrillo, owners of the hacienda Chapi, in the province of La Mar, department of Ayacucho, is a historic act of justice, comparable with the hanging of corregidor Ariaga by Túpac Amaru. We could say the same of these butchers that the Inca said about the Spanish tyrant: 'his bad behaviour made encompassing his ruin a meritorious task'. The hacienda Chapi is a vast estate, the biggest in Ayacucho, covering six villages or parts of them, among them Panto and Chupón, several days apart. It is so big that it takes nearly a week to cross it on horseback. As the owners had their armed bullies and didn't want the authorities near, the nearest civil guard post was five days from the main house. The climate is warm and the hacienda produces excellent coffee and cacao, apart from sugar cane to make rum, and coca. There are also plenty of cattle. All this production is based on unpaid labour by peasants, who, in exchange for tiny plots to grow their food, work for nothing . . . on the hacienda lands and graze its cattle. There are hundreds of families so downtrodden that none of them speak Spanish. Naturally there is no school or medical post, despite a request for them made in 1962.

In 1960 Gonzalo and Miguel Carrillo murdered a peasant whose name was Huamán. They had accused him of theft, cut up his body and hung the remains at the entrance to the farm buildings to terrorize the peasants. But the peasants, who had been demanding wages, revolted, got hold of Gonzalo Carrillo, tied him up and took him as a prisoner to the nearest police post. Naturally the authorities freed the criminal landowner and arrested the leader of the peasants, Emeterio Huamán (a relative of the murdered man), who is still in Ayacucho jail. This, and many other crimes committed by the ferocious Carrillo brothers (rapes, torturing peasants, burning huts, etc.), were reported in 1964 by the newspaper *Obrero y Campesino*.

Can there be any doubt of the justice of executing such criminals?[4]

Ricardo Letts has given the following account of what occurred:

Their first action was to execute two landowners in the mountain area of Ayacucho. They first assembled the peasants, who themselves decided to exact payment for the crimes which had gone on for many years. When this action, which took place in the middle of a battle around the farmhouse, was over, they withdrew, avoiding contact with the police. With the death of the owners and the bailiff, the Indians, who had been oppressed and exploited for centuries, were in a completely new position. They had nobody to give slave labour to, nobody to give half or three quarters of their harvest to. Effectively they now owned land in their own right, and the lands worked for the hacienda could now be worked by all of them together. This was explained to them by the guerrillas and was put into practice immediately after the action. The police, who then arrived, could do nothing. They attacked the peasants, and made themselves even more hated. They kept a detachment there to guard the empty fields (the farmhouse and other concrete symbols of the landowners' oppression had been burnt down), but they could not prevent the peasant from cultivating his plots of land and getting all the produce. No other landowner would come to take the place of the previous ones, for it was obvious he would share their fate.[5]

It was some time before the army was able to deal with this new threat. All available forces were already coping with the Túpac Amaru and Pachacutec guerrilla fronts. Thus it was not until 25 November, after the Pachacutec group had been wiped out, that it was decided to send the troops which had captured Mesa Pelada into the area where the Javier Heraud group was operating. They advanced on 6 December, and a fortnight later, on 17 December, they made contact with the guerrillas. In the resulting clash, Ricardo León, Béjar's second-in-command, was killed. There were further clashes at the end of December and the beginning of January. The Javier Heraud Front came effectively to an end with the disappearance of Béjar himself. He was subsequently captured and imprisoned.

With this, the guerrilla movement of 1965 came to an end. For some reason, the Manco Capac group in the far north on the Ecuadorean border, led by Gonzalo Fernández Gasco, never went into action at all. Six guerrillas were captured during the period between 18 October and 5 November, and they provided the army with their first knowledge that a guerrilla group was planning to operate in that area. Informed that Fernández Gasco's principal base was at Cerro Negro, three army units began to converge on the area on 11 December. But after continuing to patrol until the end of the month, and finding nothing, the search was called off. The guerrillas had retired to Ecuador.

Notes

1   In May 1962, Lieutenant Vallejos was in charge of the prison at Jauja, a town some 30 minutes' drive from Huancayo in the Department of Junín. Anxious to start an uprising, he contacted a member of the POR, a Trotskyist group, in order to have the support of a political organization. Together with a peasant leader named Mayta, they planned an uprising that would spark off a Socialist revolution. They captured the prison, but it was not long before the army caught up with them. Vallejos and Mayta were killed. For further details, see Pumaruna, 'Perú'.

2 Joint communiqué of the MIR and the ELN, 9 September 1965, quoted in Mercado, *Las Guerrillas del Perú*, pp. 181–2.

3 *The New Guerrilla Front in Ayacucho*, manifesto issued by the ELN, October 1965, quoted in Mercado, *Las guerrillas del Perú, el MIR*, pp. 188–91.

4 Quoted in Mercado, *Las guerrillas del Perú, el MIR*, pp. 186–7.

5 Pumaruna, 'Perú'.

8. THE COMMUNISTS AND THE GUERRILLAS

The attitude of the Peruvian Communist party towards de la Puente's guerrillas can only be understood in the context of its complete opposition to Che Guevara's thesis that 'it is not always necessary to wait until all conditions for revolution exist; the insurrectionary *foco* can create them'.[1] This thesis, as has already been indicated, was wholeheartedly supported by de la Puente. The orthodox Communists, however, believed that the conditions for revolution could not be artificially stimulated in this way. (Communist opposition to Hugo Blanco had, of course, been more straightforwardly anti-Trotskyist.)

In an article analysing the failure of the Peruvian guerrillas, the Peruvian Communist, César Levano, writes:

> The main conclusion is that in a country whose people suffer from poverty and landlord violence, guerrilla struggle can win popular sympathy. But this sympathy cannot be utilized and cannot develop into active support unless there are more or less mature objective conditions for revolution. The second condition for the successful growth of the guerrilla movement is a relatively high level of organization and consciousness on the part of the political organization heading the guerrilla struggle.[2]

When, on 9 June 1965, de la Puente's guerrillas first went into action, the Communists faced the difficult problem of what attitude they should adopt. According to César Levano, less than 24 hours later the Communist party declared its solidarity with the guerrillas.[3]

But there was a qualification: 'its position could be more precisely described as one of critical support for them'. And Levano added that 'the Communist party from the very outset voiced certain doubts as to the time chosen to begin the struggle, pointing out that in making this choice it was essential to take into account not only the position and mood of the peasantry in one or another district but the political situation in the country as a whole.'

Nevertheless, the Communists, though having these doubts, were always faced with the possibility of the success of the guerrillas. Hence their relationship and attitude to them was a constant preoccupation. In August 1965 the Central Committee met to make 'a careful analysis of the new situation'. In its analysis it proceeded from the following basic premises:

a) A distinction should be made between guerrilla struggle and an uprising. An uprising might in some cases become the *final stage* of a people's war.

b) For the *uprising* to take place, in other words to pass over to the seizure of power, a revolutionary situation is necessary.[4] But this condition is not essential for the *emergence of a guerrilla movement*.

c) The guerrilla movement in itself cannot engender a revolutionary situation.

d) The guerrilla movement can develop only when a revolutionary situation is maturing.

The Central Committee concluded that, although the armed struggle begun by the MIR and later joined by Héctor Béjar's ELN (15 May Movement) was 'a response to the violence against the peasants', at the same time it had to be noted that 'a revolutionary situation which would warrant armed struggle becoming the main form of struggle and the principal task of the Peruvian people did not exist in our country'.

One unfavourable factor [comments Levano] was the so-called agrarian reform. Although it began to be implemented only in areas where the peasants had in fact already taken over the land, it was obvious that it would give part of the land to the peasants and foster certain illusions among them for a time. Besides, there was increasing pressure for the nationalization of the oil wells, and in this connection hopes concerning the possibility of effective government action were revived.

It should be borne in mind that the *population generally* had not yet been convinced by their own experience of the inconsistency, defeatism and demagogy of government coalition. Moreover, the APRA–UNO coalition, too, still had a certain (though meagre) amount of political capital to draw on.[5]

The disadvantage of the guerrilla outbreak as far as the Communists were concerned was that it led directly to government repression against the Communist party. The party was, in fact, found guilty of crimes that it had not committed, and the net result was to upset its own strategy. The Central Committee noted correctly that the reactionary forces had been taking advantage of the guerrilla struggle to:

1) Unleash a campaign of repressions against all Left forces.

2) Isolate these forces from the national and democratic elements.

3) Induce the conciliatory bourgeoisie at present in power to go over to naked reaction.

4) Regroup the forces within the ultra reactionary front by patching up some differences (primarily the traditional rivalry between the APRA and the army).

All that the party had stood for, in terms of supporting the reformist policies of Belaúnde, was jeopardized by the guerrillas. Yet the party could not stand aside for fear of losing its more radical supporters. So while remaining inactive in deeds, it was reasonably vocal in favour of the armed struggle.

Needless to say [wrote Levano afterwards], the Communist party of Peru is not opposed in principle to armed struggle. Our last congress made it quite clear that, although the Communists would prefer the revolutionary process in our country to proceed without violence and bloodshed, in view of the traditional methods employed by the oligarchy and imperialism the peaceful road is hardly feasible. In all probability the road to revolution in Peru, the congress stated, will be the road of armed struggle. The methods used by the ruling circles in recent months against the guerrillas, against the struggle of the peasants and the popular movement generally merely accentuate this probability.

But lest the faithful should assume from this that the Communists were endorsing the activities of de la Puente, Levano hastily listed the MIR's mistakes, the chief of which was to fail to co-ordinate its activities with those of the Communist party:

> The mistake of the MIR was not only that the time chosen was not opportune, but also that its leadership did not take the trouble to co-ordinate action—if only outside the guerrilla movement—with other Left forces, and in particular with the Communist party. It can now be said that this is one of the most important lessons to be drawn from the guerrilla struggle. Many blunders, weaknesses and betrayals could have been avoided, the death of many a valiant fighter could have been prevented, had the groups leading the struggle not been so strongly prejudiced against our party.

It is difficult not to feel, however, in the light of what happened, that the prejudice was well placed.

The pro-Chinese Peruvian Communist party was no more enthusiastic to support de la Puente's guerrillas than the orthodox pro-Russian party had been, in spite of its ideological interest in the armed struggle. The pro-Chinese party had been founded at a conference in January 1964, but from the very first it devoted most of its time and efforts to combating the 'revisionists' rather than in promoting guerrilla warfare.[6]

When the guerrilla groups went into action in the Andes in the middle of 1965, the pro-Chinese party was initially silent. The Political Commission held meetings in September and October, but did little except to state that 'the beginning of the armed struggle in Peru marks a new stage in the progress of the revolution'.[7] It was not until 15 and 16 November, in other words after the death of de la Puente, that the pro-Chinese party held its Second National

Conference to discuss the situation and to explain why the party had not supported the guerrillas.[8] Its conclusions are worth quoting at some length:

> Social conflict in Peru has begun a higher stage through the beginning of the armed struggle, in the form of guerrilla warfare. The MIR began this struggle on its own initiative. This obvious fact must be recognized, even when we must make a proper analysis of this revolutionary movement's activities from the point of view of its class basis and aims, and of the question of whether this was the right moment to begin the armed struggle in our country.
>
> The mainly *petit bourgeois* origins of the members of the MIR, some of whose members have not passed through the stage of proletarianization; the fact that many of its members, including national leaders, began in APRA; their lack of genuine Marxist–Leninist education, and their links with Trotskyism and revisionism, have all made them sectarian, élitist and hegemonic. This is what has prevented the MIR from recognizing our party as the only Marxist–Leninist Communist party. By stating that there are only two Communist factions in the country, and that the MIR is the new uncontaminated Left, they have obstructed the development of friendly relations between our party and their movement, which in general has been hostile to us. It seems that after the Fourth National Conference of the Communist party in January 1964,[9] the MIR saw the appearance of a rival capable of snatching from it the initiative in the armed struggle and has acted accordingly. This same tendency has given rise to the appearance of other small groups who are also attempting to take over control of the armed revolutionary movement. This point of view was very influential in the decision of the MIR to begin the armed struggle, especially as they considered themselves sufficiently trained militarily. The MIR took into account the general situation of the country, but not the immediate political situation which would favour the beginning of the armed

struggle. They only took into account the subjective factors, the training of their own armed forces. However, such important factors as the feelings of the broad masses, or their grievances, were not taken into account, nor was any importance given to the problem of a united front, or the consideration that the revolution is carried out by the masses and that no revolutionary group by itself can bring the struggle to a successful conclusion. This is why we consider that the moment for beginning the armed struggle was not the most favourable one. This does not prevent us from recognizing that the guerrilla struggle has brought about a greater polarization of forces, and a sharpening of contradictions. Also it has effectively shown up the brutal and repressive nature of the pro-imperialist oligarchy. The experience gained in the struggle both from victories and defeats, will be very useful for the future development of the revolution. That is why the Peruvian [pro-Chinese] Communist party pays homage to the late leader of the MIR, Luís de la Puente Uceda, who fell in battle, and to all the revolutionaries who have offered up their lives. We consider it our duty not to allow the fire of the armed struggle to be extinguished. We hereby declare that we will make every effort to keep it burning.

It must not be forgotten that beginning the armed struggle depends essentially on the degree of maturity of the subjective conditions. It is well known that a revolutionary situation exists in Peru, made up of a set of objective conditions which demand a revolutionary solution to the fundamental contradictions of Peruvian society. Of the subjective conditions, some depend basically on the degree of fighting spirit and organization of the broad masses of the people and others on the degree of particular readiness of the revolutionary party for the armed struggle. Both are maturing. But it should be pointed out that objective conditions do not depend on wishful thinking. Subjective conditions, on the other hand, depend mainly on willingness to prepare and carry out the revolution. It is not revolutionary to wait for subjective conditions to happen by themselves, when they depend on us. That is why we must create, develop and organize them. When these subjective conditions have matured to some degree, the armed struggle may be begun with greater success. But it also happens that the counter-revolutionary forces compel the revolutionary forces to begin to act sooner than expected, if their preparatory activities are discovered. That is why it is necessary to take precautions to save one's strength.

As for the prospects for the armed struggle in Peru, they are magnificent. The objective conditions may well give rise to the subjective conditions. And although imperialism and the forces of repression are strong, the forces of the revolution (although temporarily weak), aided by the justice of their cause, the heroic traditions of our people and the support of the revolutionary forces of the world, will gradually get stronger and will finally defeat the forces of counter-revolution, given that the strength of the enemy is more apparent than real since it is based on crumbling foundations and is repudiated by the oppressed and exploited classes.

THE PERUVIAN [PRO-CHINESE] COMMUNIST PARTY repeats its general guiding principles that the only way to defeat the enemies of revolution is by means of the people's revolutionary war; that is, by co-ordinating and combining fighting with political struggle of the masses, particularly with the peasants. As was stated in the Resolution of the expanded Political Committee last October, 'the armed struggle should not be restricted to the participation of small armed groups isolated from the masses, but should count on the presence of the masses. Otherwise, even if the guerrilla units can depend on nature to survive for some time, they cannot grow sufficiently to be followed by the whole people, which also means that the workers in the cities must be organized on a class and revolutionary basis in order to take their due part in the revolutionary war. An armed struggle without the aid of the masses of workers in the country and the city may end in failure.' This statement, made before the setback suffered by the MIR on

Mesa Pelada, shows its accuracy, for one of the causes of these sad events was the weak and almost non-existent support of the peasant masses for the guerrillas in the Cuzco area. The outlines laid down in this document from the Political Committee have been ratified and remain in force.

As comrade Mao Tse-tung says, the three magic wands of the revolution are the Communist party, the united front and the armed struggle. This is derived from the fact that the Communists alone cannot carry out the revolution without the support of the broad masses. Thus the fundamental task of the party is to bring together all the oppressed classes into a broad united national liberation front. It is not just a matter of the union of revolutionary or left-wing parties. If it were only a matter of uniting the Left, this unity would not be a united front. This front must be based essentially on the workers and peasants; it must attract the broad popular masses not active in left-wing parties. Besides, it must be borne in mind that apart from the Peruvian [pro-Chinese] Communist party, there is no other revolutionary party organized nationally and with any mass support. The beginning of the armed struggle makes it absolutely essential to fight to form a united front bringing in the working class as the leading class through its party, the peasants, the *petit bourgeoisie* (craftsmen, small tradesmen, professionals, intellectuals and students) and the progressive sector of the national *bourgeoisie*.

However, it should be pointed out that a genuine united front cannot be formed with revisionists and Trotskyists, because they are not revolutionaries but agents in one form or another. They try to distort the revolution or make it fail. Apart from that, none of these counter-revolutionary groups has any support. What must be done is to seek unity amongst those who are openly fighting the enemy, and that is why the doors are open for an understanding with the MIR, despite existing differences, as it is better for them to keep away from Trotskyists and revisionists and to seek an alliance with our party and link up with the vast masses. Besides, it should not be forgotten that unity can only be forged in revolutionary mass action. Apart from common aims, we must seek to co-ordinate our actions during the course of the fight allied with the masses.

In view of the failure of the National Liberation Front[10] as a result of personalist, sectarian, anti-Communist and counter-revolutionary activity by some of its members who publicly broke with the party, it will fight to create a PATRIOTIC LIBERATION FRONT, on a broader mass base, so that this front can carry out the revolution, under the direction of the working class and its party, closely allied with the peasantry and the other oppressed classes.[11]

This is perhaps the clearest exposition available of the Chinese attitude towards the guerrilla movements in Latin America.

Notes

1 Che Guevara, *La Guerra de Guerrillas*.

2 Levano, 'Lessons of the Guerrilla Struggle in Peru'.

3 In his book, *Las Guerrillas del Perú*, Mercado states that, although he asked the Secretary-General of the party, Jorge del Prado, for a copy of the party's statement about the guerrillas, one was not made available to him (p. 146). He does, however, print a statement by the FLN—a Communist front organization led by a retired general, César A. Pando. The FLN, said the statement, published in June 1965, understood and expected the outbreak of guerrilla warfare. Nevertheless, 'it would be a mistake to believe that victory can only be obtained through the action of a select vanguard group.'

4 According to Lenin, whom Communists always fall back on when in doubt, a revolutionary situation presupposes certain objective conditions: (1) A political crisis making it impossible for the ruling classes to rule in the old way; (2) a substantial deterioration in the material conditions of the oppressed masses; and (3) the rise of a genuinely mass movement. César Levano comments: 'Obviously no such revolutionary situation existed in Peru in June 1965.'

5 UNO was the party of the ex-President, General Odría. In an unholy alliance, it joined up with APRA to oppose Belaúnde.

6 This was the first pro-Chinese splinter party in Latin America to be officially recognized by Peking. According to Chinese sources, the founding conference was attended by a majority of the old Central Committee members and by representatives from 13 out of 17 regional committees. See *Peking Review*, 14 February 1964 and 22 May 1964, and also Halperin, 'Peking and the Latin American Communists'. The leader of the Chinese party was Saturnino Paredes.

7 *Peking Review*, 7 January 1966.

8 The Chinese party called it the 'Fifth Conference', as they regarded themselves as the orthodox party and the pro-Russians as the splinter group. It appears, from pro-Russian evidence, that de la Puente's guerrillas caused some havoc within the Chinese party. César Levano writes: 'The splinter group which publishes the *Bandera Raja* newspaper adopted a different position, branding Luís de la Puente and the other leaders of MIR guerrilla detachments as adventurers. The result was that part of the students broke away from the group and formed their own "armed forces of national liberation". This organization (it did not conduct guerrilla operations) still maintains contact with our party. Later, the anti-guerrilla position of the splitters had further repercussions: one of the groups in their "central committee", headed by the lawyer Saturnino Paredes, expelled another group led by the lawyer José Sotomajor, who was charged among other things with "revisionism". Such are the results of the Left opportunism of the splitters, who at first proclaimed armed struggle as the only correct form of struggle, and later, when the bullets began to fly, beat a hasty retreat, leaving to their fate the sincere but misguided men who believed in them.'

9 The founding conference of the pro-Chinese party.

10 The front organization dominated by the orthodox Communists, not a guerrilla movement.

11 Mimeographed document giving the conclusions of the Fifth National Conference of the [pro-Chinese] Peruvian Communist party, 16 November 1965, pp. 13–18.

9. The Guerrillas Sum Up

> 'Faith in the revolution is certainly fundamental, but it is not in itself
> sufficient to permit a small vanguard successfully to confront the repressive
> forces of the bourgeois state, risking everything in the first battle.'
>
> Américo Pumaruna

The Peruvian guerrillas of 1965 were wiped out within six months of going into action. But this defeat did not put an end to the polemic within the Peruvian Left about the relative merits of the armed struggle. The MIR, which had sponsored the principal guerrilla groups, held a meeting of their Central Committee early in 1966, and came up with the following conclusions:

A) In the north our revolutionary activity did not reach the political and military levels required to begin and continue the armed struggle. Shortly before the beginning of military operations, two armed groups joined together, which meant a setback in the work in that area. On the other hand, we did not consider that it was essential either tactically or strategically to begin our actions simultaneously. In spite of this setback, both the political and military parts of our organization have stayed in the area and have achieved such a level of cohesion and entrenchment that the armed forces have been unable to destroy them. In just one of these surround-and-destroy operations, in December, about 10,000 men were engaged, plus strong forces from the Ecuadorean army. Lately our military organization has not undertaken direct fighting with the enemy, following directives from the National Command.

B) In the central area the 'Túpac Amaru' guerrilla unit carried out considerable liaison work with the local peasants, and fought energetically and competently. It suffered from weaknesses in the make-up of the party, which prevented it from making better use of the support and enthusiasm aroused by them among the peasants.

The MIR guerrillas in the central area showed that victories can be won against the forces of repression, even in very unfavourable conditions. This was proved at Yahuarina, Pucutá and in other engagements.

Analysis of the guerrilla campaign in the centre carried out in the MIR Assembly showed that the setbacks suffered by our companions were not entirely due to the fighting competence of the powerfully equipped forces of repression on land, in the air and on the rivers, but mainly to tactical mistakes by the guerrillas themselves.

C) In the south the work of building up the party, and of organizing the masses on this basis, was going ahead well, and to such an extent that there is reason to believe that had it gone on in the same way, armed action would have been well supported by the masses. However, while this work went ahead well, insufficient attention was paid to the guerrilla arm itself. The military preparations were not sufficient to allow the guerrillas to keep the initiative. Besides, a serious mistake was made when the presence there of Luís de la Puente, secretary-general of the movement, was allowed to be discovered. The enemy concentrated their attention on the area, and what was supposed to be the rearguard of the command became the front line. In spite of this, the defence of the zone, with mine-fields and guerrilla action, held the forces of repression back for some time. They suffered considerable casualties and their morale was undermined by these factors and the natural difficulties of the area.

A chance event helped the forces of repression, and played an important part in the heavy losses suffered; this was the criminal action of the traitor to his country and to the revolution, Albino Guzmán. This individual, incapable of putting up with the privations of guerrilla warfare, his morale shattered, surrendered to the forces of repression and gave away all the military secrets of the guerrilla group, thus making the enemy's task that much easier.

The traitor Guzmán was particularly competent to help the forces of repression in their aims. He was from the area and had taken an active part in the peasants' struggles under Hugo Blanco. For a long time he was one of the most outstanding members of the guerrilla force, so much so that in view of his record he was promoted by his comrades to the regional committee; as such he worked on the preparation of the guerrilla zone. All this, plus his personal knowledge of the party organization, made him the enemy's most effective weapon for locating and destroying the main group under the command of the commander-in-chief, comrade Luís de la Puente.

Although aware, days before his surrender, of the state of moral decay which the man was in, the guerrilla unit did not take the proper measures, for humanitarian reasons.[1]

Héctor Béjar, the leader of the ELN, discussed in an interview the role of the one crucial element upon which the guerrillas must depend: the peasant.

QUESTION 9: What was the attitude of the rural population to the guerrillas? Did they support or reject the guerrillas? What sort of political work did the ELN carry out among the peasants?

ANSWER: Many left-wingers are now repeating the enemy's slanders and saying that we failed because the people did not support us. Nothing is further from the truth. I am going to tell you about our own experience, since I know the work of my comrades in the MIR from first hand.

When the peasants began to realize that there were armed men in the area, their first reaction was one of curiosity. They wanted to know what it was about, who we were, what we were fighting for. They were cordial and wanted to satisfy their curiosity. Then our relationship became closer, we became friends and helped them when we could, within our possibilities. We became nurses, advisers, teachers, all sorts of things which helped us to win their confidence. Then they told us their problems. Among them we found a good number with pretty clear ideas on why they were so badly off, and many who had had some experience of fighting, for they had been miners and had tried to form unions. Their problems boiled down to one: the large estates. And naturally, they wanted us to help them to solve this problem. Their communities spent money uselessly in unending court cases which they always lost, and the hacienda workers, slaves in effect, knew perfectly well that the landlord was their first enemy. Thus our actions were always directed against the large estates in the area, leaving the army to defend the landowners.

By the end of the year, we were practically the sole authority in the area and many peasants had joined our unit or were about to do so.

All this was valuable experience for them and for us. We began to realize how far, how very far, the revolutionary or café Marxist is from the reality of Peru and its people, and why Peru has not had until now an organized and vigorous mass political movement. At the beginning, even our language was strange to them. We learnt to speak to them in a language which they understood, about things they found easily understandable. And they quickly understood the need for the revolution. Our political work was based on trying to make them understand that the revolution does not end with driving out the landlord, that there is a long way to go and that elsewhere there are other people as exploited as they are. The Peruvian peasant is slow to make up his mind, that is true, he thinks about a problem several times. But when he does make up his mind, he is serious. His determination may be simple, but it is also profound and very human. That is why I believe that the Peruvian Revolution will take not months, but years. But when it comes it will be one of the most profound and beautiful in America. The peasant must be made ready, and that is what we were doing, preparing them not only as rank-and-file members, but as revolutionary leaders.

This experience is useful not only for us, but for all the Left. Many people say that the conditions do not exist because the peasant has no political awareness, that he must first be given revolutionary political awareness. We can tell them that they do not know the peasant. Our tactics should be to adapt ourselves to the psychology of the Peruvian peasant. We cannot wait for landslide mass movements to tell us that the time is ripe to fight for power. To develop the peasant's political awareness you must live with him, but not just as a propagandist or union organizer, or as a chance visitor who arrives, gives an unintelligible speech, and then returns straight away to give his report to the party or to the leaders in the city. We must be armed to defend ourselves and to defend the peasant against the landlords and their lackeys and to show him the strength that lies in arms and organization. But we have to survive enemy repression. Survival is an obligation for the guerrilla, for in our ability to survive lies our effectiveness in showing the people that the revolution is not only necessary, but possible.[2]

Béjar's interesting analysis is a necessary corrective to the widely held belief that the Peruvian peasant possesses a 'kulak' mentality and is loth to engage in revolutionary activity. While this may have been true of the area around La Convención where Hugo Blanco and de la Puente operated, Béjar's evidence suggests that such an outlook was not so widespread in the region of the ELN's activities. His remarks point to the danger of generalizing about peasants from the results of small-scale surveys.

The MIR analysis completely ignores the question of whether the guerrillas had peasant support or not. Failure was due to 'tactical mistakes' and 'treachery'. This rather simple explanation was perhaps natural in the immediate aftermath of defeat. Nevertheless it should not be assumed from the relative ease with which the guerrillas of 1965 were crushed, that an agrarian revolution in Peru must necessarily be excluded for ever. Peasant discontent in the Peruvian altiplano is still very real, and when the moment comes it may well overflow the banks of repression that have been erected by the oligarchy and its United States allies to contain it.

The military regime installed in Peru in October 1968 has probably postponed the genuine Peruvian Revolution by stealing much of the programme of the Left. But when that revolution does eventually come, liberating the most interesting indigenous group in the continent, we may well believe that it will be, as Béjar suggests, the most profound and beautiful in America.

Notes

1   Mercado, *Las Guerrillas del Perú, el MIR*, pp. 167–9.

2   Interview with Héctor Béjar, published in *Opiniones*, the journal of the Peruvian ELN, 1967, and reprinted in 'Perú: entrevista a dos guerrilleros', *Pensamiento Crítico* (Havana), NO. 6, July 1967.

V

TRAGEDY IN BOLIVIA

'One thing is certain, irrefutable: fifty men shook an entire nation, rocked a government, deprived the imperialists and their servants of sleep, and focused the attention of the whole world upon them. These men paid for their immortality with their lives. Think what will happen when the whole country advances along the road to revolution.'

Mario Monje
Secretary-General of the Bolivian Communist Party

1. JORGE MASETTI AND THE GUERRILLAS OF SALTA

The Bolivian guerrilla episode of 1967 was a deliberate attempt to begin the continental revolution. From the very first Ernesto Guevara had been an enthusiastic proponent of this idea. For six years he had talked to Latin American revolutionaries from behind his desk in Havana. He had watched the ups and downs of guerrilla movements in countries all over the continent, and finally he decided that it was time to throw himself, together with his immense experience and prestige, back into the guerrilla struggle. As Castro explained:

> Comrade Guevara joined us during our exile in Mexico, and always, from the very first day, he clearly expressed the idea that when the struggle was completed in Cuba, he would have other duties to fulfil in another place, and we always gave him our word that no state interest, no national interest, no circumstances would lead us to ask him to remain in our country, or hinder him from carrying out that wish, that desire. And we fully and faithfully kept that promise to comrade Guevara.[1]

Initially, as was perhaps natural from even someone with such an underdeveloped sense of nationalism as Che, his thoughts turned to Argentina. It is difficult to feel that he did not occasionally have a desire to revolutionize that almost impossibly bourgeois society.[2] There is some evidence to suggest that he had some hand in the ill-fated guerrilla expedition to Tartagal and Salta, led by Jorge Masetti in 1963.

Jorge Masetti was an Argentinian journalist who had travelled to the Sierra Maestra in 1958 to interview Fidel and Che. Subsequently he wrote a book about the Cuban guerrillas called *Los que luchan y los que lloran*. After the Cuban Revolution he was invited to Havana by Che and was instrumental in setting up the Cuban news agency, Prensa Latina. He resigned in 1961, largely, it is believed, because of problems with old-guard Communists within the agency, and partly because of Cuban jealousy that he, an Argentinian, should be head of a Cuban agency.

He had always been taken with the idea of starting a guerrilla movement in Argentina. Although a former Peronist, there is no evidence that he had anything to do with the Peronist guerrilla movement of Comandante Uturuncu in Tucumán in 1959. But after leaving Prensa Latina, he devoted much of his time to planning a clandestine return to Argentina.

In June 1963 he established himself in Bolivia, in a farm close to the frontier with Argentina. With him were three Cubans, one of whom, Ricardo (or Papi), was later to play an important role in Guevara's Bolivian expedition.

In September, with a small group of men, Masetti crossed the border into the Argentinian province of Salta. His band was called the Ejército Guerrillero del Pubelo (EGP)—the Guerrilla Army of the People, and he himself operated under the name of Comandante Segundo.[3] Little is known of what happened to them. They were infiltrated by the police and most of them were captured, tortured and shot. Masetti himself was never discovered, but he was either shot or died in the jungle.

Ricardo Rojo suggests that they may have been hoping to link up with Javier Heraud's Peruvian guerrilla group which was decimated at Puerto Maldonado in May 1963. He also points to the inadequate conditions that existed in Argentina at that time for a guerrilla outbreak to prove successful. Although the military had overthrown the civilian President, Arturo Frondizi, in 1962, they allowed elections to be held in July 1963. The successful candidate was Arturo Illía, and he was permitted by the military to rule until 1966. Thus, at the time when Masetti hoped to launch his guerrilla campaign, Argentina had a reasonably moderate civilian government.[4]

Undoubtedly Guevara was interested in doing something in Argentina. It was his own country, he knew it well, and it would perhaps be possible to build constructively on the failure and mistakes of Masetti. In addition, he had the support of the Cuban, Ricardo, who had been involved in the planning of Masetti's expedition, had survived, and was willing to have a second go.

But from the start Guevara emphasized that the struggle should have continental dimensions. If the isolated outbreaks of guerrilla warfare that had occurred up and down the continent since the Cuban Revolution had had central direction and co-ordination, their history might have been very different. If Argentine was to be the target, it was important that the struggle should rapidly spread up the Andes chain through Bolivia and Peru, and across to the tropical jungles of Paraguay and Brazil. From there it could join up with the movements already established in Colombia and Venezuela.

In 1964, when Che first began giving serious thought to the possibility of his personal return to active warfare, conditions looked promising. A military coup in Brazil had released the energies of Leonel Brizola, the Governor of Rio Grande do Sul and the brother-in-law of ex-President João Goulart. Brizola, after fleeing into exile in Uruguay, was busy canvassing the possibilities of beginning a guerrilla campaign against the gang of colonels who had taken over his country.[5] In Peru, Luís de la Puente, Guillermo Lobatón, and Guevara's brother-in-law, Ricardo Gadea, were making their separate efforts to get things going again in the Peruvian altiplano after the collapse of Hugo Blanco's movement and the disastrous death of Javier Heraud. And in Bolivia, in November 1964, the nationalist regime of President Paz Estenssoro, which had ruled since 1952, was overthrown by Generals René Barrientos and Alfredo Ovando. The possibility of a revolt against the military dictators did not seem wholly unrealistic.

Notes

1 Fidel Castro, speech at the closing session of the Tricontinental Conference, Havana, January 1966.

2 An interesting interview with Guevara in the Cabaña fortress in January 1959 throws some light on his attitude to Cuba and Argentina. 'I met Fidel and at once identified myself with his ideas and ideals. I enlisted as a volunteer in his group, not just as a doctor but as a soldier in a just cause. Earlier, I had escaped from my own country instead of fighting against the dictatorship of Perón. But there is no heroism in young people dodging their responsibilities to their own country and their own generation. I had to pay my debts in this respect, and I hope I have cancelled it in Cuba.'—Rafael Otero Echeverría, *Reportaje a una Revolución: de Batista a Fidel Castro*, Editorial del Pacífico, Santiago, 1959, p. 46.

3   This account is taken from Rojo's *Mi Amigo el Che*. Rojo maintains that Masetti's decision to call himself Comandante Segundo indicates that there was a Comandante Primero, i.e. Che Guevara. Other evidence suggests that the two Argentinians had given themselves *noms de guerre*, but that Guevara's was that of the famous Argentinian gaucho Martín Fierro, and that of Masetti's was of another famous gaucho called Segundo. There is no record of the real name of Ricardo, which is surprising, considering his importance and the fact that the bulk of the Cubans involved in the Bolivian expedition of 1967 were later identified.

4   In September 1968, the Unión de Periodistas de Cuba held a meeting in Havana, which I attended, to honour the memory of Jorge Masetti. A portrait depicting the guerrilla together with Che Guevara was unveiled by his son, and a booklet was published which reprinted some of the documents connected with the Argentinian campaign. One is an open letter to Arturo Illía, written by Masetti on 9 July 1963, from the Campamento Augusto César Sandino, and another is a letter addressed to 'Comrade Peasant', dated January 1964, from the mountains of Salta.

5   As was stated at the beginning of this book, Brazil and the struggles of Francisco Julião among the peasantry in the poverty-stricken northeast have not been included. Nor does Brizola receive more than this cursory mention. It may be useful therefore to include this brief fragment of his views, as recorded in an interview late in 1963: 'He [Goulart] and I [Brizola] met through politics, and we had the same ideas. He is a reformist, one of these people who wants to paint the walls of peasant huts and leave them looking beautiful, but who remains in possession of the big house themselves. He is not aware that the big house must become the headquarters of the local co-operative. We have had problems due to the errors committed by the Communist party and by Francisco Julião. However, we must acknowledge that Julião possesses the great merit of having awakened the most oppressed sector of the population, the peasantry. And we believe that all the errors will be overcome. We are not anti-Communist, we welcome any Brazilian who comes as a patriot to struggle for the liberation of his country. The Latin American problem must be stated in terms of national liberation. Without national liberation there can be no basic reforms, because poverty cannot be reformed.'—Interview with Brizola taken from Víctor Rico Galán, 'The Brazilian Crisis', *Monthly Review*, April 1964.

2. THE SINO-SOVIET SPLIT

'It would be too boring, too tedious, to examine the failure of the organizations or parties styling themselves, above all, "pro-Chinese". At the first stages of organization they are able to attract honest and resolute militants, thanks to their programmes and their promises. Very soon, however, their method of work, the noisy opportunism of their political line, the hypocritical sabotage of their own official line on the armed struggle, lead the revolutionary strata, principally the youth, to abandon them.'

Régis Debray, *Revolution in the Revolution?*

The year 1964, which seemed to offer so many opportunities for the revolutionaries, was also the year in which the Sino-Soviet dispute grew into a wide and irrevocable split. Its impact on Cuba and on the plans for a continental revolution could hardly have been more devastating, for many of the most militant members of the orthodox Communist parties in Latin America hived off to join the new pro-Chinese groupings. And those who had been most vociferously in favour of Comrade Castro could now only listen to the voice of Chairman Mao. Already in January 1964 the Peruvian party had split in two, and other parties, including the Bolivian, were preparing for a similar eventuality.

Throughout this difficult period within the Communist world, the Cuban leaders—novices in the matter—refrained from intervening on, either side. In August 1964, Guevara explained to a group of visiting American students:

The Sino-Soviet differences are one of the saddest developments for us. We do not take sides in these disputes. We try to use our influence to resolve them. But now that they are happening we inform the people of them and the party is discussing them. Our party's position is not to say who is right or who is wrong. We choose our position and, as they say in American films, 'any resemblance is purely coincidental'. What matters to us is the development of Socialism to live with dignity.

Without openly supporting the Chinese, the Cubans nevertheless had a marked preference for the Chinese emphasis on the armed struggle over the Russian desire for peaceful coexistence. Their own revolutionary experience, and their almost daily confrontations with American imperialism, 90 miles from their shores, left the Cubans with little choice. But economic necessity kept them firmly in the Russian camp. Whenever possible, however, the Cubans tried not to take a stand. When the Russians attempted to organize the March 1965 Meeting of Communist Parties in Moscow into a forum for expelling the Chinese from the world Communist movement, the Cubans were at first reluctant to attend. Finally, when they did go, they refused to take up a position.

The Latin American Communist parties, on the other hand, were much more closely committed to supporting Moscow. The degree of independence permitted a dependent nation was much greater than that accorded to a dependent party. Consequently when, in November–December 1964, there took place a meeting of Latin American Communist parties in Havana to discuss the joint attitude to be adopted towards the Moscow meeting, the seeds were sown of the conflict that was to develop later between Cuba and the orthodox parties of Latin America.

On this occasion their differences were patched up reasonably amicably. The Cubans agreed to oppose 'fractionalist' activity, which pleased the orthodox Communists, and they in turn agreed to support 'revolutionary fighters' in a number of named countries, which pleased the Cubans.

But the document contained a serious contradiction. Many of the revolutionaries 'subjected to severe oppression' and actually engaged in fighting, whom the Communist parties were supposed to be supporting, were the same people engaged in 'factionalist activity'. Even so, the document brought little joy to the Chinese, and it probably speeded up the fissiparous tendency within the continental Communist movement that had been observable during the previous year. Two months after the Havana conference, in February 1965, Guevara was in Peking, where he received a noticeably frosty reception. The official emissaries from the conference fared no better. The Colombian Communist, Gilberto Vieira, has explained what happened:

> The Havana conference appointed a commission of nine Latin American Communist leaders to forward to the CPSU and the Communist party of China the Latin American parties' recommendation to secure the unity of the world Communist movement by means of bilateral or multilateral discussions, a conference or conferences of all the Marxist–Leninist parties.
>
> It will not be amiss to say, without going into detail, that the commission called on the leaders of the CPSU in Moscow, and that the latter expressed full agreement with the resolution of the conference of Latin American Communist parties, adding that, if it could, the CPSU would not hesitate to put its signature under that document.
>
> After the CPSU had approved all the points of the resolution, the commission went to Peking, where it exchanged opinions and discussed points of view with a delegation of the Communist party of China. As a result of these exchanges, continued in talks with Mao Tse-tung, the Chinese leaders took the following stand:
>
> A) The Central Committee of the Communist party of China cannot terminate open polemics; it does not believe that polemics damage the interests of the world Communist movement.
>
> B) The Central Committee of the Communist party of China disagrees with the denunciation of factional activity: contained in the resolution of the Latin American parties and will not abandon its decision to support persons whom it considers anti-imperialist and revolutionary, though expelled from Communist

parties. The Central Committee of the Chinese Communist party insists on their right to found new parties. . . .

In view of this categorical disagreement of the Chinese leaders with the Latin American resolution, the commission decided to wind up its work and inform the Latin American Communist parties about its results in a special communique, copies of which were also made available to the CC CPSU and CC CPCh.[1]

Though often attracted to the activism which the Chinese line appeared to represent, the Cuban leaders at no stage showed signs of endorsing the Chinese decision to force a rupture within the Communist movement. Leftist movements in Latin America have had a propensity to split which long predates the Sino-Soviet rift, and no responsible revolutionary acquainted with this history would wish to elevate this propensity to a new doctrine. Guevara was no exception. There is no evidence that he was opposed to the decisions of the November 1964 Havana Conference and, although an activist, he was never attracted to the dogmatism of the Chinese position. In his writings, like Fidel, he berated both the Russians and the Chinese for their tiresome squabbling which could only make the revolutionary task in Latin America more difficult.

And in practice, in Bolivia, the Sino-Soviet split caused the Cuban revolutionaries their major problem. There seems little doubt that Guevara had had close contacts with various Bolivian Communists at an earlier stage during the campaign of Masetti in Argentina. Fidel Castro himself has explained that:

Che had established relations with Bolivian Communist leaders and militants before the split that occurred within the party, calling on them to help the revolutionary movement in South America. Some of those militants, with the party's permission, collaborated with him on various tasks for years. The party split created a new situation in which the militants who had worked with Che found themselves in different camps.[9]

The Cuban, Ricardo, had almost certainly been in and out of La Paz, in contact with the Bolivian Communist party, at the time when Masetti was operating in Argentina in 1963–64. Indeed, one of the many polemics that have arisen out of the Sino-Soviet split in South America is the charge by the pro-Chinese Communists that the Secretary-General of the Bolivian party, Mario Monje, was involved in sabotaging the Argentina guerrillas.[3]

And in October 1964, before the party split, Che Guevara discussed with the Bolivian Communist militant, Oscár Zamora, a plan Zamora had for setting up a revolutionary group outside the Communist party dedicated to the armed struggle. Zamora himself has left an account of this meeting:

> In September–October of 1964, a group of young Bolivian students living in Cuba and Europe agreed to begin a struggle to set up a revolutionary vanguard to seek the liberation of Bolivia under the banners of Marxism–Leninism. We thought that to do this we had to set up a Marxist–Leninist force outside the framework of the existing leadership, the Bolivian Communist party. So I went to Cuba to seek help. There Major Ernesto Guevara expressed his support in the struggle against the corrupt leaders of the Communist parties who had lapsed into revisionism. He was in support of the armed struggle in Bolivia, by the only way possible, the armed way. At no time during these conversations with Che, who was then Minister of Industries in Cuba, did he show his intention of leading armed action in Bolivia or anywhere in the world. At the end of these talks with Che, it was agreed not to tell the then leaders of the Bolivian Communist party about the decisions that had been taken, but only you [Fidel].[4]

However, this took place just at the moment when the Sino-Soviet split in Latin America was about to break out into an open rift, with the Cubans desperately trying not to take sides. And in December 1964 the Havana meeting of all the Latin American Communist parties that was designed to reach a compromise took place. Zamora continues:

> In December 1964 . . . at the time of the preparatory meeting for the conference of revisionist Communist parties, you personally told Monje of my conversations with Che, and had the

group of Marxist–Leninist students in Cuba put under the control of the revisionist party. You agreed with Monje to break off all relations with our group, which you then described as a 'fraction'. That was how you put into practice the decision of the revisionist conference to fight against the forces of Marxism–Leninism. You cannot deny these facts, since in La Paz in January 1965 Monje told me so himself, boasting of 'winning his greatest political victory'.

It is doubtful whether Guevara himself had ever made any concrete promise about Cuba's likely attitude towards his 'fractionalist' movement.[5] In any case, after the December 1964 Havana meeting, Cuba had definitely come out against splinter movements. Nothing however, could stop Zamora and his pro-Chinese colleagues from obeying the signals emanating from Peking to the effect that the best way to sabotage the 'revisionists' was to split their parties. In April 1965, at a conference held in the great tin mining area of Siglo Veinte, Zamora and his comrades, led by the miners' leader, Federico Escobar, set up the pro-Chinese Bolivian Communist party. Also present was another miners' leader, Moises Guevara, who was later to form a dissident movement of his own, hovering ideologically between the Moscow and Peking parties.

The pro-Moscow Communists in Bolivia were distinctly upset by this development and they immediately held a Congress to consider 'the divisionist activity of anti-party elements'.

According to Jorge Kolle Cueto, a member of the Central Committee, there had been 'an unprecedently large split'. It had affected 6 out of 14 districts where the Communist party was organized. In the three principal cities of La Paz, Cochabamba and Santa Cruz, the split had not been too disastrous, but in the other three areas 'time will be needed to reabsorb and re-educate the large group which supports the splitters'.

No analysis of the Bolivian guerrilla movement of 1967 can be complete without emphasizing the serious effect that the Sino-Soviet split had upon the revolutionary Left in Bolivia. Nevertheless, in many ways Bolivia was less affected than other countries, in that the Communist party was only one among many claiming to have the exclusive revolutionary formula. Organized Trotskyism has one of its strongest parties in Bolivia, the Partido Obrero Revolucionario (POR), and although it, like the Communist party, was seriously split, it had strong sympathies for guerrillas. The Partido Revolucionario Izquierda Nacional (PRIN) also had some good claims to be considered revolutionary. This had broken away from the old ruling party, the Movimiento Nacionalista Revolucionario de Izquierda (MNR), and its leader Juan Lechín, though somewhat opportunist, did not discount the possibility of guerrilla action. There is some evidence to suggest that he had a notion of what was afoot in Bolivia, but was unable to do anything concrete to help.

Notes

1   Gilberto Vieira, 'International Conference of Communist Parties will Promote Unity', *World Marxist Review*, September 1968.

2   Fidel Castro, 'Una Introdución Necesaria', *El Diario del Che en Bolivia*.

3   In July 1968, Oscár Zamora, by then head of the pro-Chinese Communist party in Bolivia, sent an open letter to Fidel entitled. 'Cuba directed the Bolivian guerrillas and is wholly responsible for their failure'. Zamora's charges, which need not be taken too seriously, made specific charges about the betrayal of guerrilla movements by the 'revisionists': 'Tartagal, Argentina. The guerrilla movement of young Argentines was betrayed by the Bolivian and Argentine revisionists. In spite of being well-informed by your embassy in La Paz and directly in Havana of the fact that Monje and his clique betrayed the Peruvian guerrilla movement, you [Fidel] personally decided to entrust Monje and his "party" with the task of meeting and training the Argentine guerrilla group on Bolivian soil. This group was met by the Argentine police at Tartagal soon after crossing the frontier. General San Román, the head of the Bolivian political police, was also informed of these events by the revisionists. When I talked with Ernesto Guevara in Havana in 1964, he agreed with me that the person responsible for the disaster of Tartagal was Monje, because of his contacts with the Bolivian police; Guevara's words were: "What happened at Tartagal was a betrayal by Monje of the Argentines, and Fidel knows this." The revisionist Communist party of Argentina was kept well informed by Monje about the guerrilla movement in spite of an agreement that they were not to be because the guerrillas were

acting outside the Argentine Communist party. The calling of a conference of Communist parties, signed by you in the name of the
Cuban Communist party, by Marío Monje and Vittorio Codovilla,
was closely connected with the need to cover up what happened at
Tartagal.'—Oscár Zamora, 'Cuba dirigió las guerrillas en Bolivia y su
fracaso le pertence íntegramente', *Los Tiempos* (Cochabamba), 14
July 1968.

4   Ibid.

5   In 1966 Guevara explained to the orthodox Communist, Marío
Monje (according to Monje's account): 'I have made few mistakes
about men in my life, and one of those mistakes concerned Oscár
Zamora. Zamora came to Cuba to ask for help and told us he would
foment fractionalism in order to take over the leadership of the
Bolivian Communist party or divide it. I said I agreed with fractionalism if it began with guerrilla warfare. Zamora agreed. He returned
to Bolivia, forgot his promise and the help he had received, and sold
himself to the highest bidder. Now we have nothing to do with him
and his group.'—Letter from Marío Monje, printed in *Presencia* (La
Paz), 25 July 1968.

'If there is a real intention to begin the struggle from some foreign country or from distant and remote regions within the same country, it is obvious that it must begin in small conspiratorial movements of secret members acting without mass support or knowledge.'

Ernesto Che Guevara, *Guerrilla Warfare*

Guevara 'disappeared' from Cuba in April 1965. He spent some months in the Congo, and probably Vietnam, before returning to Cuba to plan the Latin American Revolution early in 1966. The idea had been given additional impetus by the holding of the Tricontinental Conference in January in Havana, which brought together revolutionary leaders from Africa and Asia as well as Latin America. Guevara himself was not present, but the leaders of a number of Latin American Communist parties were, and a good deal of pressure seems to have been put on them by the Cubans to take more seriously the task of supporting revolutionary fighters, as they had promised to do at the November 1964 Havana Conference of Communist parties.

The original plan for the commencement of the continental revolution dreamt up in Cuba involved Guevara's returning to Argentina, reviving the guerrilla embers left by Masetti, working in close co-operation with Brizola in Brazil and El Chino in Peru, and using Bolivia as a refuge and a training ground.[1] By the beginning of 1966, the guerrilla movement of Luís de la Puente had been wiped out, but El Chino—a man of immense energy and enthusiasm—believed that there were enough survivors and enough new volunteers to resurrect it. In the original scheme Bolivia was given secondary importance largely because of the lack of local cadres ready to organize a guerrilla war. Nevertheless, the Bolivian Communists were urged to start developing their thoughts on how they actually planned to promote the Bolivian Revolution.

Marío Monje, the Secretary-General of the Bolivian party, had been in Cuba for the Tricontinental. He was there again five months later, in May 1966, and had an interview with Fidel Castro, of which he has left a record:

> In May 1966 in Cuba an interview was arranged for me with comrade Fidel Castro. In the course of this, after making much of my spirit of internationalism, he said that rather than approaching others he was asking for my help in protecting on his way through Bolivia a comrade whom we both knew as a good revolutionary. He had every right to return to his country, and Fidel asked me personally to choose four trusted comrades to protect him on his way through and if possible to go with him afterwards. I agreed to this request, and he asked me to keep it to myself. Then he offered the Bolivian Communists unconditional help, saying that he was in favour of the Bolivian revolution being run by Bolivians; he promised not to get mixed up in the internal affairs of Bolivia and to retain the students who had been trained in Cuba and now wanted to return to their country. I thanked him for all this.
>
> When I returned, I informed the National Secretary of the request and the agreement we had made, as well as the offers.[2]

In addition to providing four men, Monje was also asked 'to co-ordinate with Brizola the matter of Brazil'.[3]

It will perhaps help to explain Monje's subsequent tortuous attitude if it is recalled that, during this trip to Havana, he was given $25,000 for the purpose of promoting the Bolivian Revolution.[4] The Bolivian Communist party was never very rich, and to some extent Monje's co-operation with the Cubans over a programme with which he was not wholly in agreement seems to have been due to his lack of financial independence from Cuban funds. There was always a danger from the Communist point of view that the Cubans might choose to channel their activities through other revolutionary groups in Bolivia.

Subsequent to Monje's journey to Cuba in May, Ricardo was sent to La Paz to begin organizing, in company with the four Bolivians provided by Monje, the Bolivian aspect of the projected continental struggle. At no stage does the Communist party appear to have been given details of what was being planned in Havana, nor did anyone know that Che Guevara was going to be an integral part of the plan.

Some time between May and July 1966, the basic strategy was changed. It was decided that Bolivia, rather than Argentina, was the country 'that had the best conditions'.[5] Consequently Bolivia was to become the headquarters of the continental revolution. Instead of the struggle beginning in Argentina and spreading northwards into Bolivia, it was decided to begin in Bolivia and spread northwards into Peru. Apart from the fact that Bolivia seemed a more obvious choice than Argentina, it is clear that the Cubans had extreme difficulty in locating any groups in Argentina who looked as though they were capable of launching a guerrilla *foco*.

There is some evidence to suggest that the Peruvians had hoped that priority would be given to Peru. When told of the change in plan, 'El Chino' was distinctly disappointed. The Cubans felt, however, that too many things had been left unexplained after the collapse of the Peruvian guerrilla of 1965. Since there was more than a hint of betrayal, it is clear that the Cubans did not feel justified in recommending Guevara to begin operations from there.[6] It is quite possible that this also explains why Bolivia was chosen rather than a country like Venezuela or Colombia where guerrilla movements had proved their staying-power. Quite apart from the fact that Guevara obviously wanted to begin somewhere new, rather than to poach on the territory of an existing movement, the risk of treachery was perhaps marginally less in a movement that could be started from scratch than in one which was well-established and also well-infiltrated.

After the failure of the Bolivian campaign, many people questioned the suitability of Bolivia for a successful guerrilla struggle. At the time, however, it seemed almost a perfect choice. 'Bolivia,' wrote Régis Debray in 1965, 'is the country where the subjective and objective conditions are best combined. It is the only country in South America where a Socialist revolution is on the agenda.'[7]

Writing in the *Guardian* in April 1967, ten days after the first ambush, I tried to explain why Bolivia had been chosen:

> If you were a Latin American guerrilla leader—say, someone with Cuban experience nicknamed 'Che'—which country would you choose for your new revolutionary base? Venezuela is

no longer a very attractive spot. The anti-terrorist forces are well in control, and only just before Easter one of the chief guerrilla leaders, José Saher, was killed in the province where his father is governor. Guatemala is too small to be an effective 'second Cuba', and there, too, the leadership has been hit by disaster. A key figure, Luís Turcios, was killed mysteriously in a motor accident at the end of last year. In Colombia violence is endemic and could be turned only with difficulty into genuinely revolutionary channels. In Peru the guerrillas have faded out, with one leader dead and the other locked safely away.

And that, until last week, was the sum total of all guerrilla activity in Latin America. But just one glance at the map should have shown the careful observer that there is one country where, if the conditions were right, guerrillas could operate from a strategic base of unparalleled value.

'Bolivia,' explained the respectable Santiago newspaper *El Mercurio* in a recent leading article, 'offers excellent opportunities for guerrilla action. Its territory includes most difficult terrain, both in the areas of sierra and high plateau as well as in those of tropical forest; its material backwardness makes the population receptive to demagogy: the absence of modern communications hinders the activities of the government's military forces. And, from Bolivia, the guerrillas can infiltrate through the heart of South America, for it has frontiers with Argentine, Paraguay, Brazil, Peru and Chile, and the borderlines cross areas that are isolated and difficult to reach.'

The newspaper might have added, though it refrained from doing so, that Bolivia's average *per capita* income is barely £30 a year, that the country is solely dependent on one unstable source of income—the sale of tin—and that 70 per cent of the population is Indian. A similar proportion is illiterate. Surely a paradise for revolutionary guerrillas.

. . . If the guerrillas can sustain themselves . . . there seems no reason why they should not be able to create that permanent 'revolutionary foco' of which Che Guevara has always dreamed. Such a base on the South American mainland would revive the flagging spirits of *Fidelistas* far from Bolivia itself.[8]

In July, two Cubans, Pombo and Tuma, arrived in La Paz bringing
further details about the change of plan.[9] It was to be an uphill struggle to persuade the Bolivians that the revolution had to begin in
Bolivia and not in Argentina. Immediately on arrival, the two Cubans
made contact with Ricardo and a series of political discussions began.
First they discussed the new scheme with the four members of the
Bolivian party who had been allotted by Monje to help Ricardo at the
request of Fidel in May. The most important of these four were two
brothers, Coco and Inti Peredo. The four were in favour of launching
a guerrilla war, but they very quickly revealed to the Cubans the lack
of enthusiasm for the scheme on the part of the party leadership.

However, on 28 July, Ricardo had a meeting with Monje and he
emerged reasonably optimistic. In a report to Guevara he wrote that
Monje 'seems committed and has proposed to go along with the plan,
although he proposes doing so by means of an uprising in the capital
that would serve as an awakener simultaneous with the struggle in the
mountains. For the latter he has promised twenty of his best men with
whom he will start work.'[10]

Ricardo thought, however, that it was high time for Monje to be told
that Guevara himself was to be involved in the project, and Pombo comments in his diary that a number of points in the discussions with the
party could only be cleared up personally by Guevara on his arrival.

A week later Monje's apparent enthusiasm had completely evapo-
rated. When Ricardo asked him for more men in addition to the twenty
that had been promised, Monje replied 'What twenty?' and added that
'he was having trouble with the rest of the Central Committee, which
was putting pressure on him not to enter the armed struggle, feeling
that the recent elections [in July] had been a success for them because
they had gotten 32,000 votes, about double what they had previously
obtained.' Pombo comments bleakly:

> From the little progress we were making, one could see that
> there was something in the air; more precisely, a great deal of
> uncertainty about the decision to join in the struggle. In fact,
> it is a dead issue; and we face the problem that there is little
> enthusiasm for the affair. In fact Mbili [Ricardo] has to keep
> breathing down people's necks just to get anything done at
> all; tremendous apathy. We are the ones who are doing all the
> organizing, and they aren't helping us at all.[11]

On 19 August there was a further meeting between Monje and Ricardo. Far from producing extra men, Monje in fact threatened to withdraw the four who were actually working with the Cubans. Again the chief problem seemed to be, not Monje himself, but other members of the Central Committee who were openly hostile to any kind of guerrilla struggle.

At the same time, as the discussions proceeded with the Bolivian Communist party, the Cuban emissaries were also in constant contact with the organizers of the planned Peruvian *foco*. El Chino's representative in La Paz was a Peruvian leftist called Julio Dagnino Pacheco, known as 'Sánchez'. He was first told of the major strategic decision that had been taken to begin the struggle first in Bolivia and then in Peru at the end of July. It was arranged that some men from El Chino's group should be sent for training in Bolivia, as had already been planned. Under the new scheme, however, the Peruvian recruits could expect to be trained chiefly under actual battle conditions, and would be involved in the initiation of warfare in Bolivia. Subsequently they would be withdrawn, together with a number of Cubans, to launch the projected *foco* in Peru. El Chino was not happy about the decision to begin the Bolivian *foco* first, but as the Cubans controlled the purse strings their decision had to be final.

Apart from Sánchez and Monje, the Cuban organizers in La Paz were also in indirect contact with Moises Guevara, the miners' leader from Oruro who led a small group of Communist dissidents which had split away from the pro-Chinese Communist part of Zamora and Escobar. It appears that Moises Guevara was brought into the Cuban scheme largely because he had already been in contact with El Chino's Peruvian group. At any rate, Sánchez had had some dealings with him in which the Peruvian had tried to ascertain how the Bolivian was planning to put his professed belief in the armed struggle into practice. On 23 August, at a moment when relations between the Cubans and Monje and the orthodox Communists were at their most difficult, the possibility arose of relying more heavily on Moises Guevara. But no one was very certain of his calibre or trustworthiness.

Pombo commented in his diary that day:

> We discussed what should be done in the event that using [Moises] Guevara should be approved. Sánchez suggested not entrusting Guevara with knowledge of the designated place for the zone of operations and concentration, etc. The best

thing, he suggested, although it might cost a little money, would be to put his organization to a practical test. For this purpose, he could be asked to assemble his people in Cochabamba, ready to revolt. He would be given fifteen days to do this, and asked to find out how much it would cost for fares, house rentals, etc. In this way, we would ascertain if he really has any people who are ready to revolt.

But this plan was not carried out, and the uncertainty about Moises Guevara remained. Ricardo thought that he was 'a trouble-making prick incapable of really revolting'. Sánchez thought that he was 'of some value'. Pombo concluded eventually:

> We cannot fail to recognize that he has stated his decision to fight openly for our line, guerrilla warfare. That his is a group of working class extraction (miners); peasants, people who are dedicated to fight. Almost all of the militants are ready to join in the struggle, twenty men.

The reliability of Moises Guevara would not have been of such crucial importance had it not been for the fact that, at the beginning of September, a further emissary from Che in Cuba, Pacho (Alberto Fernández Montes de Oca), arrived in La Paz with new directives. Firstly, Che intended to rely more on the group of Moises Guevara than on the Communist party proper. Secondly, he wanted the initial *foco* to begin in the Beni, which was in the north of Bolivia and had access to Peru, rather than in the south of the country, where there was access to Argentina and Paraguay. And thirdly, Régis Debray, a young Frenchman who had been a philosophy professor in Havana and had visited Bolivia in 1964, was being sent to the country from Havana to examine the choice of site for the *foco* and to ascertain the trustworthiness of Moises Guevara.

The news was not well received by the Cubans who were already in La Paz. In the first place, Ricardo felt that he was personally committed to the orthodox Communists. All his dealings had been with them. They had not been uncooperative, and he hardly knew Moises Guevara and his group. Secondly, the choice of zone of operations had already been made: the Cubans had decided that the area of Santa Cruz was more suitable than the Beni, and a farm had already been bought by Coco Peredo on the Río Ñancahuazú in July.

Confused by these new commands from Havana, the Cubans in La Paz prepared a memorandum for Che, outlining their activities to date:

We want to let you know that all our relationships for the organization of the dance have been established with the party and with Estanislão [Monje]. . . . By giving priority to the negotiations with the Guevara group, we have been placed in a difficult position. In addition, because of what preceded this, we do not feel that this was the right thing to do because we could organize a unified, central command which would include both the party's and [Moises] Guevara's people.[12]

The Cubans also explained in their report to Guevara why they had chosen the zone of Ñancahuazú. It was tropical, inhabited, suitable for constructing caves, and economically important:

The Ñancahuazú property is located in the south-west region of Santa Cruz province, in a mountainous area of exuberant vegetation but scant water in the general area. The property itself has plenty of water. Ñancahuazú is in a canyon between the Serranías de las Pirirendas to the east and the Serranías Incahuasi to the west; their highest peaks are its eastern and western borders. These ranges join up further south and continue into the Salta range in Argentina. The farm is bounded on the north by the Iripiti property, unoccupied, owned by the same man who sold us the farm, Remberto Villa, who lives on a farm called Terrazas near Lagunillas, about 20 kilometres from Ñancahuazú; on the south by the farm of Ciro Algarañaz, who raises pigs. The property is 255 kilometres from Santa Cruz on the Santa Cruz–Camiri road, and is relatively isolated. It can be reached without going into Lagunillas, which is 25 kilometres from Ñancahuazú taking a side-road about six kilometres south of Gutiérrez. . . .

The farm is 1,227 hectares, and has a considerable amount of timber. On this basis the legal cover plan is to raise pigs and later on to build a sawmill.

An important point is that, towards the north, it is possible to travel to Vallegrande through a mountainous and heavily wooded area; from there on the woods become sparser. Towards the south it is possible to go through terrain of similar nature to Argentina.[13]

The Communists, however, were giving the Cubans a much greater headache than the location of the property at Ñancahuazú. Régis Debray had arrived in September and, as well as exploring the Beni with a view to examining the desirability of establishing a *foco* there, he was also in contact with the pro-Chinese Communists. It was not long before this reached the ears of Marío Monje, and in the middle of the month he demanded to see Ricardo to ask for an explanation. He told the Cuban that he didn't like the contracts that Debray appeared to be making with the pro-Chinese splinter groups.

The Cubans explained to Monje with some anger that they knew nothing of Debray's mission, but that they were not at all pleased with the activities of the Communists. 'We took the opportunity to point out a few things,' Pombo writes grimly in his diary:

1) They have shown no confidence in guerrilla warfare.

2) They have made no efforts to organize themselves; rather, they view it all as not solving anything. They added that they had been concentrating all their efforts toward a general uprising and considered guerrilla warfare as secondary. We asked them what they had done to date: they replied 'Nothing'. We told them we could not sit around twenty years waiting for them.[14]

Relations between the Cubans and the Bolivian Communists continued to be extremely strained, with Monje—doubtless under pressure from his Central Committee—trying to back out of the commitments he had already made. At the beginning of October a clarifying message arrived from Che Guevara in Cuba which seemed to reverse the decisions that had been brought by Pacho:

We are not sure at all of [Moises] Guevara. We are only collaborating without commitment. Don't worry about the political relations between us, Estanislão and [Moises] Guevara. The important thing is to ensure the necessary conditions.

Continue relations with Estanislão, avoiding arguments. Aid requested will be considered later.

The present farm [Ñancahuazú] is good. Get another, but don't transfer the arms to it until I notify you.[15]

At this stage it appears that Che Guevara was anxious that no final decision about the relations with the Communist party be taken until his arrival in Bolivia. This was timed for early in November.

Notes

1 'El Chino'—Juan Pablo Chang—was a Peruvian who had been involved in the planning of the ELN guerrilla in Peru in 1965 and earlier, but he had not participated in the fighting.

2 Letter from Marío Monje to the Central Committee of the Bolivian Communist party, 15 July 1968, printed in *Presencia* (La Paz), 25 July 1968.

3 *Pombo's Diary*, 28 September 1966. This diary is printed in Daniel James (ed.), *The Complete Bolivian Diaries of Che Guevara and Other Captured Documents*, Stein & Day, New York, 1968. The problem with this diary is that it has so far only been printed in English. A Spanish version, printed in *Presencia*, was, I believe, taken from the English version and not from the Spanish original.

4 *Pombo's Diary*, 24 October 1966.

5 Ibid., 28 September 1966.

6 Ibid., 6 August 1966.

7 Debray, 'Latin America'. And *The Economist*, 12 August 1967, wrote: 'If this is really one of Fidel Castro's "new Vietnams" it is, at least psychologically, a potential triumph. No South American country is worse conditioned than Bolivia to face guerrilla warfare.'

8 Richard Gott, 'Latin America: the Next Revolution', *Guardian*, 6 April 1967.

9 Pombo, the nickname of Harry Villegas Tamayo, was one of the few survivors. Tuma, a very close comrade of Guevara's, has never been identified.

10 *Pombo's Diary*, 30 July 1967.

11 Ibid., 8 August 1967.

12 Ibid., 10 September 1967.

13 Ibid., 11 September 1967.

14 Ibid., 24 September 1967.

15 Ibid., 4 October 1967.

Bolivia

25. Ernesto Che Guevara with two peasant children.

26.1. Colonel Zenteno Anaya (*right*) and General Alfredo Ovando Candia (*foreground*), Vallegrande, 9 October 1967.

26.2. Major 'Pappy' Shelton of the US Army, at the US training camp at La Esperanza, near Santa Cruz.

27.1. A CIA agent, Eduardo González, climbing into a jeep at Vallegrande, 9 October 1967.

27.2. CIA man González nervously looks around, apparently aware that he is being photographed with a telephoto lens.

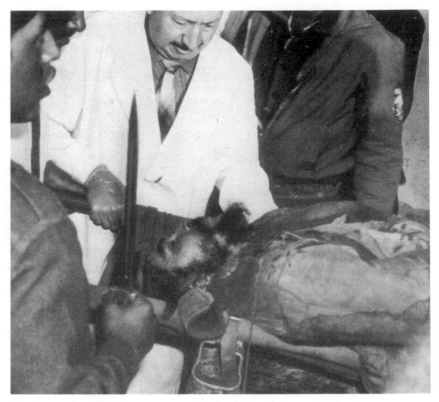

28–31.2. The following five photographs were taken by Brian Moser of Granada Television at Vallegrande on Monday, 9 October 1967, about 6 hours after Guevara was shot.

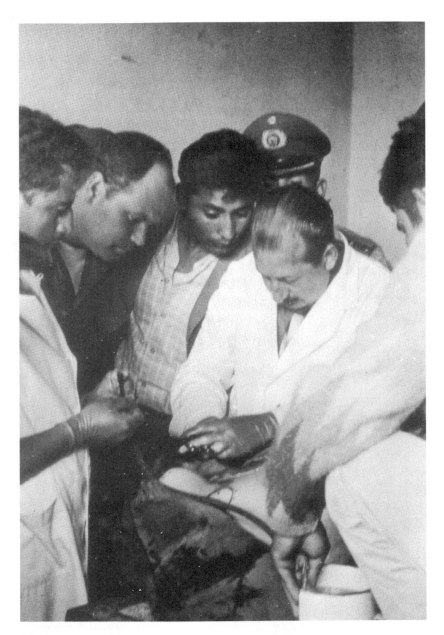

29.

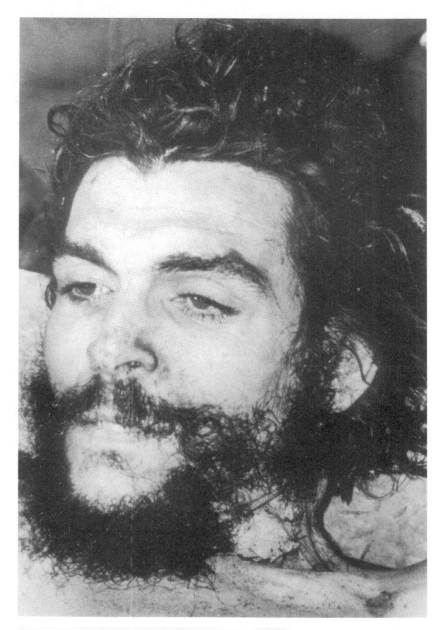

30.

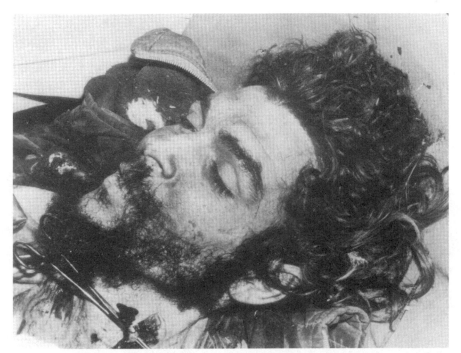

31.1.

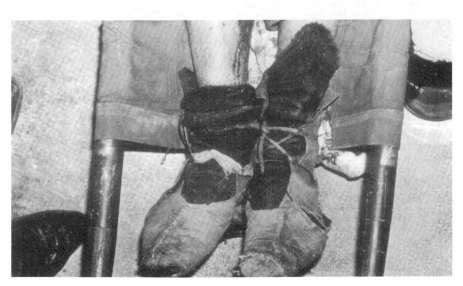

31.2.

32. Defeat of the Revolution? From the roll in Guevara's rucksack.

At the beginning of November 1966, a Uruguayan businessman, Adolfo Mena González, arrived in São Paulo having flown in from Spain. He made his way from Brazil to La Paz, where he secured from President Barrientos' director of press and information, Gonzalo López Munoz, a credential claiming that he was 'a special envoy from the Organization of American States who is making a study and collecting information on the economic and social relations obtaining in the Bolivian countryside'. The credential further asked all national authorities and private individuals 'to co-operate with Sr Adolfo Mena in order to facilitate his investigations'.

Armed with this document, Mena, a balding, bespectacled middle-aged man, continued with several companions to Cochabamba, Bolivia's second most important city, which lies between the cold Andean altiplano and the tropical zones of eastern Bolivia. There Mena made contact with a bushy-moustached Bolivian student called Jorge Vásquez Viaña. Vásquez, then nearly 28, was the younger son of one of Bolivia's most distinguished historians, Humberto Vásquez Machicado, and he had for some time been a student in Germany. He was a militant of the Bolivian Communist party.

Vásquez provided two Japanese Toyota jeeps, with which the eastern part of Bolivia abounds, and the four of them set out on a two-day journey to the small town of Lagunillas in south-east Bolivia. Lagunillas consists of a central square with a few streets leading off it. The buildings are quite impressive, though in varying stages of decay. Their boom-time was in the 1920s, when the town was the centre of an important cattle-raising region. But that came to an end in the 1930s with the Chaco wars between Bolivia and Paraguay, and the town has been in a state of decline ever since. One cause of Lagunillas' decay has been the growth of Bolivia's oil industry based in Camiri, an hour and a half's drive by jeep to the south. Camiri, a thriving town of some 20,000 inhabitants, has all the prosperity and vitality that Lagunillas lacks. Camiri owes its dynamism in good measure to the forethought of Humberto Vásquez Machicado, who, together with a group of Bolivian nationalists, set up the Yacimientos Petroliferas Fiscales Bolivianos—the Bolivian State Petrol Industry—in the late 1930s.

Once past Lagunillas, Jorge Vásquez left Adolfo Mena and one jeep hidden beside the road, and drove on with the others to a farm he had acquired, an hour and half's drive to the north along a sandy track, close to the banks of the Río Ñancahuazú. The area around Ñancahuazú is characterized by hundreds of knife-edge hills bunched together and separated only by deep, impenetrable ravines filled with thick tropical vegetation. Vásquez's farmhouse, known as the Casa Calamina, was a small two-roomed hut with a corrugated-iron roof.

Having left his visitors at the house, Vásquez returned along the road to Lagunillas to pick up Adolfo Mena and the contents of the other jeep. This complicated arrangement was necessary in that halfway along the road from Lagunillas to the Casa Calamina was another farm called El Pincal, whose owner, Ciro Algarañaz, was highly suspicious of Jorge's activities, believing him to be engaged in the illicit fabrication of cocaine. This area of Bolivia, which is less than 150 miles from the border with Paraguay, is renowned for its hospitality to smugglers. Too many jeeps travelling up and down the road to the Casa Calamina might well have led Ciro Algarañaz to believe that here was a profitable business in which he might take a hand.

On the second drive back to the Casa Calamina, Adolfo Mena told Jorge that he was in fact Ernesto Che Guevara, apparently lost to the world since April 1965, when he had disappeared from Cuba.

> On learning of my identity [Guevara commented dryly in his diary that night], Bigotes[1] almost ran off a cliff, leaving the jeep stranded on the edge of a precipice. We had to walk about twenty kilometres and arrived at the farm somewhat after midnight.

On arrival at the farm at Ñancahuazú, Guevara devoted himself to a number of crucial revolutionary tasks. Although his lieutenants had performed several preliminary activities, there was still much to be done. Contacts with the Argentinians and the Peruvians were still in a rudimentary form, and the guerrillas' urban network left much to be desired.[2]

Plans for the establishment of a Peruvian *foco* were already in preparation before Guevara's arrival in Bolivia. Indeed, El Chino had been champing to get started several months before. He was now waiting to see Che in order to co-ordinate plans. At the end of November, Ricardo brought news that El Chino was in the country, and was anxious to send 20 Peruvians down to the Bolivian *foco* for training.

El Chino arrived at the camp on 2 December. After a day's discussion, it was decided that he should return to Cuba to report on the situation. It was agreed that he should be given some weapons and that five Peruvians should be sent to the Puno area, on the other side of Lake Titicaca, which forms the frontier between Bolivia and Peru, to arrange for arms to be smuggled across the border. Within a couple of months, after the Bolivian guerrilla had begun to activate itself, El Chino would send two, possibly five, Peruvians down to Ñancahuazú for training.

After his trip to Havana, El Chino returned to Ñancahuazú in March 1967, bringing two Peruvians as promised. Guevara comments in his diary on 20 March:

> I had a preliminary talk with El Chino. He wants $5,000 a month for 10 months, and Havana has told him to talk it over with me. . . . I said that I agreed in principle, but they must start fighting within the next six months. He thinks he can manage with 15 men under his command in the Ayacucho area. We also agreed that he would take five men with him now and 15 more later; they would be sent armed and trained for combat.

Guevara planned to give him $30,000, which would have financed him over the six-month preparatory to beginning the guerrilla struggle. To Fidel, Guevara wrote somewhat caustically that El Chino 'doesn't seem much like a guerrilla leader, but that's his problem'.[3]

The arrangements for an Argentinian *foco* were rather less advanced. The chief go-between used by the Cubans for organizing a basis in Argentina was an Argentinian girl of German origin called Tamara Bunke, known as 'Tania'. She had been established in La Paz for some considerable time, and seems to have played an important role in organizing the preliminary stages of the Bolivian *foco*.[4] In December, Guevara writes of his intention to send her to Buenos Aires to make contact with two left-wing Argentinians, Jozami, a journalist, and Ciro Roberto Bustos, a painter. Tania was to contact them and bring them to Ñancahuazú for discussions. But by the end of January there was still no news of them.

It subsequently turned out that Tania did make contact with Jozami, but he was not in a position to come:

> Tania made the contacts and the people came, but according to her, they made her travel in their jeep as far as here; she was planning to stay for one day, but things became complicated. Jozami could not stay the first time and he did not even contact us the second time because Tania was here.[5]

However, Bustos made the journey down to Ñancahuazú at the beginning of March, and Guevara made the following arrangement with him:

> I proposed that at present he should act as a kind of co-ordinator with the groups under Jozami, Gelman and Stamponi, and that he should send me five men to begin training. . . . If they accept, they should begin to explore in the north of Argentina and send me a report.

If plans for the Argentinian and Peruvian *focos* were still in a rather underdeveloped state when Guevara first arrived in Bolivia, the same was true of the Bolivian *foco* itself—especially as regards its organizations in the urban areas. 'The network is still in its infancy,' wrote Guevara on 2 December, and at the beginning of January the guerrillas were still only discussing the most rudimentary arrangements for the urban network. At a meeting in Ñancahuazú at the end of the year, duties were allotted to the Peruvian contact, Sánchez, who had been working with the Cubans in La Paz, and it was decided that Humberto Vásquez (the brother of Jorge) and another Bolivian, Rodolfo

Saldaño, should also be left in La Paz. The treasurer of the movement was to be a Bolivian girl, Loyola Guzmán, who was a member of the Young Communists. She too was to stay in La Paz, but her sister was to be stationed in Camiri. Another contact was to be placed in Santa Cruz, and one somewhere near Sucre.

Guevara was obviously not very impressed with earlier arrangements that had been made, and on 15 January he notes in his diary that he stayed in the camp writing notes for the cadres in the city. By 22 January they were finished.[6] A few days later Loyola arrived in the camp and was given the document to take back to La Paz.

More important than any of these problems was that of recruiting men for the guerrilla itself. By the end of the year, the Ñancahuazú *foco* had acquired its full complement of 17 Cubans, friends of Guevara who had agreed to accompany him on this historic effort to promote the continental revolution. To find Bolivians proved to be more difficult, and was one of Guevara's constant preoccupations in the early months. Admittedly he had once written that with a base of 30 or 40 men it would be possible to start a guerrilla unit, but unless he could get more Bolivians, the *foco* would be dangerously reliant on the Cubans from the very start. There is some evidence to suggest that the Cubans were meant to be there chiefly in a training and advisory capacity, and that the base at Ñancahuazú was to be used as a training base for guerrilla fighters who would subsequently branch off to the *focos* in Peru and Argentina.

Part of the reason for the failure to recruit Bolivians was the fact that Guevara was relying on no major political organization in the towns. There were, in fact, cadres from the Communist party ready and waiting to join the guerrillas, but they could not move until they got the go-ahead from Monje. This could not be obtained until after there had been political discussions between Monje and Guevara. As it was, Guevara, continually notes the failure to find more Bolivians. 'The Bolivians are good,' he writes at the end of December, 'although few in number.' A month later the refrain is the same: 'The incorporation of Bolivian fighters has proved harder to accomplish than the rest of our programme.' The situation was to remain the same, and in fact the guerrilla force was always under strength.

Notes

1 *Bigote* is the Spanish for 'moustache'. It was the nickname of Jorge Vásquez. He was also known as Loro.

2 There are no references in Guevara's diary to the possibility of making contact with Brizola and the Brazilians. In fact a Brazilian *foco* was begun in Rio Grande do Sul at about the same time as the Bolivian. After a week, however, the Brazilian guerrillas had to give up. They had contracted the bubonic plague and were forced to surrender—a horrifying picture of the natural hazards that can be encountered in South American jungles.

3 From a note written by Guevara to Fidel, 'coded and written in invisible ink'. It was read out at the trial of Régis Debray by the prosecutor, Colonel Iriarte, and published in *Presencia*, 14 November 1967.

4 It has frequently been maintained that Tania was a Russian spy. Some stories go as far as to suggest that she was Guevara's lover and that she was responsible for the betrayal of the guerrilla force. There is not a shadow of evidence for these charges, and there seems little doubt that the story was invented by the CIA. The original story was printed in the German paper *Welt am Sonntag*, which is noted for its sensationalism rather than its sober reporting of news, and it purported to reveal how Gunther Maennel, a man who had defected from East Germany in 1961, had recruited Tania as an agent to keep an eye on the activities of Guevara. Even if this were true in 1961, which seems highly improbable, it would be difficult to draw any valid conclusions from it about Tania's likely behaviour in 1966–67. Antonio Arguedas, the former Bolivian Minister of the Interior, has explained to me how his attention had been drawn to this article by his CIA contact in La Paz, and how he was instrumental in having the story printed in the Bolivian paper, *El Diario*. Benjamin Welles, a State Department correspondent of the *New York Times*, also printed it, and it was taken up and publicized in a highly sensational and inaccurate piece by Daniel James in the London *Observer*. The story that Tania was Guevara's mistress seems to have been invented by James.

5 *Guevara's Diary*, 21 March 1967.

6 These lengthy instructions for the organization of an urban network to support rural guerrillas have been published in Havana and in the edition of Guevara's Bolivian diaries published by Siglo XXI, Mexico City. I have not yet seen them translated into English.

5. THE NEW 'GRITO DE MURILLO'

'At noon we drank a toast to mark the historical importance of the date.
I replied, marking this moment as the new "Grito de Murillo"
of the continental revolution. I stressed the point that our lives were
insignificant faced with the fact of the revolution.'

Ernesto Che Guevara, 31 December 1966

Guevara's overriding concern during the first six weeks in the encampment at Ñancahuazú was the attitude of Monje and the Communist party. Until the co-operation of the Communists was secured, it was difficult to take any major decisions about the future continental struggle. Everything was held up. Guevara had been rather put out by the arrival at Ñancahuazú of El Chino, who was champing to begin the guerrilla struggle in Peru, yet nothing could be done until things had been settled with Monje.

Monje himself has left an account of the uneasy situation that prevailed in the last few months of 1966. He maintains that while he was going ahead with preparations for guerrilla warfare in Bolivia, the Cubans and Régis Debray were actually making plans that bypassed the orthodox Communist party:

After the elections, in August and September, when we were preparing to make our help available, and when we were selecting and training our military units and setting up the military arm of the party, I had a feeling that elsewhere there was another plan going forward in the country, that there was being set up a conspiracy beside the party apparatus and that I was being misinformed from all sides. The journeys around the country made by a European intellectual increased my suspicion. Finally I summoned an emissary of Fidel Castro and told him that I did not agree with what appeared to be going on in the country and that I would not tolerate foreign interference. I pointed out that this was a violation of the agreement proposed by Fidel, and I added that I would bring all this to the notice of the political committee of the Bolivian Communist party. The emissary replied that no agreement was being broken, that they were simply taking precautions, and that the journeys of the European intellectual had nothing to do with it.

In October I told the political committee of what I thought was going on. The political committee decided to send a delegation to Cuba to discuss the situation and make our position known—that the Bolivian revolution had to be run by Bolivians; we suggested a conference of Communist and workers' parties of Latin America; we also restated our support of the stand of the international communist movement.[1]

Monje had an invitation to a Communist party congress in Bulgaria. He took advantage of the trip to call in at Havana on the way home, together with the prominent Bolivian Communist, Jorge Kolle Cueto.

In December I arrived in Havana and had another talk with Fidel Castro, and told him of my concern about what was happening in the country. He answered, apologizing for the attitude of the emissary with whom I had spoken, and again stated that he completely agreed with me that the Bolivian revolution should be run by Bolivians. I told him that I definitely intended to take the matter up and I impressed on him the need for another conference of Communist and workers' parties. Then, he invited me to have a talk with comrade Ernesto Che Guevara, who he said was in a country bordering on Bolivia. Later I would be told of the place of the meeting, somewhere on the frontier. I enthusiastically accepted the invitation. As for the proposed conference of parties, he said that that would depend on any agreements reached with comrade Guevara.

He again told me to keep the talk a secret and only to talk about it afterwards. He criticized me for not having kept the earlier interview a strict secret.

After this discussion, Fidel sent the following cable to Guevara:

Czo No. 24

Dear Ramón: Stanislão's [Monje's] journey was to ask us to clarify whether Papi's [Ricardo's] actions were directed internally or towards the south and whether or not the agreement with me was to help the south and to leave internal plans in his hands. He also repeated complaints about Papi, saying that he had not fulfilled his agreement to help him in his plans. This situation created confusion and Kolle took advantage of it to press Stanislão to leave the party at short notice. He was thinking of doing this anyway as he was planning to leave with his military group and carry out an insurrection without compromising the party or at least with it neutral. He saw that if he had to depend on the party there would be no insurrection. In this situation we agreed that he would postpone leaving the party until he had talked with you. He thinks it better to join you from his position of secretary-general rather than from outside. You will decide what is best from an on-the-spot analysis. I suggested that he should talk with you since you are the strategic leader of this operation whose beginning cannot be exactly foreseen. Unexpected events might make it begin in Stanislão's territory, rather than in the south. Mentioning your name impressed him immensely and he answered decidedly that he would follow you anywhere and help you in every way possible, arranging the talk tentatively for between 25 and 30 December; Papi would fix the exact time and place. For his information I told him the interview would be outside the country. I cannot say what Stanislão's final attitude will be but he might bring in some good people. . . . The bearer of this message is the leader of the group of ten sent by Stanislão and controlled by Inti. The rest leave at the end of December, see if you can fit them in. Greetings. Leche. 14 December.[2]

Towards the end of December 1966 Monje returned to La Paz. Accompanied by Ricardo, Tania and the Peruvian contact Sánchez, he then made his way down to Ñancahuazú. His encounter with Guevara was unfortunate. The chief exponent in Latin America of the virtues of guerrilla warfare had to argue with a minor Communist functionary. But in their relative strengths, the two antagonists were more or less equal. Guevara had the vision and the mystique and 20 men already established in the jungle. He also had access to funds. Monje, however, controlled the party machine.[3]

It was a historic meeting. It represented the final rejection by the Communists of the thesis which had brought the Cuban revolutionaries to power. And it marked the beginning of a new era both in Latin American and in world politics, an era which saw the end of the Communist party's hegemony over the Left. Guevara had given a pithy version of what was discussed:

> The conversation with Monje began with generalities, but he quickly came down to his fundamental premise, stated in three basic conditions:
>
> 1) He would resign as party leader but would obtain its neutrality, and cadres would be brought for the struggle.
> 2) He would be the political and military leader of the struggle as long as the revolution was taking place in Bolivia.
> 3) He would handle relations with other South American parties, trying to persuade them to support liberation movements (he mentioned Douglas Bravo as an example).
>
> I answered that the first point was a matter for his own judgement as party secretary, although I considered his position to be a great mistake. It was vacillating, accommodating and would protect the good name in history of those who should be condemned for their crookedness. Time would prove me right.
>
> On the third point, I told him I had no objection to his trying but that he would fail. To ask Codovilla to support Douglas Bravo was equivalent to asking him to support an insurrection within his own party. Time again will tell.
>
> As for the second point, I could not accept it under any conditions. I was to be the military chief and I would not

accept any ambiguities on this matter. Here the discussion ended and we talked in a vicious circle.[4]

Monje has given two accounts of the meeting, both of which offer some idea of the lines along which his own mind was working, even if they may be somewhat inaccurate when he comes to reporting exactly what Guevara said. According to Monje, Guevara said the following:

> I wanted to make some things clear to you beforehand, to prevent any future ill-feeling between us. In fact we deceived you. I would say that it is not Fidel's fault; it was part of my plan. He asked you to do something at my request. At first I had other plans and then I changed them. I am here, this is my liberated zone and I am not leaving it even if I only have the people who came here with me. Please excuse the comrade whom you talked to [Fidel's emissary] he is very good, completely trustworthy, but he is not a politician and couldn't have told you my plans. I know he was very rude to you. . . . I waited impatiently for you, I badly wanted to speak to you about many things, but chiefly because I wanted to ask you to stay with us, to lead the rising as its political head.

After this rather startling preliminary, discussions began. The following is also Monje's version:

> We began to talk. I put to him the conditions which are already well known, but which should be explained in detail. The vicious circle which Guevara refers to in his diary arose over the idea that the Bolivian revolution should be run by Bolivians, and that revolutionaries from other countries could collaborate unconditionally and when necessary. Afterwards we talked about differences in our plans for the revolution, and also about the fact that a political bureau cannot be subordinated to a military command, and thus the political commander of the revolution cannot be subordinated to the military commander. Finally we discussed the need to organize party cells within the revolutionary army, the part the political bureau and the political head should play in the choice of political commissars, promotions and planning of operations, etc. etc.

As we were unable to agree, I asked that Fidel Castro should be allowed to intervene. Guevara replied that he always set himself a target, made plans and carried them out, despite all obstacles, sweeping away anybody in his path. 'You can think what you like about that, it's not like you, who think of political principles; call my principles what you like, even personal ones. The fact of the matter is that I must be the Number One.'

He asked me if my position was flexible. I said no. Then I asked him the same question, and he also replied no.

Monje, ever anxious to justify his own position, has elaborated on this account:

When comrade Guevara first broached the subject, he said that no matter where he was born or had acquired his best experience, he considered Latin America, the whole continent, to be his country; as a revolutionary, he would fight anywhere to drive out American imperialism and build Socialism. His initial intention had been to start the fight somewhere else, in another country, but he had concluded that Bolivia had good possibilities: a difficult economic situation for the masses, increasing hunger and poverty, severe imperialist exploitation and oppression, great fighting spirit among the people, weak reactionary and repressive forces, an incompetent government, political instability, etc. etc. This was a favourable situation to set up a guerrilla group, a revolutionary group that would step up the people's struggle. The guerrilla group would have the advantage of bringing together anti-imperialist forces and drawing them into armed fighting; the spread of the fighting and the open intervention of imperialism and other foreign forces would allow the creation of new centres in other countries, with guerrilla warfare spreading all over the continent. The struggles might last ten or fifteen years, but by any other method Bolivia might unfortunately be one of the last countries to be liberated. In view of all this, comrade Guevara asked me to join the struggle as political head, while making it clear that as military head he would be in absolute command.

I replied that I would join on three conditions: 1. The holding of a conference of Communist and workers' parties of the continent, to co-ordinate action against the attacks of American imperialism. 2. The setting up of a broad political front in the country, with all the peoples' and anti-imperialist groups, including the Bolivian Communist party, which would organize a single revolutionary command. 3(a). The revolutionary plan for Bolivia should be related to mass experience and consciousness and should not be based solely on the guerrillas. 3(b). The political or military leadership could be in my hands or in those of whoever chose the revolutionary command, but anyway the military leadership should be subordinated to the political leadership. To help in the struggle I would resign from all my political posts, which I intended to do anyway.

As a counter to the guerrilla plan I drew one up which I considered more in keeping with the Bolivian situation and whose main points are as follows: training of the Bolivian Communist party and other revolutionary forces for the armed struggle; the bringing together, organization and militarization of the people's armed forces on a national scale; the co-ordination of simultaneous action in the cities, mines, countryside and the mountains; beginning the struggle at a time of acute political crisis, and not simply as the continuation of a strike or as a response to government repression.

Comrade Guevara played down the first two points with pessimistic remarks; but he accepted them, saying that for him the third point was the most valuable. He said that my plan would mean a long period of training, a large revolutionary organization, and an endless wait before the struggle would begin. He also said that he was afraid that if my plan was carried out and was successful it might be limited to one country, forgetting the interests of other countries, and that if so I would almost certainly concentrate on consolidating the revolution in Bolivia, making a deal with imperialism on access to the sea.[5]

I, for my part, pointed out that his plan could not be carried out without taking into account existing conditions and the people's experience; his plan would lead to hasty action, sacrifices, the failure of the guerrillas and an easy victory for Yankee imperialism and the reactionary bourgeois government. Finally I made it clear that the political or military leadership involved carrying out a plan, the application of a line, and that therefore the military leadership should be subordinated to the political leadership.

Our points of view were in complete opposition and it was impossible to reach [an] agreement on the problems discussed. In view of this, and considering that it was unnecessary to discuss details, I gave up the conversation.

More than a year later, in January 1968, Monje presented a report to the Bolivian Communist party explaining in great detail exactly what had been discussed at Ñancahuazú. He gave details of six points that he said he had enumerated to Guevara. Almost all of them are directly opposed to the ideological line followed by Guevara and the Cuban Revolution. Guevara's position can be summarized as follows: firstly, the Latin American Revolution will take place on a continental scale; secondly, each Latin American country has broadly similar characteristics which give it a revolutionary potential; thirdly, Cuba shared these characteristics and the Cuban Revolution has thus provided a revolutionary pattern that is likely to prove successful; fourthly, the Sino-Soviet dispute is a hindrance to revolutionary activity: neutrality is the only correct position to adopt towards the squabblers; fifthly, the political decisions in the revolutionary war must be in the hands of the military commander; and sixthly, revolutions are caused by the decisions of men who take advantage of existing conditions.

On each one of these crucial points that made up Guevara's ideological outlook, Monje took up an opposing position:

Guevara was trying to put his revolutionary theory into practice in our country. I tried to explain to him why we had a different idea about the likely course of the Bolivian revolution. Some of the reasons that I explained to him are as follows:

Undoubtedly the peoples of Latin America have many links, many common problems and tasks; their destinies are tightly bound together; the people are similar from south of the

Río Bravo (Mexico) to Patagonia (Argentina); to prove this it is sufficient to look at the past and see the two great empires: the Aztecs in what is now Mexico and the Incas in what is now Peru, and with them the Mayas, Chibchas, Araucanians, etc., and many other tribes; all these peoples lived on a similar economic, political and cultural level, although their languages and customs were somewhat different; the feudal powers of Spain and Portugal got hold of this continent, conquered its peoples with fire and the sword, and interbred with them; they imposed more advanced methods of production, overcoming previous differences, and to some extent unifying the continent.

I then pointed out to him that after three centuries of Spanish and Portuguese rule, the final struggles against the colonists began in 1809 and took some fifty years, but that most countries gained their independence between 1820 and 1830, some a little before and some a little later. After the Spanish and Portuguese colonialists had been driven out, several countries were created, not entirely at the whim of a person or a group. There are economic, political and cultural reasons for the birth of these countries, factors which led to the splitting up of the continent in spite of so many common problems, ties and revolutionary aspirations.

When these countries were set up, existing differences were accentuated, there were fratricidal struggles, bloodshed and dismembering of countries. Chauvinistic nationalism and revanchism were encouraged, because the ruling classes were trying to consolidate their domination, capitalism was expanding and imperialism was becoming more ferocious. Today all the Latin American countries, with the exception of Cuba, are living under capitalist régimes with traces of feudalism. But there are economic, political and cultural differences which make no difference to the common ties and tasks for the peoples of this continent. Faced by this situation, Yankee imperialism is acting according to an overall continental strategy, supporting its puppets in each country, who in turn support each other by supporting imperialism. It follows that the attitude of the peoples must be to form a single front against imperialism. But we should not be led to generalize about the possibilities of victory for the revolution in every country at once or even in only one. The situation in Latin America includes both possibilities for revolution. The important thing is to get on with the revolution in one country if it is necessary, and in more than one if it is possible; without losing sight of the international aspect of the movement, it can well be started within one country. Anyway, this should be the first step; later as the revolution develops, this may change.

Monje then elaborated a second point to Guevara, which he resumes as follows:

The area that is now called Bolivia was originally inhabited by indigenous tribes. They were controlled by the Aymará people, who had arrived at the stage of primitive Communism.

The whole area was then controlled by the Quecha people. It became part of the Inca Empire, with its capital in Cuzco, in what is present-day Peru. The empire extended from the south of present-day Colombia to the north of present-day Argentina and Chile. When the Spanish colonists arrived, they found these peoples in a transitional stage between primitive Communism and a higher mode of production. The Spanish colonists imposed capitalism by force. This territory and its people first became part of the Viceroyalty of Lima (Peru). Later—with some degree of autonomy as the Audiencia of Charcas—it became part of the Viceroyalty of Buenos Aires (Argentina).

In the Spanish colonies in general, political divisions were almost imperceptible, so that revolutionaries could act anywhere with no importance given to where they had been born or lived. Túpac Amaru acted in a region overlapping Peru and Bolivia. The revolutionaries kept contacts both with Buenos Aires and with Lima. During the colonial period in that part of the continent, certain economic, political and even cultural elements appeared, differentiating it from other regions and allowing the foundation of the country of Bolivia. Later, in

150 years of independence, firstly under a feudal oligarchy and later under imperialism, differences with other countries became more acute and ill-feeling and conflicts arose which directly benefitted the common enemy. Despite this, and despite the fact that our country is the most backward of all those that border it and is under heavy imperialist pressure, it managed to make considerable liberal changes which have not been achieved in some others, and this should not be forgotten when drawing up a revolutionary plan.

The third point I mentioned was the following: Mankind is developing in one direction: after capitalism comes Communism. Imperialism is the highest stage of capitalism as Socialism is the first stage of Communism. Nobody disputes this. The road from Socialism to Communism was opened by the Russian people on 7 November 1917. Today a third of mankind lives under the banner of Socialism. People have arrived at it from different points, overcoming a series of obstacles and difficulties, learning from failures and setbacks. The victory of the Socialist revolution is the result of the victory of the proletariat over the bourgeoisie, the basic capitalist class, on the basis of particular historical conditions.

In 1871 the Communards of Paris won an initial victory owing to the defeat of the French army and the weakening of the *bourgeoisie* at the hands of the Prussian army and *bourgeoisie* in a capitalist war. However, the enemies in the war (but class brothers) quickly signed a truce to face up to the working class and save the capitalist régime. Thus the Prussian *bourgeoisie* and army helped the French *bourgeoisie* and army to crush the Paris Commune. In Russia, in 1905, the defeat of the Tsarist army at the hands of Japanese militarism made possible the rising of the Russian working class, who won some early successes. But the governments of both countries hastened to come to terms in order to face up to the revolution and defeat it. Both imperialist forces got together to prevent the victory of the Russian working class and their allies the peasants. In 1917, the first imperialist world war was the setting for revolution. The defeat of the Tsarist army and the weakening and discrediting of the Russian imperialist bourgeois forces made possible the great revolutionary rising of the Russian proletariat. The action of the Communist party at the head of the Russian proletariat, chose the right moment to rise and thus guaranteed victory. The Russian revolution gave great prestige to the role of the party and showed insurrection to be the best road to Socialism. The setting of the Chinese revolution was not exactly the same. It was made up of the increase in disputes between the imperialists which led to the Second World War and by the existence of the first Socialist country, the Soviet Union, on its borders. This allowed the Chinese to carry out a prolonged civil war which ended in victory. In the civil war not only the party won prestige, but also the People's Army.

The setting of the Cuban revolution is different again. It is composed of the contradiction between Socialism and imperialism on a world scale, plus contradictions between the imperialists, although these are not as strong as before, due to the existence of the Socialist camp. This is the setting for guerrilla warfare, with limited objectives at first, but with every possibility of developing later. The role of the Communist party is weakened here and a large-scale armed revolutionary movement came to the fore, which later became more radical and consolidated.

These are the three most illustrative examples of peoples' struggles for their liberation, without ignoring the experience of other people in Europe and Asia whose revolutionary processes without doubt have unique characteristics. That is why we can say that the peoples of the fourteen Socialist countries have won their victories each in its own way, so we could talk about fourteen examples, not three. Under the leadership of the working class in alliance with the peasants, all these peoples defeated the bourgeoisie and reaction, basically by means of armed struggle, under the leadership of a political force capable of mobilizing the masses in accordance with the particular conditions in each country. These revolutions have had a common denominator with individual numerators.

All this shows that each way to carry out the armed struggle has been unique and that none of them has been repeated, so that it is a mistake to generalize. As Marxist–Leninists, we cannot expect repetition of the same concrete historical conditions which would allow us to make absolute generalizations about the way to revolution. On the contrary, it is clear that new ways must be sought and developed. This has been shown by history.

The fourth point put to Guevara by Monje was that recognition of the fact that revolutions take different forms makes it possible to understand the disputes which have arisen with the international Communist movement:

The desire for the swift victory of the forces of Socialism over imperialism demands unity between all anti-imperialist forces, especially between Communists, and this demand makes it necessary to take sides to force unity, to prevent the split from widening as a result of neutrality. This is essential and cannot be put off.

The victory of the Russian revolution brought into being the Soviet Union, which by means of building Socialism and Communism has become a world in all fields cannot mean a return to capitalism. Men do not fight for rewards in heaven but to live better on earth. A better organized society is the greatest attraction and stimulus for mankind; that is why the Russian policy of peaceful co-existence must not be confused with conciliation.

The Communist party of the Soviet Union is without doubt the guardian of Marxism–Leninism, the meeting place of the international Communist movement. But this does not mean, just like that, that the CPSU is the party which knows most about the problems of the revolution in all countries. It is simply recognition of its role as the leader in the struggle against imperialism. Besides, the CPSU has never claimed that right. It is unacceptable for the Chinese Communist leaders to ignore this. There is no doubt that the people have had many successes, many victories. But that does not give those leaders any right to set themselves up as judges of other peoples. They claim to be the best heirs of the founders of the Soviet Union and yet criticize it bitterly; they say that they agree with the workmen, but not with the work, when the work is what a workman is known for. But the Socialist course of the revolution is irreversible, and although it may be slow and painful, we must look forward to the Chinese people rejoining the family.

In the face of these disputes between the two great Socialist powers which have given rise to other lesser ones between other Socialist countries, caused, as was the first quarrel, essentially by opportunism, our immediate task is to achieve unity as the situation is more favourable to capitalism than to Socialism. The imperialists will always be more afraid of a united revolutionary front than a divided one.

The fifth point raised in the discussion concerned leadership, and this was not by chance. Subordinating the political head to the military head is different from subordinating the military head to the political head. The problem of revolution is basically political, although military factors play a part in the solution. In no case can politics be completely and permanently subordinated to military thinking. The political problem is related to the party and the military problem to the army. It should be said in passing that when we talked about the role of the party and the revolutionary army, we bore in mind the situation of both forces, the party and the guerrillas and the need to make changes in order to bring them up to the level of the situation. Finally, the open or disguised subordination of the party to the army meant one point of view, and the subordination of the army to the party, another. The military as part of politics and not politics as part of the military is the right approach to revolution.

The sixth point dealt with was that revolutions cannot be planned and pre-determined by decree, by a simple act of will. They come about, grow and mature with a combination of factors, not all of which depend on men's will. Men can contribute to its ripening, and make it happen faster, but they can't set time periods for it. Revolutions arise from concrete historical conditions and not from men's wishes alone.[6]

It is doubtful whether Monje actually said all this at the time. It is a thought-out rationalization of his reluctance to involve himself with Guevara's plans. But the debate, whatever its exact course, ended in complete deadlock. There was no middle way that could accommodate the opposing views.

When the discussions were over, Guevara allowed Monje to go down to talk to the assembled Bolivian guerrillas, many of whom were Monje's personal friends who were sad that the situation appeared to have reached the parting of ways. According to Guevara's account, Monje 'spoke with all of them and gave them the alternative of either staying or supporting the party; they all chose to stay and this seemed to be a blow to him'.

At noon the entire company drank a toast to celebrate the significance of the decision taken to go ahead without the formal support of the Communist party. Guevara compared the occasion with the '*Grito de Murillo*'—a cry that had launched the first independence of Latin America. The second continental revolution had begun.

Monje left for La Paz the following day. Guevara told his guerrilla band that they would 'unite with all those who wanted to make the revolution', but he foresaw 'difficult moments and days of moral anguish for the Bolivians' among the guerrillas. Guevara himself clearly half expected and welcomed the break. For him the Communists were running true to form. In his diary he noted: 'Monje's attitude can slow down our development on one side, but it may contribute on the other by freeing me from any political compromise.' And at the end of January, as the situation becomes a little clearer, he writes:

> The party is now taking up arms against us and I do not know what it will lead to, but it will not stop us and perhaps in the long run it will prove a good thing (I am almost sure of this). The most honest and combative men will be with us, even if they have to go through a more or less serious crisis of conscience.

Finished with Monje, Guevara then began to make arrangements to interview Moises Guevara, the dissident Chinese-line miners' leader from Oruro. Moises Guevara arrived at Ñancahuazú late in January and seemed willing to fall in with the conditions that Che put forward.

These were that Moises Guevara should dissolve his own group and allow it to be absorbed into the guerrilla movement, and that there should be 'no polemics about the subject of international or national disagreements'. According to Che's account, Moises Guevara 'accepted everything very sensibly' and agreed to bring the first group of men to Ñancahuazú in February.

Notes

1   Letter from Monje, printed in *Presencia* (La Paz), 25 July 1968.

2   Text plus photocopy printed in *El Diario* (La Paz), 31 October 1967. 'Ramón' was the code-name for Guevara (taken from a short story by Julio Cortazar); 'Leche' was that for Fidel.

3   In his diary for 15 November 1966, Pombo explains the point about Guevara's financial hold over Monje: 'Mongo [Che] told us about the points he is going to outline to Stanislão [Monje] . . . That he has no political power in Bolivia. He does, however, feel he has enough experience to direct military operations and control finances. Because this is where the money is needed. We could ask help from China and the USSR, explaining to the Chinese that without any political commitment on China's part, we could send [Moises] Guevara [to China] with a letter from us to Chou En-lai and we could also send Marío [Monje] with a companion to the USSR, so they will at least tell us how much they will contribute.'

4   *Guevara's Diary*, 31 December 1966.

5   Bolivia is unique in Latin America in being wholly landlocked. It lost its sea coast on the Pacific to Chile during the War of the Pacific in 1879. It has been the aim of successive Bolivian governments to secure the return of its maritime province.

6   'Las divergencias del P. C. Boliviano con Che Guevara', *Punto Final*, NO. 49, 27 February 1968.

6. Betrayal and Action

'The guerrilla fighter ought never to permit himself a single useless
word, even with his own comrades in arms, since the enemy
will always try to introduce spies into the ranks of the guerrilla
band in order to discover its plans, location, and means of life.'

Ernesto Che Guevera, *Guerrilla Warfare*

The first months in the camp at Ñancahuazú had been designed for
training. Once the encampments had been constructed and the caves
for equipment dug out, military exercises could begin. On 21 January
Guevara reports: 'We fought a mock battle; it failed at certain points,
but in general it was satisfactory. We must work harder on the retreat,
which was the weakest part of the exercise.' Then, at the end of
January, he planned a long route march. The object was to explore the
area north of Ñancahuazú and north of the Río Grande and to make
contact with the local peasantry to discover where they could find people on whom they could rely.

In practice the march proved disastrous. It revealed the extreme
weakness of the guerrilla force when confronted with the problems of
existence in the jungle. When the guerrillas tried to return to this zone
some months later, the army knew that they had been there earlier
and were waiting for them. The inhabitants of entire villages were
taken away for questioning, and the area was sown with informers
dressed as peasants.

The route march was designed to take six weeks. Guevara took
most of the guerrilla band with him, a group consisting of 15

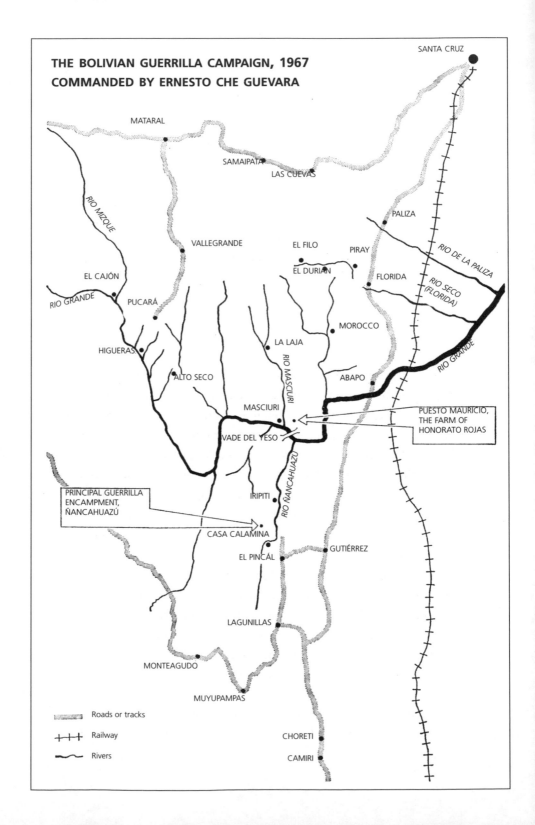

**THE BOLIVIAN GUERRILLA CAMPAIGN, 1967
COMMANDED BY ERNESTO CHE GUEVARA**

SANTA CRUZ

MATARAL

SAMAIPATA

LAS CUEVAS

PALIZA

RIO MIZQUE

VALLEGRANDE   EL FILO

PIRAY

RIO DE LA PALIZA

EL DURIAN

FLORIDA

RIO SECO
(FLORIDA)

EL CAJÓN

RIO GRANDE   PUCARÁ

MOROCCO

HIGUERAS

LA LAJA

RIO MASCIURI

RIO GRANDE

ALTO SECO

ABAPO

MASCIURI

VADE DEL YESO

PUESTO MAURICIO,
THE FARM OF
HONORATO ROJAS

PRINCIPAL GUERRILLA
ENCAMPMENT,
ÑANCAHUAZÚ

IRIPITI

RIO ÑANCAHUAZU

CASA CALAMINA

GUTIÉRREZ

EL PINCÁL

LAGUNILLAS

MONTEAGUDO

MUYUPAMPAS

Roads or tracks

Railway

Rivers

CHORETI

CAMIRI

Cubans and 12 Bolivians. In the camp at Ñancahuazú he left two
Cubans, Antonio and Arturo, and two Bolivians, Camba and El Ñato.
They were to await the arrival of a group of eight Bolivians recruited
by Moises Guevara, who were scheduled to arrive in the middle of
February, and a further five Bolivians who were on their way back from
training in Cuba.

Guevara left elaborate instructions for those who remained in the
camp:

> to make contact at least every three days; while there are four
> of them, two will be armed; the post must not be deserted for
> one moment; the new recruits will be instructed along general
> lines, but they must not know more than is absolutely neces-
> sary; the camp will be cleared of all personal things, and the
> weapons will be hidden in the forest, covered with a canvas;
> the reserve of money will stay in the camp all the time, to be
> kept on one of the men; the tracks already opened are to be
> patrolled as well as the streams nearby.

The 27 guerrillas set off on 1 February. They marched steadily
northward and on 8 February they built a raft and crossed the Río
Grande—at that season in flood. On the other side of the river, close
to where the Masicuri flows into the Río Grande, they met their first
peasant, a man called Honorato Rojas. Eventually he was to betray
the guerrillas and to cause the deaths of many of them. At the time,
however, he seemed reasonably friendly. But Guevara had his
doubts: 'The peasant was a typical sort, capable of helping us, but
also incapable of realizing the dangers that might crop up, and thus
potentially dangerous.'

For a month the guerrillas wandered around the area north of the
Río Grande talking to peasants. They were careful, however, only to
contact those who they were told were likely to be friendly. But on the
return journey to the encampment at Ñancahuazú in March, the
leader of the vanguard—a Cuban called Marcos—finding that his men
were faint with hunger decided to take them to the house of an
employee of the Yacimientos Petroliferas Fiscales Bolivianos—the
Bolivian Petrol Company. With an amazing disregard for the rules of

guerrilla warfare, they arrived at the house—the man's name was Epifanio Vargas—carrying their rifles and pretending to be a group of Mexican geologists. A more improbable story it would be hard to invent. Later in the month, when he heard what had happened, Guevara was furious and demoted Marcos from his position as leader of the vanguard. But the damage had been done. When Marcos' group left his house, Vargas followed them along the trail back to Ñancahuazú. Losing track of them, he continued to Camiri and denounced the presence of strange armed men in the area to the authorities.

But the rest of the guerrilla band, returning exhausted and hungry under the leadership of Guevara, had worse news in store for them on their return to the main camp at the end of the third week in March. During their absence in February, Moises Guevara's eight recruits had arrived. ('Very sub-standard,' Che commented later; 'two deserters, one prisoner who "squealed", three who had to be expelled, two feeble.') Two of them, Vicente Rocabado and Pastor Barrera, stayed for three weeks and then decided that they had had enough. Debray has explained what happened:

> On 11 March, before anyone was thinking of military operations, two men from Moises Guevara's group, detailed to go out hunting, left the guerrillas' central camp at seven in the morning, took their rifles and went down to the river. But instead of going right, to the east, to the hunting grounds, they disappeared to the west, towards Camiri. They were the first two deserters.
>
> Before they could get to La Paz, where they were heading for, to 'give in their report', as they said, they were arrested in the area, on 14 March.
>
> On the same day they made very detailed statements as one of them happened to have had previous contact with the DIC and the political police.[1] He says in his confession, and I quote, 'He had joined the guerrillas to seek information, thinking he would be rewarded for reporting it.' His written statement appears in the evidence, pages 30 et seq. As they

could not be read in public, I would ask the officers to read them carefully. They will find there an exact description of the guerrilla organization; the number reconnoitring around Vallegrande with Che (thirty men), the nationality of the guerrillas, names, plans, the position of the camp, paths, the existence of radios, etc. . . . You will find there not only the presence of Che with his pseudonym Ramón, but also when and how he came to Bolivia, his diguise, his work, his belongings, how they were waiting for him at the main camp, etc. . . . Antonio, then head of the camp, had treated them as ordinary comrades, hiding nothing, even showing them the complete set of photographs which were still secret and which Che and his companions had been taking since November. So without waiting for him to return, they left. They themselves have stated how they immediately acted as guides for the army on land and from the air, and were then sent to General Headquarters in La Paz, before 23 of March, to complete their report. Then, as if there could remain any doubt, Choque-Choque, also from Moises Guevara's group, was captured without resistance on the 17th. He confirmed what his comrades said and was immediately used as a guide, to show the army how to reach the camp and how it was defended. . . .

The third source of information which enabled the army to build up a complete picture of the guerrilla situation before Ñancahuazú was the guide Vargas, a uniformed civilian who fell in the ambush of the 23rd while guiding the military column towards the camp. This man from Vallegrande had been unwisely visited by Marcos, leader of the vanguard, and all his armed men. They introduced themselves to him at the beginning of March as foreign geologists, in order to buy food, as there was a real famine amongst the guerrillas exploring the area with Che. This Vargas was suspicious and followed them from Vallegrande to Ñancahuazú and then went straight off to tell the commander of the IV Division in Camiri. This, added to Algarañaz's repeated reports and the sudden appearance of Marcos and the vanguard before his labourers, naturally made the army get moving and begin an offensive. On 16 March, they fought their way into Coco Peredo's house (the Casa Calamina) with the loss of one soldier dead. In the next few days the army, having pinpointed the camp, put out patrols further and further. Reconnaissance planes flew over the zone all day. The guerrillas were not only cut off with very little food, since the farm and the road to Camiri were blocked, but they were caught unprepared and scattered for Che and his men, who had said that they would be back at the Ñancahuazú camp on 1 March, took three weeks to get there. Messengers were sent to them to warn them of this unforeseen situation. Meanwhile, Marcos, who was in charge of the central camp, helped by Antonio, decided to abandon it, as he didn't have enough men to defend it, and to withdraw. On the 20th, when Che arrived, he found the guerrillas retreating before the army's advance. He considered this retreat to be a sign of defeatism. He removed Marcos from his post, brought everybody back to the main camp, and decided to defend it against any army attack. To cut off the advance, he sent a small group of six men to take up a position about three quarters of an hour from the camp, in the Ñancahuazú ravine. What happened before the ambush of the 23rd had a decisive and fatal influence on the later course of the campaign.[2]

Guevara got back to the central camp at Ñancahuazú on 20 March. 'A climate of defeat prevailed,' he noted in his dairy, 'there is a terrible impression of total chaos; they do not know what to do.' The previous day he had received warning that something was wrong, for they had seen a small aeroplane circling above them. Before his arrival, the other Cubans had taken a decision to withdraw before the army's advance, rather than to organize an attack. Guevara was furious. 'Whoever heard of retreating before ever making contact with the enemy.' He organized an ambush in the narrow ravine of the Ñancahuazú, and early in the morning of 23 March an advance party of the army's forces fell into it. In the gorges of the river the army had little chance against the hidden guerrillas. Six soldiers and a lieutenant were killed and a further seven captured, including a major and a captain.

Although the ambush was a complete success from the guerrilla point of view, there is no doubt that the guerrillas were not fully prepared to begin a guerrilla campaign. They were few in number, their contacts with political organizations in the city were still in a very rudimentary form, and they were all extremely exhausted after a tough training march. Guevara had commented in the middle of March that he himself was very weak, and the morale of the men was low. On the other hand, he had clearly envisaged the possibility of a premature discovery. 'The plans are,' he had written at the end of November, 'to wait for the rest of the men (from Havana), to increase the number of Bolivians up to twenty at least and to start operating.' By March, his guerrilla force had its complement of 20 Bolivians. At the end of January, he had written: 'Now begins the actual guerrilla phase'; and a month later: 'The next stage will be that of combat and certainly decisive.'

Inevitably, considering the scale of their operations, the story would eventually have got out. Indeed, it is surprising that the guerrillas managed to survive undetected for so long. Early in March rumours were flying round La Paz to the effect that something strange was going on in the south-eastern corner of the country. The Catholic daily paper, *Presencia*, gave currency to the rumour that armed bands were forming in the Santa Cruz region (250 miles to the north of Lagunillas), organized by POR, PRIN and the pro-Chinese Communist party.[3] This news was immediately denied by the government, but after two weeks of further rumours about guerrillas and unusual troop movements, *Presencia* came out with a major headline on 21 March announcing that Castro-Communist guerrillas were operating in the country. News reaching the outside world the following day described a clash between guerrillas and the army. The guerrillas, it was said—surprisingly accurately—were led by a Cuban and two Bolivians.[4]

The news of the major ambush on 23 March was not released immediately, and it was not until 27 March that President Barrientos finally gave details of the clash in a nation-wide broadcast. He said that Guevara was connected with the guerrillas.[5]

The interim commander-in-chief of the armed forces, General Jorge Belmonte Ardiles (General Ovando was in Europe returning from a trip to Washington), confirmed this to the press, saying that he had been told of Guevara's presence by two guerrillas. From the very beginning, therefore, the Bolivian authorities were able to present the guerrilla outbreak as something essentially foreign. The official government communiqué on the ambush stated that: 'the national territory has been invaded by an armed group made up of diverse nationalities, the majority adhering to the Castro-Communist line. They have been joined by a number of extremist political sectors within the country.'

The guerrilla deserters had done their work well. They told the army that Guevara had been in the camp at Ñancahuazú on two occasions and was expected back any day. Guevara himself commented in his diary on 27 March:

> The news broke today, taking over most of the programmes on the radio and producing a host of communiqués, including a press conference by Barrientos. . . . It is obvious that the deserters or the prisoner talked, but we do not know how much they said and how it was put. Everything seems to indicate that Tania has been identified, which means that two years of good and patient work are lost. It is very difficult for people now to leave the area. . . . In the evening we had a staff meeting in which we worked out our plans for the future.[6]

It was decided to go ahead with the prosecution of a guerrilla war. The band of guerrillas gave themselves the name of the Bolivian National Liberation Army. The first thing they had to do was to construct a new cave into which they could put all their belongings—the transmitter, medicines, guns and munitions. The deserters had done their work so well that the existing caves were obviously known to the army. But dynamiting through the cliffs took time, especially as it was not possible to do it while there was a reconnaissance plane flying around. The task of dynamiting new caves was given to Moises Guevara, who, as a former miner, was expert in the manipulation of dynamite. But he did not finish the job till 1 April, and it was two more days before the guerrillas had finished transferring their goods and were finally ready to abandon camp. They left on 3 April.

The army had in the meantime been exploring close to the Casa Calamina. The very day after the guerrillas had evacuated their principal camp, 4 April, the army crossed the river from south to north and, with information received from the deserters, arrived at the camp. A few days later the first two journalists arrived, from the Santiago *Mercurio* and the London *Times*. The *Times* correspondent, Murray Sayle, gave the following account of the encampment:

> We found a fully equipped field kitchen with a big oven capable of baking bread for at least a hundred men. Near it were healthy gardens, growing vegetables, and a butcher's shop where mules had been cut up with machetes. From the condition of the meat I judged that the camp had been evacuated no more than three days ago.
>
> A little further along the trail, under the dense canopy of trees and creepers, was a well-equipped field hospital. I found empty packets of antibiotics, surgical dressings and instruments manufactured in Italy, Britain, West Germany and the United States. The canvas covering of the big hospital tent had been taken away, but I saw an operating table and seats for patients to wait outside, all made of jungle timbers bound together with creepers. . . .
>
> A hundred yards further on was the dormitory area. In this area were more than 50 home-made hand-grenades. These had been welded up in a clandestine factory somewhere from empty fruit juice cans and lengths of gas pipe filled with sticks of dynamite and fired by detonators. . . .
>
> Among the rubbish neatly raked from the dormitory area I found a picture of Dr Che Guevara taken in a jungle and a copy of a speech by General Vo Nguyen Giap, of North Vietnam, translated into Spanish.
>
> The guerrillas' camp showed every sign of an orderly evacuation, as nothing of value had been left behind and attempts had been made to burn all documents. Judging by a pile of spent cartridge cases, one part of the camp had been used for weapons training.

Meanwhile the guerrillas had moved north-east in the direction of the village of Gutiérrez, and on 10 April there was a major clash with the army near Iripiti, actually on the banks of the Ñancahuazú. It was another victory for the guerrillas. Ten Bolivian soldiers were killed, including two officers, and 30 under the command of Major Ruben Sánchez were captured. But one Cuban—El Rubio—was killed in the ambush.

After the first ambush on 23 March, the army and the Bolivian government had been in a state of confusion, unable to decide what to do or how seriously to treat the guerrilla menace. Barrientos sent the head of the air force, León Kolle Cueto (the brother of the Communist leader Jorge Kolle), on a mission to the neighbouring countries of Argentina, Paraguay, Peru and Brazil. But many observers seemed to think that Bolivia was exploiting the guerrillas to secure international sympathy at the coming inter-American meeting of Heads of State in Punta del Este—and to get increased United States aid.[7]

The second clash at Iripiti forced everyone to take the guerrilla threat less lightly. The Americans began to send in equipment, helicopters and advisers, and the government clamped down firmly on leftist groups in the country. On 12 April five United States military experts arrived from Panama to establish an anti-guerrilla training school, but it was estimated that six months would be needed to produce one battalion of 'Rangers'. The same day the Bolivian government put most of south-east Bolivia under martial law, and the Communist party and the Trotskyist POR were banned.

In fact the Americans had been quietly investigating the guerrillas during the previous month. When *Presencia* first announced the rumour early in March that guerrilla bands were operating in the Santa Cruz area, four members of the permanent United States Military Mission in Bolivia, accompanied by a Cuban exile working for the CIA named Aurelio Hernández, flew down to Santa Cruz to examine the reality of the reports on the spot.[8] A month later, the head of the mission, Colonel Joseph P. Rice, with Major Robert 'Pappy' Shelton, arrived in Santa Cruz to look for a place to begin anti-guerrilla training. On 19 April it was announced that anti-guerrilla training would begin at the deserted sugar mill of La Esperanza, north of Santa Cruz, with Major Shelton in charge.

Because of the emergency, the annual recruiting programme scheduled for April had taken place in late March, and so with 600 Bolivian raw recruits, some 20 United States Special Forces, and a few CIA-sponsored Cuban exiles, 'Pappy' Shelton began the task of beating out an anti-guerrilla force.

Notes

1 Although Vicente Rocabado had been a police informer, he had not been deliberately infiltrated into the guerrilla. When he was captured, however, he realized how useful his information could be to the police. He had an exceptionally good memory and gave an extremely accurate description not only of the camp and the caves, but also of the guerrillas and their various jobs. When asked why he had joined the guerrillas, he told the Minister of the Interior, Antonio Arguedas, 'If you had a mother-in-law like mine, you too would join the guerrillas.'

2 Debray trial at Camiri: defence statement.

3 There is a good résumé of the first few months of guerrilla activity in *Presencia* (La Paz), 6 August 1967.

4 *El Diario Ilustrado* (Santiago), (ANSA cable), 22 March 1967.

5 This was according to Jorge Canelas, the AP correspondent in La Paz, whose dispatch was printed in *El Mercurio* (Santiago), 28 March 1967. The text printed in *Presencia* on the same day does not mention Guevara by name. On 1 April, Barrientos told the press that he personally thought that Guevara was dead (UPI cable, *El Diario Illustrado*, 2 April 1967). He continued to make conflicting statements throughout the ensuing months.

6 It is this reference that has led to the accusation that Tania 'betrayed' the guerrillas. In fact she had left her jeep at Choreti, outside Camiri, and had proceeded to the camp at Ñancahuazú by other means. Overtaken by events, it became impossible for her to leave, since she was too well known in Camiri and the surrounding area. In fact, of course, the damage had been done, by the three deserters, long before the army found her jeep.

7 See Gott, 'Latin America: the Next Revolution'.

8 In all there were about half a dozen Cuban exiles working for the CIA in Bolivia during 1967. Although the Minister of the Interior,

Antonio Arguedas, knew of their activity, they did not come under his control. They operated separately, in close contact with the American military headquarters at La Esperanza.

'The main difference between Régis Debray and myself is that
the places I felt called to held the future of the world. You understand,
I went to Asia, that was the future of the world. If not I would
have gone to Russia. That was still the future; but the future of the
world is not Bolivia. Régis Debray went there for nothing.
Times have changed.'

André Malraux, quoted in *Le Monde*, 27 October 1967

The mobility of the guerrillas was considerably affected in the first weeks after the ambush by the presence among them of a number of 'visitors' whom it had not been planned to enrol as combatants. Early in March the chief contacts with Peru and Argentina had arrived—El Chino and Ciro Roberto Bustos—for discussions with Guevara, and with them was the French revolutionary philosopher, Régis Debray, who had already been in the country late the previous year.

Régis Debray was born in Paris on 2 September 1940, the second son of Georges and Janine Debray. He was a lawyer, she a prominent conservative politician. Throughout the war the family lived in Paris. Always a bright and studious child, Régis received the philosophy prize in the Concours Général at the age of sixteen, and the following year he began preparing for the exam to enter the École Normale Superieure. In 1959, at the age of eighteen and a half, he passed first into this exacting school.

As a reward his parents sent him off on a trip to the United States in July 1959. While he was in Miami, he found a boat that took him on a brief trip to Cuba, then in the first year of the Revolution. He returned to Paris in November to begin his studies at the École Normale.

He travelled to South America for a few months in 1961, and then in July 1963, having taken his degree in philosophy, he set off to make a film about Venezuela for French television. There he met a Venezuelan revolutionary, Elizabeth Burgos, whom he later married in Camiri in February 1968. He then began a long journey through all the countries of Latin America, except Paraguay, travelling by land, and he did not return to Paris until the end of 1964. There, after reflecting on his experiences, he settled down to write his first long essay on Latin America, called 'Castroism: the Long March of Latin America', which was published in Jean-Paul Sartre's *Les Temps Modernes* in January 1965.

While in France he went back to his philosophy studies, taking a further degree in July 1965. For a few months he went to teach at the University of Nancy. Then in January 1966 he returned to Cuba, under the Franco-Cuban technical and cultural co-operation agreement, as Professor of the History of Philosophy at the University of Havana. While there, he collected the material on the Cuban revolutionary war that enabled him to write his long essay, *Revolution in the Revolution?* which was published in Havana in January 1967. It immediately made a great impact in Cuba and in the rest of the continent, for it articulated many of the Cuban criticisms of the orthodox Communist parties which, until then, had been voiced only privately. Debray returned briefly to Paris in August on his way to Bolivia, where he spent September exploring the Beni.

He returned to Cuba, but in February 1967 he left Havana once again and made his way to Santiago, Chile. From there he went to Antofagasta and caught the train that crosses the Atacama desert and climbs up to the altiplano and to La Paz.

Debray arrived at Ñancahuazú at the beginning of March, ostensibly as a journalist. Later he explained what he had been doing:

> I was sent here by M. Maspéro [the French publisher] and by the Mexican magazine *Sucesos*. It was M. Maspéro who gave me instructions how to get here. The idea of my trip was to

interview Che Guevara. . . . I entered Bolivia in the first few
days of March. In accordance with the instructions given me
by M. Maspéro, I met a Bolivian—a certain Andrés—one
Tuesday at six in the evening. I had the same instructions as
Sr Bustos. We came together after we had been introduced to
a woman, whose name I later learnt from the press, who introduced herself to me with the name of Tania. It was she who
brought us here.[1]

When they got to the camp at Ñancahuazú, however, Guevara was
still on his exploring trip north of the Río Grande. Debray had to wait
for two weeks before he could get his interview. Later, he explained
the nature of his activities in the camp:

Without going into the details of my role, I want to underline
that when I got to the main camp in order to share in the ideals
of the Bolivian guerrillas to the full, I asked to share the duties
and hardships of guerrilla life, standing guard inside and outside the camp, helping in the kitchen, in the house and in other
everyday tasks. So I asked to be put on the duty roster, like anyone else, according to the order of my arrival, because as a revolutionary I could not, nor did I want to, be considered as a
mere visitor staying in a hotel, arms folded and sleeping well,
while my comrades tired themselves out bringing me food and
watching me sleep. This continued until I was able to talk with
Che on 10 March. In spite of having come as a journalist, I personally asked Che at that time to bring somebody else to do my
work, to stop considering me as a visitor and to let me join the
guerrillas, after consulting the Bolivians there. But he refused,
saying that my task of informing the outside world of his presence there and his aims was as important as fighting. Then it
was decided that I should leave the area as soon as possible, and
that while I could and should go on taking part in the everyday
chores of the camp, I could not, nor should I, be considered as
a guerrilla fighter.[2]

Guevara was not enthusiastic about the idea of Debray becoming
a combatant. 'I don't find him in sufficiently good physical condition,'

he wrote to Fidel, and in his diary he commented: 'He came to stay with us, but I asked him to go back to France to organize a network to help us from there; on his way he could go to Cuba, which would coincide with his wish to get married and have a son by his comrade.'

After the first ambush, on 23 March, it became necessary for the guerrillas to divest themselves of those who were not there as combatants. Debray explains:

> Suddenly the situation became more complicated. Communication with the outside world was already difficult. Of the four visitors in the camp, Che decided that Bustos and I should be the first to leave, by way of Gutiérrez, and a more cautious plan was drawn up for El Chino and Tania, as they were more important for the revolution. After the Gutiérrez attempt failed, I talked to Che again about joining the guerrillas, and he alluded to my lack of experience of living in the jungle, and said that for him one peasant from the area was better than ten intellectuals from the city. This convinced me that I would be more useful outside than inside, especially in those moments of isolation, and I decided to leave the guerrillas as I had arrived—just as a visitor. . . .
>
> If at the beginning of April when I urged Che to let me join the guerrilla unit immediately, he had answered: 'You're physically fit, capable, used to jungle warfare and living in the country; your journalist's work can be done by somebody else later; there is no hurry for that, stay here with us.' Then I would have stayed, with pleasure, as a combatant, as a guerrilla fighter, ready to fight wherever and whenever I was ordered to. What more could a revolutionary wish for than to be under the orders of Che. Unfortunately, I fell ill at that time, because of malnutrition, as my initial statement shows, and Che didn't have much confidence in my physical fitness.[3]

The first plan made by Che was to evacuate the 'visitors' through the village of Gutiérrez, which lies to the east of the Río Ñancahuazú on the main road from Camiri to Santa Cruz. This fell through because they discovered that the village had been taken over by the

military. After the ambush at Iripiti, the guerrillas moved south-west.
It was hoped that Debray and Bustos at least would be able to leave
through the village of Muyupampa and then make their way out of the
guerrilla zone towards Sucre or Cochabamba.

In the early hours of 20 April, Debray and Bustos left the guerrillas, together with George Andrew Roth—a freelance Anglo-Chilean
photographer who had arrived the previous day—and the three of
them made their way down to Muyupampa.[4] In the main street of the
village they were picked up for questioning by the DIC—the Bolivian
Criminal Investigation Department. A few minutes after their capture,
Debray was identified by Salustio Choque Choque—the former miner,
soldier and recent deserter from the guerrillas who had already
proved his worth to the army. He claimed that he had seen Debray in
the camp at Ñancahuazú, and he denounced him to the army as a
guerrilla. The three men were then handed over by the DIC to the
military authorities.

Luckily for them, there happened to be a journalist from *Presencia*
in the town. Otherwise they might well have disappeared without
trace. He took photographs of them. They were fortunate, for the first
cables coming out of La Paz on 21 April said that an Argentinian and
an Englishman had been captured after a clash with the guerrillas,
and that a Frenchman, 'René Debré', had probably been killed.[5] The
report added that 'Debré' occupied a very important position in the
Communist hierarchy in Havana.

All journalists were ejected from Muyupampa and Camiri and the
other towns of the guerrilla zone at this stage, so there was no detailed
information of what had happened. But it was finally announced that
all three men were alive. It seems fairly clear that the army had
received an order to kill Debray, but that this was later rescinded. The
three men were beaten up, dumped in various prisons in the Camiri
area, and held incommunicado until the beginning of July. Later, Roth
was released, while Debray and Bustos were both sentenced to 30
years' imprisonment.

During the first six weeks of its existence, the ELN had been able
to make an impact, both nationally and internationally, out of all proportion to its actual strength. And with the capture of Debray a veritable

legion of foreign correspondents—especially from France—descended on the scene. Even President de Gaulle sent a letter to President Barrientos asking for clemency for Debray, But the guerrillas themselves, though doubtless pleased with the publicity, were by no means in such a strong position as some of the press reports would have led one to believe.

Notes

1   In fact 'Andrés' was invented by Debray and Bustos 'to put the authorities off the track'. See Luís González and Gustavo Sánchez, *The Great Rebel: Che Guevara in Bolivia*, Grove Press, New York, 1969, p. 83.

2   Letter from Debray to his judges, 12 October 1967.

3   Debray, defence statement, Camiri.

4   Roth has told his story in *Ercilla* (Santiago), September 1967, and also in the *Evergreen Review*.

5   AP cable in *El Mercurio* (Santiago), 22 April 1967.

One of the major disasters caused by the premature beginning of the guerrilla action and the subsequent isolation from the city was the breaking off of contact with the Bolivian Communist party. When Monje had left the camp at Ñancahuazú at the beginning of January, he had said that he would hand in his resignation as Secretary-General of the party the following week, and the possibility of further discussions between the Communists and the guerrillas remained. However, later in the month Guevara learnt that Monje had not only not resigned but that he had also spoken 'with three men who were coming from Cuba and dissuaded them from joining the guerrillas'. The decisions of the party, however, were now chiefly in the hands of Jorge Kolle Cueto and Simón Reyes, and these two journeyed to Havana in February to discuss the matter further with Fidel. Late in January Guevara received a message from Cuba announcing that the two Bolivians were expected: 'Fidel warns that he will hear what they have to say and that he will be severe with them.' On 14 February Guevara received details from Havana of the meeting:

> We decoded a long message from Havana. Its main point was the news of the interview with Kolle. In the interview he said that he had not been informed of the continental scope of the task; as this was the case, they would be willing to collaborate on a plan; they would like to discuss its details with me: Kolle himself, Simón Rodríguez and Ramírez would come. I am also informed that Simón has stated his decision to help us, regardless of what the party decides.

The message Guevara received reads as follows:

> In the Kolle-Simón talks recently held, Kolle said that Monje
> had told the secretariat [of the Communist party] that the
> operation was on a national scale and that this was causing
> confusion. It was made clear to Kolle the continental scale and
> strategic content of the operation. This removed confusion
> about the operation and he agreed to demand leadership of
> the operation on a national level. He asked to speak to you to
> discuss their collaboration and participation in the operation.
> Kolle, Simón and Ramírez will come to see you. They are leav-
> ing immediately . . . favourable impression. . . . I think some-
> thing can be done . . . he wants economic help and training
> for his men. We will tell you the result.[1]

Guevara was obviously not very impressed by this new overture
from the Communists, and he comments in his diary at the end of the
month: '. . . the party's attitude continues to be two-faced and hesitant,
to say the least, although there is still one point to clear up, which may
be decisive, when I speak with the new delegation.' What annoyed
Guevara most was the fact that, at the very moment when the leaders
of the Communist party appeared to be making overtures to the guerrilla leadership, they were expelling from the youth movement any
young Communists who showed signs of being interested in supporting the guerrillas. Loyola Guzmán, for one, the guerrillas' treasurer, had
fallen a victim to this kind of intra-party purge, as had others who were
actually with Guevara in Ñancahuazú. In March, Guevara told the assembled company what he thought of the new Communist initiative:

> I referred to Kolle's project to come here and discuss what is
> to be done simultaneously with the expulsion from the
> Communist Youth of those members present with us. The
> facts matter here; words that don't coincide with facts are
> unimportant.

Nevertheless, he clearly hadn't ruled out the idea of seeing them.
Debray has confirmed this:

> When Bustos and I left the guerrillas, Che was waiting for the
> arrival of other people from outside, I mean La Paz, real mes-
> sengers. Unfortunately they never came. No guerrilla could

leave the group to do anything in the city, on Che's strict orders. Che's political and military strictness became one of the main reasons for the guerrilla's failure, for after once coming into the jungle, he allowed no combatant to go back to the plains. And as they couldn't go from the plains to the jungle either, there was this terrible misunderstanding, each side waiting for the other to come to decide very urgent matters.[2]

Yet, from the public statements of the Communist leaders in La Paz, it appears that they were not over-anxious to re-establish contact with Guevara, once guerrilla warfare had actually broken out. In a statement of 30 March, issued over the signature of Marío Monje and Humberto Ramírez, the secretariat of the party called for 'solidarity' with the guerrillas, but confirmed that the political line of the party had not been altered in any degree by the outbreak in the south-east of the country:

Bolivians!

Guerrilla warfare has begun in this country. . . .

The Communist party expresses its solidarity with the struggle of the patriotic guerrillas. The most positive aspect of this stand will doubtless be that this struggle will help to show Bolivians the best way to follow to achieve revolutionary victory.

The question of joining the ranks of the guerrillas falls outside the scope of party organization and discipline, since Bolivians have the right and the obligation to contribute to the people's struggle in the way they see fit.

The Communist party of Bolivia has its own line, passed at its Second Conference, and will continue to keep to it and develop it. It has never hidden its intention of seizing power by the means which concrete historical conditions and necessity impose, bringing about a popular anti-imperialist government at the service of the Bolivian people, with the sole condition of the action and participation of the broad masses led by their own party and at the most favourable moment. *The present situation does not fundamentally change the line and aims of the Bolivian Communists*; but it does demand greater efforts, sacrifices and discipline.[3]

In the light of this document, the appeal issued by the urban network of the ELN a month later, at the end of April, from the zone of Ñancahuazú, should be seen as a direct call to Communist militants to ignore the directives of their party: 'The National Liberation Army calls on the Bolivian people to close ranks, to forge the closest unity without distinction of political colours.'

This document was the only appeal published by the guerrilla movement during the campaign. In an interview with a Chilean journalist published in May, Jorge Kolle Cueto explained why:

> It so happened that the guerrillas in the eastern part of the country went into action with the regular army before they were supposed to. This means that the guerrillas began fighting before the movement in the cities and the mines got off the ground. Nor did it coincide with the disintegration of the present government.

The Chilean journalist then began to question the Bolivian Communist in more detail. It is a revealing interview:

JOURNALIST: I have the impression that, until now, the guerrillas have lacked the support of mass action in the urban part of the country.

KOLLE: At present the political forces of the left-wing parties are having talks designed to open a large-scale mass movement bringing in the political parties, the miners, factory workers and the advanced middle classes, not only from the point of view of actively supporting and collaborating with the guerrillas, but also in order to put forward economic, social and political claims which will raise the fighting spirit of the masses to the level needed to take power. . . .

JOURNALIST: Don't you think that the delay in starting mass actions in the cities may prejudice the very survival of the guerrillas?

KOLLE: The survival of the guerrillas is a strategic military problem that has been well studied. We have never considered the possibility of the guerrillas being crushed by the army. This part of the problem depends a great deal on tactical plans as far as the number of operations are concerned. And anyway, the initiative has always been ours.

JOURNALIST: How long would it take to prepare mass actions in the cities?

KOLLE: This problem is closely linked to the political crisis the country has undergone since the overthrow of the MNR government. That party is now split into several groups and it is now necessary to make certain positions clear and to bring the most determined sectors into the fight. In the PRIN, on the other hand, the miners, in spite of being in a majority, have to fight their own internal battles with the middle-class intellectuals who want to be on good terms with everybody from the army to the United States embassy. This has slowed up the process of anti-imperialist political unity which we are urging.

JOURNALIST: Does this mean that the guerrilla are not the most important part of the plan?

KOLLE: It means that the guerrillas, insurrection, is one way of fighting, but obviously it isn't the only activity we are undertaking. These are combined actions which depend one on the other. You must understand that the guerrillas will get stronger and stronger as the fighting spirit of the urban masses, miners and peasants rises.

JOURNALIST: Would you consider that the outbreak of guerrilla warfare in Bolivia is a triumph for the Cuban line within your party?

KOLLE: We believe that guerrilla warfare has broken out in Bolivia at the right moment. We consider that each Communist party must work out its problems according to the conditions for the struggle in each country. We hope that our mass action will contribute to political unity amongst Latin American Communists and destroy once and for all the doubts and suspicions about positions—for example, the supposed position of the so-called Moscow-oriented parties, allegedly opposed to solving political problems by military means. This is obviously not true. Peaceful co-existence is a policy for the Soviet Union and the United States, as they are trying to avoid a thermonuclear war, but that does not mean that peaceful co-existence obliges us Communists to give up the class struggle or the struggle against imperialism in our countries. This is well shown by our present stand supporting the guerrillas.[4]

But in spite of Kolle's insistence that his party was supporting the guerrillas, the fact remains that neither he nor the party was prepared to accept the guerrilla proposal, namely the formation of a broad anti-imperialist front with its focal point in the mountainous jungle of Ñancahuazú, rather than in the mines or La Paz. Debray cannot have been surprised. In *Revolution in the Revolution?* he writes:

> it is very difficult for such a front to crystallize before the armed struggle, if it is to be a genuine revolutionary front and not an alliance set up for the duration of an election or a pact among bourgeois groups to recapture their lost power. The formation of a broad anti-imperialist front is realized through the people's war.[5]

Throughout April and May, Guevara seems to have been too taken up with military matters to pay much attention in his diary to whether or not the Bolivian Communist party had offered its support . . . But at the end of May he writes, without further comment, that 'through Kolle, the party offers its collaboration, apparently without reservations'. This was probably a reference to the Chilean interview, which he may well have heard on the radio.

In the middle of June, Guevara's guerrilla group found a boy, Paulino, who seemed prepared to help as a messenger. They asked him to take a number of messages to Cochabamba—the nearest large town. Through him they hoped to make contact with the city and the party. At the end of the month, Guevara writes:

> The lack of contact extends to the party, although we have made an attempt through Paulino that may bring some results. . . . Our most urgent task is to re-establish contact with La Paz, to restock our medical and military supplies and to recruit about fifty to a hundred men from the city, even if the number of combatants is never more than ten or fifteen people in action.

In the middle of July, returning to Paulino's village, the guerrillas found no sign of him. The army had passed through the area in their absence. The guerrillas questioned Paulino's acquaintances: 'They didn't know what Paulino was up to, except that the army was looking for him for having been our guide.'

This was the guerrillas' last effort to make contact with the city. But Guevara continued to listen anxiously to the radio for news of what was happening in the country as a whole. The purpose of a guerrilla *foco*, it is worth repeating, is not to create a revolution, but to create the conditions for a revolution. Guevara believed that the insertion of a group of men into an already explosive political situation could have a positive result. During the early months, he obviously felt that everything was going according to plan. At the end of May he reported: 'From a military point of view, these new battles, with losses to the army and none to ourselves . . . mean success.' And in the middle of June he writes:

> The interesting thing is the political convulsion in the country, the fabulous number of deals and counter-deals which are in the air. Seldom has the possibility of the guerrilla as a catalyst seemed as clear.

A month later, on 14 July, he writes in similar vein:

> The PRA and the PSB are withdrawing from the revolutionary front [of Barrientos] and the peasants are warning Barrientos about an alliance with the Falange. The government is rapidly disintegrating. It's a pity we do not have a hundred more men at this moment.

The following week he mentions that 'the news is about a tremendous political crisis and I don't see where it is going to end'. In June government troops had taken over the mining areas on the altiplano, and this, together with the existence of Guevara's guerrillas, had caused a political crisis in La Paz of major dimensions. Had the Communist party or some other urban-based party been ready and able to take advantage of this situation, the Ñancahuazú *foco* might have served its purpose. But the pusillanimity of the opposition politicians in La Paz was such that they were not able to grasp the opportunity offered them.

Guevara's other thesis was that a guerrilla *foco* could trigger off American intervention. In the early days he was optimistic about this. In April he writes:

> The Americans have announced that the military advisers sent to Bolivia were part of an old plan and had nothing to do with the guerrillas. Perhaps we are present at the first episode in a new Vietnam.

And at the end of the month he concludes:

> It seems certain that the Americans will intervene here in strength. They are already sending helicopters and, apparently, Green Berets. . . .

Later on, however, at the end of July, he seems to guess that American intervention may have adverse effects on his guerrilla theory: 'the political crisis in the government grows,' he writes, 'but the USA is handing out small credits which are a great help by Bolivian standards and serve to ease the discontent.' Perhaps this was an aspect that Guevara forgot when formulating his thesis about the necessity of creating the 'second Vietnam' in Latin America. The United States has many strings to its bow, and not all of them are military.

Notes

1 From a document read by the Bolivian Minister of the Interior, Antonio Arguedas, at a press conference in La Paz, 30 October 1967. Text in *El Diario* (La Paz), 31 October 1967.

2 I have translated the word *'llanos'* as 'plains'. In guerrilla terminology, however, it usually means the city, as opposed to the rural areas where the guerrillas operate.

3 Quoted in *El Siglo* (Santiago), 29 April 1967. (My italics.)

4 Jorge Kolle Cueto interviewed by José Gómez López for *Flash* magazine; quoted in *El Siglo* (Santiago), 14 May 1967.

5 Debray, *Revolution in the Revolution?* p. 125.

Guerrilla strategy during the first three weeks of April had been largely dictated by the need to get rid of the 'visitors'. The clash at Iripiti on 10 April had occurred as they were trying to make their way towards Gutiérrez. This exit being closed, the guerrilla group moved towards Muyupampa. Guevara's plan was to operate there for a while and then to retreat to the north, presumably to the area that he had been exploring in February, north of the Río Grande. But during the difficult period when the guerrilla group was trying to shed Debray and Bustos, they mislaid the rearguard led by the Cuban Joaquín. In addition to Joaquín, the rearguard contained two Cubans and five Bolivians. They parted company from the main group on 15 April, Joaquín's instructions being 'to make a show of strength in the zone so as to keep down the enemy's mobility'. 'He was to wait for us,' Guevara noted in his diary, 'for three days; after that he was to remain in the zone without any head-on fighting and wait for our return.' Guevara's group continued on towards Muyupampa. On 16 April, Guevara discovered that Tania and a Cuban, Alejandro, were lagging badly. They both had high temperature, and so it was decided to leave them with another Bolivian and the Peruvian doctor to join the rearguard. The following day, peeved by the slow speed of the march, Guevara, gave orders for the four slowest Bolivians to drop behind to join Joaquín. Moises Guevara too was poorly, and he also joined the rearguard.

Joaquín's group by this time consisted of 17 men, many of them ill and in need of recuperation. Free of them, Guevara's group of 12

Cubans, 2 Peruvians and 13 Bolivians was able to move with greater speed. Nevertheless, 27 men was a trifle small for a guerrilla group, and Guevara became extremely anxious when, after a few days, there appeared to be no sign of Joaquín. The strategy of the succeeding weeks and months was dictated by the need to find the missing group. They were destined never to reunite.

Throughout May, Guevara's group remained in the area of the Ñancahuazú, searching for Joaquín. At the end of the first week they returned to one of their old camps to restock with food, which had run very low. The soldiers had left the camp but they were well-installed in the Casa Calamina. At the end of the month the group began moving north along the railway-line which, for some of the way, serves as the main road between Camiri and Santa Cruz. Guevara had concluded that Joaquín had moved to the north and that it would be easier to find him north of the Río Grande.

He now began to operate within a rough quadrilateral, bordered on the north by the asphalted road from Santa Cruz to Cochabamba, in the west by the bad but passable road from Mataral through Vallegrande to Pucara, to the south by the Río Grande, and to the east by the Santa Cruz–Yacuiba railway-line. The area has two important rivers, both of which flow into the Río Grande: the Masicuri, flowing south, and the Florida, west. The whole region is mountainous, covered in jungle and broken up by deep ravines. There are virtually no roads, only paths and occasional beaten tracks. Very few people live there.

The Eighth Division of the Bolivian army, under the command of a former Foreign Minister, Colonel Joaquín Zenteno Anaya, kept a battalion in Abapo and a company in Masicuri Abajo to prevent the guerrillas from crossing the Río Grande. But on 10 June, without opposition, the guerrillas managed to slip across the river. However, a peasant got word through to the military headquarters in Abapo, which hastily dispatched a group of 90 soldiers southwards. There was a minor clash the following day.

After this engagement, the army assumed that the guerrillas had crossed the river again to head back to Ñancahuazú. But, in fact, they doubled back and continued their move northwards. On 19 June they reappeared near the village of Morocco, where a number of peasants lived. But two of them were intelligence officers disguised as peasants who had been sent down from the main base at Vallegrande to Morocco, with a view to keeping a check on the guerrillas' movements. They were captured by the guerrillas, but released two days later. Whereupon news got back to Vallegrande that the guerrillas had moved north again. The army caught up with them on 26 June and there was a clash near Piray. One soldier was killed and two wounded. On the guerrilla side, one of Guevara's closest colleagues, Tuma, was killed, and Pombo was wounded and had to be taken off on a mule.

The Bolivian authorities became quite alarmed at this stage, since Piray was not far from the Cochabamba–Santa Cruz road, and indeed not far from Santa Cruz itself. But instead of continuing their march north the guerrillas moved west, into an area where many rivers meet. This is a totally impenetrable and inaccessible region where, according to Colonel Zenteno, they could have remained for years without being discovered. On 3 July a campesino told the military unit at Bermejo that the guerrillas were in this very difficult country.

Three days later, on 6 July at 10 o'clock in the evening, the guerrillas moved into Las Cuevas, on the Santa Cruz–Cochabamba road. Hearing of this, the authorities in Santa Cruz telephoned the military unit in Samaipata to move along the road to Las Cuevas. The guerrillas, however, were listening in to the telephone conversation and were therefore aware of the troop movements. They commandeered an old bus, and at 12.30, just after midnight, arrived in Samaipata. The officer in charge there was at that moment issuing ammunition to his troops. He heard the sound of a lorry and, without picking up his rifle, went out to see what it was. It was the guerrillas.

In a subsequent scuffle a rifle went off and a soldier was killed. The guerrillas stopped at the telegraph office on the main road, tore down the telephone and inquired where they could find drugs. They wanted antibiotics and something for asthma.

After this venture into Samaipata, which was a great publicity coup, the guerrillas retired to the impenetrable area to the south, and disappeared for a fortnight. On 19 July they were located in El Filo, and on 27 July there was quite an important clash in El Duran. One guide was killed and a soldier injured, but the guerrillas had no losses. There was another clash further south on 30 July. The army lost four dead and six wounded owing to a bungle by the commander of the vanguard. The guerrillas lost two dead, Raúl and Ricardo, and one wounded, Pacho. And they left 10 huge rucksacks behind.

In the meantime, Joaquín's group had continued to operate in the area of the Ñancahuazú, south of the Río Grande. Their mobility was impeded by the presence of Tania, for whom it had proved impossible to secure an escape route, and also by the continued illness of some of the members. On 20 July, however, after a battle which the group had had near Ticucha, the first desertion took place. Two Bolivians from the altiplano, Chingolo and Eusebio, little more than boys, managed to escape during the confusion of the fight. They set off towards Sucre, but in the village of Chullayacu, near Muyupampa, they tried to sell a rifle. The peasants, perturbed, told the army, and the pursuit of the deserters began. In Monteagudo they managed to sell the rifle to the local schoolmaster for five dollars. They continued on their way, and while pausing for a swim in the waters of the Río Monteagudo, they were surprised by Major Ruben Sánchez, the same officer who had been captured by the guerrillas after the ambush at Iripiti.

Initially the two boys denied having been guerrillas, but a little persuasion with a rifle soon made them reveal that they had indeed been members of the guerrilla band. They then began to co-operate with the army in revealing where the caves of Ñancahuazú were to be found—that is to say, those that had been built *after* the ambush of 23 March. They led the army to the first cave on 4 August. The other two were found during the next few days.[1]

The discovery of these caves was one of the gravest setbacks received by the guerrillas. In his diary Guevara commented after hearing the news over the radio, 'It is the hardest blow they have inflicted on us.' Only five days before he had sent three men to return to Ñancahuazú to open up one of the caves to secure the medicines that he needed and which they had been unable to obtain during the assault on Samaipata. Now he would have to overcome his asthma without any medical assistance. This was bad news personally for Guevara, but the implications of the capture of the caves was serious for the entire guerrilla band. They now had nowhere where they could return to to

find provisions or arms for new recruits. Not only did the army capture Guevara's medicines, but also the supplies and radio equipment
that would be vital to any future development of the guerrilla. They
were now isolated and alone.

Even more important was the capture of photographs and documentary evidence concerning the urban net. In particular, there was a
photograph of an attractive girl guerrilla seated between Inti and Coco
Peredo. It was of Loyola Guzmán, the treasurer of the guerrillas' urban
organization who had visited the camp at Ñancahuazú in January. She
was soon identified and captured, and, with the material they found in
her house, together with that from the caves, the authorities had little
difficulty in winding up the guerrillas' support group in the towns.

The only hope the guerrillas had by the middle of August for survival, let alone for success, was to reunite their forces. And by some
magic circumstances both Guevara's group and that of Joaquín began
converging on the house of Honorato Rojas, the peasant they had visited in February. Neither group knew that this was the intention of the
other, but towards the end of the month, Guevara from the north and
Joaquín from the south were steadily marching towards each other.

On 30 August, Joaquín's group appeared just north of the Río
Grande, at Honorato's ranch, Puesto Mauricio, on the east bank of the
Masicuri, just where it flows into the Río Grande some way upstream
from the Ñancahuazú. At six o'clock in the evening, the dogs began to
bark in the little farm, and three or four guerrillas appeared. They
found three peasants there eating their evening meal. The guerrillas
bought a few things, holding the peasants prisoner. But they did not
know that these peasants, like those that Guevara's group had encountered earlier, were in fact soldiers in disguise. One of them managed
to escape, and he walked through the night with no shoes to La Laja,
where he arrived the following morning to find the officers of the
army group there playing volleyball. The guerrillas meanwhile withdrew to the hills behind the ranch.

The troops based in La Laja hurried back to Puesto Mauricio,
where Honorato told them that he had agreed to show the guerrillas
where to cross the river the following day. Joaquín was presumably
planning to double back to Ñancahuazú. The officer placed six men

on one side of the river and 29 on the other, and the soldiers waited from six o'clock in the morning till five o'clock at night. Then one guerrilla, Braulio, appeared. He crossed the river and looked to see if all was well. Then he waved to the others to follow—10 in all. When they were all in the river, the shooting began. They tried to throw off their rucksacks to fire back, but it was impossible in the breast-high water. The last two, Tania and Joaquín, were able to fire back, but only momentarily. The entire group was annihilated. Later their bodies were taken to Vallegrande. It was a major victory for the Bolivian army The very next day, Guevara's band arrived at the place. Unable to join up with Joaquín's group, Guevara moved towards Citanas, and finally, on 24 September, they entered the small hamlet of Alto Seco.

At five o'clock in the morning, when the first villagers appeared, they found that their whole village had been taken over by the guerrillas, who were occupying strategic positions. The first thing the guerrillas did was to ask for the telephone, which was in the house of the magistrate. They entered the house and cut the line, although in fact the telephone had not been working for some weeks.[2]

About an hour later the guerrilla 'chief' arrived. The local peasants said that he came on a mule. He was of medium height, with long hair. It seemed that he was ill, as they had to help him to dismount.

The guerrillas bought food and clothing and then set up camp about 200 metres from the village in an abandoned and half-destroyed house. There were about 20 of them, and they spent the day resting.

That evening, at 8.30, they organized a meeting in the school, presided over by Inti Peredo and Che Guevara. 'You must think that we are mad,' said Inti, 'to fight like this. They say that we are bandits, but in fact we are fighting for you, for the working class, for the workers who earn little, while the soldiers get large wages. You are only working for them. What have they ever done for you? Why, only just now we cut the telephone thinking that it worked. Now it appears that it didn't even work. Here you don't have water, you don't have electric light. You have been abandoned like all Bolivians. That's why we're fighting.'

Inti finished by appealing to anyone who wanted to, to join up with them to fight until 'the final overthrow of Barrientos'. But Guevara interrupted him: 'We want you to come of your own free will, not by force. We never use force, but anyone who wants to come will be well received.'

Then Che began his speech. Perhaps trying to raise the morale of his own men, rather than seeking to impress the villagers, he said that the bodies of Tania and Joaquín and the other guerrillas killed in the ambush at the end of August and exhibited by the army in Vallegrande were false. 'The army says that it has killed Joaquín and our other comrades. But this is a lie, it's only army propaganda. The corpses they showed in Vallegrande were brought from the cemeteries. They didn't kill guerrillas. This I can assure you, because only a couple of days ago I was in communication with Joaquín.'

After talking for half an hour, Che wound up his speech. 'In every country we shall continue fighting to liberate it from American oppression. You have heard tell of Santo Domingo. It is a country like Bolivia. There, the Americans went in and killed many peasants who were only asking for a better life. The same will happen here. That's why we're fighting.'

But later in the evening, one of the peasants approached a young beardless guerrilla and asked whether he could join up with them. 'Don't be crazy,' came the reply. 'Can't you see that we've had it? Why, we don't even know how to get out of here.'

Che and Coco had in fact been discussing in great detail with the villagers the various routes through the area, and they had also tried to pick up information about the whereabouts of the army. The following day, they sallied forth in the direction of Higueras, but there, on 26 September, they ran into the Bolivian army. Coco and two others (including the Cuban, Miguel) were killed.

Things were made more difficult for the guerrillas at this stage owing to the fact that Colonel Zenteno had thrown into the fight an additional 600 fresh Bolivian 'Ranger' troops who had just finished their training by United States Special Forces at La Esperanza. Consequently, the whole area where the guerrillas were operating was saturated with troops. In addition, the army was assisted by two former guerrillas. One, Antonio Rodríguez Flores (León), was a deserter. The other, Orlando Jiménez Bazán (Camba), was captured the day after Coco's death, having been separated from the other guerrillas and having run out of ammunition. Both gave information about the whereabouts and the situation of the guerrillas. From their evidence there seemed little doubt that the remaining group had wanted to break away. They had bought clothes and razor blades in Alto Seco. But it was also clear that they were encircled and had only the slenderest chance of escape. They managed to hold on for 10 days in the area of Higueras, but on 8 October, at 1.30 in the afternoon, they ran into a group of soldiers.

Notes

1   This account comes from Darc, 'Dos canillitas hirieron de muerte a la guerrilla boliviana', *Confirmado Internacional* (La Paz), NO. 2, February 1968.

2   This account is taken from Edwin Chacón, '52 horas de ocupación guerrillera en Alto Seco', *Presencia* (La Paz), 4 October 1967.

10. The Capture and Death of Che Guevara

> 'The guerrilla fighter must never for any reason leave a wounded
> companion at the mercy of the enemy troops, because this would be
> leaving him to almost certain death. At whatever cost he must be removed
> from the zone of combat to a secure place. The greatest exertions
> and the greatest risks must be taken in this task.'
>
> *Ernesto Che Guevara*, Guerrilla Warfare

On the morning of Sunday, 8 October 1967, the guerrilla group of 17 led by Che Guevara, lay hidden in the Quebrada del Yuro, a narrow wooded canyon leading down to the Río Grande—the great river that rises in the heart of Bolivia and flows down into the Amazon. Noticing the troop movements on the bare heights above, they realized that they had allowed themselves to be caught in an extremely difficult position. Apparently encircled, the only possible line of escape lay down the valley to the Río Grande. Guevara commented that if they got involved in a fight before one o'clock, things would go badly, but if they could hold on without exchanging fire till four o'clock, they would be safe and could escape under cover of nightfall.

He called for six volunteers who, if necessary, would give covering fire while the main body of the group tried to make their way down the floor of the canyon. From the volunteers he chose Inti Peredo, who had become the leader of the Bolivians in the group since the death of his brother, Coco, two weeks before. He also selected two other Bolivians, Dario and Nato, and three Cubans Pombo, Beningo and Urbano. Pombo had been his bodyguard for more than eight years.

Hardly had this suicide squad moved into position before firing began, some time shortly after one o'clock. The main group led by Guevara, promptly began slipping down the valley towards the Río Grande. But unknown to them, the circle was in fact complete, and it was not long before they ran into the soldiers guarding the entrance to the valley. Paradoxically it was the group that had volunteered for the most dangerous task that managed to escape. Guevara's group, which should have had an easier job, ran into far superior forces.

Guevara himself was shot in the leg and tried to escape with the aid of Willy, a Bolivian from the mines. 'We tried to help him,' said Pombo, who later escaped to Chile, 'but it was impossible. We were few and they were many.'

Che and Willy were captured, together with Pacho and El Chino, who were also wounded. Although a Bolivian officer radioed for a helicopter, it was thought unsafe for it to land in the canyon since the fighting was still going on. The prisoners were taken to the nearby village of La Higuera. There, a helicopter arrived from the military headquarters at Vallegrande, bearing with it a Bolivian colonel and Felix Ramos, a Cuban exile employed by the CIA who had been working in conjunction with the United States army base outside Santa Cruz for some months. Ramos, who is believed to have known Guevara in Cuba, interrogated him but without securing any information.

Although a decision had been taken in principle by the military authorities to shoot Guevara if he were captured—as occurred with 90 per cent of the guerrillas that fell into the hands of the army—the Bolivian soldiers were not anxious to fulfil the order until they had direct authorization from La Paz. This was not immediately forthcoming, and consequently Guevara spent the night in La Higuera. Had he been flown out alive to Vallegrande, where there were two or three local and foreign correspondents, it would have been impossible to sustain what was later to become the official story, namely that he had been wounded in battle and died of his wounds.

At dawn the following morning, the commanding officer of the area, Colonel Joaquín Zenteno, arrived from Vallegrande by helicopter to ensure that the prisoner really was Guevara. Shortly before nine o'clock the helicopter set off from La Higuera to Vallegrande bearing the bodies of two Bolivian soldiers shot in the fighting the previous day. Later in the morning it returned to La Higuera bearing the order of execution, sent by radio and signed by the President, General Barrientos, and the Commander-in-Chief of the armed forces, General Ovando. Guevara, who had been accommodated in the village schoolroom, was then shot by an insignificant Bolivian sergeant, Mario Terán. Willy and the other prisoners were dispatched likewise almost immediately afterwards.

At one o'clock, Zenteno returned to Vallegrande and gave waiting journalists the news that Che was dead, and at five o'clock in the evening the ever-active helicopter brought his body from La Higuera to be laid out in the laundry of the hospital in Vallegrande. Here the operation was left in the hands of another CIA man, Eduardo González, also a Cuban exile, while Ramos remained in the background.[1]

That Monday and the following day, full facilities were given to journalists to inspect the body, but on Wednesday it had disappeared, giving rise to the speculation that the Bolivian authorities were trying to ensure that it should not be examined by Guevara's brother who had arrived belatedly on the scene from Buenos Aires. There were a whole series of unverifiable rumours that the body had been buried or burnt, and that the hands and head had been cut off. In fact the body was taken away from Vallegrande in the middle of Tuesday night in a small plane, accompanied by two Bolivian officers and one CIA man. Its ultimate destination remains unknown. Perhaps, as some suggest, it was spirited away to the American base in Panama. Probably it was thrown out of the plane in some desolate spot. All that is certain is that it will never be found.

The Bolivians discourage inquiry. Senior officers who have told journalists too much have been reprimanded or denied promotion. Junior ones have been sent on scholarships abroad. The schoolroom at La Higuera, bearing the marks of Guevara's execution, is closed and is scheduled to be destroyed. But while the physical evidence is removed, a powerful myth survives.

Of the group of 17 guerrillas in the Quebrada del Yuro on Sunday morning, seven were dead by midday the following day. Apart from those assassinated with Che, two Cubans—Arturo and Antonio—and a Bolivian—Aniceto—had been killed during the fighting on Sunday afternoon. Of Che's group of 11, only four remained—Paolo and Chapaco (Bolivians), Eustaquio (Peruvian) and Moro (Cuban)—sometimes known as 'El Medico'.

This group of four was never able to reunite with the group of six led by Inti Peredo. While Inti's group managed to break through the circle drawn by the army, the four remained inside it. They clashed twice with the army on 12 October, killing four soldiers and a guide at Potrero El Naranjal. But on 14 October they were captured on an island, El Cajón, situated at the junction of the Río Mizque with the Río Grande. They had been trying to cross the river. That night they were shot while sleeping in captivity.

Inti's suicide squad proved the most fortunate. They remained within the area for more than a month, only suffering one loss—El Ñato—who was killed in a clash 15 kilometres south-east of Mataral on 15 November.

The survivors, three Cubans and two Bolivians, struggled to Cochabamba, where they were hidden by supporters. Inti and Dario, the two Bolivians, chose to remain in Bolivia, but the three Cubans—Pombo, Benigno and Urbano—accompanied by two other Bolivians from the city, journeyed to the altiplano and crossed into Chile in February 1968. From there they were allowed to return to Havana.

Just how revolutionary was Bolivia during Guevara's guerrilla campaign? If it was, it possessed a unique characteristic among revolutionary countries in that it had had a revolution which was real enough only 15 years before.

After 1952 the upper classes fled, the army was disbanded and, by means of enfranchisement and agrarian reform, large numbers of Indians—the pre-dominant element in the population—were brought into the framework of a modern society. But the direction of the revolution was at best uncertain, and the leaders soon fell out among themselves. The Movimiento Nacional Revolucionario, the great party that had pioneered these changes, splintered under the corrupting pressures of power. After 1964, when a coup brought Barrientos and Ovando to power, the MNR leaders retired into exile.

The effect of the agrarian reform, and the precise attitude of the peasants towards it, are of some importance, since the miners—the other potentially radical element in Bolivian society—were effectively out of the struggle during the guerrilla campaign. In the early months the miners appeared to be solidly supporting the guerrillas. Propaganda in favour of the armed struggle poured out from the radio station in the mines. In the great tin mine at Siglo Veinte there was a shooting range within the mine, and miners were training for guerrilla warfare. At union meetings, miners were urged to give money to the guerrilla cause.

But in June 1967 President Barrientos clamped down. The army moved into the mines. Dozens of innocent people as well as miners were shot. The radio transmitters were silenced. The miners' support for the guerrillas was more tacit than active, although a large proportion of the army—which might have been diverted to the guerrilla zone—was needed to keep them neutralized.

The peasantry was more of an unknown quantity, for it is difficult to make any valid generalizations about the impact of the agrarian reform initiated after the 1952 Revolution. It reached certain regions successfully, but in others it was abortive, and in some places it never penetrated at all. It would be surprising if things were otherwise. The problems of subsistence agriculture are such that they cannot be solved simply by the passing of a law.

More serious than simple backwardness was the fact that, since 1964, when Barrientos drove his old leader, Víctor Paz Estenssoro, from the country, the old landowners in some places began creeping back, from Argentina and elsewhere, to reclaim their hold over the peasantry. There were indications that in some areas, the administration of the law began to benefit the landlord more than the peasant, and in some cases peasants were having to buy their land, instead of acquiring it by right. Unobtrusively, radical leaders of peasant unions were replaced by more pliable men.

All this, if it had taken place on a large scale, could have been an important element in the growing disaffection of the population, although it is not difficult to conclude that much of the peasantry was too cynical, if not actually demoralized by unkept promises, to be an effectively radical political force. The bulk were probably happy with the gains already made, and were content for the time being to support Barrientos. He could never openly oppose the achievements of the 1952 Revolution, which he had helped to make, however much he tried to bring back the pre-1952 men to bolster his own rather shaky political position. In certain areas, Barrientos was actually able to rally armed peasants to demonstrate against the guerrillas—though these rallies may well have been staged.

The fact that the agrarian reform can in some circumstances operate against the peasant affords an all too obvious parallel with the situation in South Vietnam in the 1950s when the land reform, by reinforcing the power of the landlords, actually increased the alienation of the peasantry from the Diem regime.

And like Vietnam, Bolivia has been propped up, both financially and militarily, by the United States. Its economy has been in the hands of Americans ever since 1952, while military assistance began in 1958, under President Siles Suazo, just at the time when the miners were being deprived of their weapons and the People's Militias—set up by Paz Estenssoro—were being dissolved.

The Americans trained two regiments at Viacho (La Paz) to look after the capital. Then one alpine battalion was trained and based at Challacollo (Oruro) to look after the mines. A Ranger battalion was placed in Cochabamba to look after the peasants, and a river-experienced group was set down in the far north at Riveralta, since the Americans were led to believe that this was the area where guerrillas crossed from Brazil to Peru. Finally, in 1967, a further Ranger battalion was trained at La Esperanza outside Santa Cruz. In 1965 anti-guerrilla training began, although then it was called 'counter-insurgency'. Later it turned into 'internal defence and development'.

Nor should one underestimate the United States' contribution to intelligence work within Bolivia. The guerrillas' urban network was not discovered by the unaided efforts of Bolivian intelligence. Nor did the Bolivians think up the idea of sowing the guerrilla zone with soldiers dressed up as peasants. And the overwhelming evidence of Guevara's presence in Bolivia, that the Bolivian Foreign Minister presented to an OAS conference in October, was almost certainly prepared by men who were not Bolivians. On the day that Guevara died, and the week before as well, the CIA was well-represented in Vallegrande.

It is easy to conclude that, with the death of Guevara and the annihilation of the Bolivian guerrillas, the strategy of the armed struggle in Latin America is over. But this would be to overestimate the guerrillas. The prospect for violent revolution has never looked particularly good anywhere on the continent. Before March 1967, when the Bolivian guerrillas first became news, guerrilla movements were in a state of retreat. In Peru they had been wiped out. In Venezuela, Colombia and Guatemala, they were on the defensive, facing internal dissensions as well as the external enemy. And yet in spite of these discouragements, many people remained prepared to support the armed struggle. The guerrilla outbreak in Bolivia and the foundation of the Organization for Latin American Solidarity (OLAS) gave encouragement to them, and the failure of the first and the apparent impotence of the second is unlikely to deter those with revolutionary fire in their bellies. For such people, the death of Guevara will be an inspiration and a challenge, rather than proof that the strategy is wrong.

Some have suggested that Guevara was mistaken to choose Bolivia, arguing that the peasants there are essentially conservative and anxious to hold on to the few gains which they secured from the Revolution of 1952. But this is to miss the point. The armed struggle in the strategy of Guevara was designed to 'create the conditions' for a successful revolution. Only Mao insists that the guerrillas must move around 'like fish in the water'.

In eastern Bolivia, there is very little 'water'. The guerrilla zone was no-table for its lack of population. It is true that some of the peasants that the guerrillas did encounter were hostile to them, but probably no more so than those in Cuba during the first six months in the Sierra Maestra. The initial stages of the guerrilla *foco* are invariably the most difficult—in Argentina the *foco* in Salta was destroyed even before it had emerged from the secret stage.

One could perhaps argue, not that the peasants were too conservative and lacking in land hunger, but that the guerrillas were too intellectual. On one occasion Joaquín's small group had gone to a farm to buy food from the peasant who lived there. They tried to win him over to their cause:

'When the National Liberation Army triumphs,' they said, 'you will have tractors, schools and even a university.'

'What's a university?' asked the peasant.

The spokesman for the guerrillas replied that it was a place where high school students went to study.

'And who are high school students ?'

'Those who have finished secondary school'.

'And where are they going to come from?'

'They will have to come from you yourselves.'[2]

And the guerrillas went on their way, leaving behind one mystified peasant. It would be wrong, however, to conclude from this rather sad story of mutual incomprehension that the guerrillas were completely mistaken in their approach to what needed to be done in Bolivia. Had they survived longer, one would be in a better position to judge whether the country, in spite of having had a revolution in 1952, is still in a potentially revolutionary situation. As it is, this is only a matter for conjecture. Certainly, however, it is reasonable to assert that the gains of the peasants as a result of the land reform are by no means secure. Today the peasants are indifferent; tomorrow they will have to fight if they are to retain their rights, for the government of Barrientos, whatever its outward appearance, was fundamentally hostile to peasant interests. It was equally hostile to the miners. The situation in the mines remains an almost textbook case of capitalist oppression: the army moved in, wages were halved, and the trade unions were destroyed. Discontent has been widespread and it lacks an effective outlet.

In these circumstances, the guerrillas' analysis of Bolivia's revolutionary potential was not so wide of the mark. Their mistake, perhaps, was to fail to explain how the spark provided by their *foco* was going to set the country ablaze. In their efforts to 'create the conditions' for revolution, they chose an indifferent area which made their lives in the jungle even more hazardous than is usual in guerrilla warfare. Even Che Guevara, the most important exponent of guerrilla warfare since Mao and Giap, the most romantic revolutionary figure since Leon Trotsky, and perhaps the greatest Latin American since Bolivar, found the task beyond him.

Notes

1   Reuter's correspondent, Christopher Roper, and I, who were in Vallegrande that day, were told that the balding CIA man in charge of operations was Ramos, and Roper put this name in his story. However, Antonio Arguedas has made clear to me that Ramos was in fact in La Higuera. The man we saw all day in Vallegrande was González.

2   *El Diario* (La Paz), 19 August 1967.

EPILOGUE

DEFEAT OF THE REVOLUTION?

'With the exception of only a few chapters, every more important
part of the annals of the revolution . . . carries the heading:
Defeat of the Revolution!

'What succumbed in these defeats was not the revolution. It was the pre-
revolutionary traditional appendages, results of social relationships
which had not yet come to the point of sharp class antagonism. . . .

'In a word: the revolution made progress, forged ahead, not by its
immediate . . . achievements, but, on the contrary, by the creation of
a powerful, united counter-revolution, by the creation of an opponent
in combat with whom, only, the party of overthrow ripened
into a really revolutionary party.'

Karl Marx

The debate about the value of guerrilla warfare in promoting revolutionary change in Latin America and elsewhere is one that is now firmly
rooted in the history of the latter half of the twentieth century. The purpose of this book is not to terminate that debate with overwhelming
arguments, but rather to provide material that will make it more fruitful
and conclusive. For the debate cannot be ended while, in Venezuela,
Colombia and Guatemala, the guerrilla struggle continues. This book
deals with the major guerrilla movements that have arisen in Latin
America since the Cuban Revolution, and it would be easy to conclude, as
Marx was tempted to do after the experience of 1848–49, that 'with the
exception of only a few chapters, every more important part of the
annals of the revolution . . . carries the heading: Defeat of the Revolution!'

In the 10 years since Fidel Castro marched on Havana, there has been no repeat performance in the countries discussed here, but this does not necessarily mean that in other, often-ignored countries, the *foco* theory or a variant of it might not meet with more immediate success. Can one feel sure that, in tiny Nicaragua, where a Somoza rules with the viciousness of a Batista, the seeds of a successful rebellion have not already been sown?

> In mid 1967, a band of young men, most of them members of the Frente Sandinista de Liberación Nacional (FSLN), went to the mountains of north-central Nicaragua and began to train, gather ammunition, and cache food. A small contingent of well-trained Nicaraguan National Guard troops with prior experience in the Dominican Republic caught up with the guerrillas and killed fifteen. Of the dead, ten were identified as active members of the FSLN. Some of them had been trained in Cuba, others in Eastern Europe.
>
> Subsequently, there was an outbreak of Communist terrorism in Nicaragua's cities. In León the homes of Liberal (government) party politicians were bombed, and in Managua a sergeant in the Office of National Security was gunned down in the street. . . .
>
> In view of these incidents, it would appear that the FSLN can still carry out at least isolated terrorist incidents—whether or not it is presently capable of finding a guerrilla force as it did in 1967.[1]

Could these be the heirs to Augusto Sandino? And in Social-Democratic Uruguay, the 'Switzerland' of Latin America, the '*Tupamaros*'—the spiritual descendants of the great Inca chieftain Túpac Amaru who was burnt at the stake in the eighteenth century for rebelling against Spanish role—are already making their presence felt:

> There remains little doubt in the minds of experts that little Uruguay, with a population of more than 2.5 million, has become the home of a well-disciplined and potentially effective guerrilla movement of about 1,000 men that includes members of the nation's élite. It appears to have extensive ties in other Latin American countries, including Cuba.

Furthermore, there are strong indications that the *Tupamaros* represent a new approach to guerrilla warfare in Latin America—an emphasis on urban guerrilla activity that its advocates hope will work better than the pattern followed by Ernesto Che Guevara in rural areas of Bolivia and elsewhere.

The *Tupamaros* have dealt Uruguay's democratic government a series of massive shocks during the last year—and the repercussions have been felt in Washington. They have blown up radio stations, carried out a series of bank robberies, stolen weapons and dynamite, and organized a variety of strikes and riots. . . .

The core of the group represents the political and professional élite of Uruguay. *Tupamaros* are believed to hold key positions in government ministries, banks, universities and powerful unions.[2]

And in Mexico, where a terrified government gunned down hundreds of students under the eyes of foreign journalists in the city before the Olympic Games in October 1968, the scene is surely set for further revolutionary outbursts.

In other words, however scientific we try to be, the current state of our knowledge of the social processes in Latin America is not sufficiently advanced to allow us to plot with any degree of accuracy the shape of the future. It is reasonable to assume that, when the revolution comes, it will come at a time and from a quarter that is least expected. But even an orthodox Communist writer, leaning over backwards not to be over hostile towards the guerrillas, has deigned to admit that a group of men, without ideological formation or a proper understanding of the conditions of the country, might take to the hills and provoke a revolution. This could happen if the conditions were ripe but not apparent:

Of course, there is always the possibility that a group of revolutionaries might decide to take armed action, irrespective of the concrete situation on the fronts of the class struggle. Such action might coincide with a situation when the objective conditions are ripe (it is a question, first of all, of the sentiment of the masses) for armed struggle. In that case, the armed struggle can rely on the support of the masses, can become a decisive factor in the political life of the country and [can] grow into a victorious revolution. Experience shows that launching the armed struggle in these circumstances, that is, when still gathering strength, becomes an important factor accelerating the revolutionary process.[3]

Nevertheless, without ruling out the possibility of future success, some conclusions must be drawn from the relative failures of the last 10 years.

First, one must be clear what failure the guerrilla movements are guilty of. They are not guilty, as many maintain, of failing to create the revolution. This has not been their immediate objective. Their aim has been to create *the conditions* for revolution. There is a subtle and important distinction between these two positions. The guerrilla attitude is not so much that Latin America is ripe for revolution, but rather that it *needs* a revolution. The task of the revolutionary, therefore, is not to go up to the hills, where he will be immediately recognized by the starved and oppressed masses as their saviour, but rather to go out into the countryside, as the *narodniks* did in Russia in the nineteenth century, to *stir up* the passive peasantry to understand the nature of the wrongs they are obliged to suffer. With the people aware and mobilized, revolution would then be on the agenda. But in many countries in Latin America this type of activity is impossible except with gun in hand. Political agitation, the organization of peasant unions and the holding of strikes is often illegal. The power of local landowners, reinforced by that of the state, is used to repress incipient signs of rebellion. Debray has explained the problem in one of his early essays:

> Illiterate peasants, without newspapers and radios, suffocated by centuries of 'social peace' under a feudal régime, assassinated by the *latifundistas*' private police at the first sign of revolt, cannot be awakened or acquire political consciousness by a process of thought, reflection and reading. They will reach this stage only by daily contact with men who share their

work, their living conditions and who solve their material problems. Thrown into a revolutionary war, they acquire practical experience of resistance to repression and also of a limited agrarian reform in a liberated zone: the conquest from the enemy of a small area of fertile land belonging to the *latifundista* is better propaganda for agrarian reform than a hundred illustrated pamphlets on Ukrainian *sovkhoses*.[4]

It is true that the guerrillas have little to show for their efforts so far, but then neither do the Communist parties of the continent—which have been operating for much longer—nor indeed the more idealistic supporters of the Alliance for Progress—who have far larger sums of money at their disposal. The failure of the guerrillas, therefore, must be seen in the context of the failure of all the groups interested in seeing social and economic change in Latin America.

What, then, are the specific reasons for the guerrillas lack of success so far in creating the conditions for revolution? It is best to start with the most obvious:

1. *United States intervention*. According to Arthur Schlesinger Jr in his work on the history of the Kennedy years, the growth of United States interest in guerrilla warfare was almost the single-handed work of President Kennedy and Walt Rostow. The President first began to take an interest in guerrilla warfare in May 1961 after the Laotian crisis. It was 'an old preoccupation from Senate days'.[5] Anti-guerrilla instruction soon became 'a personal project' of his, and he asked Rostow to discover what the army was doing about it:

> He was soon informed that the Special Forces at Fort Bragg consisted of fewer than a thousand men. Looking at the field manuals and training literature, he tossed them aside as 'meagre' and inadequate. Reading Mao Tse-tung and Che Guevara himself on the subject, he told the army to do likewise. (He used to entertain his wife on country weekends by inventing aphorisms in the manner of Mao's 'Guerrillas must move among the people as fish swim in the sea'.) He asked General Clifton, his military aide, to bring in the army's standard anti-guerrilla equipment, examined it with sorrow and ordered

army research and development to do better. Most important of all, he instructed the Special Warfare Centre at Fort Bragg to expand its mission, which had hitherto been largely the training of cadres for action behind the lines in case of a third world war, in order to confront the existing challenge of guerrilla warfare in the jungles and hills of underdeveloped countries. Over the opposition of the army bureaucracy, which abhorred separate élite commands on principle, he reinstated the Special Forces' green beret as the symbol of the new force.[6]

Other enthusiasts of counter-guerrilla warfare, according to Schlesinger, were Robert Kennedy and Richard Bissell of the CIA.[7] And in the autumn of 1961, a Counter-Insurgency Committee, to develop 'the nation's capability for unconventional warfare', was set up under the chairmanship of General Maxwell Taylor.

This new emphasis on anti-guerrilla warfare took place against a background of increased American military interest in Latin America that had already, under the pressure of the Cuban Revolution, been awakened in President Eisenhower's day. At that time, the United States had set up 'Southern Command' based in the Canal Zone of Panama—United States territory since 1903. This command, together with the European Command, Middle East Command and Asian Command, still makes up the four continental military commands of the United States. It consists of a general staff of 500 or 600 officers from the army, navy and air force; underground offices, logistic bases, storage of equipment, including nuclear weapons, and numerous training schools: guerrilla warfare, counter-subversion, infantry, parachute, etc. Since 1962, more than 20,000 officers from all Latin American countries have been there to learn new ways of fighting subversion.

The Special Forces (Green Berets) also have one of their four world training bases in Panama. (The other three are in Vietnam, Okinawa and West Germany.) In 1965 alone, these forces made 52 special anti-subversive missions in Latin America, including parachute drops into guerrilla zones.[8] In the course of 1966 and 1967, these forces assisted the Guatemalan army and even suffered several losses at the hands of the guerrilla. In 1967, a Special Forces training camp was set up outside Santa Cruz in Bolivia under the command of

Major 'Pappy' Shelton, for the purpose of training a Bolivian 'Ranger' battalion and for keeping an eye on the Bolivian anti-guerrilla operation. Two Special Forces units have also been operating in Venezuela. Towards the end of 1967 they were also to be found in Nicaragua.

Although the Vietnam experience has taught the Americans to be reticent in involving their own troops on a large scale, they do have active military and intelligence missions throughout Latin America. The CIA played an important role in bringing the Bolivian *foco* to a speedy conclusion.

Much emphasis has been placed by counter-insurgency experts on the 'civic action' programmes, and these do seem to have had some value in Guatemala in depriving the guerrillas of peasant support. In general, however, it seems that they are only successful in providing soldiers with something to do.

A major disadvantage for the guerrillas is that the army is nearly always several stages higher up the escalation ladder than they are. No guerrilla group possesses napalm. It is not too difficult to conclude that the anti-guerrilla experts now know very much more about the conduct of guerrilla warfare than most guerrillas do themselves.

2. *Lack of unity on the Left*. The Latin Left has rarely been united, and the guerrillas have signally failed in their aim to unite the Left around them. Castro is constantly emphasizing the need for unity, and there is some reason to believe that guerrilla groups used to receive Cuban aid only on condition that they made unity with other groups a very high priority. In fact, however, unity in Cuba itself was not achieved by the revolutionary movement in the pre-revolutionary period. Fidel managed to impose the 26 July Movement as a dominant force, but there were other *caciques* who did not take their orders from him. At least in Cuba, however, every revolutionary group was doing something, which somehow or other advanced the cause of the revolution. In Latin America today, too many revolutionary groups are either contemplating their navels or attacking one another.

It is reasonable to conclude that a guerrilla movement is likely to fail in the preliminary stages unless it has the backing and support of an existing political organization. In practice, this has meant the support of the Communist party—though there have been exceptions.

The failure of the movements in Peru, the movement in Bolivia and the extreme weakness of the MR13 movement in Guatemala, can be put down very largely to the lack of a properly organized political base. Cuba itself, of course, was an exception, as is the ELN of Colombia. With the reversal of the position of the Communist party, this support and backing is not at present forthcoming to guerrilla groups. This, though not necessarily fatal in the case of established groups like the FALN of Venezuela or the FAR of Guatemala, has certainly made things more difficult.

3. *Lack of commitment on the Left*. Contrary to established belief, Latin American universities are not full of students ready to take to the hills at the drop of a hat. The greatest problem for the guerrillas has not been securing peasant support, but luring intellectuals from the cities to organize the guerrillas. This problem has been the constant preoccupation of the Cubans, as the following remarks by Fidel Castro indicate:

> In the vast majority of the countries in Latin America, better conditions exist for making the revolution than those that existed in Cuba. If revolutions do not occur in these countries, it is because conviction is lacking in many of those who call themselves revolutionaries. . . .
>
> Revolutionaries of conviction, who feel a cause deeply, who have a theory and are capable of interpreting that theory in accordance with the facts, are, unfortunately, very few. But if and when there are men with such convictions, even though they be only a handful, then, where the objective conditions for revolution exist, there will be revolution. For history makes the objective conditions, but man creates the subjective conditions.[9]

Part of the lack of conviction on the part of those who might otherwise be out in the hills is due to the inadequate case that the guerrillas make out for their own position. Although the Cuban Revolution had an initial impact in proving that revolution was possible and could be sustained in Latin America, this became a diminishing asset when it was not followed by a further success. The missile crisis and the prolonged war in Vietnam appeared to show that the Soviet Union was not prepared to take risks to protect its allies, while the American landings at Santo Domingo seemed to indicate that the United States was not prepared to accept the emergence of anything remotely resembling another Cuba. As Guevara pointed out in 1961, 'imperialism has learnt the lesson of Cuba. . . . It will not again be taken by surprise in any of our twenty republics.'

The guerrillas have tried to turn this undoubted fact to their advantage by actually welcoming foreign repression in the hope that this in turn will provoke a nationalistic reaction. Guevara was well aware that guerrilla wars are best carried out against a readily identifiable enemy, preferably foreign, who will arouse a people's latent sense of nationalism. His plan to 'create Vietnams' was drafted with this in mind. But in practice the United States has been able to crush guerrilla movements in Latin America with the maximum of brutality and the minimum of physical involvement.

4. *Ignorance of the detail of local conditions.* In Bolivia, for example, the guerrillas do not seem to have realized that the Camiri–Vallegrande area had been a military area since the time of the Chaco War. Far from being hostile to the military, the local population had got used to them. In Peru, de la Puente's guerrillas were isolated in an area that was easy to cut off from the rest of the country. Others operated on land that belonged to the Cerro Pasco Company, where conditions were completely different from those on adjacent lands.

This is part of a general ignorance. Very few studies have been made of the situation in the Latin America countryside, with the exception of the CIDA reports. The more one looks at the problem, the more one is led to conclude that, in fact, conditions vary not just from country to country, or from province to province, but from valley to valley. Guerrillas may find support in one hamlet but not in another for reasons which are not always immediately apparent. In Bolivia, you cannot even generalize about peasants who live within the 100-mile radius of Camiri, Masicuri and Santa Cruz. All operate under differing systems of land tenure and are in varying stages of misery. To suggest, as many do, that the peasants in the zone were not revolutionary because Bolivia passed a land reform law in 1952, ignores the detail that the reform in many areas was never carried out.

* * *

The fact is that, contrary to widely held beliefs, neither the peasants nor the urban masses—the two major groups in Latin American society— are particularly revolutionary, in spite of the unspeakable conditions in which both groups live. The peasants often live outside modern society, largely unaffected by the central government except in a negative sense, their horizons limited to the village or valley in which they live. When they do prove rebellious, governments have had little difficulty in keep- ing them quiet. In Peru repression, coupled with a limited land reform, soothed the revolutionary ardour that had been awakened. In Venezuela and Bolivia, the governing parties absorbed alert peasants into the gov- ernmental machine. In Colombia, peasants were encouraged to fight each other rather than their landlords. And in Guatemala sheer brute repression, with United States encouragement, has been sufficient to keep potentially rebellious peasants under control.

The urban proletariat ought to be revolutionary. The conditions of life of those who live in the *callampas* of Santiago, the *favelas* of Rio, the *barriadas* of Lima or the *ranchos* of Caracas, are miserable. The wretched inhabitants are constantly reminded in their daily lives of the gap between rich and poor. If anybody in Latin America were to be affected by the revolution of rising expectations, it should be they. Yet, in practice, the urban dweller, employed in services more than in man- ufacturing, apes the manners of the class above—seeking to join it rather than to supplant it.[10] His interest in revolution is strictly limited.

But if both the peasantry and the urban masses are not immediate- ly combustible material for the revolutionary fire, why is it that the guer- rillas have concentrated on the countryside and not on the towns?

For this, there are a variety of reasons: First, of course, it must be recognized that the guerrillas have not ignored the towns. One has only to think of Guevara in his encampment at Ñancahuazú writing detailed instructions for the urban cadres, or of Douglas Bravo in Venezuela, constantly preoccupied by the situation in Caracas, or of the urban activity of the guerrillas in Guatemala, avenging, blow for blow, the deaths of their comrades, to realize that the towns play an important, though not a predominant, part in guerrilla strategy. Guerrilla emphasis on the countryside is due partly to the success that the Cuban revolutionaries in the Sierra Maestra had in catalysing the urban struggle in Santiago de Cuba and Havana. Partly also it reflects the disillusionment with several decades of orthodox Communist emphasis in the towns. Experience has at the same time shown, in Caracas and Santo Domingo (and in the mining areas of Bolivia), how easy it is for the repressive forces to bottle up urban insurgents and make them impotent.

Urban rebellion moreover implies a brief bloody battle preceding the rapid seizure of power. Guerrilla theory, however, demands a long educational war in which the conditions for a successful revolution are created. The apathetic masses will become aware. But if the conditions for revolution do not exist today, they will not exist next week after an urban rebellion has brought a 'revolutionary' group to power. Thus a revolutionary government that takes power through an urban coup will be confronted with the same problem that confronts the guerrilla today: how to convert an apathetic, alienated peasantry into a revolutionary force. Since the peasantry in Latin America has to be mobilized sooner or later, the guerrillas argue that it is better to start now, that is, before the final seizure of power by a revolutionary movement.

The importance of the peasantry in the future development of Latin America is, perhaps, the single most important contribution made by the guerrillas to development theory. With the exception of a few avant-garde economists, the guerrillas are the only group which has latched on to the crucial role that the peasantry will be called upon to play if Latin America is to move out of its present backwardness.

So that although I wrote above that the guerrillas' failure must be seen against the general failure of both reformists and revolutionaries, it is important to emphasize that, alone of these groups, the guerrillas have isolated the vital factor of the peasantry. The most rudimentary knowledge of Latin America indicates that rapid industrialization is no substitute for the proper organization of agriculture. There is no prospect at present of industry, either as it is now or until the end of the century, providing jobs for those who pour in from the land to the towns. The introduction of capital-intensive techniques might conceivably solve the continent's food problems in the short run, but would only serve to accelerate the trend that drives unemployed men from the land to under-employment in the city. Only an agrarian revolution that mobilizes the peasants and keeps them on the land can provide a stable basis for industrialization. To imagine that Latin

America can jump from prehistory to the Welfare State without an agrarian revolution is wishful thinking—unhappily subscribed to by the vast majority of those who deal professionally with the problems of Latin American development. Cuba is unique in Latin America in concentrating on its agricultural sector, and the Cuban-inspired guerrillas are unique in foreseeing the crucial importance that this sector holds for development.[11]

Finally, it is now clear that, even if the guerrilla experience of Latin America during the last 10 years is only to have a limited impact on the continent in the future, it has become of enormous importance outside. Latin America, which has for so long copied the ideas of other continents, is for the first time exporting something. Che Guevara has become a political symbol with a world-wide application. Already Negro movements in southern Africa—notably in Rhodesia and the Portuguese colonies—have drawn the conclusion that the guerrilla struggle is the only way to wear down the white governments that oppress them. And as a result of the historic journey of Stokeley Carmichael to the OLAS Conference in Havana in 1967, guerrilla movements have a new significance which is not merely confined to the southern half of the Hemisphere. 'In the United States,' writes an American historian, 'the New Left in general more and more identifies itself with Castro, Guevara, Régis Debray and Ho Chi-minh; many of the new radicals speak of "guerrilla warfare" against "colonialism" at home; and in fact they see the black militants, as the black militants see themselves, as the revolutionary vanguard of violent social change.'[12] The same tendency can be noted in western Europe.

This development may well be of major importance for Latin America, for such is the continent's external dependence that it is doubtful whether it is even capable of making a revolution on its own. A successful rebellion against the domination of the United States can only come about when the United States itself decides that the game is not worth the candle. The internal disintegration of the advanced capitalist world is therefore an important prerequisite of revolution on the fringes of the American empire. After events in Paris and Chicago, such a development does not seem beyond the bounds of possibility. Recent happenings seem to suggest that the United States is more powerful in Bolivia than in Berkeley, and finds it easier to use the Marines abroad than at home.

But the Latin American guerrillas have started an important chain-reaction. What happened in Paris in May 1968 could not have taken the form it did had it not been for events in Bolivia the previous year. Guevara and Debray have between them eroded the faith of the younger generation in the orthodox revolutionary Left, and a great new revolutionary force is now emerging in the urban areas of the world. And the ideas that were given a new impetus by what happened at Ñancahuazú are now returning to Latin America, transformed by what happened in Paris. The Mexican student rebellion preceding the Olympic Games in 1968 was directly influenced by the May Revolution in France and this type of activity—a growing revolt against the bourgeois values among the student avant-garde in Latin American cities—may well be the pattern of the future.

In the meantime, although the guerrilla movements will probably continue without any major successes in the immediate future, they are already laying the groundwork for future changes. One of the characteristics of the Cuban Revolution noted by Professor Hugh Thomas was that Castro 'did have behind him a real revolutionary tradition, a tradition which was firmly rooted in the previous 60 years of Cuban politics, almost the whole of which had been passed in perpetual crisis'.[13] He concludes that the revolution itself 'was the culmination of a long series of thwarted revolutions'. A *New York Times* correspondent, writing in 1965 about the Venezuelan guerrillas, pointed out that many analysts believed that they were 'accomplishing a long-range, admittedly minimal objective. This is to establish a presence—even if it is shifting and nonoperational—that frustrates the army, reflects on the government, and above all keeps alive a revolutionary mystique that has deep though dormant roots in Venezuelan politics.'

Historians in the next century, picking their way through the failed and bogus revolutions that litter the history of Latin America, may well come to feel that the small groups fighting in the mountains against impossible odds in fact played a crucial role in nourishing a genuine revolutionary tradition that eventually proved successful.

Notes

1 *The New Strategy of Communism in the Caribbean*, report of a special study mission by Armistead I. Selden Jr, Subcommittee on Inter-American Affairs of the Committee on Foreign Affairs, November 1968, p. 10.

2 Malcom W. Browne, 'A Small Élite Rebel Band Harasses Uruguayan Régime', *New York Times*, 23 January 1969.

3 Schafik Handal, 'Reflections on Continental Strategy for Latin American Revolutionaries', *World Marxist Review*, April 1968.

4 Debray, 'Latin America'.

5 Arthur Schlesinger Jr, *A Thousand Days*, p. 309.

6 Ibid., pp. 309–10.

7 No one should have illusions about the late Robert Kennedy's radicalism with regard to Latin America. His friend and colleague, Richard Goodwin, writing in the *New Yorker* after the death of Guevara, maintained that the Americans were right to have intervened in Bolivia, but that the Bolivians were wrong to shoot Guevara—a typical liberal compromise.

8 'Le Dispositif militaire anti-subversif en Amérique Latine', *Problèmes d'Amérique Latine*, NO. 7.

9 Fidel Castro, speech of 26 July 1966. See also Richard Gott, 'Latin America's Vietnams Short of Guerrillas', *Guardian*, 19 June 1967.

10 See Claudio Velíz (ed.), *The Politics of Conformity in Latin America, passim*.

11 Here, regretfully, I have to part company with Hugh Thomas, who writes that 'the increased Cuban emphasis on agriculture does make some sense in a fertile island, but affords no worthwhile message for countries such as Mexico, Peru or Bolivia, whose soil one cannot see supporting any more people.'—Hugh Thomas, 'Cuba's Ten-year Revolution Still Experimenting', *The Times*, 17 February 1969.

12 Christopher Lasch, 'The Trouble with Black Power', *New York Review of Books*, 29 February 1969.

13 Hugh Thomas, 'The Origins of the Cuban Revolution', *The World Today*, October 1963

POSTSCRIPT

GUERRILLA MOVEMENTS AFTER CHE GUEVARA'S DEATH

The defeat of the Bolivian movement led by Che Guevara, and his capture and death in 1967, brought a dramatic end to the first phase of Latin America's experience of guerrilla struggle in the decade after the Cuban Revolution of 1959. That period had been rich in hope and tragedy, as a generation of inexperienced political idealists embarked on utopian schemes to repeat the success of Fidel Castro's guerrilla army in establishing a revolutionary regime. The Bolivian defeat seemed to indicate the end of an era.

Yet the process unleashed throughout the continent in the 1960s did not come to a halt with Guevara's death. Some of the guerrilla movements that were to flourish in the 1970s, like the Sandinistas in Nicaragua and the Tupamaros in Uruguay, had already received a fleeting mention in the original edition of this book, published in 1970.[1] Several others discussed in this book, like the FARC and the ELN in Colombia, continued almost unchanged into the twenty-first century, still far from victory but successful in avoiding defeat. The various movements in Guatemala regrouped endlessly, and soldiered on until the 1990s, although the country suffered from greater repression than other parts of the continent.

Fresh groups emerged elsewhere, in both familiar and unexpected places, and often with different tactics and ideologies. Some of these new movements sought to operate in the cities, others among the indigenous peoples in the mountains. Yet whatever their arguments and differences, nearly all were inspired by Guevara's example and sought to fulfil his last message to the Tricontinental organization set up in Cuba in 1967:

Wherever death may surprise us, let it be welcome, provided that this, our battle cry, may have reached some receptive ear, and another hand may be extended to wield our weapons, and other men may be ready to intone our funeral dirge with the staccato singing of the machine-gun and fresh battle cries of war and victory.[2]

This unusual and eloquent appeal struck a chord all over Latin America, and was listened to—and acted upon—long after Guevara's death. His message was to be resurrected time and again throughout the continent: in the busy streets of Buenos Aires, Sao Paulo, and Montevideo; in the impenetrable jungles of the Amazon; in the hills and scrublands of Central America; and in the mountains of the Andes. It was only finally silenced in the 1990s, after two further decades of pitiless military repression. The armed forces in Latin America, alarmed by the potent force of Guevara's legacy and urged on by successive governments in the United States, seized power in many countries, and slaughtered the guerrillas in a general war against their populations. As Régis Debray had once prophesied, a revolution occurred in the counter-revolution.

The initial reaction of many would-be revolutionaries to the death of Guevara was not to abandon his strategy of revolutionary guerrilla war, but to question his emphasis on the countryside. The rough country folk in the Bolivian region of Ñancahuazú had not come to his assistance, and elsewhere in the continent the peasants were already draining away from the rural areas, moving into the slums and shanty towns of the big cities. Might not these immense urban concentrations provide the sea, in the classic image of Mao Zedong, within which the guerrilla armies could swim? This was the conclusion drawn in the late 1960s by a new generation of revolutionaries in the south of South America—in Brazil, Argentina and Uruguay.

Brazil

In 1968, Carlos Marighela, a veteran Brazilian communist, split away from the orthodox pro-Soviet Brazilian Communist Party (BCP), and adopted the concept of the revolutionary *foco* developed by Guevara and Debray, transferring it from the country to the city. Marighela argued that small groups of *urban* guerrillas, injected into the potentially explosive cities of Latin America, would have a greater political impact than bands of rural guerrillas lost in the Brazilian jungle. Brazil had been under military rule since 1964, and civilian democracy had been crushed. Armed resistance of some kind appeared to be the only political option.

With this urban emphasis, although sympathetic to the example of the Cubans and the legacy of Guevara, Marighela organized a small band of urban guerrillas. He called them the Action for National Liberation (ALN), and planned a revolutionary war that would start in the city and move out later to the rural areas. In 1969 the ALN began robbing banks, both to raise money for weapons and to provide subsistence funds for its activists. In September that year, in a theatrical coup that foreshadowed new developments in the tactics of guerrilla warfare, Marighela's group kidnapped Charles Burke Elbrick, the US ambassador. Elbrick was set free only after the government had agreed to release 15 imprisoned revolutionaries.

Brazil was not an easy country in which to sustain a guerrilla war, whether urban or rural. With the military firmly in control (and they had further clamped down on civilian political institutions in 1968), the guerrillas had little chance of success. The armed forces considered themselves to be involved in an internal war and, after the Elbrick kidnapping, retribution against Marighela's group was swift. Marighela himself was captured and killed in November 1969, and subsequent fierce repression caused his movement to peter out in the course of 1970. Yet his influence remained significant for some years, his writings on urban guerrilla warfare being widely published.[3]

Another group within the BCP had split off a few years earlier, in support of the Chinese position in the Sino-Soviet dispute. This group, calling itself the Communist Party of Brazil, continued to promote the notion of insurgency in the countryside. In a document of 1969, it envisaged the organization of 'a people's army' that would start by establishing bases in the rural areas, although seeking also to collaborate with urban groups. The party launched a guerrilla war in 1972 along the banks of the Araguaia river, on the frontiers of the states of Tocantins and Pará, but it was soon lost in the immense spaces of central Brazil, It was rapidly and brutally crushed in a large but secret military operation that was not known about widely until many years later.[4]

Argentina

At about the same time that Marighela was organizing an urban guerrilla movement, two revolutionary groups in Argentina began thinking along similar lines. One called themselves the Montoneros, a strange alliance of formerly right-wing Catholics with formerly right-wing supporters of Juan Perón, the President deposed in 1955 who lived in exile in Madrid. In the early 1970s the Montoneros moved to the extreme Left, and organized themselves as a well-armed political group. Believing that genuine revolutionaries could not ignore the social legacy of Perón, they campaigned for his return to Argentina, in tandem with the *Juventud Peronista*, the radicalized youth wing of the Peronist movement. Perón did indeed return briefly to Buenos Aires in 1972, and he came back again the following year to be elected President. He died in 1974, and was succeeded by the Vice-President, his wife Isabella Martínez.

A second Argentine group, the Revolutionary Army of the People (ERP), led by Mario Roberto Santucho, emerged in the late 1960s from a more orthodox Trotskyist background. 'We rejected the rural guerrilla strategy,' said an ERP militant in 1971. 'The war is where the masses are, and Argentina is mostly urban.'[5] The ERP established itself in the industrial cities of the provinces: in Córdoba and Rosario. The Montoneros and the ERP were at odds with each other politically, but they both embarked on a strategy of urban insurrection, seeking funds through the kidnapping of rich businessmen, and raising their public profile by assassinating prominent and unpopular political figures.

Largely as a result of their actions, a state of imminent insurrection developed in the country between 1973 and 1976. With political connections deep in the Peronist movement, the Montoneros engaged in what amounted to a civil war within Peronism during the brief reign of Perón's wife, Isabella, from 1974 to 1976. Meanwhile the ERP, having held itself aloof from the Peronist infighting, established a guerrilla *foco* in 1974 in the northern Andean province of Tucumán, the scene of the activities of an earlier Cuban-backed guerrilla movement of Jorge Masetti in 1963.[6] A successful campaign against them was unleashed in the province by the armed forces in 1975, and Santucho was killed the following year. Isabella Perón was overthrown by a military coup in 1976 led by General Jorge Videla, and the subsequent

'Dirty War' crushed all resistance. Both the Montoneros and the ERP were obliterated.

Uruguay

In the late 1960s a comparable movement, operating in the urban areas, had arisen in Uruguay. They called themselves the Tupamaros. Their origin lay in the early years of that decade, when Raúl Sendic, an inspired union activist, had organized sugar workers in the country's impoverished northern provinces.[7] The rather moderate political impact of isolated actions in the countryside led Sendic to believe that revolutionaries needed to work in the urban areas, specifically in Montevideo, and in 1968 the Tupamaros began attacking economic targets in the capital city. First they kidnapped rich businessmen for ransom, and then, in 1970, they executed Dan Mitrione, a police torturer from the United States. In 1971 they captured the British ambassador, and held him for eight months.

The Tupamaros lasted for barely two more years, since fierce repression led to the round-up and capture of its principal leaders, including Sendic. The Uruguayan armed forces seized power in 1973, and further armed actions became impossible.

Urban guerrilla actions in the late 1960s and early 1970s, in Brazil, Argentina and Uruguay, made a significant impact on local politics and attracted an international audience for events in Latin America. The outside world had never taken much interest in the rural guerrillas of the 1960s, but the actions of the urban guerrillas made headlines everywhere, especially in the United States. Yet a conservative reaction was not long in coming. With the coup against Salvador Allende in Chile in September 1973, military rule prevailed there and throughout most of South America for more than a decade.

Nicaragua

While the countries of the Southern Cone—Argentina, Brazil, Bolivia, Chile, Paraguay and Uruguay—were under military control throughout the 1970s, the guerrilla phenomenon revived in Central America, first in Nicaragua. The Sandinista National Liberation Front had been set up originally by Carlos Fonseca Amador in 1961, inspired by the Cuban example. The Sandinistas sought to organize a political movement to overthrow the dictatorship of General Anastasio Somoza, long an American pillar in Central America. They formed a guerrilla group in the hills in 1967, but it was swiftly destroyed. Not until the 1970s did they begin to make a substantial political impact. In 1974 they engaged in the theatrical seizure of the house of a minister in a wealthy suburb of Managua, securing the release of political prisoners in exchange, and a large ransom. Yet the Sandinistas were soon divided among themselves about strategy and tactics, and they failed to consolidate their position. Fonseca was captured and shot in 1976.

The Sandinistas split into three groups. One, called the Prolonged Popular War, led by Tomás Borge and Bayardo Arce, advocated the accumulation of forces in the countryside. Another, the Proletarian Tendency, led by Jaime Wheelock, advocated armed actions in the cities. A third group, the Third Way (or Terceristas), led by Daniel Ortega, sought alliances with groups other than the traditional left. All three groups came under pressure from Castro in Cuba to unite, but not until 1978, when the Somoza regime showed signs of its inherent weakness, did they begin to make military headway, with supporters of each group involving themselves in armed and strike actions across the country. Under Cuban pressure, the three groups did eventually amalgamate to form the Sandinista National Directorate in March 1979, four months before a small guerrilla army finally captured Managua, on July 19. Somoza fled into exile, and was eventually assassinated in Paraguay.

The victory of the Sandinistas appeared as a carbon copy of the Cuban Revolution, and it seemed to justify Guevara's faith in the revolutionary potential of guerrilla warfare in the countryside. Yet despite the surface similarities, the defeat of Somoza was more the result of pressure from a broad coalition of forces in town and country than a specific victory for the guerrilla army. The Sandinista success, however, was perceived, both in Managua and in Washington, as a triumph for the Cuban Revolution and as an extension of Cuban (and Soviet) influence into Central America. The United States, during the administration of Jimmy Carter, had not strenuously tried to prevent the overthrow of Somoza, but with the victory of Ronald Reagan in 1980, Washington perceived the Sandinistas as a new cold war enemy in the American Hemisphere. Soon the United States was intent upon destroying them. By supporting the 'contras', the right-wing armed opposition to the Sandinista government, the Americans paved the way to a civil war in Nicaragua, and to the eventual defeat of the Sandinistas at elections held 10 years later in 1990.

El Salvador

One effect of the Sandinista victory in 1979 was to put fresh hope into comparable left-wing movements in Central America, notably in El Salvador and Guatemala, countries that were also under oppressive military rule.[8] The Communist Party of El Salvador had suffered the same divisions as occurred elsewhere in Latin America in the 1960s, as a result of the Sino-Soviet split. Many left the pro-Soviet party to set up groups favourable to the Chinese or the Cuban model. One prominent dissident was the Communist leader, Cayetano Carpio, who left the party in 1970 to set up a guerrilla group, known as the Farabundo Martí Popular Liberation Forces (FMLN). Farabundo Martí had been a Communist leader in the 1930s. Similar small guerrilla armies were formed in El Salvador in the 1970s, though with serious differences of ideology and tactics. These included the ERP, led by Joaquín Villalobos, and National Resistance (RN), set up after the ERP had assassinated Roque Dalton, a well-known poet and activist.

These groups eventually came together in December 1979 under the umbrella of the FMLN. Once again, as in Nicaragua, the pressure for unity came from Castro in Cuba. The FMLN launched its first military offensive in January 1981, 10 days before the inauguration of President Reagan in Washington. Effectively controlling the provinces of Morazán and Chalatenango, the FMLN guerrillas fought for a decade, but failed to make a nationwide impact against the Salvadoran army, backed to the hilt by the United States. In an unexplained incident in April 1983, Cayetano Carpio's second-in-command, known as Ana María, was killed by her comrades, and he committed suicide later the same day.

After the collapse of the Sandinista government in neighbouring Nicaragua, the terms of a peace agreement were negotiated in 1992 that ended the guerrilla war. The FMLN became a legal political group that took part in elections, albeit without success.

Guatemala

The guerrilla movements in Guatemala had been in serious decline at the end of the 1960s, although they engaged in several serious urban actions in 1970, including the kidnap of the Foreign Minister and the German ambassador. A serious period of repression unleashed by Colonel Carlos Arana Osorio, elected President that year, led to their collapse. The assassination in 1972 of six leading members of the Communist Party (PGT) marked a low point in the history of the Guatemalan left.

Yet grassroots mobilization against the military regime continued. After the catastrophe caused by the earthquake of 1976, the indigenous communities were obliged to organize in the absence of any governmental authority. They became more political, and three new guerrilla groups emerged: the Revolutionary Organization of the People in Arms (ORPA), the Guerrilla Army of the Poor (EGP), and the revived Rebel Armed Forces (FAR). In the late 1970s, all three groups met with an astonishingly favourable reception from the indigenous population in the rural areas, and undertook several spectacular operations, kidnapping wealthy ranchers and assassinating prominent military figures.

Yet once again the regime turned to fierce repression, and the years between 1978 and 1982 saw military offensives in several provinces, and many massacres. A *coup d'état* in March 1982 brought the sanguinary General Efraín Ríos Montt to power, signalling the start of an all-out military effort to crush the insurgency. The guerrilla groups united in a new umbrella organization, the Guatemalan National Revolutionary Unity (URNG), and the war continued for a further decade. Peace negotiations began in 1994 and concluded under the auspices of the United Nations in 1996.

Peru

An unusual and powerful political movement appeared in Peru in the 1970s that also engaged in guerrilla war. The Shining Path, or *Sendero Luminoso*, owed little to Cuba or to the memory of Che Guevara. Its origins lay in the pro-Chinese split from the pro-Soviet Peruvian Communist Party in 1964, and its presiding genius was Abimael Guzmán, a philosophy lecturer at the university in Ayacucho in the Andes. Guzmán had visited China in 1965, and became convinced of the similarities between Chinese and Andean societies. He took over Peru's pro-Chinese party, the Red Flag, and made it his own. He also paid homage to José Carlos Mariátegui, the early Peruvian Marxist in the 1920s, who had written of how 'Marxism–Leninism will open the shining path to revolution'.

Shining Path operated originally in the 1970s as a left-wing political movement within the universities in the cities of the Andes, but it moved out into the countryside in 1980 and prepared for a 'peoples' war' on the Chinese model. Espousing extreme violence with opponents and with its own dissidents, it campaigned with a degree of religious intensity comparable to that of the Christian evangelical movements already gaining support in the Andes. Shining Path rapidly expanded throughout the Andes and soon began organizing in the slum cities surrounding Lima. It blew up electricity pylons, to discredit the government, and assassinated local community leaders to assert its hegemony.[9]

Shining Path extended its influence in the country throughout the 1980s, with the government seemingly powerless to intervene. The situation changed in 1990 after the election as President of Alberto Fujimori, who gave the military a free hand to curb the guerrillas. They did so in a fierce and bloody war. Guzmán was captured in Lima in September 1993, and his movement did not long survive his trial and imprisonment. Some 70,000 people were killed or 'disappeared' in the course of the war, according to a report from the Truth and Reconciliation Commission published in 2003.

A smaller guerrilla movement also operated in Peru in these years, the Túpac Amaru Revolutionary Movement (MRTA). This was a typical pro-Cuba movement, the lineal successor of the MIR of Luís de la Puente in the 1960s, once closely involved with the left-wing of the ruling APRA party.[10] Their first actions occurred in 1984, when they bombed restaurants of the Kentucky Fried Chicken chain. Víctor Polay, their leader, was captured in 1989, but the movement continued for some years with little impact. Their most spectacular operation was the occupation of the Japanese embassy in Lima in December 1996, when they held 72 hostages for four months. The armed forces were finally permitted to storm the building in April 1997, under the orders of the Fujimori government, rescuing all but one of the hostages, and killing or executing the guerrillas.

Mexico

An armed rural movement of a completely different kind emerged in Mexico in the 1990s, in the southern state of Chiapas. The Zapatista Army of National Liberation (EZLN) was the brainchild of a figure who called himself 'Subcomandante Marcos', another university professor, who had rooted himself among the Lacandón Indians in the previous decade. On 1 January 1994, the Zapatistas seized five municipalities in Chiapas, creating an extraordinary degree of national and international interest.

They were the heirs to, yet different from, an earlier generation of pro-Cuban revolutionaries that had taken to the hills in the late 1960s. Two groups, the National Revolutionary Civic Association (ACNR), led by Génaro Vázquez Rojas, and the Party of the Poor (PP), led by Lúcio Cabañas Barrientos, had arisen in the period after the student Tlatelolco massacre in Mexico City at the start of the Olympic Games in 1968. Both groups had considerable indigenous support, and their support came initially from people affected by government repression in the coastal state of Guerrero. Their fighting troops were always small and they failed to make headway outside the state. They did not survive the death of their leaders in the early 1970s, yet their memory lived on in a society that has long honoured those who contribute to its revolutionary traditions.

The Zapatistas, following in their footsteps, began to organize in the 1980s, but from the first they had a different agenda from the old pro-Cuban groups in Latin America. Mexico, after all, had a powerful revolutionary tradition of its own, and the strongly nationalist Zapatistas drew on it in their support for landless farmers. Aware of the revolutionary activities of the powerful indigenous movements in neighbouring Guatemala, they began to champion the cause of the indigenous peoples of Chiapas.

The Zapatistas were a new kind of political movement. Largely pacifistic, after their initial armed actions in Chiapas in 1994, they swiftly made international alliances with the burgeoning anti-globalization movement that arose in that decade. They also took advantage of new technologies, including the mobile phone and the internet, to ensure that a wider audience, in Mexico City, Paris and New York, was kept abreast of their activities and of the thought of Subcomandante Marcos.

The international support that the Zapatistas secured ensured that the Mexican government was obliged to negotiate with them. The government was unable to engage in the kind of 'Dirty War' that had destroyed guerrilla movements elsewhere in Latin America. Yet the Zapatistas failed to secure the support of the wider Left within Mexico, at a time when the decades-old revolutionary government of the Institutional Revolutionary Party (PRI) was beginning to lose ground. The EZLN remained within the boundaries of Chiapas, making a virtue of their relative failure with the slogan of 'changing the world without taking power'.

Colombia

The guerrillas in Colombia have remained the most long-lasting of all such movements in Latin America, and Manuel Marulanda, the leader of the Colombian Revolutionary Armed Forces (FARC) in the 1960s, has survived in the same position into the twenty-first century. The past 40 years have seen several major changes, at home and abroad, that have made an impact on the guerrilla movements but have not affected their ability to survive. The first change has been the development in the production of the raw material of cocaine and heroin, fuelling the drug markets of the United States and Europe. The land devoted to growing cannabis, coca and poppies has grown five-fold since the 1960s, and the guerrilla movements have been protecting the rural workers on these plantations.

The second change has been the growth of paramilitary organizations, first sponsored by the drug barons and then by the state, that have revived the pattern of civil war that has been a particular Colombian phenomenon since the nineteenth century. Coupled with the growth of the paramilitaries has been the US-designed Plan Colombia, a military aid package first established in 1999, that has made Colombia the fifth largest recipient of US aid in the world.

The third change has been the collapse of the Soviet Union in 1991 and the corresponding loss of influence of the Colombian Communist Party, once the principal backer of the guerrillas of the FARC. The death in 1990 of Jacobo Arenas, the talented Communist leader, left Marulanda as the FARC's sole commander.

Although negotiations between the guerrillas and the government have been a feature of the past 25 years, an unfortunate experience in the 1980s has left the FARC a reluctant participant. After a ceasefire was signed in May 1984, the FARC was encouraged by the authorities to establish a legal political party, the Patriotic Union (UP), and to put forward candidates in the elections in 1985. This was reasonably successful experience, and the FARC secured six senators, 23 deputies and several hundred local councillors.

Yet the outcome was disastrous. After coming out into the open and putting their heads above the parapet, many of the UP supporters were singled out and killed. More than 4,000 left-wing activists and organizers were assassinated in the year after the elections. The FARC guerrillas retired to their safe territories in the rural areas and vowed not to make the same mistake again.

Bolivia

The death of Guevara appeared to mark the end of guerrilla struggle in Bolivia, but several left-wing revolutionaries continued to believe in the strategy. In July 1970, a group of university students from La Paz, many of them Catholics, set up a guerrilla base in the area of Teoponte, in the valleys south-east of La Paz, a gesture perceived as a homage to Guevara and as a continuation of his movement. The guerrillas of Teoponte were inexperienced both politically and militarily, and their group was brutally crushed within months.[11] Then, after a brief period of radical nationalist rule in the early 1970s under General Juan José Torres, Bolivia joined the other southern countries of Latin America in a prolonged period of military rule in which armed opposition became impossible.

In the 1980s, as indigenous political movements began to establish themselves, some of them developed an armed wing. The Túpac Katari Guerrilla Army (EGTK), named after Túpac Katari, an Indian rebel at the end of the eighteenth century, was the first indigenous guerrilla movement in Bolivia, organized originally in 1984. Its first armed action took place in 1991, when it blew up an electric pylon in El Alto, outside La Paz.

Among the leaders of the EGTK was Felipe Quispe, known as 'El Mallku', the head of the Pachakuti Indigenous Movement, and Alvaro

García Linera, a sociologist who became Vice-President of the country in 2006. A military crackdown in 1992 caused the group to disintegrate, and many of its supporters, including Quispe, were imprisoned.

A second indigenous guerrilla group, the Zarate Willka Armed Forces of Liberation (FALZW), was set up in 1989, taking its name from an Indian rebel at the end of the nineteenth century. An indigenous and anti-imperialist movement, the FALZW began its public activity with an attack on Mormon missionaries in 1989. Its leaders were arrested the following year, and the movement collapsed, merging with other groups with a similar indigenist agenda.

Conclusion

The 40 years after the death of Guevara were marked by a growth in urban guerrilla warfare, increasingly effective military repression, and the emergence in the Andean countries of powerful indigenous movements. While Guevara remained an international revolutionary icon, his specific message had become blurred. By the beginning of the twenty-first century, the panorama had been irrevocably changed. Peasant insurrections and guerrilla movements had disappeared into history. Yet with the election in Venezuela in 1998 of Hugo Chávez, a left-wing colonel with a revolutionary programme, many of the political themes once espoused by Guevara were again placed at the top of the continental agenda.

The creation by Chávez of a new international movement, known as 'Bolivarianism' after Simón Bolívar, the nineteenth century Liberator of Latin America, appeared to revive the early ambitions of the Cuban Revolution. Fidel Castro himself had survived for nearly half a century at the head of a revolutionary government, to become widely regarded as perhaps the greatest Latin America figure of the twentieth century. With the subsequent election in 2006 of Evo Morales as the first indigenous President of Bolivia, this 'Bolivarian' movement began to gather strength. Morales' Vice-President, Alvaro García had once been an activist in the Túpac Katari guerrilla movement, while many of Chávez's ministers were survivors of the guerrilla campaigns in Venezuela of the 1960s. The guerrilla movements of the 20th century Latin America has become lost in mists of history, but their legacy was now firmly rooted in the developing politics of the continent.

Notes

1   See above, *Defeat of the Revolution?* p. 358.

2   John Gerassi (ed.), *Venceremos: The Speeches and Writings of Che Guevara*, Weidenfield & Nicolson, London, 1968, p. 424. The Tricontinental was the shorthand title for the Organization of the Solidarity of the Peoples of Africa, Asia and Latin America, established by Cuba at a conference in Havana in 1965. Ben Barka, its Moroccan organizer, who was assassinated in Paris in October 1965 before the conference took place, had told a preliminary meeting that 'the two currents of the world revolution will be represented there: the current that emerged from the October Revolution and that of the national liberation revolution'.

3   Carlos Marighela, *For the Liberation of Brazil*, Penguin Books, London, 1971. In some foreign editions the book was called *The Mini-manual of the Urban Guerrilla*.

4   See Taís Morais and Eumano Silva, *Operação Araguaia: Os Archivos Secretos da Guerrilha*, Geracão Editorial, São Paulo, 2005.

5   James Petras, 'Questions to a Militant of the PRT–ERP', *New Left Review* (London), NO. 71, January–February 1972, quoted in Daniel Castro (ed.), *Revolution and Revolutionaries: Guerrilla Movements in Latin America*, Scholarly Resources Inc., Wilmington, 1999.

6   See above 'Masetti and the Guerrillas of Salta'. See also Jon Lee Anderson, *Che Guevara: A Revolutionary Life*, Bantam Press, New York, 1997, pp. 573–94.

7   Alain Labrousse, *The Tupamaros: Urban Guerrillas in Uruguay*, Penguin Books, London, 1973.

8   James Dunkerley, *The Long War: Dictatorship and Revolution in El Salvador*, Junction Books, London, 1982.

9   Simon Strong, *Shining Path: the World's Deadliest Revolutionary Force*, HarperCollins, London, 1992.

10 See above, 'Luís de la Puente and the MIR'.

11 Gustavo Rodríguez Ostria, *Teoponte: la otra guerrilla guevarista en Bolivia*, Grupo Editorial, La Paz, 2006.

(Events in countries outside those covered by the book are indicated by italic type.)

1958

January	GUATEMALA	Elections won by General Ydígoras
	VENEZUELA	Overthrow of Pérez Jiménez, organized by Fabricio Ojeda's 'Patriotic Junta'
April	CUBA	Failure of General Strike ordered by 26 July Movement
May	VENEZUELA	US Vice-President Richard Nixon visits Caracas and his car is smashed up
	COLOMBIA	Alberto Lleras Camargo elected president
June	PERU	Hugo Blanco sets up as a peasant union organizer in the Valley of La Convención
		General de Gaulle becomes President of France
August	CUBA	Carlos Rafael Rodríguez, a leading Communist, joins Fidel Castro in the Sierra Maestra
December	VENEZUELA	Romulo Betancourt wins elections; rioting in Caracas

1959

January	VENEZUELA	Castro visits Caracas
	CUBA	Fidel Castro marches into Havana; Batista flees to Santo

		Domingo
April		*Unsuccessful rebellion in Panama*
May	CUBA	Castro visits Buenos Aires
June	CUBA	Agrarian Reform Law passed
		Unsuccessful rebellion in Nicaragua and in the Dominican Republic
July	PERU	Luís de la Puente visits Cuba
August	VENEZUELA	Anti-government demonstration in Caracas
		Unsuccessful invasion of Haiti
October	PERU	APRA Rebelde (MIR) withdraws from APRA
November		*Guerrillas briefly appear in Paraguay; Mikoyan visits Mexico*
December		*Peronist guerrillas in Tucumán, Argentina, led by Comandante Uturunku*

1960

January	COLOMBIA	MOEC founded by Antonio Larotta
		President Eisenhower visits Argentina, Brazil, Chile and Uruguay
February	CUBA	Visit by Mikoyan
March	CUBA	Eisenhower orders CIA to train Cuban exiles
April	VENEZUELA	MIR withdraws from Acción Democratica
June	CUBA	US oil refineries expropriated
August		*Conference of Latin American Trotskyists held in Santiago, Chile*
September	CUBA	First Declaration of Havana
October	GUATEMALA	Students denounce presence of anti-Castro Cubans planning invasion of Cuba
	VENEZUELA	Six members of MIR arrested on charges of subversion; rioting in Caracas
	CUBA	Castro speaks at the United Nations
November	GUATEMALA	Military uprising involving Turcios Lima and Yon Sosa
	PERU	POR congress in Arequipa votes in favour of guerrilla warfare

	CUBA	Guevara visits Peking
		John F. Kennedy defeats Richard Nixon for the Presidency of the U.S.
December	CUBA	Peru backs off diplomatic relations

1961

January	CUBA	United States breaks off diplomatic relations
April	CUBA	CIA-backed exiles invade at the Bay of Pigs and are repulsed
		Latin American Trotskyists meeting in Buenos Aires agree to support and organize peasant movements in Peru, Brazil and Guatemala
May	COLOMBIA	Antonio Larotta killed
		Assassination of President Rafael Trujillo in Dominica
June	PERU	Arrival of Argentine Trotskyist cadres and formation of 'Revolutionary Front'
July	GUATEMALA	Alejandro de León captured and killed
August	CUBA	Guevara attends inaugural meeting of Alliance for Progress, Punta del Esto, Uruguay
		President Quadros of Brazil resigns
September	VENEZUELA	Further split in Acción Democratica
October	VENEZUELA	Rioting in Caracas
November	PERU	APRA Rebelde presents draft Agrarian Reform Law to Congress
December	PERU	Formation of FIR; branch of Banco Popular raided

1962

January	CUBA	Cuba expelled from the OAS
February	GUATEMALA	MR13 goes into action; rebellion in Guatemala City
	VENEZUELA	Various guerrilla fronts are opened
	CUBA	Second Declaration of Havana
March	GUATEMALA	Formation of '20 October

		Front' under Colonel Paz Tejada
		Guerrillas briefly appear in Ecuador; President Frondizi of Argentina deposed by military
April	PERU	Trotskyist cadres captured in Cuzco
May	VENEZUELA	Military uprising at Carúpano; Communist party and MIR suspended
	COLOMBIA	Dr Guillermo León Valencia elected president
June	VENEZUELA	Military uprising at Puerto Cabello
	PERU	Haya de la Torre wins presidential elections; APRA Rebelde becomes the MIR
July	PERU	Military coup
		Algeria independent
October	VENEZUELA	Saboteurs destroy power stations at Maracaibo
	PERU	Meeting between Hugo Blanco and Luís de la Puente
	CUBA	Missile crisis
November	GUATEMALA	Air force rebellion crushed
December	GUATEMALA	Foundation of the FAR, which grouped the guerrilla fronts with the Communist party
	VENEZUELA	IV Plenum of Communist party supports strategy of armed struggle
	PERU	Hugo Blanco involved in the shooting of a policeman

1963

February	VENEZUELA	FALN formally established
March	GUATEMALA	President Ydígoras overthrown by Colonel Perata Azurdia
	PERU	Agrarian Reform Decree applying to La Convención
May	PERU	Hugo Blanco captured; Javier Heraud killed
June	PERU	Fernando Belaúnde wins presidential elections

	BOLIVIA	Jorge Masetti establishes his Argentinian guerrilla group on a Bolivian farm
July		*Arturo Illia elected President of Argentina*
August	BOLIVIA	Mining strike in Catavi *Jorge Masetti establishes the EGP in Salta, Argentina; Nuclear Test Ban Treaty*
November	VENEZUELA	Deputy head of U.S. military mission kidnapped; Venezuelans capture arms coming from Cuba *Assassination of President Kennedy*
December	VENEZUELA	General election, won by Raúl Leoni and Acción Democratica, boycotted by the Left

1964

January	VENEZUELA	Domingo Alberto Rangel of MIR approves guerrilla struggle
	PERU	Setting up of a pro-Chinese Communist party, the first in Latin America
February	PERU	Luís de la Puente speaks in the Plaza San Martín, Lima
March	CUBA	Guevara addresses UNCTAD in Geneva
April		*President Goulart of Brazil deposed by the military*
May	COLOMBIA	Attack on Marquetalia begins
	BOLIVIA	Paz Estenssoro elected president—unopposed
July	VENEZUELA	New front opens in Bachíllex province
	COLOMBIA	Marulanda issues a peasant manifesto; ELN begins —in secret
	PERU	MIR policy document published, highly critical of peaceful coexistence
October	GUATEMALA	Leadership of the Edgar Ibarra Front (Turcios) approves the Trotskyist trend of MR13

	VENEZUELA	Douglas Bravo elaborates 'combined insurrection' strategy *Khruschev replaced by Kosygin and Breshnev in the USSR*
November	BOLIVIA	Paz Estenssoro overthrown by Generals Barrientos and Ovando *Johnson defeats Goldwater in the U.S. presidential elections*
December	GUATEMALA	MR13 issues First Declaration of Las Minas
	CUBA	Meeting of Latin American Communist parties, Havana; Guevara addresses the United Nations

1965

January	COLOMBIA	ELN goes into action
February	GUATEMALA	Head of U.S. military mission shot
	COLOMBIA	'Independent republic' of El Pato eliminated by government troops
	CUBA	Guevara visits Peking, and addresses Afro-Asian solidarity conference in Algiers *US begins bombing North Vietnam*
March	GUATEMALA	Break between MR13 and FAR; Communist party gives active support to guerrillas
	COLOMBIA	Camilo Torres outlines his 'Platform for a Movement of Popular Unity' *World Communist parties meet in Moscow*
April	VENEZUELA	VII Plenum of Communist party gives priority to legal struggle
	BOLIVIA	Pro-Chinese Communist party set up at a conference in Siglo Veinte
	CUBA	Guevara 'disappears' from Cuba *Revolution and U.S. intervention in the Dominican Republic*
May	GUATEMALA	Deputy Minister of Defence shot
	COLOMBIA	Government imposes state of siege (lifted December 1968)

	BOLIVIA	Juan Lechín deported; general strike; state of siege
June	COLOMBIA	Camilo Torres leaves priesthood
	PERU	MIR guerrillas go into action
		Ben Bella of Algeria deposed by Colonel Boumedienne
July	COLOMBIA	Pro-Chinese Communist party set up
August	PERU	Constitutioned guarantees suspended
September	PERU	MIR and ELN sign a joint communiqué, and ELN goes into action
October	GUATEMALA	Mario Méndez Montenegro, leader of the Revolutionary party, shot
	VENEZUELA	Douglas Bravo outlines his grievances with the Communist party
	PERU	Luís de la Puente killed
		Indonesian Communists massacred
November	VENEZUELA	The Communist party rejects Bravo's views
	PERU	Pro-Chinese Communist party holds conference to explain why it did not support the guerrillas
December	VENEZUELA	Douglas Bravo and Fabricio Ojeda set up a new FALN/FLN
	COLOMBIA	Camilo Torres joins the ELN guerrillas

1966

January	PERU	Lobatón killed
	CUBA	Tricontinental Conference, Havana
February	COLOMBIA	Camilo Torres killed
March	GUATEMALA	26 prominent Communists arrested and later killed; Julio César Méndez Montenegro wins elections
	VENEZUELA	Venezuelan Communist leaders released from prison
April	COLOMBIA	The FARC formerly inaugurated

May	GUATEMALA	Yon Sosa finally breaks with the Trotskyists
	VENEZUELA	Douglas Bravo expelled from the Communist party
	BOLIVIA	Marío Monje discusses Bolivia with Fidel Castro
June	VENEZUELA	Fabricio Ojeda captured and killed
	BOLIVIA	'Ricardo' begins organizing in La Paz; General Barrientos elected president
		President Illia of Argentina deposed by General Ougania
September	BOLIVIA	Debray arrives in Bolivia, departs and returns again in March 1967
October	GUATEMALA	Turcios Lima killed and succeeded by César Montes
November	BOLIVIA	Guevara arrives at Ñancahuazú
December	BOLIVIA	Showdown between Guevara and Marío Monje

1967

March	VENEZUELA	Julio Iribarren Borges kidnapped and shot; Castro attacks Communist party
	BOLIVIA	First ambush at Ñancahuazú
April	CUBA	Che Guevara's letter to the Tricontinental published
June	BOLIVIA	Government troops occupy tin mines and impose state of siege
	CUBA	Kosygin visits Cuba
		Israel invades Egypt
July		*Leonel Brizola sentenced in absento to nine years' imprisonment in Brazil*
August	BOLIVIA	Annihilation of Joaquín's group of guerrillas
	CUBA	OLAS conference
October	BOLIVIA	Che Guevara captured and killed
November	BOLIVIA	Regis Debray sentenced to 30 years' imprisonment

1968

January	Guatemala	FAR breaks with Communist party; head of U.S. military mission shot
	COLOMBIA	EPL goes into action; government renews diplomatic relations with Russia—broken since 1948
	CUBA	Aníbal Escalante and other Communists arrested
March	GUATEMALA	Communist party sets up its own FAR; Archbishop of Guatemala kidnapped
April	GUATEMALA	Head of 'Mano Blanca' shot
July	BOLIVIA	Antonio Arguedas, Minister of Interior, admits sending copy of Guevara's diary to Cuba
August	GUATEMALA	US Ambassador John Gordon Mein killed in a kidnapping attempt
		Russia invades Czechoslovakia
October	PERU	President Belaúnde deposed by General Juan Velasco; IPC nationalized
November		*Nixon beats Humphrey in the US presidential elections*

1969

January	BOLIVIA	State of siege declared
March	GUATEMALA	Decree of 1955, prohibiting trade with Communist countries, revoked
	VENEZUELA	President Rafael Caldera of Christian Democrats takes office
April	VENEZUELA	Communist party legalized; Communists released from prison; offer of amnesty to guerrillas; renewal of diplomatic relations with Russia
	BOLIVIA	President Barrientos killed in an aircrash; succeeded by Vice-President Siles Salinas
June	PERU	Agrarian Reform Law published
September	BOLIVIA	President Siles Salinas deposed by General Ovando; Inti Peredo killed

		US Ambassador to Brazil, Burke Elbrick, kidnapped and released in exchange for 15 political prisoners
October	BOLIVIA	Gulf Oil nationalized
December	GUATEMALA	'State of alarm' decreed
		Brazilian guerrilla leader, Carlos Marighela, killed

BIBLIOGRAPHY

GENERAL

Books

Willard F. Barber and C. Neale Ronning, *Internal Security and Military Power*: *Counter-insurgency and Civic Action in Latin America*, Ohio State University Press, 1966.

Alberto Bayo, *150 Questions for a Guerrilla*, translated by H. Hartenstein and D. Harbour, 3rd edition, 1965.

Andrés Cassinello Pérez, Operaciones de Guerrillas y Contra-guerrillas, Compañía Bibliográfica Española, Madrid, 1966.

Oscár Delgado (ed.), *Reformas Agrarias en la América Latina*: *procesos y perspectivas*, Fondo de Cultura Económica, Mexico City, 1965.

Theodore Draper, *Castroism*: *Theory and Practice*, Pall Mall Press, London, 1965. Norberto Frontini, *Los Guerrilleros de Salta*, Buenos Aires, 1966.

Eduardo Galeano, *Reportajes*, Ediciones Tauro, Montevideo, 1967.

John Gerassi, *The Great Fear in Latin America*, Collier Books, New York, 2nd printing, 1966.

Boris Goldenberg, *The Cuban Revolution and Latin America*, Allen & Unwin, London, 1965.

Carlos María Gutiérrez, *En la Sierra Maestra y otros reportajes*, Ediciones Tauro, Montevideo, 1967.

Gerrit Huizer, *On Peasant Unrest in Latin America*, a collection of notes for the ILO–CIDA study on the role of peasant organizations in the process of agrarian reform in Latin American countries, CIDA–Panamerican Union, Washington, D.C., June 1967.

Jean Lartéguy, *Les Guérilleros*, Raoul Solar, Paris, 1967.

Neil Macaulay, *The Sandino Affair*, Quadrangle Books, Chicago, 1967.

Luís Mercier Vega, *Las Guerrillas en América Latina*, Editorial Paidos, Buenos Aires, 1968.

Juan M. Vivanco, *Subversión en América Latina*, Federación Iberoamericana de Escritores, Miami, 2nd edition, 1968.

David Wise and Thomas B. Ross, *The Invisible Government*, Jonathan Cape, London, 1965.

Articles

Richard Armstrong, 'How the Communists Plan to Win Latin America', *Saturday Evening Post*, 29 June–6 July 1963.

Mehdi Ben Barka, 'National Revolution in Africa and Asia', *Revolution*, VOL. I, NO. 3, 1963.

Malcolm Deas, 'Guerrillas in Latin America: A Perspective', *World Today*, February 1968.

Henri Edmé, 'Revolution en Amérique Latine?', *Les Temps modernes* (Paris), May 1966.

Adolfo Gilly, 'A Guerrilla Wind', *Monthly Review*, November 1965.

John Gittings, 'Latin American Guerrillas', *Pacific* (Sydney), May–June 1967.

Francisco Julião, 'Marxistes et marxologues', *Révue internationale du socialisme* (Rome), October 1967.

Jean Lartéguy, 'Les Guerrilleros: (2) portrait d'un maquisard', *Paris Match*, 26 August 1967.

Leslie J. Macfarlane, 'Guerrilla Revolution: a Romantic Illusion?', *Government and Opposition*, VOL. III, NO. 3.

Edgardo Mercado, 'La politica y la estrategia militar en la guerra subersiva en America Latina', *Revista Militar del Perú*, December 1967.

James Petras, 'Revolution and Guerrilla Movements in *Latin America*: *Venezuela, Guatemala, Colombia and Peru*', in *Latin America: Reform or Revolution?* ed. by James Petras and Maurice Zeitlin, Fawcett Books, New York, 1968.

Clea Silva, 'Los errores de la teoría del foco', *Monthly Review (en castellano)*, December 1967.

Tad Szulc, 'Exporting the Cuban Revolution', in *Cuba and the United States*, ed. by John Plank, Brookings Institution, Washington, D. C., 1967.

Geoffrey Warner, 'Latin America', in *Survey of International Affairs 1959–1960*, ed. by Geoffrey Barraclough, Oxford University Press, 1964.

Ted Yates, 'The Undeclared War', NBC news script, 15 June 1966.

CUBA

Books

Rafael Otero Echeverría, *Reportaje a una Revolución: de Batista a Fidel Castro*, Editorial del Pacífico, Santiago, 1959.

Carlos Franqui, *Cuba: El libro de los doce*, Ediciones Era, Mexico City, 1966.

Articles

Robin Blackburn, 'Prologue to the Cuban Revolution', *New Left Review*, NO. 21, October 1963.

Ernesto Che Guevara, 'Cuba: Exceptional Case or Vanguard in the Struggle against Colonialism?', *Monthly Review*, July–August 1961. (Translated from *Verde Olivo*, 9 April 1961.)

Javier Pazos, 'Cuba—"Long Live the Revolution",' *New Republic*, 3 November 1962.

Hugh Thomas, 'Middle-class Politics and the Cuban Revolution', in *The Politics of Conformity in Latin America*, ed. by Claudio Véliz, Oxford University Press, 1967.

Hugh Thomas, 'Why Democracy Failed in Cuba', *Observer*, 9 February 1964.

Hugh Thomas, 'The Origins of the Cuban Revolution', *World Today*, October 1963.

CHE GUEVARA

Books

Hugo Gambini, *El Che Guevara*, Editorial Paidos, Buenos Aires, 1968.

Ernesto Che Guevara, *Obra Revolucionaria* (*Prólogo y selección de Roberto Fernández Retarmar*), Ediciones ERA, SA, Mexico City, 1967.

John Gerassi (ed.), *Venceremos: the Writings of Che Guevara*, Weidenfield & Nicolson, London, 1968.

Ernesto Che Guevara, *La Guerra de Guerrillas*, Ediciones MINFAR, Havana, n.d. (1960?); translated as *Guerrilla Warfare* by J. P. Morray, Monthly Review Press, New York, 1961.

Ernesto Che Guevara, El Diario del Che en Bolivia, an edition of *Punto Final* (Santiago), NO. 59, July 1968.

Daniel James (ed.), *The Complete Bolivian Diaries of Che Guevara and Other Captured Documents*, Stein & Day, New York, 1968.

Ernesto Che Guevara, *Testamento Politico*, Publicaciones Peruanas, 'Inti', Lima, November 1967.

Ricardo Rojo, *Mi amigo el Che*, Editorial Jorge Alvárez, Buenos Aires, 1968.

Gregorio Selser, *Punta del Este contra Sierra Maestra*, Editorial Hernández, Buenos Aires, 1968.

Carlos J. Villar-Borda, *Che Guevara: su vida y muerte*, Editorial Gráfica Pacific Press, Lima, 1968.

Harold and Hugo Martínez, *Che, Antecedentes Biográficos del Comandante Ernesto Che Guevara*, PLA, Santiago, 1968.

Articles

Pepe Aguilar, 'Rojo escribe un libro amarillo', *Punto Final*, NO. 64, 24 September 1968.

Eduardo Galeano, 'Che Guevara—the Bolivar of Our Time?', Monthly Review, March 1966.

Eduardo Galeano, 'Magic Death for a Magic Life', *Monthly Review*, January 1968.

Norman Gall, 'The Legacy of Che Guevara', *Commentary* (New York), December 1967.

Adolfo Gilly, 'La renuncia del Che', *Arauco*, October 1965.

Adolfo Gilly, 'Respuesta a Fidel Castro', *Arauco*, February 1966.

John Gittings, 'Roads to Revolution: A Guerrilla's Diary', *Far Eastern Economic Review* (Hong Kong), 15 August 1968.

Ernesto Che Guevara, 'Guerra de guerrillas: un metodo', *Cuba Socialista*, September 1963.

I. F. Stone, 'In Memory of an Ardent Revolutionary', *World Marxist Review*, November 1967.

Lee Lockwood, 'The End of a Guerrillero', *New York Times Book Review*, 25 August 1968.

'Los falsos amigos del Che', *Punto Final*, NO. 62, 27 August 1968. (A letter written from Salta prison by two of the survivors of the Argentine guerrilla, Juan Héctor Jouve and Federico Evaristo Méndex.)

Anne Philipe, 'Che Guevara parle', *Le Monde* (Paris), 2/3 January 1963.

I. F. Stone, 'The Spirit of Che Guevara', *New Statesman*, 20 October 1967.

RÉGIS DEBRAY

Articles

Luís E. Aguilar, 'Régis Debray: where Logic Failed', *Reporter*, 28 December 1967.

Robin Blackburn and Perry Anderson, 'The Ordeal of Régis Debray', *Observer*, 27 August 1967.

Janine Alexandre Debray, 'Jules Régis Debray, mi hijo', *Los Tiempos* (Cochabamba), 26 August 1967.

Régis Debray, 'Le Castrisme: la longue marche de l'Amérique Latine', *Les Temps modernes* (Paris), NO. 224. January 1965. Translations: 'Latin America: the Long March', *New Left Review* (London), NO. 3, October–December 1965, a somewhat abbreviated text; 'El castrismo: la marcha de America Latina', *Punto Final* (Santiago), NO. 30, June 1967.

Régis Debray, 'América Latina: algunos problemas de estrategia revolucionaria', *Casa de las Américas*, NO. 31, July–August 1965.

Régis Debray, 'Revolución en la Revolución?' *Casa de las Américas* (Cuadernos series), January 1967. Translations: *Revolution in the Revolution?* Joint Publications Research Service, United States Government (JPRS 40, 310), 20 March 1967. *Revolution in the Revolution?* Monthly Review Press, London and New York, 1967, translated from the author's French and Spanish by Bobbye Ortíz.

Lee Hall, 'Debray: Prophet of Revolution in a Fight for Life', *Life Magazine*, August 1967.

THE SINO-SOVIET DISPUTE

Books

Luís E. Aguilar (ed.), *Marxism in Latin America*, Alfred A. Knopf, New York, 1968.

Robert K. Furtak, *Kuba und der Weltkommunismus*, Westdeutscher Verlag, Cologne and Opladen, 1967.

Alain Joxe, *El conflicto chino-soviético en América Latina*, Editorial Arca, Montevideo, 1967.

Andrés Suárez, *Cuba: Castroism and Communism, 1959–1966*, MIT Press, New York, 1967; see also Foreword by Ernst Halperin, p. xi.

John Gittings, *Survey of the Sino-Soviet Dispute: a Commentary and Extracts from the Recent Polemics, 1963–1967*, Oxford University Press for Chatham House, 1968.

Articles

Raymond Carr, 'The Cold War in Latin America', *Cuba and the United States*, ed. by John Plank, Brookings Institution, Washington, D. C., 1967.

Herbert S. Dinerstein, 'Soviet Policy in Latin America', *American Political Science Review*, March 1967.

Eduardo Galeano, 'The Communist Schism in the Outskirts of the World', *Monthly Review*, May 1963.

Martin D. Gensler, 'Los aliados incompatibles', *Problemas de Comunismo*,

July–August 1967.

Edward González, 'Castro's Revolution, Cuban Communist Appeals and the Soviet Response', *World Politics*, October 1968.

Ernst Halperin, 'Peking and the Latin American Communists', *China Quarterly*, NO. 29, January–March 1967.

Ernst Halperin, 'Las operaciones de Pekín en la América Latina', *Problemas del Comunismo*, November–December 1966.

Ernst Halperin, 'Le Communisme en Amérique Latine', *Problèmes d'Amérique Latine 4*, La Documentation Française: Notes et Études Documentaires, NO. 3360, 3 February 1967.

Robert F. Williams, 'Open Letter to Fidel Castro', *Vanguard* (New York), October–November 1966. (Reprinted in *Global Digest* (Hong Kong), December 1966.)

Louis L. Wiznitzer, 'Sino-Soviet Rivalry in Latin America', *New Republic*, 1 December 1962.

OLAS

Books

Guillermo Atias, *Después de Guevara*, Ediciones Plan, Santiago, 1968.

Arid Collazo, *La OLAS, el camino revolucionario de los trabajadores*, Editorial Diálogo, Montevideo, 1968.

Albert-Paul Lentin, *La Lutte tricontinentale: impérialisme et révólution après la conference de La Havana*, François Maspéro, Paris, 1966.

OLAS: Premiere conférence de l'organization latino-américaine de soldarité, François Maspero, Paris, 1967.

Articles

David Alexander, 'Un nouvelle internationalisme révolutionnaire', *Les Temps modernes* (Paris), March 1967.

Domingo Amuchástegui, 'Tattica e strategia rivoluzionaria in America Latina', *Terzo Mondo* (Milan), October–December 1968.

Gregorio Goldenberg, 'The Mro-Asian Peoples and Latin America', *Monthly Review*, June 1964.

D. Bruce Jackson, 'La Gente de Quién en La Habana ?', *Problemas del Comunismo*, May–June 1966.

Paul F. Power, 'The Peoples' Solidarity Movement: Evolution and Continuity', *Mizan*, January–February 1967.

'La Strategie revolutionnaire en Amérique Latine: de la tricontinentale a la Conférence de l'OLAS', *Problèmes d'Amérique Latine 7*, La Documentation Française: Notes et Études Documentaires, NO. 3454, 12 January 1968.

R. Otero, 'The First OLAS Conference: Delegates' Notes', *World Marxist Review*, October 1967.

GUATEMALA

Books

Eduardo Galeano, *Guatemala, Clave de Latinoamérica*, Ediciones de ia Banda Oriental, Montevideo, 1967.

Miguel Ydígoras Fuentes, *My War with Communism*, Prentice-Hall, Englewood Cliffs, N. J., 1963.

Nathan L. Whetten, *Guatemala: the Land and the People*, Yale University Press, 1961. *Turcios Lima* (biography and documents), Ediciones Tricontinental, Havana, December 1968.

Articles

Richard N. Adams, 'Receptivity to Communist–fomented Agitation in Rural Guatemala', *Economic Development and Cultural Change* (Chicago), VOL. V, NO. 4, 1957.

Camilo Castaño, 'Avec les Guérrillas du Guatemala', *Partisans*, NO. 38, July–September 1967.

Orlando Fernández, 'Situación y perspectivas del movimiento revolucionario guatemalteco', *Pensamiento Crítico* (Havana), NO. 150 April 1968.

José Manuel Fortuny, 'Guatemala: the Political Situation and Revolutionary Tactics', *World Marxist Review*, VOL. X, NO. 2, February 1967.

Jon Frappier, 'Guatemala Military Camp under Liberal Command', *Viet Report* (New York), April–May 1968.

Eduardo Galeano, 'With the Guerrillas in Guatemala', in *Latin America: Reform or Revolution?* ed. by James Petras and Maurice Zeitlin, Fawcett Books, New York, 1968.

Manuel Galich, 'Causas internas de una derrota: la revolución guatemalteca en 1954', *Tricontinental*, NO. 2, 1967.

Adolfo Gilly, 'The Guerrilla Movement in Guatemala', *Monthly Review*, Part I: May 1965; Part 2: June 1965.

Adolfo Gilly, 'Elecciones en Guatemala', *Arauco*, August 1965.

César Montes, 'Una ruptura lógica y necesaria', *Punto Final*, NO. 53, 23 April 1968.

'Le Guatemala', *Notes et Études Documentaires*, NO. 3127, 13 October 1964.

'Elections au Guatemala: 6 mars 1966', *Problèmes d'Amérique Latine 3*, La Documentation Française: Notes et Études Documentaires, NO. 3317, 9 September 1966.

Luís A. Turcios Lima, 'Discurso en la conferencia tricontinental', *Pensamiento Crítico* (Havana), NO. 150, April 1968.

Julio del Valle, 'Contra la tendencia conservadora en el Partido', *Pensamiento Crítico*, NO. 1, February 1967.

Julio del Valle, 'Guatemala bajo d signo de la guerra', *Pensamiento Crítico* (Havana), NO. 15, April 1968.

Nathan L. Whetten, 'La Reforma Agraria (1952–54) y la contra–reforma (1955–)' (en Guatemala)', *Reformas Agrarias en América Latina*, ed. by Oscár Delgado, Fondo de Cultura Económica, Mexico City, 1965.

M. A. Yon Sosa, 'Breves apuntes históricos del Movimiento Revolucionario, 13 de Noviembre,' *Pensamiento Crítico* (Havana), NO. 15, April 1968.

VENEZUELA

Books

Avec Douglas Bravo dans les maquis vénézuéliens, Dossiers Partiesans, François

Maspéro, Paris, 1968.

Manuel Cabieses Donoso, *¡Venezuela, Okey!* Ediciones del Litoral, Santiago, 1963.

John D. Martz, *Acción Democratica: evolution of a modern political party in Venezuela*, Princeton University Press, 1966.

Moses Moleiro, *El MIR de Venezuela*, Guairas, Instituto del Libor, Havana, 1967.

Fabricio Ojeda, *Hacia el poder revolucionario*, Havana, 1967.

Robert J. Alexander, *The Venezuelan Democratic Revolution*, Rutgers University Press, 1964.

La Batalla de Carúpano: Venezuela en pie de lucha (Praga, 1963, pp. 104).

Articles

Marío Cerda Gutiérrez, 'La guerrilla crece en Venezuda: entrevista con Francisco Prada', *Punto Final*, NO. 46, 16 January 1968.

James D. Cockroft, 'Venezuela: Class Stratification and Revolution', *Mexico Quarterly Review* (Mexico City), VOL. II, NO. 3, July 1965.

James D. Crockcroft and Eduardo Vicente, 'Venezuda and the FALN Since Leoni', *Monthly Review*, November 1965.

Alberto Domingo Rangel, 'Guerrilla in Venezuela', *Monthly Review*, February 1964.

René Dumont, 'Betancourt's Venezuela Hesitates over Agrarian Reform', Chapter 2 of *Lands Alive*, Merlin Press, New York, 1965.

Jesús Faria, 'From the History of the Communist Party of Venezuela', *Peace, Freedom, and Socialism (World Marxist Review)*, December 1967.

Frente de Liberación Nacional 'El paso de la guerra corta a la guerra larga', February 1966, reprinted in *Estrategia* (MIR), Chile, NO. 8, April 1967.

'La resistencia armada se recupera', *Izquierda* (MIR), Venezuela, NO. 13, February 1967, reprinted in *Estrategia* (MIR), Chile, NO. 8, April 1967.

John Gerassi, 'Latin America: the Next Vietnam?', *Viet Report* (New York), January–February 1967.

Gobierno y Nación defienden en Venezuela el régimen democratico: Actos contra el terrorismo comunista, Publicaciones de la Secretaria de la Presidencia de la República, Caracas, 1964.

Jean-Claude Guénier, 'Luttes au Vénézuela', *Partisans* (Paris), April–June 1967.

Germán Lairet, 'Una nueva etapa en la lucha armada en Venezuela', *Cuba Socialista*, July 1965.

John R. Mathiason, 'El campesino venezolano', in Frank Bonilla and José A. Silva Michelena, *Cambio Político en Venezuela*, CENDES, Venezuela, 1968.

Marcel Niedergang, 'Vénézuela: miracle ou illusion?', *Le Monde* (Paris), 24/25/26 March 1965.

Fabricio Ojeda, 'La revolución verdadera: la violencia y el fatalisamo geopolitico', *Pensamiento Crítico* (Havana), NO. I, February 1967.

Raymond J. Penn and Jorge Schuster, 'La Reforma Agraria en Venezuela', *Reformas Agrarias en la América Latina, ed. by Oscir Delgado*, Fondo de Cultura Económica, Mexico City, 1965.

Teodoro Petkoff, 'Como nos fugamos del cuartel San Carlos', El Siglo (Santiago), 21 May 1967.

Anne Philipe, 'Le Vénézuela: un pays riche, un peuple pauvre', *Le Monde* (Paris), 19/20/22 March 1966.

'L' expérience démocratique au Venezuela', *Problèmes d'Amérique Latine 6*, La Documentation Française: Notes et Etudes Documentaires, NO. 3423, 29 September 1967.

Programme of Action of the National Liberation Front, published by the London Committee of the NLF of Venezuela, n.d. (? 1964).

Juan Rodríguez, 'The New in the Political Line of the Communist Party of Venezuela', *World Marxist Review*, September 1967.

'Venezuela: nueva etapa operativa', *Tricontinental*, NO. 6, 1968.

'Venezuela: vanguardia 0 elecciones', *Tricontinental*, NO. 6, 1968.

Eduardo Vicente, 'The Venezuelan FALN', *Studies on the Left*, Winter 1965.

Yen Erh Wen, 'Armed Struggle Flames in Venezuela', *Peking Review*, VOL. vi, NO. 13, 29 March 1963.

COLOMBIA

Books

Colombia en pie de lucha, Editorial Paz y Socialismo, Prague, 1966.

Comité Central del Partido Comunista de Colombia, *Treinta años de lucha del partido comunista en Colombia*, Ediciones Paz y Socialismo, Bogotá, 1960.

Enrique Cuellar Vargas, *13 Años de Violencia*, Ediciones, Cultura Social Colombiana, Bogotá, 1960.

Diario de un guerrillero colombiano, Editorial Freeland, Buenos Aires, 1968.

Robert H. Dix, *Colombia: the Political Dimensions of Change*, Yale University Press, 1967.

Orlando Fals Borda, *Campesinos los Andes*, Editorial Iqueima, Bogotá, 1961.

Orlando Fals Borda, *La Subversión en Colombia*, Ediciones Tercer Mundo y Departamento de Sociología, Universidad Nacional, Bogota, 1967.

Vernon Lee Fluharty, *Dance of the Millions: Military Rule and Social Revolution in Colombia, 1930–1956*, University of Pittsburg Press, 1957.

Eduardo Franco Isaza, *Las guerrillas del llano*, Librería Mundial, Bogotá, 1959.

Germán Guzmán Campos, *La Violencia en Colombia*, Ediciones Tercer Mundo, Bogotá, 1962.

Germán Guzmán Campos, *Camilo: Presencia y Destino*, Servicios Especiales de Prensa, Bogotá, May 1967.

Norberto Habegger, *Camilo Torres: el cura guerrillero*, Editorial A, Pena Lillo, Buenos Aires, 1967.

Pat Holt, *Colombia Today—and Tomorrow*, Pall Mall Press, London, 1964.

Alonso Moncado Abello, *Un aspecto de la violencia*, Bogotá, 1963.

Diego Montaña Cuellar, *Colombia: país formal y país real*, Editorial Platina, Buenos Aires, 1963.

Cristian Restrepo Calle (ed.), *Camilo Torres: Biografía, Plataforma, Mensajes*, Ediciones Carpel-Antorcha, Medellín, April 1966.

José María Nieto Rojas, *La batalla contra el comunismo en Colombia*, Empresa Nacional de Publicaciones, Bogota, 1956.

Camilo Torres Restrepo, *Obras Escogidas*, Provincias Unidas, Montevideo, 1968.

Camilo Torres: Liberación o Muerte, Instituto del Libro, Havana, 1967.

Luís Torres Almeyda, *La Rebelión de Galán el Comunero*, Bucaramanga, Imprenta del Departamento, 1961.

Articles

Germán Arciniegas, 'La violence en Colombie', *Problèmes d'Amérique Latine* La Documentation Française: Notes et Études Documentaires, NO. 3247, 21 December 1965.

Norman A. Bailey, '*La Violencia* in Colombia', *Journal of Inter-American Studies*, October 1967.

Alvaro Delgado, 'The Working Qass and Labour Movement in Colombia', *World Marxist Review*, September 1967.

Alvaro Delgado, 'Freedom to Colombian Patriots', *World Marxist Review*, April 1967.

Orlando Fals Borda, 'Violence and the Break-up of Tradition in Colombia', in *Obstacles to Change in Latin America*, ed. by Claudio Véliz, Oxford University Press for Chatham House, 1965.

Ernest Feder, 'The Rational Implementation of Land Reform in Colombia and its Significance for the Alliance for Progress', *America Latina* (Rio de Janeiro), Centro Latinoamericano de Pesquisas en Ciencias Sociais, January–March 1963.

Rafael H. Gaviría and Calarca Moeschamp, 'La lutte en Colombie', *Partisans* (Paris), April–June 1967.

Adolfo Gilly, 'Guerrillas and "Peasant Republics" in Colombia', *Monthly Review*, October 1965.

Adolfo Gilly, 'Camilo, Guerrillero', *Arauco*, January 1966. (Written before Camilo's death.)

Alberto Gómez, 'The Revolutionary Armed Forces of Colombia and their Perspectives', *World Marxist Review*, April 1967.

Eric Hobsbawm, 'The Revolutionary Situation in Colombia', *World Today*, VOL. xix June 1963.

Ronald H. McDonald, 'Political Protest and Alienation in Voting: the Case of Colombia', *Interamerican Economic Affairs*, VOL. xxi, NO. 2, Autumn 1967.

Mario Menéndez Rodriguez, 'El Ejército de Liberación Nacional de Colombia'. *Sucesos*, NOS 1777–81 (partially reprinted in *Punto Final*, NO. 34, August 1967).

Diego Montaña Cuellar, 'Los problemas estratégicos y tácticos de la revolución en Colombia' (political thesis submitted to the Colombian Communist party), *Punto Final* (supplement), NO. 47, 30 January 1968.

Marcel Niedergang, 'La Guérilla Révolutionnaire en Amérique Latine', *Le Monde* (Paris), 8 February 1965.

Francisco Posada, 'La violencia y la vida colombiana', *Documentos Políticos* (Colombian Communist party review), May–June 1967.

'Un pays inquiet qui manifeste sa volonte de progres', *Tribune de Genève*, 20 January 1967 (Articles and Documents, 7 April 1967).

'Colombie: la situation politique apres les elections generales de 1966', *Problèmes d'Amérique Latine 4*, La Documentation Française: Notes et Etudes Documentaires, NO. 3360, 3 February 1967.

Russell W. Ramsey, 'The Colombian Battalion in Korea and Suez', *Journal of Inter-American Studies*, October 1967.

Gilberto Vieira, 'La Colombie à l'heure de Marquetalia', *Démocratie Nouvelle* (issue entitled *Où va Mister Johnson*), July–August 1965.

Richard S. Weinert, 'Violence in Pre-modern Societies: Rural Colombia', *American Political Science Review*, June 1966.

Robert C. Williamson, 'Toward a Theory of Political Violence: the Case of Rural Colombia', *Western Political Quarterly*, March 1965.

PERU

Books

Héctor Béjar, *Perú 1965: apuntes sobre una experiencia guerrillera*, Casa de las Américas, Havana, 1969.

Hugo Blanco, *El camino de nuestra revolución*, Lima, 1964.

François Bourricaud, *Poder y sociedad en el Perú contemporáneo*, Paidos, Buenos Aires, 1967.

Gonzalo Añi Castillo, *Historia Secreta de las Guerrillas*, Ediciones 'Mas Alla', Lima, 1967.

Silvestre Conduruna, *Las experiencias de la última etapa de las luchas revolucionarias en el Perú*, Ediciones Vanguardia Revolucionaria, Lima, 1966; *Estrategia* (Santiago), NO. 3, 1966.

Las Guerrillas en el Perú y su represión, Ministerio de Guerra, Lima, 1966.

Ricardo Letts Colmenares, *Reforma Agraria Peruana*, Lima, 1964.

Ricardo V. Luna Mendoza, *The Role of the Modern Peruvian Left* (unpublished thesis submitted to the Department of Politics of Princeton University, April 1962).

Carlos Malpica, *Guerra o muerte al latifundio*, Lima, 1963.

Carlos Malpica, *Los dueños del Perú*, Ediciones Ensayos Sociales, Lima, 3rd edition, 1968.

Marío A. Malpica, *Biografia de la revolución: historia y antologla del pensamiento socialista*, Ediciones Ensayos Sociales, Lima, 1967'

Rogger Mercado, *Las guerrillas del Perú, el MIR: de la prédica ideológica a la acción armada*, Fondo de Cultura Popular, Lima, 1967.

Nahuel Moreno (Hugo Bressano), *La revolución latinoamericana*, Ediciones Chaupimayo, Lima, 1962.

Hugo Neira, *Cuzco: Tierra y Muerte*, Ediciones Problemas de Hoy, Lima, 1964.

Hugo Neira, *Los Andes: Tierra o Muerte*, Editorial Zyx, Santiago, 1968.

R. J. Owens, *Peru*, Royal Institute of International Affairs, Oxford University Press, 3rd printing, 1966.

James L. Payne, *Labour and Politics in Peru*, New Haven, Conn., 1965.

Luís de la Puente Uceda, *La Reforma del Agro Peruano*, Ediciones Ensayos Sociales, Lima. 1966.

Tenencia de la tierra y desarrollo socio-económico del sector agricola: Perú, Panamerican Union, Washington, D. C., 1966.

Victor Villanueva, *El Militarismo en Perú*, Lima, 1962.

Victor Villanueva, *Hugo Blanco y la Rebelión Campesina*, Editorial Juan Mejía Baca, Lima, 1967.

Articles

Héctor Béjar, 'Bilan d'une guérrilla au Pérou', *Partisans* (Paris), NO. 37, April–June 1967.

'Hugo Blanco Correspondence', *International Socialist Review*, Spring 1965.

David Chaplin, 'Peru's Postponed Revolution', *World Politics*, April 1968.

Wesley W. Craig Jr, 'The Peasant Movement of La Convención, Peru: Dynamics of Rural Labour Organization', paper presented to seminar on peasant movements in Latin America, Cornell University, December 1966 (mimeograph).

Norman Gall, 'Letter from Peru', *Commentary*, June 1964.

Norman Gall, 'Peru's Misfired Guerrilla Campaign', *Reporter*, January 1967.

Adolfo Gilly, 'Los sindicatos guerrilleros del Perú', *Marcha*, Montevideo, August 1963.

André Gunder Frank, 'Hugo Blanco Must Not Die', reprinted speech, University of Toronto, January 1967.

Eric J. Hobsbawn, 'Problèmes Agraires à La Convención (Pérou)', address presented to the International CNRS Conference on Agrarian Problems in Latin America, October 1965 (mimeograph).

Ricardo Letts Colmenares, 'Breve reseña contemporánea de la lucha por la reforma agraria', *Economía y Agricultra* (Lima), February 1964.

César Levano, 'Lessons of the Guerrilla Struggle in Peru', *World Marxist Review*, VOL. ix, NO. 9, September 1966.

Jacqueline Eluau de Lobatón, 'Tras las huellas de Lobatón', *Punto Final*.

Livio Maitán, 'The Revolt of the Peruvian Campesinos', *International Socialist Review*, Spring 1965.

Marcel Niedergang, 'Guerre de guérillas au Pérou', *Le Monde* (Paris), 24/25 August 1965.

James Payne, 'Peru: the Politics of Structured Violence', *Journal of Politics*, May 1965.

'Pérou: le président Belaúnde à mi-course', *Problèmes d'Amérique Latine 5*, La Documentation Française: Notes et Études Documentaires, NO. 3383, 19 April 1967.

Américo Pomaruna (Ricardo Letts Colmenares), 'Perú: revolución, insurrección, guerrillas', *Pensamiento Crítico* (Havana), NO. 1, February 1967.

Luís de la Puente Uceda, 'The Peruvian Revolution: Concepts and Perspectives', *Monthly Review*, VOL. xvii, NO. 6, November 1965.

Aníbal Quijano O., 'El movimiento campesino del Perú y sus líderes', *América Latina* (Rio de Janeiro), VOL. viii, NO. 4, 1965.

Milton C. Taylor, 'Problems of Development in Peru', *Journal of Inter-American Studies*, VOL. ix, NO. 1, January 1967.

BOLIVIA

Books

Luís González and Gustavo Sánchez, *The Great Rebel: Che Guevara in Bolivia*, Grove Press, New York, 1969.

Mariano Baptista Gumucio (and others), *Guerrilleros y generales sobre Bolivia*, Editorial Jorge Alvárez, Buenos Aires, 1965. (Including articles by Ted

Córdova-Claura, Sergio Almáraz and Simón Reyes.)

Philippe Labreveux, *Bolivia bajo el Che*, Colección Replanteo, Buenos Aires, 1968.

Edgar Millares Reyes, *Las Guerrillas: teoría y practica*, Biblioteca Universidad de San Francisco Javier, Sucre, Bolivia, 1968.

Ruben Vásquez Díaz, *La Bolivie à l'heure du Che*, Maspero, Paris, 1968.

Cornelius H. Zondag, *The Bolivian Economy 1952–65: the Revolution and its Aftermath*, Praeger, New York, 1966.

Articles

Dare, 'Dos canillitas hirieron de muerte a la guerrilla boliviana', *Confirmado Internacional* (La Paz), NO. 2, February 1968.

Casto Ferragut, 'La Reforma Agraria (en Bolivia)', *Reformas Agrarias en América Latina*, ed. by Oscár Delgado, Fondo de Cultura Económica, Mexico City, 1965.

Antonio García, 'La Reforma Agraria y el desarrollo social de Boli-via', *El Trimestre Económico* (Mexico City), July–September 1964.

Richard Gott, 'Guevara, Debray and the CIA', *Nation* (New York), 20 November 1967.

C. A. M. Hennessy, 'Shifting Forces in the Bolivian Revolution', *World Today*, May 1964.

'Informe ténico sobre la documentación subversiva', *El Diario* (La Paz), 23 September 1967.

'La Situation politique en Bolivie, novembre 1964–fevrier 1966', *Problèmes d' Amerique Latino 2*, La Documentation Française: Notes et Études Documentaires, 17 June 1966.

Ramíro Otero, 'The Communists of Bolivia in the Fight for Unity of the Popular Forces', *World Marxist Review*, April 1967.

Alfredo Ovando Candia, 'Una descripción documentada de la acción guerrillera roja', *El Diario* (La Paz), 23 September 1967.